PERSONALITY

A PSYCHOLOGICAL INTERPRETATION

PERSONALITY

A PSYCHOLOGICAL INTERPRETATION

GORDON W. ALLPORT

ASSOCIATE PROFESSOR OF PSYCHOLOGY
IN HARVARD UNIVERSITY

NEW YORK

HENRY HOLT AND COMPANY

To my Mother

To my Mother

PREFACE

As a rule, science regards the individual as a mere bothersome accident. Psychology, too, ordinarily treats him as something to be brushed aside so the main business of accounting for the uniformity of events can get under way. The result is that on all sides we see psychologists enthusiastically at work upon a somewhat shadowy portrait entitled "the generalized human mind." Though serving well a certain purpose, this portrait is not altogether satisfying to those who compare it with the living individual models from which it is drawn. It seems unreal and esoteric, devoid of locus, self-consciousness, and organic unity—all essential characteristics of the minds we know.

With the intention of supplementing this abstract portrait by one that is more life-like, a new movement within psychological science has gradually grown up. It attempts in a variety of ways and from many points of view to depict and account for the manifest individuality of mind. This new movement has come to be known (in America) as the *psychology of personality*. Especially within the past fifteen years has its progress been notable.

Since it is young, this movement finds difficulty in evaluating its first achievements. Its research is plentiful but piecemeal; its theories are numerous but conflicting. Yet every year more and more psychological investigators are attracted to it, and colleges at a rapid rate are adding the study of personality to their psychological curricula. The result of this rising tide of interest is an insistent demand for a guide book that will *define* the new field of study—one that will articulate its objectives, formulate its standards, and test the progress made thus far.

In attempting to write such a book I have sought above all else to respect the many-sidedness of the subject-matter of this new science. An account written exclusively in terms of any single school of psychological doctrine would be far too narrow. Better to expand and refashion one's theories until they do some measure of justice to the richness and dignity of human personality, than to clip and compress personality until it fits one closed system of thought.

In striving for adequacy and balance I have tried to make a special ally of common sense which, I believe, affords precisely the hypotheses and insights that it is the duty of the new psychology of personality to verify and (if possible) improve. I have likewise borrowed liberally from many types of psychological writing, past and present. But whatever I have appropriated I have tried to assimilate within a single and coherent theoretical frame.

This goal of adequacy means, of course, that I cannot accept whole-heartedly each and every partisan point of view. The endocrinological approach, for example, is a specialty with many enthusiastic supporters. So too is psychoanalysis. Their danger is their one-sidedness, their monosymptomatic bias. Though I borrow from these approaches I cannot subscribe to them as adequate.

Similar is the case of the currently popular statistical methodologies. Many believe these are indispensable in supplying the factual ground for the science of personality. Sometimes they are useful; but many times they are not. In any event, mere arrays of statistics are never capable of self-interpretation. It is for this reason that I have preferred in most cases to state the results of research as clearly as possible in words, proceeding at once with the interpretation of the results. If the argument is sound, statistics can do no more than symbolize the fact; if the argument is unsound, statistical elaboration can never make it sound and may even increase the confusion. So, at a time when in many quarters mathematical symbolizing enjoys exaggerated favor, I prefer for clarity's sake to stick to the verbal method of exposition and argument, especially since it seems to me the only one wherewith to co-ordinate the field as a whole.

From another direction I may be called to task for overlooking the close relationship between personality and culture. But such criticism can arise only from a misunderstanding of my purpose. I do not deny that personality is fashioned to a large extent through the impact of culture upon the individual. But the interest of psychology is not in the factors *shaping* personality, rather in personality *itself* as a developing structure. From this point of view culture is relevant only when it has become *interiorized* within the person as a set of personal ideals, attitudes, and traits. Likewise, culture conflict must become *inner* conflict before it can have any significance for personality. Why is it that in our times, when Western culture is sadly disorganized, our personalities are not correspondingly disorganized? The enthusiastic determinist might reply: "They are. Our institutional anchors are lost and each of us is either drifting or breaking to pieces." But such a reply would be wholly unrealistic. Are personalities in fact any more disorganized now than formerly? Is there any sure evidence for an increase of insanity? It is doubtful. Certainly, it is impossible to hold that disorganization of personality today is *proportional* to the rapid shattering of cultural forms. Cultural determinism is one of the monosymptomatic approaches; it has a blind spot for the internal balancing factors and structural tenacity within personality.

There is also in some departments of social science a tendency to define personality as one man's influence upon others, as his status in the group, or as his "social stimulus-value." With such definitions psychology cannot possibly operate. If it tried to do so its datum would evaporate, and there would be left only the notoriously conflicting images that men have of one another. The psychology of personality must regard its subject-matter as wholly objective and accessible. To be sure, the task of judging personality correctly, of reading motives aright, and of representing adequately the change and variation of which each person is capable, complicate the study enormously, but still a stable biophysical frame of reference must be assumed.

Psychologically considered the important fact about personality is its relatively enduring and unique organization. The central problem of the psychology of personality therefore concerns the nature of this structure and its composition in terms of sub-structures or units. The elements and bonds sponsored by traditional psychology do not serve as adequate means for depicting the structure of individuality. Part III devotes itself entirely to this question, and it is here that the chief novelty of my own position lies. Chapters 11 and 12 on *traits*, especially if taken in conjunction with Chapter 7 on the autonomy of motives, supply, I believe, a theory that is concretely applicable to the infinitely varied forms of personal existence, and at the same time abstract enough to serve as a unifying principle for the new branch of science.

To sum up, my purpose is twofold: (1) to gather into a single comprehensive survey the most important fruits of the psychological study of personality, and (2) to supply new co-ordinating concepts and theories where they will equip this new department of psychology for a more adequate handling of its endlessly rich subject-matter.

The beginnings of this book lay in certain researches I undertook seventeen years ago. Ever since that time it has been in the process of development and completion. From start to finish my constant and loyal collaborator has been Ada L. Allport, my wife. The material has been presented many times in my classes. Through their interest, discussion, and willing participation in experiments my students have contributed to its final content and form more than they know. In certain chapters I have benefited much from the advice and assistance of my friends, H. D. Spoerl, C. E. MacGill, D. M. McGregor, R. P. Casey, C. M. Harsh, and H. Werner. Especially deep is my indebtedness to my brother, F. H. Allport, for significant help with some of the crucial portions of the argument, and to Hadley Cantril who has carefully read and criticized the entire manuscript. I wish also to acknowledge the kind assistance of R. T. Fuller in drawing the illustrations, and of Miss Dorothy Telfer in preparing the manuscript for publication.

G. W. A.

August, 1937.

CONTENTS

CONTENTS

CONTENTS

CONTENTS

Part V: Understanding Personality

CHAPTER XVIII

THE ABILITY TO JUDGE PEOPLE

CHAPTER XIX

INFERENCE AND INTUITION

CHAPTER XX

THE PERSON IN PSYCHOLOGY

Part I

THE APPROACH TO PERSONALITY

CHAPTER I

PSYCHOLOGY AND THE STUDY OF INDIVIDUALITY

Die Natur scheint Alles auf Individualität angelegt zu haben.
—*Goethe*

THE outstanding characteristic of man is his individuality. He is a unique creation of the forces of nature. Separated spatially from all other men he behaves throughout his own particular span of life in his own distinctive fashion. It is not upon the cell nor upon the single organ, nor upon the group, nor upon the species that nature has centered her most lavish concern, but rather upon the integral organization of life processes into the amazingly stable and self-contained system of the individual living creature.

In daily life, in our direct contacts with our fellows, the pre-eminence of individuality is recognized readily enough. During our waking hours and in our dreams people appear to us as definite and individual. The man in the street is never in danger of forgetting that individuality is the supreme characteristic of human nature. It seems to him self-evident. But with the scientist the case is different. Of the several sciences devoted to the study of life-processes, none, peculiarly enough, recognizes as its central fact that life processes actually occur only in unified, complex, individual forms. Sciences find the very existence of the individual somewhat of an embarrassment and are disturbed by his intrusion into their domains. They pretend to deal with Nature, but are oblivious to the fact that Nature, as Goethe said, seems to have planned everything with a view to individuality.

SCIENCE AND THE SINGLE CASE:
"*Scientia non est Individuorum*"

Why is it that science and common sense part company over the fact of human individuality? The answer is that science is an arbitrary creed. It defines itself as a systematic attempt to trace order in nature through the discovery of regularities and uniformities *characteristic of a whole class* of objects. By choice, therefore, scientists have pre-occupied themselves with generalized truth, with occurrences that are common to events of one class. A "class," to be sure, is a question-begging concept, for it in turn is an abstraction designed to cover common occurrences. So it turns out that the "order in nature" which the scientist seeks is after all quite a circular matter.

The order that is manifested in the single organism through the inter-relation of its bodily and mental processes is overlooked; it is not considered to be of legitimate scientific concern. The individual is regarded only as an *instance* or *example* of a universal principle; the search is always for broader and more inclusive formulations. "A description of one individual without reference to others may be a piece of literature, a biography or novel. But science? No." [1] *Scientia non est individuorum.*

There is a typical procedure the scientist feels compelled by convention to follow. He starts always with a certain professional attitude toward nature. The fact that this attitude is only one of many kinds of attitude of which he is capable, demonstrates at the outset a certain arbitrariness in his method of study. First, he makes a critical discrimination of his subject matter, isolating from the individual who confronts him a chosen segment of behavior. This procedure is termed *abstraction*. He then observes the recurrence of this segment and its conditions in many members of a hypothetical class. Finding uniformity in the event and its attendant conditions, he makes a *generalization* or a law, and then, if he is a thorough investigator, he will submit his law to repeated tests and so establish it securely by *empirical verification.* [2]

The discovery of a law by this procedure is like finding a single thread running from individual nature to individual nature, visible only through the magical spectacles of a special, theoretic attitude. In everyday life, the scientist, like anyone else, deals effectively with his fellow men only by recognizing that their peculiar natures are not adequately represented in his discovery. The single functions which they have in common are deeply overshadowed by the individual use to which they put these functions. The piling of law upon law does not in the slightest degree account for the pattern of indi-

---

[1] M. Meyer, *Psychol. Bull.*, 1926, 23, p. 271.
[2] These stages of scientific labor are described repeatedly in treatises on the scientific method; see, for example, A. Wolf, *Essentials of the Scientific Method,* 1925.

viduality which each human being enfolds. The *person* who is a unique and never-repeated phenomenon evades the traditional scientific approach at every step. In fact, the more science advances, the less do its discoveries resemble the individual life with its patent continuities, mobility, and reciprocal penetration of functions.

Starting with an infinitely more complex subject-matter than the other biological sciences, but with the same presuppositions, the psychologist has isolated his fragmentary elements, has generalized and verified his findings in the manner of the austere elder sciences. He has succeeded in discovering orderly processes in the "generalized mind," but the phenomenon of individuality, so deliberately excluded, returns to haunt him. Whether he delimits his science as the study of the mind, the soul, of behavior, purpose, consciousness, or human nature,—the persistent, indestructible fact of organization in terms of individuality is always present. To abstract a generalized human mind from a population of active, prepossessing, well-knit persons is a feat of questionable value. The generalized human mind is entirely mythical; it lacks the most essential characteristics of mind,—locus, organic quality, reciprocal action of parts, and self-consciousness.

This exclusion of the individual from pure psychology has led to many anomalies. It has, for example, often been pointed out that the psychologist, in spite of his profession, is not a superior judge of people. He should be, but his ascetic and meager formulae derived from "generalized mind" do not go far in accounting for the peculiar richness and uniqueness of minds that are organic and single. The study of psychological laws is not sufficient training for the comprehension of personal forms of mental life. Science is commonly considered to give men control over nature, but in the psychological field there is no "generalized mind" to be controlled. There are only single, concrete minds, each one of which presents problems peculiar to itself. In ordinary life we deal with our acquaintances, not by applying abstract laws, but by studying their individual natures.

Still, with considerable tenacity, psychologists have held to convention, abstracting from minds initially organized such properties as suit their convenience, and their convenience is determined largely by scientific tradition. They are absorbed by the shadow of Method rather than by the individual objects upon which the shadow lies. To take a single example, the method of paired-comparison recommends itself as an objective and quantitative technique for studying judgments of the affective value of colors. In order to employ it the subject is brought into the laboratory, and all variables other than color are controlled. He is shown two pure colored lights at a time, and states his preference. From a complete series of such judgments, the relative affective rank for each color is determined. Another subject is called in, and then another. The goal is to find out how in the "generalized mind" one color takes precedence over others in affective value. This particular attempt long ago had to be given up, for it was soon found that the generalized mind had no uniform preference. Individuals differed too markedly. Even the single individual has no constant affective response toward, say, green. Green light has a different value in the dark room of the laboratory and in a traffic signal; it has still different values as a property of an apple or a running brook, in a friend's cravat or in an enemy's automobile. Its pleasantness depends upon the observer's interest, his memories, his mood. There is no affective value in abstract greenness. There are only *personal* experiences, and these determine the meaning and value of this contingent quality green.

The founder of experimental psychology, Wilhelm Wundt, admitted that "there is no psychological law to which the exceptions are not more numerous than the agreements." [3] The exceptions, he recognized, result from the persistent intrusion of living individuality into the experimenter's fragile abstractions. He then decided, with unassailable logic, that the direct study of this intruding fact is a necessary extension of psychological science.

Now it is not to be doubted that here in the study of concrete individuals original talent and happy instinct must in the last analysis produce the best results, and that without these gifts a psychological analysis . . . is impossible. But this does not mean that scientific consideration and practice would not be in a position to render essential service. . . . Such a combination of methods is the task of a practical psychology, namely, a characterology, which should investigate the basic and typical forms of individual character with the aid of principles derived from a general theoretical psychology, and a study of the relation and interaction of mental elements. Such a characterology Bacon has already demanded as a propaedeutic to politics and history. Unfortunately one cannot say that since Bacon any essential progress has been made in the task. But one may indeed prophesy that a solution will depend above all else upon a full development of psychologi-

[3] *Phil. Studien*, 1886, 3, 204.

cal analysis and an overcoming of the one-sided intellectualistic and metaphysical tendencies in psychology.[4]

It is evident that the founder of experimental psychology perceived the dilemma, even though he did not offer a clear-cut solution. Previously he had misappropriated the term "individual psychology" for what is today called general psychology. From individual psychology, therefore, curiously enough, he ruled out the study of the single individual, and consigned this important problem to "characterology." [5] Although Wundt was right in his belief that general psychology has much to contribute to the study of single individuals, and right too in his statement that up to his time little progress had been made, he was nevertheless quite wrong in suggesting that the individual has no place in psychology proper, but only in a special science of characterology or "practical psychology." He was wrong in holding that psychology should establish the laws, and characterology account for the exceptions.

APPROACHES TO THE INDIVIDUAL WITHIN THE SCIENCE OF PSYCHOLOGY

More important than Wundt's passing comments are those movements arising within the broad province of psychology as a protest against the prevalent neglect of the individual. Each of these movements, in greater or less degree, has attempted to improve the situation, and has exerted marked influence: *differential psychology, psychography, psychoanalysis, typology, Gestalt psychology*, the *psychology of Verstehen, purposive psychology*, and *personalistic psychology*. Each deserves a critical note.

Differential Psychology. In the early part of the nineteenth century astronomers created wide-spread interest by their accidental discovery of individual differences in reaction time. In the recording of the time of the transit of stars, it appeared that there were innate differences in the speed with which the visual impression led to a simple motor reaction such as the pressing of a key. Psychologists became concerned with the problem, and the study of the "personal equation" in reaction time entered Wundt's laboratory.[6] Individual differences in reaction time, however, turned out to be only one kind

---

[4] *Logik*, II, 4, 1, (3), (b). The reference to Bacon is in the *Advancement of Learning*, VII, 3.

[5] See also, W. Wundt, *Logik*, II, 4, 2, (2), (a).

[6] E. G. Boring, *History of Experimental Psychology*, 1929, pp. 133-156.

of individual difference. Everywhere the personal equation was found. Having commenced with reaction times, Wundt, with some reluctance, was compelled to admit the study of other individual differences. His reluctance, of course, came from his preconception of psychology as a science dealing with universal and not with individual characteristics of mental life.[7] Then came Galton with a totally different outlook. His primary interest lay precisely in the differences between people, in their intelligence, imagery, and character. It is really Galton who deserves to be called the founder of differential psychology.[8]

Differential psychology has become perhaps the most active branch of the science. Its attachments to the traditional outlook, however, remain very close. Its method is by no means radical. Its first step is completely orthodox. It does just what general psychology does: selects a single attribute or function that can be conveniently isolated for study. It is concerned with the single attribute and not with the complex individual. The second step establishes the range and distribution of this attribute within the population of subjects employed. A third step is often added to discover the degree of covariation between two or more of the functions or attributes thus isolated.[9]

In three important ways differential psychology fails to be an adequate method for the study of individuality. (1) Its interest, like that of general psychology, centers in the function or attribute that is isolated for study and not in the men possessing these functions. The individual is only a means, not an end. (2) The approach is as distinctly elementaristic as in traditional psychology; it is "from beneath" in terms of the elements of mind, and not "from above" in terms of their organization and patterning. In this respect differential psychology differs markedly from characterology.[10] (3) The implication is that the sum-total of an individual's scores on the isolated functions constitutes his individuality. The psychograph, with its separate plottings, is the utmost that the psychology of individual

[7] E. G. Boring, *History of Experimental Psychology*, 1929, p. 319.
[8] *Ibid.*, p. 478.
[9] The chief tool of differential psychology is statistics. The range of individual differences in respect to a single variable is expressed usually in terms of mean or standard deviations. The co-variation of two simple variables is expressed by a coefficient of correlation. When more than two variables are employed the principle of correlation is extended with the aid of such complex devices as multiple correlation, partial correlation, factor analysis, and the like.
[10] W. Stern, *Differentielle Psychologie*, 3d edit., 1921, p. 12.

differences has achieved in depicting the organization of mind (cf. pp. 10-12).

Mental tests are a typical achievement of differential psychology. Individuals are discovered to vary "normally" in some function (such as intelligence, perseveration, or introversion), and the degree of a person's variation above or below the mean is considered to be his score. It is quite clear that the chief interest here is in one elementary attribute at a time. The peculiar patterning of attributes within the single person is not considered.

Although the outlook of differential psychology is so limited, many psychologists are still inclined to regard it as the method *par excellence* for the study of individuality. Boring writes, "The psychology of individual differences because it deals with the particular and not with the general, tends to be practical." But differential psychology does not deal with the *particular* at all, but rather with *variations in the general.* Dodge acclaims the great advance of differential psychology over the older psychology of the "average" man: "Treating each individual as a special combination of capacities, accomplishments and tendencies, has been far more productive than treating individuals as though they were all alike or as though they belonged to mutually exclusive types." But actually, differential psychology has not at all treated the individual as a special *combination* of capacities, accomplishments and tendencies. It has done nothing more than to imply that a person is a simple sum-total of his departures from the average.[11]

The reasons for the favored position of the psychology of individual differences are fairly obvious. In the first place it readily lends itself to standard experimental procedure, demanding only that enough cases be obtained to secure a reliable measure of the distribution of differences. In the main it asks just what general psychology asks, that one function be abstracted at a time from the total complex person, and that these functions be observed and measured with accuracy. In the second place, it is a purely quantitative method, and rarely deals with more than one or two variables at a time. Although there is a tendency in recent years to develop mathematical techniques whereby more variables can be simultaneously treated, the

[11] The quotation from Boring is taken from his *History of Experimental Psychology*, p. 520; the quotation from Dodge, *Conditions and Consequences of Human Variability*, 1931, p. 6. This confusion concerning the province of differential psychology is discussed by Allport and Vernon, *Studies in Expressive Movement*, 1933, p. viii.

utmost that has been achieved still falls far short of the complete pattern of individuality. Even the most modern extension of differential psychology, "factor analysis," seeks to discover only that which is *common*. Individual distinctiveness arising from the arrangement and organization of these factors remains completely untouched.

The method of group comparison is a branch of differential psychology. In the study of the psychological differences between the sexes, between races, or between two age-levels, it is customary for the investigator to compare the mean scores and the distribution of scores of the two groups in respect to one isolated function at a time. Here again the method lies, both in respect to its objective and its technique, well within the limits of traditional psychology.

Figure 1 (modified from Stern) represents these methods. It is easy to see that both general psychology and differential psychology deal with abstracted attributes, considered common to all men, and represented on the horizontal dimension. The vertical dimension, where individuality is represented, is not served by the methods of either general or differential psychology.

General psychology pursues the horizontal dimension, ideally without regard to individual differences, narrowing its object of investigation wherever possible until variability is no longer a factor, or until it is found to take the form of a "chance" distribution.

Differential psychology likewise deals with the horizontal dimension, but is concerned with the range and dispersion of variation. One branch of this method is *correlational* psychology, another *factor analysis*, which characteristically follows through two, or sometimes more, functions (*e.g.*, a, b, c, d). As a result the coexistence of these functions in the mental life of men may be demonstrated. By this method it may be shown that certain functions are more commonly related in a population than certain other functions. But the patterning of the individual functions in the *individual* case is never directly considered.

The *method of group comparison*, a branch of differential psychology, is concerned with the differences between groups of subjects in respect to any one or more of the functions. The separation of the sexes in Figure 1 illustrates the possibilities in the field of sex differences. Racial psychology employs the same method.

Psychography. This movement is a direct offspring of differential psychology. It assumes that the individual is the sum-total of his scores on all the separate, measurable, psychological functions. In

Figure 1, for example, Paul is represented by plotting his standings in respect to functions a, b, c, d, m, n, o, *etc.*[12] This method is the last resort of those who believe in differential psychology, but who find that a single score in terms of deviation from the average fails

Examples of Elementary Functions	Paul	Peter	Henry	John	Mary	Lucy	Patricia	Jane
general intelligence	a....	....	....	....	....	....	....	....
mechanical aptitude	b....	....	....	....	....	....	....	....
rote memory	c....	....	....	....	....	....	....	....
retentivity	d....	....	....	....	....	....	....	....
auditory threshold	m....	....	....	....	....	....	....	....
red-green acuity	n....	....	....	....	....	....	....	....
muscle tonus	o....	....	....	....	....	....	....	....
affective range	u....	....	....	....	....	....	....	....
perseveration	v....	....	....	....	....	....	....	....
gregariousness	w...	....	....	....	....	....	....	....
political prejudice	x....	....	....	....	....	....	....	....

FIGURE 1

A Scheme for the Comparison of Methods

to represent the individual. Having found nothing admirable in one unit, they try many units.

Toulouse's study of Poincaré may be taken as an example.[13] Although himself an experimental psychologist, Toulouse was not content with the study of mind-in-general, or as he said, of what is "common to an imbecile and to an Aristotle." For this reason he undertook, in terms of deviations from the average, an analysis of the psychological functions of a single individual. He chose the gifted

[12] Cf. Stern, *op. cit.*, pp. 327-371.
[13] E. Toulouse, *Henri Poincaré*, 1910.

mathematician Poincaré as his subject. He determined that Poincaré
had a memory span of eleven digits, that his associations with numbers were prolific, that he had superior auditory imagery, and possessed a relatively stable synaesthesia (*audition colorée*), that he
suffered from insomnia, had a fondness for music and not for hunting, and that he seemed obsessed by his work. Surveying his efforts
Toulouse admits that the genius of Poincaré was somehow provok-
ingly absent from his "synthesis." [14]

Toulouse neglected especially the dynamic factors involved in
the mental life of his subject. Interests, drives, values, and motives,
complexes, sentiments, desires, and ambitions were slighted. A modern
psychograph would be stronger for its inclusion of such material.
But no psychograph escapes from the implication that the individual
is merely the sum of separate functions which are studied in terms
of deviations from the average.

Psychoanalysis. Unlike psychographic methods, psychoanalysis
does not hold a quantitative view of mental organization. It seeks to
understand *patterns* of desire and conflict. Since it deals in prolonged
sessions with the examination of single persons it would seem at first
sight to be a true science of individuality. Its method is clearly
superior for disclosing the interlocking of dispositions and capacities
in each individual life, and for tracing the dependence of present outlooks upon past experiences.

But in spite of its valuable contributions (to be considered in
Chapter VI) psychoanalysis fails to fulfill all the requirements of a
science of individuality. (1) Like general psychology it is preoccupied with the search for universal causes. The properties of the unconscious, it holds, are archaic and therefore the same for all people.
The desires of the infant, his fixations, joys, fears, and the stages
of development through which he passes are prescribed; the three-
fold division of the self: the super-ego, the ego, and the id permit
no variation; the behavior of people follows a conceptualized standard and has essentially uniform significance. (2) Psychoanalysis is
doctrinaire. The System is sacrosanct. Its design is traced upon the
patient, and then—*mirabile dictu*—is discovered to exist there. The
danger of fascination with theory is not unrecognized by psycho-

[14] Even before Toulouse undertook his psychography B. Pérez attempted similar
"synthetic" portraits, stressing qualities of temperament and dealing with ordinary
individuals rather than genius. His results were no more satisfactory. Cf. *Le
caractère de l'enfant à l'homme,* 1892.

analysts themselves. No doubt in their practice many of them indi-
vidualize the lives of their patients more than they do in their theory.
It is likewise common for one school of psychoanalysis to accuse
another of slavery to creed; but it is not apparent which school is
free to cast the first stone. (3) Psychoanalysis is not an eclectic movement; it has made virtually no contact with any other branch of
psychology. The somewhat fantastic metaphors it employs show how
little it has profited from the antecedent labors of psychological
science. Much is known to general psychology about the unconscious
operations of the mind, the processes of remembering, forgetting,
dreaming, inhibiting, learning, reasoning, self-knowledge, and even
about the mechanisms of motive and desire, and all of this knowledge
psychoanalysis should, but does not, employ. No school of psychology can afford such splendid isolation.

(4) The detachment of psychoanalysis from general psychology
is due to its one-sided interest in the problems of psychopathology.
Its doctrines have considerable pertinence in the study of the psycho-
neuroses. Without modification, however, they are applied repeatedly
to healthy mental processes; balance is interpreted in the same way
as lack of balance; the sane are represented by the insane. The view
that normality may be studied through the lens of abnormality is remarkably common, but it is none the less debatable. Even if it be
sound, the equation should be reversible, and the study of normality
should illuminate the field of abnormality. But this possibility is persistently overlooked.

(5) Finally, the bulk of personal motives and traits which comprise the individual are not, as psychoanalysis claims, necessarily
rooted in the unconscious. They cannot all be understood simply by
the art of deep-sea diving. Even where links are correctly traced
between present trends and the experiences of childhood, they have
often been so long rusted and broken that they are not, as analysts
maintain, the bonds in the present structure of an individual's life;
in neurotics, perhaps, but in most people, no. Traits and interests,
like plants, are capable of casting aside the shell of the seed from
which they grew. Their direction of growth is upward into the
future, and not downward into the past. In short, conscious motives
and manifest behavior are of as great significance as are repressed
motives and latent dispositions.

Typologies. Any doctrine of types is a halfway approach to the
problem of individuality, and nothing more. The typologist is ob-

viously dissatisfied with a psychology of mind-in-general. He wishes to account for variety in human nature. It seems, however, that the task fatigues him, for he stops on the way somewhere between the abandoned "average" mind and the undiscovered fact that each individual is unique. It is difficult to disprove any given doctrine of type, particularly if "mixed types" are admitted, as they usually are. A type means nothing more than that certain people resemble other people *in some respect*. One may say, there are three types of people: those who use a convex tooth brush, those who use a concave, and those who use a straight tooth brush, plus, of course, the mixed type which uses sometimes one kind and sometimes another (or none at all). This is a valid typology if one is interested in tooth brushes. Similarly, there are people who are extroverted, those who are introverted, and those who are both. This, too, is true, if one is interested in extroversion and introversion. But the weakness lies in the narrowness of the interest. Should the investigator concern himself *both* with the habits of brushing teeth and with extroversion, he would find that a given individual belongs to more than one type. And if he is interested in *all* aspects of behavior, the individual turns out to have innumerable, unco-ordinated memberships. The patterning of these memberships within the person himself is overlooked.

Figure 2 illustrates the fact that typological psychology has a tangential, and not a direct, bearing upon individuality. John, let it be supposed, is validly classified in four types. He resembles Messrs. A, B, C, D in physical features, and he resembles other individuals (E, F, G, H) in respect to his introversion, still others in imagery, and others in vocational interests. Each classification is correct, but John as an individual is almost untouched. His mental functions have been related to similar functions in *other* individuals, and have not been related within the organic field of his own nature to one another. Similarly every other individual escapes total inclusion; each is of a type only with respect to *some one segment* of his nature. Like general psychology, typology deals with abstracted attributes; its only advantage is that the abstracted attributes it selects are not regarded as universally distributed; only certain people have them.

Here and there a typologist will argue that *his* schema is inclusive, that when John is fitted into *his* system, John's position will be determined not only for one mental function but for all. The typology of Kretschmer (cf. pp. 73-76), it is sometimes claimed, is *complete*. If

John has such and such a physique, he must have such and such a temperament, together with a certain outlook upon life, a characteristic form of fantasy, and a particular manner of adjusting to the world. But such claims are made also for other typologies which do

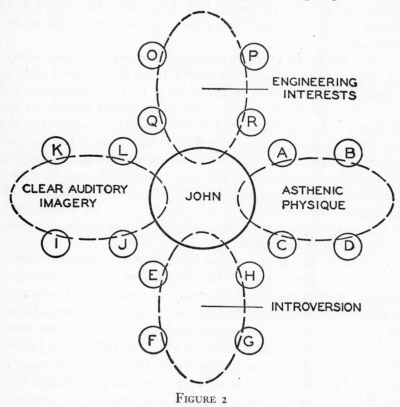

FIGURE 2

Typology *vs.* Individuality
(Dotted ellipses signify types; solid circles, individuals)

not overlap with Kretschmer's at all. Typologies that are independent of one another cannot each be all-embracing. Every typological doctrine tends toward extravagance. In reality types are valid only for a limited characteristic; they embrace a segment of individuality, but never the total individual.[15]

Gestalt Psychology. During the past twenty years there have been many rebels within the ranks of general psychology attacking its

[15] Some of the most influential historical doctrines of type are described in Chapter III, and the critique of the concept is resumed in Chapter XI.

long-entrenched assumption that elements abstracted from individual experience are the proper data of the science. Not every opponent of elementarism, to be sure, is a *Gestalt* psychologist, but they all agree well enough that the time has come for a new emphasis upon the totalities and patterns of mental life. The special movement known as *Gestalt* psychology has four clear implications for the study of individuality.

1. It deliberately shifts its emphasis from the traditional study of single segments of behavior abstracted from their natural setting to the study of the net-work of functions as they interpenetrate in the life of the organism. It may be instructive, writes Köhler, to study one hundred hearts together, but functionally considered a single heart has more in common with a pair of lungs than it has with other hearts.[16] Both general psychology and the psychology of individual differences have, as it were, studied hearts removed from their natural setting. A psychology of individuality will study the functions of an organism as they are related to other functions of the *same* organism, and not as they are related, through abstraction, to the activities of entirely different organisms.

2. Another crucial innovation lies in Lewin's distinction between genotypes and phenotypes.[17] The former are causal categories, the latter are descriptive. When similarity of *appearance* is observed in the behavior of different individuals the similarity in question may be said to constitute one phenotype, but not necessarily one and the same genotype. What appears to be the same effect may be due to radically different causes. For example, two individuals may have introverted natures (and thus belong to the same phenotype), but for very different reasons, one because of hereditary determination, and the other because of certain harsh experiences. Conversely, the same genotype, say an attack of infantile paralysis, may in the pattern of one individual's life result in shyness, self-consciousness, and an attitude of defeat, in another the result may be compensation, vigor, and accomplishment. This distinction provides a more flexible treatment of individuality, for, according to it, the "same" cause, in the context of different lives, may produce contrasting effects instead of uniformity.

3. Such an emphasis upon the individuality of motivational sys-

[16] W. Köhler, *Gestalt Psychology*, 1929, p. 351.
[17] K. Lewin, *Gesetz und Experiment in der Psychologie*. Reprinted from *Symposion*, 1927, 5, 375-421.

tems .s an improvement over the standard classification of impulses and drives advanced by psychoanalysis and by instinct-psychology. It provides also a corrective to the overemphasis upon the *origin* of traits. According to *Gestalt* psychology, the form of behavior may be determined by goals whose attainment lies in the future as well as by events of the past. Early habits are at best only one factor in a large system of forces determining at any given moment the form that individuality will take.[18]

4. A final bearing of *Gestalt* theory upon the study of individuals lies in its doctrine of the nature of understanding. Not only is the person well-structured, but he is *perceived* as well-structured. Elementarism fails to account both for the organization of the individual mind and for the way in which it is understood by others. The argument has far-reaching significance, but it is too complex for discussion here. It will be considered in detail in Chapter XIX.

The Psychology of Verstehen. This related school of thought is even more radical than *Gestalt* psychology. According to it there must be two separate and distinct psychologies, one to deal in the historic way with *elements* and the other to deal only with *structures;* there is no common ground between them. The psychology of elements "destroys the meaningful totalities of life," whereas the psychology of structures seeks deliberately the meaningful relation between the acts and experiences of the person.[19] The second method is the better, for it attempts to *understand* each unique mental life, without destroying its integrity.

This is a drastic remedy for psychology's ailment. Much would be lost by discarding altogether the methods of general and differential psychology. Properly modified and adapted they can be employed in the study of individuality, and their past accomplishments in this direction are not altogether negligible. The problems of individuality are so complex that no legitimate method can be excluded. It would be foolish to repudiate the assistance of the psychology of elements wherever it may be accepted with profit. Psychology needs a broadening of outlook, not a schism.

[18] This virtue of *Gestalt* psychology turns out sometimes to be a limitation, for so complete is its emphasis upon "forces actually at work at a given moment" that it has difficulty in treating the consistency of the individual over a period of time. Disposition, latency, continuity, and the life-history are neglected problems. Even K. Lewin's *Dynamic Theory of Personality*, 1935, deals almost entirely with the behavior of the individual in momentary (contemporaneous) "fields of force."

[19] E. Spranger, *Types of Men*, trans. 1928, chap. i.

Purposive Psychologies. Wherever the conception of goal or purpose is paramount in psychology, there lies the implication that a personal life is involved. It is not, however, correct to assume that all dynamic psychologies are interested in the problem of individuality. In fact most of the doctrines of instinct, desire, need, propensity, attitude, or drive have been strictly within the tradition of the psychology of mind-in-general. Nevertheless, the purposive outlook makes the transition to individuality easier. Commencing in his *Dynamic Psychology* with an acceptance of the doctrine of common instincts, R. S. Woodworth arrives ultimately at a doctrine of the individuality of motive. Each person in the course of his life modifies his common hereditary equipment of impulses in ways that are peculiar to himself; he likewise develops new and autonomous interests. With the acceptance of this doctrine the ground is obviously prepared for a dynamic psychology of the *individual*. This is a point of view of crucial significance and is developed at length in Chapter VII of this volume.

Personalistic Psychology. The logical culmination of interest in the individual is the creation of a personalistic psychology. The chief tenet of this school of thought is that every mental function is embedded in a personal life. In no concrete sense is there such a thing as intelligence, space perception, color discrimination or choice reaction; there are only *people* who are capable of performing such activities and of having such experiences. It is improper to speak of the growth of skill, of vocabulary, or of knowledge; there is no growth excepting in the *person;* it is as part of *his* development that skill is enhanced, that vocabulary and knowledge are extended. Nor can motives ever be studied apart from their personal setting, they represent always the striving of a total organism toward its objective.

It is an interesting fact that the most prominent representative of personalistic psychology, William Stern, was in past years the leading figure in the study of differential psychology. It was in fact his perception of the limitations of the psychology of individual differences, based upon long experience, that led him to attempt a more adequate formulation of the psychology of individuality.[20] Personalistic psychology is still a relatively new school. Its guiding lines have been laid, but it awaits the rounding out that factual research alone

[20] W. Stern, *Differentielle Psychologie*, 3d ed., 1921, p. 12; *History of Psychology in Autobiography* (ed., C. C. Murchison), Vol. I, 1930, pp. 360 f.; *General Psychology from the Personalistic Standpoint*, trans. 1937.

can give. Since, in a sense, this volume itself is a contribution to the same line of thought, further consideration may be postponed until all the evidence is assembled. The final chapter will return to the problem.

EXTENDING THE HORIZONS OF PSYCHOLOGY

This chapter has dealt with a paradox. The scientific method, it is said, cannot study individuals. Yet within the province of scientific psychology several radical movements in the past fifty years have been focusing their interest with varying degrees of success upon the individual. Must it therefore be said that psychology, because of its growing interest in this subject, is becoming less and less scientific?

Definitions are always arbitrary, even those in science. Therefore anyone who wishes to restrict the meaning of the sacred phrase, "the scientific method," to the three-fold process of analysis, abstraction, and generalization is at liberty to do so. If the psychologist wishes to accept the same narrow definition, he too is free. But in doing so he must not transform what is merely an artifice of method into a doctrine of reality. Memory, intelligence, reaction, perception, sensation, volition, and all like processes are real only in so far as they are organic; they are nothing more than *attributes* of personal activity. General psychology may, if it chooses, treat them as data, but the abstraction thus committed should be acknowledged. Titchener, a most ascetic methodologist, defined psychology as the study of experience considered as *dependent upon the experiencing person*.[21] It would be impossible to devise a definition more satisfactory from the standpoint of personalistic psychology! But Titchener was so faithful to the narrower traditions of science that he did not appreciate the implications of his own definition. He sought only general laws of experience *abstracted from* the person. The logic of nature forced him to recognize the pre-eminence of the individual, but the conventions of science forced him to forget it.

John Stuart Mill argued strongly that all definition in science must be "progressive and provisional," for "any extension of knowledge or alteration in the current opinion respecting the subject-matter, may lead to a change more or less extensive in the particulars included in the science." [22] At the present time current opinion in

[21] E. B. Titchener, *Text-book of Psychology*, p. 8.
[22] J. S. Mill, *System of Logic*, Book I, chap. viii, Sect. 4.

psychology favors the inclusion of the phenomenon of individuality. Therefore, no frozen definition should be allowed to interfere with the progress of investigation. Novel and somewhat daring methods will be required, and they should not be prejudged. The horizon is expanding. Yet there are no grounds for scientific dismay. The psychologists now bent upon the study of individuals are not likely to forget the rules they have learned in the laboratory for diminishing the risk of error in their observations. Simply because they wish a more liberal conception of science and of its methods, they do not therefore demand abolition of controls and a return to mysticism.

Consider for a moment the method of experiment. It is the most serviceable technique of the exact sciences. At first glance it might seem inapplicable to the study of individuality. For one thing in order to secure suitable controls it is customary to isolate a *simple* segment of behavior for experiment, whereas individuality can never be secured a second time in the same way. The organism changes, and each direction of change influences all the interdependent functions. Doubt concerning the suitability of experiment for the study of the person has been expressed by Stern,

> The more exact [for general psychology] an experiment is—that is, the more elementary and isolated the phenomenon, and the more constant the conditions—the greater is its artificiality and the greater its distance from the study of the individual. Methods must above all else be suited to the problem in hand, and the problems set by general psychology and by the psychology of the individual are quite different.[23]

An experiment, as everyone knows, involves exact observation and such control as admits of the isolation and the variation of conditioning factors. As a result of these requirements experiments frequently seem *lebensfern,* far removed from the study of the individual. *But they need not be.* In recent years there have been satisfactory experiments dealing with complex levels of behavior—studies of gait and handwriting, vocal expression, personal style of work, and individual modes of thought, intuitive (non-analytical) judgments, and many other unorthodox subjects. In these studies, as Chapter XVI will show, the standards of experimentation have been well preserved, and yet the investigations conducted at a new level of complexity. If the experiments are not susceptible of exact repeti-

[23] W. Stern, *Differentielle Psychologie*, p. 34.

tion, neither, strictly speaking, are those of elementaristic psychology. Organisms continually change, and this fact must necessarily alter the behavior of elements as well as of patterns.

To be sure, some problems of individuality completely elude the experimental method. One cannot approach experimentally such experiences as embarrassment, remorse, falling in love, or religious ecstasy. Wherever experiment is feasible it is to be preferred, where it is not, the problems still remain, and other methods must be employed. Psychology is not exclusively experimental in its method, but neither for that matter is the eminently respectable science of astronomy.

Will a science treating individuals be able to evolve laws? The answer depends upon the conception of law. As law is ordinarily understood, it will not. If a law is a statement of an invariable association common to an entire class of objects, then, as Stern says, "individuality is the asymptote of the science that seeks laws."

General laws have value in depicting the common ground upon which all individual minds meet. But this common ground is really a no-man's land. When the investigator turns his eyes upon the individual he finds that in him all laws are modified, or as Wundt would have it, exceptions always occur. But a more liberal interpretation of the nature of law, considering it to be *any uniformity that is observed in the natural order,* is equally possible. In this sense, each person by himself is actually a special law of nature, so too is any structural occurrence within the pattern of his life. Though individuality is never twice repeated, it represents nevertheless order in nature. If it were possible to grasp the complex totalities within a single individual life, to understand their formation, reciprocal action, directional tendencies, and dynamics—even though the discovery should have no wider application—it would be an achievement quite as significant as the establishment of any *common* law.

As long ago as 1858, Samuel Bailey foresaw that the preoccupation of psychology with mind-in-general would result in the neglect of the single individual. Accordingly he proposed that *two* sciences be recognized.

> In reference to the division concerning Individual and Personal Character, I may remark that it would be advantageous on several accounts to keep it distinct from Psychology, which, when confined to its proper objects, is chiefly occupied with describing, classifying and bringing under general laws, the phenomena of consciousness

common to all mankind, and deals with Individual Character only incidentally and briefly—too briefly for the importance of the subject.[24]

Bailey's advice that characterology be kept distinct from psychology has never been observed in English speaking countries. On the continent, however, something of the kind has taken place. Since Bahnsen's work of 1867 a tradition of independent characterology has flourished. But its independence of psychology has unfortunately meant a greater dependence upon guess-work, figurative discourse, and esoteric metaphysics. The advice to study "personal character" without the aid of a general and experimental psychology is dark counsel.

The proposal to distinguish sharply between the study of general principles and the study of the individual case has taken many other forms. The philosopher Windelband, for example, proposed to separate the *nomothetic* from the *idiographic* disciplines.[25] The former, he held, seek only general laws and employ only those procedures admitted by the exact sciences. Psychology in the main has been striving to make of itself a completely nomothetic discipline. The idiographic sciences, such as history, biography, and literature, on the other hand, endeavor to understand some *particular* event in nature or in society. A psychology of individuality would be essentially idiographic.

The dichotomy, however, is too sharp: it requires a psychology divided against itself. As in the case of the two psychologies (the analytical and the descriptive) advocated by Dilthey and Spranger, the division is too drastic. It is more helpful to regard the two methods as overlapping and as contributing to one another. In the field of medicine, diagnosis and therapy are idiographic procedures, but both rest intimately upon a knowledge of the common factors in disease, determined by the nomothetic sciences of bacteriology and biochemistry. Likewise, biography is clearly idiographic, and yet in the best biographies one finds an artful blend of generalization with individual portraiture. A complete study of the individual will embrace both approaches. Half a century ago this same conclusion was reached by the French psychiatrist, Azam. The science of character, he wrote, "cannot proceed by generalities, as does psychology, nor by individualities, as does art. It occupies an intermediate posi-

24 S. Bailey, *Letters on the Philosophy of the Human Mind*, 1855-58, II, 265.
25 W. Windelband, *Geschichte und Naturwissenschaft*, 3d edit., 1904. See also, R. Eisler, *Wörterbuch der philosophischen Begriffe*, 1904, p. 512.

tion." [26] One should now add that this "intermediate position" will fall properly within the scope of a *broadened* psychology.

The psychological study of individuality will continue in the manner of general psychology to employ experimentation, not on the simple level to be sure, but on the level of traits, interests, and the personal idiom. It will be interested in the laws of learning and in all genetic principles, but will attempt to co-ordinate these in the nexus of individuality. It will employ critical standards of observation, avoid the impressive single instance, and profit from all other hard-earned lessons of psychological science. But the interest will be broader. It will embrace the problem of intra-individual consistency as well as inter-individual uniformities; it will not be content with the discovery of laws pertaining to mind-in-general, but will seek also to understand the lawful tendencies of minds-in-particular. But there is no need for two disciplines. Psychology can treat both types of subjects. Its position will be stronger for having enlarged its horizon. The individual has now taken his place within this horizon, and he has come to stay. To study him older methods will be adapted and new ones invented, as exact as the subject will permit.

If there are psychologists who in the face of this growing movement still declare that the study of the individual is not and never can be a part of science, they must now be left alone with their views. The psychological study of individuality is being undertaken with profound seriousness; no blind loyalty to an anachronistic ideal can prevent it. One may call it science or not science, as one chooses. Long before the method of natural science attained its commanding position with psychology paddling in its wake, there was an ancient meaning of *Scientia*. It prescribed no method; it set no limits; it signified simply *knowledge*.

[26] É. Azam, *Le caractère dans la santé et dans la maladie*, 1887, p. vi.

CHAPTER II

DEFINING PERSONALITY

But this word *persona* has rolled along with wonderful bounds, striking right and left, suggesting new thoughts, stirring up clouds of controversy, and occupying to the present day a prominent place in all discussions on theology and philosophy, though few only of those who use it know how it came to be there.

—*F. Max Müller*

In the previous chapter the term *individuality* was used to signify the separateness and uniqueness of each human being. But mere separateness and uniqueness are not the psychologist's chief concern. Wasps and mice, trees and stones possess this elementary distinction. In addition to separateness and uniqueness a human being displays *psychological* individuality, an amazingly complex organization comprising his distinctive habits of thought and expression, his attitudes, traits and interests, and his own peculiar philosophy of life. It is the total manifold psycho-physical individuality, commonly referred to as *personality*, that engages the attention of the psychologist.[1]

The term "personality" expresses admirably this interest of the psychologist, and yet it is a perilous one for him to use unless he is aware of its many meanings. Since it is remarkably elastic, its use in any context seldom is challenged. Books and periodicals carry it in their titles for no apparent reason other than its cadence, its general attractiveness, and everlasting interest. Both writer and reader lose their way in its ineffectual vagueness, and matters are made much worse by the depreciation of the word in the hands of journalists,

[1] The question whether animals have personality in the psychologist's sense should probably be answered in the affirmative, for animals like people manifest individuality in their patterns of habit and expression. See, F. Schwangart, *Jahrbuch der Charakterologie*, 1928, 5, 101-140; also T. Schjelderup-Ebbe, in *A Handbook of Social Psychology*, 1935, chap. xx; D. Katz, "Characterology and Animal Psychology," *Univ. Maine Stud.*, 1930, No. 14, pp. 28-59. Nevertheless, the mental individuality of lower animals is too rudimentary to serve as a prototype of human personality, and for that reason will not be considered in this volume.

beauty doctors and peddlers of gold bricks labeled "self-improvement."

"Personality" is one of the most abstract words in our language, and like any abstract word suffering from excessive use,[2] its connotative significance is very broad, its denotative significance negligible. Scarcely any word is more versatile.

> Let us take such a word as *Person*. Nothing can be more abstract. It is neither male nor female, neither young nor old. As a noun it is hardly more than what *to be* is as a verb. In French it may even come to mean nobody. For if we ask our concièrge at Paris whether anybody has called on us during our absence, he will reply, "Personne, monsieur," which means, "Not a soul, sir." [3]

The only way to re-vitalize such a frayed concept is to trace its history. There is no single correct definition of "personality"; usage has sanctioned too many. Some of the meanings are psychological, some are not. The first task is to distinguish between them. The second is to select from among available psychological definitions one that best fits the phenomenon dealt with in this volume.

There is probably no single word of greater interest to philologists. To bring within a few pages the fruits of their investigations is a hazardous undertaking, but the only practicable alternative is to omit entirely historical conceptions, thereby isolating the present day psychology of personality from the history of human thought, a very common, but nevertheless very undesirable, practice.

The terms *personality* in English, *personnalité* in French, and *Persönlichkeit* in German closely resemble the *personalitas* of medieval Latin. In classical Latin *persona* alone was used, but its meanings are in so many respects equivalent to those of the modern terms that our historical sketch must commence with *persona* itself.

ETYMOLOGY AND EARLY HISTORY OF "PERSONA"

Persona originally denoted the theatrical mask first used in Greek drama and adopted about a hundred years before Christ by Roman players. (Legend has it that a popular Roman actor was responsible for the importation to hide his unfortunate squint.) The Greek designation for mask was *prosôpon*, a word having a vague resemblance to

[2] Thorndike lists *personality* in the eighth thousand of English terms arranged in order of frequency. E. L. Thorndike, *The Teachers' Word Book*, 1921.
[3] F. Max Müller, *Biographies of Words*, 1888, pp. 32 f.

persona. Several authorities regard the Latin term as a direct derivation from the Greek.[4] Critics of this theory point to the improbability
of such a marked alteration occurring in the form of the word. To
escape this difficulty other philologists favor its derivation from *peri
sôma* (around the body), and still others from the Etruscan and Old
Latin word *persum* (head or face).[5] Some trace its origin from the
Latin *per se una* (self-containing).[6]

The antecedent of *persona* favored by most authorities, however,
is the Latin phrase *per sonare* (to sound through).[7] According to this
theory the term had reference to the large mouth of the mask or
perhaps to a reed device inserted into it for projecting the voice of
the actor. Those who hold this view concede that from the very
beginning *persona,* by a metonymic change, referred not so much to
the vocal aspects of the mask as to its visual properties.

Whatever its antecedents may have been, no philologist denies
that *persona* at one time designated the theatrical mask. But drama
and life, the actor and the role, the assumed and the real character, are
too intimately related to withstand confusion. In rapid succession all
within classical times, a series of extensions and transformations took
place, converting this concrete noun into one that is abstract and
multiple in meaning. In the writings of Cicero (106-43 B.C.), probably not long after the word first appeared, are found at least four distinct meanings of *persona:* [8]

(a) as one appears to others (but not as one really is);
(b) the part someone (*e.g.,* a philosopher) plays in life;
(c) an assemblage of personal qualities that fit a man for his work;
(d) distinction and dignity (as in a style of writing).

[4] See H. Rheinfelder, "Das Wort 'Persona,'" *Zsch. f. roman. Philol.,* 1928,
Beiheft 77, pp. 22 ff.

[5] These various theories may be readily traced through Rheinfelder, *op. cit.,*
and Müller, *op. cit.*

[6] While this derivation is generally rejected it is of interest to observe its
emphasis upon the *unitary* nature of the person. Cf. S. Schlossmann, *Persona und
Προσῶπον im Recht und im christlichen Dogma,* 1906, p. 13 ftn.

[7] Among the writers accepting this derivation are: A. Trendelenburg, "Zur
Geschichte des Wortes Person," *Kantstudien,* 1908, 13, pp. 4 ff.; Müller, *op. cit.;*
J. B. Greenough and G. L. Kittredge, *Words and Their Ways in English Speech,*
1902, p. 268.
There is only one significant objection to this theory, namely, a conflict in
vowel quality. In *per sonare* the *o* is short, whereas in *persona* it becomes long.
Such alteration in the quality of root vowels is somewhat rare, although, as Müller
points out, by no means unknown.

[8] Cf. Müller, *op. cit.,* pp. 38 f.

The first meaning, of course, has the original significance of the mask; the second suggests real status, not the mere pretence; the third signifies the inner psychic qualities of the player himself; and the final meaning connotes importance and prestige which later were conveyed by the derivative term *personage*.

These early transformations are summarized in Figure 3. Starting with *Persona* as Mask, the four earliest derivative meanings are listed

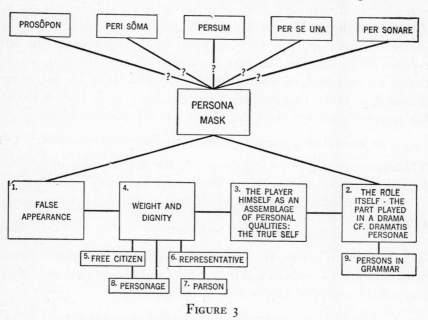

FIGURE 3

The Early Derivative Meaning of *Persona*

and numbered. Each serves as a radiant point for later semantic change. From them it is possible to derive all of the fifty types of definition listed in this chapter. Nearly all of these definitions are still in current use as accepted meanings for *person* or *personality*. It would be impossible to claim that the lines of connection here drawn are in every detail historically accurate. What is intended is a chart of relations of *meaning* rather than an exact chronology of change.

The first logical extension of *Persona* as Mask refers then to

$$\text{external appearance (not the true self).} \qquad (1)$$

The adjective *personatus* meant provided with, or wearing, a mask. Unlike *persona* it never took on the meaning of the true self. It was always fictitious, counterfeit, a pretense. The meaning is preserved today in Jung's doctrine of "persona" and in some popular definitions of personality (see p. 42).

The second root meaning signifies the

> character or role which the player assumes in the drama.   (2)

In German one may hear the phrase *"Er hat seine Person gut gespielt."* This meaning is likewise preserved in the still current phrase *dramatis personae.* The theater-goer of today is, however, not quite certain whether the *personae* are listed in the right or in the left column of his program; he does not know whether the parts in the drama are indicated, or whether the *personal names* of the actors are intended, or both. This confusion was possible even in ancient Rome, for *persona* often indicated the player himself, considered as

> an individual possessed of distinctive personal qualities.   (3)

This meaning, of greatest importance in the development of psychological definitions, appears as the third usage in Cicero's writings.

The fourth derivation, likewise found in Cicero, has the significance of

> prestige and dignity.   (4)

This meaning was eagerly assimilated into the Roman caste system, wherein some individuals had legal rights and obligations, and others did not. Hence *persona* was used to indicate

> the free born citizen (as distinguished from the slave).   (5)

Still in classical Latin, the term came to mean

> a representative (one who stands for a group or institution),   (6)

whence the Latin expression *persona grata.* The representative of the church came later to be called its

> parson (Anglo-Saxon, *persoun*).   (7)

Important persons, possessed of prestige and dignity (4) came also to be known as

> personages.   (8)

As a latter day example, the family name McPherson derives from the cluster of meanings expressed in definitions (5), (6), (7), and (8).

A by-path was created by the Latin grammarian Varro (116-26 B.C.) who early spoke of the

persons in grammar, (9)

a metaphor based upon the resemblance between dramatic and syntactical roles.

These definitions, as well as all those that follow, can be ordered according to their position in a continuum of meanings ranging from the external (false, mask-like) manner to the internal (true) self. This double and contradictory reference is the outstanding characteristic of the term *persona,* and of the contemporary term *personality* as well. *Personality means that which is assumed, non-essential, false, as well as that which is vital, inward, and essential.* Which meaning the psychologist should choose will be discussed later.

THEOLOGICAL MEANINGS

The choice of certain Church Fathers who used the term to designate

the Members of the Trinity (10)

markedly advanced the equivalence between *persona* and the inner (true) self. Many writers have speculated upon the remarkable transformation of a word which originally meant *assumed* manner, and came to have the *opposite* significance of *inner* nature, substance, and even essence.[9]

By the third century A.D. the elements of the Trinity were designated as *Personae.* At first there seemed to be danger here of an heretical error; for did not *persona* signify variable appearance, a mask-like pose? Would not a Deity assuming three alternative roles be forced to abandon two of them while representing the third? That such heresy was avoided is due no doubt to the flexible connotation of the term itself which made it possible to *think* of substance while *speaking* of masks; the Deity indeed subsisted in three Persons, but each shared the same essence. Although the matter was thus settled to the satisfaction of the Church Fathers, later theologians continued for

[9] Cf. C. Webb, *God and Personality,* 1919, *e.g.,* p. 20 and p. 36; A. Trendelenburg, *op. cit.,* p. 12; R. Hirzel, "Die Person," *Sitz. d. kön. Bayer. Akad. d. Wissenschaften,* 1914, 10, p. 53. P. Carus, *Personality,* 1911, p. 18; H. Rheinfelder, *op. cit.,* p. 165.

long to discuss the paradox of varied appearance and single substance.[10]

PHILOSOPHICAL MEANINGS

Through associating the concept of Person with true essence the
early theologians helped prepare the way for the celebrated definition
given by Boëthius in the sixth century:

Persona est substantia individua rationalis naturae. (11)

Taking the substantial nature of the person for granted Boëthius adds
the attribute of rationality, thus breaking ground for a long line of
subsequent philosophical definitions of personality.

The definition given by Boëthius was satisfactory to virtually all
the philosophers of the Middle Ages. St. Thomas Aquinas exalted the
person above every other reality observed in nature; nothing, he
thought, was superior in dignity to the beings who possess rational
individuality.[11] The cultivation of personality was not explicitly emphasized in medieval ethics, but inasmuch as man should live a life that
is rational, the growth of personality was clearly an implied good.[12]
In this manner the emphasis was gradually taken from Aristotle's
belief that the individual existed for the good of the species, and came
to be placed upon respect for the integrity and value of the individual. This trend reached its culmination in later romanticism and in
personalistic ethics.

Christian Wolff emphasized as the chief criteria of the person

self-consciousness and memory.[13] (12)

This view is not unlike that of Leibnitz who defined a person as a

substance gifted with understanding.[14] (13)

[10] Cf. S. Schlossmann, *op. cit.*

[11] For the place of personality in Scholastic philosophy of value see E. Gilson,
"L'ésprit de la philosophie médiévale," chap. x of *Le personnalisme chrétien*, 1932.

[12] Classical Latin employed only *persona, personalis* (adj.) and *personaliter*
(adv.). The substantive *personalitas* is not found until medieval Latin (Rheinfelder,
op. cit., pp. 155 ff.). It was a characteristic of nouns based upon the adjectival root
and formed in this way, that they gained somewhat in abstractness. The difference
in meaning, however, between *personalitas* and *persona* should not be exaggerated.
The break in the form of the word does not correspond to an equally sharp change
of meaning.

[13] "*Persona* dicitur ens, quod memoriam sui conservat, hoc est, meminit, se
esse idem illud ens quod ante in hoc vel isto fuit stato." *Psychologia rationalis*, 1734,
sec. 741, p. 660.

[14] G. W. Leibnitz, *Hauptschriften zur Grundlegung der Philosophie* (ed. by
E. Cassirer), 1906, Vol. II, p. 184.

Locke stressed still more the attribute of self-consciousness.[15] A person for Locke is

> a thinking, intelligent being, that has reason and reflection and can consider self as itself. (14)

In more recent times Windelband has reinforced Locke's definition. Personality is

> individuality which has become objective to itself. (15)

This capacity is possessed in varying degrees by different individuals, so that one man may possess more personality than another.[16]

Rickert returns to the purely metaphysical conception of personality as essence.[17] The true personality is to a large degree

> the indivisible center, and only in the periphery do the processes of alteration take place. (16)

Since these philosophical definitions with their varying emphasis upon rationality, self-consciousness, and the subjective core of a man's being, are indistinguishable from various parallel conceptions of the Self, some writers explicitly equate personality with

> Selfhood.[18] (17)

Personeity was used by Coleridge in the nineteenth century as equivalent to selfhood, but the term did not take root.

Other philosophical definitions consider personality as an *ethical* rather than a metaphysical conception. There are writers, for example, who regard it as the ideal and perfect attribute of Being, never fully attained by human kind. To Lotze, for example, personality was

> . the ideal of perfection (18)

reached only by God though approached in varying degrees by men.[19] This is likewise Webb's view: personality is "suggested by what we find in men" but "only imperfectly realized in them." [20]

---

[15] *An Essay Concerning Human Understanding*, Book II, chap. xxvii, sec. 9.
[16] W. Windelband, *An Introduction to Philosophy*, trans. 1921, p. 281.
[17] H. Rickert, *Die Grenzen der naturwissenschaftlichen Begriffsbildung*, 3d ed., 1921, p. 237.
[18] Cf. Roberta Crutcher, *Personality and Reason*, 1931, p. 75.
[19] H. Lotze, *Microcosmos*, 4th ed., 1897, p. 682.
[20] Webb, *op. cit.*, p. 21.

Also one psychologist, William Stern, has maintained that the fully fashioned personality is that at which men aim but never fully attain.[21] The significance of this doctrine lies in its emphasis upon the continuous growth and development of all personal characteristics. The personality is always striving for greater completeness in accordance with its own ideals. This point of view might be phrased as

> the person being formed by unattained ideals   (19)

The conception of personality as an ideal is exalted still further in Romanticism.[22] Goethe, for example, regarded personality as the

> supreme value.[23]   (20)

Like Goethe, Nietzsche and William von Humbolt, who spoke often of personality, would not have man sacrifice his integral, entire self to any one part of his nature.

A somewhat more sedate expression of the ethics of personal integrity is found in Kant. "Everything in creation, except one thing, is subject to the power of man, and can be used by man as a means to an end; but man himself, man the rational creature, is an end in himself. He is the subject of moral law and is sacred by virtue of the autonomy of his individual freedom. . . .

> Personality exhibits palpably before our bodily eyes the sublimity of our nature." [24]   (21)

The so-called ethics of self-realization, placing higher value upon the development of the individual personality than upon any other goal, has, of course, a Kantian origin. One illustrative definition will suffice. "Personality is

[21] William Stern, *Die menschliche Persönlichkeit*, 1923, p. 20.

[22] For an exposition see T. J. McCormack, "Personality, A Study in the History of Verbal Meanings," *Ment. Hygiene*, 1931, 15, 34-44.

[23] "Volk und Knecht und Überwinder,
      Sie gestehn zu jeder Zeit:
      Höchstes Glück der Erdenkinder
      Sei nur die Persönlichkeit."
            West-östlicher Divan, Buch Suleika.

[24] *Kritik der praktischen Vernunft, Kant's gesammelte Schriften*, Bd. V. (Reimer Verlag), 1908, p. 87.

that quality in every man which makes him worth
while, aside from the uses to which he may be put by
his fellows." [25]
(22)

Kantian ethics is commonly considered likewise to be a starting
point for personalistic doctrines. Some of these take a voluntaristic
turn. Thus Hetherington and Muirhead define personality as

"that form of individuality . . . which is rendered possible by the possession of mind and will. To be a person
is to be one and indivisible, but it is a unity that is
achieved, not by the suppression of natural instincts,
temperament, and capacities, but by the permeation of
them with a common spirit—the power of finding freedom, not *from* them but *in* them." [26]
(23)

Personalistic philosophies agree (a) that the personality is of supreme value, (b) that persons are to be distinguished metaphysically
from things, and (c) that subjective experience is the final psychological court of appeal. According to Bowne, "personality can never
be construed as a product or compound; it can only be experienced
as a fact." [27]

"The essential meaning of personality is selfhood, self-
consciousness, self-control, and the power to know.
These elements have no corporeal significance." [28]
(24)

On the other hand, Stern, though a personalist, does not deny corporeal significance to personality, but declares the person to be "psychophysically neutral,"

a multiform dynamic unity.[29]
(25)

The personalistic position has importance for psychology in so
far as it focuses attention upon the organization of the individual
mental life; but its significance becomes metapsychological when, for
example, it treats institutions, nations, or God as "persons." This
super-individual realism is illustrated in Kant's doctrine that

[25] M. F. Adler, in *Essays in Honor of John Dewey*, 1929, p. 8.
The ethics of self-realization is expounded by James Seth, *A Study of Ethical
Principles*, rev. ed., 1904; J. Dewey and J. H. Tufts, *Ethics*, 1908; R. C. Cabot
The Meaning of Right and Wrong, 1933.
[26] H. I. W. Hetherington and J. H. Muirhead, *Social Purpose*, 1918, p. 104.
[27] B. P. Bowne, *Personalism*, 1908, p. 264.
[28] *Ibid.*, p. 266.
[29] W. Stern, *Die menschliche Persönlichkeit*, p. 4.

"A person is a rational being with rights; if he has duties too, he is a man; if not, he is a God." [30]   (26)

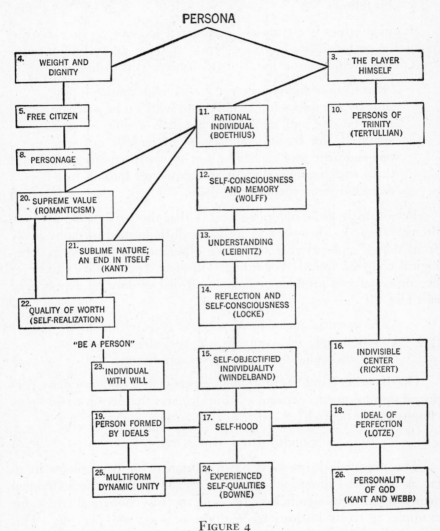

PERSONA

4. WEIGHT AND DIGNITY

3. THE PLAYER HIMSELF

5. FREE CITIZEN

11. RATIONAL INDIVIDUAL (BOETHIUS)

10. PERSONS OF TRINITY (TERTULLIAN)

8. PERSONAGE

12. SELF-CONSCIOUSNESS AND MEMORY (WOLFF)

20. SUPREME VALUE (ROMANTICISM)

21. SUBLIME NATURE; AN END IN ITSELF (KANT)

13. UNDERSTANDING (LEIBNITZ)

14. REFLECTION AND SELF-CONSCIOUSNESS (LOCKE)

22. QUALITY OF WORTH (SELF-REALIZATION)

"BE A PERSON"

15. SELF-OBJECTIFIED INDIVIDUALITY (WINDELBAND)

16. INDIVISIBLE CENTER (RICKERT)

23. INDIVIDUAL WITH WILL

19. PERSON FORMED BY IDEALS

17. SELF-HOOD

18. IDEAL OF PERFECTION (LOTZE)

25. MULTIFORM DYNAMIC UNITY

24. EXPERIENCED SELF-QUALITIES (BOWNE)

26. PERSONALITY OF GOD (KANT AND WEBB)

FIGURE 4

Some Inter-relations of the Philosophical Meanings of Personality

These varied philosophical conceptions of personality may greatly enrich the psychologist's view of his problem, even though in many instances they extend far beyond his professional sphere. In particular, definitions (11), (12), (14), (19) and (25) suggest the

[30] C. C. J. Webb, *Kant's Philosophy of Religion*, 1926, pp. 181 f.

attributes of *rationality, self-consciousness, conative striving,* and *absolute uniqueness* that ought surely find their way into the psychologist's store. With the metaphysical and ethical conceptions he will have less to do. Figure 4 summarizes the expansion of meaning of personality in the hands of theologians and philosophers. Again it must be said that the connecting lines in the diagram do not necessarily represent historical currents of *influence* but serve primarily to call attention to similarities or extensions of *meaning.*

JURISTIC MEANINGS

It was established by Justinian that a slave was not a person. Slaves were held to be a-personal. Only freeborn men had the dignity of persons; see Definition (5). It was against such social discrimination that the Christian moralists raised their cry. Each man, they insisted, is a person. Although yielding finally to this moral suasion, the juristic conception of the nature of the person began with the Roman Code. Since, according to this Code, only freeborn citizens could be bearers of rights, claiming the privileges and protection of law, it followed that a person was

any individual enjoying legal status.   (27)

In time the individual's material possessions with which the law likewise had concern came to be known as his *personalty.*

In modern times, in civilized countries, *all* individuals may claim the protection of law, and hence the standard legal conception of the nature of the person has broadened out, showing clearly the influence of Christian moral doctrine: today a person at law is "any being having life, intelligence, will, and separate individual existence, distinguished from an irrational brute and inanimate thing; a human being, as including body and mind; an individual of the human race; a living person, composed of body and soul; a man, woman, or child; a moral agent; a self-conscious being; the whole man." [31] This generous definition makes person equivalent to

the living human being in his entirety.   (28)

In the course of its development the law came to embrace not only the rights and duties of *individual* human beings, but of whole

[31] *Corpus Juris* (ed. by W. Mack & D. J. Kiser), 1929, Vol. 48, sec. i, pp. 1037 f.

groups of people, of "corporations." There grew up therefore the conception that a person might be

an incorporated group of people. (29)

Such a group, to be sure, is generally designated as an "artificial person,"[32] though there are some who argue that corporate groups are "real" enough from a philosophical point of view.[33]

Closely related to this juristic conception of the "group person" are many of the group-mind doctrines found in idealistic philosophy. An illustration may be taken from Royce:

> "A genuinely and loyally united community which
> lives a coherent life is in a perfectly literal sense a
> person."[34] (30)

Similar is the statement quoted by a newspaper from an address given by Nicholas Murray Butler, president of Columbia University, "Each nation is a moral personality with a mind and heart and soul." Such definitions extend the concept of personality far beyond the individual-organic locus with which the psychologist prefers to deal. Nevertheless it is necessary to note these trans-individual definitions, for they serve as a background to the numerous sociological conceptions next to be reviewed. The preceding juristic definitions as well as the sociological definitions that follow are summarized in Figure 5.

SOCIOLOGICAL MEANINGS

Definition (28) held that person may mean simply an individual human being. When we ask, for example, "How many persons were there?" nothing more is intended than an inquiry concerning the number of living beings who were present. Person in this sense means then a human "unit of mass." More especially since the word *personality* came into use (in English in the fourteenth century) the term *person* has been freed for this simple usage. Oddly enough, as Max Müller has pointed out (p. 25), the same term in French means not only a single human being, but likewise

[32] Beals defines a corporation as an "artificial person, created by law as an entity independent of the natural person or persons composing it, and endowed by the law that creates it with the power of acting as such independent person." J. H. Beals, *The Law of Foreign Corporations*, 1904, p. 7.

[33] Cf. F. Hallis, *Corporate Personality*, 1930, p. 240.

[34] From a letter to Mary W. Calkins printed in *Papers in Honor of Josiah Royce*, 1916, p. 67.

no human being. (31)

Here is no doubt an instance of what philologists call "condensation," and comes about through the fact that in the expression *ne personne* the *ne* is phonetically lost.

Many times emphasis is placed upon the physical portion of the self, as in such phrases as "to injure the person" or "to expose one's person." One definition, therefore, must be in terms of

the bodily self. (32)

A variant of the same definition places special emphasis upon physical *presence*, as in the phrase "will appear in person." This expression once seemed redundant, but it is less so now in the days of cinema and radio when partial appearance or appearance *not* in person is possible.

A curious blending has appeared between Definition (28)—the single human individual—and an inversion of Definition (4), weight and dignity. The result is

an expression of contempt (33)

as in the phrase "That person!" In this case it seems almost as though an individual were scarcely human; if a person at all, then certainly devoid of the dignity and worth that a true *personality* would possess.

The term *personality* like "person" has also one connotation of disparagement, as in the expression "Do not indulge in personalities," spoken when the listener wishes to interrupt slander or incrimination. This meaning is frequently encountered in eighteenth century English literature. It might be defined as

revealing qualities of others in offense to good taste. (34)

Proceeding again from Definition (28) we find that sociologists, thinking always of society at large, regard the person, not merely as an individual being, but, to use Eubank's expression,[35] as

the ultimate granule of the human group. (35)

It is characteristic of all sociological definitions of personality that they deny to it the attribute of self-sufficiency. In one way or another personality is always considered a reflection of, or dependent

[35] E. E. Eubank, "The Concept of the Person," *Sociol. & Soc. Res.*, 1927, 12, p. 363.

upon, the social ground. One succinct and fairly typical statement says that personality is

the subjective side of culture. (36)

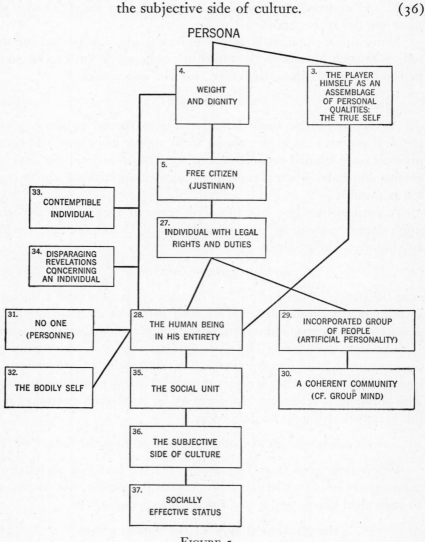

FIGURE 5

Juristic and Sociological Meanings

This view, expressed by Faris [36] and others, overlooks completely the part played by biological determinants (by intelligence, temperament, and physical heredity) and considers the subjectification of the

[36] E. Faris, "The Concept of Social Attitudes," *J. Appl. Sociol.*, 1925, 9, 404-409.

customs and social traditions within a single human life as the whole story. It is obviously a one-sided view.

There are other, better balanced, sociological definitions; some in fact are intricately synthetic: the following definition by E. W. Burgess, for example,[37]

> Personality is the integration of all the traits which determine the role and status of the person in society. Personality might, therefore, be defined as social effectiveness. (37)

This definition seems to contain remnants of all the original Ciceronic usages!

EXTERNAL APPEARANCE (BIOSOCIAL DEFINITIONS)

Definitions of personality in terms of the outer appearance of a man, that is, in terms of his "stimulus value" for others, are as common as they are troublesome. They have, to be sure, the virtue of etymological fidelity, for of all the various types of definitions they cling most closely to the original meaning of *mask*, signifying

> deceptive masquerade or mimicry. (38)

Cicero, in one context of his writing, asked, "Why should I walk around like a *persona?*"—why, that is, should he assume an appearance false to his nature, pretending to be that which he was not? It has already been shown that *persona* means not only what a man *is* (3), but likewise precisely the opposite: what he is *not* (1)! This ambiguity has never been overcome even in modern definitions of personality. In Latin it was somewhat lessened in certain contexts through the adoption of the derivative participle *personatus* to mean exclusively wearing a *false appearance*. In English we have the verb "to personate"; more commonly, "to impersonate."

Now, in everyday life it is often necessary to mask the true self, to present to the world an appearance of conventional fitness. For this common practice of wearing a conventional mask Jung has preserved in his system of psychology the original term *persona*, defining it as

[37] Contained in *Proc. of the Second Colloquium on Personality Investigation* (Johns Hopkins University Press), 1930, p. 149.

"a mask of the collective mind, *a mask that disguises individuality* . . . a stage part spoken by the collective mind."[38]   (39)

Many of the popular definitions of *personality* are of the same type as Jung's definition of *persona*, and it is here that confusion arises. Is personality a solidly organized system of traits and sentiments or is it the mask of a poseur presented to a critical world? Is it the *moi profond et essentiel* of Bergson, or is it the *moi superficiel?*[39]

Colloquial speech, influenced by the idols of the theater and the market-place, equate personality with charm, with "It," with

superficial attractiveness.   (40)

A cosmetic advertisement claims that a certain lipstick will confer "personality" upon its user. In this instance personality is not even skin-deep![40]

Popular definitions have two serious defects. First, they refer only to some portion of the intricate pattern of personal life, generally to the vitality, expansiveness, or expressiveness of the individual. Secondly, they invariably consider personality only in terms of its influence on other people, and never in terms of its subjective or interior organization.

This second deficiency is found frequently in the writings of psychologists who embrace the *biosocial* view of personality. The biosocial view stands in sharp contrast to the *biophysical* conception represented in this volume, which holds that personality, psychologically considered, is what an individual *is* regardless of the manner in which other people perceive his qualities or evaluate them.

As an example of the biosocial view, two definitions will serve. One considers personality to be those "habits or actions which successfully influence other people."[41] According to this narrow definition the secret schemes, frustrations, worries, and private aspirations that never become socially effective are not parts of personality. Another definition speaks of "the sum-total of the effect made by an individual upon society."[42] These views would deny personality to

[38] C. G. Jung. *Die Beziehungen zwischen dem Ich und dem Unbewussten*, 1928, p. 64.
[39] H. Bergson, *Essai sur les données immédiates de la conscience*, 19th ed., 1920, pp. 97-106.
[40] For a discussion of popular definitions see A. A. Roback, *Personality, the Crux of Social Intercourse*, 1931, chap. i.
[41] E. G. Flemming, *J. Educ. Sociol.*, 1933, 7, p. 409.
[42] H. C. Link, *The Return to Religion*, 1936, p. 89.

the solitary hermit or to Robinson Crusoe (at least before the advent of Friday). They would also invite a perilous distinction between "more" and "less" personality, for it is obvious that individuals have various degrees of social effectiveness. A queen of the movies seen by millions of people on the screen would have incomparably "more" personality than the complex and tortured poet dwelling in attic obscurity. In contrast, the biophysical view would argue that each human being has "as much" personality as any other. The effectiveness of a life is indeed a problem (best handled in social psychology), but it is by no means a criterion for the existence of personality. A solitary dweller on a desert island, unknown to any other mortal, has a full-fledged (and intensely interesting) personality.

The biosocial views are best summarized in the brief definition proposed by May. According to him personality is a man's

social-stimulus value. (41)

"It is the responses made by others to the individual as a stimulus that define his personality." [43]

In favor of this view it is sometimes urged that only through the judgments of other people are our personalities known at all. As we appear to others so must we be, for there is indeed no other criterion of our natures. A man's personality is what others think of him; it is, in short, his reputation.

If this reasoning be sound then it might as truthfully be said that a fish, a tree, or a star can be defined only in terms of their "social stimulus value," for is it not through their stimulus-giving properties that the scientist comes to know them? Philosophers have repeatedly made this same point in insisting that the scientist's own perception is ultimately the definitive test of existence. But it is none the less certain that the scientist safely *infers* that fish, trees and stars do exist outside of his own mind. Should he persist, because of his errors of sense or of judgment, in regarding the fish as an eel, or the tree as twice too large, or the star as a ball of cheese, the essential nature of these objects would still remain unchanged. It is so with personality. Our only basis for *knowing* people is their stimulus-properties. But our errors of judgment and perception do not change their personalities any more than a star becomes a savory because it is misperceived

[43] M. A. May, "The Foundations of Personality," chap. iv of *Psychology at Work* (ed. by P. S. Achilles), 1932.

by the scientist who has a taste for cheese. If it is here objected that
the criterion for truth is always social, that the greatest agreement
among the greatest numbers is the only possible test, the proper reply
is that whatever holds for *stars* holds also for personality. Personality

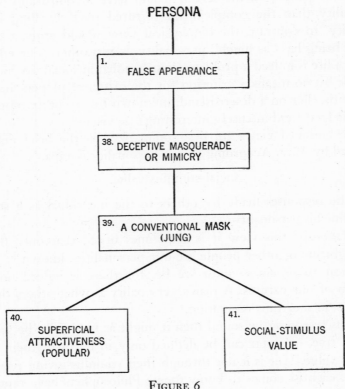

FIGURE 6

Biosocial Definitions (in Terms of External Appearance)

is just as objective a fact as any other event in nature; there are no
special grounds to single it out for biosocial definition.

It is not helpful to the psychologist therefore, to assume that personality is merely an impression made by one individual upon others.
Unless the investigator approaches personality as directly as he would
any other objective event he will be swamped by considerations of
reputation, rumor, gossip, erroneous evaluations, and social effectiveness. If the biosocial view were followed to its logical conclusion it
would not be necessary to study the perceptions, reactions, prejudices
and interests of the personality in question at all, but rather the per-

ceptions, reactions, prejudices and interests of everyone else in his social circle! [44]

PSYCHOLOGICAL MEANINGS

Even in classical times *persona* had the meaning of *an assemblage of personal qualities* (3). In English by the seventeenth century this usage was firmly established. It is this tradition more than any other that serves as background for all current biophysical definitions of personality. It contains no reference to drama, to pretense, or to mere reputation. It is, nevertheless, a broad conception that allows a number of varying points of stress. Indeed it is rare to find one psychologist who will accept another's definition, even though both agree that personality is a biophysical event. In spite of the multiplicity of definitions it is possible to assort them into five basic classes.[45]

1. *Omnibus Definitions.* Perhaps the commonest type of definition is the one that starts with the phrase, "Personality is the sum-total of . . ." In place of "sum-total" we sometimes find equally nondescript expressions such as "composite," "aggregate," "ensemble," "congeries," or "constellation." Typical examples are: "the sum-total of the reactions of an individual to all the situations which he encounters"; [46] or "a constellation of the following event patterns—somatic reactions, autistic reveries, adjustive thinking, and object orientations." [47] One of the best known omnibus definitions is that of Prince: "Personality is

> the sum-total of all the biological innate dispositions, impulses, tendencies, appetites, and instincts of the individual, and the acquired dispositions and tendencies— acquired by experience." [48]

(42)

[44] Sensing the paradox in this position May adds to his biosocial view the statement that it "does not deny the reaction side but insists that the stimulus side be included in the picture," and adds that "fully 90%" of research investigations deal with personality as an objective fact, *i.e.*, "take the reaction point of view" (*op. cit.*, pp. 84 f.). It appears then that the biophysical position taken in this book is acceptable not only to the majority of psychologists, but even, in part, to Professor May himself.

[45] For a somewhat fuller treatment of these five classes see G. W. Allport and P. E. Vernon, "The Field of Personality," *Psychol. Bull.*, 1930, 27, pp. 681-687.

[46] L. G. Lowrey, in *Proc. Second Colloquium on Personality Investigation*, 1930, p. 151.

[47] H. D. Lasswell, *ibid.*, p. 151.

[48] Morton Prince, *The Unconscious*, 2d ed., 1924, p. 532.

The confusion resulting from this view of personality as an omnibus piled high with all manner of unarranged impedimenta can be seen in Menninger's definition—which seems almost satirical. He writes, "Of course personality is used to describe almost everything from the attributes of the soul to those of a new talcum powder. As we shall use it, it means the individual as a whole, his height and weight and loves and hates and blood pressure and reflexes; his smiles and hopes and bowed legs and enlarged tonsils. It means all that anyone is and all that he is trying to become." [49]

Such omnibus definitions render absolutely no service to science. They are glib and reckless, and at best define merely by *enumeration*. They omit the most outstanding phenomenon of all mental life, namely, the presence of *orderly arrangement*. The mere cataloguing of ingredients defines personality no better than the alphabet defines lyric poetry.

2. *Integrative and Configurational Definitions.* Unlike the omnibus definitions this second class stresses the *organization of personal attributes*. A simple formulation of this type is that of Warren and Carmichael: [50]

> the entire organization of a human being at any stage
> of his development. (43)

A more complex definition still placing primary stress upon organization, but a secondary stress upon distinctiveness or uniqueness, is that of MacCurdy: [51]

> an integration of patterns (interests) which gives a
> peculiar individual trend to the behavior of the or-
> ganism. (44)

Similar is the definition of A. Gesell: "the pervasive superpattern which expresses the integrity and the characteristic behavioral individuality of the organism." [52]

3. *Hierarchical Definitions.* These are known by the demarcation of various levels of integration or organization, usually with the image of a capstone, or innermost self, to dominate and to center the pyra-

[49] K. Menninger, *The Human Mind*, 1930, p. 21.
[50] H. C. Warren and L. Carmichael, *Elements of Human Psychology*, 1930, p. 333.
[51] J. T. MacCurdy, *Common Principles in Psychology and Physiology*, 1928, p. 263.
[52] In *Proc. Second Colloquium on Personality Investigation*, 1930, p. 149.

mid of personal life. The prototype for conceptions of this sort is to be found in James's classic treatment of the four levels of the Self.[53] Self is essentially the personality "viewed from within." (James's preference for the *Self* was not unnatural in the introspective era in which he wrote. He used the term *personality* only in referring to the phenomena of dissociation, hysteria, and multiple personality popularized by the French school.) [54]

There is first the *material* Self, including the body, one's possessions and one's family and friends whom one cherishes. There is next the *social* Self determined by the recognition one obtains from one's associates. Regarding this level James made his famous statement that a man "has as many different social selves as there are distinct groups of persons about whose opinion he cares." [55] As though feeling that he had here dangerously dismembered the personality, James hastened to the third level, the *spiritual* Self that unifies so far as is possible man's discordant tendencies. A fourth level, The Pure Ego (the knower, the Self of Selves), is required by certain philosophical systems, but is not, according to James, psychologically distinguishable from the third level. With this hierarchical scheme as a model many authors have treated personality in a similar way, McDougall, for instance, and Bridges, Heider, Blondel, Martin, and many others.[56] All of them offer their conception in terms of

> levels or layers of dispositions, usually with a unifying
> or integrative principle at the "top." (45)

4. *Definitions in Terms of Adjustment.* Biologists and behaviorists are inclined to view personality as an evolutionary phenomenon, as a mode of survival. According to them personality is the "whole-organism-in-action." The point of view is most fully developed by Kempf [57] whose conception, in essence, is

> the integration of those systems of habits that represent
> an individual's characteristic adjustments to his environ-
> ment. (46)

There is so much that is manifestly true and important in this conception that it will receive fuller discussion in Chapters IV and V.

[53] William James, *Principles of Psychology*, 1890, Vol. I, chap. x.
[54] Cf. Th. Ribot, *The Diseases of Personality*, 2d ed., trans. 1895.
[55] *Op. cit.*, p. 294.
[56] See G. W. Allport and P. E. Vernon, *Psychol. Bull.*, 1930, 27, p. 684.
[57] E. J. Kempf, "The Autonomic Functions and the Personality," *Nerv. & Ment. Dis. Monog.*, 1921, No. 28.

5. Definitions in Terms of Distinctiveness. Schoen writes, "If all the members of any one social group acted alike, thought alike, and

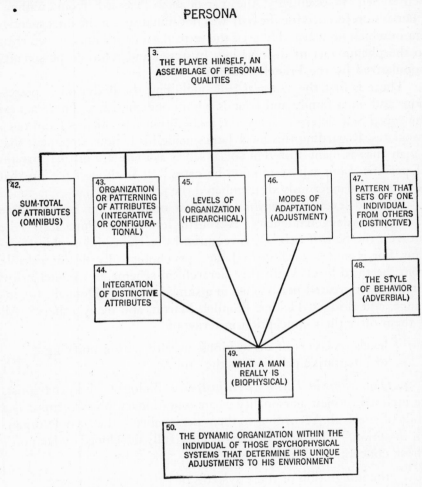

FIGURE 7

Psychological Meanings

felt alike, personality would not exist," and hence proposes as his definition,

> "Personality is the organized system, the functioning whole or unity of habits, dispositions and sentiments that mark off any one member of a group as being different from any other member of the same group." [58]   (47)

[58] M. Schoen, *Human Nature*, 1930, p. 397.

A similar definition is Wheeler's, "that particular pattern or balance of organized reactions which sets one individual off from another." [59]

An early and somewhat singular use of the term to indicate distinctiveness in the functioning of a *single* organ, is Mitchel's phrase "absolute personality of the eye," employed in connection with the long-standing problem of the "personal equation" or individual differences in reaction time.[60]

Another variant of definitions of this type is Woodworth's.[61] This author believes that every act of the individual is *colored* by personality. Personality is not substantive, it is *adverbial;* it is the style of life. "Personality refers not to any particular sort of activity, such as talking, remembering, thinking or loving, but an individual can reveal his personality

in the way he does any of these things." (48)

These psychological definitions thus far considered are summarized in Figure 7 which serves likewise as the frame of reference for Definition (50) offered as the guide for the author and reader of this volume.

A DEFINITION FOR THIS BOOK

From this long survey of past and present usage what may we conclude? Since there is no such thing as a wrong definition of any term, if it is supported by usage, it is evident that no one, neither the theologian, the philosopher, the jurist, the sociologist, the man in the street, nor the psychologist, can monopolize "personality." For the psychologist, to be sure, some definitions seem to be more serviceable than others. Completely unsuitable are biosocial formulations in terms of social reputation or superficial charm (40) and (41). The distinction between reputation (social effectiveness) and the true personality is one that will be observed rigidly throughout this book. Omnibus definitions (42) must likewise be rejected. More helpful are those conceptions that ascribe to personality a *solid organization* of dispositions and sentiments. Valuable likewise are definitions that refer to the *style of life*, to *modes of adaptation* to one's surroundings. to *progressive growth* and development and to *distinctiveness*.

[59] R. H. Wheeler, *The Science of Psychology*, 1929, p. 34.
[60] Cf. E. G. Boring, *A History of Experimental Psychology*, 1929, p. 140.
[61] R. S. Woodworth, *Psychology*, 1929, p. 553.

Might we not merely say that, psychologically considered, personality is

what a man really is?   (49)

This terse expression states the essential biophysical position, and is acceptable enough in principle. Yet it is too brief and vague as it stands. The following amplification seems to serve the purpose better:

PERSONALITY IS THE DYNAMIC ORGANIZATION WITHIN THE INDIVIDUAL OF THOSE PSYCHOPHYSICAL SYSTEMS THAT DETERMINE HIS UNIQUE ADJUSTMENTS TO HIS EN- VIRONMENT.   (50)

This formulation contains the seeds of the hierarchical, integrative, adjustive, and distinctive classes of definitions described above. In a sense, therefore, *it represents a synthesis of contemporary psychological usage.* But each portion of the definition is chosen for a particular reason, and these reasons must be made clear if the definition is to be accurately understood.

Dynamic Organization. To escape from the sterile enumerations of the omnibus definitions it is necessary to stress active organization. The crucial problem of psychology has always been mental organization (association). It is likewise the outstanding problem dealt with in this volume. Hence "organization" must appear in the definition. Yet this organization must be regarded as constantly evolving and changing, as motivational and as self-regulating; hence the qualification "dynamic." Organization must also imply at times the correlative process of *disorganization,* especially in those personalities that we are wont to regard as "abnormal."

Psychophysical Systems. Habits, specific and general attitudes, sentiments, and dispositions of other orders are all psychophysical systems. In later chapters these dispositions will be ordered within a theory of *traits.* The term "system" refers to traits or groups of traits in a latent or active condition. The term "psychophysical" reminds us that personality is neither exclusively mental nor exclusively neural. The organization entails the operation of both body and mind, inextricably fused into a personal unity.

Determine. This term is a natural consequence of the biophysical view. Personality *is* something and *does* something. It is not synonymous with behavior or activity; least of all is it merely the impression that this activity makes on others. It is what lies *behind* specific acts and *within* the individual. The systems that constitute personality are in every sense *determining tendencies*, and when aroused by suitable stimuli provoke those adjustive and expressive acts by which the personality comes to be known.

Unique. Strictly speaking every adjustment of every person is unique, in time and place, and in quality. In a sense, therefore, this

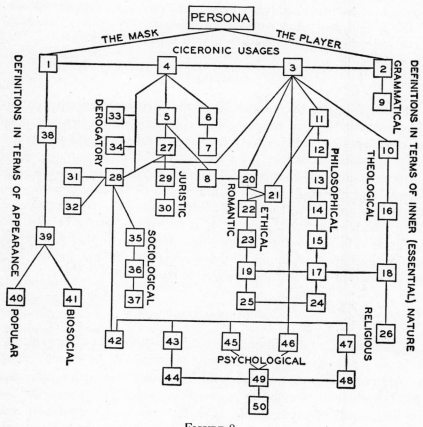

FIGURE 8

Summary View of the Definitions of Personality

criterion seems redundant. It becomes important, however, in our later discussions of the problem of *quantitative* variation among individuals in respect to the so-called "common" traits (see Chapter XI), and is therefore emphasized in the definition.

Adjustments to His Environment. This phrase has a functional and evolutionary significance. Personality is a mode of survival. "Adjustments," however, must be interpreted broadly enough to include maladjustments, and "environment" to include the behavioral environment (meaningful to the individual) as well as the surrounding geographical environment.

Above all, adjustment must not be considered as merely reactive adaptation such as plants and animals are capable of. The adjustments of men contain a great amount of spontaneous, creative behavior toward the environment. Adjustment to the physical world as well as to the imagined or ideal world—both being factors in the "behavioral environment"—involves *mastery* as well as passive adaptation.

SUMMARY

Figure 8 relates by number all of the fifty representative definitions contained in this chapter. The connecting lines, it must once more be repeated, indicate only meaningful relations, and not necessarily historical sequences. The reader will observe that in general the more "outer," more superficial definitions fall to the left, the more "inner," metaphysical definitions fall to the right. The definition to which this volume will adhere (50) represents the convergence of many trends of semantic change. It is perhaps as nearly central and synthetic in its significance as any single definition could be. It represents a distillation of much of the speculative thought in past ages and of much of the scientific research in recent times.

CHARACTER

Character is a term frequently used as a synonym of personality. It has a history as long and nearly as intricate. As employed by Theophrastus it possessed much of the same adverbial significance that Woodworth ascribed to personality. It was the "engraving" of the individual, his style of life as determined by his dominant trait (see pp. 56 ff.). There is no historical reason why the term should not be used interchangeably with personality, as indeed it frequently is. But in modern psychology there are two divergent lines of meaning both of which give an independent significance to the term, thereby lessening the practice of equating the terms.[62]

Many writers identify character with some special phase of per-

---

[62] For various meanings of character see L. Klages, *The Science of Character*, transl. 1929, pp. 38 ff.; W. McDougall, "Of the Words Character and Personality," *Char. & Pers.*, 1932, 1, pp. 3-16; also J. B. Watson, *Psychology from the Standpoint of a Behaviorist*, 1919, p. 392 ftn.

sonality, making it a subdivision of the whole. For example, it is said that personality may be viewed as intelligence plus character,[63] or as intelligence, temperament, and character.[64] Since personality is never an additive phenomenon such statements serve to characterize neither personality nor character.

Whenever character is considered to be a subdivision of personality, it is nearly always identified with volition in some way; thus, "the degree of ethically effective organization of all the forces of the individual," [65] or "an enduring psychophysical disposition to inhibit impulses in accordance with a regulative principle." [66] Large numbers of writers hold this view; for all of them character is the aspect of personality that engenders stability and dependability, that is responsible for sustained effort in the face of obstacles, or works for remote ends rather than those that are nearer in time but of less worth. This is the meaning endorsed not only by many psychologists but by the church, by educators, and by common speech as well.

With due respect to the prevalence of this usage one must still question the wisdom of separating the volitional faculty from the remainder of personality. Activities involving "will" emanate from the most complex systems of personality, but not from any one area that can be arbitrarily designated as *character*. When a man shows "character" by resisting temptation, or when it is said that the aim of education should be the "development of character," what is really meant is that the man has behaved, or the child should be trained to behave, in ways that are approved by prevailing social and ethical standards. The exercise of "will" in each case is a phenomenon of personality. *Character enters the situation only when this personal effort is judged from the standpoint of some code.* If will-power is shown in a man's behavior, then will-power is in his personality; if constancy, inhibition, self-respect, the power of "prolonging the vestibule of desire," or of "keeping the selected motive dominant throughout life" characterizes his behavior, then these talents are important features of his *personality*. Social standards as well as psychology are brought in when we label such conduct "character."

On all sides one encounters confusion of psychology with ethics. The layman asks the psychologist, "How ought I bring up my child?"

[63] G. G. Fernald, *J. Abnorm. Psychol.*, 1920, 15, p. 1.
[64] E. Kahn, *Psychopathic Personalities*, 1931, p. 32.
[65] W. S. Taylor, *J. Abnorm. & Soc. Psychol.*, 1926, 21, p. 86.
[66] A. A. Roback, *The Psychology of Character*, 1927, p. 450.

And the psychologist is presumptuous enough to tell him; although no psychologist *qua* psychologist can tell how a child ought to be brought up. The most he can do is to disclose human nature as it is, and then, *after a moral code has been chosen*, find out means of incentive and training that will achieve the end desired. Unreflectingly many psychologists, particularly mental hygienists, pose as experts in ethics, for do they not speak with assurance about the desirability of "mental adjustment"? Strange to say, it is often the Behaviorist, the most "rigidly scientific" in his ideals for psychology who traffics most unguardedly in ethics. The child "should" grow up without complexes and conflicts; he "ought" not have fears. Such "guidance" is not psychology at all; it is pure ethics, springing from an uncritical acceptance of the normative ideal of "perfect adjustment." Were the psychologist not guided by this particular code (popularized by mental hygiene), but rather by an ethics of perfectionism, self-realization, or rationalism (to name only a few alternatives) he would have to recast completely his advice and prescriptions.

Therefore, instead of defining character as the volitional aspect of personality, it is sounder to admit frankly that it is an ethical concept. Sir John Adams writes, "Character is the moral estimate of the individual, an evaluation." Defined in this way, the psychologist does not need the term at all; personality alone will serve. *Character is personality evaluated, and personality is character devaluated.* Since character is an unnecessary concept for psychology, the term will not appear again in this volume, excepting in quotations from other writers, or in a clear historical context.[67]

Biologists are still able to employ the term as meaning a distinguishing attribute, for example, in the phrase "inheritance of an acquired character." If it were not for the unhappy invasion of psychology by ethics this simple and pristine meaning would still be serviceable. One would speak, for example, of the "characters of a personality," meaning, of course, distinctive determining tendencies. Although this usage is now unfortunately impossible, the word *characteristic* remains unspoiled, both as an adjective and as a substantive. It is an admirable word to express the graven marks of individuality and can be employed in psychology without ethical connotation. It is especially serviceable as a generic term to cover habits, traits, attitudes, and interests, in so far as they are distinctive determining tendencies

[67] In the following chapter, for instance, it is convenient to employ the term *characterology* in its broad historical sense, as the science of the characteristics of men.

of the individual. It is a curious fact that *characteristic* should have kept its primitive and psychologically useful meaning, whereas its root-form has gathered so much ethical moss.

TEMPERAMENT

The classical doctrine that ascribed peculiarities of temperament to the humors of the body has persisted throughout the ages so that the meaning of the term has varied but little. The term found its way into English in the Middle Ages along with the doctrine of the humors. It meant then and still means a "constitution or habit of mind, especially depending upon or connected with physical constitution." Today in America psychological writers stress particularly the constitutional basis; for them temperament is the "internal weather" in which personality develops; it is the subjective climate provided by native physiological and kinetic endowment. The usage of the term in Great Britain is somewhat different, tending to equate temperament with personality, as in the phrase "temperament tests" (rather than "tests of personality").

Temperament, like intelligence and physique, might be said to designate a certain class of raw material from which personality is fashioned. Strictly speaking there is no temperament apart from personality, nor any personality devoid of temperament. It is merely convenient to employ the term in speaking of dispositions that are almost unchanged from infancy throughout life (dispositions saturated with a constant emotional quality, with a peculiar pattern of mood, alertness, intensity, or tonus). The more anchored a disposition is in native constitutional soil the more likely it is to be spoken of as temperament.

It is seldom doubted today, any more than it was among the ancients, that temperament is dependent somehow upon the biochemical constitution. Work dealing primarily with glands, physical build, or blood composition (to name only a few popular fields of contemporary study) frequently claims to be seeking the biological foundations of *personality*. And so it is—indirectly; but first of all it is seeking the physical correlates of *temperament*. There is danger of exaggeration in labels such as "Glands Regulating Personality," "Biological Foundations of Personality," "Physique and Character." The implication in these titles is that no factors other than the constitutional need be considered. It would clarify the problem if biologists and endocrinologists would drop the term personality altogether, and speak exclusively of temperament. It is in this latter field of research that their efforts and those of the psychologist can be most directly joined.

The following definition of temperament fits standard psychological usage and meets the requirements of this book. *Temperament refers to the characteristic phenomena of an individual's emotional nature, including his susceptibility to emotional stimulation, his customary strength and speed of response, the quality of his prevailing mood, and all peculiarities of fluctuation and intensity in mood; these phenomena being regarded as dependent upon constitutional make-up, and therefore largely hereditary in origin.*

CHAPTER III

A BRIEF HISTORY OF CHARACTEROLOGY

THE term *Characterology* as employed in this chapter refers to all the diverse schemes advanced in the past to account for, or to depict, forms of human individuality. The word itself was first employed by J. Bahnsen in 1867.[1] But in spite of its relative recency it serves very well to designate all the forerunners of the modern psychology of personality.

The fact that each human being is unique and distinctive has always caused astonishment and comment, provoking some of the greatest thinkers throughout the ages to theorize and to observe. Employing as they did the language of pre-scientific psychology some of their formulations now seem quaint and old-fashioned. But our efforts today are faltering enough, so why should we dismiss these venerable contributions with amusement or condescension?

The reader will find in A. A. Roback's *Psychology of Character* (1927) a rich record of past descriptions of human types, and of methods, postulates, plans and projects for the discovery of the basic principles of the development and activity of personality.[2] While there is no reason to attempt another complete history of the subject, certain authors emerge from the past with whose contributions readers of this book must be familiar. It is convenient to classify these outstanding figures as representative of six different schools of thought. Three have their sources in ancient Greece, *viz.*, *literary characterology, humoral psychology*, and *physiognomy;* three are of modern origin: *phrenology, ethology*, and *experimental characterology*. Within these movements we shall pay particular attention to

---

[1] J. Bahnsen's work is in two volumes, entitled, *Beiträge zur Charakterologie*, and was republished in 1932. For a discussion of the term, see W. Stern, *Differentielle Psychologie*, 3d ed., p. 11, and E. Utitz, *Charakterologie*, 1925, p. 8.

[2] Likewise a chronological table of the leading events in the history of characterology will be found in *A Bibliography of Character and Personality* compiled by the same author in 1927. This volume also contains 3,300 classified references to literature in the field. A shorter history of characterology is offered by J. Jastrow, *Pop. Sci. Mo.*, 1915, 86, 590-615.

the contributions having lasting value, and pass lightly over their erroneous by-paths.

"Character writing," as it is technically called, is a minor literary form originating in Athens. Some say Aristotle invented the form, for proof pointing to his characterization of the Magnanimous Man in the *Nichomachean Ethics*. Others hold that the originator of the form was Theophrastus, Aristotle's pupil and successor at the Lyceum. Whoever the actual inventor, it is certain that Theophrastus' crisp, brilliant, detached representations of human types brought him lasting fame and established a model for innumerable imitators in the past two thousand years.

A successful "Character" is a brief descriptive note which so aptly depicts a common type of human being that it is recognized and appreciated by the readers of any age and in any land as a simplified but essentially correct image. Descriptions of particular individuals are not Characters; they are Portraits. Actually, of course, Characters and Portraits shade into one another, and certain Portraits, notably those of La Bruyère, possess such universality of application that they belong with the productions of Theophrastus. Strictly speaking a Character is a *type*, drawn by the accentuation of some dominant disposition or trait. The 30 Characters of Theophrastus follow a rigid style of composition. Each commences with a brief definition of the dominant trait, and continues with typical instances of the operation of this trait. The numerous imitators of Theophrastus depart in varying degrees from this rigid formalism, so much so at times that they virtually forsake the tradition of Character writing.

It is a peculiarity of Theophrastus' Characters that all present somewhat vicious or at least unpleasant types of personality. Whether he found the good man too dull to write of, whether he wished to hold up to the Athenians their own mean and sordid conduct, or whether the 30 sketches which survive are only a portion of those written, are all possibilities for conjecture. The text of his work suffered considerably from Byzantine interpolation but has now been purified, and several good translations are available.[3] It was part of the Byzantine

---

[3] R. C. Jebb, *The Characters of Theophrastus*, 1909; R. Aldington (ed. and trans.), *A Book of Characters*, E. P. Dutton and Co., 1925; C. E. Bennett and William A. Hammond, *The Characters of Theophrastus*, 1902; Francis Howell, *The Characters of Theophrastus*, 1824. (The last two have physiognomical sketches.)

tradition that Theophrastus wrote his Characters when he was 99 years old.[4] It is not difficult to find in the shrewd observations and detachment of the sketches reasons for assigning them to a writer of venerable age and rich experience. The following example (from Aldington's translation) demonstrates the style of Character writing in the hands of the Greek master. Though written 2,200 years ago it is applicable to some of our acquaintances today.

THE PENURIOUS MAN

Penuriousness is economy carried beyond all measure. A Penurious Man is one who goes to a debtor to ask for his half-obol interest before the end of the month. At a dinner where expenses are shared, he counts the number of cups each person drinks, and he makes a smaller libation to Artemis than anyone. If someone has made a good bargain on his account and presents him with the bill he says it is too much.

When his servant breaks a pot or a plate, he deducts the value from his food. If his wife drops a copper, he moves furniture, beds, chests and hunts in the curtains. If he has something to sell he puts such a price on it that the buyer has no profit. He forbids anyone to pick a fig in his garden, to walk on his land, to pick up an olive or a date. Every day he goes to see that the boundary marks of his property have not been moved. He will destrain on a debtor and exact compound interest. When he entertains the members of his deme, he is careful to serve very small pieces of meat to them. If he goes marketing, he returns without having bought anything. He forbids his wife to lend anything—neither salt nor lamp-wick nor cinnamon nor marjoram nor meal nor garlands nor cakes for sacrifices. "All these trifles," he says, "mount up in a year." To sum up, the coffers of the penurious men are moldy and the keys rust; they wear cloaks which hardly reach the thigh; a very little oil-bottle supplies them for anointing; they have hair cut short and do not put on their shoes until midday; and when they take their cloak to the fuller they urge him to use plenty of earth so that it will not be spotted so soon.

In all ages and in all lands there have been penurious men. The skill of Theophrastus consists in his selection of such universal types, in his choice of illustrative incident, and in his economy of expression. By the addition of one bit of penurious behavior to another he has exemplified the dominant trait and has at least by implication given us

[4] But the dates of his life are given by modern authorities as 372-287 B.C.

a theory of the structure of personality. It is clear that to him penuri-ousness as a personal trait is a dynamic and directive force, a true mainspring of conduct. It is stable, predictable, self-consistent, and compulsive. In the case of the penurious man nineteen samples of conduct exemplify the inner trait; they seem to issue directly and unambiguously as motor manifestations of inner disposition; they are not at all "specific habits" unrelated to one another, but form a coherent and meaningful style of life, which to be understood must be referred to the *central trait*.

Whether he is in business or at home, whether he is entertaining his friends or making his toilet, whether he deals with his wife, his servants, his friends, his debtors, his neighbors, or his deity, the man is dominated by his penurious nature. His conduct does not "depend upon the situation" nor has he "as many social selves as there are individuals who recognize him." He is consistently parsimonious. It is safe to predict that in new situations he would react in the same way. Note well: The man did not have merely a "habit" of wearing his tunic short, and another habit of examining the boundary marks of his property, and another of going to market without spending any of his money. Each activity is merely one manifestation of a *central* motive.

The persistence of the theory that a personality is known best through its dominant trait is found in the long line of followers of Theophrastus. A list of the more eminent Character writers would include many names famous in the history of literature: John Earle, Samuel Butler, Ben Jonson, John Donne, Richard Steele, Joseph Addison, Samuel Johnson, Jean de la Bruyère, the Marquis de Vau-venargues, and George Eliot. In America Character writing has been recently resumed. By entitling his book of character-sketches *En-caustics* (1926), Stark Young has made an admirable and deliberate translation of Theophrastus' Χαρακτήρ.

Although Jean de la Bruyère (1645-1696) confined himself to Portraits, they were so universalized that they have taken their place with the very greatest of Character writing. Issued originally as satire of the manners and personalities of his times, these sketches are ap-plicable to human beings in any age or land. An illustration (from Aldington's translation) will show how much less formal was his writing than that of Theophrastus, and how he contrives his effects without explicitly naming a dominant trait.

GITON

Giton has a fresh complexion, a full face and bulging cheeks, a fixed and assured gaze, broad shoulders, a projecting stomach, a firm and deliberate tread. He speaks with confidence; he makes those who converse with him repeat what they have said and he only moderately enjoys what is said. He unfolds an ample handkerchief and blows his nose noisily; he spits to a great distance and sneezes very loudly. He sleeps by day, he sleeps by night; he snores in company. At table and in walking he occupies more room than anyone else. He takes the center and walks with his equals; he stops and they stop; he walks on and they walk on; all regulate themselves by him; he is not interrupted, he is listened to as long as he likes to talk; his opinion is accepted, the rumors he spreads are believed. If he sits down you will see him settle into an armchair, cross his legs, frown, pull his hat over his eyes and see no one, or lift it up again and show his brow from pride and audacity. He is cheerful, a hearty laugher, impatient, presumptious, quick to anger, irreligious, politic, mysterious about current affairs; he believes he has talents and wit. He is rich.

In this sketch it is difficult to name the central trait in Giton's nature, if indeed only one trait is indicated, but it is not difficult to comprehend the man and to recognize him among our own acquaintances. A peculiar *style of life* permeates Giton's every activity. Certainly he is extroverted, expansive, ascendant, conceited, selfish, and socially insensitive; but these traits are not separate and distinct springs of action; they flow together in a *style* of expression. La Bruyère does not dissect his character but holds the mirror for his full reflection.

There are other features of this sketch of interest to modern psychology. Giton has a physique that somehow seems thoroughly congruous with his temperament;[5] he also enjoys economic security which enhances his self-assurance. By giving the reader these two bits of "explanatory" (genetic) information the author enhances enormously the reader's understanding of Giton's personality. Theophrastus described the ruling passion. La Bruyère by adding a small amount of genotypical data draws a fuller portrait. Another feature of interest is the selective artistry of the author. Undoubtedly Giton had many contradictory aspects of nature, sets of interests and forms of conduct not here disclosed. All *types*, however, must

[5] The significance of the pyknosomic physique is discussed on pp. 73 f.

be simplifications; so too must all Portraits if they are to be symbolic of an entire range of personalities. A full-length picture would inevitably introduce elements of uniqueness and would sacrifice its universality in the interest of the individual case.

Character writing, then, for all its virtues of brevity and compactness, and for all the beauty of its prose sonnets, is a limited medium. At its best it produces stylized and simplified depictions of human nature, universal in their significance but for that very reason remote from the vital individuality of living people. Few character writers, it should be added, follow Theophrastus and La Bruyère in keeping the psychological interest uppermost; the majority drift off into the by-paths of burlesque, preciosity, or moral censure.

Still greater treasure for the psychologist lies in the world's store of drama, biographies, poetry, and fiction. After reading the magnificent studies of personality written by literary genius the psychologist feels ineffectual and a bit foolish. He may even agree with Zweig that writers like Stendhal, Amiel, Tolstoy, Carlyle and Proust are "giants in observation and literature, whereas in *psychology* the field of personality is worked by lesser men, mere flies, who have the safe anchorage of a frame of science in which to place their petty platitudes or minor heresies." [6]

Since literature and psychology provide the two most important methods for the study of personality the comparison between them must be pursued somewhat further. It may be true, as Zweig alleges, that the psychologist is heavy-handed and unimaginative, whereas the literary artist captures the subtleties of personality with precision and delicacy. It may even be true that whenever the psychologist succeeds in spite of his scientific clichés in representing personality with fidelity, he seems then to be saying only what some literary genius has already said more agreeably and artfully. Psychology would seem to come off very badly in the comparison, for only a pedant could prefer his own scientific analysis to the glorious characterizations of Dickens or Ibsen. Yet on the other hand, only an esthetic bigot can deny that there is a place for some scientific complement to the undisciplined artistry of literature in the attempt to understand, and even to depict, personality.

[6] Stefan Zweig: *Adepts in Self Portraiture: Casanova, Stendhal, Tolstoy.* Trans. 1928. For another comparison somewhat more respectful toward the attainments of psychology see Max Eastman, *The Literary Mind: Its Place in an Age of Science,* 1931.

The subject matter of literature is entirely idiographic. It is the single person, the "particular truth" that stands revealed. Whatever broader applications literature may have are merely implicit and are usually debatable. The psychologist, on the other hand, has an inescapable interest in the discovery of general principles, of laws of human behavior. In recent times, as Chapter I explained, some psychologists have grown dissatisfied with the exclusively nomothetic outlook of their science, and have approached more closely the problems of individuality hitherto consigned to literature. But there remains, however, a difference: the literary writer cares primarily for the individual case, leaving to the reader the task of generalizing the insight he gains. The psychologist, while studying the single, is never content until he himself has made appropriate generalizations. The generalizations are not, or should not be, concerned only with the operations of an hypothetical "average" mind. Their aim is rather to state explicitly the principles by virtue of which unique personalities are created by nature and understood by men.

Another important difference exists in the *context* in which personality is studied. The literary investigator may give the full social setting and portray the cross-currents in which his character develops, confining himself to complex levels of personality. He develops his character in the stream of life. The psychologist likes to disregard the complexities of the social setting, to fasten the personality as-it-is for analysis, to reduce so far as possible the confusion of surrounding variables, and to seek the elementary features of conduct which can be separately studied. He prefers the laboratory or the clinic to the stream of life. Here, of course, lies a serious danger. Too much analysis and control may destroy his datum. But with due care his method of isolation brings many significant rewards.

The effects of literature are gained by skillful selection and exaggeration. The *petits faits vrais* are made prominent, currents unsuited to the interests of the author are omitted. And yet the very incidents that heighten the character may to a degree falsify it. This distortion is common in both fiction and biography. The psychologist, however, is permitted no artistic accentuation, and illustrative incident must not be used until it is known to be both recurrent and diagnostic. *Exaggeration apropos* is not allowed. Also, in the arbitrary scope of a work of literature a lack of discipline not permitted science is shown. The telling may begin anywhere, and leave off abruptly; it may be simplified as much as the author desires to secure an effect. The psychologist must give reasons for his beginnings and his endings, as well as for his inclusion and his exclusion.

The artist strives to be entertaining and engaging, to communicate his own images, to express his own biases. One measure of his success is the responsiveness of his readers. The psychologist is permitted only to discover and record. His primary aim may be to instruct but never to entertain. His work must exclude his own bias, be true to the scientist's conception of fact, and his success is measured by sterner criteria than the reader's applause.

In gathering material, the writer draws from his casual observation of life, the psychologist from controlled investigations. The writer may present his observations in epigram and in pretty phrases, the psychologist must use exact and standard terminology. In literature rapid and bold inferences may be made, in psychology the inferences requiring proof step by step are slowly and cautiously drawn. It is unnecessary for a literary work to be "proved" or submitted to the test of repetition; it is even unnecessary for the author to be completely consistent in his own statements. He need not fit his observations into a conceptual system for the purpose of testing a general theory. All these requirements bind the psychologist. "The scientist must submit to the judgment of others, not merely the conclusions which he reaches, but also the premises with which he began and the methods which he uses in developing his work from them; but the artist, within very wide limits, at least, is allowed to choose whatever premises he likes, and as a result, it is by no means necessary that all good artists should agree to anything like the same extent that all good scientists must agree." [7]

Freed from the bondage of scientific terms, the writer can speak recklessly of the course of nature. He can ascribe causes and assign correlates at random. One of his characters may have "menial blood in his veins," another a "weak chin." A hand may possess "a wonderfully cruel greed" and a blond head "radiate fickleness." Such undisciplined metaphors give cadence and inspire a kind of bland credulity, but for science they are mere idle phrases. Recently a famous professor of literature in describing a character wrote, "The nose, almost invariably the index of mental power, was perfect in fullness, straightness, and strength." No psychologist could write such a passage without being torn limb from limb by his professional colleagues!

[7] Joseph W. Krutch, *The Modern Temper*, Harcourt, Brace, 1929, p. 152.

Psychology will not supplant literature, nor will the hauteur of artists hinder the growth of psychology. The two methods are distinct and complementary. If psychology today is discovering only what literature "has always said" it is nevertheless giving precision and general application to the ancient truths. Less enjoyable, it is more disciplined; less subtle, it is more verifiable; less artful, it is more exact.

HUMORAL PSYCHOLOGY

Even more ancient than Character writing and closer in spirit to modern science is the doctrine of the humors and their corresponding temperaments. This is the oldest characterological theory of which there is any record. Growing out of the four-part cosmogeny of Empedocles it has had an almost unbroken history.[8] With relatively few changes it has endured from the dawn of history down to the latest text-book in psychology.

In the following table the development of the doctrine in classic times is reviewed. Its original logic rested upon the belief that man is a microcosmic reflection of nature. He should therefore in his own being express all the properties of the cosmos.

Cosmic Elements	Their Properties	Corresponding Humors	Corresponding Temperaments
Empedocles cir. 450 B.C.		Hippocrates cir. 400 B.C.	
Air	warm and moist	Blood	Sanguine
Earth	cold and dry	Black Bile	Melancholic
Fire	warm and dry	Yellow Bile	Choleric
Water	cold and moist	Phlegm	Phlegmatic

The classical doctrine ascribed peculiarities of temperament to the "humors" of the body. In the light of modern physiology and endocrinology the list of specific "humors" advanced by Hippocrates has been completely abandoned, but the principle of psychophysical cor-

[8] Taken together the following references reconstruct the whole interesting story: Ben Jonson, *Every Man Out of His Humor*; V. Laehr, *Literatur der Psychiatrie, Neurologie und Psychologie von 1459-1799*, 3 Vols., 1900; A. A. Roback, *A Bibliography of Character and Personality*, 1927; L. Klages, *The Science of Character*, pp. 144-149; W. B. Pillsbury, *The History of Psychology*, 1929, 37-44; P. Malapert, *Le Caractère*, 1902; A. A. Roback, *The Psychology of Character*, chap. iii and Pt. II; W. Stern, *Differentielle Psychologie*, Appendix I.

respondence remains. Chemical substances, notably the hormones, are now known to affect the working of the nervous system in ways that were only dimly surmised by the ancients. Modern science has shown these substances to be even more powerful, more numerous, and more varied in their influence than Hippocrates supposed.

Later variations of the theory took the form of subdividing or renaming the temperaments, and of modernizing the conception of humors. The doctrine profoundly influenced medicine, especially down to the time of Harvey's discovery of the circulation of the blood. It likewise influenced literature and art. It was reworked by Kant, Wundt, Ribot, Fouillée, Ribéry, Azam, Malapert, Paulhan, by Höffding, Bahnsen, Herbart, Külpe, Ebbinghaus, Meumann, Spurzheim and Klages. It has claimed the attention of intellectual giants as well as charlatans, and still survives in a modified form in our new era of research.

There are two principal reasons why interest has been so persistent in this venerable approach to temperament. In the first place, the happy guess that temperament, the emotional groundwork of personality, is conditioned above all else by body-chemistry has been increasingly borne out in modern research.[9] In the second place, the four-fold classification of temperament is still useful, because of certain fundamental dimensions of emotional response that it implies, a fact that Wundt, of all the writers on the subject, seems most clearly to have perceived.[10] According to Wundt men may differ in the characteristic *speed* of emotional arousal, or in the characteristic *intensity* of the response. The four temperaments are essentially the resulting combinations in a two dimensional scale of emotionality.

	Strong	Weak
Quick Slow	choleric melancholic	sanguine phlegmatic

The definition of temperament offered on page 54 recognizes as important distinguishing factors in temperament these Wundtian dimensions of *strength* and *speed*. But *breadth* and *depth* are likewise

[9] A readable presentation of the case is R. G. Hoskins, *The Tides of Life*, 1933.
[10] W. Wundt, *Grundzüge der physiologischen Psychologie*, 5th ed., 1903, Vol. III.

important variables, and it so happens that the classical types may be ordered under these dimensions as well.

	Deep	Shallow
Broad Narrow	choleric melancholic	sanguine phlegmatic

Or still another dimensional arrangement may be made in terms of predominant affective tone, pleasantness and unpleasantness, paired with the kinetic dimensions of excitement and calm.

	Pleasant	Unpleasant
Excited Calm	sanguine phlegmatic	choleric melancholic

In short, because of their elasticity the temperaments fit into various dimensional or quantitative schema, thereby satisfying the requirements of various investigators. Originally, the temperaments had merely a qualitative coloring; the choleric being *irascible*, the sanguine, alertly *hopeful*, the melancholic, *sad*, and the phlegmatic merely *apathetic*. But these colorings, it turns out, fit nicely into a number of modern dichotomous schemes.

The longevity of the theory is thus due in part to its flexible nature and in part to its implicit recognition of the underlying effect of body-chemistry. In this way the venerable conception of temperament still serves a purpose. But the gain is not great; sounder and newer formulations are now needed.

PHYSIOGNOMY

The art of discovering characteristics of personality from the outward appearance, and especially from the configuration, cast, or expression of the face, is called *physiognomy*. Probably mankind has always practiced this art. The oldest treatise on the subject is one entitled *Physiognomonica* attributed, probably incorrectly, to Aristotle.[11] Ancient though it is it refers to three methods each having its special adherents in the still more distant past. The first method sought resemblances in appearance between men and animals and assumed that when the form of a man is reminiscent of that of a particular animal he must be endowed with some of the same psychic qualities. The man who looks like a fox must be sly. The second method was a kind of racial typology. The man who is excessively pale or dark should be judged a coward, for—the author asks—are not Ethiopians dark and women pale, and both alike cowardly? The third method took as its basis the facial expressions engendered by emotion, and sought in the face muscular *traces* of angry, fearful, or lustful habits of thought and expression.

The author of this ancient treatise gives a list, "a complete list," of the sources from which physiognomic signs are drawn. They are: "movements, gestures of the body, color, characteristic facial expression, the growth of the hair, the smoothness of the skin, the voice, condition of the flesh, the parts of the body, and the build of the body as a whole." He adds, "But inferences drawn from the parts of the body are less secure than those based on facial expression of character and movements and gesture. In general it is silly to rely on a single sign: you will have more reason for confidence in your conclusions when you find several signs all pointing one way." From this treatise several valuable suggestions emerge, especially the requirement that signs must be consistent with one another if they are to sustain a judgment, and the suggestion that signs which spring from active habits of expression are more to be trusted than simple structural characteristics which are innate and unchanging. The author is keen likewise in his observation that certain states of mind have no recognizable bodily counterparts. The specific content of a man's knowledge or belief, for example, are not physiognomically revealed.

With the Aristotelian revival in the thirteenth century physiognomy became once more popular, and has in fact had an unbroken history since that time. The quantity of literature on the subject is far more striking than its quality, for the practical nature of its appeal brought it early under the patronage of quacks and charlatans, where unfortunately it has largely remained. So great were its abuses in the

[11] This treatise which covers only 24 pages is translated by T. Loveday and E. S. Forster and appears in the *Opuscula*, Vol. 6, of the Works of Aristotle (ed. by W. D. Ross), 1913.

eighteenth century that George II by an act of parliament deemed all persons pretending to have skill in physiognomy rogues and vagabonds, to be publicly whipped or sent to houses of correction. A similar law had been passed in the sixteenth century in the reign of Queen Elizabeth.[12]

The crusade against fraudulent physiognomists is still being waged, not so much by law as by professional psychologists. It may seem strange that the "impractical" psychologist should be forced to protect "hard-headed" business men from these charlatans, but such is the case. Dunlap has given four reasons why popular systems based on physiognomy appear to succeed.[13] The first is that the actual value of the readings is rarely checked; the second, that a few, though not many, of the physiognomists make surprisingly good guesses based on indications which they do not really understand, but falsely ascribe to their own systems.[14] An additional reason is found in the clever salesmanship of the analysts (to which even businessmen are not immune). Finally, the "experting" is done at the instance of some director who soon loses interest, and pigeonholes the results. But the physiognomist goes on to the next job with a lordly fee in his pocket, and impresses his new clients with his reputation for having successfully served the first corporation. So the cycle continues.

The shadowy history of systems of physiognomy may be disregarded in favor of the challenging fact that men have always found some indirect assistance in their judgments of others through the observation of their physical expressions: their eyes, their cast of countenance, their facial play, their posture, build, and manner. Even excluding all actual movement, the body at rest retains traces of its habits of exercise, the face seems to betray one's way of life. There is also theoretical justification for judgments based on physiognomy: growth is largely regulated by the glands of internal secretion, so too is the emotional life. Physical features therefore may logically be expected to reveal peculiarities of temperament.

In Figure 9 are presented certain traditional drawings of the facial types supposed to correspond to the four temperaments. (The

---

[12] *Encyclopedia Britannica*, 11th ed., Vol. 21, p. 550.

[13] K. Dunlap, "Reading of Character from External Signs," *Sci. Mo.*, 1922, 15, 2, 153-165.

[14] F. Gall, the phrenologist, probably gave the correct interpretation of this point when he asserted that the apparent success of practicing physiognomists came from their judgments of muscular expression, posture, and movement, and not from the cast of the facial features. F. Gall, *On the Functions of the Brain*, 1835, Amer. trans., Vol. V, p. 266.

combining of humoral psychology and physiognomy is commonly encountered.) Noteworthy is the ease with which judges who are

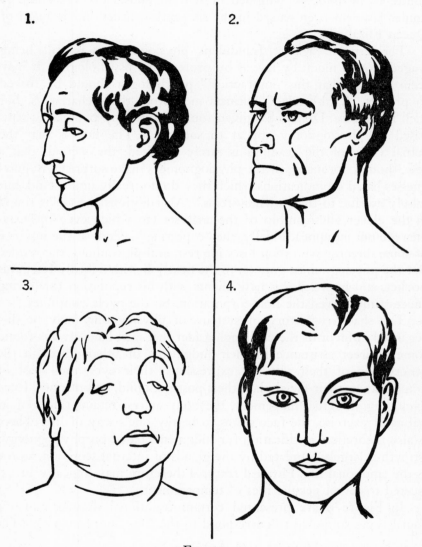

FIGURE 9

Physiognomic Representations of the Four Temperaments

familiar with the characteristics of the four temperaments can recognize them in these drawings. Shown to several hundred judges, the percentage of correct designations was as follows:

No. 1. Melancholic 83%
No. 2. Choleric 86%
No. 3. Phlegmatic 81%
No. 4. Sanguine 80%

The commonest errors are the confusions between the two intense temperaments (melancholic and choleric) and between the two un-emotional temperaments (phlegmatic and sanguine). It may rightly be objected that both the pictures and the temperaments are presented in their extreme forms, and that moderate or mixed instances would certainly not be so easily recognized. It is also true that stereotypes and verbal habits aid in correct judgments. Number 1 looks like the traditional love-sick poet who is by reputation *melancholic*. Similar associations may be recorded for the others. Number 2 appears to be a "fighter" clearly endowed with *choler;* Number 3 is sleepy, flaccid, and *phlegmatic;* Number 4, because of the suggestion of vacuous optimism, is judged *sanguine*. But these inferential and associative judgments are ultimately physiognomic, for whence came our stereotypes of the melancholy poet, the fighter, the sluggish beef-eater, and the shallow optimist if not through actual experience of just such correlations between physical and temperamental characteristics?

There are two entirely different types of physiognomic diagnosis. There is first that based on *bony structure*, and second that based on *muscular set*. Since bony structure cannot be changed by experience, it would not seem to be a promising index to personality, for personality is largely a product of education, experience, conflict, and adaptation to the environment. Heredity alone gives us our bony structure; but it alone does not give us our personalities. Therefore, the correlate of bony structure or constitutional build is *temperament*, the native factor in personality. Muscular set, the second criterion, is the agency of movement and is in turn influenced by habits of movement. The professional work of the sailor, the blacksmith, the clergyman, the teacher and the prize-fighter create diverse patterns of muscular strength and flaccidity, specialization and exercise. It is from these muscular sets, therefore, that we seek information regarding the acquired factors in personality, the products of *experience*. Needless to say in the physiognomic judgments of everyday life we do not distinguish the separate diagnostic significance of the

bony structure and of the musculature, but this distinction is necessary as a first step in physiognomic theory.

The drawings in Figure 9 depend for their effect upon both the
bony and the muscular structure. Considering first the muscular
structure, it may be pointed out that the crucial facial lines in Number 1 are the vertical furrows in the brow, and the downcast eyes.
The former feature is present characteristically in states of unpleasantness and during thought. Both features would be expected
in a temperament which is slow to be excited, but intense when
aroused.[15] In Number 2, the choleric nature is betrayed both by the
heavy seaming of the face, the result of frequent emotional seizure,
and by the forward direction of the eyes, displaying the attentiveness
required for prompt reaction. In Number 3, the facial lines do not
follow the muscular divisions of the face; they are due to fat rather
than to feeling. The eyes are inattentive, and suggest the slowness
which is characteristic of the phlegmatic temperament. Number 4
has a smooth face, devoid of muscular traces of intense emotional
experience, and wide open eyes, indicating a readiness for quick response; these are the two distinguishing features of the sanguine
person. The analysis thus far is strictly in the psychological tradition
of Piderit, Wundt, Boring and Titchener.[16] Popular physiognomists
would undoubtedly wish to add more detailed readings based on the
height of the brow, shape of the ears, contour of the nose, color of
the eyes or hair, but so far as is known these features yield absolutely no reliable positive correlations with characteristics of personality.[17]

Personality is only one of four determinants of facial expression,
and it is by no means easy to "see through" the effects of the other
three influences and find the reflection of the true personality. First
of all there is the limitation placed by constitutional build. Faces may
be short or broad, with thick lips or thin, with deep-set or protruding
eyes. The play of expression is constrained by such native structures

[15] There is some evidence in favor of the view that pleasant emotions are quick
to arouse, while the unpleasant are slower to arouse and perhaps more enduring.
F. H. Allport, *Social Psychology*, pp. 85-94. This fact would explain why the slow
melancholic temperament should suffer from a characteristically negative (unpleasant) feeling tone as well as from latency and perseveration of response.

[16] Cf. E. G. Boring and E. B. Titchener, "A Model for the Demonstration of
Facial Expression," *Amer. J. Psychol.*, 1923, 34, 471-485.

[17] Cf. Cleeton and Knight, "Validity of Character Judgments Based on External
Criteria." *J. Appl. Psychol.*, 1924, 8, 215-231. Also Paterson and Ludgate, "Blonde
and Brunette Traits: a quantitative study," *J. Pers. Res.*, 1922, 1, 122-128.

of the countenance. Although, as will soon be shown, the native structure itself may have some slight significance for personality (as a means of indicating racial or endocrine types), it is at the same time often a misleading mask. A face, for instance, with coarse or repulsive features may blind the observer to the play of wistful or friendly expressions.

Another "non-personal" determinant of facial expression is provided by the primary emotions, such as fear, anger, amusement, disgust, universal among men, and essentially the same from country to country and from age to age. This common instinctive groundwork underlying facial expression is not related to individuality but results from a common biological constitution. Consistent with their preoccupation with mind-in-general, it is in this field that psychologists have expended most of their efforts.[18]

A third interlocking influence is the presence of conventional (racial and regional) standards of expression which individuals (even children) adopt, and through which they actually come to resemble their fellows.[19] It has been frequently noted that to the occidental eye, Orientals "all look alike," and conversely, incredible though it may seem to us, Orientals have complained that Americans are hard to differentiate by their faces. These racial similarities are due in part to constitutional type but also in part to the *assumption* of standard expressions. It is usually difficult for the foreigner to recognize the play of individuality within the racial pattern.

There are also *customs* which require affected facial expression. The tired hostess, whatever her inner conflict, must assume the "awfully glad" look when her guests arrive. A gentleman, according

[18] For instance, there is plentiful research bearing upon the ability of judges to recognize common and basic emotional expressions in the face. This work derives primarily from Darwin whose interest, of course, was confined to the serviceable vestigial habits *common to all men* and recognizable in all races and in all individuals. Actually, however, experiments show a surprisingly low degree of success in identifying emotional expressions unless the judge is aided by knowledge of context and stimulus. Landis helps to explain these poor results by demonstrating that there is after all the important variable of *individuality*. For any single person the manner of expressing, say, disgust or mild amusement, is quite constant, but from individual to individual there is marked variation (C. Landis, *J. Comp. Psychol.*, 1924, 4, 447-509). To be sure, in states of intense emotional involvement the expression conforms more closely to the norm for the human race. Emergencies always have a way of leveling personal forms of expression to a form common to the species.

[19] The role of this unconscious imitation of expression was recognized by the philosopher, Immanuel Kant, who pointed to the curious fact that congenial married couples grow to have a similar cast of features. *Anthropologie*, Part I, sec. 32.

to Lord Chesterfield, must "never show anger." In the ancient cultures of the Orient, even more severe masking is required. Lafcadio Hearn speaks somewhere of his amazement at seeing the tortured and tragic expression on the usually placid face of his Japanese valet when the latter thought he was unobserved. All of our various social masks (of "interest," "friendliness," and "equanimity") belong to the conventionalized group of expressions whose purpose seems to be to smooth the path of social intercourse by submerging the often turbulent life beneath. It requires a shrewd observer to distinguish in facial expression the difference between assumed interest and real absorption, between authentic self-assurance and the pose of bravado.

But behind the universal, instinctive expressions common to all mankind, and behind racial and conventional standards, there exist true differences in facial lines and casts of countenance that can be attributed only to *individual* habits of thought and emotion. In order to practice the arts of physiognomy one must find means, if one can, of distinguishing the effects of each of these influences in order to read through the "outer" determinants to the "inner." At present the situation is simply this: we *know* that facial cues are revelatory of "the life within" but we find these cues obscured by the influence of such "non-personal" accidents as membership in a common species, hereditary structure, race, and convention.

Physiognomy, as has been pointed out, deals not only with the problem of muscular expression, which has just been discussed, but also with the almost wholly independent problems of *bony structure* and *constitutional habitus*. It is only in recent years that psychologists have interested themselves in this second class of problems. In novels and dramas, various psychophysical relationships have long been assumed. Julius Caesar says:

> Let me have men about me that are fat;
> Sleek-headed men, and such as sleep o' nights:
> Yon Cassius has a lean and hungry look;
> He thinks too much: such men are dangerous.
> *Julius Caesar*, Act I, sc. 2.

It was not Shakespeare, however, who inspired the psychological laboratories, clinics, and other psychometric centers to work on this problem. The credit goes to a German psychiatrist, Ernst Kretschmer, whose brilliant book *Physique and Character*, published first in

German in 1921, provoked a flood of investigations, which have confirmed *in part* his striking claims.

Kretschmer presented evidence that in mental hospitals elongated and frail "asthenic" physiques were found most frequently among dementia praecox patients, and that short and rounded "pyknic" physiques were most frequent among manic-depressive patients. Reduced to its barest statement, this was Kretschmer's finding.

Dissatisfied, however, with so bald a statement of the correlation, Kretschmer elaborated this single finding into a theory of the relationship between physique and *normal* personality, proceeding from the common premise that the abnormal is merely an exaggeration of the normal (cf. pp. 13, 76). Thus elaborated the theory requires that tall, slender physiques wherever found be ordinarily associated with such schizothymic qualities as introversion, formalism, idealism and romanticism ("normal" variants on the syndrome of dementia praecox). Correspondingly, physiques which are rounded, heavier, shorter, with larger body cavities should belong to individuals who in the main are cyclothymic; sometimes moody, but often jovial, and predominantly extroverted, realistic, and objective (reflections of the manic-depressive make-up).[20] Kretschmer distinguishes two additional types of body-build, the athletic and the dysplastic, both of which, like the asthenic, are supposed to be associated with the introverted pattern of personality.

A more detailed exposition of Kretschmer's contentions and of the investigations which they have provoked would be beyond the scope of this chapter.[21] Passing directly to a summary evaluation of the evidence to date, it is unfortunately necessary to report that the exuberance of Kretschmer's claims and the enthusiasm of his many disciples need correction and restraint. Taken at the pathological level the evidence is favorable enough, though not as favorable as

[20] In the schematic drawings in Figure 9 the reader has already noted the slender and delicate (asthenic) physique of the melancholic temperament (No. 1). The physical-mental correlation here indicated by the humoral theory is quite in agreement with Kretschmer's doctrine. The hormones are, according to both theories, responsible for the fragility of the bodily structure and for the introverted, idealistic, withdrawing attitude. Somewhat less clearly perhaps the drawing of the phlegmatic type (No. 3) depicts the pyknic physique, and the traditional conception of this temperament is not incompatible with Kretschmer's picture of the extroversion and realism found in this physical type.

[21] Reviews of the literature on this subject may be found in L. Polen, "Körperbau und Charakter," *Arch. f. d. ges. Psychol.*, 1928, 66, 1-116 (a complete bibliography up to 1928); O. Klineberg, *Race Differences*, Harper, 1935, pp. 56-66.

Kretschmer claims.[22] At the normal level there are many totally negative investigations.[23]

The good and the bad points of this type of modern physiognomy can be best understood, not by citing the conflicting evidence, but by examining the presuppositions of the work. Kretschmer's original hypothesis, it will be shown, is in part unsound, and therefore should not be expected to yield uniformly positive results.

In the first place, Kretschmer's theory requires that "character" be innately determined. But is it? Is it not rather the *temperament* (the emotional ground upon which "character" develops) that is closely controlled by the chemistry of the body and therefore associated with physical build? Kretschmer should not have attempted to write of "physique and character," nor of physique and personality.

[22] According to Kretschmer the incidence of physiques among the two classes of psychotics in a group of over 4,000 cases in mental hospitals is as follows:

Constitutional Type	Circular Insanity (Per cent of cases)	Schizophrenia (Per cent of cases)
Pyknic and pyknoid	66.7	12.8
Leptosome (asthenic) and athletic	23.6	66.0
Dysplastic	0.4	11.3
Atypical	9.3	9.9

(From O. Klineberg, *op. cit.*, p. 69.)

On the other hand critics have pointed out that age is an uncontrolled influence in this table; (*e.g.*, C. R. Garvey, *Psychol. Bull.*, 1933, 30, 567, 739). Schizophrenia generally strikes early in life when the body is still slender. The average age of manic-depressives is higher, and with age many physiques become pyknic.

[23] One example may be briefly described. P. S. Cabot, employing a group of 200 boys in late adolescence, for whom anthropometric records of growth were available for twelve preceding years, undertook to check on Kretschmer's claims. ("The Relation between Characteristics of Personality and Physique in Adolescents," forthcoming in *Genet. Psychol. Monog.*) For the physical criterion he employed various types of anthropometric indices which seemed fairly to represent the asthenic, pyknic, and athletic physiques; he also used ratings of these physiques based upon impressions of the boys' appearance. On the side of personality his criteria consisted of dozens of rating scales, tests, and questionnaires all pointed in such a way as to obtain the optimum information concerning each boy's personality (with special reference, of course, to Kretschmer's claims regarding introversion, withdrawing, autism, leadership, realism, objectivity, and the like).

The results of the investigation offer little support for any of Kretschmer's contentions. The differences in personality shown by each physical type seemed, on the contrary, just about what one would expect according to a wholly different theory. *Those boys who had solid and substantial physiques (whether pyknic or athletic) seemed on the whole to develop personalities that were extroverted, outgoing, realistic, and dominant. In short, a "good" physique disposes the boy to develop strong traits of self-expression.* Social acceptability and physical vitality, or else compensation, seem to be the determining factors. These factors, all of them dependent upon the *interaction* of the boy's constitutional make-up with environment, are so outstanding as to cast serious doubts upon the *native* predetermination of personality required by Kretschmer's theory.

but rather of physique and *temperament.* Had he done so he would not have entered the hazardous claim that the *finished portraits* of a personality can be paralleled by corresponding physical types. Dealing with temperament he would have been on safer ground, for emotionality and physique must indeed be expected in some basic way to correspond (since both are partially the products of the glands of internal secretion). There is a marked difference between traits that are the product of *all* formative influences (such as extroversion, dominance, leadership, autism, and the like) and the simpler and more basic qualities of temperament (cyclothymia, melancholy, euphoria, phlegmatism). It is in this second group of features, and not in the first, that he should have sought his correlations.[24]

Kretschmer's strong nativistic bias leads to a further difficulty when the question of hereditary mixtures is concerned. Constitutional habitus is clearly not a Mendelian unit, neither is "character" a unit trait. Considering our long lines of mixed ancestry, it is remarkable that he should find so many pure types to illustrate his theory.[25] Actually, of course, most people are extreme neither in physique nor in temperament; the types are mixed. And yet if Kretschmer has failed to solve the riddle of the inheritance of temperament and body-build, so too has every other investigator; one cannot be too critical on this account.

All the inadequacies of the concept of "types" are realized in the Kretschmerian scheme as it stands at present (cf. pp. 13-15). For example, Kretschmer takes his departure from the two major forms of functional mental disturbance (dementia praecox and manic-depressive psychosis). He finds two corresponding physiques. But what would he do if he added to his basic list of "character types" other clinical forms of disturbances in personality, for example the epileptoid, the paranoid, or the psychopathic inferior? And why, in his theory, should such utterly different physical types as the dysplastic

[24] The only results supporting Kretschmer's theory have come from mental hospitals where one finds the effect of extreme temperamental (emotional) disturbance upon the psychosis. It is not the psychosis itself, however, that corresponds to the constitutional type, but rather the *temperament* underlying the psychosis.

[25] The averaging out, through mixed inheritance, of all extremes in physical build, is, however, to some extent prevented through a curious phenomenon of assortative mating. C. B. Davenport has shown that slender men tend to marry slender women to an extent exceeding chance expectation by 50%; fleshy men and fleshy women marry to an extent exceeding chance by 80%. Hence the children of these marriages tend, to some extent, to perpetuate the more or less pure asthenic and pyknic physiques. *Proc. Assoc. Res. Nerv. & Ment. Dis.,* 1934, 14, 21-27.

and athletic be lumped together with the contrasting asthenic physique, and all three then be expected to parallel the schizothymic mental make-up?

Empirical evidence has thus far failed to prove that Kretschmer's correlation occurs anywhere else than in cases of mental disease. He believes, nevertheless, that what holds for the extremes must hold as well for the means. But should it? Is the normal personality simply an undistinguished edition of the mentally diseased? We do not hold this view in reference to *organic* conditions. There is no continuum of states from cancer to no-cancer. The patient either has a malignant growth or else he hasn't; there are no intermediate conditions. Similarly a diseased mind is in many respects functionally quite different from (and not merely an exaggeration of) the normal mind.

The belief in the perfect continuity of the normal and abnormal, which most psychiatrists and psychologists share with Kretschmer, has resulted in the rapid multiplication of studies of disordered people, partly because, confined as they are to institutions, they are easily accessible, and partly because the extreme nature of their disorders makes them more interesting and more spectacular. Actually the number of studies of neurotic and psychotic personalities far exceeds the number devoted to normal personality, although, of course, the ratio in the world at large is precisely the opposite. The uncritical carrying over of the point of view of the mental hospital into the world outside has made, as in Kretschmer's case, for serious one-sidedness in the psychological study of *normal* personality. This charge is justified, even though occasionally the discoveries of psychopathology may be of indirect aid to the psychology of normality.

Returning to Kretschmer's theory specifically, we conclude that extreme glandular *imbalance* may affect physique and temperament in significant ways, whereas normal conditions of glandular *balance* leave a greater play for environmental and experiential determinants. What slight effect constitutional type may have in the development of the personality of *normal* people seems to be totally overlaid by the more important determinants of education and social experience. In cases of abnormality the imbalance is so extreme as to dominate the picture.

Before summarizing this somewhat lengthy discussion of physiognomy, we should pay our respects to the most famous physiognomist of all times, Johann Kaspar Lavater (1741-1801).[26] Many details of his system are not helpful, for in some respects they resemble the contentions of modern "quack" physiognomists; certainly his tendency to combine his readings of personality with moral preachment may be overlooked.[27] It is Lavater, however, who expressed most clearly the exceedingly important hypothesis that all of the features of the body are ultimately congruent and consistent. Their forms of expression all proceed from a central, unified personality, and therefore they must be harmonious among themselves, and must all betray the organization of personality within. Laughing eyes, he says, do not occur without a laughing mouth, nor, if we are shrewd enough to see it, without corresponding "mirthful" qualities in the gait, handwriting, and postures of the body. He is emphatic in this view: "Everything in man is progressive; everything is congenial. Form, stature, complexion, hair, skin, veins, nerves, bones, voice, walk, manner, style, passion, love, hatred: one and the same spirit is manifest in all." This contention has recently provided a problem for laboratory research, and its approximate correctness in the field of expression has been experimentally demonstrated.[28] What is especially important in Lavater's system, then, is his emphasis upon the radical consistency of personality both in its inward aspects and in its expression.

In conclusion, physiognomy, although it has had a checkered and in part a disreputable career, is an important branch of the psychology of personality. But scientific knowledge lags behind naive belief and credulous practice. Only a few fairly certain principles can as yet be entertained:

1. The bony structure of the body (constitutional build) is related to personality through the medium of temperament, for both the physical habitus and temperament are products of bodily chemistry.

[26] His chief work, *Physiognomische Fragmente zur Beförderung der Menschenkenntniss und Menschenliebe*, issued in 1783-87 in three volumes, has many times been republished. Still earlier editions of this work appeared in 1772 and 1775 under different titles. A good secondary account will be found in E. Utitz, *Charakterologie*, pp. 55-60.

[27] Goethe in both his *Gespräche mit Eckermann* and in *Dichtung und Wahrheit* describes vividly Lavater's evangelical manner of practicing his art upon street crowds and in churches.

[28] G. W. Allport and P. E. Vernon, *Studies in Expressive Movement*, 1933. The matter is discussed further in Chapter XVII of the present volume.

2. In cases of extreme glandular imbalance there are likely to be severe upsets of emotion, and corresponding changes in personality. But "thyroid" personalities or "enuchoid" personalities occur *only* in serious cases of glandular dysfunction.

3. Within the normal range of glandular functioning (and bodily build) other causative influences are vastly more important factors in determining the development of personality than is the "constitutional type."

4. Within this normal range, physical build is associated only *indirectly* with personality. Strong bodies, well-formed, and socially approved, predispose people (especially in youth) to develop extroverted, realistic, sociable traits; conversely, frail, malformed, or markedly atypical physiques tend (in response to social and environmental standards) to produce introverted, intellectual, or autistic personalities. This finding takes care of much of Kretschmer's evidence, but offers a totally different theory (one that is environmentalistic rather than nativistic) to account for the association of physique and personality *within the normal range*.

5. The musculature of the body reflects better than its bony structure the influence of life-experiences, and hence from facial and postural sets more certain inferences concerning personality can be made than from constitutional build (for example, a highly educated person or a degenerate can more readily be identified by muscular sets than by constitutional build).

6. In making inferences from muscular set and facial expression it is necessary to "read through" such non-personal determinants as racial membership, local customs, and the universal patterns of instinctive emotional expression. Personality is only one of the factors that affect the cast of features, or posture and movement.

7. There is considerable consistency among the expressive features of the body.

These conclusions are taken up again and extended in Chapter XVII.

PHRENOLOGY

Unlike the preceding three schools of characterology, phrenology is exclusively a modern doctrine; it is less than a century and a half since it was first promulgated by Franz Joseph Gall (1758-1828).[29] Even more than physiognomy it has had its disreputable side, as a lucrative "racket" for vainglorious mountebanks. Although its influence, enormous in the past, now is waning, phrenology still has its devotees. Even today there are phrenological practitioners and magazines that thrive by simplifying and perverting some of the older teachings, none too sound in themselves, by infusing them with the popular idols of success, wealth, and fascination. But it is not with this slum of psychology that we need concern ourselves. Phrenology has another, less familiar, but more significant side.

The story of the origin, premises, growth and decline of phrenology has many times been told.[30] It need not be repeated here. Nor is it necessary any longer to take time to refute the specific assumptions upon which Gall founded his eccentric system: their weakness is entirely transparent to the modern psychological reader.[31] But even

[29] The popularity of phrenology immediately commenced with Gall's first lectures in 1796. It spread rapidly through the enterprising salesmanship of Gall's assistant, Johann Gaspar Spurzheim (1776-1832), who, however, separated from his master in 1815, and wrote many independent works, lecturing widely in England and on the continent. Spurzheim came to America in 1832, lectured to large audiences, was well received at Harvard, and died in Boston.

Gall's chief work appeared in four volumes between 1810 and 1819, and was entitled, *Anatomie et physiologie du système nerveux en général, et du cerveau en particulier, avec observations sur la possibilité de reconnoître plusieurs dispositions intellectuelles et morales de l'homme et des animaux par la configuration de leur têtes.* In 1822-25 Gall published a revised edition in six volumes under the title, *Sur les fonctions du cerveau,* etc. The six volume American edition, *On the Functions of the Brain,* etc., was published in 1835.

The name "phrenology" was invented by Dr. Thomas Forster and was adopted by Spurzheim in 1815. Gall himself never used the term, but referred to his doctrine as "organology," "cranioscopy," or more often as "the physiology of the brain."

[30] Interesting and discriminating accounts are those of E. G. Boring, *A History of Experimental Psychology,* 1929, chap. iii; M. Bentley, "The Psychological Antecedents of Phrenology," *Psychol. Monog.,* 1916, No. 92; C. Blondel, *La psychophysiologie de Gall,* 1913; McQ. De Grange, *The Science of Individuality,* 1923; H. D. Spoerl, "Faculties *versus* Traits: the Solution of Franz Joseph Gall," *Char. & Pers.,* 1936, 4, 216-231.

[31] These assumptions, or "laws" as they were often called, are stated briefly in the following way:

(a) mental faculties are innate;
(b) the brain is the organ of mind;
(c) the form and size of the brain are distinguishable by the form and size of the head or skull;

though we can afford to disregard the many spurious features of the system along with its curious history, there still remain three positive contributions in Gall's work deserving respectful consideration today.

In the first place, there is an acceptable postulate underlying Gall's organology, namely, that mind and body are not two independent entities, but are inextricably related. In one way or another virtually all of the contemporary work on personality shares with Gall this implicit faith in psychophysical parallelism. Furthermore, it was Gall himself who brought this philosophical conviction into fashion among characterologists. To be sure, it does not specifically advance our knowledge to hold that an individual's psychic attributes are rooted in some way in the physiological functions of his body. The view, however, becomes important when it is regarded as a framework for more detailed theorizing and research. Probably no modern investigator doubts that through scientific discovery patterns of personality will be found to parallel patterns of somatic response. "Engrams," "neurograms," "physiological vectors," "visceral-cortical tracts" are some of the terms nowadays proposed to aid in establishing this correlation. It was Gall's intention to create through his biological studies a conceptual unification of the mind-body relationship as an aid in understanding human personality. Most investigators of the present day would like to do the same thing.

In the second place, phrenology rendered timely service by calling attention to the phenomenon of individual differences. Psychology in the early nineteenth century was interested almost exclusively in mind-in-general. Gall recognized that human beings differ widely in their personal tastes and mental qualities, and yet he hoped, as many psychologists of the present day hope, to discover basic variables that might account for the apparently limitless varieties of human personality. He struggled persistently to establish a final list of the essential, or as he called them the "primitive," characteristics of human nature.

> (d) the mind possesses distinct faculties and the brain is composed of distinct organs, and each mental faculty is manifested through a distinct cerebral organ;
> (e) the size of each organ can be estimated during life, and the size, other things being equal, is a measure of power;
> (f) each organ, when predominantly active, impresses the body with certain uniform attitudes and movements, called its "natural language." (From George Combe, *Lectures on Phrenology*, 1847, p. 63.)

Of these assumptions only (b) and (f) are by any stretch of the imagination acceptable to modern psychologists, and these not in the sense Gall intended.

What is more, in seeking these radical elements (which turned out to be the famous twenty-seven faculties) Gall employed an empirical method. He was, as he thought, decidedly positivistic in his procedure. He compared innumerable skulls, studied genius, labored in asylums for the insane, reasoned inductively, and with the most honest of intentions criticized and revised his own work constantly. He obeyed, much more faithfully than most of his contemporaries, the canons of scientific method, and yet he committed absurdities. His failure should be a warning to the devotees of positivism that a *method* in itself is never a certain guarantee of truth.

Today with different instruments a similar positivistic search is being made for the "primitive" or basic elements of personality. Instead of being the audacious quest of a single investigator, handicapped by an assistant as headstrong as Spurzheim, the modern project has been the subject of a call for international co-operation of all the psychologists who are interested in applying statistical methods to the problem. The method, like Gall's, is to be empirical, but every assistance of modern tests and experimentation together with the aid of mathematics are to be utilized.[32] It is "factors" rather than "faculties" that are sought, but the intent of the search is similar. Whether this modern endeavor will meet with greater success than Gall's remains to be seen. Part III of this volume will define some of the serious problems that must be faced in any attempt to discover the ultimate unitary traits of human nature.

The third meritorious contribution of Gall's work is the most important, but least understood of all. It has to do with the nature of the units of personality (the "faculties") with which he dealt. In contemporary psychology there is, of course, a prejudice against faculty psychology in all its forms—an unfortunate fact since such a totalized prejudice prevents balanced criticism and discriminating judgment. As a matter of fact there are many varieties of faculty psychology, and Gall's is seriously misrepresented when it is identified with other faculty psychologies current in the early nineteenth century. Cast by his critics into the same camp as Wolff, Stewart, Reid, and Hutcheson, Gall has been unfairly sentenced with them to oblivion.[33]

[32] C. Spearman, X[th] Congress of Psychology, Copenhagen, 1932. A recent report on this co-operative research is K. J. Holzinger, "Recent Research on Unitary Mental Traits," *Char. & Pers.*, 1936, 4, 335-343.

[33] Wundt, for example, claimed that Gall produced simply a physiological caricature of Wolff's faculties (*Gehirn und Seele*, 2d ed., 1906, 145-148). Similarly, James asserted that Gall "took the faculty-psychology as his ultimatum on the mental side,

The charge that Gall was imitating the faculty psychologists of his time is false. Time and again he inveighed against Wolff, and other continental psychologists. He regarded their a priori lists of faculties as totally worthless, and pursued what he thought was a strictly empirical, and far sounder, method of discovering the really radical units of character. For one thing, he sought faculties that would be independent of one another. No other faculty-psychologist claimed independence for his faculties, and none sought as Gall did to establish the faculties inductively and empirically through a direct examination of innumerable individual cases. But the chief difference between Gall's psychology and that of the others lay in the fact that he sought with the aid of his "faculties" to account for the *differences between men.* "We need faculties," he wrote, "the different distribution of which shall determine the different species of animals, and the different proportions of which explain the difference in individuals." [34] All other faculty psychologists aimed to establish *universal faculties,* such as would account for the mental operations of all men. They were not interested in individual differences at all, certainly not in the problem of the organization of unique personalities. In envisaging this problem, Gall was a century ahead of his time.

The point at issue is important enough to deserve an illustration. "Perception," for example, does not appear in Gall's list of faculties; it does appear in Reid's and Stewart's (cf. lists in table p. 84). It seemed self-evident to the latter that perception is a basic power of all minds, and so it is. But for Gall, the very universality of Perception disqualified it as a radical (differentiating) faculty. He would say that such a basic process is common to the exercise of *all* the

and he made no farther psychological analysis" (*Principles of Psychology,* I, 27). How could these famous founders of modern psychology reconcile their charges with Gall's own repeated condemnation of faculty psychology as it was known to him? (Cf. Gall, *On the Functions of the Brain,* Vol. III, pp. 82-86.)

James lays the disrepute of phrenology largely to the vagueness and vastness of its faculties which, he thought, not only lacked analytic finesse but were conceived as so many separate self-active "souls" or homunculi. To James, as to the modern specificists, the faculties should have been analyzed into smaller, sensorimotor, elements. "A science of mind must reduce such complex manifestations as 'philoprogenitiveness' to their *elements*" (*Principles,* I, 27).

It is true that Gall did not analyze his 27 functions into elements, but his failure to do so is the very reason why his list of human qualities seems more in keeping with the structured character of personality as we know it in actual life than do the motley assortments of habits, conditioned reflexes and other sensorimotor elements out of which recent psychology has vainly attempted to create a scientific characterology.

[34] Gall, *On the Functions of the Brain,* Vol. I, p. 88.

faculties; its role is merely attributive; it is not a characterological unit. On this ground he repudiates not only Perception, but many other universal faculties proposed by his contemporaries. He wrote, for example, "We nowhere find that a man or a woman has become celebrated by the Understanding and the Will, by Attention, Comparison, Desire. . . . Every man, except an idiot, enjoys all these faculties. Yet all men have not the same intellectual or moral character." [35] What is needed, he concludes, is "primitive" units which will account for the distinctions, and not merely the resemblances, between human beings.[36]

Most of Gall's disciples did not perceive the significance of his distinction between the nomothetic, or universal attributes of mind, and the concrete, differentiating, faculties which he so arduously sought to discover. His followers, of whom Spurzheim is a good example, were attracted by the pseudo-practical applications of phrenology. An exception to this rule is von Struve who re-states the issue clearly: "When I accurately specify each of the thirty-five phrenological qualities of a man,[37] I have laid the foundation for a graphic account of character from which its direction can be traced both in its larger and in its detailed aspects, and in relation to intellectual and moral factors. But when, with the old school, I speak in general only of the life of experience, feeling, and the like, they throw little light upon the matter." [38] Another shrewd reader of Gall was Thomas Hyde, who, as a senior in Harvard College, presented an honor's thesis to William James comparing the merits of phrenology and psychology, then a young experimental science. He concluded that, "the establishment of primitive powers was chiefly the work of phrenology," whereas psychology "seems better able to detect the general or universal rather than the specific or individual." Hence, he concludes, "after a careful consideration of the claims of each, we gave our adherence to phrenology." [39] This essay, we are

[35] *Loc. cit.*

[36] The opposition between "universal faculties" and "primitive faculties" is discussed more fully by H. D. Spoerl, "Faculties or Traits: The Solution of Franz Joseph Gall," *Char. & Pers.*, 1936, 4, 216-231. This study shows an excellent appreciation of the significance of Gall's work for the psychology of personality. The readiness of most psychologists to confuse Gall's conception of the faculties with those of his predecessors is due to their pre-occupation with mind-in-general. They fail to understand that Gall's ultimate interest was mind-in-particular.

[37] Gall's original list of twenty-seven faculties was increased to thirty-five by Spurzheim and to forty-two by Combe and other followers.

[38] G. von Struve, *Phrenologie in und ausserhalb Deutschland*, 1843, p. 51.

[39] Thomas A. Hyde, *How to Study Character*, 1884, pp. 170 f.

told, was favorably commented upon by James, but the crucial distinction it drew between universal and characterial faculties was apparently unappreciated by James, for it did not find its way into his own critique of phrenology.

Thomas Reid, 1780	Dugald Stewart, 1827	Franz Joseph Gall, 1810
Active Powers	*Active Powers*	*Determinate Faculties*
Self-Preservation		
Maintenance of Habits	Propensity to Action and Repose	
Hunger and Thirst	Hunger and Thirst	
Lust	Sex	Instinct of Generation (1)
	Acquired Appetite for Drugs	
	Desire of Society	
Instinct of Imitation	Instinct of Imitation	Mimicry, Imitation (25)
Language		Verbal Memory (14)
Desire for Power	Ambition	Vanity, Ambition (9)
Self-Esteem	{ Self-Love / Self-Confidence }	Pride, Self-Esteem (8)
Desire of Knowledge	Desire of Knowledge	Educability (11)
Confiliate Affection	{ Parental Affection / Filial Affection	Love of Offspring (2)
Gratitude	Gratitude	
Pity and Compassion	{ Pity / Sympathy	
	Universal Benevolence	Good Nature (24)
Esteem of the Wise and Good	Desire of Esteem	
	Veracity	
Friendship	Friendship	Friendship, Attachment (3)
Sexual Affection	Sexual Affection	
Public Spirit	Patriotism	
Emulation	Desire of Superiority	
Rational Resentment } Animal Resentment }	Resentment	Courage, Self-Defense (4)
Transcendent Good	Interest	
Duty	Sense of Duty	
Veneration	Veneration	Theosophy, Religion (26)
	Hope	
	Decency, Regard to Character	Firmness of Character (27)
Imagination (—invention)	Imagination	Poetry (23)
	Instinct for Construction	Mechanical Aptitude (19)
	Sense of Similarity and Contrast }	Wit (22)
	Sense of the Ridiculous }	
Beauty	Memory for Colors	Sense of Colors (16)
	Time	
	Music	Music (17)
		Wish to Destroy (5)
		Cunning (6)
		Sentiment of Property (7)
		Cautiousness (10)
		Mathematics (18)
Intellectual Powers	*Intellectual Powers*	
The Five Senses and Their Faculty of Perception	The Five Senses and Their Faculty of Perception	
	Form	Memory for Persons (13)
Size and Novelty	{ Size / Novelty	
	Locality	Local Memory (12)
	Language	Memory for Languages (15)
Memory	Memory	
Judgment and Reason	Judgment and Reasoning	Comparative Sagacity (20)
Abstraction	Abstraction	Metaphysical Depth (21)
Conception	Conception	
	Attention	
Moral Taste	Moral Taste	
	Association of Ideas	

COMPARATIVE TABLE OF FACULTIES

(From H. D. Spoerl, *op. cit.*, Duke University Press, p. 222. Gall's numbering of the **faculties** is in parentheses; he alone used numbers.)

As clear as Gall's intention was, it must be admitted that he was not uniformly successful in his achievement. Some of the faculties listed in Spoerl's table all too obviously parallel the Scottish faculties, and thereby reflect the same abstractions from the generalized mind, rather than clear-cut characterial units. *Memory for languages* is one example; *color sense* is another. Gall would undoubtedly reply that he had accepted such of these faculties as seemed to him to be *qualities* whose quantitative variation did actually account for differences in character; when intense, these attributive faculties actually operate as characterial (differentiating) faculties as well. Whatever the merits of this reply, Gall is guilty of confusing passive (intellectual) faculties, *viz.*, aptitudes and skills, on the one hand, with active, conative integrations of character, on the other. Actually it is only the latter that fit his requirements for "primitive" units.

It is easy enough in retrospect to see what Gall should have done in order to accomplish his admirable purpose of constructing a psychology of individuality. He should have rejected the term "faculty" as too heavily freighted with a meaning wholly foreign to his own. He should have then distinguished not only in theory between the universal and the characterial method of analysis, but should have followed his conviction more consistently in practice. Only by so doing could he show that the former faculties represented an undesirable abstraction, and that the latter followed in principle the concrete personal organizations of nature. He would have had to eliminate intellectual aptitudes and talents from his list more completely than he did, and confine himself to such personal-conative systems as are nowadays referred to as interests, sentiments, values, and traits. This step would have led him away from his two other most serious errors, namely, the assumption that each of the units he chose is independent of all other units, and the equally false assumption that every radical quality of character is inborn and "resists education."

Gall's belief that personality is naturally organized into more or less systematized dispositions, each of which expresses individuality of adaptive behavior, is altogether acceptable. If shorn of its many false embellishments (the myth of corresponding organs, its nativistic bias, its numerical listings, and its occasional and inconsistent concessions to the prevailing faculty psychology of the day) it would then serve as an admirable starting point for a modern psychology of personality founded upon a clear conception of the nature of traits.

ETHOLOGY AND THE STUDY OF SENTIMENTS

Under the title of "Ethology" John Stuart Mill proposed the formation of "an exact science of human nature." [40] It should deal, he maintained, with human character, and be established upon the secure foundations of a general and abstract science of psychology. Its material should consist of the empirical wisdom of common sense, descriptions of personal patterns of conduct, but its explanatory principles must be derived from the science of psychology. This distinction between descriptions of character and explanations of character is of considerable importance. [41]

Only the *explanatory* principles in characterology, according to Mill, can be derived from the science of psychology. Its *data* must be drawn from life and not from experiment. Experimentation with human character, he thinks, is impossible. To prosecute such studies it would be necessary to bring up and to educate individuals in complete isolation, with every conditioning factor known and controlled from infancy to a mature age. (Mill's requirements for an experiment were much more exacting than those of the present day!) There are, however, innumerable collections of proverbial wisdom concerning human characteristics which are to be found in maxims, adages, and in the literature of all ages. These empirical generalizations affirm tendencies, not facts. It is, for example, said that bodily strength tends to make men courageous; not that it always makes them so; it will do so only if no counter-influence intervenes. Now an accumulation of such empirical wisdom becomes valuable when it can be referred to psychological laws, and in this way be checked by placing it in a framework of "causal" explanations. "Unless we have resolved the empirical law into the laws of the causes on which it depends, and ascertained that those causes extend to the case which we have in view, there can be no reliance placed in our inferences." [42] The really scientific truths, then, are not these empirical laws, but the causal laws which explain them.

Mill realizes that general psychology alone is not equipped to deal

---

[40] J. S. Mill, *System of Logic*, 1843, Book VI, chap. v.

[41] The distinction is the same as Lewin draws between the *phenotype* ("the immediate perceptible appearance") and the *genotype* ("genetic conditioning"); cf. p. 16. Throughout the psychology of personality the opposition between *appearance* and *cause* constantly recurs.

[42] Bk. VI, chap. v, sec. 2.

with character. It merely supplies a statement of laws useful in explaining the development of character. This view is the same as
Wundt's (pp. 6 f.), who regarded the science of "characterology" as
a supplement to general psychology. Mill wrote before Bahnsen had
coined the term "characterology," and therefore was unable to profit
from it. He says,

> A science is thus formed, to which I would propose to give the
> name of Ethology, or the Science of Character, from ἠϑος, a word
> more nearly corresponding to the term "character," as I here use it,
> than any other word in the same language. The name is perhaps
> etymologically applicable to the entire science of our mental and
> moral nature; but if, as is usual and convenient, we employ the name
> Psychology for the science of the elementary laws of mind, Ethology
> will serve for the ulterior science which determines the kind of char-
> acter produced in conformity to these general laws, by any set of
> circumstances, physical and moral.[43]

Referring to the accumulated maxims concerning character, and
to the great advances of general psychology, Mill asserts that the
creation of this new science has at length become practicable. "The
empirical laws, destined to verify its deductions, have been formed in
abundance by every successive age of humanity, and the premises for
the deductions are now sufficiently complete." [44]

What were these premises which were sufficiently complete?
What causal principles did psychology at the time of Mill have to
offer? When this question is asked it becomes clear immediately why
Ethology made no advance for fifty years after Mill published his
program. Associationism, the principle by which fragmentary states of
consciousness aroused other fragmentary states, was the sole "explanatory" tool of psychology, and woefully inadequate to account for the
galaxy of human interests, motives, conflicts, and passions which are
the essential forces in the formation of character. Psychology in Mill's
time was intellectualistic, Apollonian, and not until the influence of
Schopenhauer, Darwin, Freud, and McDougall had altered its point
of view radically, training its vision upon the irrational motives of
men, were the premises sufficiently complete to permit a realization
of Mill's proposal.

It was Alexander Shand who put Mill's method to its only ade-

[43] *Ibid.*, sec. 4.
[44] *Ibid.*, sec. 6.

quate test. Following Mill's instructions he assembled countless proverbs, maxims, and literary statements concerning human nature. But for his "premises for deduction" he accepted not the laws of association but the theory of sentiments.[45] Apart from his use of this new type of psychological explanation, his method follows Mill's proposal exactly. He deduces 144 laws for the "foundations of character," under the guidance of his basic law that "Every sentiment tends to form a type of character of its own."[46] The individual laws refer to the typical courses which the major sentiments take in human life, for example,

> (Law 116) *Hope tends always to make the future appear better than the present.*

He then "verifies" each law by common wisdom and adages to conform to Mill's requirement that "verification *a posteriori* must proceed *pari passu* with deduction *a priori*."[47] In the case of this particular law, Shand offers among other proofs the authority of Shakespeare:

> True hope is swift, and flies with swallow's wings,
> Kings it makes Gods, and meaner creatures kings.

The outstanding weakness of Shand's procedure is his arbitrary selection of supporting proverbs and maxims. However much of an advance it was to insist upon dynamic and emotional factors as the foundations of character, reliance solely upon sentiments limited unduly the genotypical background with which psychologists of character must work. As for proverbial wisdom, it is notoriously ambiguous. Every proverb affirming one type of occurrence, seems to engender another negating it. It is said that "as a twig is bent, so inclines the tree," but also that "a young monk makes an old devil." Goethe wrote, "The weak often have revolutionary sentiments"; but G. B. Shaw has maintained that "a man who is not a revolutionary by twenty is an inferior."

The positive contribution of Shand is his recognition of systema-

[45] In *Mind*, in 1896 Shand published an article giving the outlines of his theory, but it was not until 1915 that his book *Foundations of Character* appeared. Between these dates Stout and McDougall had made important contributions to the theory of sentiments. Cf. W. McDougall, "Organization of the Affective Life. A Critical Survey," *Acta Psychologica*, 1937, 2, 233-346.

[46] *Op. cit.*, p. 123.

[47] Mill, *op. cit.*, chap. v, sec. 6.

tized emotional dispositions as the functional units of which the personality (or as he prefers to call it, the character) is composed. Like
Gall, he sought units that would differentiate men from one another
in respect to those complex affective and conative functions which
are the ultimate systems of adaptive behavior. His interest basically,
however, is nomothetic, for he hopes through the compounding of
the *same* common sentiments in all men, with the aid of the *same* one
hundred forty-four laws, to account for all manifestations of individuality. His approach is significant for his selection of the dynamic
unit of the sentiment, but it is not completely personalistic; and his
neglect of all psychological aids other than the concept of sentiment
is short-sighted.

Similar to Shand's, but resting upon a more adequate psychological groundwork, is McDougall's theory of personality. Here again
"sentiment" is the cardinal concept. The sentiment is itself a com-
plexly organized affective tendency, springing from instinct and emotion, but attached by experience to a certain object or class of objects. In themselves the various sentiments may obstruct one another
or conflict with one another unless they are brought into one single
system within which their impulses are harmonized. This embracing
integration is the "character," and is achieved through the development of a master sentiment of "self-regard," which takes the form of
a self-conscious devotion to certain selected ideals with which the
person identifies himself. Not only does this devotion to certain ideals
dominate and harmonize all other sentiments, but it is capable of extension and change so that a continuous and consistent growth of personality is assured. Failure to organize the system of sentiment-units
into a hierarchy with the sentiment of self-regard "at the top," leads
to mental conflict, neurosis, and in extreme cases to psychosis.[48]

Two other writers of the past century, preceding Shand and
McDougall, placed stress upon the role of dominant interests or "ruling passions" in conferring form and unity to personality. One of
these, Alexander Bain, was well acquainted with the history of characterology. He wrote both appreciatively and critically of his predecessors, and even prepared an original translation of the *Characters*
of Theophrastus.[49] Mill's provocative plan for Ethology inspired him
to offer an alternative program for characterology which would be,

[48] W. McDougall, *Outline of Abnormal Psychology*, 1926, esp. pp. 525 f.
[49] Alexander Bain, *On the Study of Character*, 1862.

he thought, "more in accordance with the present state of our knowledge of the human constitution."

The foundations of Bain's doctrine were the three venerable faculties of Emotion, Volition, and Intellect, derived originally from Plato's tri-partite division of the human soul. By Bain these faculties were viewed as so many channels for the flow of "psychic energy." Each man has a characteristic amount of this energy, which may either be wasted or turned to account. When it is not merely expended at random (as in play) it is purposefully directed into emotional, volitional (muscular) or intellectual activity. A man's nature thus is determined by the predominance of one or the other of these three channels. "Human nature being limited, if one's vitality runs very much to the active organs, less will go to the other parts." [50] This "steam-boiler" conception results inevitably in a doctrine of types, with the result that there are men who are *mental*, others who are *motor* ("men of action"), and still others who are *vital* (sensual).

Popular and commercial characterology of today employs this same three-fold distinction, often supplementing the types with reckless physiognomic parallels. For instance, it is said that the mental type possesses an elongated or triangular face, the motor type, square and aggressive features, and the vital type, a round and flabby countenance.

Bain's fallacy lay in assuming a constant amount of "psychic energy" which if drained into one channel would necessarily flow in deficient qualities through other channels, shaping the personality in accordance with its flow. The resulting typology seems too scanty in its permutations and unconvincing in its selection of channels and in its theory of energy. It has, however, the merit of recognizing as the central problem in the psychology of personality the study of dominant motives and interests.

The other characterologist who emphasized the importance of the dominant interest or "ruling passion" is Charles Fourier (1772-1837). His analysis of human passions served him as a basis for the elaborate social philosophy and doctrine of reform for which he is famous.[51]

The intricacies and eccentricities of Fourier's classification of human types are fascinating. He was obsessed by the possibility of

[50] Alexander Bain, *op. cit.*, p. 201.
[51] Charles Fourier, *The Passions of the Human Soul*, trans. 1851, two volumes. See also A. A. Roback, *The Psychology of Character*, chap. x.

distributing mankind into regional and vocational groups according to his own elaborate scheme of character types. The fundamental "passions" of men are of three classes (sensuous, affective, distribu-

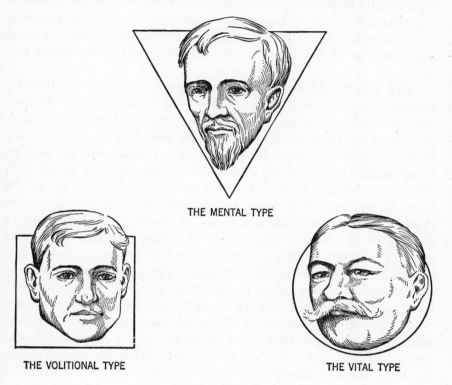

THE MENTAL TYPE

THE VOLITIONAL TYPE

THE VITAL TYPE

FIGURE 10

Physiognomic Parallels to Bain's Types (as offered by popular "character analysis"). The oversimplification is apparent from the selection of extreme physiques, and from the use of accentuating boundary lines and goatee. No proof is offered for the validity of the types.

Reprinted by permission from *Psychology*, 1925, 4, p. 41.

tive), but these must further be divided into 12 orders, 32 genera, 134 species, 404 varieties. When recast into types of character there are 810. Two-thirds of these types are "monogynes," that is, individuals who have only one dominant motive, a few are "digynes" (with two dominant motives). Rarer and rarer become men of multiple motives and the attendant insight and wisdom, though occasion-

ally (twice in 29,222 cases) an "omnigyne" is encountered. By further computation, a condition of character exists four times in three
billions of people which must be called the "Super-omnigyne." Speaking modestly of his own accomplishment in discovering this classification, Fourier writes, "This exalted degree has this singular property
of discovering, almost by inspiration, the laws of harmony. I must
necessarily be of this degree, since I have arrived at it without any
help"!

Men may be classified not only in respect to the number but also
according to the nature of the leading motives they possess. Motives
are either "dominant" or "tonic." The former are the guiding purposes, and the latter confer color, flavor, and style on the execution
of the purpose. A certain king of Saxony, Fourier tells us, used to
write on the last day of the year a plan for his activities during each
day of the ensuing year. "On the first of March I shall go to the
hunt; on the second of April, I shall spend the day fishing; on the
third of May I shall hold a Council of State. . . ." According to
Fourier this methodical king had a "dominant" of ambition, and a
tonic of "stability." This quaint doctrine contains one lesson of importance. No psychology of personality can be written exclusively
in terms of purposes, goals, needs, or instincts. These "dominants"
leave completely out of account the *manner* or personal *style* through
which the purpose is achieved. There are many *ways* in which men
may express ambition. Personality involves not only purpose, but also
certain habitual and individual modes of attaining the chosen goals;
not only the dominant determinants, but the tonic determinants as
well. The necessity for such dual determination was clearly seen by
Fourier; it is recognized likewise in Stern's specification of both the
Richtungsdispositionen and the *Rüstungsdispositionen* in personality.
The relation between such "driving traits" and "directive traits" is
discussed more fully in Chapter XII.

Fourier thought that he had invented a "science of concrete
charm, applicable to the wants of the whole human race," that would
"put an end to its long endured miseries." If society were organized
so as to employ the talents of its members according to his plan of
classification, great increases in production would result. For example,
the proceeds of six months' sale of hen's eggs, when poultry raising
was in the hands of the proper monogynes, would pay off the British
national debt!

Eccentric as it is, Fourier's scheme has three merits. In the first place, it serves as a warning against over-elaborate typologies. Divisions and sub-divisions soon get out of hand, and neither the author nor the reader can work with a typology whose ramifications exceed his own range of manipulation. The temptation with every typology as soon as its inadequacies are apparent is to elaborate it through sub-division. The process ultimately leads to the swamps of confusion. A second, more positive, contribution is Fourier's emphasis, in common with Shand, McDougall, and Bain, upon the *dominant motive* as the integrative and distinguishing factor in personality.[52] Lastly, Fourier's distinction between dominant and tonic "passions" recognizes both as important phenomena, not wholly independent of one another, yet by no means identical.

THE BEGINNING OF EXPERIMENTAL CHARACTEROLOGY

During the nineteenth century the literature of characterology was rich in observation and hypothesis, but no writer prior to 1884 proposed to apply the newly developed experimental methods of psychology to the study of personality. Physiognomists and phrenologists, it is true, had spent much time examining people, but for their purposes it mattered little whether the people they studied were dead or alive; in no case did they conduct their examinations under what today would be called "controlled conditions."

John Stuart Mill, it will be remembered, repudiated the experimental method as unsuited to the study of personality. His science of Ethology could have been pursued by a recluse without so much as a glance at another human being, nor even at himself, provided he had access to the world's literature of proverbs and to treatises in theoretical psychology. Even the rapidly growing interest in experimental psychology, which in 1879 materialized in a psychological laboratory at Leipzig, was concerned not at all with personality. The nearest approach it made was the "personal equation" in reaction times, and in other equally simple, nomothetic functions.

It was Sir Francis Galton (1822-1911), the pioneer in so many psychometric fields, who for the first time proposed explicitly that the standards of experimentation be applied directly to the study

[52] The aphorism, "A man is what he loves," fits this type of theory very well. It is endorsed by many characterologists today. (Cf. Havelock Ellis, *The Dance of Life*, 1923, p. 336; also E. Stern, "New Ways of Investigating the Problems of Personality," *Psyche*, 1923, 3, 358-366.)

of personal, particular forms of behavior. After satisfying himself through his previous work on genius and twins, and through his introspective studies of his own behavior that all of man's actions "seem clearly to lie within the province of normal cause and consequence," he reached the conclusion that "the character which shapes our conduct is a definite and durable 'something,' and therefore that it is reasonable to attempt to measure it." [53] One method of measurement, advocated by him, was the rating of complex human qualities. Schoolmasters especially, he pointed out, had an enviable opportunity to count the frequency and estimate the intensity of their pupil's responses of anger, fear, loyalty, and ambition. Norms were to be established for the development of character at successive ages. Many statistical methods, especially those of correlation, likewise made available for the first time by Galton, were to be employed in these investigations. This advance in empiricism, now accepted by the great majority of investigators, alone would have entitled Galton to a preeminent position in the history of characterology. But his proposal to employ actual experiment is still more radical.

Observation is a slow process, especially while waiting for critical episodes of life to appear. But "emergencies need not be waited for; they can be extemporized; traps, as it were, can be laid." Galton gives the following example,

> Thus when two persons have an "inclination" to one another, they visibly incline or slope together when sitting side by side, as at a dinner-table, and they then throw the stress of their weight on the near legs of their chairs. It does not require much ingenuity to arrange a pressure gauge with an index and dial to indicate changes in stress, but it is difficult to devise an arrangement that shall fulfill the threefold condition of being effective, not attracting notice, and being applicable to ordinary furniture. I made some rude experiments, but being busy with other matters, have not carried them on, as I had hoped.[54]

This humorous, but nonetheless reasonable, proposal marks the beginning of experimental characterology. The special problem with which it was concerned, expressive movement, has, regrettably enough, advanced little since Galton's ingenious suggestion. But his faith in experimental procedures has, in the main, triumphed.

[53] F. Galton, "Measurement of Character," *Fortnightly Rev.*, 1884, 42, 179-185.
[54] *Op. cit.*, p. 184.

The invention and spread of experimental techniques after Galton's time are scarcely yet matters of history. Experimentation is the very tissue of contemporary research, and its story must be told in every subsequent chapter of this volume.

SUMMARY

Out of the long and varied past this chapter has selected only those characterological doctrines that have some special significance for the contemporary study of personality. In a few cases ancient and persistent blunders have been discussed, but for the most part positive contributions have been recorded.

Theophrastus saw that the small every-day acts of men are remarkably congruent with one another. To him the "elements" of personality were not specific and fragmentary; on the contrary, the only unit of any consequence to him was the *dominant trait* from which a man's every habit derives its significance. La Bruyère failed to specify, as Theophrastus did, what dominant traits his characters possessed, but he drew portraits reflecting an equally consistent style of life. The physical qualities, the manners, bearing, and address of his subjects constitute an intricate but unified pattern.

With greater freedom, poetry, drama, and fiction portray not only the consistencies but the inconsistencies of human nature. So artful are its masterpieces of characterization that psychology, by contrast, seems clumsy and inept. But standards of objectivity and verifiability strengthen the case for psychology. Clumsy exactness is a wholesome antidote to undisciplined felicity. Either alone is one-sided; but taken together, the two methods provide a well-rounded equipment for the student of personality.

Humoral psychology, the longest standing of all doctrines of human nature, owes its longevity partly to the uncontroverted claim that there is a correspondence between the chemistry of the body and emotional make-up, and partly to its implicit recognition of certain fundamental dimensions of temperament.

Physiognomy too maintains that some relationship between temperament and the skeletal structure should be expected. Today we would say that this correspondence is due to the dependence of both physical development and emotional excitability upon the action of the hormones. In recent times Kretschmer and his many followers have proposed a nativistic physiognomy based upon this logic; but they overlook the influence of experience upon muscular development. Beside the constitutional type we must know the significance for physiognomy of the common instinctive patterns of emotional expression, the influence of custom and convention, and the effect of personal experience in determining posture, and also movement. Lavater held that ultimately all expressions must be consistent with one another because all alike proceed from the unity and harmony of a man's own inner nature.

Phrenology stresses even more specifically the correlation between a man's personal qualities and his bodily structure. The correlations are most certainly not what Gall believed them to be. Yet Gall's cardinal error, "organology," has blinded critics to his positive contributions, leading them to read in his work the prevalent faculty psychology of his time, which he had, in fact, expressly repudiated. Gall must be credited not only with helping to establish the hypothesis of psychophysical parallelism from which most modern work on personality proceeds, and with creating a new interest in the psychical differentiations between men, and with the adoption of positivistic methods (however far astray they led him), but he must be credited especially with the important distinction between universal (nomothetic) faculties and characterial (primitive) faculties. Seeking a psychology to account adequately not for the similarities among men but for the differences between them, he arrived, somewhat confusedly, to be sure, at the first systematic conception of traits.

In proposing Ethology as an exact science of human nature, Mill envisaged clearly the interdependence of psychology, literature and common sense. Like Wundt, Mill would base his characterology firmly upon psychology, but allow it new methods and greater latitude. Shand and McDougall find in the "sentiments" an adequate basis for a psychology of personality, a more satisfactory foundation than the older associationism. Bain offered a still simpler conception of the energic flow, later revived and modified by Jung and by Kempf. Gradually conation and emotion came to bear the central emphasis. Now with the added support of Freud it is unlikely that the study of personality will ever slip back into the intellectualistic formulations of the past.

Fourier's eccentric doctrine acts as warning against elaborate typologies. Fourier, however, does call attention to the rich variety of motives playing decisive roles in the development of personality. Furthermore, the distinction he draws between "dominant" and "tonic" traits anticipates an important modern distinction between the driving motives of life and the directive or expressive styles of execution.

Fifty years ago an entirely new era began in characterology when Sir Francis Galton argued for the first time for direct experimentation, at the same time contributing many novel and now indispensable techniques. Mill had declared experimentation in the field of personality to be impossible, and many skeptics have since agreed with him. Nevertheless, it is not Mill's view but Galton's that has prevailed, and that seems destined to dominate the psychology of personality during the twentieth century.

Part II

THE DEVELOPMENT OF PERSONALITY

CHAPTER IV

FOUNDATIONS OF PERSONALITY

Nature, then, has generated and fashioned man's body in such a way that some parts of it were perfect at birth, others were formed as its age increased, without much use of external and adventitious aids. Now in other respects she made the mind as perfect as the body, endowing it with sense capable of perceiving things, so that little or no assistance of any sort was needful to supplement them. But that faculty which is highest and most excellent in man she left lacking . . . she furnished merely the rudiments; nothing more.

—Cicero

ONLY the rudiments of that "which is highest and most excellent in man" are given at birth. The fully fashioned social and moral being, the developed adult personality, waits upon the process of growth. The nature of growth is the critical problem for the psychology of personality. For above all else it must know how the biological organism it finds at birth becomes transformed into the adult person able to take his place in the highly complex social activities of the civilized world surrounding him.

As yet no pooling of the resources of physiological, genetic, comparative, and social psychology can give a complete answer. There are gaps as well as contradictions in the evidence. Knowledge of heredity is meager; the problems of instinct, maturation, and learning, though fairly well formulated, are unsolved. Adding to the difficulty, what seems to hold true for one child does not always hold true for another—the *weights* of the factors involved in growth apparently vary from case to case.

Take, for example, a typical problem of the influence of the home environment. Great though it undoubtedly is, it seems to operate in *antithetical* ways. The novelist, Sinclair Lewis, in the following passage about two brothers has brought out this issue most clearly:

"My father," said Ora, "was a sloppy, lazy, booze-hoisting old bum, and my mother didn't know much besides cooking, and she was too busy to give me much attention, and the kids I knew were a bunch of foul-mouthed loafers that used to hang around the hoboes up near the water tank, and I never had a chance to get any formal schooling, and I got thrown on my own as just a brat. So naturally I've become a sort of vagabond that can't be bored by thinking about his 'debts' to a lot of little shop-keeping lice, and I suppose I'm inclined to be lazy, and not too scrupulous about the dames and the liquor. But my early rearing did have one swell result. Brought up so unconventionally, I'll always be an Anti-Puritan. I'll never deny the joys of the flesh and the sanctity of Beauty."

"And my father," said Myron, "was pretty easy-going and always did like drinking and swapping stories with the Boys, and my mother was hard-driven taking care of us, and I heard a lot of filth from the hoboes up near the water tank. Maybe just sort of as a reaction I've become almost too much of a crank about paying debts, and fussing over my work, and being scared of liquor and women. But my rearing did have one swell result. Just by way of contrast, it made me a good, sound, old-fashioned New England Puritan." [1]

The same fire that melts the butter, hardens the egg.

But in spite of variations from case to case, there is one law to which there are no exceptions: *every personality develops continually from the stage of infancy until death, and throughout this span it persists even though it changes.* Each succeeding stage of development emerges, in very complex ways, from the stages existing previously. This process of transition from one stage to another is in some measure clarified by our present knowledge. Though far from complete, this knowledge is extensive enough to demand our attention during the present chapter and the four succeeding.

HEREDITY

Human beings in common with all other living creatures are subject to the laws of heredity. What these laws are, and to what degree they determine a man's physique, temperament, mentality, and personality are subjects of controversy. The force of this controversy can easily be seen by placing in opposition two extreme statements.

Heredity and not environment is the chief maker of men. . . . Nearly all the misery and nearly all the happiness in the world are due

[1] *Work of Art*, by Sinclair Lewis, copyright, 1934, pp. 310 f., reprinted with permission from Doubleday, Doran and Company, Inc.

not to environment. . . . The differences among men are due to differences in the germ cells with which they are born.[2]

With this statement a behaviorist's notorious challenge may be compared:

> Give me a dozen healthy infants, well formed, and my own specified world to bring them up in and I'll guarantee to take any one at random and train him to become any type of specialist I might select—doctor, lawyer, artist, merchant, chief, and yes, even beggar-man and thief, regardless of his talents, peculiarities, tendencies, abilities, vocations, and race of his ancestors.[3] There is no such thing as an inheritance of capacity, talent, temperament, mental constitution and characteristics.[4]

But even such an extreme environmentalist as the author of the last quotation cannot and does not deny the inheritance of *physical* structure. If a child resembles his parents physically the fact is ascribed to the operation of determinants in the germ-plasm; but if a child has habits, handwriting, emotional outbursts, or esthetic sensibilities similar to his parents', the author claims that *training* is sufficient to account for the resemblance.

> Yes, there are hereditable differences in form, in structure, but the mere presence of these structures tells us not one thing about function.[5]

> The behaviorists believe that there is nothing from within to develop. If you start with the right number of fingers and toes, eyes, and a few elementary movements that are present at birth, you do not need anything else in the way of raw material to make a man, be that man genius, a cultured gentleman, a rowdy or a thug.[6]

Muscles, heart, glands, nerve-tissues, cortex, all are inherited as structure, but so long as they are "normal" they do not predetermine function; psychology can therefore disregard them.

This is a remarkable doctrine, one that asks us in effect to admit that *gross* (abnormal) defects of structure set limits upon function, and at the same time to deny that all other peculiarities of structure determine idiosyncrasies of function. The logic is amazingly faulty.

[2] A. E. Wiggam, *The New Decalogue of Science*, 1923, p. 42.
[3] J. B. Watson, *Behaviorism*, W. W. Norton & Co., 1925, p. 82.
[4] *Ibid.*, pp. 74 f.
[5] *Ibid.*, p. 77.
[6] J. B. Watson, *Psychological Care of Infant and Child*, W. W. Norton & Co., 1928, p. 41.

Even though glands, for example, be regarded as structure, their structural differences obviously produce differential *functions* (*viz.*, differences in temperament). Likewise, intelligence and adaptive reflexes though closely bound to inherited nerve structure, also represent an important *functional* inheritance.

Most psychologists tend whenever possible to stress the operation of environmental forces, even though they seldom state their case in as extreme a form as Watson, and even though they may not be behaviorists. There are two reasons for this. In the first place, the plasticity of the child, the rapidity of his learning, the subtle course of conditioning, the ease of "slanting," give unlimited possibilities for the acquisition of peculiarly personal habits of response. With a natural preference for causes that are apparent rather than for those that are hidden (and therefore only inaccurately inferred), the psychologist in nearly every instance chooses to ascribe personal characteristics to conditioning, imitation, trauma, or some other form of *learning*. Since the possible variations of environmental influence are infinite in number, they can easily account for *all* the differences between human beings. Why invoke an explanation in terms of heredity? It often seems superfluous.

Another matter seriously worries the psychologist. He knows that function invariably involves the integration of afferent, central, and efferent nervous pathways. In this circuit are many synapses, but synapses are *non-cellular*. They are indefinite junctions between neuronic cells. The laws of heredity, on the other hand, presuppose *material* determiners that reside in *material* substance. Does heredity also provide "tendencies" in the synaptic regions? If so, how? It would be far easier to regard only cell-structure as inherited and to ascribe all *synaptic* connections to the influence of learning or "neurobiotaxis."[7] This dilemma worries the psychologist, though for some reason it does not seem to worry the geneticist. One reads, for example, the words of Jennings:

> Temperament, mentality, behavior, personality—these things depend in manifold ways on the genes.[8] It may be safely said that there is no type of characteristics in which individuals may differ that has not been found to depend on genes.[9]

[7] Even the reflexes that an infant displays at birth are, according to Holt, learned *in utero*. (E. B. Holt, *Animal Drive and the Learning Process*, 1931.)

[8] H. S. Jennings, *The Biological Basis of Human Nature*, W. W. Norton & Co., 1930, p. 36.   [9] *Ibid.*, p. 154.

To illustrate the theory of genes, the evidence for which he claims to be "positive, inescapable, conclusive," [10] he refers continually to such functional and highly complex personal characteristics as laziness, stupidity, slowness, lack of industry, ambition, patience, and genius.[11]

Jennings, however, does not claim that these complex personal characteristics are genetic units, nor that they are determined exclusively by heredity. The manner in which genes play their part is in the highest degree complex. In the Drosophila at least fifty pairs of genes co-operate to produce the usual red color of the eye.

> By changing any one of the fifty genes of the fruit-fly that take part in producing the eye color, the color is altered; eyes of other color are produced; or there is no pigment in the eye; or it is structurally imperfect. The same situation is found for all characteristics, in the fruit-fly or in ourselves. Any feature or characteristic, structural, physiological, or mental, can be changed or made defective by altering any one of the many different genes that co-operate to produce it.[12]

A gene, we are told, is not a hypothetical unit with mystic properties, but an actually separable part of the elongated chromosomes.[13] Since genes enter into the production of every bodily cell it is not unthinkable that every structural characteristic receives its initial determination from them. It is, to be sure, a leap from the determination of bodily structure to the determination of the functioning personality, but since function is undoubtedly intricately dependent upon structure (Watson to the contrary notwithstanding), Jennings' claim that heredity affects the traits of personality, though vague enough, is not untenable.

This doctrine of genetic determination does not state that personality is inherited, but rather that *no feature of personality is devoid of hereditary influences.* It means simply that if the genes are altered the personal characteristics are altered, not that personal characteristics are determined solely by the genes. In fact, it admits that while every characteristic is influenced somehow by the genes, the same characteristic may be influenced also by the surrounding conditions, by temperature, by the physical environment, and in human beings, by the complex social environment. Even the young Amblystoma has the possibility of two diverse careers, as an aquatic or as a land animal, depending upon his early surroundings. Similarly, each human indi-

---

[10] *Ibid.*, p. 36.
[11] *Ibid.*, e.g., pp. 20 f.

[12] *Ibid.*, p. 17.
[13] *Ibid.*, p. 61.

vidual so far as heredity is concerned has the possibility of *many* careers, and of *many* personalities, whose realization will depend upon the exigencies of his physical and social environments.

There is then an embarrassing array of causes that may be drawn upon to explain a given personality. The gene theory provides by its flexibility more than enough permutations to account both for family resemblances and for individual distinctiveness. On the other hand the environment, in connection with the subtle operations of human learning, provides equally limitless possibilities. Since every quality is probably influenced by the original determinants inherent in the genetic system, and at the same time by the course of life in an actively stimulating environment, it becomes impossible to ascribe with finality any single feature of personality either to heredity or to experience. Both are always involved. This point of view might be expressed as an equation: *Personality* $= f$ *(Heredity)* $\times$ *(Environment)*. The two causal factors are not added together, but are interrelated as multiplier and multiplicand. If either were zero there could be no personality.

The persistent reader may ask, which is on the whole more important? For given individuals, or for given groups of individuals, the question is at least theoretically possible to answer. Within a family where very similar environmental influences exist for each member, the differences between siblings are probably due, paradoxical as it may seem, chiefly to heredity. Unless the children inherited quite different genes from the myriad combinations which their parents had to offer, they might be expected, because of the similarity of their environments, to be much more alike than they are. The same principle holds true in other homogeneous groups. For example, dull people, Jennings thinks, are on the whole determined relatively more by their heredity than bright people, for the latter learn with ease, adjust variously and with great delicacy to the environment, while the unintelligent plod along changelessly with such qualities and manners as spring from their original natures.[14]

The genes supply one set of conditions for development, the environment another. In any given individual the environmental and genetic conditions may reinforce one another, to produce a trained and talented statesman, for example. Or they may conflict to produce a talented but untrained statesman, or one trained but untalented. In-

14 H. S. Jennings, *The Biological Basis of Human Nature*, 1930, p. 181.

numerable combinations result, each affecting the structure of personality.

There is yet another complicating consideration: characteristics induced by genes may also be induced by environmental forces. (In personality, for example, one individual may be reclusive and retiring because of inborn qualities, another because of conflict with the environment.) This consideration, if followed logically, means that one personality may be relatively more a product of heredity, and another of environment. In some cases the decision might be reached after an intensive analysis of the life-history; but it would be impossible to formulate a general rule regarding the weight of the two factors in every life. In one case training seems markedly to outweigh the influence of heredity; in another the stress seems to be reversed.

Besides the conclusion that in different lives the operation of heredity plays very different roles, there is another fairly certain fact important for the psychology of personality, namely, that the more directly a quality is bound to structural inheritance the less modifiable it is. The three principal raw materials of personality, *physique*, the endowment of *intelligence*, and *temperament*, are genetically determined through structural inheritance, and are only slightly altered by conditions existing subsequent to birth. They are the effective agencies of heredity entering the process of growth at every stage to influence the development of traits and attitudes. Sometimes they accelerate the molding influence of the environment; sometimes they place limitations upon it; but always their force is felt.

THE BEGINNINGS OF PERSONALITY

The newborn infant *lacks* personality, for he has not yet encountered the world in which he must live, and has not developed the distinctive modes of adjustment and mastery that will later comprise his personality. He is almost altogether a creature of heredity. In fact, if it were not for two complicating considerations we might equate the observable equipment of the neonate with the endowment of his inheritance. The complicating considerations are, first, the probable existence of *pre-natal learning*, and secondly, the fact that some aspects of inheritance are latent and require time for their *maturation*.

Regarding pre-natal learning little needs to be said, for however many adaptive responses the child may learn *in utero*, he does not learn them in the environment in which he must live, and it is only

---

A LIFE PRINCIPLE or PROTOPLASMIC IRRITABILITY
(Vitalistic Postulate)   (Mechanistic Postulate)

---

reflected in

A STREAM OF ACTIVITY

---

differentiated at birth into

MASS ACTION (Gross patterns of movement, often called "random activity"), *e.g.*, extension, retraction, indeterminate squirming, accompanying vocalization, etc.

SPECIFIC REFLEXES: breathing, sucking, swallowing, digestive and eliminative sequences, grasping, sneezing, Babinski, etc.

---

set into motion and sustained through

SIMPLE SENSITIVITY (stimulation of extroceptive, introceptive, or proprioceptive sense organs)

SEGMENTAL DRIVE (tensions), *e.g.*, hunger, thirst (cf. pp. 114-118)

[GOAL-SEEKING PROCESSES: instincts, needs, entelechy (cf. pp. 112-114)]

---

employing

INNATE INDIVIDUAL EQUIPMENT: sensory capacities, nervous plasticity and retentivity (INTELLIGENCE); glandular and chemical tonicity (TEMPERAMENT); muscular and skeletal structure (PHYSIQUE); special capacities, skills, and sexual functions, to mature later

ADAPTIVE MECHANISMS (potentialities for modification of the stream of activity), *e.g.*, maturation, conditioning, integration, inhibition, differentiation, and all other agencies for modifying behavior during the course of the individual's interaction with his environment (cf. Chapters V-VIII)

FIGURE 11

The Beginnings of Personality: The Situation at Birth

with the distinctive adjustments to the *post-natal* world that the problem of personality is concerned. For our purposes, therefore, the congenital and the hereditary equipment of the child may both be regarded together as the one primordial source of personality, observable, in part, in the stream of activity at birth.

Less easily disposed of is the problem of maturation. Not every inherited tendency is observable at birth. Throughout life there is a subtle procession of ripening events, so much obscured by the effects of training that no one can tell just what develops in response to maturation and what comes from teaching. This problem will be considered in some detail in the next chapter, but its existence makes it difficult for us to formulate an initial account of the "Givens" of personality, as a starting point for a genetic theory of development. But since, in spite of the difficulty, a beginning must be made, an *approximate* schedule of the equipment of the infant at birth is offered in Figure 11.

The origin of the stream of activity here portrayed may be viewed either as a manifestation of a vitalistic urge (*Horme, Will, Élan Vital*), or of an equally mysterious though more scientific-sounding principle of "Protoplasmic Irritability." Some Original Cause or Source of Animation is assumed explicitly or implicitly by all biological and psychological sciences. Life exists in individual forms. This fact, unexplained and perhaps inexplicable, is the starting point for these sciences.

Recent studies of early infancy make a convenient distinction between two manifestations of the observable stream of activity.[15] There is, first of all, a type of diffuse, massive movement involving large regions of the body. Owing to the basic physiological opposition of flexor and extensor muscle patterns (which have the original property of inhibiting each other while they are active) this mass action can frequently be characterized either as retraction (abience) or as extension (adience); while some of the random squirming that takes place, as in twisting, thrashing, pounding movements, makes such complex use of the musculature that it cannot readily be classified either as retractive or extensive.

From one study of the first ten days of life we are given the following picture:

[15] Cf. E. Dewey, *Behavior Development in Infants*, 1935. K. C. Pratt, "Specificity and Generalization of Behavior in New-born Infants: A Critique." *Psychol. Rev.,* 1934, 41, 265-284.

The infant maintains continuous body movement with such speed and excessiveness that the experimenter, even when using a specially devised code, cannot keep up with the infant. The body squirms, twists, rolls, and bends. The back arches, the hips sway, and the head rolls from side to side or is thrown back. The arms slash vigorously and the legs are kicked in exaggerated extensor thrusts or are flexed sharply at ankle, knee and hip. Hands, feet, toes, and fingers are in continuous movement. Sucking and smacking sounds frequently occur, while loud crying is usually coincident with mass activity. All of this activity is more or less simultaneous and comes and goes with periodicities which appear in intervals of a few seconds to several minutes.[16]

The same investigator reports that mass activity of this type is especially prominent just previous to nursing, and occurs also from a flatulent condition, during regurgitation, intestinal disturbances, defecation and micturation.[17] That this diffuse and random movement is especially marked when there are ascertainable organic tensions is a fact of considerable importance for the theory of motivation (pp. 113 ff.).

In addition to these gross patterns of movement, so difficult to characterize, there exist many specifically adaptive responses, such as movement of the eyes toward a light, sucking, swallowing, withdrawal of a limb from noxious stimuli. The exact number of these specific reflexes is difficult to determine owing to their frequent organization into complex chains or into such large patterns or groups that their appearance approaches mass action itself. The operation of these reflexes is discussed in other texts.[18] Their importance for *personality* consists chiefly in the raw material they provide for the operation of two of the principal mechanisms of growth, *viz.*, *conditioning* (pp. 151-153) and *integration* (pp. 138-147).

What is it that sets the stream of activity into motion, that sustains it until it lapses or changes? This is the problem of *motivation*, and there is no problem in psychology more difficult to handle. The special portion of Figure 11, devoted to this topic, therefore will need much more thorough discussion. But before settling into it attention should be called to the two other "Givens" underlying the development of personality.

[16] O. C. Irwin, *Genet. Psychol. Monog.*, 1930, 8, pp. 59 f.
[17] O. C. Irwin, *loc. cit.*, and *J. Comp. Psychol.*, 1932, 14, 429-445.
[18] *E.g.*, J. B. Watson, *Behaviorism*, 1924, pp. 90-103, and F. H. Allport, *Social Psychology*, 1924, chap. iii.

First, there is the *innate individual equipment* of physique, and temperament, and general intellectual capacity including the highly complex abilities and talents that later become manifest. Such constitutional endowment has many facets, and the part it plays in personality, as already indicated, is complex indeed. The question of temperament alone, intricately tied as it is to the chemical functions of the body, is as important as it is baffling. Take, as an example, that subtle constitutional quality commonly called energy, vitality, or "pep." In various studies of leadership, of popularity, and of personal happiness this temperamental quality has been found to be decidedly significant. In common speech it is often equated with "personality." What the precise physical counterpart of vigorous and vital activity may be one does not know, though certain glands, especially the hypophysis, the adrenals, the gonads and the thyroid are thought to have more to do with it than certain others.[19]

Or take the case of the normal speed of movement (likewise an aspect of temperament, or of one phase of temperament, *viz.*, *motility*). One investigator studied the normal rates of tapping of twins, of brothers and sisters, and of parents.[20] The results show a striking correspondence in normal tapping speeds among related individuals, monozygotic twins being closest, dizygotic twins and siblings less, parents and offspring next, while unrelated individuals had only a chance correspondence with one another. Such a finding is, of course, precisely what would be expected if heredity played an appreciable part in this basic form of activity, one of many of the tap-roots of personality.

The remaining "Given" in Figure 11 consists of *adaptive mechanisms* that make it possible for the infant to vary his responses, to learn, and to bring his rich innate equipment into the most effective interaction with the demands of his environment. These mechanisms are not structures; they are merely instruments of growth, types of modifiability of which the nervous system is capable. It is capable of organizing its segmental responses into higher and more complex units through integration; of differentiating its diffuse, mass responses into more refined and successfully adaptive movements. It is capable of maturing, of being conditioned, of learning. In the following chapters all these instruments of growth will be considered in detail.

[19] Cf. P. Richter, *Amer. J. Orthopsychiatry*, 1932, 2, 345-354; D. J. Ingle, *Psychol. Rev.*, 1935, 42, 466-479.
[20] Ida Frischeisen-Köhler, *Char. & Pers.*, 1933, 1, 301-313.

MOTIVATION

In the central portion of Figure 11 there appears an entry in brackets: [Goal-seeking Processes: instincts, needs, entelechy]. The brackets call attention to the fact that this "Given" is often regarded as a superfluous assumption. Psychologists dispute as to whether the equipment of the new-born infant does or does not include a system of latent purposes. Does the primordial stream of activity contain within itself *directions* which determine its own course of development? Is there in the infant, for example, a latent propensity that will later lead him to *construct*, and another to *acquire*, one to *mate*, another to *imitate*, another to *seek companionship* of his fellows? The instinct theory asserts that there are such propensities operating "prior to experience and independent of training." An instinct "determines its possessor to perceive (to pay attention to) any given object of a certain class and to experience in its presence a certain emotional excitement and an impulse to action which finds expression in a specific mode of behavior in relation to that object." [21] Since it is obviously impossible to discern any such elaborately purposive dispositions in the conduct of the newborn infant, it has been necessary for proponents of the instinct doctrine to lean heavily on the theory of maturation which holds that this providential equipment of goal-seeking processes must take time to ripen, and that throughout life the instincts, one after another, come of age.

In recent years it has become common to reject this somewhat extravagant portrayal of human purposes. It seems to many psychologists to violate unnecessarily the requirement of parsimony in a scientific theory. Are there not many individuals who live their entire lives lacking some of these instincts, failing, for example, to become acquisitive, constructive, pugnacious, or parental in their behavior? Is it not simpler to account for these types of interest if and when they are present, than to assume that "instincts" are common to a species and then be forced to explain away the many exceptions where the "instincts" fail to put in an appearance?

Yet in one form or another many contemporary theories of personality are instinct-theories. They view personality as a matter of individual modification of universal instincts or common needs. A collector of vases is but showing a special modification or extension of

[21] W. McDougall, *Outline of Psychology*, 1923, p. 110.

his acquisitive instinct; an altruist is following the instincts of self-abasement and gregariousness (perhaps with a little of the parental propensity thrown in). But are not the purposes of different people far too diverse and too numerous to be traced to a few primal motives shared by all the species? Are the directions of striving after all innately determined? Is it not necessary to allow for the learning of *new* motives and for the acquisition of *novel* interests as personality matures? When people do seek the same goals may the fact not be explained by the more parsimonious assumption that similarly constructed individuals living in similar environment, influenced by similar culture, *would* develop similar goals and employ similar modes of obtaining them?

If so, then instincts would evaporate. They would turn out to be nothing more than constellations of emotion, habit, and foresight, better called *sentiments* or *interests,* and regarded as acquired rather than innate. Learning would then serve not merely as a way of extending and modifying purposes, but also of *creating* them. And the fact that many of these purposes are fairly common to mankind could be readily explained without recourse to a hypothesis of racial inheritance.

The question of instincts in animals should not confuse the issue, for there is such flexibility in learning, in making and breaking habits, and so much insight, foresight, and delay in response, that human goals must be viewed as different in kind from the stereotyped objectives of lower animals.

Rejecting the instinct hypothesis it becomes necessary to provide an alternative. A beginning, but only a beginning, may be made in the theory of Drive. A drive is defined as a vital impulse which leads to the reduction of some segmental organic tension. It has its origin in an internal organic stimulus of peculiar persistence, growing characteristically stronger until the organism acts in such a way as to alleviate the accumulating tension.

The doctrine of drive is a rather crude biological conception often employed as a factotum by psychologists with a simple mechanistic outlook. The hypothesis herewith offered is that the doctrine, while inadequate to account for *adult* motivation, does none the less offer a suitable portrayal of the motives of *young infants,* and for that reason serves very well as the *starting point* for a theory of motivation. After the level of infancy is passed primitive segmental drive rapidly recedes in importance, being supplanted by the more sophisticated type of motives characteristic of the mature personality, and commonly represented by such terms as *interest, sentiment, value, trait, ambition, attitude, taste,* and *inclination.* Obviously none of these motives are found full-fledged in the new-born child.

THE BIOLOGICAL THEORY OF PERSONALITY

The doctrine of drive must be set where it belongs in a well-saturated background of biological and evolutionary theory. This theory, readily intelligible to all readers of biological science, may be presented in a single sentence.[22] *The personality of an individual is the mode of adjustment or survival that results from the interaction of his organic cravings (segmental drives) with an environment both friendly and hostile to these cravings, through the intermediation of a plastic and modifiable central nervous system.*

Just as all organisms take on the form of some *species,* each of which represents a successful mode of survival in the evolutionary struggle, so too do individuals within the human species attain *personality* as the form of survival most suitable to their individual needs within the particular environmental framework provided. The central nervous system in the process of effecting the necessary adjustments between the organic cravings and the exigencies of the environment develops certain characteristic habits, attitudes, personal traits, forms of sublimation and thought, and it is these characteristic modes of adjustment that, taken collectively, comprise personality. In a sense, therefore, the central nervous system is the seat of personality.

The organic cravings which are the sole original motive power for activity are closely associated with the primitive vegetative processes having their origin in various segments of the autonomic nervous system. When the vital functions of the viscera are disturbed widespread postural changes result throughout the body, and the organism is restless and active until an equilibrium is reached. The nutritional system illustrates the situation very nicely. When the stomach is empty, its contractions bring into play glandular, cardiac and respiratory changes which with their consequent effect upon the musculature of the body create a condition of restlessness and random activity that only the ingestion of food can appease. The origi-

[22] The exposition of the biological theory given in these pages follows quite closely the formulation of E. J. Kempf, in "The Autonomic Functions and the Personality," *Nerv. & Ment. Dis. Monog. Ser.,* 1921, No. 28.

nal sucking and swallowing reflexes are nature's only provision at the outset for meeting this type of maladjustment; but as the organism grows, the central nervous system evolves elaborate new ways of effecting the adjustment. The individual learns to use language (to ask for food), to earn money (to buy food), to organize markets for barter and for efficient distribution, and to obey certain social requirements in the preparation and eating of food. All these elaborations are ultimately in order that the organic craving may be most efficiently satisfied within the restraining conditions of the environment.

The vegetative nervous system, where these cravings originate, is thought to be more primitive and more essential than the central nervous system which is primarily an agency of adjustment. The vegetative system is the master, the cerebro-spinal is the servant; the former compels adjustment, the latter effects adjustment.

Evidence for the primacy of the vegetative system might be drawn from various sources. (1) Kempf, for example, points low in the evolutionary scale (to the amoeba, for instance) where the vegetative functions are all essentially present, but without a sensori-motor system to mediate between them and the environment. The vegetative system is directly submerged in environmental media and supplied immediately with the requirements for effective survival. (2) Obviously, too, the vegetative functions of the infant are far more advanced in development than those of the higher nervous system. Indeed a child with only seven months of pre-natal life has a complete and complex autonomic development with only a few as yet undeveloped central nervous functions to serve it. (3) In some individuals the secondary nervous system never grows, and yet the individual (an idiot) may live a long time, provided only that someone else supplies the idiot's autonomic system with its requirements. (4) In older people the secondary system may disintegrate entirely as in dementia, and yet the individual will live so long as his vegetative functions are not impaired, and so long as others take over the role of his own deteriorated intellectual functions. (5) The study of the effects of fasting, of brain lesions, and of accidents to the cortex, all confirm the view that life depends not upon the integrity of the functions of the central nervous system, but on the intactness of the autonomic segments and their vital nervous centers. (6) In the case of urgent organic cravings their satisfaction takes precedence over all forms of activity. The central nervous system is compelled to serve them. Lack of oxygen, intense hunger, marked sexual tension, the need for elimination, may all defeat the "intellectual" activity of the central nervous system and compel it to find ways of satisfying the urgent craving. This list of arguments in defense of the primacy of the autonomic system reads very much like Schopenhauer's defense of the primacy of the Will over the Intellect.[23] It is an antirationalistic view of human activity that today finds much favor.[24]

Figure 12 indicates schematically the essential features of this theory. It shows that Drive is ultimately of autonomic origin, that the environment supplies both potential satisfactions as well as menaces and obstacles to the well-being of the organic system. The central nervous system receives warning of both disturbing and satisfying elements in the environment, and in general operates in such a way as to acquire the maximum of gratification for the affective cravings with a minimum expenditure of energy. Strictly speaking, of course, the central nervous system and the autonomic are not entirely independent; they constantly exchange impulses and elaborately interact. What the theory does is to call attention to their supplementary roles in adjustment, one as motivational, the other as executive.

According to this theory the most important organic cravings (drives) are the nutritional and sexual. Of these two the latter is of cardinal significance for personality, for in civilization the obstacles to the free and natural satisfaction of this craving are greater than those confronting the nutritional drive. The chief single source of personality is, therefore, the unsatisfied sexual craving that provokes continuous and circuitous efforts within the central nervous system to invent some adequate means of resolving the erotic tensions. The force of this affective craving, as is now well known, is the root of many neurotic adjustments that represent unconsciously artful but still futile attempts of the central nervous system to supply a solution for insoluble personal problems. It is not always apparent which personal characteristics are outgrowths of attempts to solve personal sexual problems, but to a trained (e.g., a psychoanalytic) eye, a manner of talking, flushing, working, saving, day-dreaming, or philosophizing may reveal the struggle.

The sexual tension, important as it is, is not the only source of

[23] A. Schopenhauer, *World as Will and Idea*, II, Appendix, chap. xix.
[24] Other authors besides Schopenhauer who are responsible for the prevailing voluntaristic or anti-rational view of motivation are Darwin, McDougall, and Freud.

traits. The doctrine of Drive recognizes others. In the case, for example, of a fear that besets an individual when confronted with some continuous menace from the environment, such as ridicule for some physical weakness—in such a case there result all manner of distinctive

AUTONOMIC NERVOUS—→ SYSTEM ←—	CENTRAL NERVOUS —→ SYSTEM ←—	THE ENVIRONMENT
segmental cravings, both avertive and acquisitive, caused directly or indirectly by the operation and interaction of organs innervated by this system:	unlearned cerebro-spinal reflexes conditioned reflexes habits and skills traits expressive movements expressive postures attitudes beliefs	potential satisfaction (*e.g.*, food, love, objects, oxygen, sunshine, water, and objects of cultivated interest) potential menace
pituitary gland pineal gland lachrymal gland dilator of pupil salivary gland hair follicles sweat glands thyroid gland thymus gland heart diaphragm liver stomach visceral arteries pancreas spleen intestine adrenal gland kidney colon bladder rectum ovary testes	compensations sentiments philosophy of life sublimations neurotic adjustments: tics regressions hysterias fixations repressions phobias compulsions all other ingredients of PERSONALITY	(painful and injurious stimuli, threatening and destructive objects) obstacles to the securing of satisfaction or the avoiding of danger

FIGURE 12

Biological Theory of Personality (Kempf)

compensations and escapes to avoid the painful tensions (inferiority feelings) that result. The frail boy who suffers a "narcissistic wound" every time he is taunted by his fellows, and finds refuge in becoming a teacher's pet; the short man who cultivates a beard, grand gestures, and a haughty bearing; the man who is excessively polite in order to escape abuse or domination by others; the scrupulous monk attempting to expiate persistent feelings of guilt: all are cases of central nervous adjustments (and forms of personality) resulting from persistent organic tensions involving fear. Personality results from the attempts of the central nervous system to establish security and comfort for the individual torn between his own affective cravings and the harsh demands of his environment.

To the objection that man's cravings are after all not exclusively nutritional, sexual, fearful, or otherwise "vegetative," the biological psychologists (Kempf, for example) reply with the behavioristic theory of conditioning. A craving may be reinstated easily by various originally indifferent stimuli which have acquired potency through their association with the effective stimulus. Take the case of attachment to one's parents, the so-called filial sentiment. At first the infant's cravings are only for bodily comfort. The mother becomes associated with this comfort; later her mere presence is sufficient to bring pleasure and her absence provokes a longing for the comfort of her companionship. Such extension and conditioning may continue until objects, tastes, ideas, associated with the mother become satisfying when they are present, and set up desire and longing when they are absent. Due to such conditioning maternal ideas are accepted with emotional conviction, and violation of parental teaching even in later life brings restlessness, pangs of conscience, and feelings of guilt.

The theory goes on to a treatment of mental conflict. Basically all drives are either *acquisitive* or *avertive*. One wishes to have something that the environment affords or to avoid something in the environment that threatens one's health and safety. This opposition leads to many types of conflict, for in the course of life the desirable is often tangled with the undesirable; the brightness of the flame attracts but its heat repels; danger is often alluring. Intelligence (a functional capacity of the central nervous system) is sometimes able to *discriminate* successfully and to attain the desirable while excluding the undesirable. But often the conflict is not intelligently resolved, and a *suppression* of the desire occurs because of the hazards attending its realization. Or the object of desire is obtained bringing with it *remorse* and *regret* because of the attendant evil consequences. Sometimes an *alternation* takes place; the individual swings back and forth from the self-indulgent to the ascetic course of conduct. Again, there may be a *compromise*, whereby a little of the desirable and a little of the undesirable are both admitted. Which method of solving conflicts the individual characteristically takes may be an important feature of his personality. Some people are nearly always headstrong, others hesitating and undecided, still others adopt the road of suppression, and some seek always the golden mean.[25]

Only in its broader outline is the biological theory described above acceptable. Personality, let it be admitted, represents the mode of survival that the individual has consciously or unconsciously worked out for himself. It is a resultant in a parallelogram of forces. But the forces are not quite so simple as the narrower statement of the biological theory would imply; for one thing the personality itself supplies many of the forces to which it must adjust!

To make the criticism more specific, there is first of all a tendency to keep the list of primary organic cravings too limited. If we concede first place among the biological motives to the nutritional and sexual tensions, there are still other original needs—for example, tensions demanding sleep, equalization of temperature, elimination, the unimpeded freedom of each organ and limb—all of which may underlie the development of important personal characteristics. In children there is clearly a craving for almost continuous muscular exercise during waking hours. Parents learn, often to their astonishment, that this vital need (not corresponding to any autonomic segment) takes precedence over nutritional demands; even when hunger is present, children frequently prefer physical activity in play to eating.

Further, the division of labor between the two nervous systems (in Kempf's theory)—one as master and one as servant, one as motive and one as agent—is far too simple. It is known for example that cortical determination plays a decisive role in the sexual behavior even of lower animals, and most obviously, of course, in the sexual and all other motives of men.[26] As soon as the earliest stages of

---

[25] Cf. E. B. Holt, *The Freudian Wish*, 1915.

[26] Cf. K. S. Lashley, *Psychol. Rev.*, 1924, 31, 192-202; also J. F. Fulton, *Muscular Contraction and the Reflex Control of Movement*, 1926, chap. xxi.

infancy are past every autonomic tension is overlaid with intellectual and volitional factors that facilitate, inhibit, or otherwise direct the course of the motive. Hence, the compartmentalization of the autonomic and cerebro-spinal nervous systems cannot be rigidly maintained.

Current emphasis upon "glands regulating personality" is an article of faith wholly in keeping with an over-simplified biological theory of personality, but it is psychologically far too narrow a conception. Granting that the chemistry of the body has much to do with the general cast of temperament, and that severe *dysfunctions* of the glands bring with them characteristic types of emotional disorder, there is still no reason to suppose that a *specific* and *proportionate* relationship exists between the chemical and psychic constitution of normal people. Tensions produced by glandular activity are absorbed into the more integral tensions that comprise *personal* motives. Suppose, for example, that there is a marked secretion from the adrenal glands. A vague emotional excitement will probably ensue; but *the way in which this excitement is handled* is a matter of deep-seated habits and attitudes, even of one's underlying philosophy of life. Chemical changes induced by disease or age, the menopause, adolescence, even hyperthyroidism and castration, are all *handled* by the individual in ways characteristic of his own preexisting personality.[27]

A final warning should be given against the acceptance of a narrow biological theory, this time in respect to its superficial con-

---

[27] Endocrine enthusiasts commit their fallacy of exaggeration chiefly because they do not distinguish between *personality* and *temperament*. They do not realize that there is a great difference between simple temperamental correlates of endocrine action (excitability, irritability, apathy, fluctuation of mood, etc.) and the much more intricate, cortically dominated, traits of personality (*e.g.*, egotism, aestheticism, pride, and suspiciousness).

A much-needed antidote to the exuberance of the endocrinologists is a study based on 1,400 autopsies by W. Freeman. Using the method of comparing the size of various endocrine glands (assuming that abnormal size indicates some variation in function) with the records of the patients' personalities, he reaches the following conclusion: "As far as determining whether an individual shall be a proud, sensitive, suspicious, paranoid individual or a timid, shut-in dreamy, schizoid person; a boisterous, jolly, hail-fellow-well-met cycloid, or a moody, pedantic, egocentric, epileptoid individual, the endocrine glands would seem to have little say in the matter." *Annals of Intern. Med.*, 9, 1935, pp. 444-450.

A general survey of the findings of endocrinology in relation to personality is offered by D. J. Ingle, *Psychol. Rev.*, 1935, 42, 466-479. Normally, this author points out, the endocrines are concerned with maintaining homeostasis, and by themselves lack potency for bringing about significant differences in personality.

ception of learning. It is all too easy to say that the primitive organic tensions become *conditioned*, and by this bit of verbal magic to think that one has accounted for all the motives of the adult person whose desires include not only nutritional and sexual satisfactions but likewise fine music, rare books, and the answer to puzzling problems in science, politics, and theology. What really happens is that an elaborate process of learning and growth intervenes between the organic wants of infancy and the cultural wants of adulthood, involving all manner of linguistic, imaginal, and rational factors that ultimately transform the segmental cravings of infancy into desires having no longer any functional connection with them, but holding in their own right an autonomous place in personal life (cf. Chapter VII).

The biological theory, then, is at its best when applied to the simpler motives of infancy. It is right in holding that there is no need to postulate an elaborate system of latent purposes underlying the restless behavior of the young child. On the other hand, as personality develops it is not possible to consider the cruder segmental motives of infancy as all-sufficient. Even though the adult, no less than the child, fulfills the requirements of survival, and fashions habits and attitudes that relate him adaptively to the world in which he must live, still the instruments he uses, and the complex roles he fills, place him beyond the reach of the cruder biological conception wherein segmental drive and conditioning are regarded as the simple and sovereign sources of personality.

PERSONALITY IN THE FIRST YEAR

Returning to the infant: the evidence then tells us that at birth he is endowed with capacities for activity of both a random-diffuse nature and of a specific-reflex order; these capacities can be activated by various forms of stimulation, and especially by tensions arising in certain autonomic-somatic segments that provoke restless movement until the tensions are resolved. He is endowed also with a distinctive physical and nervous constitution, including peculiarities of glandular function that predetermine to a large extent both his temperament and course of *physical* growth. Also in his constitutional inheritance are various incipient talents and defects that will in time manifest themselves, given suitable environmental conditions. In addition to this lavish equipment the infant has a many-sided capacity for mental growth involving numerous neuropsychic mechanisms that later must be considered in detail.

But in spite of all this equipment the newborn infant *lacks* personality. Although many of its determinants are congenital, personality as such is not inherited. Only when the original stream of activity meets the environment, acting upon it and being acted upon by it, do the first habits, conscious desires, and incipient traits emerge.

To discover the earliest manifestations of personality, two psychologically-minded parents observed a young infant attentively during the first months of life, keeping a complete daily diary. Oddly enough, for all their watchfulness, there are no certain entries concerning personality in their child until the fourth month of life. It is, of course, true that an infant in isolation cannot be viewed in respect to his individuality as easily as if he were in a group of children (or at least with one other child) of his own age. Some observers (able to compare the behavior of several infants) claim that the first faint signs of distinctive adjustment appear soon after birth.

The infant for whom the diary was kept will be called Andrew. A few excerpts reported here illustrate the difficulties of interpreting early behavior as expressive of personality. The age of the child in months and days is given before each entry.

0.1 First seen at age of 45 minutes, A. has his eyes open; much random squirming, clasping and unclasping hands. At the age of six hours, eyes wide open, blinks, yawns, and sneezes, also rejects first feeding from bottle. Aged 20 hours brought for first nursing, A. is wide awake and clearly sucking upon his arrival, showing many facial and mouth reflexes; suddenly goes sound asleep and cannot be roused for nursing.

0.2 Second time he is presented to breast A. is awake; he performs with perfection, sucking and swallowing, holding all the while tenaciously to the nipple.[28] Sucking movements take place against blanket or other objects, or frequently in the *absence* of any contact.[29] A. turns his head in well-co-ordinated fashion from right to left and back again. Coughs and hiccoughs noted.

[28] Inasmuch as A. nurses lying on his side, there is no evidence for the theory that swallowing is a conditioned response that depends upon the operation of gravity for the first stimulation of the successive ring muscles. Swallowing is entirely innate.

[29] Some behaviorists claim that the sucking response takes place only upon actual contact with breast or other objects. This entry illustrates the existence of *spontaneous* (internally provoked) adaptive behavior, and warns against the familiar bias of behaviorists that all behavior is purely *reactive*.

Already there is clear evidence both of the random mass-action and of the specific adaptive reflexes.

0.3   Foot and leg reflexes noted: when sole of foot is tickled, all five toes contract together, and again only the four little ones (positive Babinski). Prick on sole causes immediate withdrawing at knee.

0.4   Can be wakened by tickle but not by more massive movements. Grasp reflex noted in position of hands: thumbs inside. Eyes move synchronously, not independently.[30]

0.5   Seems to focus eyes on finger held 12 inches from his face, but does not follow the movement of the finger with his eyes.

0.6   Startles at sudden (but not loud) sound of electric light switch.

0.8   Quite definite fixation of eyes upon mother's face, and upon flower held in front of own face. After fixating objects for a short time there is much synchronous roving of the eyes.

0.10   When cheek is stroked lightly, muscles twitch in pattern of smile; when repeated a third and fourth time, a more diffuse bodily movement takes place, effecting a change of position and escape.

0.12   When pushed by his shoulders away from breast A. shows active resistance, a contrary movement of body (specifically at shoulders) back toward breast.

0.14   As soon as he is lifted a little way toward the breast, but before he reaches it, A. stops crying, and makes vigorous sucking movements.

This entry at two weeks is the first observed instance of possible conditioning. Andrew's preparatory adjustment for feeding seems to be the first visible example of learning. Thus far the entries have shown the dominance of sleep, random activity, and adaptive reflexes. Now that learning enters the record the possibility of distinctive modes of adjustment becomes enhanced. Up to this time there is little to distinguish Andrew from all his infant contemporaries.

0.16   Mother steps out to the baby-wagon to claim A. for his feeding. She approaches one sleeping baby (presumably A.): nurse says, "That's not your baby; that's Baby S." Mother next misclaims another sleeping baby as hers. In physical appearance the three are similar. Upon close inspection it seems that the chief visible dif-

[30] In some children this co-ordination seems to be acquired; in others it is present from birth.

> ference between A. and the others is that when crying he does
> not, as they do, display his gums.

This is the first entry of "distinctive modes of adjustment." In the
case of Andrew the first trace of personality seems to be a matter
of gums!

The earliest entries bearing unequivocally upon personality come
at the ages of three and four months.

> 3.01 A notable feature of A.'s disposition is the relatively small amount
> of crying and large amount of smiling. He is easily amused by
> sounds, grimaces, wagging fingers, playful thrusts, etc.
>
> 4.00 Characteristics at four months: healthy, good-natured, smiles
> readily and is easily amused, coy (while nursing he withdraws,
> smiles at mother, aggressively returns to breast with a kind of
> divided attention that can only be described as coy). Prophecy
> based on present characteristics: ready laugher, well-adjusted,
> *i.e.,* "normal" and "extroverted," capable of considerable temper,
> active, sensitive to rhythm, adaptable, wiry and muscular, tall,
> mischievous, with linguistic superiority.

It will be noted that some of the entries at 4.00 are in the nature of
prophecies. The qualities in question could not actually be observed,
but there seemed to be faint indications that suggested the beginnings of such qualities. It is not certain whether some of these predictions would not be duplicated for *any* infant of the same age;
nor is it certain that the parents are not prophesying wishfully or
reading into the child parental qualities. Let us follow this prospect
through.

These prophecies of the parents suggested an experiment, namely,
to check them against later records of Andrew's personality. During
the early years the parents themselves made the "follow-up" record,
but after four years of age different teachers co-operated without
any knowledge whatsoever of the entries made by the parents or by
the other teachers. Figure 13 gives the results of this comparative
study at different stages in early childhood.

According to this table the prognosis at the age of four months
is borne out in most respects. "Temper" seems to have given way to
excitability, and "mischievousness" to imaginativeness. Thus two of
the initially dominant characteristics have shifted their emphasis. Apparently a reserve, especially in school, has entered his nature, making
him more reticent and less dominant socially. But on the whole the

schedule is consistent throughout. Even at the age of nine, Andrew does not show any major characteristic not indicated in this chart. He is essentially a bright, not rugged, excitable child with marked masculine interests, adaptable to groups and friendly.

From this record two important hypotheses concerning personality in early life are suggested. In the first place, it appears that *vague and variable indications of distinctive traits are evident at an early age,* in this case at four months. The second hypothesis is of special and far-reaching significance: *from early infancy there is consistency in the development of personality.* These principles, which the following pages will further establish, show that innate determinants of personality are indeed important. They do not, however, imply that personality is nothing more than an unfolding of latent tendencies uninfluenced by environmental circumstance. As Andrew's environment becomes more diverse and more hostile, his assertiveness may be modified, or even destroyed, and his former "extroversion" may turn into a more marked withdrawing and reserve; conceivably even his gay and excitable temperament may undergo alteration. One can say only that he seems to have developed certain qualities compatible with his own temperament, but that these have been, and will continue to be, either accentuated or diminished according to the re-quirements of his environment.

There have been many other biographical studies of infants, but most of these have been concerned with the development of sensory, motor, and intellectual functions. The observer, especially if he is also the parent, is often inclined to overestimate the child's abilities, or to interpret the behavior in the light of his own adult preconceptions.[31] But even with these limitations the intensive study of the single child has its advantages over the present more popular method of an impersonal observation of masses of children, the subtleties of whose natures cannot but be lost in a maze of mechanical methods for classifying, recording and averaging. There are, however, a few studies of the early development of personality with which the case of Andrew might be compared.

Some observers have reported marked differences in the amount of activity and in the expenditure of energy not only in the first weeks but even in intra-uterine life. From the very beginning some

[31] M. C. Jones has shown that 85 per cent of these biographical studies report development more rapid than the norms established for a large representative group of infants. *Ped. Sem.,* 1925, 33, 537-585.

Prognosis at 4 mos. (parents)	Record at 12 mos. (parents)	Record at 2 yrs., 9 mos. (parents)	Record at 4 yrs., 7 mos. (teacher 1)
ready, easy laughter	laughs readily in imitation	happy and gay	
well adjusted "normal" extroverted	sociable but not affectionate	plays easily with other children	likes to be with older children
active	aggressive in friendships with other children	dominates other children; demands to be admitted to groups of older children	leads and dominates; has to be put with older children
active; capable of temper	excitable; somewhat nervous	decidedly excitable	very excitable, too tense; relaxation difficult for him; excitement may block speech
sensitive to rhythm			outstanding in school in rhythm
adaptable	regards people as agents for play; sociable	especially enjoys visitors; natural with strangers	discusses freely; good listener
mischievous	many inventions of games	people comment on his imaginative nature more than on any other quality	much originality in drawing
linguistic superiority			gets ideas quickly

FIGURE

Comparative Records of One Child's

babies seem placid and contented; others fidgety, restless and enterprising. Specifically, different patterns of feeding can be noted (e.g., the aggressive, intermittent, indolent, or impatient), and these patterns some writers believe are prophetic of a child's later temperament.[32]

One observer claims that there are differences in "social responsiveness" as early as the twentieth day,[33] but in this study social responsiveness must be taken merely to mean temperamental differ-

[32] Cf. S. and M. Blanton, Child Guidance, 1927, p. 31.
[33] H. Zoepffel, Zsch. f. Psychol., 1929, 111, 273-306.

Record at 6 yrs. (teacher 2)	Record at 8 yrs. (teacher 3)	Record at 9 yrs. (teacher 4)
almost always happy and active; easily provoked to laughter	unusual sense of humor; average amount of laughter	
without complexes or conflicts; no shyness or shame	seems sensitive but never inattentive to what is going on	well-adjusted, "sane"; has no enemies
exceedingly sociable; outstanding in any group	average in activity	plays all games vigorously, prefers active boys of masculine type as friends
jumps up and down when excited; occasional twitching in face; must be protected from exciting situations		calm and well-mannered at school (parents' note: at home entry at 6 yrs. by teacher 2 holds)
likes to sing, so much that he must be silenced in school for drowning out other children	attentive and interested in music	of all class members uses strongest colors and sharpest contours in drawing
his playmates are older; gets along well with them	fits into any group though with reserve	fits well into group situations at school
imaginative in play; very fond of stories; likes pranks and tricks	markedly original in content of drawings; amusing detail; not mischievous in school	
high in school work	high in school work	scholarship of high rank— I.Q. 140

13
Personality During Nine Years

ences in alertness and motility upon which differential social traits may *later* be founded. No distinctive social behavior as such can be observed as early as the twentieth day. But in the second half-year there are unmistakable differences in sociability. Bühler finds that some babies pay very little attention to people, whereas some are socially dependent, and still others are neither inattentive nor unduly dependent, but have what might be designated as "social ease." [34] It should be noted that, as in the case of Andrew, these earliest observa-

[34] Ch. Bühler, "The Social Behavior of the Child," *Handbook of Child Psychology,* 1st ed., 1931, chap. xii.

tions establish distinctiveness in temperament, motility, and intelligence. Traits, interests, tastes, social habits, and sentiments are unformed.

The second hypothesis, namely, that early observed differences tend to persist, likewise secures confirmation. An investigation by Shirley following the activity of twenty-five infants for two years from the time of birth, showed that certain qualities (*e.g.*, adaptability, timidity, aggressiveness) seem outstanding in a child from the early months onward.[35]

In another study it was found that infants between the ages of two and twelve months could readily be classified as those who laughed more often than they cried, those who laughed and cried in approximately equal amounts, and those who cried more than they laughed. This temperamental characteristic was found to be generally constant throughout the early months of life.[36] It would be valuable if such a study were continued beyond the first year to see whether this early affective balance is a characteristic of temperament in later childhood and in maturity.

One more study may be added to show that temperamental differences are distinguishable in the early weeks of life, and that they persist throughout infancy.[37] Monozygotic twins were chosen, strikingly alike in appearance, anthropometric measurements, hand prints, and intelligence. They were alike also in certain basic forms of emotional expression, gestures of request and refusal, vocalization, good nature and amenable demeanor. But throughout the study T was more approachable, more aggressive socially, more fearless, more vivid and reactive. By contrast C was more immobile, more introverted, cautious and fearful. A few selections from the examiners' protocol show the persistence of these differences.

*Age in
Weeks*

0   T more active immediately after birth; weight 3 oz. more than C.

6   T more responsive to material, but fusses more readily than C.

8   T more alert in fixating on objects; more reactive in prone position.

16   T cries more easily but also smiles more readily.

24   T slightly more placid during examination.

28   T vocalizes more; shows more tendency to fuss; more active.

[35] M. M. Shirley, *The First Two Years*, Vol. III, 1933, p. 219.
[36] R. W. Washburn, *Genet. Psychol. Monog.*, 1929, 6, Nos. 5-6.
[37] A. Gesell and H. Thompson, *Genet. Psychol. Monog.*, 1929, 6, No. 1.

Age in
Weeks

36 T's emotional behavior more spontaneous and vivid.

38 T gives more heed to C's material than C does to T's.

44 Vocalizations slightly more in C. Social playfulness before mirror slightly more vivid in T.

62 T more active. Slight personality difference; extensive correspondence remains.

79 T more mobile and active, but in adaptive, emotional and language behavior resemblance is extensive.

With the exception of one or two observations (at 24 and 44 weeks) T was the more reactive twin on every occasion. It is probable that the slightly different patterns of emotional nature will result in the development of increasingly distinctive personalities as soon as the social environment becomes broadened and as soon as the twins become aware of their similarities and differences.[38]

Only one study begun after the first year of life will be mentioned. It is based upon observation of 72 children between two and three years of age.[39] Two traits, negativism and distractibility, were chosen for study. Ratings were made by different observers who spent much time in watching the children. After an interval of nine weeks the ratings for these children correlated .80 for negativism and .83 for distractibility. After an interval of forty-three weeks the ratings for these children correlated .60 for negativism and .64 for distractibility. Since these correlations are based on quite independent ratings by different observers, the correspondence is undoubtedly significant. These two traits, then, seem to function persistently throughout the age-range studied. Attention should be called to the fact that these traits are primarily of the temperament-motility type.

From the evidence now in hand four important conclusions may be drawn: (1) Personality, defined as the distinctive mode of adjustment adopted by each individual in his efforts to live, is not formed at birth, but may be said to begin at birth. (2) The earliest distinctive adjustments in respect to which infants can be said to differ are in the intensity and frequency of their spontaneous activity (*motility*) and in their emotional expression (*temperament*). Both these factors are primarily products of inheritance. (3) Probably not before the fourth month is there sufficient learning and maturation to form distinctive *habits* of adjustment or rudimentary traits; but by the

[38] Cf. H. von Bracken, "Mutual Intimacy in Twins," *Char. & Pers.*, 1934, 2, 293-309.

[39] F. L. Goodenough, *J. Juv. Res.*, 1929, 13, 204-219.

second-half of the first year adaptive responses to the physical environment and to people show marked distinctiveness. (4) Distinctive qualities noticed early in life tend to persist; the child seems predisposed to learn certain modes of adjustment and to reject others. Even before these adaptive forms are clearly defined an observer can often by the method of "prophecy" predict later traits. Irrespective of the methods used to study the consistency of early development the evidence is positive in virtually every case.

This last conclusion, however, should not be regarded as implying that personality is fixed once and for all during the first year of life. No one's destiny is determined so early. Later circumstances affect personality profoundly. Ill health, a marked change in home conditions, or traumatic experiences, may actually reverse the course of development indicated during the first year of life. Furthermore, in early infancy there are certain conditions that prevent the formation of dispositions as stable as those to be formed later. There is, for example, a low degree of retentivity for conscious experiences, in fact such a low level of consciousness itself that the child has no distinct self-awareness. Consciousness of self later plays a primary role in organizing personality. Then too, though the infant learns rapidly, he also forgets rapidly. Habits, the balance wheel of personality, are readily lost. Furthermore, his emotional life is not graded, being almost incapable of moderate response. The propensity for an all-or-none type of emotional activity prevents his learning discriminative affective responses or the development of a hierarchy of likes and dislikes. His capacity for conceptualization is slight. There are, then, plenty of reasons why personality should be less stable, less predictable, and less consistent in the early months of life than at any later time. It is indeed never again as unorganized and unstructured as in infancy. But since even in the first year of life it is neither completely unorganized nor unstable, one must expect the maturing personality to show even greater self-consistency.[40]

[40] This chapter endeavors to *interpret* evidence drawn from modern investigations, in terms of its theoretical and systematic significance for the development of personality. Readers desiring a broader background of fact are referred to an excellent summary of research (1920-1935): M. C. Jones and B. S. Burks, "Personality Development in Childhood," *Monog. of the Soc. for Res. in Ch. Devel.*, 1936, Vol. I, No. 4.

CHAPTER V

BASIC ASPECTS OF GROWTH

Das Geeinte zu entzweien, das Entzweite zu einigen, ist das
Leben der Natur.

—Goethe

IT is easy enough to mark off arbitrarily stages in the progressive
development of personality from infancy through senility. One
could distinguish the periods of babyhood, childhood, adolescence,
maturity, and senescence, or make finer subdivisions according to
choice. But whether there are seven ages of man as Shakespeare held,
or three as the Sphinx would have it, or five, or nine, or seventy,
is a rhetorical and not a psychological question. For the single *person*
there is only *one* consecutive, uninterrupted course of life.

It is easy enough, too, to commit another psychological abstraction and speak of the separate "mechanisms of growth" whereby personality advances from one stage to another, for example, "conditioning," "the law of exercise," or "the law of effect." But here too the
homogeneity of the process of growth is misrepresented. As Goethe
points out nature continually unites and divides, builds up and tears
down, organizes and disorganizes, in such a complex way that no
single mechanism can be considered to operate independently.

But if instead of speaking of separate mechanisms of growth as if
they were so many *dei ex machina*, the psychologist distinguishes
merely *aspects* of the total process, his analysis will be better justified
and less subject to misrepresentation. It is only with aspects that the
psychologist *can* deal. With the total, homogeneous phenomenon of
growth he has nothing to do. For at bottom this phenomenon is
simply an unexplained property of all *living* substances, a problem
for the philosopher not the psychologist. An aspective rather than a
substantive analysis of the process, then, is the safest one to follow.

In planning such an aspective analysis, however, there is no
authoritative guide. The list of aspects here distinguished will serve

as well as any. Their adequacy will be seen as they are followed through in detail in this and in subsequent chapters.

A List of Various Aspects of Growth Significant in the Development of Personality

Differentiation
Integration
Maturation
"Learning"
Self-consciousness
Suggestion
Self-esteem
Inferiority and Compensation
Psychoanalytic "mechanisms"
Functional Autonomy
Sudden Reorientation: trauma
Extension of Self
Self-objectification: insight and humor
The personal *Weltanschauung*

DIFFERENTIATION

In the previous chapter it was pointed out that much of the infant's initial behavior is random and diffuse, mere "mass action." From this matrix in some way specialized skills and precise adaptive responses gradually become *differentiated*. A crude prototype is the case of the amoeba. This animal has no organs, no differentiated parts. By changing its entire shape it produces a mouth, a hand, a foot, or an arm, whenever they are needed. Its reactions are total. Higher in the phylogenetic scale the various biological functions sooner or later become specialized and assigned to more permanent segregated systems for which specific *structures* develop. These structures execute in a more adaptive way the responses originally made by the clumsy and inefficient pre-structuralized whole.[1]

Not only do structures become progressively specialized through the development of limbs and executive organs, but so too do nervous functions and all the adaptive patterns of behavior. From the massive

[1] The evolution of such special structures in the life-history of an organism, and their growth and self-repair under the domination of integral functional needs, have been described by G. E. Coghill, *Anatomy of Behavior*, 1929.

retraction or outreaching innervations supplied by the undeveloped brain of the infant, and from the random twisting and squirming produced by the dissipation of nervous impulses, the child gradually attains greater refinement in movement. Vocal habits, pleading, coaxing, facial expression, gesture, reaching, and later, working, spending, saving, collecting, repairing, commanding, dissimulating, combating, adapting socially—become his differentiated and more efficient patterns of behavior, proceeding from, and substituting themselves for, the original, inaccurate, total responses of his whole body.

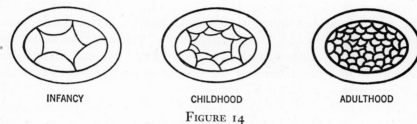

INFANCY   CHILDHOOD   ADULTHOOD

FIGURE 14

The Differentiation of Functional Systems

A psychological account of differentiation is given by Lewin.[2] "The child to a greater extent than the adult is a dynamical unity. The infant acts first with its whole body and only gradually acquires the ability to execute part actions." Unlike adults, Lewin goes on to say, the young child has only slight functional firmness in the boundaries of the various systems. In the adult, movements, mannerisms, attitudes and traits are more definitive, more fixed, less confused with unrelated tendencies. This course of development may be represented diagrammatically in the manner of Lewin (Figure 14). The boundaries between the functional systems are weak in infancy, causing the child to react as a whole; likewise the barrier between the child and his environment is less firm, leaving him a prey to all manner of environmental stimuli that later in life will be inhibited. The weakness of this barrier likewise prevents the development of sharp self-consciousness in the first year or two of life.

Motor tensions in a child are far more totalized and imperative than in a self-controlled (well-differentiated) adult. A child of three, for example, who is "set" to respond in some particular way cannot

[2] K. Lewin, "Environmental Forces in Child Behavior and Development," *Handbook of Child Psychology*, 1st ed., 1931, chap. iv.

delay his response even until the starting signal is given.[3] And every parent knows the exasperating insistence of a child who must wait twenty minutes to be read to, or who expects to leave for the circus in an hour. There is little capacity for delay. There is likewise little capacity for graded response. When the child acts he uses much more of his body than does the adult. When he is pleased he jumps up and down; when he is angry he is "mad all over." His emotional behavior is not differentiated, and nearly all of his activities are accompanied by "synkinesis" (auxiliary but meaningless movement).[4] Especially when he reads, writes, talks, or practices on the piano, he wriggles or fusses. Precise co-ordination and patient skill are beyond him. The whole development of neurodynamics, writes Luria, consists in the creation of a "functional barrier" reducing the excitation from the total nervous system to certain limited systems that enable the child to mobilize accurately the amount of energy and the precise reaction patterns required by the situation.[5]

Differentiation, involving as it does the selection of precise adaptive movements in place of gross and indecisive activity of the whole body, obviously depends upon the operation of inhibition. The inhibition of antagonistic or useless movements is the first step in acquiring adaptive skill. A certain amount of inhibition is automatic, since the effective innervation of one muscular system will perforce inhibit an antagonistic system. It is therefore not strictly true to say that the infant's activity is *ever* completely undifferentiated. Inhibition occurs in the earliest movements of the limbs and the first expression of emotion. The child cannot thrust his leg forward and retract it at the same time, nor can he smile and cry. Curious effects are seen when the two innervations are struggling for the final common path, but ultimately one or the other will prevail or else the child must remain in a tense state of suspended animation.

Ultimately, thanks to the refinements of inhibition, not only actions executed by antagonistic muscle systems come to suppress one another, but also auxiliary, wasteful, and irrelevant actions become eliminated. There is growing precision; each act increases in skill and in adaptive value even while it decreases in area, spread, and in the

[3] A. R. Luria, *The Nature of Human Conflicts*, trans. 1932, chap. x.
[4] Cf. G. W. Allport and P. E. Vernon, *Studies in Expressive Movement*, 1933, pp. 16-21.
[5] A. R. Luria, *op. cit.*, p. 342. The doctrine of differentiation is in essence a modern statement of the Spencerian principle that the process of life consists in breaking down diffuse *homogeneity* into coherent *heterogeneity*.

consumption of energy. With the aid of selective inhibition the random vocalizations of the infant become reduced in range and variety until there remain only the narrower patterns of vocal response serviceable for communication and symbolic thought. Gross and violent emotional expression becomes reduced through inhibition until in the adult nothing overt but a subtle gesture, a lifted brow, or a well-chosen word may remain. Inhibition destroys the amorphous and monotonous character of early behavior, and generates greater diversity in activity and greater firmness in the boundaries between activities.

The chief lines of support for the doctrine of differentiation (or *individuation*, as it is sometimes called) have not yet been enumerated. Working with human fetuses secured through abortions, Minkowski discovered that only in the older fetuses were there any signs of segmental reflex action, and that even in these there was a great predominance of slow, asymmetrical and arrhythmical mass activity. When stimulated cutaneously these organisms seemed to respond with their entire muscular equipment.[6] Coghill's work with the *Amblystoma* is well known. He has shown that the specific reflex activity of the forelimbs, legs and gills occurs after, and as a derivative of, diffuse bodily movement. In the embryo of the *Amblystoma*, for example, the predominant type of activity is an S-like swimming reaction. This method of locomotion puts stress upon certain segments of the body, and by so doing seems to cause nerves to invade those regions, while this invasion in turn seems to determine the location of the limbs. The local limb reflexes thus derive from the more unified preceding reaction of the total organism. To state the theory in his own terms:

> Organ systems must be secondarily attained by a process of individuation within a totally integrated system, and the development of the behavior patterns must be effected, not by an integration of independent reflexes, as is usually considered, but by a process of individuation within a total organismic system which is from the beginning of reaction integrated as a whole. The basic principle, therefore, in the development of the nervous system of vertebrates appears to be *the maintenance of the integrity of the individual while independencies are growing up within it, and are, so to speak, struggling*

[6] An accessible account of this work is given by G. E. Coghill, *J. Gen. Psychol.*, 1930, 3, 431-435. The literature on the field as a whole is summarized by L. Carmichael, *Handbook of Child Psychology*, rev. ed., 1933, chap. i.

*for ascendancy among themselves and for dominance over the indi-
vidual.*[7]

Irwin studied the movements of infants during the first ten days
of life in a situation enabling him to keep constant the external stimulating conditions.[8] The records were taken continuously, 24 hours a
day, for four infants. It appears that segmental responses are less conspicuous than mass action, and that any segmental response becoming intense tends to irradiate until it involves all visible organs of response, so that "literally everything seems to be going at once." It is
an inescapable conclusion that since mass activity is the prevailing
mode of response in early life, learning must proceed at least in large
part, as specialization or individuation of this crude activity. The
author also contends that an organismic theory of development
through differentiation is far preferable to the older theory of sum-
mated, compounded, chained or integrated specific reflexes.[9]

The physiological process by which habits and dispositions become differentiated within a loose primitive field of response is by
no means clear. Why should useless movements be inhibited? Why,
for example, does the infant at first reach with arms, feet, and head
for an object; then with arms alone, and finally with *one* arm? The
problem is to account for the fact that afferent impulses gradually
cease to spread to any excepting certain preferential paths. Smooth
and effective movement gradually obliterates diffuse and random
movement, except for occasional synkinesis, or "nervous" movement,
persisting in the form of personal mannerisms. Undoubtedly the process is enormously complex. Some authors have stressed the successive
myelinization of motor and sensory nerve tracts and nuclei, or other
temporal differences in the maturation of motor and sensory segments.[10] Some speak of differential rates of metabolism favoring first

[7] G. E. Coghill, "The Growth of Functional Neurones and Its Relation to the
Development of Behavior," *Proc. Amer. Phil. Soc.*, 1926, 65, 51-55.
Coghill has made specific application of his theory to the structure of personality: "The higher and more complicated expression of this conflict concerns the
integrity of personality. Here it is chiefly the cerebral cortex that is the seat of
conflict between the partial and total patterns of integration. The various components
of the personality, according to this hypothesis, just as local spinal reflexes, develop
by individuation within the mechanism of total integration, and their normal function depends upon their subordination to that mechanism," *J. Genet. Psychol.*, 1936,
48, p. 19.
[8] O. C. Irwin, *Genet. Psychol. Monog.*, 1930, 8, No. 1.
[9] O. C. Irwin, *Psychol. Rev.*, 1932, 39, 189-201.
[10] F. Tilney and L. Casamajor, *Arch. Neurol. & Psychiat.*, 1924, 12, 1-66. O. C.
Irwin, *Psychol. Rev.*, 1932, 39, pp. 189-201.

one locality and then another, until specialized and regional response has supplanted diffuseness.[11] Other behavioristically inclined writers emphasize the different intensities and different periods in which certain environmental stimuli become effective,[12] or call upon "neurobiotaxis," the "reflex circle," and "algebraic summation" of competing and antagonistic motor impulses.[13] It is safest to assume that all the resources of physiology will be required to give a complete account of this intricate process. In addition the psychological law of effect according to which successful adaptive movements are retained and unsuccessful ones lost will be called upon.

In the meantime, the significance of the doctrine of differentiation for personality must not be lost sight of. The concept of the reflex-arc, which it opposes, arose as a consequence of the cell theory in biology. Just as the cell was accepted as the structural unit, so the functional co-ordination of sensory, central and motor neuronic cells into a simple arc was regarded as the unit of behavior. The cell theory held the organism to be a sum-total of intricately connected cells. When this notion was abandoned in favor of a more systemic theory, the reflex theory of nervous activity fell into disrepute. Today, therefore, differentiation, in spite of its vagueness, is a principle usually preferred by genetic psychologists to the specious simplicity of integration. Even behaviorists have swung into line. "Simple reflexes," write Lashley and Ball, "elaborated by a combination in chain reflex arcs have proved of little value for an understanding of the more intricate problems in psychology." [14]

Some writers fear that enthusiasm for the doctrine of mass action as the original form of behavior, and the belief that from it are derived more specific, segmental reflexes and habits, may go too far.[15] A controversy is on foot. Although the conditioning and compounding of simple reflexes seems to be an inadequate theory of growth, that there is still such a *cementing* or *integrating* process cannot be denied. *Dissociation* as a law of development cannot entirely supersede the more ancient law of *association*.

This dispute is of special significance for the problem of consistency in personality. If, as implied in the diagram of Lewin's theory

[11] C. M. Child, *Individuality in Organisms*, 1915; and *Physiological Foundations of Behavior*, 1924.
[12] Z. Y. Kuo, *Psychol. Rev.*, 1932, 39, 499-515.
[13] E. B. Holt, *Animal Drive and the Learning Process*, 1931.
[14] K. S. Lashley and J. Ball, *J. Comp. Psychol.*, 1929, 9, 7-107.
[15] Cf. I. Pavlov, "The Reply of a Physiologist to Psychologists," *Psychol. Rev.* 1932, 39, 91-128.

(Figure 14), personality comes in time to have finer, more differen-tiated, and firmer divisions, would it not follow that personality is never again as unified as it is in early infancy? Would it not be ex-pected that each individual grows more and more specific in his con-duct and less and less of a consistent unit? Differentiation, as the sole mechanism, would produce a kind of entropy or dissipation of per-sonality. That movement, language and emotional expression become more subtle and precise no one can deny; and this fact is of exceed-ingly great importance for the development of personality. But these specializations once acquired seem to influence one another and to join together into a closely-knit and expanding organization. The course of nature, as Goethe said, is not only to divide what is united, but also to unite what is divided. Integration is fully as important a principle as differentiation.

INTEGRATION

Integration, like differentiation, is sometimes considered to be the supreme principle of growth. Both genetic psychology and mental hygiene make wide use of it, and in the latter field especially it has been exalted to the place of the most solemn Om. Whatever condi-tion makes for mental health is called "integrative," whatever con-dition makes for mental difficulty is called "disintegrative." The dev-otees, of course, never doubt that integration is an unalloyed good, and disintegration an incarnation of evil.[16] But it is not always clear to what psychophysical process all this incantation refers.

The original significance of integration is best understood by re-ferring to the cell theory in biology. The initial fact is that a human body contains about ten trillion cells, over nine billion of which are found in the cortex. Somehow out of this bewildering array of ele-ments a relatively unified and stable personal life is constructed. The single cells cohere in such a way as to lose their independence of function. From the many there emerges the one; the motto implicit in integration is *e pluribus unum*.

Even though a person's life exhibits contradictory trends, even though the unity is never complete and final, it is nevertheless obvi-ous that the number of totally independent qualities is not very great.

[16] Cf. W. H. Burnham, *The Normal Mind*, 1924, and *The Wholesome Per-sonality*, 1932. In spite of their over-emphasis these books are to be recommended for the profusion of concrete applications of the principle of integration to the development of personality.

Probably only a very few specific segmental reflexes remain unassociated with the complex activities of that great integrative organ, the cortex. Within this organ the links and combinations are of such profusion that every function seems joined in some way and to some degree with almost every other function.

Just as those who choose to regard the behavior of the newborn baby chiefly as mass action, prefer as a consequence to endorse the doctrine of differentiation, so do those who see the infant's equipment at birth consisting chiefly in specific reflexes, prefer the doctrine of integration.[17]

The doctrine of integration easily lends itself to a conception of hierarchy in personality. The simplest possible integration would be of two nerve cells functioning together as a simple reflex arc because of some synaptic affinity between them. Whether or not there are any reflexes involving as few as *two* neurones is not known. C. S. Sherrington, the physiologist who above all others is responsible for the concept of integration, regards this limiting case of integration as a "convenient though improbable abstraction." Similarly, at the opposite extreme, where from a final perfect integration a completely *unified* personality is supposed to emerge, one meets another convenient though improbable abstraction. But between these ideal limiting cases there is ample room for the operation of actual integration. In ascending order of complexity one might distinguish a hierarchy of the levels produced by integration as follows:

> *Conditioned reflexes,* the simplest learned forms of adaptive behavior involving substitution of associated stimuli for congenitally effective stimuli, with the result that the individual performs innate acts to altered stimulus situations.

> *Habits,* integrated systems of conditioned responses, involving altered responses as well as an extended range of effective conditioning, leading to fairly stereotyped forms of response in the face of recurrent situations of a similar type.

> *Traits,* more dynamic and flexible dispositions, resulting, at least in part, *from the integration of specific habits,* expressing character-

---

[17] V. M. Bechterev (*General Principles of Human Reflexology,* trans. 1932), and J. B. Watson (*Psychology from the Standpoint of a Behaviorist,* 1919), are two writers who regard personality above all else as an integration of separate reflex arcs. Bechterev holds that the combining of reflexes is the only guide needed, and Watson speaks of the reflex level of functioning as occurring first in infancy, followed, through virtue of integration, by the conditioned reflex level and by the habit level. Personality, for Watson, is synonymous with the integration of an individual's manual, visceral and laryngeal habits.

istic modes of adaptation to one's surroundings. Belonging to this level are the dispositions variously called sentiments, attitudes, values, complexes, and interests.

Selves, systems of traits that are coherent among themselves, but are likely to vary in different situations. (Cf. the statement of James that a man "has as many different social selves as there are distinct *groups* of persons about whose opinion he cares.")

Personality, the progressive final integration of all the systems of response that represent an individual's characteristic adjustments to his various environments. (Considered as a *perfect* integration this level represents the ideal final stage, never actually attained.)

A relatively simple case may be taken as an illustration of the way the mechanism of integration is supposed to operate. The newborn infant has the reflex capacity of withdrawing the arm when the hand is brought into contact with a dangerously hot object. In creeping around the room, perhaps at the age of 10 months, he reaches out and touches a hot radiator, quickly withdrawing the arm to avoid the painful contact. Next time he sees the radiator he withdraws "in advance," inhibiting the impulse to touch its shiny surface. This is a simple instance of conditioning.[18] At the same time it is an elementary case of integration: the sight of the radiator, originally unconnected with the withdrawing tendency, is now effectively integrated with it, with the result that one somewhat elaborated functional system is created. What is more important, the burned child usually avoids the hot radiator *ever after*, without periodic rebuilding or reinforcing of the integration. *Once established, the system of avoidance continues to operate as a dynamic whole.* This *functional autonomy* of systems acquired through integration is often found, and turns out to be one of the most important principles in the psychology of personality (cf. Chapter VII).

Usually integration is portrayed in quasi-physiological terms—a perilous proceeding. That there are physiological correlates of integration involving complex spatial, temporal, histological, and electrochemical factors no one will deny. But since integration implies *functional* joining of nervous pathways, taking place presumably in the region of the synapse, and since this entire process lies still in the

[18] The law of the conditioned reflex may be stated as follows: Whenever a stimulus has a motor outlet, any stimulus occurring simultaneously will tend to acquire the same motor outlet; after sufficient repetition (sometimes one occasion is enough) the second stimulus alone will suffice to produce a discharge in that motor outlet.

limbo of scientific mystery, all accounts of integrative growth in physiological terms are at the present time highly speculative. The characteristics of integration are known far better through psychological investigations.[19]

To escape from the deceptive snares of pseudophysiology it will be safer to take from now on a frankly psychological approach to the whole course of growth, and here specifically to the

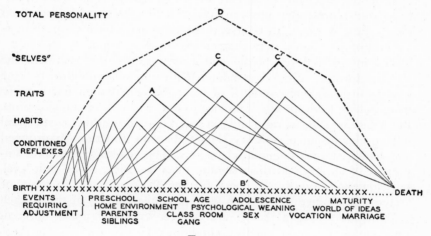

FIGURE 15

A Schematic Representation of Integration

problem of integration. In so doing a diagram will be helpful in summarizing the various phenomena that psychologists have classed as instances of integration (or of disintegration). Remembering always that integration is only one aspect of growth, and not the whole story, it becomes possible nevertheless to draw from it much help in understanding the development of personality. The significant features of Figure 15 may be analyzed under ten headings.

[19] Indeed, for that matter, the study of all the aspects of the development of personality may be said to be more advanced on the psychological level than on the physiological. "To reject the resource of psychological analysis and construct the theory of the mind solely on such data as physiology at present affords, seems to me a great error in principle, and an even more serious one in practice. Imperfect as is the science of mind, I do not scruple to affirm that it is in a considerably more advanced state than that portion of physiology which corresponds to it; and to discard the former for the latter appears to me an infringement of the true canons of inductive philosophy. . . ." J. S. Mill, *System of Logic*, Bk. VI, chap. iv, Sec. 2. This judgment made one hundred years ago is as appropriate today as when it was first written.

(1) *The Hierarchical Organization of Personality*. Integration means that from disparate units of behavior larger and more inclusive integers are formed. The actual functional scope of these new integers may be narrow or broad. A conditioned reflex represents an integration of two or more sensory pathways (or types of excitation) with one common motor outlet; at the other extreme, personality itself represents an hypothetical integer including in a functional unity all the varied systems of behavior possessed by one individual. For convenience intermediate levels may be distinguished, *e.g.*, *habits*, *traits*, and *selves*, representing progressively widening integers of generalized dispositions. Actually, of course, these levels are arbitrary since inclusiveness of *any* degree may characterize an integration.

The inborn reflexes, before and after conditioning, represent the simplest form of adjustive response. With time most of these become intricately joined into systems of habits, which though not entirely independent, have specific reference to one class of stimulus situations. But habits are still too rigid and too specific to serve as the most typical structural units in personality. Habits become functionally grouped and saturated with common characters. The resulting, and most important of all levels in the structure of personality, is the trait-level. It is sometimes possible to speak further of organization in terms of "selves," for sometimes, though seldom, whole systems of traits (each system constituting a "self") are evoked separately under different environmental or psychological conditions. Finally, there is the theoretical possibility of a thoroughly unified system of personality at the top of the pyramid. Whether this theoretical possibility is ever attained will be discussed later.

(2) *The Chronological Character of Integration*. The base-line of the figure is roughly chronological. It represents the process of separate adjustive acts that the individual is compelled to perform from birth to old age. An approximate division of this line into important "ages" of life is indicated. The pre-school environment is ordinarily constant and is responsible for calling out the initial and basic adjustments that form some of the habits enduring for a lifetime. Entering school introduces the child to many new and critical situations. Here he must adjust to individuals outside the family. As he approaches adolescence there is the "gang" and his own status among his contemporaries. Adolescence itself brings a welter of physiological and social emergencies. Breaking away from the ties of home, perhaps leaving the shelter of home for good, precipitates a new crisis. A special section on the chart indicates the flood of intellectual, emotional and social experiences that follow an induction into the world of abstract thought, of industry, or that attend religious conversion. Such ex-

periences, intangible though they are, have a profound effect on the maturing personality.

As maturity advances there are other adjustments to be made, to one's occupation, to one's partner in marriage, and to one's newly founded family. When this period is passed the personality is virtually finished. "If you have an adequate picture of the average individual at thirty you will have it with few changes for the rest of that individual's life—as most lives are lived." [20] By the age of thirty the "character" has "set like plaster, and will never soften again." [21] The verdict is perhaps too pessimistic and overdrawn, for some personalities seem to change markedly after the age of thirty. But in principle the judgment is sound, and is admitted to the diagram by assigning on the base line relatively small space after this age for the further integration of *new* qualities of personality.

(3) *Richness of Personality.* The length of the base line is a measure of the range of experiences encountered in the course of life. It indicates the variety of adjustments the individual is forced to make. For some individuals the crises of life are lightly passed over; they bring no strain and leave no mark. In many cases, for example, the highly significant introduction to the abstract world of ideas never takes place. Some persons find it easier to keep an integrated view of life, because life has put few demands in their way. The country grandmother, lovable though she is, possesses only a few dominant habits and traits. She worries neither about the dictates of fashion nor the collapse of Capitalism; it is less important to her that the universe is wearing down than that her kitchen needs refurbishing. A few simple attitudes and rules of life serve her. She performs her daily duties, trusts in God, and drinks tea of herbs that she has gathered. Compared with an educated citizen of the world, buffeted about by discordant doctrines, torn by conflicts, personal and cosmic, her personality is not many-sided and rich, though in all probability it is better integrated.

(4) *Incompleteness of Integration.* By virtue of integration the rudimentary forms of adjustment in infancy commence to interlace, to form higher units with the passage of time. But the process is highly irregular. The weight of the various adjustments entering into higher units varies markedly. A bitter disappointment or grief, or a timely success may become the focal point for all future organization and thus serve to *set* a habit or a trait. On the other hand, many (perhaps most) of one's experiences in life are never adequately integrated; they occur—a passing adjustment is made—but then

[20] J. B. Watson, *Behaviorism*, 1924, p. 223.
[21] W. James, *Principles of Psychology*, 1890, I, p. 121.

the matter is dropped and forgotten. One's assimilated experience (*Erlebnis*) does not keep pace with one's passing and transient experience (*Erfahrung*).

Bergson has said that personality is a knife edge pressed against the future. Constantly we encounter new events to which we must respond, but in responding we do not always *incorporate* the action into the permanent structure of our personalities. Rather we let our earlier habits and our previously formed attitudes and traits suffice, not troubling to alter our integrations to embrace the new features of the environment or the new evidence that we have encountered. Diagrammatically expressed, there are innumerable x's on the base line that never contribute to broadening a pre-existing integration or to the creation of one that is new and more adequate.

This fact is of paramount importance. It is well known that men ordinarily direct their behavior by inappropriate habits, by stereotyped ideas, and by hollow verbal symbols. Most people do not learn as much from their own experience as they think. There seems to be an inertia in the process of integration. A few conventional habits, some fossils of ancestral political-economic beliefs, a handful of superstitions, a vocabulary of clichés, a simple *Weltanschauung*, serve most people to their satisfaction.

The rule seems to be that unless some strong desire exists to alter an unsatisfactory habit or trait, or unless the demands of the world are so insistent that one cannot possibly continue to use his former equipment, or unless for some other reason an individual is genuinely pliable and open-minded, his personality will continue to employ its rough and ready devices for meeting the demands of life, thus avoiding the necessity for integration.

(5) *Regression and Dissociation.* Two types of disintegration reflect the difficulty of maintaining a progressively unified set of attitudes and traits sensitive to the successive demands of life. Sometimes when an individual encounters harsh experiences, difficult or impossible to adjust to, his personality reverts or regresses to earlier levels of integration. This *regression* has both its normal and its abnormal manifestations.[22] It is not uncommon for a woman, finding it impossible to meet the demands of her married life, to return temporarily to the protective home of her parents; or for an adult defeated in some emotional encounter, to give way to tantrums or to coaxing; or for the Old Grad or the Legionnaire to seek to regain temporarily at a reunion the more carefree habits and outlook of his youth; or for an

---

[22] A many-sided treatment of the subject is that of F. L. Wells, "Social Maladjustments: Adaptive Regression," in the *Handbook of Social Psychology*, 1935, chap. xviii.

aged person partially childish, to resume the memories and even the habits of his early years. In *abnormal* instances usually after severe traumatic defeat, there is sometimes complete regression: a personality tumbles like a house of cards, leaving the victim as helpless as an infant.[23]

The process of *dissociation* occurs when some self-coherent system fails to integrate with the remainder of the personal life, becoming instead an independent "complex," a logic-proof organization that resists the healing incursion of common sense and of other potentially neutralizing experiences. A phobia, an amnesia, an anxiety neurosis, are examples. Such separate systems indirectly affect the normal and primary systems controlling the personal life, causing severe conflict and giving rise to neurotic symptoms familiar enough in these post-Freudian days.[24] Such systems are often like mental cancers. In the diagram an attempt has been made to represent an independent, dissociated system of this sort in the minor integration marked (A).

(6) *Infantilism.* Occasionally one meets someone who refuses to grow up, to "be his age." Having found an earlier level of integration emotionally adequate, or perhaps for some reason fearing (probably unconsciously) to assume the burdens of adult estate, this person remains behind in development. This failure to grow is a counterpart of regression where maturity, once attained, is surrendered; in infantilism, maturity is not reached.

A few years ago a freshman in college, the only son of a self-made man, was summoned before the dean for failure in his work. The dean asked if he was '28, meaning the class of 1928. The boy replied, "Oh, no, sir, I'm only 18." By the Freudian theory this might be regarded as a significant and ominous misunderstanding. Indeed, it developed that the boy who appeared like a fifteen year old, was attempting to win his way by an attractive smile, by coaxing, by childish appeals for sympathy, rather than by mental exertion and study. Consultation with the parents revealed that this mode of adjustment was always used by the boy at home, with marked success. In the diagram it is as though the personality had developed only to point (B) instead of to (B'), the point suitable to the boy's age. On the dean's advice the lad was sent out to earn his own living and make his own way, with the result that in a few years the boy's personality caught up to his years. This is a minor and not a spectacular case of infantilism. But it is of just such slight deviations that the variant patterns of normal personality are composed.

[23] A dramatic and highly instructive case of this order is offered by W. McDougall, Case 24 in *Abnormal Psychology*, 1926, pp. 285-289.

[24] An excellent case of a dissociated phobic system is given in the autobiography of W. E. Leonard, *The Locomotive God*, 1927.

(7) *The Nature of Traits.* Figure 15 also gives a hint concerning the nature of traits. It is apparent from the diagram that traits are more inclusive than habits, being compounded of them and of the underlying, still more specific, modes of adjustment. Traits appear gradually in life, becoming strengthened or refashioned as the base line of experience is extended. They are not wholly independent of one another. In fact, any specific instance of conduct may result from the confluent operation of several traits, and it may in turn contribute to the reorganization of these same traits. Traits are simply nodal points in the structure of personality, regions of adaptive stress, foci of adjustment (cf. Chapters XI and XII).

(8) *Multiple Selves.* Different situations, as William James pointed out, and as sociologists constantly reiterate, may call into play different combinations and proportions of traits. At home a man may seem domineering, testy, and gruff; at work, considerate, tactful, even obsequious. His two major environments accent different complements of traits in one and the same personality.

When the case is very extreme, when, like Dr. Jekyll and Mr. Hyde, the same individual has utterly incompatible and functionally separated integrations one may speak of *dual personality*. In rare cases more than two such independent systems have been clinically recorded; these are *multiple personalities*. In Figure 15 the possibilities of "selves" turning into multiple personalities is indicated by the pyramids (C and C').

In general, however, the situation is reversed. Even the man in the above illustration probably shows more characteristics that are alike in his two environments than are unlike. The case for the existence of separate and distinct selves is easy to exaggerate. James is partially responsible for this exaggeration because of the quotable aphorism, a man "has as many different social selves as there are distinct *groups* of persons about whose opinion he cares," [25] which decidedly overstates the case.

(9) *Rigidity versus Flexibility.* Is the well-integrated person able to vary his behavior as occasion demands, or is his character really set like plaster? Some writers regard integration as synonymous with petrification: "With the perfection of reaction patterns achieved during advancing years, personality becomes better integrated, but a heavy price is paid: imagination fails and intellectual sterility ensues." [26]

It is true that by its very nature integration reduces the irregular

[25] *Principles of Psychology*, 1890, I, p. 294.
[26] J. T. MacCurdy, *Common Principles in Psychology and Physiology*, 1928, p. 263.

and random nature of adjustment by providing definite guiding systems within which responses are prepared. The drifter, the soldier of fortune, the person who readily takes on the complexion of his environment, cannot be said to have a firmly integrated personality. No one, as William James remarked, can at one time be a bon vivant, a philosopher, a tone poet, a lady-killer, and a saint; such diverse integrations could not keep house together in the same tenement of clay. Even if these phases *succeeded* one another in the course of life the picture would still be one of pathological disunity.

Yet integration does not necessarily mean rigidity in personality. Flexibility may exist side by side with integration. It all depends upon the nature of the integration itself. If immature, rutted, intolerant systems have developed and become set, they will not readily bend to new experiences nor be modified by them. But if a system is held somewhat tentatively, or if it is broad and ample in scope, the integration itself will not preclude adaptability in conduct and progressive change in personality.

(10) *The Unity of Personality*. Rarely does one encounter a person who seems to be completely integrated with only one dominant philosophy of life from which every attitude, trait, and individual act *must* proceed, and for whom perfect prediction of conduct is possible. Occasionally a literary writer argues for such a case.[27] And there are some psychologists who contend that if a personality is rightly understood it will always be found to lie under the domination of one controlling goal, *one* ruling passion, possessing (to borrow Professor Wertheimer's term) one *radix*. To allow for the possibility of such a supreme, all-inclusive integration, the pyramid in Figure 15 is closed with a dotted line (D). But the problem of the unity of personality is not to be disposed of so easily. In Chapter XIII we shall return to it.

MATURATION

Maturation may be defined as the ripening of innate behaviorial tendencies in the absence of training and experience. The ripening may involve a native process of *differentiation*, of *integration*, or of both. Since the visible equipment of the infant at birth is relatively meager (Figure 11), supplying only a partial demonstration of the child's hereditary endowment, the conception of maturation has of

---

[27] For example, a statement from a London newspaper: "Einstein is all of a piece. . . . His social behavior, his political views, his general interests, all seem to be the spontaneous manifestations of a profoundly integrated nature. There is no division in him." Another instance is Chesterton's keen characterization of Tolstoy, cited on pp. 190 f.

necessity been embraced by those who are interested in the native factors in growth. It is obvious that the more one leans on heredity the more must one depend on maturation. Instinct-psychologists are an instance in point; since the newborn infant shows no visible signs of a parental, acquisitive, or gregarious propensity, they have to rest their case for these instincts upon the latent powers of maturation. Opponents of this doctrine reply that subtle and socialized types of learning account for the appearance of these "instincts" later in life.[28] The subject requires further consideration.

At the outset it must be granted that there is indisputable evidence in favor of two kinds of maturation, though neither of these has any very specific relation to the traits of personality. In the first place, it is clear that the nervous system as a whole ripens in its capacity for the retention of experience and for intelligent adaptation to new situations. Intelligence is certainly not complete at birth. Normally it increases in "power" through adolescence, probably later. Likewise, certain intellectual capacities—talents for art, music, mathematics, and the like—we must admit as inborn and as undergoing maturation. This type of growth-from-within parallels, approximately, physical growth. There is also an obvious ripening of glandular functions, most notably those regulating sexual development. Granting all this physical, intellectual, and sexual ripening, there are still no proofs of the unfolding of innately determined instincts nor of pre-ordained traits of personality. However important the intellectual capacity and sexual drive may be in the development of traits, still no adaptive trait is ever given in advance. The ripening sexual impulses, for example, will be met within the framework of pre-existing attitudes and fears, and will be affected by traits acquired well before the onset of puberty.

Another type of maturation indisputably occurs—an object of much investigation in recent years—the unlearned ripening of motor co-ordinations and capacities such as creeping, walking, climbing, swimming, laughter, and vocalization. The ingenious development of the method of co-twin control has contributed to this research. Identical twins (with presumably equivalent heredity) are separated for the purposes of experiment. One receives an intensive course of train-

[28] A statement of the case for maturation from the standpoint of instinct-psychology is given by W. McDougall, *Outline of Psychology*, 1923, chaps. iv and v. The case in opposition is stated by F. H. Allport, *Social Psychology*, 1924, pp. 44-48. A criticism of the opposition is offered by R. S. Woodworth, *J. Abnorm. & Soc. Psychol.*, 1925, 20, pp. 94-98.

ing during the early months of infancy, say in walking or in climbing; the other remains untrained, or perhaps is, so far as possible, prevented from learning. The results commonly show that at a given age both infants will perform these chosen functions almost equally well; it was growth from within, not outer training that developed the ability.[29] It would seem that until certain nerve tracts myelinize, or certain nerve centers mature, these activities are impossible, but that once the inner processes of growth have prepared the appropriate nervous mechanisms these motor functions appear regardless of experience or training.

Besides the method of co-twin control, careful observation of babies supplies plenty of ground for the same conclusions. The evidence is of two kinds.[30] In the first place, all babies seem to go through the same stages of development (*e.g.,* in locomotion and vocalization) regardless of efforts to change the order of the appearance of these stages. The length of a given stage for some babies may be long, and for others short, but the order is the same. In the second place, the development of such functions appear with a suddenness not at all common in motor learning. This suddenness is unlike the occurrence of "insightful" behavior, for it occurs when there is a minimum development of appropriate anatomical structure, and when there has been a complete absence of training.

If, in line with available evidence, the process of maturation is regarded as limited to the general ripening of somatic and nervous structures, and to the ripening of a few rather specific locomotor and vocal functions, it cannot be regarded as one of the *direct* fashioners of personality. Gesell is in danger of overstating the case when he asserts that "maturation must be granted a basic role even in the patterning of personality and career." [31] A man's personality and career are not due primarily to what ripens within him but to the manner in which he lays hold of these maturing functions and incorporates them into what he has already learned.

It is sometimes said of a grown man that he more and more resembles his father as he gets older. Tastes, mannerisms, and attitudes

---

[29] Illustrative experimental studies of this order are: M. B. McGraw, *Growth; A Study of Johnny and Jimmy*, 1935; L. C. Strayer, "Language and Growth: The Relation of Early and Deferred Vocabulary Training," *Genet. Psychol. Monog.,* 1930, 8, No. 3; A. Gesell and H. Thompson, *Infant Behavior, Its Genesis and Growth,* 1934.

[30] M. Shirley, *The First Two Years*, 3 Vols., 1931-1933.

[31] A. Gesell. *The Guidance of Mental Growth in Infant and Child,* 1930, p. 292.

repeat the parental pattern, even though the direct parental influence has many years been removed. Might it not be that inherited traits lie dormant and rise to take form within the personality many years after childhood and after the period of general maturation have passed?

It is of course a possibility, but still there are two strong adverse arguments. (1) How does one know that subtle learning has not taken place, that ideals early implanted take their form when appropriate situations arise? From her own training the daughter learns how to bring up children, but she cannot put this knowledge into effect until she has children of her own; nor can a son or daughter follow the parents' example in household management, citizenship, or club membership until there is an opportunity to do so. (2) As the physique and its inherited deficiencies reach their mature expression, certain appropriate forms of adjustment must occur; but it is the physique and its deficiencies, and not the forms of adjustment that mature. An inclination to obesity or to baldness, may be a late consequence of heredity, and as one comes to look more like the parent, it is likely that similar physical demands, *provided* the environment too is similar, will lead one to act more like the parent. "Like father, like son," is a proverb not merely of heredity and maturation, but also of example and learning.

Maturation contributes to the development of personality by bringing out every inherited feature (pp. 107-109 and Figure 11). These features include physical structure, peculiarities of temperament and talent, the general capacity for intelligent modification of behavior, peculiarities of physical growth and decay, the latent sexual functions, and numerous specific locomotor and vocal patterns. All these develop by virtue of an inherent maturational capacity. But none of these qualities are in themselves independent units of personality. They *contribute* to the formation of personal dispositions, but their influence must be combined with the demands made by the environment upon the individual. Goals and purposes are not inherited, unless one grants that vague primordial need-to-live. Special interests and so-called "instincts" develop, as do traits and attitudes, through the many-sided effort of the individual to find a balanced position for himself in the world he has to live in. Maturation presents him with new internal situations to which he must adjust; but excepting at a rudimentary motor level it does not provide him with ready-made instruments for the task.

"LEARNING"

Taken broadly, the field of learning includes every form of acquisition and modification that occurs in the course of growth. Every way of learning is at the same time a way of building or of changing one's traits, and hence, at first glance, it seems reasonable to equate the problem of the development of personality with the problem of learning. But traditionally in psychology what is called "learning" is a somewhat narrower problem; though even in its narrower sense it forms one of the longest and most disputed chapters in psychology. Since the account here must be kept within bounds, only three of the most pertinent applications of "learning" to personality will be reviewed, viz., *conditioning, efferent modification*, and *imitation*. The three succeeding chapters, taking a broader view of learning, will amplify the account.

Conditioning. At times this concept is employed in the loosest possible way, as a pseudo-explanation of all learning. Properly used, however, it refers only to the extension of the range of stimuli that will arouse a given response. The law of the conditioned reflex, stated on p. 140, deals only with the fact that a relatively simple response originally initiated by a certain stimulus, A, is now initiated by another stimulus, B, that has occurred frequently in connection with A. It is important to note that the *response* is not altered by the conditioning, but is simply reinstated by a series of secondary (conditioned) stimuli. Conditioning is thus at most a theory of "afferent" learning; it explains why a wider and wider range of stimuli are reacted to, but not how the reaction itself becomes modified, made more precise and adaptive.

Any theory of personality requires some principle to account for the widening of one's tastes, interests, desires and aversions, in the course of growth. *Conditioning* serves the purpose, in part, although one may reasonably debate whether it is any great improvement upon its predecessor, the venerable doctrine of the *association of ideas*, or whether it will not eventually be replaced by some more discriminating theory of mental organization.

In discussing the biological theory of personality (pp. 114-121) the principle was applied to the rapidly widening range of stimuli that arouse *drives*. The primitive segmental tensions, the theory maintains, are easily conditioned, so that acquisitive behavior is aroused not only by a few prepotent stimuli to which the infant responds reflexly, but by a wide range of desirable objects in the environment. Conversely, the negative valences of the environment, the range of objects that are rejected and avoided, is extended through the same principle.

A simple illustrative case might be the establishment of liking for a certain color. Suppose a man decorates his room in blue, is also unusually fond of blue in clothes, and plants many blue flowers in his garden. This taste is an ingrained characteristic of his personality; he has an acquired disposition to perceive, to seek out, and to respond

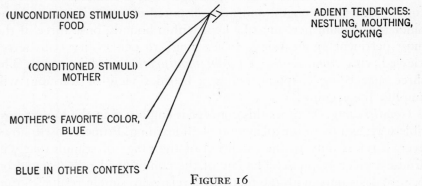

FIGURE 16

Development of a Taste Through Conditioning

to this color in a favorable way. A hypothetical account of the case in terms of conditioning might lie in the association of this color through two or three connecting links to some *original* cause of favorable or adient behavior, as suggested in Figure 16. Such a process of conditioning, or association through contiguity in time, might account also for a person's liking of certain poems, churches, songs, pictures, vocations, philosophies of life, or traits of personality, or for his repugnance to certain foods, races of people, or philosophical and moral doctrines.

That conditioning is not the whole of learning is easily seen from a glance at Figure 16, for certainly when he is mature this man does not respond in the *same* way as he did in infancy. He does not commence to mouth or suck or nestle when confronted by the blue fabrics or blue flowers, although this type of response is all that the doctrine of conditioning taken by itself would expect. Plainly the process of learning involves not only an extension of the range of effective *stimuli*, but also an alteration in the *response*; there is not only *afferent* learning, but *efferent* learning as well.

There are several difficulties with the doctrine of conditioning even as a theory of afferent learning. For one thing, it implies that *any* stimuli occurring simultaneously with a pre-existing effective stimulus will acquire the same motor outlet. This implication is manifestly false, for innumerable surrounding concurrent stimuli fail to act as conditioners. Strong emotion or deliberate effort on our part seems to enhance the chances of successful conditioning, but the mere temporal contiguity the law assumes is insufficient. Furthermore, the conditioned reflex as it is discovered in the laboratory—the only place where it is known thoroughly—is a capricious affair. It is easily extinguished, dies if it is not reinforced by the original unconditioned stimulus at intervals. Competing conditioned stimuli not infrequently cause the experimental animal in laboratory situations to fall asleep. So far as we can observe none of these capricious phenomena exist in the conditioned responses of normal human life.

All in all, it is best for the present to think of conditioning as a broad principle, crudely formulated, and too coarse for precise application in the field of personality. By itself it does not do justice to the many selective functions of the human mind that have the power of limiting and directing the course of conditioning. On the other hand, as a rough modern equivalent for the indispensable principle of association, it has its uses, and seems to express rather more dynamically than the older law the fact that stimuli associated with active systems often forge a functional bond with these systems.

Efferent Modification. Two of the familiar and traditional laws of learning are *frequency* and *recency*. The former simply restates the adage "practice makes perfect," and the latter calls attention to the obvious fact that we tend to remember recent events and newly acquired skills better than those of long ago. Though undoubtedly valid, these principles cannot account for change in behavior. By themselves they would produce complete stereotyping of conduct; an act recently performed would be repeated and the more it was repeated the stronger would become the tendency to continue it!

Within the traditional psychology of "learning" the *improvement* in adaptive behavior has been left to the *law of effect*, according to which successful modes of response are retained and unsuccessful modes are lost. Since success is usually accompanied by pleasure, and failure by pain, the law is often stated in a hedonistic fashion: *pleasure stamps in, pain stamps out*. Troland has cast this theory into a quasi-physiological form. Successful acts, he believes, characteristically result in stimulation of "beneceptors," giving to the organism pleasurable sensations, and sending back to the cortex characteristic afferent excitations having the property of enhancing the conductivity of the motor pathways then in action. In this way successful acts are "stamped in." Conversely, "nociceptors" are stimulated by acts that bring baleful consequences to the organism, or at least consequences immediately disagreeable. The return afferent impulses from these sense organs have the property of heightening the resistance at the motor centers, so that the same act is less likely to be repeated a second time.[32]

According to this hedonistic formulation, personality results from the retention of those modes of adjustment that have yielded pleasure, and from the habitual avoidance of events that bring displeasure. "Strong personalities are those which have been consistently built upon a coherent foundation, in which the pull of pleasure and the push of pain are in the same direction, when this is the direction which leads to success." [33] Since for most personalities, the pull and push are not in the same direction, the individual can only obtain the best possible hedonistic balance, the greatest possible pleasure with the minimum of pain. In any case the operation of the law of effect is thought to be quite automatic. Responses yielding pleasure are retained; those resulting in pain are abandoned. Personality grows through the production of tentative trial-and-error acts, some of which are selected by the Great God Pleasure for establishment, and some by the Great God Pain for banishment. If this picture were true mortals should be more content with their personalities than they are, for all annoying and unsatisfactory habits and traits in oneself would be automatically eliminated.

The chief fault of hedonism is that it confuses the *by-product* of a complex process with the process itself. Pleasure usually *accompanies* successful striving, but it is not necessarily the goal of the striving. It is more often an *indicator* that a successful mode has been discovered. There is no evidence that this mode is automatically selected for preservation. The hedonists' account of personality as a jellification of pleasure-giving habits is far too simple.

A more liberal interpretation of the law of effect is offered by the doctrine of *Insight*, whereby human beings are credited with the ability to survey and organize the confused field that confronts them,

[32] L. T. Troland, *Fundamentals of Human Motivation*, 1928.
[33] L. T. Troland, *Mystery of Mind*, 1926, p. 171.

intelligently comprehending the potential relationship of the various factors to one another, and finally adopting the course of behavior most suitable to their needs. By virtue of this ability one line of conduct is understood to be more suitable than another and is accordingly adopted. (It must be assumed, of course, that what every individual is doing is to strive always for a more effective relationship between himself and his behavioral environment.) Even though insight may *fail* in its attempts to change the modes of adjustment or even though it may render them *less* suitable, still the very existence of insightful behavior presupposes that intelligent effort and evaluation underlie the phenomena of change in personality.

This doctrine has the advantage of offsetting the merely mechanical laws of learning with a recognition of the oft-forgotten human capacities for foresight, planning, and problem solving. But by itself it gives a somewhat rationalistic view of the developing personality, and needs to be tempered with a recognition that not all the "closures" formed in personality are intelligent structurations of the field. Many of them, as observed earlier, are clichés, complexes, and stereotyped habits with which the individual bludgeons his way through a psychological environment too subtle for him to meet in a truly insightful way.

Imitation. A child's personality, and to a less extent an adult's, is fashioned in part through imitation. That is to say, many modes of adjustment are taken over more or less ready-made from other persons who serve the imitator consciously or unconsciously as models for conduct. In the latter part of the nineteenth century this form of learning received so much emphasis that a simple and sovereign "instinct of imitation" was postulated as underlying the acquisition of all mental and motor dispositions. Imitation was conjured up to explain *everything* (which was decidedly over-working the trick). Nowadays, instead of assuming one special *power* of imitation operating relentlessly on all occasions it is better to distinguish at least three different processes, all imitative in their effects, but independent in their manner of operation.

The first is a kind of conditioned reflex imitation, sometimes called the "echo principle." [34] It is significant chiefly in the first year of life,

[34] E. B. Holt, *Animal Drive and the Learning Process*, 1931, states the principle as follows: "A child will learn to echo back any action of another, provided that another's performance of the act stimulates any of the child's sense-organs at a moment when the child is engaged in a (random) performance of the same act" (p. 112).

for to it may be ascribed the first linguistic forms that the child adopts as well as many early conventional gestures (of refusal, acquiescence, good-by, etc.). The stages are three: (a) an infant performs an act (*e.g.*, a vocalization) quite "accidentally" (*i.e.*, without social reference); (b) an adult reading into it some social significance, performs the same act at the same time in the child's presence (in reality the adult imitates the child); (c) thereafter, by the principle of conditioning, the child may repeat the act when he hears or sees the adult performing it. Unquestionably, the first words that a child learns to speak are acquired in precisely these three stages.[35] Even later in life some simple forms of imitation seem explicable in the same way (*e.g.*, laughing when another laughs, or yawning when another yawns).

A second early form of imitation is less certainly established; it may even be reducible to the first, though it is rather unlikely. To illustrate, "an infant of a few months, lying in the mother's arms, showed signs of restlessness and anxiety and wept silently when the mother became disturbed by a reference in the conversation." Again, "an older child showed anxiety (shyness) when the mother was perturbed by the presence of a stranger at the door. In such situations there seems to be some direct method for translation of attitudes, without the necessity of experiencing them. As a working premise, only, it may be assumed that, through vision or direct contact, a mimetic capacity in the individual is stimulated, and that he then takes into his own muscles the postures and tensions of the person observed or felt; and translates them in terms of muscular and glandular activity." [36] This unconscious mimicry of "muscle tensions" in others is not well understood and needs further investigation. It has been assumed to play an important part in our understanding of other personalities (Chapter XIX), and likewise to account for the growing resemblance between persons constantly associated with one another (*e.g.*, husband and wife).

The third form of imitation is the conscious and deliberate copying of the behavior of another. It appears toward the close of the first year. A few instances from the psychological diary of little Andrew enlighten the point.

[35] F. H. Allport, *Social Psychology*, 1924, pp. 181-188.
[36] S. and M. Blanton, *Child Guidance*, 1927, p. 26.

8.28 A. watches intently father smoking his pipe. When father offers A. the pipe (properly cleaned), A. puts the stem into his mouth and *blows* vigorously.

According to the theory of conditioning, Andrew should have *sucked* the stem (as he would a nipple or pacifier). Actually Andrew imitated the father blowing out the smoke. The resemblance of his action to the *puff* of smoke he had been watching demands explanation in terms of insight—a deliberate attempt to reconstruct or to duplicate the stimulus-situation *as understood*. He could not, of course, know that smoking required sucking as well as blowing. This is the first of a long series of similar instances in this particular child's history.

14.8 A. always objects to having his nose wiped, but takes handkerchief out of his mother's apron pocket, puts it to his own nose and snuffles.

20.0 The doctor gave A. great discomfort by depressing his tongue with a spatula while examining his throat, causing A. to wriggle, cry, and reject the object. Fifteen minutes later, left to himself, A. picks up the spatula and puts it down his throat just as the doctor had done.

In these instances Andrew is seen deliberately reinstating situations that originally caused annoyance or pain. Instead of rejecting the stimuli associated with this annoyance, he returns to examine them and to reinstate in part the annoying situation, quite contrary to the doctrine of conditioning and to the hedonistic law of effect. The desire to comprehend, to execute a meaningful act shows that learning through insightful imitation may transcend the mechanical principles alleged to account both for learning and for conditioned reflex imitation.[37]

Advancing to later childhood, deliberate copying becomes a more and more important factor in the growing personality, especially, for example, in the adoption of prejudices, beliefs, and attitudes of one's elders.

A. (now nine years of age) heard many discussions of politics prior to a presidential election. Wondering about the merits of the various political parties, he came to his father and asked, "Daddy, what are *we?*"

[37] It is not uncommon to find this insightful imitation combined with the unconscious mimetic form of imitation described above. It often happens in personal relationships that each of two friends imitates the other more than he realizes.

It seemed never to occur to the lad, who in much of his behavior is very independent, that he might decide the issue for himself. He had learned that the assumption of his parents' attitudes was a fairly safe procedure when needing a guide. He begged to have his mind made up for him on a troublesome issue; he wished to imitate his parents' partisanship. In so doing he is planting the seed for many later qualities in his personality. He may continue merely an uncritical "inheritor" of his parents' views, or, when childhood is past, he may rebel, adopting different views, perhaps after rebellion to return again to the point of view of his parents. In any case his entire life is affected by his conservative imitation of parents in his early years. The story can be duplicated in every child's life, not only in the adoption of a political outlook, but likewise in religious affiliation, occupational and racial loyalties, moral and esthetic codes.

This type of insightful imitation lasts throughout life. When another person seems to us to have worked out a happy solution of the problems that confront us, we often try to adopt *in toto* this solution, including sometimes the qualities of personality that make the solution possible. Such imitation is a labor-saving device for us, a short cut in the development of our own personalities. Certainly it is sincere if unintentional flattery to the individual we imitate.

CHAPTER VI

THE SELF AND ITS CONSTRAINTS

O F the whole of our own natures we are never directly aware, nor of any large portion of the whole. At any single moment the range of consciousness is remarkably slight. It seems only a restless pencil point of light entirely insufficient to illuminate the edifice of personality. Yet, for all its feebleness, it provides each of us with the one and only sure criterion of our personal existence and identity. The past is drawn out in successive and overlapping conscious moments, backwards, twenty, thirty or forty years to early childhood, and the future extends, vaguely but still intimately, before us in each overlapping moment of planning and imagination. It is through this dovetailing of the successive moments of consciousness with their imbrication of temporal reference and content, that we arrive at the conviction that we do somehow possess consistent personalities surrounding the momentary conscious core. Unless we postulated for ourselves a permanence of personality we could not possibly account for the many identical threads running through our conscious states.[1]

CONSCIOUSNESS OF SELF

Consciousness and self-consciousness are not identical. Not all experience possesses ego-reference.[2] Some of it simply occurs, the sub-

[1] It is nowadays fashionable to distrust the evidence of immediate experience. Behaviorists, logical positivists and psychoanalysts have joined the discrediting chorus. Each individual, they say, is aware of so little, his introspection is so faulty and unverifiable, he is so given to self-deception, that direct awareness must not be admitted as a scientific datum of any importance. It is following this line of reasoning that the Unconscious or the physico-chemical Bodily Constitution has been proposed as the true matrix of personality, the only region worth exploring. This reasoning has something to commend it, but even so, the *core* of the objective method is still the reliance each scientist places upon the testimony of his own fugitive and overlapping conscious states. He can work with the Unconscious or with Bodily Constitution only as they are distilled into his own consciousness. And what is more important, his acceptance and rejection of evidence, his devotion to his own standards, are bound to the still more subjective core of his personality, *viz.,* his *self-consciousness.*

[2] K. Koffka, *Principles of Gestalt Psychology*, 1935, p. 328. Koffka treats the *Ego* both as a phenomenal object (the direct object of knowledge) and as the phe-

ject not feeling that the experience is somehow tied to *his* interests, to *his* memories, and to *his* personal life (though a slight shift of attitude can change almost any state of consciousness into a state of self-consciousness). Genetically this fact is of considerable importance, for it is agreed that in the young child the consciousness of self is a gradual and difficult achievement, whereas consciousness of a less personal order is no doubt present from birth. What the earliest consciousness, devoid of self-reference, is like, is difficult to imagine. Readers of William James are by now persuaded that it must be a "big, blooming, buzzing confusion"; though, as a matter of fact, it may not be so at all, but rather a consciousness of sharply segregated figures upon dim backgrounds as Gestalt theory would prefer to have us believe. In any case, the young infant seems quite unaware of himself as a *self*. He treats his own body as if it were foreign to him; his toes are his toys, and he may claw his own face until it bleeds. He has no "bodily" self, no "social" self, and no "material" self. The boundary between him and not-him, between his and not-his is unestablished. There is, as Koffka would say, little or no Ego-organization.

Until the child has a fairly definite conception of himself as an independent person he cannot conceptualize his relationship to the surrounding world, and hence lacks the subjective nucleus for the development of his own personality. By bringing the consciousness of the self only slowly into focus during the first three or four years of life nature seems to withhold from the individual the very keystone to his structure of personality.

Several conditions are responsible for the infant's lack of self-consciousness. There is the well-known deficiency in his memory-life. Recognition, which occurs much earlier than recollection, is not clearly present until the latter part of the first year, and then it fails if the interval of time involved is more than three or four weeks. As for recollection, it is rare indeed to find accessible memories reaching back before the age of three, and never into the first year of life.

nomenal ground against which many of our perceptions occur. The term "self-consciousness" has the same double reference, and may be considered essentially synonymous with Koffka's Ego. But there are two reasons for preferring the former term. (1) Philosophy has previously equated Ego with the *Knower*, whereas Koffka, disregarding the nominative form of the Latin pronoun, equates it with the *Known*, with the empirical *Me*. (2) At the core of the Ego, thus conceived, Koffka places the *Self*, a sub-system where are located the deeper layers of the Ego, and strongly emotional states of personal reference (p. 342). This division does not seem to be necessary. The difference being entirely one of degree it can be ruled out in favor of one consistent account of the genesis and nature of the *consciousness of the self*, whatever its layers may be.

Why are early memories so impermanent? One answer is that infantile experiences are not verbalized, and cannot therefore be held as concepts in consciousness. Another answer invokes maturation, holding that the areas of the cortex involved in conscious memory are undeveloped (specifically—unmyelinized), and therefore unable to hold "traces" of experience. Motor areas, on the contrary, are in an advanced state of development during the early months of life, for it is well known that motor habits once learned are readily retained. Still another answer claims that recall depends upon the child's ability to place an event in some context familiar to him, and that there is too little of this apperceptive context in early life to serve as a preservative of early experience. A fourth theory, the psychoanalytic, holds that the infant upon encountering the "reality principle" represses into the unconscious all memories of his self-indulgent life up to that date. However it comes about, this fugitive condition of memory in early childhood is most certainly a handicap in the development of self-consciousness.

Another handicap arises from the ungraded and undifferentiated character of the infant's emotional responses. Affectively he behaves whole-heartedly or not at all. He does not evaluate the stimulus according to the degree of its importance in relation to his own needs and desires. He laughs and cries excessively, almost as an automaton. Such behavior can only be accounted for by assuming a virtual all-or-none operation in response to stimuli, devoid of the grading effects of inhibition that would intervene if each stimulus were tested out by its relevance for the self.

Still another drawback is the child's deficiency in language. His concepts, expressing the relationship between himself and his surroundings, are but dimly formed, for as yet he lacks the capacity for sharply sculpturing thought with words. One illustration: in his "collective monologues" the two-year-old often confuses quite sadly the first, second, and third persons. He may be overheard to say to himself, "You be careful, William get hurt. No! I won't get hurt." He is first, second and third person all at the same time! It is especially difficult for him to learn the correct use of pronouns; he cannot learn by imitation, for he has to realize that each pronoun has a different reference when used by himself. Although it would not be correct to date the dawn of self-consciousness from the correct use of the personal pronouns (around two and a half years of age), still the confusion undoubtedly signifies to some extent the difficulty the child is having with his sense of his own individuality.

Even after self-consciousness is partially established the child readily surrenders his own identity in play. He may lose it so completely that he becomes angry with his parents if they fail to recognize his transformations.[3] Even at the age of four or five the self is by no means firmly encapsulated. The child continues to confuse himself with his surroundings, to take the role of others in play, and to identify his private fantasies with objective fact. He does not customarily feel himself, as does the adult, to stand out against all that is foreign to him, distinguishing in thought and act that which is himself from that which is not.[4]

The factors contributing to the growth of self-consciousness have often been discussed.[5] During the nineteenth century the account was given most often in sensationalistic terms. The infant receives, pre-

[3] This depersonalization of the self by children is called by J. Pérès, *autoscopie*, *J. de Psychol.*, 1926, 23, pp. 558-566.

[4] But even adults in some respects behave as does the child. Most striking are those practices among primitive peoples that indicate a merging of the sense of self with a consciousness of the surrounding world. The primitive medicine man through incantation feels that he "becomes" the rain; the father in couvade identifies himself with his wife at childbirth; injury to one's personal property causes a feeling of illness; one keeps one's secret name and one's totemic animal sacred as means of self-protection. Parts of one's bodily self, *e.g.*, the hair or finger-nails, also are sometimes treated as equivalent to the whole self. All such practices of identification, projection and sympathetic magic indicate that the primitive person, like the child, feels himself to be extensible, variable, and capable of merging with events outside of his physical body. (Cf. H. Werner. *Einführung in die Entwicklungspsychologie*, 1926, Book II, Pt. 4.)

And even among civilized people there seem to be differences in the degree to which the individual closes himself off from his environment. Lewin points out a peculiar difference in this respect between the typical German and the typical American. Only in the most superficial layers of his personality does the German expose himself freely and un-selfconsciously to his environment. He, more often than the American, associates his daily activities with his own Ego; he becomes emotionally aroused if his theories and ideas are assailed, confides little in his associates, and even keeps his office door closed and his callers waiting in order to enhance his own feeling of pride and worth. The typical American on the other hand does not mind if newspapers publish a good deal concerning his private life, if people see him at work in his office, if unexpected interruptions deflect him from his momentary purposes, or if he is addressed without title or formality by somewhat casual acquaintances. The ego-systems of the American are not so readily aroused; he is not so instantly and intensely conscious of himself as is the typical German. He allows himself to bend and adapt to the pressures of his surroundings without feeling as quickly as the German that these pressures are intrusions. The latter is more markedly *self-conscious* (K. Lewin, "Some Social-Psychological Differences between the United States and Germany," *Char. & Pers.*, 1936, 4, 265-293).

[5] Comprehensive accounts may be found in H. Taine, *On Intelligence*, trans., 1889, II, Bk. 3, chap. i; W. Preyer, *Mental Development in the Child*, trans., 1893, chap. ix; P. Janet, *L'evolution psychologique de la personnalité*, 1929.

sumably, a stream of organic sensations from the internal organs of his body, from his muscles, joints and tendons. This coenesthetic core becomes further elaborated with the sensory impulses of touch, taste, smell, sight and hearing. The fusion of sensory impressions, particularly around the kinesthetic sense of postural strain and position, originates the sense of self. This theory is wholly congenial to empiricism, to the belief that at birth the infant is a *tabula rasa* upon which the sense of self along with everything else has yet to be engraved. William James found evidence for this sensationalistic theory in his observation that for the adult the reportable experience of selfhood is usually reduced to a matter of postural strains and stresses, centering especially in the head.[6] Some people, he found, locate the self in the facial furrows between the brows, so that midway between the eyes the introspective self resides. Following a less sensationalistic view, a more abstract location is suggested by Koffka. The self (or Ego) is that which lies between *right* and *left*, between *before* and *behind*. The self is the point of reference in all temporal experience too, for it lies as well at the exact junction of *past* and *future*.

The conscious recognition of *recurring* experiences (the sense of *familiarity*) contributes to the development of self-consciousness. When an experience is felt as *similar* to a preceding experience, there is always at the same time a vague sense of time-binding, and for the individual the person having this conjoint experience of *then* and *now* can only be himself.

Then there are certain symbols providing *anchorage points* for selfhood, of which the most important is one's name. A proper name is a mark put upon the individual at birth, first acquiring significance for him in the second year of life. The name becomes a more and more strategic point of contact between the self and the outer world. With the name comes the formality of receiving salutations and address from others, and with this formality comes a sense of self-importance and of position within the social hierarchy. The importance of this symbol of the self is revealed in the magical practices of primitive peoples where the mere pronouncing of a person's name with maledictions is thought sufficient to inflict actual injury upon him. Even in civilized societies a man's good name is to him a sacred possession.[7]

---

[6] W. James, *Principles of Psychology*, 1890, II, p. 301. Cf. also, E. L. Horowitz, "Spatial Localization of the Self," *J. Soc. Psychol.*, 1935, 6, 379-387.

[7] An experimental investigation dealing with the problem of the justifiability of homicide, revealed that a man's honor (*i.e.*, the regard in which his name is held) is

To possess a name is only one step in achieving social status. Everyone feels more at home (*i.e.*, less self-conscious) in certain groups than in others: this is because habitual status in a group provides a familiar frame of reference. Outside this frame a person is likely to feel uncomfortably aware of himself. The professor speaking at a labor-meeting is much more self-conscious than in his classroom; the farmer who finds himself in a city drawing room is similarly ill at ease. One loses oneself only in surroundings that are familiar and in groups where the role one plays is habitual, or else in certain situations (a crowd, for example) where each participant is inconspicuous and safely anonymous.

In childhood, clothing, ornamentation, and special grooming contribute their share to self-consciousness. Investigators have observed that little children speak more frankly and with less inhibition when unclad. It is as if self-consciousness were a garment as readily shed as shoes. Apparently the Nudists in abolishing clothing hope to regain some of the child's freedom from the oppressive burden of self-consciousness. Before Hitler officially instituted "morality" into Germany, Nudist colonies were more numerous there than in any other country, perhaps because self-consciousness, as Lewin observed, is an oppressive national characteristic. But if it is difficult for the child to take on the burden of self-consciousness, it is even more difficult for the adult to lay it aside.[8]

Finally, all experiences of pain, frustration, and especially of social ridicule engender acute states of self-consciousness that leave permanent effects. Whenever one is unable to achieve, or to continue in, a condition of friendly relation with the environment, he must perforce pay attention to his own shortcomings, and thereby become acutely aware of the incompatibility between himself and the physical and social world outside, and of his isolation. In pleasure, when everything is going well, this separation is not felt; but pain is always referred to the self.

considered second in importance only to the immediate physical safety of himself and of others closely associated with him. Violation of one's honor is considered a far more justifiable cause for homicide than invasion of one's property and material possessions (Cf. G. W. Allport and R. L. Schanck, *Char. & Pers.*, 1936, 2, 195-205).

[8] Self-consciousness in its popular sense of embarrassment is a hypertrophy of the natural awareness of self, intensified by frequent failure and consequent experiences of shame. It is a common and chronic condition in many personalities. In one study, one-third of a general population of adults reported it as their main handicap in life and chief source of worry (A. A. Roback, *Self-consciousness, Self-treated*, 1936, p. 41).

The advent of self-consciousness in childhood is gradual, and its growth continuous, but a certain critical stage is reached around the age of two. Its symptom is the period of negativism that is as distressing to parents as it is interesting to psychologists.[9] Children at this period commonly resist persuasion, more often than not disobey, and generally protest against interference with their own designs. They say "No" much more often than "Yes." One little boy, not yet three, made a daily visit to his grandmother's house across the street to announce (apropos of nothing), "Grandma, I won't!" Such impulsive contrariness augments the sense of selfhood through the aggressive exercise of self-determination. The child regards outsiders as threats to his initiative, choice, and freedom of execution. Against all of these, prompted by his new and disturbing sense of personal integrity, he rebels. A similar counter-suggestibility occurs sometimes in adult personalities. Apparently as a matter of principle they immediately disagree with every proposal or assertion. Spontaneously they say "No"; they may later think the matter over to find that they would have preferred to say "Yes." As a mode of preserving one's integrity such negativism is far more appropriate to the two-year-old than to the adult.

There are likewise pathological types of regression and dissociation in self-consciousness, cases of psychogenic loss of personal identity. In some instances the loss takes the form of a splitting of self-consciousness into independent regions, as in fugues and other amnesias; the patient by surrendering his continuous sense of identity lops off areas of his life that are distasteful to him, or for which he is unable to assume further responsibility. In completely regressive states a patient seems to commit a kind of psychological suicide in order to escape entirely from the oppressive burden of some intolerable feature of his system of selfhood.[10]

[9] The onset of this period is sometimes placed earlier for female and later for male children (D. M. Levy and S. H. Tulchin, *J. Exper. Psychol.*, 1923, 6, 304-322; 1925, 8, 209-224). An experimental study of the stages of childhood negativism is described by M. M. Reynolds, "Negativism of Pre-school Children," *Teach. Coll. Contrib. to Educ.*, No. 288, 1928.

[10] Cf. M. Abeles and P. Schilder, "Psychogenic Loss of Personal Identity: Amnesia." *Arch. Neurol. Psychiat.*, 1935, 34, 587-604.

SUGGESTION

It would be impossible to estimate how large a portion of anyone's personality is acquired through the instrumentality of suggestion, but it must be a very sizable part, because—if for no other reason—a remarkably close relationship exists between suggestion and learning by means of language.

Chiefly through speech the child takes over his beliefs and norms of conduct from adults. For example, as soon as he is able to understand and obey he hears from his parent a series of mandatory rules: (a) "You must take this medicine," (b) "You must be quiet while I am speaking," (c) "You must not talk about such things outside the family," (d) "You must attend Sunday School." Assuming that the child has already learned the obligatory significance of propositions introduced by the injunction *must*, he now obeys for the simple reason that this word has a mysteriously imperative character. The word, perhaps, is spoken in an emphatic tone of voice, and may have been originally accompanied by physical coercion. Whatever its history it acquires with time its unquestioned and irrational sanction.

The child is unable to see that there are a good many different reasons why he "must" behave in prescribed ways. In the case of the first of the prescriptions set down above the penalty for failure will be a natural punishment, *viz.*, ill health; in the second, the sanction is merely parental prerogative based on superior strength and status; in the third, the penalty is *social ostracism;* in the last, *divine displeasure.* Unless, or until, the child by a persistent course of questioning, asks "Why" whenever he is told that he *must* do thus and so; unless, or until, he discovers the answer and considers it a sufficient ground for conforming to the course of conduct indicated—unless or until such a time arrives, his habits of response will be shaped by suggestion. If he obeys these four rules unquestionably he will be forming the rudiments of hygienic, filial, conventional, and religious habits and sentiments, all without self-determination, merely by virtue of his own suggestibility. By the time he comes of more critical age, deciding henceforth to guide his own destiny, he is already a creature of innumerable conventional forms of behavior and outlooks, acquired by suggestion, from which he can never completely escape.

Suggestion has not as yet been defined. Simply stated, it is the adoption of a course of conduct or belief by an individual who does not engage in those processes of thought and judgment that would be pertinent to the acceptance of such a course of conduct or belief. More briefly, suggestion is *the acceptance of a proposition for belief or action in the absence of complete self-determination.*

At a rudimentary level, most conditioned responses can be viewed as elementary suggestions. An infant, given a nipple detached from the nursing bottle, sucks it with considerable show of satisfaction. At first the milk in the bottle alone brought contentment, but now by frequent association, the outward sign or symbol alone suffices (at least until hunger becomes more urgent). At a more complex level, all the verbal pronouncements accepted as gospel truth simply because one is accustomed to take words at their face value without supplementary evidence or reason, are likewise suggestions. A college teacher often finds to his surprise that his lectures, his counsel, and even his *obiter dicta* are adopted uncritically as models of conduct and belief by students in whose eyes he has prestige. However beneficial the influence may be for the student it is none the less a result of suggestion.

It is not the case, however, that all the functions of language are at the same time instances of suggestion. Words may in fact be sharp instruments for reasoning and as such aid in the formation of *self-determined* concepts. Yet, even when used with the maximum of critical discrimination a word inevitably carries with it the weight of pre-existing socialized forms of thought. The result is that the thinker, as he comes to depend on verbalized concepts, tends more and more to guide his conduct and to build his personality into conventional molds. Perhaps one chief reason why personalities within the same culture resemble one another as much as they do is the common possession of linguistic symbols that give common meanings, common evaluations, and common guidance to the thought and to the conduct of the various members of any one cultural group.

We cannot say at what age suggestion plays its chief part in the development of personality. The younger child, in spite of his negativism, is really unable to resist the weight of authority of those who teach him, and takes on his earliest social behavior almost entirely by virtue of his unwitting suggestibility. Somewhat older children, around eight or nine years of age, owing to the rapidly advancing period of linguistic development, are especially suggestible; for at this age a vocabulary is built of moral, religious, political, and esthetic concepts—all extremely significant for the development of person-

ality. Again, the college age, in some respects, is even more suggestible, for at that time submissiveness to prestige and to the printed
word has reached, through long training, such a peak that students
sometimes seem completely to lack minds of their own. Nor are
adults in their mature personalities free from the effects of suggestion:
witness the role of propaganda in shaping their political, moral, rec-
reational conduct, and its effects upon their habits of purchasing, diet,
travel, dressing, investing, war-making, and home-making.

Since suggestion is so significant an aspect of personal development it becomes important to determine whether some people are by
nature more suggestible than others, that is, whether suggestibility is
a trait existing in some fixed amount in each personality. This is a
much-investigated question, and the evidence on the whole is negative. To be sure, a few individuals seem chronically to accept any and
every suggestion offered them. Lacking the power to resist proposals
that are discordant with their own self-determined plans of action,
they give themselves up to the situation, trusting that in so doing,
things will go well, as perhaps they have in the past when the same
surrender was made. But for most people, suggestions, if habitually
accepted, would be ruinous to the integrity of traits and ideals already
established. Usually each of us is suggestible in certain ways, in directions where we have already a strong desire to believe or act in the
suggested way, or in directions where we lack knowledge and conviction. By its very nature suggestion involves only *part* of the personality; it is a species of dissociation, operating only when resistances
are weak. It is a capacity that all people have, but only in a few is it
a well-integrated disposition to adjust in a *positive* way by passing
all decisions over to some outside control. In other words it is rarely
a trait.

A similar answer must be given to the question, "Is negativism a
trait?" In a few people, yes. On p. 165 we mentioned certain adults
who seem, like the typical infant of two or three years, to be always
on guard, resisting every proposal on principle for fear they may
think thoughts or perform acts contrary to their own natures. Such
contredisant individuals there are, indubitably possessing a trait of
negativism. But ordinarily, each of us is negativistic only in specific
ways; we feel no positive urge to contradict every proposal that
comes to us: only those propositions that offend firmly established
sentiments and beliefs, or that violate mature traits, are rejected.

SELF-ESTEEM

All the philosophies of Egoism, and many others as well, stress the demand for self-aggrandizement in human nature.[11] Nothing, it is said, is ultimately sacred excepting the beloved Ego. Motives ordinarily regarded as self-sacrificing and other-regarding are at bottom merely selfish. Scratch ever so lightly the coating of hypocrisy, of social varnish, and the cave-man stands revealed. The one important instinct is the desire for power, for "masculinity," and though overlaid with sweet-sounding protests of sympathy and altruism, this root desire is biologically prepotent and ultimate. Every man is inescapably a *Machtmensch;* his most coveted experience is the enhancement of his self-esteem, and his most ineradicable trait is vanity.

Such a doctrine of human nature contains so much obvious truth that it is often accepted uncritically as a fully adequate interpretation of personality. The next chapter will show that socialization is not simply a varnish laid over personality, but involves, at least much of the time, a genuine transmutation of interests from the egoistic to the altruistic. The biological creature that we find in early childhood possesses no instincts, habits, nor sentiments that are in the remotest degree socialized or civilized. Egoism *is* the incontrovertible philosophy of early childhood. But in the process of growth and extension of interests, newly adopted codes and manners represent genuine, not superficial, alterations in personality. Nor is the transformation merely one from unenlightened self-interest to enlightened self-interest. Demonstration of this point must wait. In the present section due weight and consideration shall be given to the importance of self-esteem in directing the development of personality.

When an adult undertakes to perform a task he generally places his goal at a level not so far above his abilities that he will suffer embarrassment and humiliation if he fails, nor so far below his abilities that he will feel ineffectual and cheap upon accomplishing the task. He undertakes that amount and that kind of labor which will keep his self-esteem at a maximum.[12] It is true that some people prefer to make *certain* of success, and accordingly undertake no more than they can surely achieve. Others, more characteristically daring, bite off more

[11] For example, F. Le Dantec, *L'Egoisme,* 1918; likewise the philosophies of F. Nietzsche and M. Stirner.

[12] F. Hoppe, *Psychol. Forsch.,* 1930, 14, 1-63.

than they can chew, maintaining their self-esteem either through this act of courage or through the closeness with which their accomplishment corresponds to their ambition. They like to be surprised that they have approximated the goal as closely as they have.[13] But in every case one's level of aspiration betrays in some way the "upward tendency of the Ego."

It is likewise known that younger children ordinarily prefer to repeat tasks in which they have already succeeded, unlike older children and adults who prefer to work on tasks as yet uncompleted. Feeling that they will be humiliated if they fail to accomplish their goal, older persons persevere, while younger children avoid humiliation by demonstrating over and over again their success on a low level of accomplishment and leave difficult tasks uncompleted with no signs of embarrassment. The older person battles against outer reality to retain his self-esteem; the young child in his world of pleasure prefers to hold to his earlier and assured successes.[14]

These experimental studies all seem to bear out the traditional dicta of philosophers: "The deepest principle of human nature is the desire to be appreciated"; "Self-defense is nature's eldest law"; "By whatever name we call the ruling tyrant, Self is all in all." The centering of each life upon its own sense of integrity and self-importance is everywhere recognized. In psychology, Freud's concept of Narcissism has found a prominent place. Koffka postulates as a paramount principle of dynamic psychology "a force which propels the Ego upward." [15] McDougall has found at the heart of every personality the central sentiment of *self-regard*, playing "the most powerful all-pervasive role in the higher life of man." [16]

Now, with what are we dealing here? Is self-esteem a force, an instinct, a sentiment, or what? Is it not perhaps a self-evident principle, a psychological redundancy, equivalent to that vague, though unquestionable primordial "will to live," postulated on page 109?

---

[13] J. D. Frank, *Amer. J. Psychol.*, 1935, 47, 119-128.
[14] S. Rosenzweig, *J. Genet. Psychol.*, 1933, 42, 423-441.
[15] *Principles of Gestalt Psychology*, 1935, pp. 670 f.
[16] *Energies of Men*, 1933, p. 234. See also, *An Introduction to Social Psychology*, 1908, chap. vii, and *Outline of Psychology*, 1923, pp. 426-434. This writer believes that "self-regard" is the best name for the sentiment, whereas "self-respect, self-esteem, self-love, pride, ambition are the names of distinctive types of self-regard. Selfishness, egoism, egotism, vanity, conceit, humility, megalomania, swelled-head, bumptiousness, pushfulness, masterfulness, aggressiveness, these are some of the qualities of personality determined in the main by the composition and mode of working of the sentiment." *Energies of Men*, p. 233.

Considered in this way the psychologist cannot make use of it as an explanatory principle. To do so would be to beg the question. It must be broken open and studied in its manifold operations. One cannot treat self-esteem or self-regard as an entity; for basically co-extensive with life itself, it enters into *all* sentiments and traits, which are after all merely channels of the primordial (non-psychological) life-principle.

We must adopt a more discriminating view of the problem. Let egoism with its conscious accompaniment of self-esteem be admitted as an initial principle of life, especially manifest in the early behavior of children. Let the numerous aspects of growth discussed in these chapters represent so many ways of focalizing, channelizing, and radically redirecting this original "metaphysical" flow. Then, in order not to overstate the case for transformation, let it be admitted that in spite of all the alterations that egoism may undergo in the course of development, there frequently remains at the core of self-conscious-ness a strong element of self-seeking and vanity, which likewise may be traced in many, perhaps most, of an individual's sentiments and traits. The task of the psychology of personality is to characterize all the innumerable and variable contexts in which the element of self-esteem occurs, *including* those where it is no longer a crude factor, but is drastically altered and transformed, as well as those where its operation is as yet unsocialized and primitive.

Whatever the ultimate character of this principle, its cruder forms of expression result in extraordinary strategies of conduct. It alone is responsible for a great super-structure of masquerade built up in every life. All in the interests of self-esteem one may cover one's true emotions, put on a front, and at considerable cost avoid exposing one's weaknesses. The *persona* that develops protects one from unwelcome narcissistic wounds.

What is even more spectacular, likewise in the interest of self-esteem, is the capacity men have for deceiving *themselves*. At first sight the ability to fool oneself would seem to be a fatal invention of nature, for living would seem to require an accurate evaluation of one's own motives and capacities. Why should an intelligent person invent an eye-wash for himself? Because an eye-wash, surface treatment though it is, brings immediate relief, preventing conflicts from developing through the sense of being in the wrong, and engendering a certain bravado necessary for life, and for maintaining one's rights in the face of immediate opposition. Self-deception also enables one

for the time being to put off the admission of unpleasant truths until
one is ready to receive them.

The techniques of self-deception are numerous.[17] Psychological
usage groups them all under the single rubric *rationalization*, a term
signifying, of course, precisely the opposite of *reason*. Reason may be
defined as one's capacity to shape one's belief and conduct to accord
with one's knowledge of the world, and if one's knowledge is insufficient, the capacity to set out to acquire more knowledge pertinent to the issue in hand. Reason fits one's impulses and beliefs to the
world of reality; rationalization fits one's conception of reality to
one's impulses and beliefs. Or, as the aphorism has it, reasoning discovers *real* reasons, and rationalization, *good* reasons, for what we do.

Rationalizations range from the trivial to the grandiose. Not infrequently we do something on impulse and then call it by the best
name possible. As Emerson has said: "That which we call sin in others
is experiment for us." At the other extreme one finds elaborate systems of "metaphysical absolutes" built up to justify tenacious convictions; since these convictions would be held even in the face of plentiful contrary evidence, rationalization enters to make them seem as
reasonable as possible. According to Lotze, a man's philosophical
creed is more often than not merely an attempt to justify a fundamental view of things adopted once for all early in life. The same
thought underlies Pareto's doctrine of *derivations*. But one must be
careful. The reduction of all philosophical activity to mere rationalization is dangerous; for underneath there must be an ontology of the
Being who rationalizes, and a logic capable of distinguishing rationalization from true reasoning. It gets us nowhere to say that all philosophy is a rationalization of what the private life of the philosopher
secretly holds. For to reach such a cynical conclusion it is necessary
to trust one's own *reason* as well as the canons of logic.

Quite a different example of rationalization is that special form
known as projection. It may be defined as a type of self-deception by
which a person ascribes his own secret thoughts, wishes, and shortcomings to another person. If one can castigate others, one is thereby
saved from the painful duty of castigating oneself. "It is not hard to
observe," writes Goethe, "that in this world man feels most free from
his sins and most blameless when he can comfortably expatiate on the
same shortcomings in others." There is likewise a complementary

[17] A valuable classification and discussion are offered by R. C. Cabot, *The
Meaning of Right and Wrong*, 1933, pp. 283-347.

form of projection whereby a person does not attribute his own frame of mind to others but rather one that explains and justifies his own frame of mind to himself. Thus the over-timid child thinks that others have aggressive intentions toward him, and the paranoiac believes that others are plotting his destruction. Through such complementary projection one's personal quirks of temperament and traits receive "rational" explanation, and do not appear as unfounded and foolish as they are.

And so there are many, many methods, some direct and some indirect, for keeping self-respect and self-esteem at the highest possible level. In ordinary undertakings the level of aspiration automatically adjusts itself to serve this purpose. When the direct achievement of a high level of self-respect is not possible, roundabout tricks are resorted to: the *persona* is donned, *defenses* spring up, *rationalizations* become rife, and *projections* are unconsciously devised. But the most interesting of all the sly handmaidens of self-esteem has not yet been described—the principle of *compensation*.

FEELINGS OF INFERIORITY AND COMPENSATION

The successive rhythms of maladjustment and adjustment constitute the pulse of development. Some intrusive factor, perhaps hunger, a change in temperature, or some social demand, upsets an insecurely established equilibrium. There are resulting tension and unrest, followed, through the instrumentality of higher mental functions, by an attempt to restore the equilibrium. If a straightforward adjustment is possible the problem is met and solved, at least temporarily. And if a direct solution is unsuccessful and variations in the method of attack do not succeed, the failure sometimes is minimized, repressed, or rationalized out of the way.

Often, however, when failures are recurrent and serious they cannot be so easily disposed of. A tension not relaxed by fulfillment is present in a latent state and always ready to cause trouble whenever the desire for the unattainable goal returns. As a result a deep-seated sense of deficiency may develop and be steadily aggravated. The sense of deficiency may be due to different causes: physical incapacity, ill health, low vitality, sexual impotence, unpleasant appearance; to social inadequacy—poverty, lack of education, gaucheness, or lack of wit and self-possession; to faulty intelligence—poor memory, meager vocabulary, deficient accomplishment; or to moral conflict—

a sense of unworthiness, of guilt or of sin. As failures multiply, the source of difficulty becomes the focus of attention and concern. The sufferer feels habitual uncertainty or fear in the face of those situations that threaten to reveal to himself and others his own weakness and ineffectuality. This condition is the famous *inferiority complex*. If a definition is required, one may say that the inferiority complex is the strong and persistent tension arising from a somewhat morbid

Type of inferiority feelings	Men 175		Women 100	
	Percentage reporting persistent inferiority feelings			
	Formerly	Now	Formerly	Now
physical	60	48	56	55
social	60	58	65	65
intellectual	58	29	25	64
moral	37	17	25	18
none at all	8	10	2	9

A Table of "Inferiority Complexes"
Among College Students

emotional attitude toward one's failure to effect a satisfactory direct adjustment to his environment, owing to some felt-deficiency in his personal equipment.

Few people need to have explained to them the discomfort caused by feelings of inferiority. In one study reports from college students were secured concerning the four types of inferiority feelings described above.

Less than ten per cent of the students report that they do not know what it is to suffer from gnawing feelings of inferiority. The table shows that as students grow older they show a tendency to suffer less from a sense of inferiority. On the whole the women seem to be somewhat worse off than the men; not only do they report a larger number of such feelings, but also they show a less marked reduction in conflicts with growing maturity. In one of the categories, the intellectual, the inferiority feelings of the women have markedly *increased*, and are far more numerous than among men.[18] In both sexes the sense of social inadequacy seems to lead, but this category is not definitive, since almost any type of inferiority is reflected in *social* inadequacy. Half the students are afflicted with a sense of physical inferiority, and it was, in fact, the recognition of the role of such *organic* deficiency that led to the first psychological recognition of the complex by Adler.[19] Moral inferiorities are least frequent, probably not because of the superior virtue of the students, but because of the diminished emphasis in their generation upon moral lapses and sin.

Hidden within this table is one conclusion of importance. *Feelings of inferiority cannot be taken as an index of actual inferiority.* One notices, for example, that over one-half of the students have at one time or another suffered a sense of intellectual inferiority, an absurd situation from the factual or objective point of view. Over half the group cannot be *below* the average in intelligence; statistically they cannot be *inferior*. But more to the point, college students, it is known, are actually *superior* in intelligence to the average population. Yet they suffer because of their shortcomings in mental ability. It is also known that college students are by and large superior in physique and health, and that they have better than average social and economic advantages; and still they suffer. Inferiority feelings obviously are not based on factual inferiority but are subjective phenomena, engendered entirely by the ratio that obtains between *success* and *aspiration*. The second best chess player in the world might suffer miserably from feelings of inferiority, so too might the topmost scholar in a university whose aspirations were in excess of his great ability. As to physical inadequacy, who is not a candidate for an inferiority complex unless he is that *rara avis*, a biological millionaire? But if he were a biological millionaire he might still have inferiority feelings of a moral order because, unlike his less favored associates, he had never experienced physical suffering!

To return to the question of sex differences. The higher ratio of

[18] This curious result may have only local significance. The women in the study were students in a girls' college in the shadow of a large university attended only by men. They were dependent for all their instruction on teachers from the neighboring university, and the fact that all of the teachers were men seemed to undermine the women's confidence in the intellectual abilities of their own sex, and of themselves.

[19] A. Adler, *Organminderwertigkeit und ihre psychische Kompensationen*, 1912; also trans., 1917, *Nerv. & Ment. Dis. Monog. Series*, No. 24.

inferiority feelings among women no doubt reflects the disadvantage they feel in a "man's world." Over and above whatever handicaps they have as individuals they have extra restrictions placed upon them, especially in economic and moral spheres of activity. The following table sheds some light upon this problem. It is based upon anonymous replies from four groups, about 300 cases in all.[20]

		Percentage Replies			
		Girls		Boys	
		Working Girls	College Girls	Prep School	College
Have boys on the whole an easier time in life than girls?	Yes	77	53	63	81
	No	23	47	37	19
Did you ever wish to be of the opposite sex?	Yes	58	70	26	19
	No	42	30	74	81
Would you now like to be of the opposite sex?	Yes	30	7	0	0
	No	70	93	100	100

Table of Attitudes Toward
Opposite Sex

The majority of all groups regard the position of growing boys to be more enviable than that of girls. Nearly three times as many girls as boys at some time have wished to be of the opposite sex. Although most of the young women are now content with their role, the desire to be a male is by no means uncommon among them, especially in the population of working girls. The corresponding desire among boys is apparently non-existent. How much this last result reflects the victory of the Super-ego, preventing an honest report, and how much the general conflict on the part of women reflects a "masculine protest" in the sexual sense, cannot be decided. But whatever part these or other unconscious factors play in the results, their significance for our purposes is unaffected: girls have a harder time to make satisfactory positions for themselves in their environments,

[20] The results were obtained with the kind assistance of Miss Theresa Larkin and Mr. W. H. Clark.

and for this reason suffer more commonly feelings of inferiority.[21]

What does one do about an inferiority complex besides suffer from it? The tension it engenders, by its very nature, defies simple and direct methods of alleviation. One cannot permanently repress it, nor can one always escape it by "going out of the field." Some more sustained form of combat is required, and to this form Adler has given the name, compensation.[22]

Many forms of compensation have been described in psychological literature.[23] Only a brief characterization of each need be given here.

Direct action, or compensation in kind, occurs when through persistent attack upon the *source* of an actual inferiority it is finally for all time removed. When, as occasionally happens, the source of the deficiency is not only removed but actually converted into a source of strength, one speaks of *over-compensation.* Demosthenes, legend has it, worked so persistently to overcome his stammering that he became not merely a normal speaker but a great orator. Theodore Roosevelt whose early frailty caused him to suffer feelings of inferiority, built up his physique through systematic training, but in so doing he *over*-compensated, and emerged a lion-hunter and a roughrider (not merely a partridge hunter and a smooth rider). Everyone knows of immigrants who upon arrival in the United States felt themselves to be socially despised and inferior, but who by attacking directly their difficulties rose to remarkable heights of success. The American classic of the self-made man is nearly always a story

[21] In the home, the only niche allotted them in previous times, women did not have such exaggerated feelings of inferiority. It was *their* world, freely granted them by men. Few of the sex left the niche to compete in the "world of men." Nowadays it is the world of men in which many women are living and competing, a world of standards intrinsically alien to them as women. Slowly those standards are being modified to include them. As this occurs, as women are admitted on equal terms, the ratio of inferiority feelings may be equalized. No doubt the change will also affect the percentage of girls preferring to be boys.

[22] The psychological significance of this term is much narrower than its common usage. It is not the cosmic principle that Emerson would have it, nor is it synonymous with every attainment of equilibrium and adjustment. When, for example, a short person walks faster to keep up with a tall person, he is, in common speech, compensating for his inferior height, but *psychologically* he is in all probability merely adjusting his gait. But if at the same time he is telling tall tales of his own prowess to his companion he is probably compensating for a chronic inferiority complex now re-aroused by the contrast in heights.

[23] The gist of Adler's teaching filtered rapidly through the institutes of psychology into popular lore, psychologists assisting in the popularization. Cf. R. Dodge and E. Kahn, *The Craving for Superiority,* 1931, and W. F. Vaughan, *The Lure of Superiority,* 1928.

of compensation in kind. It goes without saying that the mental hy-
gienist regards such compensation as the most desirable form both
from the social and the personal points of view.

Substitution. Often the source of difficulty cannot be removed
by compensation in kind. One must seek satisfaction in an entirely
different direction. The hunchback cannot correct his deformity, but
he may, through application or cunning, become the power behind
a throne. The plain girl may develop a compensatory charm and wit,
or the non-athletic youth through diligence may excel at his studies.
As a young man the philosopher Immanuel Kant could not reconcile
himself to his sunken chest, restricting the free action of the heart
and lungs. He describes how this condition predestined him to hypo-
chrondria from which he suffered greatly. Little by little as it became
clear to him that nothing could be done to change his physique, he
centered his attention more whole-heartedly upon his stronger abilities. In his own words, he taught himself to be "calm and clear in the
head, although oppressed in the chest." [24]

Defense Mechanisms are compensations designed to deceive others.
Many of them are of a rather trivial order, mere habits or mannerisms
calculated to throw others off the scent. One can often recognize
defensiveness in the exaggerated handshake of a self-conscious adolescent striving to mask his own embarrassment, or in the bluster of a
bully who throws a smoke screen around his own weakness, or in
goatees, thick-soled shoes, disarming smiles, or ingratiating manners
affected in order to hide physical defects of stature or feature. More
highly organized defense mechanisms are those typical of the brag-
gart, the pathological liar, and the person who "protests too much"
in the effort to hide feelings of inadequacy or guilt.

Self-justification and Rationalization are forms of compensation
unconsciously designed not only to fool others but likewise to fool
oneself. When failure occurs, however minor it may be, the first
reaction often takes the form of self-justification. The beloved Ego
must be allowed to triumph; if it cannot do so in a realistic encounter,
it may do so in retrospect. How often conversations overheard in

[24] One might, somewhat less securely, go further in Kant's case and point out
that not merely the *fact* of becoming a philosopher, but the *nature* of his philosophical teaching bears traces of the compensatory urge. He had failed in the emotional field; that is to say, most of his emotions had been unpleasant ones of suffering and defeat. He substituted, therefore, an emphasis upon *reason*, pure and
practical, at which he himself so greatly excelled, comforting himself with the conviction that emotions, after all, were "diseases of the intellect."

the street car reduce to the simple formula: "He said to me . . . but *I* said to him!" Watch the wagging assent of heads. There is never any question as to who was right in the argument. In cultivated personalities of good insight or social training this impulsive self-justification is less often encountered (Chapter VIII).

When one slips constantly below a standard of conduct chosen for oneself (in morality or in the display of strength, wit, or grace) one usually finds extenuating circumstances to minimize the force of the failure. Sometimes the extenuation takes the form of a permanent protective rationalization. A pale non-athletic young man defended (and deceived) himself with the comforting sentiment, "I am sick of hearing about red-blooded athletes. I have decided what red blood means; it is the blood that never flows through the brain." One man who admitted that he was by nature slow, added for his own comfort, "but sure." Another with an especially cadaverous face thought it not such an affliction since it made him distinguished in appearance "like Rameses or Savonarola." The youth who decided that what he couldn't have wasn't worth having was indulging in *sour-grapes* rationalization; the man who looked like Rameses and the other who though slow was sure, were making virtues of their respective necessities in a *sweet-lemon* rationalization.

To accuse oneself, or to be accused, of dereliction and incompetence causes tension and annoyance. Better, if possible, to find an "alibi," an immediate excuse, and so close the subject. Often such a stop-gap proves adequate; suspicion of incompetence is lulled; tension is removed. It is to be sure only a *pars pro toto* closure, and may not —like direct action—permanently defeat the inferiority feeling. Sooner or later some more thoroughgoing type of compensation may have to be instituted.

Rationalization has its institutional aspect. A great many people with social and intellectual inferiority feelings find solace in the sour-grapes and sweet-lemon attitudes of journalism. They read comforting news of the stupidity of the "brain trust," the evil ways of the élite, and the uncouthness of college students. In pulp magazines and on the screen they find the homely virtues of poverty and semi-illiteracy extolled. To provide such ready-made rationalizations is one duty of the fourth-estate, committed, as it is, to giving the public what it wants. This phenomenon of institutional rationalization provides one of the principal problems of social psychology.

Autistic Thinking (*fantasy*) is compensation that occurs when an individual disregards completely the demands of his physical and social environment, withdrawing into himself to day-dream of success. A certain slim youth suffering persecution from his tougher schoolmates, fled to his room every afternoon after school to play his two favorite games. In one he was a schoolmaster, the head of a large class of boys (his own tormenters). In this role he wrote out severe assignments and administered floggings to his heart's content. In the other game he was an English country gentleman. Living in an imaginary hunting lodge he entertained titled guests and wrote fabulously large checks for his favorites.

Personalities having a marked fantasy life are *introverted*. When the process is carried further so that the outer life, conducted in a routine way, has little connection of any kind with the inner life of memory, imagination, and wish, one speaks of a *schizoid* personality.[25] Whereas to his associates the ordinary introvert may seem merely imaginative, an individual with such a marked cleavage seems definitely queer. Still more extreme cases are *schizophrenic*—pathological to such a degree that no one can tell what curious forms the imagination is taking, and to what delirious unreality the patient has surrendered himself.

Neurotic Compensation. Anyone who is ill cannot be expected to work energetically, to expose himself to disagreeable social duties, to succeed in competitive sports. In general the ill person has an acceptable excuse for, and protection from, all failure. Because this is so, there are conditions of purely psychic invalidism (usually neurasthenic or hysteric) that represent the last trump for otherwise insolvable inferiority complexes. A pseudo-malady is the last line of defense, and represents so serious an imbalance, so complete a defeat for the normal mode of life, that it belongs more properly in the field of abnormal psychology.

We see therefore that the forms of compensation range from the most deliberate and persevering attempts to remove the *source* of difficulty by compensation in kind, through a whole course of tricks involving self-justification and defensive maskings, both fraudulent and fanciful, to down-right pathological surrender. Goals that cannot be achieved through the direct channels of adjustment, are pursued through one compensatory bypath or another.

Like suggestibility, compensation is a basic potentiality of the

[25] An unusually good case of this type is that of *M. S.* in G. H. Green, *Psychoanalysis in the Class Room*, 1923, pp. 33-40.

human mind. Everyone is capable of using it. Like suggestibility it is not often a distinctive trait. A few personalities, to be sure, are so colored by their painfully evident, systematic striving to overcome their handicaps at all costs and by whatever method possible, that one may speak of a trait of compensation.[26] In these cases there is an oddly tenacious, positive quality in the program of compensation. But as with suggestibility, only rarely may compensation in a personality be identified as a trait, but it is very often a *device* through which traits develop.

PSYCHOANALYTIC "MECHANISMS" [27]

The tremendous vogue of psychoanalytic interpretations of personality may perhaps be explained somewhat as follows. Whenever there is a striking lack of proportion between an act and the apparent reasons for it, there is a presumption that some hidden and unconscious impulses guided the act. Any psychological doctrine that offers a consistent account of these impulses and their operation promises thereby to amend all the shortcomings of traditional intellectualistic psychology. Before Freud there was in general a fatal neglect of impulsive emotion and its subterranean workings. What Freud did was to insist that the neglected facts of emotion are the most important facts of all for psychology. The instant promise of such a new dynamic doctrine attracted doctors, laymen, and psychologists themselves, dissatisfied with the older intellectualistic outlook. Those who

[26] Such a case is described in the personality of *G. L., J. Abnorm. & Soc. Psychol.*, 1921, 16, 6-40.

[27] Devotees of psychoanalysis will no doubt be distressed to find here so tardy and so incomplete a review of the contributions of Freud and of his many disciples, both orthodox and dissident. There are three reasons why the account is so critical and so brief. (1) Psychoanalytic concepts are drawn exclusively from neurotic and pathological material, *i.e.*, from cases where imbalance prevails over balance, and for this reason their applicability to normal personality is in many respects questionable. (2) The portions of psychoanalytic doctrine most valid for normal personality are incorporated elsewhere in these chapters, in contexts unfamiliar to psychoanalytic theory, but more suitable. (3) The story of psychoanalysis is too familiar to require another detailed exposition. One cannot improve upon the accounts of Freud, *A General Introduction to Psychoanalysis*, trans. 1920, *New Introductory Lectures on Psychoanalysis*, trans. 1932; of G. Murphy and F. Jensen, *Approaches to Personality*, 1932; or of I. Hendrick, *Facts and Theories of Psychoanalysis*, 1934.

Such a volume as F. Alexander's *The Psychoanalysis of the Total Personality*, trans. 1930, wrongly implies that psychoanalysis is equipped to deal with the *whole* of personality. The truth is that it deals only with a fraction of the phenomena encountered in a comprehensive study of the subject. But in spite of its narrowness the bulk of all literature on the psychology of personality is written from this one point of view. It is time that the story be told in more eclectic terms!

wanted a dynamic psychology as guide had no other choice; it was a question of psychoanalysis or nothing. There have been, to be sure, minor and even major departures from the initial teaching of Freud, but broadly speaking, ever since its epoch-making formulation, psychoanalysis has served as the one and only pivot for all thorough-going dynamic psychology.[28]

In spite of its subtle secondary elaborations, the Freudian picture of personality is essentially simple. Freud does precisely what Plato and a host of faculty psychologists have done—he divides personality into three arbitrarily conceived parts. The special names for these divisions are the *Id*, the *Super-ego*, and the *Ego*, which roughly may be translated as *Emotional Impulse, Conscience*, and cognitive *Self-consciousness*, respectively. The last of these is without energy of its own; from the dynamic point of view it is weak. As the merely passive principle of conscious selfhood it is continually buffeted by three "tyrants," the objective world, the Super-ego and the Id.

Not infrequently the Ego, perceiving its own weakness, breaks out in distress, suffering vague or specific feelings of fear, *i.e.*, an "anxiety neurosis." (Anxiety, though obviously not a universal trait among normal people is a common condition among neurotics, and may be said to be the *raison d'être* for the whole theory of psychoanalysis). The mission of psychoanalysis is to strengthen the Ego by making it more cognizant of the forces of the Super-ego (the socialized conscience of which it is already partially aware), and of the Id (the unconscious store-house of instinctive impulses). If psychoanalysis can widen the Ego's field of vision, so that it is able to take over into the unified region of consciousness many hitherto hidden portions of the Id, reconciling them in the process with the demands of the Super-ego and the outer world, the patient will then face life

[28] Another explanation of the spread of psychoanalytic theory is its dramatic and imaginative character. It presents the problem of good and evil dramatized in new terms. In its simplicity it can be understood by the layman; he can participate in the objectified drama of his own conflicts which has great therapeutic advantage. It is a fresh approach, free from the religious terms which as likely as not he has repudiated (probably because his own moral growing pains have been associated and entangled with religious sanctions and restrictions). He can accept these new terms without losing caste with himself or his contemporaries. Witness how often the conversation of a "convert" to psychoanalysis is saturated with the terms of the doctrine much as the letters of our grandmothers were with a Biblical vocabulary. One might speculate as to whether a child brought up in the rigorous pattern and terminology of psychoanalysis might not, faced with severe conflicts in adulthood, find fresh and helpful vigor in the dramatic terminology of good and evil of the older religions, much as the reverse situation holds today.

more serenely, and his neurotic difficulties will presumably vanish. Psychoanalysis, says Freud, aims primarily at the reclamation of the Id by the Ego.[29] Though the goal is therapeutic, the originality of the doctrine extends beyond the practical domain into the region of theoretical psychology as well.

Its theoretical significance lies largely in the specific mechanisms that are postulated to account for the various relationships obtaining between the Id, the Super-ego, and the Ego. These mechanisms psychoanalysis describes in great detail. And yet the account often seems to the impartial reader altogether exceptional or else badly exaggerated. Derived as they are from the inductive study of unbalanced (anxious) personalities, they are not able, taken collectively, to provide a well-proportioned account of the *normal* course of development. Yet *some* of the mechanisms described, provided they are kept in perspective and not regarded as the alpha and omega of genetic psychology, have value for the study of normal lives. Elsewhere in this volume, in contexts where they are useful to the normal personality, some of these are employed (for example, *rationalization, projection, fantasy, infantilism, regression, dissociation, trauma,* the *complex,* and the *ego-ideal,* as well as the unique *methods* of investigation employed by psychoanalysis). A few other concepts must be added here.

The *pleasure principle* emphasizes the fact that immediate gratification, regardless of future consequences, is normally the demand of impulses that are not controlled by an organized and mature Ego. The pleasure principle is most apparent in the unsocialized and hedonistic behavior of the young child. The *reality principle*, a complementary concept, is the control that the Ego acquires over the pleasure principle through restraining habits and sentiments that are inevitable products of adaptation to the moral, social, and physical environments. The reality principle is simply a short-hand designation of the enormously complex process of the *maturing* of personality, of its fitting into a socialized and civilized setting. The two following chapters offer a more detailed analysis of this process.

The *unconscious* is an inclusive abstraction, referring to all the operations fashioning personality without the individual's direct knowledge. Psychoanalysis tends to populate the unconscious with a more or less standard equipment of mechanisms and content. Its

---

[29] S. Freud, *New Introductory Lectures on Psychoanalysis,* 1933, p. 112.

primary function is to serve as a store-house of the impulses rejected by the Ego. These impulses are rejected by *repression*, the process whereby the individual denies conscious and overt outlet to unwelcome or unsocialized wishes. "Everything contradictory to the ruling tendencies of the conscious personality, to its wishes, longing and ideals, and everything which would disturb the good opinion one likes to have of oneself is apt to be repressed." [30] Repression is not only a result of conscious conflict (cf. p. 119), but in turn breeds unconscious conflict, with dire symptoms that creep unwittingly into speech and behavior. One of the symptoms of repressed emotion is *symbolization*, the representation of unconscious thoughts in acceptable forms in dreams, art, metaphor, wit, or folklore. Similar is *displacement*, by which the unconscious wish is admitted to consciousness only after some acceptable distortion occurs, so that the true and original object of the impulse is supplanted by a surrogate object (the hated father, perhaps, becomes an ogre or an executioner).

Underlying all such mechanisms is the primary fact of conflict. Impulses may be antagonistic to each other (*e.g.*, the "Life" and "Death" wishes), or the wish may be in conflict with repressive standards (the Super-ego) or with the direct requirements of the environment. *Ambivalence* is a frequent consequence of conflict, the same object receiving both love and hate, aggression and fear, according to its capacity for arousing both a favorable and an avertive impulse. Unconscious conflict may lead also to *obsessional and compulsive* behavior, symptomatic of the individual's struggle for release from the conflict, but not as such intelligible to him, until interpreted by the psychoanalyst. And this is the *point d'appui* of the analytic theory and therapy.

Although the importance of conflict in the evolution of the individual personality is under no circumstances to be denied, it seems that only in exceptional cases is the psychoanalytic emphasis on its *unconscious* operation fully justified. Most conflicts, psychoanalysis to the contrary notwithstanding, are conscious in all *essential* particulars and for that reason another less esoteric portrayal of conflict seems more adequate.

The constant war between impulsive desires (psychoanalysis calls them "instincts") and various inhibitory agencies (chiefly the Super-ego) is sometimes solved by *sublimation* whereby impulses are ex-

[30] F. Alexander, *The Medical Value of Psychoanalysis*, 1932, p. 79.

pressed in socially and personally acceptable channels (*e.g.*, work, play, or art) without contingent suffering. Such *aim-inhibited* wishes (*e.g.*, nursing in place of maternity, or "latent" in place of "overt" homosexuality) play a large part in the socialization of personality. Psychoanalysis regards this as an altogether transparent substitution, and one that, so long as it is successful, keeps the individual from becoming neurotic.

Sublimation, it claims, is the device above all others that normal personalities employ to render their anti-social impulses acceptable. If this were the case, sublimation would be the most important genetic mechanism in the study of normal personality, but as the next chapter will show the maturing of normal personality is a far more complex process than simply redirecting the aim of originally unallowable wishes.[31]

Another serviceable concept is that of *identification*, applied when one person develops an emotional tie with some other person to such an extent that he behaves as if he *were* that person. The characteristics of the second individual are reproduced through conscious or unconscious imitation by the first. Identification is thought to be a large factor in the development of the child's personality, but it is also by no means uncommon in adults. Parents, for example, may identify with their own children quite as much as their children with them.

[31] Just what sublimation means in concrete application is seldom clear. The concept is confused in the minds of psychologists and laymen alike. The following fourfold analysis may help. (1) As applied to highly specific organic tensions (hunger, need for oxygen, or physiological sex processes) the concept has absolutely no applicability. One cannot sublimate starvation nor a distended sex-gland. (Cf. W. S. Taylor, "A Critique of Sublimation in Males: A Study of Forty Superior Single Men." *Genet. Psychol. Monog.*, 1933, 13, No. 1.) Local segmental tensions can only be relieved in ways specifically suited to them. (2) As applied to the distraction of attention from an unwelcome interest—by keeping otherwise occupied—the concept is really a misnomer. One reduces anger by leaving the scene of provocation and taking up some absorbing occupation; not by sublimation, but through a redirection of attention and interest. (3) As applied to the fatiguing out of generalized concurrent tensions accompanying a specific state of unrest, the doctrine has more merit. The diffuse somatic restlessness induced by thirst, sexual desire, and the like can often be reduced by irrelevant activity that fatigues the organism as a whole. (The *specific* segmental tension however is not directly relieved by such activity.) (4) As a still more complex concept, implying that an individual may without serious conflict forego some specific gratification, provided that he finds other sources of equal satisfaction, sublimation is a useful doctrine. In such instances, the individual simply disregards his unfulfilled desires, letting them atrophy, or repressing them without disaster, in the interest of an alternative plan of life that satisfies not these desires but satisfies *him* as a whole man. But in such a case the original psychoanalytic definition of the term is violated, for the individual is *not sublimating the original energy* at all. He is busy doing something quite different, namely, leading a satisfying life in spite of the lack of fulfillment of a certain desire.

It is doubtful whether any really new psychological process is here involved; imitation of an intensely emotional order seems to cover the situation.

Identification raises the problem of the *parent-image*. It is obvious that the prime factor in the development of any personality is the influence of other personalities. Of all the people who affect this development, in general the parents do so most poignantly. Psychological studies have failed to find any significant tendency for children to prefer the parent of the opposite sex (as Freudian theory assumes). Rather, both boys and girls as a rule have a greater fondness for their mothers, no doubt because of her closer association with them and her devotion to their comfort and well-being. A child seems never to be wholly indifferent to his parents, especially as he grows older. And whether his affective attitude toward them is positive or negative, the parent-image affects him enormously; and he never escapes from it. If an orphan has no memories of one or of both parents he takes the nearest lying substitutes, or else, if necessary, produces fanciful parents for his own guidance and satisfaction.

Now, the parent-image is a very concrete factor in experience, just as individual as is the parent himself. A child knows no other mother or father than his own. A father may be stern or gentle; the child's image conforms throughout life to the type; a mother may be the full-bosomed domestic type of woman or the high-strung, artistic or professional sort of mother, but to the child she is *mother*. Ordinarily the child is unquestioning in his acceptance of the parent as the parent is. To be sure, after early childhood he may compare his parents with other parents, but even if he finds his own lacking, he generally does not want to change. A lad of eight said to his mother, "I don't want you to change, for you're *my* mother." The influence of the parent is then usually *positive*, which means that standards, tastes, and characteristics of the parent are likely to be imitated. The effect is as subtle as it is profound. It has been found for instance that most parents apply to their children the same standards and practices which their own parents set for them. Thus it comes about that a household perpetuates its own inner mores for generations. If a reaction against the codes and customs of the older generation has taken place, there is in effect a negative imitation, a protest, which just as certainly shows the potency of the parent-image.[32]

[32] Cf. K. V. Francis and E. A. Fillmore, *Univ. Iowa Studies in Child Welfare*, 1934, 9, No. 2.

Especially in attitudes toward the opposite sex does the image (and therefore the parent) play a role. Men often choose wives in subtle ways like their mothers, or in rare cases where the mother is the object of ambivalent regard, wives strikingly and significantly different in type. Women choose husbands like their fathers in equally subtle ways, in so far as they have freedom of choice. Men often resent in their wives any departure from the mother-image. A man whose mother was domestic, a homemaker, is more likely to resent professional or undomestic interests in his wife; whereas a man accustomed to see his own mother in an intellectual role prefers his wife to be the same, or at least accepts it unquestionably if she assumes such a role. The wife, in turn, is frequently as quick to measure her husband by standards embodied in her father-image.

Finally, attention must be directed to the all-important psychoanalytic conception of *psychosexuality*, comprising "all aspects of love and pleasure-seeking and their mutual inter-relationships; it emphasizes unconscious wishes for sensual gratification and their conscious de-erotized derivatives, normal and abnormal, as well as wishes which culminate in complete and mature heterosexual union." [33] The concept—of which this is a typical definition—is very slippery. Taken in one way, it covers every life-serving impulse of the human being; it is Eros, and Eros is Life (opposed only by the "Death Instincts"). Such a generalized postulate of a dynamic, non-specific libido is nothing other than the harmless hypothesis of a basic Will to Live (p. 109), not unlike the doctrine of *Egoism* previously discussed in this chapter.

But such a broad, and psychologically valueless, conception of psychosexuality is not, after all, the psychoanalyst's real concern. In theory and in practice he translates it into a doctrine of sexuality in its narrower sense. In fact psychoanalysis, especially the Freudian variety, succeeds in the almost impossible task of *over*-emphasizing the role of sexual motivation and interest in the human person. This is no small accomplishment, for—in Western culture at least—sexual tensions are in fact the most important single factor in the development of most personalities (cf. pp. 116 f.), or rather *sex would be the most important single factor if there were any single factors, which there are not.*

Biological motives never operate singly. Sex in normal lives

[33] I. Hendrick, *Facts and Theories of Psychoanalysis*, 1934, p. 299.

never stands alone, it is tied to all manner of personal images, sanctions, tastes, interests, ambitions, codes, and ideals. To put the case as crisply as possible: sexuality in its stark biological simplicity is segmental in the organism, often insistent but never devoid of mental ramifications; in these ramifications it is indeed pervasive, but it is no longer mere sexuality; it becomes diffused into the major systems of interests and traits which are themselves the *fundamental* structural and functional systems of personality.

A remarkably illogical procedure seems to be responsible for over-emphasis on sex by psychoanalysts (by Freudians especially). Whatever form of behavior or thought is *ever* found in *any* life, to be associated with sex, they seem to assume to be *always* connected with sex in *every* life. This procedure produces such absurdities as interpreting the infant's bad memory (p. 161) as guilt repression (the justification being that neurotic adults are known *sometimes* to dissociate painful sexual memories of guilt from their own consciousness); or the dogma that all individuals normally have erotic attachments to the opposite sexed parent (because some neurotics report incestuous impulses). Actually what is true is that the extreme lability of sexual life makes all manner of associations and all manner of conflicts *possible;* but not every libidinous attachment or conflict of one person is to be regarded as a psychosexual peculiarity of all people. The ramifications of sexual interest are broad enough and deep enough in any life without the need to exaggerate their place by making the sexual history of certain typical neurotics the prototype for personality in general.

In any two personalities sexuality never seems to play the same role. Its attachments, its significance, and the conduct associated with it are among the most individualistic of all the phenomena of mental life. In spite of its biologically uniform aspects, in its psychological organization it is a remarkably idiosyncratic matter.

And this is why sex, as such, cannot be regarded as a single factor of motivation, nor as the basic element in personality. A life is not simply a variation on a uniform pattern of psychosexuality, but, on the contrary, the sexuality of a life can be understood only if it is regarded as one of the variations within the total and complete pattern of personality. Excepting in the most infra-personal sense there is no such concrete fact of sex; when one speaks of sex-habits and sex-adjustments one can only mean *personal* habits and *personal* adjustments, having partial but not exclusive reference to the segmental biological functions of sex. Personality, then, is not a system of formations within a matrix of sex.

What is true of sex is true of every other so-called instinct. Human motives are highly individual affairs. It misrepresents them to say that they are only changes rung upon universal themes. Motives are always dynamic formations of minds-in-particular, and they can only be understood if the course of their individual transformations is known. The following chapter is devoted to proving this important point.

CHAPTER VII

THE TRANSFORMATION OF MOTIVES *

The Me, like every other aggregate, changes as it grows.
—William James

SOMEHOW in the process of maturing the manifold potentialities and dispositions of childhood coalesce into sharper, more distinctive motivational systems. *Pari passu* with their emergence these systems take upon themselves effective driving power, operating as mature, autonomous motives quite different in aim and in character from the motivational systems of juvenile years, and very different indeed from the crude organic tensions of infancy.

One of the chief characteristics of the mature personality is its possession of sophisticated and stable interests and of a characteristic and predictable style of conduct. Convictions and habits of expression are definitely centered. Evaluations are sure, actions are precise, and the goals of the individual life are well defined.

G. K. Chesterton gives a brief but psychologically significant portrait of a thoroughly mature personality, Leo Tolstoy, in whom all motivation seems to be centered in one master-sentiment.

> Tolstoy, besides being a magnificent novelist, is one of the very few men alive who have a real, solid, and serious view of life. . . . He is one of the two or three men in Europe, who have an attitude toward things so entirely their own, that we could supply their inevitable view in anything—a silk hat, a Home Rule Bill, an Indian poem, or a pound of tobacco. There are three men in existence who have such an attitude: Tolstoy, Mr. Bernard Shaw, and my friend Mr. Hillaire Belloc. They are all diametrically opposed to each other, but they all have this essential resemblance, that given their basis of thought, their soil of conviction, their opinions on every earthly subject grow there naturally, like flowers in a field. There are certain views of certain things that they must take; they do not form opin-

* A part of this chapter is here reprinted from The Golden Jubilee Volume of the *American Journal of Psychology*, Vol. 50, 1937.

ions, the opinions form themselves. Take, for instance, in the case of Tolstoy, the mere list of miscellaneous objects which I wrote down at random above, a silk hat, a Home Rule Bill, an Indian poem, and a pound of tobacco. Tolstoy would say: "I believe in the utmost possible simplification of life; therefore, this silk hat is a black abortion." He would say: "I believe in the utmost possible simplification of life; therefore this Home Rule Bill is a mere peddling compromise; it is no good to break up a centralised empire into nations, you must break the nation up into individuals." He would say: "I believe in the utmost possible simplification of life; therefore, I am interested in this Indian poem, for Eastern ethics, under all their apparent gorgeousness, are far simpler and more Tolstoyan than Western." He would say: "I believe in the utmost possible simplification of life; therefore, this pound of tobacco is a thing of evil; take it away." Everything in the world, from the Bible to a bootjack, can be, and is, reduced by Tolstoy to this great fundamental Tolstoyan principle, the simplification of life.[1]

One must, of course, dismiss as literary exaggeration Chesterton's claim that there are only "two or three men in Europe" so well integrated that one could supply their inevitable view in anything. Among our own acquaintances we can name several more. In principle, however, if not in statistics, Chesterton is right, for the *majority* of personal lives are not nearly so unified as Tolstoy's; in few cases is the *Leitmotif* so entirely consistent. The difference is one of degree. For in nearly all mature personalities master-sentiments exist, and, however difficult the task may be, psychologists are bound to try to account for them.

FUNCTIONAL AUTONOMY

To understand the dynamics of the normal mature personality a new and somewhat radical principle of growth must be introduced to supplement the more traditional genetic concepts thus far considered. For convenience of discussion this new principle may be christened the *functional autonomy of motives*.[2]

[1] From G. K. Chesterton and others, *Leo Tolstoy*, 1903, pp. 3 f.

[2] The authenticity of this principle has been admitted by many psychological writers, but they have neglected thus far to give it a name. Its most familiar statement to date is the oft-quoted phrase of R. S. Woodworth, "mechanisms may become drives." Another clear recognition lies in the following quotation from E. C. Tolman. But neither Woodworth nor Tolman has adopted a substantive designation for the psychological process in question.

"The whole body of both what the anthropologists find in the way of specific culture-patterns and what psychologists find in the way of individual idiosyncrasies

Now, any type of psychology that treats *motives*, thereby endeavoring to answer the question as to *why* men behave as they do, is called a *dynamic psychology*. By its very nature it cannot be merely a descriptive psychology, content to depict the *what* and the *how* of human behavior. The boldness of dynamic psychology in striking for causes stands in marked contrast to the timid, "more scientific" view that seeks nothing else than the establishment of a mathematical function for the relation between some artificially simple stimulus and some equally artificial and simple response. If the psychology of personality is to be more than a matter of coefficients of correlation it *must* be a dynamic psychology, and seek first and foremost a sound and adequate theory of the nature of human dispositions.

Unfortunately the type of dynamic psychology almost universally held, however sufficient it may seem from the point of view of the *abstract* motives of *abstract* personalities, fails to provide a foundation sound enough or flexible enough to bear the weight of any *single* full-bodied personality. The reason is that all prevailing dynamic doctrines refer every mature motive of personality to underlying original instincts, wishes, or needs, shared *by all men*. Thus, the concert artist's devotion to his music might be "explained" as an extension of his "self-assertive instinct," of the "need for sentience," or as a symptom of some repressed striving of "the libido." In McDougall's hormic psychology, for example, it is explicitly stated that only the instincts or propensities can be prime movers. Though capable of extension (on both the receptive and executive sides), they are always few in number, common in all men, and established at birth. The enthusiastic collector of bric-a-brac derives his enthusiasm from the parental instinct; so too does the kindly old philanthropist, as well as the mother of a brood. It does not matter how different these three interests may seem to be, they derive their energy from the same source. The principle is that a very few basic motives suffice for explaining the endless varieties of human interests. And the psychoanalyst holds the same over-simplified theory. The number of human interests that he regards as so many canalizations of the one basic sexual instinct is past computation.

seems to consist for the most part, psychologically speaking, in acquired specifications of ultimate goals or in acquired adherences to specific types of means-objects, which latter then often set up in their own right. And such specifications and settings-up, once established, acquire a strangle hold." *Phil. Science*, 1935, 2, p. 370.

Taking the case of Tolstoy, Adler would find the style of life adopted by Tolstoy to be a consequence of his compensatory striving for power, for health, or for personal integrity in the face of an unfavorable environment. Freud might decide that the "simplification of life" was a mere ritual evolved to escape feelings of guilt derived from an unhallowed infantile love; or perhaps he would attribute it to a Death Wish. Rank would see it as a desire to return to the peaceful pre-natal life. Kempf might say that it represented a sublimational craving, sustained by a tension produced by unfulfilled love or by some danger not successfully averted. McDougall might attribute it to the combined effects of the propensities for submission and comfort. H. A. Murray might say that there was a need for submission and inviolacy. And in the language of W. I. Thomas, the wish for security or recognition, perhaps both, would be made responsible. Any of these writers, to be sure, would admit that the original motive had become greatly extended both in the range of stimuli which provoke it and in its varieties of expression. But *the common factor in all these explanations is the reduction of every motive, however elaborate and individual, to a limited number of basic interests, shared by all men, and presumably innate.*

The authors of this type of dynamic psychology are concerning themselves only with mind-in-general. They seek a classification of the common and basic motives of men by which to explain the normal or neurotic behavior of any individual case. (This is true even though they may regard their own list as heuristic or even as fictional.) The plan really doesn't work. The very fact that the lists are so different in their composition suggests—what to a naive observer is plain enough—that motives are almost infinitely varied among men, not only in form but in substance. Not four wishes, nor eighteen propensities, nor any and all combinations of these, even with their extensions and variations, seem adequate to account for the endless variety of goals sought by an endless variety of mortals. And paradoxically enough, in certain cases the few simplified needs or instincts alleged to be the common ground for all motivation, turn out to be completely lacking (cf. p. 112).

Before describing the principle of functional autonomy, its theoretical significance should stand out clearly. The stress in this volume is constantly on the ultimate and irreducible uniqueness of personality. "But how," cry all the traditional scientists, including the older dynamic psychologists, "how are we ever to have a *science*

THE TRANSFORMATION OF MOTIVES

of unique events? Science must generalize." Perhaps it must, but what the objectors forget is that *a general law may be a law that tells how uniqueness comes about*. It is manifest error to assume that a general principle of motivation must involve the postulation of abstract or general motives. The principle of functional autonomy, here described, is general enough to meet the needs of science, but particularized enough in its operation to account for the uniqueness of personal conduct.

The dynamic psychology proposed here regards adult motives as infinitely varied, and as self-sustaining, *contemporary* systems, growing out of antecedent systems, but functionally independent of them. Just as a child gradually repudiates his dependence on his parents, develops a will of his own, becomes self-active and self-determining, and outlives his parents, so it is with motives. Each motive has a definite point of origin which may lie in the hypothetical instincts, or, more likely, in the organic tensions and diffuse irritability described in Chapter IV. Theoretically all adult purposes can be traced back to these seed-forms in infancy. But as the individual matures the bond is broken. The tie is historical, not functional.

Such a theory is obviously opposed to psychoanalysis and to all other genetic accounts that assume inflexibility in the root purposes and drives of life. (Freud says that the structure of the Id *never* changes.) The theory declines to believe that the energies of adult personality are infantile or archaic in nature. Motivation is *always* contemporary. The life of modern Athens is *continuous* with the life of the ancient city, but it in no sense *depends* upon it for its present "go." The life of a tree is continuous with that of its seed, but the seed no longer sustains and nourishes the full grown tree. Earlier purposes lead into later purposes, but are abandoned in their favor.

William James taught a curious doctrine that has been a matter for incredulous amusement ever since, the doctrine of the *transitoriness of instincts*. According to this theory—not so quaint as sometimes thought—an instinct appears but once in a lifetime, whereupon it promptly disappears through its transformation into habits. If there *are* instincts this is no doubt their fate, for no instinct can retain its motivational force unimpaired after it has been absorbed and recast under the transforming influence of learning. Such is the reasoning of James, and such is the logic of functional autonomy. The psychology of personality must be a psychology of post-instinctive behavior. If, as in this volume, instincts are dispensed with from the beginning, the effect is much the same, for whatever the original drives or "irritabilities" of the infant are, they become completely transformed in the course of growth into contemporaneous systems of motives.

Woodworth has spoken of the transformation of "mechanisms" into "drives." [3] A *mechanism* Woodworth defines as any course of behavior that brings about an adjustment. A *drive* is any neural process that releases mechanisms especially concerned with consummatory reactions. In the course of learning, many preparatory mechanisms must be developed in order to lead to the consummation of an original purpose. These mechanisms are the effective cause of activity in each succeeding mechanism, furnishing the drive for each stage following in the series. Originally all these mechanisms were merely instrumental, only links in the long chain of processes involved in the achievement of an *instinctive* purpose; with time and development, with integration and elaboration, many of these mechanisms become activated directly, setting up a state of desire and tension for activities and objects no longer connected with the original impulse. Activities and objects that earlier in the game were *means* to an end, now become *ends* in themselves.[4]

Although Woodworth's choice of quasi-neurological terminology is not the best, his doctrine, or one like it, is indispensable in accounting for the infinite number of effective motives possible in human life, and for their severance from the rudimentary desires of infancy. Further discussion of the operation of the principle and a critique of Woodworth's position will be more to the point after a review of the evidence in favor of the principle.

[3] R. S. Woodworth, *Dynamic Psychology*, 1918. Equivalent assertions are those of W. Stern concerning the transformation of "phenomotives" into "genomotives" (*Allgemeine Psychologie*, 1935, p. 569); and of E. C. Tolman regarding the "strangle hold" that "means-objects" acquire by "setting up in their own right" (ftn. p. 191).

[4] "The fundamental drive towards a certain end may be hunger, sex, pugnacity or what not, but once the activity is started, the means to the end becomes an object of interest on its own account" (Woodworth, *op. cit.*, p. 201). "The primal forces of hunger, fear, sex, and the rest, continue in force, but do not by any means, even with their combinations, account for the sum total of drives activating the experienced individual" (*Ibid.*, p. 104).

EVIDENCE FOR FUNCTIONAL AUTONOMY

Let us begin in a common sense way. An ex-sailor has a craving for the sea, a musician longs to return to his instrument after an enforced absence, a city-dweller yearns for his native hills, and a miser continues to amass his useless horde. Now, the sailor may have first acquired his love for the sea as an incident in his struggle to earn a living. The sea was merely a conditioned stimulus associated with satisfaction of his "nutritional craving." But now the ex-sailor is perhaps a wealthy banker; the original motive is destroyed; and yet the hunger for the sea persists unabated, even increases in intensity as it becomes more remote from the "nutritional segment." The musician may first have been stung by a rebuke or by a slur on his inferior performances into mastering his instrument, but now he is safely beyond power of these taunts; there is no need to continue, yet he loves his instrument more than anything else in the world. Once indeed the city dweller may have associated the hills around his mountain home with nutritional and erotogenic satisfactions, but these satisfactions he finds in his city home, *not* in the mountains; whence then comes all his hill-hunger? The miser perhaps learned his habits of thrift in dire necessity, or perhaps his thrift was a symptom of sexual perversion (as Freud would claim), and yet the miserliness persists, and even becomes stronger with the years, even after the necessity or the roots of the neurosis have been relieved.

Workmanship is a good example of functional autonomy. A good workman feels compelled to do clean-cut jobs even though his security, or the praise of others, no longer depend upon high standards. In fact, in a day of jerry-building his workman-like standards may be to his economic disadvantage. Even so he cannot do a slipshod job. Workmanship is not an instinct, but so firm is the hold it may acquire on a man that it is little wonder Veblen mistook it for one. A business man, long since secure economically, works himself into ill-health, and sometimes even back into poverty, for the sake of carrying on his plans. What was once an instrumental technique becomes a master-motive.

Neither necessity nor reason can make one contented permanently on a lonely island or on an isolated country farm after one is adapted to active, energetic city life. The acquired habits seem sufficient to urge one to a frenzied existence, even though reason and health demand the simpler life.

The pursuit of literature, the development of good taste in clothes, the use of cosmetics, the acquiring of an automobile, strolls in the public park, or a winter in Miami, may first serve, let us say, the interests of sex. But every one of these instrumental activities may become an interest in itself, held for a lifetime, long after the erotic motive has been laid away in lavender. People often find that they have lost allegiance to their original aims because of their deliberate preference for the many ways of achieving them.

The maternal sentiment offers an excellent final illustration. Many young mothers bear their children unwillingly, dismayed at the thought of the drudgery of the future. At first they may be indifferent to, or even hate, their offspring; the "parental instinct" seems wholly lacking. The only motives that hold such a mother to child-tending may be fear of what her critical neighbors will say, fear of the law, a habit of doing any job well, or perhaps a dim hope that the child will provide security for her in her old age. However gross these motives, they are sufficient to hold her to her work, until through the practice of devotion her burden becomes a joy. As her love for the child develops, her earlier practical motives are forgotten. In later years not one of these original motives may operate. The child may be incompetent, criminal, a disgrace to her, and far from serving as a staff for her declining years, he may continue to drain her resources and vitality. The neighbors may criticize her for indulging the child, the law may exonerate her from allegiance; she certainly feels no pride in such a child; yet she sticks to him. The tenacity of the maternal sentiment under such adversity is proverbial.[5]

Such examples from everyday experience could be multiplied *ad infinitum*. The evidence, however, appears in sharper outline when it is taken from experimental and clinical studies. In each of the following instances some new function emerges as an independently structured unit from preceding functions. The activity of these new units does not depend upon the continued activity of the units from which they developed.

[5] Most mothers, to be sure, give their babies a somewhat warmer welcome from the start, but even so, there is little evidence that the maternal instinct is a ready-made, full-fledged and invariable possession of all women. Even those who have early learned to be fond of babies find that with practice and experience the interest becomes constantly stronger, demanding no other satisfaction for itself than its own autonomous functioning. Some women become *so* absorbed in being good mothers that they neglect being the good wives they were earlier.

1. *The Circular Reflex.* Everyone has observed the almost endless repetition of acts by a child. The good-natured parent who picks up a spoon repeatedly thrown down by a baby wearies of this occupation long before the infant does. Such repetitive behavior, found likewise in early vocalization (babbling), and in other early forms of play, is commonly ascribed to the mechanism of the circular reflex.[6] It is an elementary instance of functional autonomy; for any situation where the consummation of an act provides adequate stimulation for the repetition of the *same* act does not require any backward tracing of motives. The act is self-perpetuating until it is inhibited by new activities or fatigue.

2. *Conative Perseveration.* Many experiments show that incompleted tasks set up tensions that tend to keep the individual at work until they are resolved. No hypothesis of self-assertion, rivalry, or any other basic need, is required. The completion of the task itself has become a quasi-need with dynamic force of its own. It has been shown, for example, that interrupted tasks are better remembered than completed tasks;[7] that an individual interrupted in a task will, even in the face of considerable opposition, return to that task;[8] that even trivial tasks undertaken in a casual way become almost haunting in character until they are completed.[9]

Conative perseveration of this order is stronger if an empty interval of time follows the period of work, showing that *left to itself*, without the inhibiting effect of other duties or activities, the motive grows stronger and stronger. The experiment of Kendig proves this point, as well as that of C. E. Smith.[10] The latter investigator demonstrated that there is more success in removing a conditioned fear if the deconditioning process is commenced immediately. After a twenty-four hour delay the fear has become set, and is more difficult to eradicate. We are reminded here of the sound advice to drivers of automobiles or airplanes who have been involved in an accident, that they drive again immediately to conquer the shock of the accident, lest the fear become set into a permanent phobia. The rule seems to be that unless specifically inhibited all emotional shocks, given time to set, tend to take on a compulsive autonomous character.

3. *"Conditioned Reflexes" Not Requiring Reinforcement.* The pure

[6] As a means of fixating early habits and of providing a foundation for future learning, this mechanism has received detailed attention by E. B. Holt, *Animal Drive and the Learning Process*, 1931, esp. chaps. vii and viii.

[7] B. Zeigarnik, *Psychol. Forsch.*, 1927, 9, 1-85.

[8] M. Ovsiankina, *Psychol. Forsch.*, 1928, 6, 302-379.

[9] I. Kendig, "Studies in Perseveration" (in five parts), *J. Psychol.*, 1936, 3, 223-264.

[10] C. E. Smith, *Change in the Apparent Resistance of the Skin as a Function of Certain Physiological and Psychological Factors* (Harvard College Library), 1934.

conditioned reflex readily dies out unless the secondary stimulus is occasionally reinforced by the primary stimulus (cf. p. 153). The dog does not continue to salivate whenever it hears a bell unless sometimes at least an edible offering accompanies the bell. But there are innumerable instances in human life where a single association, *never* reinforced, results in the establishment of a life-long dynamic system. An experience associated only once with a bereavement, an accident, or a battle, may become the center of a permanent phobia or complex, not in the least dependent on a recurrence of the original shock.

4. *Counterparts in Animal Behavior.* Though the validity of a principle in human psychology never depends upon its having a counterpart in animal psychology, still it is of interest to find functional autonomy in the lower organisms. For example, rats, who will first learn a certain habit only under the incentive of some specific tension, as hunger, will, after learning, often perform the habit even when fed to repletion.[11]

Another experiment shows that rats trained to follow a long and difficult path, will for a time persist in using this path, even though a short easy path to the goal is offered and even after the easier path has been learned.[12] Among rats as among human beings, old and useless habits have considerable power in their own right.

Olson studied the persistence of artificially induced scratching habits in rats. Collodion applied to the ears of the animal set up removing and cleaning movements. Four days later the application was repeated. From that time on the animals showed significantly greater number of cleaning movements than control animals. A month after the beginning of the experiment when the ears of the rats as studied by the microscope showed no further trace of irritation, the number of movements was still very great. Whether the induced habit spasm was permanently retained the experimenter does not say.[13]

5. *Rhythm.* A rat whose activity bears a definite relation to his habits of feeding (being greatest just preceding a period of feeding and midway between two such periods) will, even when starved, display the same periodicity and activity. The acquired rhythm persists without dependence on the original periodic stimulation of feeding.[14]

Even a mollusc whose habits of burrowing in the sand and reappearing depend upon the movements of the tide, will, when removed from

---

[11] J. D. Dodgson, *Psychobiology*, 1917, 1, 231-276. This work has already been interpreted by K. S. Lashley as favoring Woodworth's dynamic theory as opposed to Freud's (*Psychol. Rev.*, 1924, 31, 192-202).

[12] H. C. Gilhousen, *J. Comp. Psychol.*, 1933, 16, 1-23.

[13] W. C. Olson, *The Measurement of Nervous Habits in Normal Children*, 1929, pp. 62-65.

[14] C. P. Richter, *Comp. Psychol. Monog.*, 1922, 1. No. 2.

the beach to the laboratory, continue for several days in the same rhythm without the tide. Likewise certain animals, with nocturnal rhythms advantageous in avoiding enemies, obtaining food, or preventing excessive evaporation from the body, may exhibit such rhythms even when kept in a laboratory with constant conditions of illumination, humidity, and temperature.[15]

There are likewise instances where acquired rhythms in human life have taken on a dynamic character. Compulsive neurotics enter upon fugues or debauches, apparently not because of specific stimulation, but because "the time has come." A dipsomaniac in confinement and deprived for months of his alcohol describes the fierceness of the recurrent appetite (obviously acquired).

> Those craving paroxysms occur at regular intervals, three weeks apart, lasting for several days. They are not weak, namby-pamby things for scoffers to laugh at. If not assuaged with liquor they become spells of physical and mental illness. My mouth drools saliva, my stomach and intestines seem cramped, and I become bilious, nauseated, and in a shaky nervous funk.[16]

In such states of drug addiction, as likewise in states of hunger, lust, fatigue, there is to be sure a physical craving, but the rhythms of the craving are partially acquired, and are always accentuated by the mental habits associated with it. For instance, eating in our civilized way of life takes place not because physical hunger naturally occurs three times a day, but because of habitual rhythms of expectancy. The habit of smoking is much more than a matter of craving for the specific narcotic effects of tobacco; it is a craving for the motor ritual and periodic distraction as well.

6. *Neuroses.* Why are acquired tics, stammering, sexual perversions, phobias, and anxiety so stubborn and so often incurable? Even psychoanalysis, with its deepest of depth-probing seldom succeeds in effecting *complete* cures in such cases, even though the patient may feel relieved or at least reconciled to his difficulties after treatment. The reason seems to be that what are usually called "symptoms" are in reality something more. They have set themselves up in their own right as independent systems of motivation. Merely disclosing their roots does not change their independent activity.[17]

[15] S. C. Crawford, *Quar. Rev. Biol.*, 1934, 9, 201-214.
[16] Inmate Ward Eight, *Beyond the Door of Delusion*, Macmillan, 1932, p. 281.
[17] The case of W. E. Leonard, *The Locomotive God*, 1927, is instructive in this regard. An intense phobia was not relieved by tracing its history backward to the start of life. Even though he could explain why he was once frightened for a very good reason (by a locomotive), the author is quite unable to explain why now he is frightened *for no particular reason*. Such neuroses, and psychotic delusional systems as well, often acquire a "strangle hold," and the task of dislodging them is usually more than therapeutic skill is equal to.

7. *The Relation Between Ability and Interest.* Psychometric studies have shown that the relation between ability and interest is always positive, often markedly so. A person likes to do what he can do well. Over and over again it has been demonstrated that the skill learned for some external reason, turns into an interest, and is self-propelling, even though the original reason for pursuing it has been lost. A student who at first undertakes a field of study in college because it is prescribed, because it pleases his parents, or because it comes at a convenient hour, often ends by finding himself absorbed, perhaps for life, in the subject itself. He is not happy without it. The original motives are entirely lost. What was a means to an end has become an end in itself.

And there is the case of genius. A skill takes possession of the man. No primitive motivation is needed to account for his persistent, absorbed activity. It just *is* the alpha and omega of life to him. It is impossible to think of Pasteur's concern for health, food, sleep or family, as the root of his devotion to his work. For long periods of time he was oblivious of them all, losing himself in the white heat of research for which he had been trained and in which he had *acquired* a compelling and absorbing interest.

A much more modest instance is the finding of industrial research that when special incentives are offered and work speeded up as a consequence, and then these special incentives· removed, *the work continues at the speeded rate.* The habit of working at a faster tempo persists without external support.

8. *Sentiments vs. Instincts.* Every time an alleged instinct can by rigid analysis be demonstrated not to be innate but acquired, there is in this demonstration evidence for functional autonomy. It is true enough that maternal conduct, gregariousness, curiosity, workmanship, and the like, have the tenacity and compelling power that instincts are supposed to have. If they are not instincts, then they must be autonomous sentiments with as much dynamic character as has been attributed to instincts. It is not necessary here to review all the arguments in favor of regarding such alleged instincts as acquired sentiments; the problem was discussed in Chapter IV.

9. *The Dynamic Character of Personal Values.* When an interest-system has once been formed it not only creates a tensional condition that may be readily aroused, leading to overt conduct in some way satisfying to the interest, but it also acts as a silent agent for selecting and directing any behavior related to it. Take the case of people with strongly marked esthetic interests. Experiments with the word-association test have shown that such people respond more quickly to stimulus words connected with this interest than to words relating to

interests they lack.[18] Likewise, in scanning a newspaper they will observe and remember more items pertaining to art; they also take a greater interest in clothes than do non-esthetic people; and when they are asked to rate the virtues of others, they place esthetic qualities high. In short the existence of a well-established acquired interest exerts a directive and determining effect on conduct just as is to be expected of any dynamic system. The evidence can be duplicated for many interests other than the esthetic.[19]

CRITIQUE OF FUNCTIONAL AUTONOMY

Objections to the principle of autonomy may be expected from two sides. Behavioristically inclined psychologists will continue to prefer their conception of organic drive with its capacity for manifold conditioning by ever receding stimuli. Whereas instinct psychology of the traditional order will be unable to accept a pluralistic principle that seems to leave purpose so largely at the mercy of learning.

The behaviorist is well satisfied with motivation in terms of organic drive and conditioning because he feels that he somehow has secure anchorage in the neural structure. (For some strange reason, the closer he approaches nervous tissue the happier the behaviorist is.) But the truth of the matter is that the neural physiology of organic drive and conditioning is no better established, and no easier to imagine, than is the neural physiology of the type of complex autonomous units of motivation we have described.

Two behavioristic principles will be said to account adequately for the instances of functional autonomy previously cited, viz., the circular reflex and cross-conditioning. The former concept, acceptable enough when applied to infant behavior, merely says that the more activity a muscle engages in, the more activity of the same sort does it engender through a self-sustaining circuit.[20] This is, to be sure, a clear instance of autonomy, albeit on a primitive level, over-simplified so far as adult conduct is concerned. The doctrine of cross-conditioning refers to subtle recession of stimuli in the process of conditioning, and to the intricate possibility of cross-connections in conditioning. For instance, such ubiquitous external stimuli as humidity, daylight, gravitation, may feed collaterally into open channels

---

[18] H. Cantril, "General and Specific Attitudes," Psychol. Monog., 1932, No. 192.
[19] H. Cantril and G. W. Allport, J. Abnorm. & Soc. Psychol., 1933, 28, 259-273.
[20] E. B. Holt, op. cit., p. 38.

of activity, arousing mysteriously and unexpectedly a form of con‚ duct to which they have unconsciously been conditioned. For example, the angler whose fishing expeditions have been accompanied by sun, wind, or a balmy June day, may feel a desire to go fishing whenever the barometer, the thermometer, or the calendar in his city home tells him that these conditions prevail.[21] Innumerable such crossed stimuli are said to account for the arousal of earlier patterns of activity.

Such a theory is highly mechanistic. It inherits, first of all, the difficulties resident in the principle of conditioning whenever it is applied to human behavior in general (cf. pp. 151-153). Further, though the reflex circle and cross-conditioning may in fact exist, they are really rather trivial principles. They leave the formation of interest and its occasional arousal almost entirely to chance factors of stimulation. They give no picture at all of the spontaneous and variable aspects of traits, interests, or sentiments. These dispositions are regarded as purely *reactive* in nature; the stimulus is all-important. The truth is that dispositions *sort out* stimuli congenial to them, and this activity does not in the least resemble the rigidity of reflex response.[22]

A variant on the doctrine of cross-conditioning is the principle of *redintegration*.[23] This concept admits the existence of highly integrated dispositions of a neuropsychic order. These dispositions can be aroused *as a whole* by any stimulus previously associated with their functioning. In this theory likewise the disposition is regarded as a rather passive affair, waiting for reactivation by some portion of the original stimulus. Here again the variability of the disposition and its urge-like quality are not accounted for. The stimulus is thought merely to reinstate a complex determining tendency. Nothing is said about how the stimuli themselves are *selected*, why a motive once aroused becomes insistent, surmounting obstacles, skillfully subordinating conflicting impulses, and inhibiting irrelevant trains of thought.

In certain respects the principle of autonomy stands midway between the behavioristic view and the thoroughgoing purposive psy-

[21] *Ibid.*, p. 224.

[22] The basic fact that complex "higher" centers have the power of inhibiting, selecting, and initiating the activity of simpler segmental responses is a fact too well established to need elaboration here. It constitutes the very foundation of the psychophysiological theories advanced by Sherrington, Herrick, Dodge, Köhler, Troland, and many others.

[23] Cf. H. L. Hollingworth, *Psychology of the Functional Neuroses*, 1920.

chology of the hormic order. It agrees with the former in emphasizing the *acquisition* of motives, in avoiding an a priori and unchanging
set of original urges, and in recognizing (as limited principles) the
operation of the circular response and cross-conditioning. It agrees
with the hormic psychologist, however, in finding that striving-from-
within is a far more essential characteristic of motive than stimulation-
from-without. It agrees likewise in distrusting the emphasis upon
stomach contractions and other "excess and deficit stimuli" as
"causes" of mature behavior. Such segmental sources of energy even
though conditioned cannot possibly account for the "go" of conduct.
But functional autonomy does not rely as does hormic theory upon
modified instinct, which after all is as archaic a principle as the conditioning of autonomic segmental tensions, but upon the capacity of
human beings to replenish their energy through a plurality of constantly changing systems of dynamic dispositions.

The hormic psychologist, however, will not accept the autonomy
of new motivational systems. If mechanisms can turn into drives, he
asks, why is it that habits and skills as they become exercised to the
point of perfection do not acquire an ever increasing driving force? [24]
The mechanisms of walking, speaking, or dressing, cannot be said
to furnish their own motive-power. One walks, speaks, or dresses in
order to satisfy a motive entirely external to these learned skills.[25]
The criticism is sufficiently cogent to call into question Woodworth's
form of stating the principle, *viz.,* "Mechanisms may become drives."
It is not an adequate statement of the case.

Looking at the issue more closely it seems to be neither the perfected talent nor the automatic habit that has driving power, but the
imperfect talent and the habit-in-the-making. The child who is *just
learning* to speak, to walk, or to dress, is, in fact, likely to engage in
these activities for their own sake, precisely as does the adult who
has an *unfinished* task in hand. He remembers it, returns to it, and
suffers a feeling of frustration if he is prevented from engaging in it.
Motives are always a kind of striving for some form of completion;
they are unresolved tension, and demand a "closure" to activity under
way. (Latent motives are dispositions that are easily thrown by a
stimulus or by a train of associations into this state of active tension.)

[24] W. McDougall, *Mind*, 1920, N. S., 29, 277-293.

[25] Though this objection is usually valid, it is not always so, for there are cases
where the liking for walks, for talking for the sake of talking, or for dressing, playing games, etc., seem to be self-sustaining motivational systems.

The active motive subsides when its goal is reached, or in the case of a motor skill, when it has become at last automatic. The novice in automobile driving has an unquestionable impulse to master the skill. Once acquired the ability sinks to the level of an *instrumental* disposition and is aroused only in the service of some other *driving* (unfulfilled) motive.

Now, in the case of the permanent interests of personality, the situation is the same. A man whose motive is to acquire learning, or to perfect his craft, can never be satisfied that he has reached the end of his quest, for his problems are never completely solved, his skill is never perfect. Lasting interests are recurrent sources of discontent, and from their incompleteness they derive their forward impetus. Art, science, religion, love, are never perfected. But motor skills are often perfected, and beyond that stage they seldom provide their own motive power. Only skills in the process of perfecting (mechanisms-on-the-make) serve as drives. With this emendation, Woodworth's view is corrected, and McDougall's objection is met.[26]

If the dynamic psychologist finds in such a pluralistic system a displeasing lack of unity, he may, without damage to the principle of autonomy, fall back upon the elemental horme. All motives—diverse as they are—*may* be regarded as so many channels of the original Will-to-Live. (Such a monistic under-pinning to a theory of motivation is preferable to a list of arbitrarily distinguished propensities or instincts.) But, as was previously pointed out (p. 109), the Will-to-Live, however acceptable it may be in the underlying metaphysics of personality, does not itself aid in the task of psychological analysis.

Only such a principle as that under discussion can provide a flexible enough account of the plurality of motives and their countless expressions in human life. Its specific advantages stand out in the following summary:

1. It clears the way for a completely dynamic psychology of *traits*, *attitudes*, *interests*, and *sentiments*, which can now be regarded as the ultimate and true dispositions of the mature personality.

2. It avoids the absurdity of regarding the energy of life now, in the *present*, as somehow consisting of early archaic forms (instincts, prepotent reflexes, or the never-changing Id). Learning brings new

---

[26] This theory embraces very easily the work of K. Lewin and his associates upon the nature of "quasi-needs." The urgency of these needs is greatest just before a goal is reached, after which time the motive subsides completely.

systems of interests into existence just as it does new abilities and skills. At each stage of development these interests are always contemporary; whatever drives, drives *now*.

3. It dethrones the stimulus. A motive is no longer regarded as a mechanical reflex or as a matter of redintegration, depending entirely upon the capricious operation of a conditioned stimulus. In a very real sense dispositions select the stimuli to which they respond, even though *some* stimulus is required for their arousal.

4. It readily admits the validity of all other established principles of growth. Functional autonomy *utilizes* the products of differentiation, integration, maturation, exercise, imitation, suggestion, conditioning, trauma, and all other processes of development; and allows, as they do not, considered by themselves, for their *structuration* into significant motivational patterns.

5. It places in proper perspective the problems of the origin of conduct by removing the fetish of the genetic method. Not that the historical view of behavior is unimportant for a complete understanding of personality, but so far as *motives* are concerned the cross-sectional dynamic analysis is more significant. Motives being always contemporary should be studied in their present structure. Failure to do so is probably the chief reason why psychoanalysis meets so many defeats, as do all other therapeutic schemes relying too exclusively upon uncovering the motives of early childhood.

6. It accounts for the force of delusions, shell shock, phobias, and all manner of compulsive and maladaptive behavior. One would expect such unrealistic modes of adjustment to be given up as soon as they are shown to be poor ways of confronting the environment. Insight and the law of effect should both remove them. But too often they have acquired a strangle hold in their own right.

7. At last we can account adequately for socialized and civilized behavior. The principle supplies the correction necessary to the faulty logic of *bellum omnium contra omnes*. Starting life as a completely selfish being, the child would indeed remain entirely wolfish and piggish throughout his days unless genuine transformations of motives took place. Motives being completely alterable, the dogma of Egoism turns out to be a callow and superficial philosophy of behavior, or else a useless redundancy.

8. It explains likewise why a person often *becomes* what at first he merely *pretends* to be—the smiling professional hostess who grows fond of her once irksome role and is unhappy when deprived of it;

the man who for so long has counterfeited the appearance of self-confidence and optimism that he is always driven to assume it; the prisoner who comes to love his shackles. Such *personae*, as Jung observes, are often transformed into the real self. The mask becomes the *anima*.[27]

9. The drive behind genius is explained. Gifted people demand the exercise of their talents, even when no other reward lies ahead. In lesser degree the various hobbies, the artistic, or the intellectual interests of any person show the same significant autonomy.

10. In brief, the principle of functional autonomy is a declaration of independence for the psychology of personality. Though in itself a general law, at the same time it helps to account, not for the abstract motivation of an impersonal and purely hypothetical mind-in-general as do other dynamic principles, but for the concrete, viable motives of any one mind-in-particular.

SUDDEN REORIENTATION: TRAUMA

A special instance of functional autonomy is the effect of abrupt shocks on the developing personality. Ordinarily the process of growth is gradual; it is like the slow reaching of tentacles in many directions, some of the movements being halted when they are found maladaptive, and others continued in directions found to make for successful survival. All of the processes of growth thus far described—with the possible exception of maturation—manifest themselves *as a rule* by this gradual operation. Yet, sometimes, this operation is abruptly altered. An entirely new direction is given to the person's aims, outlooks, and style of life. Growth at this moment ceases to be gradual and becomes, for the time being, saltatory.[28]

[27] C. J. Jung, *Psychological Types*, 1924, p. 593.

[28] One hundred years ago Charles Fourier, the self-styled "super-omnigyne" whose novel theories of personality were described in Chapter III, offered the following rhythmic scheme for representing the alternating phases of gradual and saltatory development. Over-simplified though it is, the list has some suggestive value.

Ascending {
    initial crisis—birth
    1st phase of growth—childhood
    ascending crisis—puberty
    2nd phase of growth—adolescence
}

Descending {
    climax of life—virility
    3rd phase of movement—maturity
    descending crisis—sterility
    4th phase of movement—decline
    final crisis—death
}

No one can tell what catastrophic events an individual will encounter in the course of his life, or what their impression will be
upon him. Some life-histories seem pivoted upon one decisive event,
the vision of St. Paul, for example, the illness of St. Francis, the
Italian Journey of Goethe, or Nietzsche's infection by a prostitute.
Yet similar experiences in the lives of others have no such radical
effects. It is small wonder that William James wrote: "However
closely psychical changes may conform to law, it is safe to say that
individual histories and biographies will never be written in advance
no matter how 'evolved' psychology may become." [29]

In each of the periods of life (cf. p. 131) there fall certain characteristic emergencies that the individual must meet in his struggles for
adjustment. Though these emergencies do not always result in
psychic traumas, they do sometimes serve to halt abruptly one course
of development and to start a distinctly new pattern of habits and
traits.

In infancy, there is first of all the possibility of a birth-trauma,
though in view of the immature condition of the nervous system at
the commencement of life it is difficult to see how one can attach as
much weight to this possibility as certain psychoanalysts do.[30] Be
that as it may, there are undeniably other traumas in infancy that
may leave permanent effects on personality—accidents, for example,
or illnesses (e.g., Jacksonian epilepsy or encephalitis). At any time in
life, for that matter, the traumatic effects of accident and illness may
alter the preceding direction of development and substitute an altogether different one to accord with the changed physical condition.

The pre-school child does not as a rule encounter crises outside
the home-circle, but within the home many critical experiences
may occur to redirect the whole course of development: the arrival
of a new baby with the consequent feelings of jealousy, early experiences of shame, of bereavement, or perhaps adoption into a foster-
family.

When at about the age of six the child leaves the shelter of his
home for the harder environment of the school and playground, experiences of failure, ostracism, and ridicule await him, and these may
provoke quite suddenly new forms of adjustment or else accentuate
previously insignificant traits. The sensitive child may grow definitely
morbid. Inferiority complexes may be created over night, affecting

[29] Principles of Psychology, 1890, II, 576 ftn.
[30] Cf. O. Rank, The Trauma of Birth, trans. 1929.

profoundly the subsequent course of life. In the development of most boys there is a critical "sissy hurdle" that must be met. Perhaps a fist-fight, a foot race, a "grown-up" haircut, or some act of daring does the trick. If so a "normal boy's" life lies ahead for him. But perhaps the hurdle is not successfully passed, and as a result the plan of life is radically altered; new compensations and new ideals develop.

Soon come the demands of the gang, relations to the opposite sex, religious interests. Experiences of success and failure, of remorse and guilt, of conversion, or puppy love, may be of supreme importance. Also in adolescence comes the frequently traumatic experience of leaving home, of being "psychologically weaned" from the parents. There are also new worlds to conquer, college examinations to be met, a living to be earned, where traumatic experiences of success or failure can occur.[31]

In adult years shocks due to business failure, to illness, to religious conversion,[32] to the death of loved persons, to the "descending crisis," all may make swift and profound alterations. Yet, as a rule, personality after the age of thirty is much less subject to sudden upheavals than prior to that age. Critical and abrupt changes are never so numerous as in adolescence.

Biography is full of illustrations, some of the most interesting of which concern the sudden intrusion of an *idea* into a preceding stagnant condition of thought. Gibbon dates the first occurrence of his ambition to write of the decline and fall of the Roman Empire as the evening of the 15th of October, 1764, as he sat musing among the ruins of the Capitol.[33] Alice James describes the lasting importance of an idea, conveyed to her by her literary brother when she was only eight.

[31] The crises of adolescence are interestingly dealt with by L. S. Hollingworth, *The Psychology of the Adolescent*, 1928. But in combating the "widespread myth that every child is a changeling, who at puberty comes forth as a different personality," the author seems to risk the opposite error of underestimating the frequency with which radical alterations of personality do occur in the period of *Sturm und Drang.*

[32] Conversions, though much more numerous in adolescence, as a rule leave a more marked impress upon personality if they come later in life. A well known example is the case of Count Tolstoy. A profound religious experience at the age of fifty resulted in a radical shift of his whole plan of life and was responsible for the development of the new and firmly knit master-motive described by Chesterton (pp. 190 f.).

[33] G. B. Hill (editor), *The Memoirs of the Life of Edward Gibbon*, 1900, p. 167.

I remember so distinctly the first time I was conscious of a purely intellectual process. . . . We were turned into the garden to play. . . . Harry suddenly exclaimed: "This might certainly be called pleasure under difficulties!" The stir of my whole being in response to the exquisite, original form of his remark almost makes my heart beat now with the sisterly pride which was then awakened, and it came to me in a flash—the higher nature of this appeal to the mind, as compared to the rudimentary solicitations which usually produced my childish explosions of laughter, and I can also feel distinctly the sense of self-satisfaction in that I could not only perceive but appreciate this subtlety, as if I had acquired a new sense, a sense whereby to measure intellectual things, wit as distinguished from giggling, for example.[34]

Sometimes casual remarks made by other people, especially people toward whom because of prestige one is suggestible, have lasting influence. A certain freshman in college, coming from an uncultured home with exclusively economic aspirations, had a marked supercilious attitude toward all intellectual activities. Badly adjusted to college, with poor habits of study, and as nearly illiterate as a college youth can be, he had special difficulties with his course in English composition. One day when his weary instructor was giving him a periodic berating, the boy countered with one of his customary defenses, "I don't like English, and I never did like it, and never shall." The instructor, bored but still didactic, remarked, "It isn't English I'm talking about at the moment, it's your life." The effect was wholly unpredictable. The thrust struck home. The lad not only reformed his precarious ways, but became devoted to the subject, obtained a high grade, made Phi Beta Kappa, and eventually became a teacher of English!

An older woman traces her life-long devotion to poetry largely to an episode in her Virgil class in high school. She was performing a routine translation, difficult and dreary. The teacher trying for the thousandth time to give significance to the monotonous task, asked how the passage would be expressed in the Bible. Happily the girl caught the allusion, and spontaneously revised her translation, "Incline thine ear unto my supplication." Her artistic success on this occasion was a traumatic experience, a dawn of poetic beauty, to which she was ever after devoted.

These "chambers of maiden thought," as Keats has called them,

[34] *Alice James, Her Brothers—Her Journal*, Dodd, Mead, 1934, p. 166.

are usually entered—if they are entered at all—as the personality approaches maturity. The experience may be due to books read, or to
sermons and lectures heard, to the influence of friends, parents, or
teachers; it may lead further into the chambers of abstract thought
and scientific research. It is, of course, not always traumatic in nature,
but may be a gradual growth, or turn out to be merely abortive.
However entered, if it is entered at all, the world of ideas is a factor
that shapes the more complex reaches of personality, and not infrequently it is the most important factor of all.

Quick turns do then occur in personality and permanently hold
the stage; the next step is to explain them. Probably the answer must
be given in terms of the adaptive process.[35] A crisis is brought about
by an exceedingly intense emotional stimulus. Why it is intense for
the particular individual depends almost wholly upon the present condition of susceptibility of that individual (a confluence of his own
temperament and previous relevant experiences). The crisis throws
into new relief the factors in a situation that was already, perhaps
unconsciously, of some importance to him. But though the shift
occurs upon some pre-existent familiar ground the old familiar pre-
formed habits and traits no longer meet the need. The crisis imperi-
ously demands new and more concordant systems. It is so urgent that
it cannot be set aside, and since it cannot be admitted into the older
setting, a new setting must be swiftly prepared. Sometimes as in the
case of a religious or moral conversion, the majority of the previous
habits and attitudes may have to be radically altered. As a result the
"new" personality seems utterly different from the old.

It is the nature of traumatic experiences that they are always
specific, that is to say, they can be dated and defined, but their
effects are always generalized, spreading into many, or sometimes all,

---

[35] One type of psychological writing, the *dialectical*, finds no difficulty whatever in accounting for the phenomenon of sudden reorientation. It holds that the
entire course of life is a matter of conflict, personality being constantly assailed by
tendencies to act and by negations of these tendencies, with its goal always the
synthesis of these conflicting impulses if possible. Sometimes the synthesis is gradual,
but it often comes as a sudden change. Especially when one of the conflicting factors is *suddenly* introduced it is normal to expect a *Katastrophenreaktion* (Künkel),
whereby a novel convergence of the old and the new takes place. Good examples
of the dialectical method applied to personality are found in F. Künkel, *Vitale
Dialektik*, 1929, K. N. Kornilov, "Psychology in the Light of Dialectical Material-
ism," in *Psychologies of 1930*, chap. xiii, W. Stern, *Allgemeine Psychologie auf personalistischer Grundlage*, 1935. Dialectic runs the danger of overestimating the prevalence of sudden, and underestimating the occurrence of gradual, change.

of the recesses of personality. The newly created interests are promptly charged with dynamic power, displacing older formations, and henceforth serving as functionally autonomous systems, guiding the further development of the personality until they in turn are gradually or suddenly transformed.

CHAPTER VIII

THE MATURE PERSONALITY

Nothing requires a rarer intellectual heroism than willing-
ness to see one's equation written out.

—*Santayana*

T HE distinctive richness and congruence of a fully mature personality are not easy to describe. There are as many ways of growing up
as there are individuals who grow, and in each case the end-product
is unique. But if general criteria are sought whereby to distinguish a
fully developed personality from one that is still unripe, there are
three differentiating characteristics that seem both universal and indispensable.

In the first place, the developed person is one who has a variety
of autonomous interests: that is, he can lose himself in work, in contemplation, in recreation, and in loyalty to others. He participates
with warmth and vigor in whatever pursuits have for him acquired
value. Egocentricity is not the mark of a mature personality. Contrast
the garrulous Bohemian, egotistical, self-pitying, and prating of self-
expression, with the man of confident dignity who has identified himself with a cause that has won his devotion. Paradoxically, "self-
expression" requires the capacity to lose oneself in the pursuit of objectives, *not* primarily referred to the self. Unless directed outward
toward socialized and culturally compatible ends, unless absorbed in
causes and goals that outshine self-seeking and vanity, any life seems
dwarfed and immature.

Whenever a definite objective orientation has been attained, pleas-
ures and pains of the moment, setbacks and defeats, and the impulse
for self-justification fade into the background, so that they do not
obscure the chosen goals. These goals represent an *extension of the
self* which may be said to be the first requirement for maturity in
personality.

The second requirement is a curiously subtle factor complementing the first. We may call it *self-objectification*, that peculiar detachment of the mature person when he surveys his own pretensions in relation to his abilities, his present objectives in relation to possible objectives for himself, his own equipment in comparison with the equipment of others, and his òpinion of himself in relation to the opinion others hold of him. This capacity for self-objectification is *insight*, and it is bound in subtle ways with the *sense of humor*, which as no one will deny, is, in one form or another, an almost invariable possession of a cultivated and mature personality.

Since there is an obvious antithesis between the capacity for losing oneself in vigorous participation and the capacity for standing off, contemplating oneself, perhaps with amusement, a third, integrative, factor is required in the mature personality, namely, *a unifying philosophy of life*. Such a philosophy is not necessarily articulate, at least not always articulate in words. The preacher, by virtue of his training, is usually more articulate than the busy country doctor, the poet more so than the engineer, but any of these personalities, if actually mature, participates and reflects, lives and laughs, according to some embracing philosophy of life developed to his own satisfaction and representing to himself his place in the scheme of things.

These are the three conditions for the optimum development of personality; each needs more detailed consideration. But before settling to this discussion it is necessary to examine the competence of psychology to deal with such complex mental conditions as are here involved.

When the academic psychologist attempts to account for such intricate formations as these he faces a dilemma. He himself lives and works primarily in professional circles, among persons trained to use their minds and abilities. It is too easy to assume that such men are representative of the majority of personalities, and to overlook those with gross limitations, occurring more frequently in an unselected population. He might easily romanticize the situation by compounding a representative personality on too high and subtle an emotional and mental level. He must not, in his interest in mature personalities, be unrealistic and forget the restrictions on the development of personality resulting from low intelligence, uncontrolled emotion, infantilism, regression, dissociation, stereotypes, autism, suggestibility, and many other entirely human, but none the less abortifacient conditions.

On the other hand, even though the number of completely mature personalities tested by these three criteria, may be few, it is still necessary to account *adequately* for such as do exist, and for the multitude of others well along on the road to maturity. This necessity leads us to the second horn of the dilemma, the one on which most psychologists, without realizing it, are already impaled.

They are impaled because they apply the (as yet) crude tools of psychology to material too delicate to be cut and shaped with their aid. For instance, methods and concepts well enough designed to explain the automatic reactions of decorticated cats or simple skin reflexes, are often superimposed upon the vast pattern of mature personality, and declared to overspread it exactly. The results are ridiculous, and are responsible for the view of so many educated people that psychology is a sappy science.

Even the psychologist who honestly desires not to underestimate the complexities of personality finds himself limited by the crudity of the tools within his professional store. As a result he puts the entire strain of investigation upon a few inadequate implements where it would be better to forge new ones.

That the available store of concepts and methods is actually insufficient can be demonstrated by a cursory review of the major limitations of the various branches of psychology concerned with personality. Here it is not a question of the validity of the concepts nor of their suitability for *special* problems, but rather of their *adequacy* in dealing with the subtle characteristics of genuinely mature personalities.

Physiological psychology manifestly fails to specify neural equivalents for complex personal functions, for such subtle processes, for example, as ambition, loyalty, self-criticism, or humor.

Behaviorism of the classical order provides at best a blue-print of non-related excursions and meaningless movements of a mindless organism. Its concepts are better adapted to segmental responses than to fully integrated patterns. Whether the newer "operational behaviorism" can improve the situation remains for it to demonstrate.

Structural psychology of the older introspective order, since it is not interested in conation, can account for no single *dynamic* event in the entire sphere of personality.

Functional psychology, like structural, is preoccupied with mind-in-general, and though it treats instincts, adaptation, the stream of thought, and other vital functions, it does not do so in a personalized, concrete way.

Gestalt psychology, for all its advantageous emphasis on wholeness, has as yet dealt chiefly with *momentary* patterns of conduct, and tends to neglect the problems of lasting structure.

Mathematical psychology, with the aid of highly trained and subtle minds, produces only a caricature of such minds by holding that they can all be reduced to a few basic and *common* factors, or can be regarded as measurable deviations from one standard pattern.

Differential psychology, likewise occupied with the distribution of single qualities in a population, cannot treat the patterning of these differences into individual dynamic formations.

Freudian psychology never regards an adult as truly adult.

Dynamic psychology often commits this error of Freudianism, and usually regards adult motives as variations upon one monotonous standard pattern.

Hormic psychology, promising though it is in its recognition of sentiments, is cramped by preoccupation with the uniform instincts presumed to underlie these sentiments.

Psychiatry and other practical arts of dealing with *whole* men come closer to adequacy, but as yet they are deficient in conceptual formulation, and do not advance the theoretical psychology of personality. Such formulations as they have are derived principally from the study of disease rather than health.

Personalistic psychology also puts its emphasis on totality, but as yet its theories are broad and philosophical, failing to provide specific implements for bringing the concrete complexities of single personalities under inspection (cf. Chapter XX).

Verstehende psychology is the only school of psychological thought that *flatters* human personality, finding it just as sublime as the ideal types produced in the minds of pre-Hitler German professors. It thereby weakens its own effectiveness; and commits in addition the fault of bifurcating psychology, refusing to utilize the results of any investigations other than its own (pp. 17, 231).

This uncomplimentary survey does not deny that each of these branches of psychology has its own distinctive merit in the study of personality, but it does deny that any one of them is at present fully equipped to handle the problems of maturity in personality as defined in this chapter. The psychology of personality cannot at present come to roost under any one of them. In time some may expand and show greater adequacy (promising signs exist especially in the last five and in *Gestalt* theory). But the required progress will come only if criticisms concerning *inadequacy* are taken to heart. In the meantime new trails must be blazed. A beginning may be made by returning now to further consideration of the three attributes of mature personality with which up to now psychology has so inadequately dealt.

EXTENSION OF THE SELF

The sense of self built up so laboriously in infancy (cf. pp. 158-165), sharpened and strengthened especially during the period of negativism, must not be regarded as fully formed in the first three, nor in the first ten years. It continues to expand with experience, with emotional involvements, frustrations, discriminative adjustments, and insight. Owing to the special psychic isolation typical of adolescence the sense of self at that time is exceedingly poignant. But neither does development stop here. The introversion of the self at this period of life merely prepares for further expansion later on.

Take that most celebrated of all periods in life, the time of falling in love, when both the organization and the sense of self are extended. Falling in love condenses into one sharply personalized sentiment all sorts of previously unrelated dispositions: specific sexual tonicity, assertive and submissive tendencies, habits, ambitions, esthetic interests, family sentiment, and often too religious interest and emotion. Most important is the fact that this intimate surge involves some *other* person. What is of interest to another becomes vital to oneself. Hitherto self-sufficient, the lover finds himself no longer so. The welfare of another is more important than his own. In this way the self is extended.

And still the process goes on. Possessions, friends, one's own children, other children, cultural interests, abstract ideas, politics, hobbies, recreation, and most conspicuously of all, one's *work*, all lead to the incorporation of interests once remote from the self into selfhood proper. What one loves becomes a part of him. And anything one can admire, feel sympathy for, appreciate, revere, deliberately imitate, or become unconsciously identified with, may become *introcepted* into the personality, and remain ever after a vital part of it.[1]

[1] The term *introception*, originated by W. Stern, stands for the adoption by an individual of cultural standards (conventions, morals, ideals) into his own personal system of motives and desires, or the incorporation of the interests and values of other human beings into his own life. The socialized person introcepts the standards of his group, the devout churchman introcepts the teachings of his faith. What was at first outer and perhaps alien becomes inner and dynamic. (Cf. *Allgemeine Psychologie*, 1935, p. 102.)

The concept of introception is not strictly speaking a psychological concept, but ethical, signifying the transformation of *heterotelesis* into *autotelesis*. The *psy-*

Introspectively the self is extended and widened; objectively a personality is evolved and matured.

In the conversation of a truly mature personality his discourse does not seem to spring from biologically bound dispositions as much as from his acquired autonomous interests. It has been said cryptically that the sign of cultivation in a man is his ability to talk for half a day without betraying his occupation. Such demonstration of an extended range of interests is not necessarily the pose of superior breeding; if it be sham, as McDougall has pointed out, it is easy to detect; a solidly constructed system of sentiments, even to an untrained observer, has a very different appearance from the mask of a poseur.

Now Freud, as might be expected, gives a very different interpretation of the maturer interests of men: "The Super-ego answers in every way to what is expected of the higher nature of man." Let us grant that a person is not mature unless he gives due respect to the codes of the society wherein he lives, acts with good taste and abides by the law, suffering pangs of conscience when he violates the rights of others and when remiss in his prescribed duties. But is this activity of the Super-ego all there is to the "higher nature" of a man? Not at all, for left to itself the Super-ego would produce a personality completely caked with custom and shackled by tribal mores. Conventionality is not the same as maturity.

The genuinely mature person has an Ego-ideal as well as a Super-ego. The former sets a goal that leads to a creative pattern of life, whereas the latter alone leads to static and stupid conventionality. It is a complete give-away of Freudian ideology that these two concepts are often considered synonymous. In psychoanalytic theory the poor Ego has no recourse but to surrender to one of its two tyrants, the Super-ego or the Id, or to compromise with both as best it may. The Ego-ideal, on the contrary, is the plan that the developed personality is able to evolve for defeating, by transcending, both the unsocialized urges of the Id and the dullness of the Super-ego, leading thereby to a new level of personal freedom and to maturity.

Intelligent and perspicacious *planning* for the future is always a significant feature of any mature life. The individual imagines things as they might be, even picturing his own personality as he would

chological counterparts of introception are many, including imitation and all other forms of learning, traumatic effects, suggestion, identification, imagination, and above all (since introcepted values become motives) *functional autonomy*.

like it. This planning for the future determines the subsequent development of personality quite as effectively as do the forces of the past. It is not only the *vires a tergo* that create a style of life, but also the plans, ambitions, ideals, and images that mediate goals projected into the *future*. Every mature personality may be said to travel toward a port of destination, selected in advance, or to several related ports in succession, the Ego-ideal always serving to hold the course in view. That which lies ahead in one's life is at every moment dynamically taking shape, not merely by virtue of the push of this habit and that stimulus, but because the course of development is being steered in a certain direction by the Ego-ideal itself.

The importance of this concept of *directionality* in mature personalities is clearly brought out by the investigations of Dr. C. Bühler and her associates.[2] In their study of approximately two hundred life-histories, the most definite conclusion was that each life seemed definitely ordered and steered toward some selected goal; each person had something quite special to live for. Each had a characteristic *Bestimmung* and *intention*. The style, of course, varied; some staked everything upon one single great objective; others varied their goals from time to time, but goals there always were. A supplementary study of would-be suicides showed that life becomes intolerable to those who can find nothing to aim at, no goal to seek.

In childhood the objectives are at first lacking altogether; in adolescence they are vaguely defined; early maturity brings definiteness of plan; and the remainder of the active years of life are spent in the pursuit. The *Bestimmung* is not, of course, unceasingly effective. Sometimes it weakens, and often it is defeated by uncontrollable factors. Lives plagued by bad luck may be forced to alter their objectives and to take a more modest goal (to lower their levels of aspiration). Sometimes, on the other hand, there is grim persevering in the face of insuperable obstacles, a decision to continue in the selected road, *quand même*. Some defeated personalities seem bound to life merely "by indignation," but even this emotional focus serves as a goal for combat.

It is perhaps a defect in Bühler's study that she deals so exclusively with geniuses who of necessity are distinguished for their *Bestimmung*. They could not have made their marks upon the world unless

---

[2] C. Bühler, *Der menschliche Lebenslauf als psychologisches Problem*, 1933; also E. Frenkel, "Studies in Biographical Psychology," *Char. & Pers.*, 1936, 5, 1-34. Additional details concerning these studies are given in Chapter XIV.

they were endowed with unusual purposes, persistence, and vigor. But in the more ordinary lives of average people the principle may be found to operate in only slightly less degree. Unassuming lives revolve around unassuming foci of interest—a comfortable home, a routine vocation, perhaps the pursuit of health or of a health-cult. In such cases the degree of maturity may not be as marked as in the genius, but without some sustained goals somewhere, a personality remains childish.

SELF-OBJECTIFICATION: INSIGHT AND HUMOR

To live without self-deception has been the ideal of many. When Phaedrus, walking with Socrates, asked some question concerning a local legend, Socrates replied, "Now, I have no leisure for such enquiries. Shall I tell you why? I must first know myself, as the Delphian inscription says; to be curious about that which is not my concern, while I am still in ignorance of my own self, would be ridiculous." [3]

Knowledge of oneself is called *insight*. The term is an extension of the psychiatric usage according to which a mental patient who knows that *he* (and not everybody else) is suffering from disorientation and aberration, is credited with insight. Also in the domain of normal personality insight means freedom from self-deception. [4] It is the trait that Lord Chesterfield claimed for himself when he wrote to his son, "I know myself (no common piece of knowledge, let me tell you). I know what I can, what I cannot, and consequently, what I ought to do."

When he wrote these self-confident lines Chesterfield probably did not realize that most human beings feel equally sure of *their* superiority in this same "uncommon" piece of knowledge. Others may lack insight, but not *I!* In one study 96 per cent of the students in various courses in psychology thought that they possessed average or better than average insight, only 4 per cent admitting possible deficiency. Unlike Socrates they were not willing to profess ignorance of themselves. One feels that living with oneself naturally results in a thorough acquaintance. But such familiarity may also work in the opposite way, by hardening one to his defects of memory and intelli-

---

[3] Plato, *Phaedrus*, 229.

[4] This usage is not to be confused with two quite different psychological meanings of the term, *viz.*, sudden learning ("learning by insight"), and clear comprehension ("he has good insight into human nature").

gence, to his defenses and rationalizations, and to his own impulsive justifications of his deeds.

Some people, to be sure, seem to make a point, even a virtue, of admitting their defects, perhaps writing their Confessions "objectively" for the world to read. But the chances are that they guard some secret tabernacles against prying eyes, even their own. Perhaps it is nothing of major importance that is withheld, only an incident of meanness or shame; but it would be too humiliating to disclose, or even to face.[5]

The *value* of insight seems never to be questioned. No writer makes out any case for self-deception. Not infrequently insight is exalted to the highest place among the virtues, or therapeutically is regarded as a panacea for all mental ills. Now, admitting that insight is a *prerequisite* for almost any intelligent change in oneself, it still does not follow that self-knowledge is synonymous with virtue, as Socrates would have us believe. The transformation of personality does not take place *automatically*. What insight does is to make past mistakes intelligible so that one is not condemned through ignorance to repeat them. Furthermore insight removes needless worries by showing their groundlessness (unless through functional autonomy they have become firmly set). But for any basic change, insight must be supplemented by a new orientation, a vigorous plan for the future, a new and effective motivation.

How is the psychologist to tell whether or not an individual has insight? According to an old adage, "Everyman has three characters:

(1) that which he has,
(2) that which he thinks he has,
(3) that which others think he has."

Ideally, insight is to be measured by the ratio between the second item and the first, for what a man thinks he is in relation to what he really is provides a perfect definition and therefore an admirable index of his insight. Practically, however, proof positive of what a man *is* in the biophysical sense is difficult to obtain; ultimately, therefore, the most practicable index of a man's insight becomes the ratio between the second and the third items, the relation of what a man thinks he is to what others (especially the psychologist) think he is.

[5] An interesting discussion of the shortcomings of Confessions and other self-revelations as psychological documents is given by Stefan Zweig, *Adepts in Self-Portraiture*, 1928, pp. xvi-xviii.

If the man objects that all the world, including the psychologist, is *wrong* about him, he cannot of course be disproved, but in such a case the evaluation of his insight becomes virtually impossible.

Psychologists know that there are certain correlates of insight, qualities that people of good insight possess. For example, those who are aware of their own objectionable qualities are much less likely to attribute them to other people, that is, they are less given to projection than are those who lack insight.[6] Also, people of good insight are known to be more intelligent than the average.[7]

But the most striking correlate of insight is the *sense of humor*. In one study where a number of subjects rated one another on a large number of traits, the correlation between ratings on insight and humor turned out to be $+.88$, the highest in the whole series. Such a high coefficient means either that personalities with marked insight are also distinguished for their humor, or else that the raters were not able to distinguish between these two qualities. In either case the result is important. Again one thinks of Socrates, and recalls the legendary association of these two qualities in his personality. It has been told how at a performance of Aristophanes' *Clouds* he stood up in order that the amused audience might better compare his face with the mask that was intended to ridicule him. Having objectified himself, he was able to view the caricature of his comic physique as an esthetic and detached event, and to aid the jest by laughing at himself.

The sense of humor must be distinguished sharply from the cruder sense of the comic. The latter is a common possession of almost all people, children as well as adults. What is ordinarily considered funny—on the stage, in comic strips, on the radio, or in ordinary life—consists usually of absurdities, horse play or puns. The laughter provoked in these cases has a very different explanation from amusement due to subtleties of true humor. For the most part the comic consists in the degradation of some imagined opponent, as Aristotle, Hobbes, and many others have pointed out. Or it consists of the abrupt and sly release of some suppression, as in the case of risqué stories. There may be other thematic elements (fear, aggression, hate), which cause laughter when people are permitted by the joke to vent some troublesome and semi-conscious tension.[8] Then there is

---

[6] Cf. R. R. Sears, *J. Soc. Psychol.*, 1936, 7, 151-163.

[7] P. E. Vernon, *J. Soc. Psychol.*, 1933, 4, 42-57.

[8] Cf. H. A. Wolff, C. E. Smith, and H. A. Murray, *J. Abnorm. & Soc. Psychol.*, 1934, 28, 341-365.

the laughter of good spirits, easily provoked in children or in adults at play. But none of these forms of fun correspond to the humor we are speaking of. They are not related to insight.

True humor has been defined by the novelist Meredith as the ability to laugh at the things one loves (including of course oneself and all that pertains to oneself), and still to love them. The real humorist perceives behind some solemn event, himself for instance, the contrast between pretension and performance. That which he values becomes, for the time being, vain show. There is a sudden shift of emphasis; for the moment all the world's a stage where nothing really matters, and where the actors, including oneself, can be viewed with the detachment of Olympus.

Humor of this type seems to have a development entirely parallel to that of insight. A young child lacks both. He cannot see himself as others see him, and his mirth is seldom directed toward himself. He laughs readily enough, but usually at the minor misfortunes of others. At this stage the degradation theory of laughter clearly applies. In adolescence, insight is but rarely attained, not because the youth is as unmindful of himself as is the young child, but for the opposite reason, in his intense seriousness he lacks perspective. There are feelings of acute self-consciousness and of inferiority, largely because a sense of proportion has not developed. His failures and eccentricities do not amuse him; he is much more likely to weep about them than to laugh. In some adolescents, to be sure, this condition of storm and stress is much less marked than in others.

Typically then, childhood is marked by freedom from self-examination, an implicit "I don't care." In adolescence, when personal values first become deep and significant, there is a profound "I do care" attitude. But in maturity, a sensitive and intricate balance is attained, peculiar to each life, between caring and not caring, between valuing and recognizing the vanity of value. Only at this mature stage can the individual both pursue his course diligently and at the same time apply the advice of Mark Twain's *Mysterious Stranger:*

> Your race in all its poverty has unquestionably one really effective weapon—laughter. Power, money, persuasion, supplication, persecution—these can lift a colossal humbug—push it a little—weaken it a little century by century; but only laughter can blow it to rags and

atoms at a blast. Against the assault of laughter nothing can stand.
You are always fussing and fighting with your other weapons. Do
you ever use that one? No, you leave it lying rusting.

To achieve a sense of humor as well as insight requires a high
level of intelligence. It is only the most intelligent who prefer their
humor objective and realistic, based on the exact relationships obtaining in their lives. People less intelligent prefer humor derived from
their own repressions and reflecting marked thematic elements.[9] Insight does away, in large part at least, with the dynamic power of
these thematic elements. If one knows one's inferiorities, jealousies
and unsocial desires, one is less likely to take pleasure in their autistic
triumph through a mere joke. It requires intelligence to see oneself
in perspective, and like Socrates to be amused at one's own pomposity
and pretensions.

The reason why the attainment of insight and of humor march
hand in hand is probably because they are at bottom psychologically
a single phenomenon—the phenomenon of *self-objectification*. The
man who has the most complete sense of proportion concerning his
own qualities is able to perceive their incongruities and absurdities
in other than their customary frames of reference. Yet perspective
does not mean superciliousness. Values have their place, even though
they be viewed at times in strange and incongruous settings where
their pretensions and incongruities are disclosed.

As with insight, almost everyone claims a sense of humor as his
special and peculiar possession. The same students who were asked
to evaluate their own insight in comparison with that of other people
(cf. p. 220) were also asked to estimate their sense of humor. Ninety-
four per cent replied that it was as good or better than the average!
Stephen Leacock has observed the same conceit, reporting it in *My
Discovery of England:*

> A peculiar interest always attaches to humor. There is no quality of
> the human mind about which its possessor is more sensitive than the
> sense of humor. A man will freely confess that he has no ear for
> music, or no taste for fiction, or even no interest in religion. But I
> have yet to see the man who announces that he has no sense of humor
> In point of fact, every man is apt to think himself possessed of an ex-
> ceptional gift in this direction. . . .

[9] Cf. C. Landis and W. H. Ross. *I. Soc. Psychol.*, 1933, 4, 156-175.

But, after all, it is perfectly natural for each of us to think himself superior in both insight and in humor. One cannot readily admit in himself deficiencies that he cannot observe, nor can he readily concede that an event is beyond his sense of humor if he can see nothing funny in it. If he could, he would already have insight and, no doubt, be amused by the whole situation!

THE UNIFYING PHILOSOPHY OF LIFE

Humor in one respect, but in one respect only, is like religion. By setting a frame of reference that is at variance with the ordinary mundane frame of reference, both have the peculiar ability of precipitating the ordinary worries and mischances of life into new and sane patterns. Humor, like religion, shatters the rigidity of literal-mindedness. To view one's problems humorously is to see them as trivial and of no consequence; to view them religiously is to see them in relation to a divine scheme that gives them changed meaning. In humor things are not at all earnest or purposive, but pompous and out of step; in religion there is no such thing as incongruity. Thus setting up novel standards, both religion and humor, albeit in very different ways, bring perspective.

Since the events of life cannot possibly be regarded at any one time as of great moment and as trivial, it follows that a personality cannot be *at one time* both reverent and jesting. Yet at bottom the mature person may be profoundly religious and still have the capacity for humor. He may even joke and pray about the same disturbing events in his own life—though never at the same time. At bottom he is an absolutist, but a certain delicate balance of interests makes it possible for him also to be on occasion as fun-loving as any pluralist. Max Eastman depicts the situation:

> Mahomet boasted that with faith and prayer he could make a mountain get up and come to him. And when a great crowd of his followers had assembled, and all his incantations failed, he said: "Well, if the mountain will not come to Mahomet, Mahomet will go to the mountain." And so we strive with all our energy and ingenuity to make the course of things do us pleasure, and as the course of things continually disappoints us, we say: "Very well, I will find a special pleasure in the disappointment!" That is our sense of humor. Humor is Mahomet going to the mountain.[10]

[10] *The Sense of Humor*, Charles Scribner's Sons, 1922, p. 25 f.

And yet what keeps the religious person from becoming a cynic—as all thoroughgoing humorists must be—is the conviction that at bottom something is more important than laughter, namely, the fact that he, the laugher, as well as the laughter itself, has a place in the scheme of things according to the dispensations of a Divine Intelligence. When this most important of issues is decided, there is still plenty of room for jesting. In fact a case might be made for the potentially superior humor of the religious person who has settled once and for all what things are of ultimate value, sacred and untouchable, for then nothing else in the world need be taken seriously. He can readily concede that the bulk of worldly happenings are ludicrous, that men and women, including himself, are given to amusing vanities, actors on a stage set with human artifices. To him nothing in their coming and going is of consequence, *except* their ultimate salvation. Most things they do are merely laughable. Beyond the reach of humor lies one and only one serious purpose to which humor must give way whenever the two are in conflict.[11]

Religion is the search for a value underlying *all* things, and as such is the most comprehensive of all the possible philosophies of life. A deeply moving religious experience is not readily forgotten, but is likely to remain as a focus of thought and desire. Many lives have no such focus; for them religion is an indifferent matter, or else a purely formal and compartmental interest. But the authentically religious personality unites the tangible present with some comprehensive view of the world that makes this tangible present intelligible and acceptable to him. Psychotherapy recognizes this integrative function of religion in personality, soundness of mind being aided by the possession of a completely embracing theory of life.

Besides the religious, there are many other unifying philosophies. Though less embracing in their scope, they too serve as autonomous systems wherein every detail tends to corroborate every other detail under some fundamental conception of value. Take for instance the *esthetic* philosophy of life. The poet says of himself,

> For beauty have I striven,
> My blood flowed in my song.

[11] It is only the core and aim of a religious faith that are beyond the reach of humor. All human foibles related to the religious intention are possible sources of amusement, examples being the incongruities due to human failing in the act of worship. Plenty of amusing episodes occur in church. It is only the ultimate aim of the acts of worship that, for the religious person, lies beyond the scope of humor.

All else for him is ordered under this one value and derives importance from it. He does not mean that he always achieves beauty, that he does not at times produce ugliness, nor that he cannot laugh at himself and his failures. He does mean that neither incompetence, backsliding, nor mirth, are able to defeat permanently this one unifying idea. It is the dynamic idea, not his skill with its mortal failings, that unifies his life.

Such a view contrasts sharply with the genetic over-emphasis of other dynamic psychologies that regard motivation as sessile to the roots of the past. Take striving for poetic beauty. One psychoanalyst claims that far from being a self-sufficient interest, love of poetry is simply an expression of oral eroticism, "a chewing and sucking of beautiful words and lines." [12] Hence this poem is not a forthright and honest account of its author's philosophy. His true philosophy is hidden from him; it consists of nothing more than the desire to secure oral gratification by sucking. The same dispute is in process regarding the nature of religious interests. Freud declares himself "perfectly certain" that this particular class of "illusions" springs from infantilism of the mind.[13]

Which interpretation is correct? Are esthetic and religious philosophies of life due to a flatulent condition of the Id that "never changes"; or are they precisely the opposite, autonomous master-sentiments that give objective coherence and subjective meaning to all the activities of their possessors' lives? By now the reader is in a position to decide for himself.

By and large psychology has done little to give systematic setting to all these various dynamic formations that represent the apex of development in the mature personality. With time, no doubt, when the errors of excessive elementarism and geneticism are cleared away, and the principle of functional autonomy is substituted as a general guide, the situation will improve.

In the meantime the one school of psychological thought that has concerned itself exclusively with these phenomena, and actually succeeded in *flattering* human nature (a thing psychology seldom does) is the school of *Verstehendepsychologie* of Dilthey, Spranger, Jaspers, and other German authors.

The method of this school is strikingly original. It consists in the postulation of *ideal* types, representing ultimate and absolutely co-

[12] A. A. Brill, *Imago*, 1933, 19, 145-167.
[13] S. Freud, *New Introductory Lectures on Psychoanalysis*, 1933, p. 225.

herent patterns of value, unifying any personality capable of following one of them consistently. Though *Verstehendepsychologie* admits that no individual is perfectly self-consistent (the types representing merely "schemata of comprehensibility" to aid in understanding), still the effect of the method, since it portrays only ideal types, is one of flattery.

The various authors of this school each present different ideal types, the best known being the six of Spranger.[14] Two of these value-directions, the *religious* and the *esthetic*, have already been mentioned as common instances of unifying philosophies of life. The four others completing the list are the *theoretical*, the *economic*, the *social*, and the *political*. The list is purely a priori, but it provides one of the few available hypotheses for the empirical psychologist interested in the question of master-sentiments.[15] The following summary describes the six ideal types as Spranger sees them.[16]

1. *The Theoretical.* The dominant interest of the theoretical man is the discovery of *truth*. In the pursuit of this goal he characteristically takes a "cognitive" attitude, one that looks for identities and differences; one that divests itself of judgments regarding the beauty or utility of objects, and seeks only to observe and to reason. Since the interests of the theoretical man are empirical, critical, and rational, he is necessarily an intellectualist, frequently a scientist or philosopher.[17] His chief aim in life is to order and to systematize his knowledge.

2. *The Economic.* The economic man is characteristically interested in what is *useful*. Based originally upon the satisfaction of bodily needs (self-preservation), the interest in utilities develops to embrace the practical affairs of the business world—the production, marketing and consumption of goods, the elaboration of credit, and the accumulation of tangible wealth. This type is thoroughly "practical" and conforms well to the prevailing conception of the average American business man.

The economic attitude frequently comes into conflict with other values. The economic man wants education to be practical, and regards unapplied knowledge as waste. Great feats of engineering, sci-

---

[14] E. Spranger, *Types of Men*, trans. 1928.

[15] The empirical validity of these types is discussed in Chapter XV.

[16] E. Spranger, *op. cit.*, pp. 109-246, 37-106, 319-347. The condensed description given here is reprinted from P. E. Vernon and G. W. Allport, *J. Abnorm. & Soc. Psychol.*, 1931, 26, 231-248.

[17] It must not be thought that a high degree of talent or attainment is necessary to qualify a person for classification in this, or in any, type. Even the most undistinguished personalities are to be known not by their achievements but by their interests and intentions.

entific management, and "applied psychology" result from the demands which economic men make upon learning. The value of utility likewise conflicts with the esthetic value, excepting when art serves commercial ends. Without feeling inappropriateness in his act, the economic man may denude a beautiful hillside or befoul a river with industrial refuse. In his personal life he is likely to confuse luxury with beauty. In his relations with people he is more likely to be interested in surpassing them in wealth than in dominating them (political value) or in serving them (social value). In some cases the economic man may be said to make his religion the worship of Mammon. In other instances, however, he may have regard for the traditional God, but inclines to consider Him as the giver of good gifts, of wealth, prosperity, and other tangible blessings.

3. *The Esthetic.* The esthetic man sees his highest value in *form* and *harmony*. Each single experience is judged from the standpoint of grace, symmetry, or fitness. He regards life as a manifold of events; each single impression is enjoyed for its own sake. He need not be a creative artist; nor need he be effete; he is esthetic if he but finds his chief interest in the artistic episodes of life.

The esthetic value is in a sense diametrically opposed to the theoretical; the former is concerned with the diversity, and the latter with the identities of experience. The esthetic man chooses with Keats to consider truth as equivalent to beauty, or else to agree with Mencken, that "to make a thing charming is a million times more important than to make it true." In the economic sphere the esthete sees in the process of manufacturing, advertising, and trade, a wholesale destruction of the values most important to him. In social affairs he may be said to be interested in persons but not in the welfare of persons; he tends toward individualism and self-sufficiency. Esthetic people often like the beautiful insignia of pomp and power, but oppose political activity when it makes for a repression of individuality. In the field of religion they are likely to confuse beauty with purer religious experience.

4. *The Social.* The highest value for this type is *love* of people, whether of one or many, whether conjugal, filial, friendly, or philanthropic. The social man prizes other persons as ends, and is therefore himself kind, sympathetic, and unselfish. He is likely to find the theoretical, economic, and esthetic attitudes cold and inhuman. In contrast to the political type, the social man regards love as itself the only suitable form of power, or else repudiates the entire conception of power as endangering the integrity of personality. In its purest form the social interest is selfless and tends to approach very closely to the religious attitude.

5. *The Political.* The political man is interested primarily in *power.*

His activities are not necessarily within the narrow field of politics; but whatever his vocation, he betrays himself as a *Machtmensch*. Leaders in any field generally have high power value. Since competition and struggle play a large part in all life, many philosophers have seen power as the most universal and most fundamental of motives (cf. p. 169). There are, however, certain personalities in whom the desire for a *direct* expression of this motive is uppermost, who wish above all else for personal power, influence, and renown.[18]

6. *The Religious*. The highest value for the religious man may be called *unity*. He is mystical, and seeks to comprehend the cosmos as a whole, to relate himself to its embracing totality. Spranger defines the religious man as one "whose mental structure is permanently directed to the creation of the highest and absolutely satisfying value experience." Some men of this type are "immanent mystics," that is, they find in the affirmation of life and in active participation therein their religious experience. A Faust with his zest and enthusiasm sees something divine in every event. The "transcendental mystic," on the other hand, seeks to unite himself with a higher reality by withdrawing from life; he is the ascetic, and like the holy men of India, finds the experience of unity through self-denial and meditation.

One advantage of such portraits (even though they are too perfect in consistency to exist in real life) is the antidote they provide against excessive emphasis upon genetic factors and segmental analysis. Spranger's classification offers a *starting point* for empirical investigations of those complex philosophies of life that serve more than anything else to confer unity upon the mature personality.

There are several reasons why the guidance of this particular school of thought cannot be followed in every respect. In the first place, its preoccupation with the ideal exalts human nature too highly; the types are obviously exaggerations. For a better balance the whole doctrine must be translated into empirical terms. Since the various authors do not agree on the number or the nature of these types, they can be considered at best to represent only *some* characteristic philosophies of life. There are others that might be named, especially of the more earthy type. Hedonistic, sensual, and vital values are the

[18] The following telegram sent by Mussolini to the American ambassador on the occasion of Lindbergh's flight to France, shows the manner in which the routine acts of a person are influenced by his dominant values. Note the number of expressions indicative of Mussolini's interest in *power*: "Please accept the shouts of enthusiastic admiration which at this moment ring from the hearts of all the people of Italy exulting over the superb oceanic flight by Lindbergh. A superb human will took by assault space and subjugated it. Matter once more bowed to the mind and the wizard[ry] of men, to the glory of Lindbergh and his people."

foci of development in many personalities, *but* neglected by Spranger. Furthermore, these *Lebensformen* are at best only *categories* of value. There are many individual patterns possible within each, many kinds of social interests, for example, each producing a different course of development in personality. All typologies are too broad, and this is no exception. Individuality becomes lost in such coarse classification.

Finally, this school of the *Geisteswissenshaften* is irreconcilably antagonistic to the contributions of all other branches of psychology, refusing not only to admit their divergent theories, but also their corrective empiricism. Such aloofness is fatal. Though each branch of psychology considered by itself has limitations, their combined resources must be pieced together critically to give even an approximately adequate account of the development of personality.

Part III

THE STRUCTURE OF PERSONALITY

Part III

THE STRUCTURE OF PERSONALITY

CHAPTER IX

THE SEARCH FOR ELEMENT

THE progress of any science, it is said, depends in large part upon its ability to identify *elements* which, in the combination found in nature, constitute the phenomenon that the science has set out to examine. Without its table of elements, chemistry could not exist; without the discovery of the cell, biology would be little better off than primitive animism; physics, while it has discarded one set of elements after another, comes again in the quantum theory to another type of element.

The suspicion with which many natural scientists view psychology arises in part from their belief (entirely correct) that the elementary processes of mind have not yet been identified. Not that psychology has neglected the search for basic units with which to work. It has embraced hopefully many possibilities: faculties, ideas, instincts, reflexes, sensations, images, affects, factors, dimensions, and others—but the shifting of the lists, according to the predilections of the various investigators, has prevented a common meeting ground. Partly as a result of this failure to agree there has set in a reaction against the search for "mental atoms." The doctrine of the *whole* has won popularity. Yet the search for units has not in fact been abandoned. Only a shift of conception regarding the nature of the elements has occurred. Psychic atoms are denied, but psychic *structures* are affirmed, and these structures turn out to obey certain principles of organization, and to be composed in turn of substructures, discoverable through the process of orderly analysis. And so even in its modern configurational phase, psychology is engaged as ever in the same difficult search for unit structures. For without some guiding hypothesis concerning the most suitable level of analysis, only wavering and ambiguous results can be achieved.

The present chapter, first in a series devoted to this pivotal scientific problem, surveys the principal kinds of elements thus far proposed by psychologists as methods for "breaking down" personality into units suitable for purposes of comparison, measurement, and description.

PRACTICAL AND A PRIORI CLASSIFICATIONS

A psychologist or psychiatrist faced with the practical task of counseling or therapy sometimes devises a schedule of components of personality for his own guidance in dealing with his clients or patients. The result is a list of distinguishable aspects of personality that he considers fundamental. Since the counselor uses the same list for all personalities, he is committing himself to a *uniform* schedule of elements; to all cases he applies the same rubrics. But such classifications are usually nondescript, consisting in a *potpourri* of units without a thought as to what the essential nature of a unit may be. Convenience and practical utility are the only guides; there are no other principles underlying the selection. A few representative citations will illustrate this kind of classification.

The Eugenics Record Office has issued a *Trait-Book* containing a list of approximately 3,000 characteristics that might conceivably be hereditary according to the principle of unitary characteristics.[1] But the non-comparable nature of the items shows the lack of underlying psychological or genetic theory. What logic of elements could possibly apply to such a mixture as *albinism, eczema, love of fishing, aggressiveness, religiosity,* and *ingrowing toenails?*

Of a different order, but still nondescript in composition, are the numerous guides to self-study, or charts for aiding in the complete description of a personality.[2] One and all these schemes have a practical aim; they disclose aspects of personality that a more casual approach is not likely to discover. But they are so diverse, they overlap in so few points, and are so seldom supported by any theory of the relation of the chosen units to one another, that they contribute nothing to the search for a suitable logic of elements.

[1] Eugenics Records Office (N. Y.: Cold Spring Harbor), *The Trait-Book*, 1919.
[2] There are many such available guides, decidedly useful in the descriptive study of personality, but not consistent even with themselves in their conceptions of the nature of the structure of personality. G. S. Amsden, *A Guide to the Descriptive Study of the Personality*, 1924 (N. Y.: Bloomingdale Hospital Press); F. H. Allport, *Systematic Questionnaire for the Study of Personality*, 1925 (Chicago: Stoelting Co.); J. O. Chassell, *The Experience Variables Record*, 1928 (Rochester: Univ. of Rochester Medical School); F. L. Wells, "The Systematic Observation of Personality," *Psychol. Rev.*, 1914, 21, 295-332; W. Baade, O. Lipmann, W. Stern, "Fragment eines psychographischen Schemas," *Zsch. f. ang. Psychol.*, 1909, 3, 191-315; G. Heymans and E. Wiersma, "Beiträge zur speziellen Psychologie auf Grund einer Massenuntersuchung," *Zsch. f. Psychol.*, 1906, 42, 81-127, 253-301; 1919, 80, 76-89; A. Huth, *Exakte Persönlichkeitsforschung*, 1930; A. Lasurski, *Über das Studium der Individualität*, 1912.

At a higher level of complexity are certain schemes setting forth alleged major divisions of personality. Thus for McDougall, personality is constituted of five major components: *disposition, temperament, temper, character,* and *intellect.*[3] Since any one of these factors is assumed to vary independently of the others, a doctrine of five initial complex units results. A conception similar in principle but wholly different in the selection of components, is that of Klages who holds the major constituents of personality to be *sensation, motion, apprehension, will, contemplation,* and *expression.*[4] Each may be studied by itself, for each is fundamental. A similar level of analysis is offered by S. Beck in his conceptualization of the four factors in personality that may be studied with the aid of the Rorschach test: *form perception, organizing energy, affective drive,* and *creative activity.*[5] Taken together these factors are thought to constitute the whole of personality. The curious feature of these coarse analyses is that in each case the rubrics chosen are claimed to cover the entire personality. Yet there is between the schemes scarcely any overlap!

Boven makes a similar attempt. He distinguishes three broad divisions or *assises* of personality.[6] These are: *dispositions* (innate temperamental factors), *traits* (acquired emotional attitudes), and *linéaments* (acquired philosophical attitudes). The dichotomies implied in this sequence between what is native and what is acquired, between what is emotional and what is intellectual, make the scheme artificial from the start.

Such practical and a priori conceptions as these show that much of the search for elements in personality is a product of solitary thinking. Each writer dives into the recesses of his own mind and pulls up what for him is a useful scheme of analysis, but one unlike that of any other writer. The units chosen by any one author are nondescript enough, but when they are compared with the units chosen by other authors, the result is complete darkness and confusion.

UNIFORM (NOMOTHETIC) ELEMENTS

The justification of any scheme of analysis is always to be found in the purpose for which the analysis is made. A system of elements is "true" in so far as it fulfills the avowed intention of the analyst. The principal reason why psychologists do not agree with one another

[3] W. McDougall, *Energies of Men,* 1933, chap. xxiv.
[4] L. Klages, *The Science of Character,* trans. 1928.
[5] S. J. Beck, *Amer. J. Orthopsychiat.,* 1933, 3, 361-375.
[6] W. Boven, *La Science du Caractère,* 1931.

in their lists of elements is that each is animated by a slightly different intention. Until the purpose of an analysis and the psychologist's aim are clearly specified (as they seldom are) it is not possible to argue about the suitability of one set of elements or another. For certain purposes it is fitting to view mind as a congeries of ideas, for other purposes, as a network of neural arcs, or as a system of vectors, or as an hierarchy of sentiments. Mind is capable of being all things to all psychologists according to their personal lines of interest.

Yet where *personality* (mind-in-particular) is concerned the criteria involved in the selection of elements become narrowed. This is especially true if investigators subscribe to a limiting definition of personality. Suppose, for example, that they agree with this volume in considering personality as always distinctive and unique, as possessing strongly individualized motivational systems, and as representing an individual's style of adjustment and mastery within his behavioral environment. If the intention of the investigator is to depict with maximum fidelity the structure of personality as here defined, then certain classes of elements will be far more suitable than others. Let us consider some of the possibilities.

Faculties. The oldest theories of the composition of personality were all in terms of faculties. Well into the nineteenth century, the differences between men were ascribed to the varying strength of the "Powers of the Mind" (Attention, Will, Sagacity, and the like). The mere naming of these powers seemed to the early psychologists to render them somehow fixed and self-active.

It will be noted that any doctrine of faculties assumes the elements of personality to be the same as the elements of mind-in-general. The belief is that by combination these universal faculties will produce in action all possible expressions of personality. Even Gall who deliberately sought characterial faculties to replace the more intellectualistic faculties of his predecessors, kept this belief. Faculties for him were uniform for all men. They were also innate and independent of one another. So many indefensible assumptions are here involved that neither Gall's guidance nor that of any other faculty psychologist can be accepted (cf. pp. 81-85).

The Elements of General Psychology. When in the eighteenth century the French Sensationalists conceived the person to be the sum-total of his sensations, they were postulating the units of personality in terms of general psychology. Most psychologists today do precisely the same. For some, personality is a bundle of conditioned reflexes, for others the sum-total of a man's habits, or his pattern of images and feelings, or the configuration of some other dimensions or factors converging in one organism. According to his own habits of thought, each psychologist tends to think of individuals as combinations of whatever abstractions he happens to favor for psychological analysis.

This procedure, common as it is, is wholly unsuitable for the psychology of personality. For one thing such abstract units are not distinctively *personal*. Nor do they give any clue as to what kind of organization unites them into a concrete pattern of a single life.

Dynamic Elements of the Nomothetic Order. When the irrational force of "instinct" and impulse in mental activity became fully recognized, the elements of personality were sought in urges or desires. But though the complexion of the elements was thus altered, the principle remained the same. Personality was now considered to be the individual pattern of instincts and wishes, forces of the Id and Super-ego, or of desires and needs. All these doctrines hold in common the belief that men are formed in the same mold. There must be, so it is assumed, a finite number of stable forms of motivation, just as there is a finite number of chemical elements. These theories deny the possibility of an infinite number of goals toward which people strive, and an unlimited number of ways in which these goals are achieved.[7]

If it were not possible to approach still closer to the unique substructures of the individual personality, this class of theories would lead to the most progress. The nomothetic doctrine of *needs* as developed by Murray is especially promising.[8] This author maintains, entirely correctly, that "No therapeutist, or indeed, anyone who has to deal in a practical way with human beings, can get along without some notion of motivational force (instinct, need, drive, impulse, urge, inclination, wish, desire, or what not)." Of these alternatives he selects for emphasis the *need* which he regards as a directional force within the organism. When a need becomes active, a characteristic trend of behavior will usually ensue, even in the absence of the customary stimuli. Conversely, unless a need is present, responses to specific stimuli do not occur. Needs are recurrent, and whenever active produce a stress towards equilibrium. If suppressed they initiate the phenomena of displacement and fantasy described in Chapter VI.

[7] Cf. G. Murphy, *Amer. J. Orthopsychiat.*, 1932, 2, 315-334.
[8] H. A. Murray, *J. Psychol.*, 1936, 3, 27-42.

In some respects this doctrine is like the more familiar psychology of instincts, though it has the great advantage of being free from nativistic commitments.

> Since behavior is an important part of personality the science of personology cannot advance much further without a classification of the more important trends of behavior, or needs. In constructing such a classification, however, it is not necessary to limit oneself to needs which appear to be inherited. Which of the needs are innate, and to what extent, is another question—one for further observation and experiment.[9]

Murray enumerates several basic needs, in respect to which he believes all people may be profitably compared. The following are illustrative of his list:

Abasement	Dominance
Achievement	Exhibition
Acquisition	Recognition
Affiliation	Retention
Aggression	Seclusion
Autonomy	Sentience
Construction	Sex
Deference	Succorance

Such a provisional classification has considerable value. It is heuristic; it yields orderly hypotheses that can be examined one at a time. It centers research, and gives coherence to the interpretation of data. Though free from the rigidity of instinct-doctrines, the approach is dynamic and places suitable emphasis upon the goal-directedness of behavior. It leads to flexible and penetrating depictions of personality.[10]

However, certain criticisms of this analytical scheme are in order, in so far as it is intended to serve as a theory of the *structure* of personality. Needs are uniform elements and few in number; to them must be traced all motives of all men. The theory says, in effect, that objects of desire may vary from person to person, but the *kinds* of desire do not. Men may want different things, but there are only a few reasons why they want them. Two men, for instance, may be animated by a strong need for abasement; one perhaps becomes a sexual masochist, the other a well-disciplined monk. Does it not seem

[9] H. A. Murray, *J. Psychol.*, 1936, 3, p. 42.
[10] See the forthcoming volume, H. A. Murray, *et al.*, *Explorations in Personality*.

unnecessarily abstract to assume one common need in these contrasting cases? Both men, to be sure, wish to abase themselves, but still a world of difference lies between their respective dispositions. Even the admission that other needs may be simultaneously present to alter the desires of each man, does not yield a concrete and life-like picture of his motives. Universalized needs fail to depict with exactness the special foci of organization existing in each individual life. Desire is always integral with its object, and its resulting forms are far more varied than such a limited list of needs would allow. In short, needs are *disembodied* and *de-personalized* to a greater degree than is justified in elements that are to serve as the radicals of personality.

Not only are needs conceived as separable from the objects sought, but as separable also from the capacities invoked in attaining these objects, and separable even from the shadings of taste and predilection that in real life are integral with all motivation. Here again they are too abstract. One cannot, without considerable violence, distinguish the *direction* of the motive from the equipment it uses in skill and habits, from its attendant attitudes and tastes, and from its object-attachment. According to Murray, the need employs varying "actones" (*modi operandi* of adjustment, peculiar to the individual or to the specific occasion). But is such a separation between end and means possible? Does any person have an abstract need for abasement? Is he not likely rather to be driven by an integral desire to serve such and such a cause, to obtain a special form of masochistic gratification, or to surrender himself to a certain type of religious experience? The need is not one for abasement in the abstract, but for a special, personalized form of self-surrender, in which the actones play an integral part with the need. (Sometimes, to be sure, the felt need is vague in respect to its goal-object; one feels that one would like to surrender oneself to something but does not know precisely how and wherefore. But even such vagueness of desire is still personalized. The attendant actones, images, goals, such as they are, though not clearly defined, are integral with the need. Vagueness of motive is not, after all, the same as abstractness of motive.)

The point seems to be admitted when Murray writes, "Every need is associated with traces (or images) representing movements, pathways, agencies, goal objects, which, taken together, constitute a *need integrate*." [11] Now, this conception of a need integrate is a great

---

[11] H. A. Murray, *J. Psychol.*, 1936, 3, 37.

improvement over the skeleton need. It fulfills well our demand for a unit of analysis that is concrete, life-like, and personal, provided only that the need integrate is understood to be not merely a momentary organization but a mental structure that endures and is a constant characteristic of the person. It is no doubt true that *comparisons* between individuals cannot be made quite so readily on the basis of individual need integrates as on the basis of common needs; but comparison is only a secondary goal of the psychology of personality. The primary goal is the representation of the single life with maximum fidelity.

Factors. For the past decade a conception of elements widely favored by psychometricians has been that of factors. Applied first by Spearman to the search for components of intelligence, the factorial approach has been varied and improved, and is now frequently applied to the problem of the composition of personality. No one seems seriously to have questioned whether intelligence, an obviously artificial construct of the nomothetic order, might, in principle, offer a different type of scientific problem from the vital and integrated personality. No doubts of this order are raised; it is simply assumed that if general and special factors can be identified as the constituents of intelligence (that is, if certain common factors are found to account for the inter-correlation of various tests purporting to measure intelligence), then an attempt should be made to reduce personality also to a few basic and uniform components, shared by all men. The search has already been carried out in many directions. There are attempts to isolate the basic patterns of vocational interests, for example, and to discover a few basic descriptive adjectives that can be applied to personality as designations of the fundamental ways in which men may differ, displacing the thousands of descriptive terms now loosely applied. Commonest of all are the applications of factor analysis to assorted batteries of "personality tests" in order to see what "unitary" factors will emerge from them.

The technical formulae employed in factor analysis and their modes of application are far too specialized for discussion here.[12] It is necessary, however, to consider the *kind* of element that factor analysis offers as the root component of personality.

A factor is an empirical, a posteriori construct or generalization.

[12] Instructive explanations of the aims and techniques of factor analysis may be found in L. L. Thurstone, *The Vectors of Mind*, 1935, and J. P. Guilford, *Psychometric Methods*, 1936, chap. xiv.

It is defined completely by its mode of derivation. Starting always with a battery of tests or ratings, heuristically presumed to cover the function that is the object of study, the factorial description of these tests reduces the scores of all the diverse items to the smallest number of independent variables. The overlap is consolidated, and the number of non-correlating factors discovered is assumed to provide the list of elements basic to the function.

To take an illustration, suppose the topic of irritation or annoyance is the one the investigator wishes to study. He administers to a large population of subjects a questionnaire containing a wide range of pertinent items, hundreds of them, presumed in some way to be diagnostic of "annoyability." One individual may report, for example, that he can't endure people who sniffle, and that he is annoyed also by falling dandruff, smutty stories, crooked teeth, and aggressive salesmen. Other individuals likewise indicate their personal aversions. With suitable statistical treatment it turns out that when all the annoyances of all the people are correlated with one another, they are found to fall into certain major clusters. These clusters are operationally defined by the component items themselves. Since it is normal and convenient to name these clusters, they are finally christened by the investigator with whatever generic terms seem to him best suited to embrace the component items. In the case of annoyances, one investigator finds that the basic factors seem to be irritation at irregularities in personal appearance, at violations of the mores, offenses against one's own ego, and annoyance at minor mishaps.[13]

The merits of such a procedure, extended to all the areas of personality, are said to be great. For one thing, it is believed that a finite number of variables will be discovered, so that personality can at last be reduced to a schedule that might resemble the periodic table in chemistry. If basic elements of this order are discovered, then and only then can scales be invented for the accurate measurement of personality. Instead of relying on homemade devices developed by solipsistic ingenuity, scales would be developed for common use by all psychologists, measuring the same components in all personalities. At last a common psychological yard-stick would be available. A man's psychograph, constructed of scores on these "essential traits of mental life," would be directly comparable with the psychograph of every other personality. Finally, it is said, rather speculatively to be

---

[13] C. M. Harsh, *An Inventory Study of Categories of Annoyance* (Univ. Calif. Library), 1935.

sure, that perhaps the factors eventually discovered—since they are common to all men—will be found to correspond in some way to the genetic units governing inheritance, and to basic and uniform structures within the human nervous system.

But there are difficulties with this conception of elements, enough difficulties to disqualify it under the theory of personality advanced in this volume.

1. The initial assumption of factor analysis, shared by all other nomothetic theories, is open to challenge. Is it reasonable to assume that all people (or even those belonging to one "type") do in fact possess the same basic constitution of personality? Must the foci of organization in all lives be the same? Must the factors, excepting for their differential weighting, be identical?

An entire population (the larger the better) is put into the grinder, and the mixing is so expert that what comes through is a link of factors in which every individual has lost his identity. His dispositions are mixed with everyone else's dispositions. The factors thus obtained represent only *average* tendencies. Whether a factor is really an *organic* disposition in any one individual life is not demonstrated. All one can say for certain is that a factor is an empirically derived component of the *average* personality, and that the average personality is a complete abstraction. This objection gains point when one reflects that seldom do the factors derived in this way resemble the dispositions and traits identified by clinical methods when the *individual* is studied intensively.

2. A second difficulty arises in the naming of factors. When the non-correlating clusters are isolated, they are often found to contain a most curious mixture of items, making no psychological sense. One such cluster, for example, contains the following hodge-podge: special acuities and pulchritude, combined with drive, but having some negative relation to empathy and to spacial facility! Can any conceivable psychological sense be made of it? It is not always true that such meaningless mixtures are obtained, but the composition of any factor is likely to give some trouble in the selection of a suitable name. It is no solution to this problem for the investigator to resort to the compromise of an initial letter, *w, p, o, s, e,* or *m,* as though he did not quite dare pronounce the names of his factors out loud. It seems easier and more fashionable to defend an abstract symbol than to argue boldly for such substantial elements as *will, perseveration, oscillation,*

social withdrawing, emotionality, and *masculinity.* And yet, if this modern version of faculty psychology has virtue at all, it must lie in its ability to identify the true and fundamental components of personality which it set out to find. Up to now it has proved difficult to translate the confident products of mathematical derivation into an equally self-assured language of theoretical psychology. In brief, factors often seem remote from psychological fact, and as such they risk the accusation that they are primarily mathematical artifacts.

3. Another ground for disagreement lies in the assumption that *independent* factors are the desideratum of any theory of elements.[14] Not only are all men supposed to have precisely the same basic elements in their personalities, but in each life these elements are to be regarded as independent of ("freed from the influence of") all other elements.

Such an assumption is highly artificial. So interwoven is the fabric of personality that it seems almost impossible to think of any patterns that are wholly unrelated to others.[15] The picture of the elements of personality offered by the theory of "pure" or independent factors, and the contrasting picture offered by a theory of focal, but overlapping traits (cf. pp. 326 f.) are suggested in Figure 17.

4. Finally it should be pointed out that no reconciliation is possible between the doctrine of *functional autonomy* developed in Chapter VII and the doctrine of factors. According to the former, the course of individuality is one of greater and greater divergence from the relatively standard pattern of infancy. The dynamic substructures of which a personality is composed are unique integrations formed in the individual course of experience and heredity. As each sub-structure develops it becomes a system of energy *sui generis,* obtaining, as Tolman has said, a "strangle hold" in its own right. Now there may be a few *primary* strangle holds in the science of wrestling, but in the science of personality it is quickly discovered that the strangle holds in each life are unique. The factorial approach mis-

---

[14] Cf. the statement of I. Lorge, "To be useful in psychology a trait must be regarded as freed from the influence of other traits." *J. Educ. Psychol.,* 1935, 26, p. 278. If strict independence is required, then Lorge is correct in acclaiming the method of factor analysis, for no other method will reach this objective.

[15] It is said that the assumption of strict independence of factors is not indispensable to the theory of factor analysis. (J. P. Guilford, *Psychometric Methods,* 1936, p. 512. See also by the same author a general defense of factor analysis, *Am. J. Psychol.,* 1936, 48, 673-685.) Thus far, however, the search has been almost entirely for non-correlating, independent "unitary traits" and the chief merit of the method is claimed to be precisely this discovery of non-correlating units.

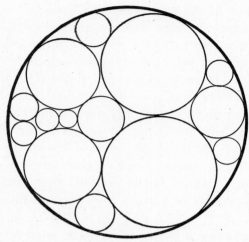

(a) The *factorial conception* of the single personality as a system of independent elements, the elements being the same in different personalities, though varying in prominence.

(b) The *trait-conception* of a single personality as a system of focal but interde-pendent sub-structures, the units being essentially different in every personality

FIGURE 17

Two Contrasting Views of the Nature of the Elements of Personality

takenly assumes that they are uniform, though varying in weight.[16]

One variation in the factor technique correlates "individuals" rather than "qualities" (cf. p. 383). A typological picture results. Thus, in a study of esthetic taste certain people are found always to prefer softer, pastel tones, and others to prefer saturated, bright colors.[17] To find that only certain people have the same taste, the same interest, or the same pattern of qualities, is an improvement on the contention that all people must be compared on identical variables. But "types" are still not individuals, and the method offers no real solution to the problem of the neuropsychic elements in any single personality.[18]

[16] At bottom, of course, this disagreement—as is always the case with conflicting conceptualizations of data—is due to different *intentions*. Different theorists have quite different ends in view. Speaking in defense of factors Thurstone writes, "The final choice of a set of primary reference traits or faculties must be made in terms of the discovery that a particular set of reference traits renders most parsimonious our comprehension of a great variety of human traits." (*The Vectors of Mind*, p. 48.)

But the *intent* to find the most parsimonious frame of reference under which the great variety of human qualities may be ordered, is itself an arbitrary intention. From the dynamic point of view it is also an ill-advised goal, at least so it seems to R. C. Tryon, who writes:

"No one may object to mathematical-factorists employing the rule of parsimony in order to simplify their problem. One must realize, however, that the factors which come out of the analysis are *chosen* from many possible sets, and that the rule of choice is *arbitrary*. Now, it happens that the 'law' of parsimony is not a natural law, but a rule agreed upon among men to simplify their thinking. With reference to the psychobiological causes of individual differences, nature does not appear, however, to work parsimoniously but rather most prodigally. As will be shown later, the experimental evidence from psychological and genetics laboratories indicates that a very large number of causes determine mental differences. Hence, the employment of the rule of parsimony to select out a parsimonious set of factors would appear to depict a fiction *if* such a depiction is urged as a representation of psychobiological causes." (*Psychol. Rev.*, 1935, 42, 427 f.)

Differing both from Thurstone's intent to discover a parsimonious set of mathematical components and Tryon's intention to discover genetic components of endless multiplicity, the desire of the present volume is to discover a type of element (trait) that will account without artificiality or undue multiplicity for the self-consistency of each individual personality. It is not so much a matter of being right or being wrong. It is rather a matter of selecting units that will best represent the structure of personality as personality is defined in this volume.

[17] W. Stephenson, *Char. & Pers.*, 1935, 4, 17-24.

[18] It is possible that the future will bring a method of factoring the components of the single personality considered by itself. In this case a great advance would be made, for then it would be possible to determine the cardinal factor for each life separately. All the overlap of the focal traits would be consolidated, and the primary saturating factor would stand revealed. It would then be possible to tell how much of the individual life was influenced by this central factor, and how much is dissociated from it, and organized around subsidiary factors.   •

To accomplish this purpose each individual would have to be considered as a "population" and the agreement of his acts with one another would be determined in reference to some postulated "intra-individual continuum." (Cf. F. H. Allport, *Char. & Pers.*, 1937, 5, 202-214.)

The various factorial techniques undoubtedly have value for certain types of problems in psychology and in sociology. But they are not qualified to pick out the elements of human personality according to the criteria laid down above. Factors fall short of our demand for a doctrine of elements that will offer as close an approximation as possible to the natural cleavages and individualized structural arrangements of each single life. The search must go on.

STIMULUS-RESPONSE ELEMENTS (SPECIFICITY)

The doctrine of stimulus-response elements is not necessarily nomothetic; it holds that "personality is made up of thousands of independent and specific habits." Whether these habits are regarded as common to all individuals is not stipulated; one specificist may think that they are, another that they are not. It makes no great difference. The point now at issue is different from those previously examined. For whether or not specificists think of common or unique habits, they all *pulverize* personality into minute constituent elements. The following quotations give the spirit of specificity.

> A widespread misconception of conduct is that it is an expression of traits. It is assumed that everyone's personality is made up of traits which are characteristics of the personality. These traits cause one to act in certain defined ways. . . . It has been found that no one acts perfectly consistently with regard to a trait as would be the case if conduct was an expression of inner traits.[19]

> Over and over, a battery of tests designed to measure traits such as persistence, or aggressiveness, or honesty, yields results so unreliable and undependable (when compared with other criteria) that one is led to question the actual existence of the general traits.[20]

> Because of all these complicating factors the study of personality becomes extremely difficult, and the analysis of "personality traits" must be limited to the particular situation and conditions under which they are shown.[21]

> A trait is a specific behavior tendency which must be defined in terms of a particular stimulus and a particular response.[22]

The specificist contends in brief that the essential element in the structure of personality is the habit, and that no organization of a

[19] P. M. Symonds, *The Nature of Conduct*, 1928, p. 320, by permission of The Macmillan Company, publishers.
[20] H. C. Lehmann and P. A. Witty, *Am. J. Psychol.*, 1934, 46, p. 490.
[21] F. L. Goodenough, *Developmental Psychology*, 1934, p. 444.
[22] F. A. Perrin and D. B. Klein, *Psychology, its Methods and Principles*, 1926, p. 363.

higher level (such as is suggested in the ordinary usage of the term "trait") exists.

This doctrine, virtually unknown in the psychological theories of other lands, has wide currency in America. Why? One answer is historical: in this country the reaction against faculty psychology was particularly violent. Specifically, it was the teaching of William James and E. L. Thorndike that led to a conception of conduct largely in terms of habit. Experiments seemed to confirm their teaching: children had no general powers of the mind that might be educated *in toto*. It was found, for example, that young children could not learn cleanliness when taught as an abstract principle, but only definite habits of cleanliness, such as brushing the teeth, changing soiled clothing, or washing behind the ears. It may be laborious to instill habits one at a time, but only in this way—according to the educators—can the child learn. (This problem is so complex and far-reaching in its implications that it will be treated more fully in the next chapter.) From this educational dictum, the habit-psychologists found it easy to reach the conclusion that personality is composed of "countless specific habits." The acceptance of specificity was also made easier by its congeniality to behaviorism, the theory recently prevailing in the American' psychological ethos, with its reflex pathways and conditioned response, its objectivity, simplicity, and practicality.

Since the doctrine of specificity holds that the individual will do in each situation just what he has been trained in that situation to do, and nothing else, many American sociologists have likewise favored the view, for they too put the weight largely on the *situation*. If conduct is determined by habits inflexibly bound to the environmental stimuli, then the road is clear for the ecological and cultural determination of personality. A sociologist wishing to "explain" personality in terms of cultural causation has a much easier time with the simple theory of habit than with a doctrine of more complex elements in which intricate internal and subjective factors are predominant.

Such are the historical reasons for the doctrine. But its exponents, being devotees of the experimental method, require proof of specificity. Near at hand they find instances enough that men are not perfectly consistent in their traits. A man may be neat about his person, slovenly about his desk; saintly on the Sabbath and diabolic on weekdays; timid at the office, tyrannical at home. It looks in these cases as if it were indeed the situation alone that determined the nature of his behavior. The elements are stimulus-bound habits, and not traits. But the trouble with this type of casual evidence is that there is much of the same order to counterbalance and contradict it. We know people who are almost *always* neat, shy, tactless, cynical, or officious; and we predict their behavior correctly in novel situations for which there are no specific habits available.

Hence, the specificists cannot rest their case merely upon cursory observation. They invoke experiment. Most frequently they invoke the monumental study of the *Character Education Inquiry*, directed by H. Hartshorne and M. A. May. This research is justly famous for its ingenious methods, its extensiveness (being probably the largest experimental project ever carried out in the field of personality), for its accurate and painstaking treatment of results. The reports comprise three large volumes.[23] By setting before hundreds of children concrete tasks in which they had opportunity to react in an individual manner, it was possible to study from the records of their behavior the evidence for and against the existence of such alleged traits as *deception, helpfulness, co-operativeness, persistence,* and *self-control.* The final conclusion was that such qualities as these are "groups of specific habits rather than general traits." [24] This imposing investigation is so influential, and so often cited as evidence for the specificist's position, that its results and interpretations must be examined with care.

1. Our first discovery is that the low correlations found between the tests employed prove only that children are not consistent *in the same way,* not that they are inconsistent with *themselves.* This is an exceedingly important discovery.

In studying dishonesty, for example, children were presented with tasks giving them repeated opportunities to be deceitful—to steal pennies, to correct their school papers to their own advantage, to cheat at games, to lie about their cheating. When the records for the entire population of children were studied it was found that there was little tendency for the youngsters to be uniformly honest or dishonest in all types of behavior. For example, the correlation between the score

---

[23] H. Hartshorne and M. A. May, Vol. I, *Studies in Deceit,* 1928; Vol. II, *Studies in Service and Self-Control,* 1929; Vol. III (with F. K. Shuttleworth), *Studies in the Organization of Character,* 1930. A useful secondary account of the methods and findings is contained in P. M. Symonds, *Diagnosing Personality and Conduct,* 1932, chap. ix.

[24] *Op. cit.,* Vol. III, p. 1.

for stealing pennies (which by itself turned out to be a fairly consistent habit) and the scores for telling lies about their cheating (which by itself was another rather consistent *habit*), was only $+.132$. Clearly, the dishonest habit aroused by one of these situations is quite independent of the dishonest habit in the other. The children who steal do not necessarily lie. There is no common trait existing in all children *in the same way*. But, on the other hand, the habit of

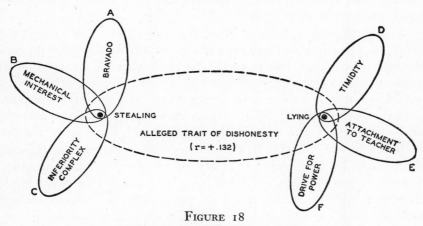

FIGURE 18

Critique of One Statistical Conception of Trait

(Dotted ellipse represents the trait as conceived by investigators in the Character Education Inquiry, solid ellipses, possible personal traits overlooked by them.)

stealing pennies may, in each child's life, be an integral part of *some* trait, even though it is rarely related to the habit of lying. Figure 18 shows the possibility.

It may be that child A steals pennies because he has a consistent personal trait of *bravado* based upon his admiration for the gangsters he reads about in the tabloids and sees on the screen; child B steals because he has a persistent *interest in tools and mechanics* that drives him to buy more equipment than he can honestly afford; child C, suffering from a gnawing *feeling of social inferiority*, steals pennies to purchase candy to buy his way into favor with his playmates. Child D does not steal pennies, but he lies about his cheating, not because he has a general trait of dishonesty, but because he has a general trait of *timidity* (fear of consequences); child E lies because he is afraid of hurting the feelings of the teacher whom he adores; child F lies because he is *greedy for praise*. Each of these children behaved as he did toward these tests, not because he had specific habits, but because he had some deep-lying and characteristic trait. All that the C.E.I. discovered was that the particular trait of honesty as defined in the usual ethical terms and tested in various conventional situations, was not one of which the children possessed constant individual degrees, especially in the face of perhaps a stronger tendency of each child to express some trait other than honesty through the behavior of lying and stealing. The children did not all have the *same* trait, but they had nevertheless their own traits.

2. The investigators based their research upon *social and ethical concepts*. The methods used were not devised from the point of view of child psychology, but from the point of view of society and its conduct values. Our culture places a premium upon honesty, service, and self-control, but these items in the social code seldom correspond precisely to the form of mental organization found in adults, and still less to the unsocialized dispositions of childhood. In terms of the distinction drawn in Chapter II, the investigators confused their research at the outset by selecting *characterial* rubrics for their starting point. A study of *good* qualities and *bad* qualities is not the same as a study of natural qualities. The study of personality is difficult enough without complicating it at the beginning with ethical evaluation.[25]

3. Whenever moral standards are involved, the question of the *age* of the subjects is of greatest importance. Older children and adults learn gradually the requirements of social custom; they come to know what is meant by honesty in their culture, by service, and by self-control. What is more, they may *introcept* these prevalent ideals into their own lives and guided by these standards, may develop integrated dispositions roughly corresponding to the ideals. This is the process of socialization. According to the principle of functional autonomy such acquired traits may in time become exceedingly dynamic, causing sharp pangs of conscience whenever their dictates are violated. But such socialized traits should not be expected in the younger child. Much of the evidence of the C.E.I. indeed demonstrates their gradual development with age. The older child more frequently than the younger guides his conduct in accordance with the social ideal.

[25] It should be pointed out that the investigators obtained their most consistent results with the trait of *persistence*, which, for example, showed the greatest progressive integration with age. This trait is the only one in the schedule that seems entirely free from extraneous definition in terms of social code; it is an authentic *psychological* conception.

The evidence shows likewise that the children grow more and more consistent in respect to the *positive* social ideals, but not in respect to vices or anti-social conduct.[26] In other words, the pressure of the environment leads gradually to *conformity* with the social code, and the conformity is flexible and generalized. Only wrongdoing is specific. This result is just what one would expect in the course of normal socialization when emphasis in training is placed upon virtuous ideals, and only occasional lapses are allowed.

4. Some arbitrariness is always involved in the interpretation of complex statistical results. Surveying the myriads of intercorrelations between the children's scores on many tests, one is struck by the prevailingly positive association that is revealed. The coefficients are low, to be sure, but even so, why should they be positive? Considering the various insufficiencies of the methods used, and the preoccupation with conduct common to a whole population of children, to the exclusion of conduct characteristic of each child, it is surprising that the results were even slightly positive. What do these low positive correlations mean? Some investigators say specificity, others generality. No one knows. Hartshorne and May have chosen "to follow the evidences of specificity to their logical conclusion." [27] This, in the face of the fact (reported on the same page) that "the twenty-three tests used in securing our total character score, for example, intercorrelate +.30 on the average." Instead of deducing specificity from this matrix, Maller, an associate in the Inquiry, finds it adequate evidence for postulating a "c" factor of character which is present in all behavior, saturating it with general quality and common strength.[28] The hypothesis of a general factor of character (derived from the same data!) is of course the complete antithesis of the doctrine of specificity. Here is a pointed illustration of the fact that correlational methods *per se* solve no problems, simply because all coefficients (o and 1.00 perhaps excepted) are intrinsically ambiguous and need evaluation.

5. Finally, whether specificity or generality is found in the structure of personality depends to a large extent, not only upon the interpretation of quantitative evidence, but upon the methods used. Employing large populations of children and myriad tests is a very dif-

[26] *Op. cit.*, Vol. III, p. 375.
[27] *Op. cit.*, Vol. III, p. 364.
[28] J. B. Maller, *J. Soc. Psychol.*, 1934, 5, 97-101. C is defined as the readiness to forego immediate gain for the sake of remote but greater gain.

ferent procedure from studying more intensively the behavior of fewer subjects at a more mature age. It is astonishing what different results this latter method brings when applied to the same problem of the self-consistency of the traits of *honesty* and *deceit*.

At the Harvard Psychological Clinic, D. W. MacKinnon set for his 93 adult subjects a series of difficult problems whose solutions were to be worked out in solitude during an hour's experimental session.[29] The answers to these problems lay before the subject in pamphlets, and certain answers the subject was permitted to consult if he chose; the remainder of the answers were forbidden to him. Through a one-way screen the experimenter observed each instance where the subjects violated the prohibition. Approximately half of the subjects were violators and half non-violators.

The first evidence of trait-consistency comes from the experimenter's predictions, made after approximately a five minute interview with each subject. On the basis of first impressions he prophesied which subjects would violate the prohibition and which would not. This method was employed with 74 of the subjects. The prophecy proved to be correct in 69 per cent of the cases. The success was greater in the case of non-violators (a fact that suggests the finding of Hartshorne and May that integration—or spread of a trait—is greater for the honest than for the dishonest subjects).

Of the 34 violators, correct predictions were made for only 62 per cent. What of those violators for whom false predictions were made? The error, it appeared, was due chiefly to the fact that the unexpected violators were also atypical violators. That is to say, they were the ones who later showed unmistakable signs of guilt (not shown by *typical* violators). Excepting for the deed itself the atypical violators behaved like the non-violators. They were, it seems, really honest people, who under the stress of the experimental situation had yielded to the temptation, violating their own customary standards. The very fact that they showed guilt, remorse, and repression following the violation suggests that in general they had a dependable trait of honesty.

The typical violators, on the other hand, were consistent with themselves. They lied to the experimenter more frequently than did the non-violators or the atypical violators. They lied even about the answers they were permitted to consult! These subjects also denied that they were ordinarily troubled by guilt (only 29 per cent admitted feelings of guilt in everyday life as compared with 75 per cent of the

[29] D. W. MacKinnon, "The Violation of Prohibitions in the Solving of Problems," to be published in *Explorations in Personality* (H. A. Murray, *et al.*).

non-violators). They maintained that they would not feel guilty "even if they had cheated!"

The honest subjects also presented a consistent picture. They were not only recognized as such (in the majority of cases) on first acquaintance, but they did not lie about consulting the permitted answers. They also showed little tendency to blame the experimenter for giving them such hard problems, or to be unduly aggressive (both of which characteristics were found in the violators). They admitted suffering from guilt whenever in everyday life they violate their own standards of conduct.

Such results entirely contradict the hypothesis of specificity. There are honest people, dishonest people, and atypical people—honest in most respects, but not always capable of resisting temptation. An intensive study of this sort, then, leads to the discovery in most instances of generality in the trait of trustworthiness; whereas the extensive (statistical) study of the C.E.I. gives the honors to specificity! Murphy and Jensen are perhaps right when they say, "Honesty is either a general characteristic or a set of specific habits, depending upon your interest and your emphasis." [30] They might have added, "depending also upon your method, and upon the particular individual you happen to be studying."

SUMMARY OF ARGUMENTS AGAINST SPECIFICITY

The doctrine that all behavior (and therefore personality) is composed entirely of countless specific habits is, for several reasons, unacceptable.

1. In the first place, the chief evidence adduced for it has come from procedures that may be incapable of discovering higher units of organization in personality. The study of moral qualities is a case in point. Are they the place to look for maximum personal integration? With advancing socialization, to be sure, the psychological make-up of a person may become centered in such a way as to correspond in some degree with social norms, but transgressions from these norms do not prove that all conduct is specific. Such transgressions may occur because of profoundly consistent dispositions, more fundamental to the person than the conventional codes. Example:

A boy of ten, accustomed to the respect of his own playmates at home, found himself for the summer among older boys who looked

[30] G. Murphy and F. Jensen, *Approaches to Personality*, 1932, p. 385.

down upon him as an outsider and as a punk. He felt frustrated and chagrined. One day a member of the gang proposed "swiping" a few bars of candy from the corner store. At first the lad's habits of honesty prompted him to resist the suggestion, but when the gang ridiculed him, his *major* desire for admiration and social standing became aroused. Alone he undertook the larceny, and in a few moments emerged from the store with a plentiful supply of chocolate bars. The less stable habits of honesty were destroyed by a stronger and more organized *trait*. The boy was consistent enough with himself, but his consistency did not happen to correspond to the social ideal.

The error of probing for consistency in the wrong place (and failing to find it, pronouncing in favor of specificity) has been likened by G. B. Watson to the absurdity of asking whether a person using the public library has a trait causing him to take out only books with red or with blue covers. Of course he hasn't. If only the bindings were studied, no consistency should be expected. But if the *subject-matter* of the chosen books was investigated, well organized traits of interest would appear.[31] Unless consistency is sought in the right direction, consistency will not be found.

2. A related error lies in employing exclusively the results of *mass investigation*. Statistical methods are ordinarily applied only to those variables to which all people may be ordered. If many people do not happen to fit the variable then the illusion of specificity results. Low correlations between habits of behavior (as demonstrated in Figure 18) mean at the most that different individuals are not all consistent *in the same way;* they never prove that the individual is not consistent with himself *in his own way.*

3. The danger of resting the theory of specificity upon studies of young children has been mentioned. Children show less integration, as a rule, than adults. The evidence presented by specificists usually shows, in fact, that older children are more consistent than younger children.

4. The evidence from "personality tests" is by no means as favorable to the doctrine of specificity as some writers imply (cf. quotation from Lehmann and Witty, p. 248). If a scale possesses reliability (internal consistency) the fact can signify only one thing, namely, that people respond to related diagnostic items in a way characteristic of themselves; their response shows that they are in varying degrees habitually *ascendant, extroverted, persevering,* or *radical.* Reliability

[31] G. B. Watson, *Char. & Pers.*, 1933, 2, p. 69.

of a many-itemed scale is *prima facie* evidence for some kind of generality in conduct.

This fact is all the more arresting when one considers that a standardized scale, in order to achieve reliability, requires that all the subjects be self-consistent in respect to the *same common* variable. Figure 18 showed that consistency in respect to a common variable may be negligible without proving the case for specificity, since each individual has his own peculiar traits with which he may be self-consistent. But when, as is the case with these scales, high reliability is found in *common* variables as well, the evidence for the existence of complex units of organization mounts even higher.

5. If we become intentionally naive and ask whether any specificist in daily life can believe and be guided by his theory, we discover swiftly that he cannot. To be in keeping with his own doctrine he would *never* be entitled to apply descriptive adjectives to persons. He could not say that his friend is trustworthy, affable, or humorous; that his child is high-strung, dominant, or sociable; that his wife is kind or tactful. In the midst of an argument for specificity, in a passage commenting on the filling out of questionnaires, one author makes a fatally contradictory observation, "The truthful person finds it very difficult to be untruthful"—a statement, of course, not of specific habits but of traits! No one can for long live or think according to the sparse concept of specificity.

6. Everything that is known concerning the integrative action of the central nervous system is incompatible with the doctrine of specificity. Belief in the "neural groove," wherein a specific habit was once supposed to reside, has been abandoned. Though little enough is known concerning the neural equivalents of generalized dispositions, the trend of evidence so far as it goes favors such a theory rather than one of insulated habits.

CONCLUSION

Thus far our search for basic psychological components of personality has not seemed very rewarding. A number of schemes have been examined and, though each has its merits for certain purposes, none serves the end we here have in view. None is concerned with the strictly individualized units of personality that are the true carriers of individuality in behavior. For the most part they are nomothetically conceived, having as their aim the facilitating of comparisons between one person and all others in respect to some one common aspect of personality. Other schemes that are not necessarily nomothetic are for the most part specificistic in conception or highly miscellaneous and of no theoretical value. At any rate none of the schemes considered in this chapter defines the level of complex but well-structured *personal* dispositions that can serve as the most suitable tool of analysis.

More promising is the doctrine of sentiments, discussed on p. 89, where individuality of affective organization is better allowed. Helpful too are certain conceptions drawn from Gestalt Psychology, such, for example, as Wertheimer's *radix*, Koffka's *ego-systems*, Lewin's *regions, tension-systems, inner personal strata*, and the like. In one way or another these various conceptions suggest improved units of analysis. The special merits of some of these proposals will be considered later and their applications discussed. In the meantime one more critical duty lies ahead, before the ground is completely cleared for a constructive theory of traits.

CHAPTER X

THE THEORY OF IDENTICAL ELEMENTS

THE problem of the organization and structure of *personality* is not separate from the more inclusive problem of *mental organization*, but is merely one phase of it. The only real difference is that whenever interest centers in personality, the emphasis is on the *lasting* or *permanent* characteristics of mental organization; whereas in the older association psychology, and in the modern study of perception, learning and thinking, it is a question of the organization of mental content into somewhat more transient sequences and constellations. But if one could tell precisely how temporary arrangements come about in the human mind, one would probably have the key to the more permanent arrangements, and *vice versa*. At all events, in the present stage of psychological knowledge, it is impossible to pursue the problem of the organization of personality apart from the more inclusive problem of mental organization. As the years pass this problem is less frequently formulated in the older terms of the "laws of association," but whatever guise it takes, the issue is still the same, and it is the pivotal issue of all psychological science.

The most prevalent doctrine of mental organization in American psychological theory is the doctrine of identical elements, or, as it is often called, of "partial identity." According to it the consistency of an individual's conduct is due to his ability to discern minute elements or aspects of an environmental situation that are identical with elements or aspects of situations encountered previously, and to make a corresponding response wherever these elements occur. To this so-called *"transfer"* in conduct Symonds has given the name "confact" (a term corresponding to "concept"—which, according to the doctrine of partial identity, arises likewise through the ability of mind to detect minute perceptual identities). Both concepts and confacts "are responses to a single element which may be common to a number of otherwise varying situations. . . . A concept is a mental or verbal response, whereas a confact is a conduct response." [1]

[1] P. M. Symonds, *The Nature of Conduct*, 1928, p. 167.

Truthfulness, courage, loyalty, frugality, generosity, kindliness, and other alleged traits are to be explained by the capacity of an individual to respond with the same sequence of habits to identical elements in otherwise varying situations. For example, a boy must never be thought to develop a *trait* of courtesy. Rather he "learns to take off a specific cap when coming in a specific door and in the presence of his mother. But in time he may take off his cap or hat or whatever he has on his head when entering any door, in any house whatsoever, whether or not in the presence of a person." [2] Courtesy, then, is nothing more than the repetition of the same habits over and over again when provoked by stimuli previously associated with these habits, or when there is partial identity in different stimulus fields, or when the habits themselves are related by means of some common bond. Such a tenuous principle of organization naturally leads to the conclusion that "generalization of conduct does not extend as far as most people suppose, with the result that conduct for the large masses of people remains unorganized, a rather loose bundle of unrelated and dissociated habits." [3]

A diagram will make the theory clear. The boy in the illustration has learned, by dint of drill, that when he enters an outside door (*a*) in his own home (Stimulus Field I), he should take off his cap (Habit 1), wipe his shoes (Habit 2), greet the occupants (Habit 3). Now, entrance doors have something in common (identical elements in different stimulus fields): they all provoke the boy to perform the same three habits (as, for example, when he enters a neighbor's door, *a′*, Stimulus Field II. A misinformed observer might remark that here is a *courteous* lad. Not at all; he has no general trait; his three habits are automatically set into motion whenever he encounters identical elements in different fields.

Now, the habits themselves are also capable of having identical features, so that the arousal of one may arouse another (by virtue of redintegrative action, cf. p. 203). Thus, greeting the occupants of the house (Habit 3) might through some commonly associated verbal components—for example, "Hello, how are you?"—set in motion a further inquiry concerning their health (Habit 4), which in turn by virtue perhaps of some commonly associated facial expression, might suggest a friendly smile (Habit 5). Finally a friendly smile through

[2] P. M. Symonds, *The Nature of Conduct*, 1928, p. 294.
[3] *Ibid.*, p. 325.

further specific association leads to some additional act of "courtesy" such as asking his friend out to play (Habit 6).

Thus it is that identical elements in the stimulus fields, or in the neuropsychic structure, are responsible for the quasi-consistency of the boy's conduct. What is denied is that any generalized disposition

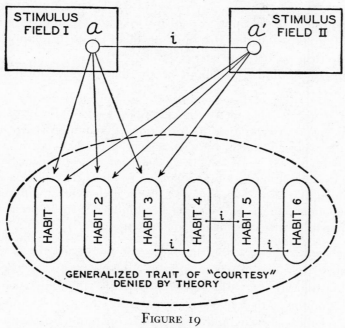

FIGURE 19

The Theory of Identical Elements

Identity may reside either in corresponding elements of the stimulus fields, or else in some neuropsychic components of the habits. Solid connecting lines (*i*) indicate such identities. Arrows show lines of stimulation, and the dotted ellipse represents the hypothetical trait of "courtesy" denied by the theory.

exists to which the name "courtesy" might be properly attached. The boy is basically a creature of specific habits. Whatever relation there may be between the six habits here enumerated is due entirely to some still more minute and specific components of these habits, in short, to some identical elements.

This, then, is the picture of the structure of personality according to the theory of partial identity. It is a serious question whether the terms "generalization" and "integration" can be applied at all to such a thread-like connectionism. It is an even more serious question whether the inward cohesion in the structure of personality can be accounted for in this way.

PARTIAL IDENTITY AND LEARNING

Any law of learning is at the same time a law of the development of personality (cf. p. 151). Now, one of the outstanding problems in the psychology of learning is *transfer of training;* and, as might be expected, it turns out that this same problem is equally important for the theoretical psychology of personality.

Suppose it should come about—as the theory of identical elements avers—that

> Training the mind means the development of thousands of particular independent capacities, the formation of countless particular habits, for the working of any mental capacity depends upon the concrete data with which it works. Improvement of any one mental function or activity will improve others only in so far as they possess elements common to it also. The amount of identical elements in different mental functions and the amount of general influence from special training are much less than common opinion supposes.[4]

Suppose such is the case. What then is the picture of the developing personality? It is one in which specific adjustments to specific stimuli are the outstanding fact—the recurrence of the same movement in the face of stimulus situations that are partially the same; sequences of closely related habits would be set into operation; throughout the process a marked rigidity would prevail. In training a child it would be of no avail to teach him general principles and abstract ideals, for his models of conduct can never be anything but specific.[5] Novel situations would leave the child bewildered and impotent, or throw him back upon "instinct," unless some familiar item in the novel situation rescued him from the dilemma by reinstating an available habit, or habit sequence. The picture is one of invariance of the stimulus; invariance of the mental set, and invariance of the response.[6]

[4] E. L. Thorndike, *Principles of Teaching*, Seiler, 1906, p. 248.

[5] The modern movement of "character education" has been greatly influenced by this belief. In its literature one reads remarkable dicta, for example, to the effect that no child can be taught virtue except "by doing specific things in specific situations." As an example of this literature, see H. Hartshorne, *Character in Human Relations*, 1932.

[6] But usually a habit that is reinstated invariantly appears merely inappropriate and ridiculous. There is a familiar story about an old soldier coming from the vil-

Suppose this theory of learning is false. Suppose it is only the young child or the mentally undeveloped who must be taught in terms of habits, and taught in this way only because his capacity for generalization has not matured. Suppose that with time these specific habits can become authentically generalized, and thus replaced by much more fluid and flexible dynamic dispositions, of the order of traits. Suppose that the maturing individual represents such traits to himself subjectively as *ideals* of conduct. A youth, for instance, accepting courtesy as an ideal worthy to guide his conduct, would not thereby be bound by six habits nor sixty, nor only by such habits as have among themselves partial identities. If suddenly removed to China, where courtesy requires the inversion of most of his habits, he would readily enough readjust them and behave in a fashion that would reverse his specific habits and yet be consistent with his general ideal. Habits would not be a ball and chain, but would readily atrophy or even reverse themselves, whenever the stable and generalized dispositions of personality demanded.[7]

Returning to the problem of transfer, psychology, we may say, has passed through two distinct periods in reference to this important question, and is now slowly emerging into a third. The first period

lage store. A wag shouted the command *Attention!* and the old soldier leaped to position, dropping his basket of eggs. In every particular the old man was manifesting transfer through the medium of identical elements. The command was the element common to two life settings; of itself it reinstated a previously formed habit. But such behavior is as comic as it is rare. (Bergson based a whole theory of laughter upon such "mechanical inelasticity.")

[7] Some time ago habit training was introduced into prisons on the assumption that good habits made good citizens. The prisoners were taught hygienic habits, vocational habits, and were paid wages that they were forced to share regularly with their families. During a long period of incarceration the prisoners received an impressive amount of such habit training, which was designed in such a way that identical elements in the world outside the prison should cause these salutary habits to function when the prisoner was freed.

The policy did not work. The study of S. and E. T. Glueck (*500 Criminal Careers*, 1930) shows that 80 per cent of the men discharged from a reformatory where many approved methods of habit training were in use, were not reformed five to fifteen years later, but continued in their course of crime. The gradual training of habits and reconditioning, with reliance upon identical elements within and without the prison walls to effect the transfer, produced few reformations, if any at all. To a prisoner with a dominant anti-social outlook, or other antagonistic traits, such habit training is worthless, for he is in no frame of mind to put it to use. On the other hand, in those rare cases where the dominating attitude and goals are altered, habit training is of secondary importance. The reformed prisoner will find ways of learning to live more hygienically, of taking care of his family, of fulfilling his responsibilities, provided only that his interests and ideals are altered. And they are not altered by mere routine drill.

was characterized by blind faith in limitless transfer, wherein it was assumed that any type of training improved mental power in general, or at least the power of some broad faculty of the mind, such as reasoning ability or memory. Even today, in less "progressive" schools, teachers believe, and assure their students, that the study of geometry or Latin, though unsavory in itself, is valuable because it automatically trains "logical power," or "memory," or perhaps "will-power." [8]

It was Thorndike who, following the suspicions of James, Hinsdale, and others,[9] made a devastating attack upon this widespread theory of "formal discipline," and instituted the second epoch. In 1901 he published, in collaboration with R. S. Woodworth, one of the earliest experimental investigations of the problem.[10] This study, according to Gates,

> resulted in a complete overthrow of the older educational theory of formal discipline. In place of this doctrine was offered the theory of transfer of training, which, in brief, states that improvement in thinking, reasoning, neatness, honesty, and the like, is to be found in the development of innumerable particular habits, and that these habits are likely to remain imbedded in the situation in which they are developed. A corollary to the theory is that such habits transfer from a situation in which they were developed to other situations roughly in proportion to the degree to which the two settings have elements in common.[11]

Thorndike himself saw the following educational consequences in this early experimental work.

> By doubling a boy's reasoning power in arithmetical problems we do not double it for formal grammar or chess or economic history or theories of evolution. By tripling the accuracy of movement in fingering exercises we do not triple it for typewriting, playing billiards or painting. The gain of courage in the game of football is never

[8] Instances of the older pedagogical literature of this type are C. Aiken, *Methods for Mind Training*, 1889, and J. Payot, *The Education of the Will*, trans. 1909.

[9] Cf. W. James, *Principles of Psychology*, 1890, I, 666-668; B. A. Hinsdale, "The Dogma of Formal Discipline," *Proceed. N. E. A.*, 1894.

[10] *Psychol. Rev.*, 1901, 8, 247-261, 384-395, 553-564. All citations from the work of E. L. Thorndike in this chapter are perforce from his earlier publications. In neither *Human Learning*, 1931, nor *The Fundamentals of Learning*, 1932, is there an explicit defense (or repudiation) of the theory of identical elements.

[11] A. I. Gates, quotation from chap. iii of *Psychology at Work* (ed. by P. S. Achilles), McGraw-Hill Book Company, 1932.

equaled by the gain in moral courage or resistance to intellectual obstacles. The real question is not, "Does improvement of one function alter others?" but, "to what extent, and how, does it?"

The answer which I shall try to defend is that a change in one function alters any other only in so far as the two functions have as factors common elements. . . . To take a concrete example, improvement in addition will alter one's ability in multiplication because addition is absolutely identical with a part of multiplication, and because certain other processes—e.g., eye movements and the inhibition of all save arithmetical impulses—are in part common to the two functions.[12]

Thorndike's influential theory may be summarized as follows. Each mental operation is by nature a distinct process, beginning with a stimulus that traces a neural path until a motor adjustment is achieved. The neural path once traversed is now in a state of reduced resistance, and will function more readily when stimulated again. The various stimulus-situations of life frequently have features in common, so that in what seems to be a new situation, there are really elements present that have been present before. This duplication of features in two stimulus-situations is responsible for whatever improvement is manifested in the second response. The second response will be made more quickly or more accurately, that is, will show transfer-effect in proportion to the amount of overlap.

In the case of arithmetic, practicing addition should show a greater amount of transfer to the learning of multiplication than to the learning of division, for the reason that the first two processes have more elements in common ($c, d, e,$ and $f,$ in Figure 20); whereas addition and division have fewer factors in common (only e and f).

One weakness of the diagram is immediately apparent, namely, that the "elements" constituting each mathematical operation are by no means elementary (though derived from Thorndike's own analysis of arithmetical operations). But, as will later be shown, this dubiety concerning the nature of elements is inherent in the theory itself. For the moment all that is required is to grasp the intent of this theory, and to appreciate its influence upon doctrines concerning the structure of personality. As instances of this influence the following quotations will serve.

Character traits are not general traits available to apply to all sorts of situations—but rather the reverse—a specific thing in each situation. . . .
Psychology no longer recognizes honesty, e.g., as a general trait which

[12] *Educational Psychology*, Teachers College, 1903, pp. 80 f.

once "acquired" would make one honest in whatever he did—rather is it true that we come to be regarded as honest by the way we respond to individual situations. . . . Our interest has shifted from "being good" to "doing good," from "being honest" as an intangible abstrac-

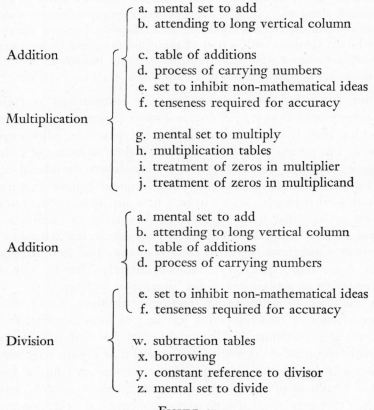

Addition
- a. mental set to add
- b. attending to long vertical column
- c. table of additions
- d. process of carrying numbers
- e. set to inhibit non-mathematical ideas
- f. tenseness required for accuracy

Multiplication
- g. mental set to multiply
- h. multiplication tables
- i. treatment of zeros in multiplier
- j. treatment of zeros in multiplicand

Addition
- a. mental set to add
- b. attending to long vertical column
- c. table of additions
- d. process of carrying numbers
- e. set to inhibit non-mathematical ideas
- f. tenseness required for accuracy

Division
- w. subtraction tables
- x. borrowing
- y. constant reference to divisor
- z. mental set to divide

FIGURE 20

Some Hypothetical Elements Involved in Different
Arithmetical Operations

tion to "doing honestly" in the concrete situations, or from "being neat" to "doing neatly" in action.[13]

We all know that individuals may be courteous, kind and generous in company or in business relations, and at the same time be rude, cruel, selfish at home. An unscrupulous business man may be the very essence of honesty in his relations with his friends, his club, his church. The kind doting father may be an employer of children

[13] From a memorandum issued by one of the leading "character forming" agencies in America.

under sweat-shop conditions. So kindness, honesty, generosity are not traits that transfer from one set of circumstances to all others.[14]

EXPERIMENTAL WORK

A problem so central in educational theory and practice has naturally been submitted time and again to experimental investigation. Since the classic experiment of William James (1890) there have been upwards of three hundred experimental reports devoted to the subject. James was interested in the possibility of training memory. Putting it to test, he memorized 158 lines of Hugo's *Satyr*, and then for practice, memorized the entire first book of *Paradise Lost*. After this intensive training he returned to Hugo's poem; another 158 lines required 151½ minutes, as compared with the 132 minutes required for the first 158 lines. There was manifestly no transfer, but James doubted the results since he was fatigued at the time of the second test. Later repetitions of the experiment fully justified his doubts.[15]

The customary procedure in all modern experiments on transfer is to compare the gain for a practiced group of subjects with the gain (if any) for a control group, the latter being in every respect equal to the experimental group, and like it, tested at the beginning and end of the experiment, without, however, any specific training in the interval. The procedure is:

Training Group: test in Function 1; training in F 2; retest in F 1.
Control Group: test in Function 1; no training in F 2; retest in F 1.

When the numerous published experiments are compared with one another little agreement is found in their results, no doubt because of the widely different conditions under which the experiments were conducted, the different types of material they employed, and the different mental functions studied. In spite of this disagreement, there are few dissenting voices to the conclusion that transfer *does* take place, in varying amounts, depending on circumstances. Transfer fails only when some extraneous condition (such as James's fatigue) precludes it, or when the tested and the trained functions stand in some kind of antithetical relation to one another, bringing about interference instead of the expected aid; the latter condition is known as "negative transfer." The experimenters' *explanations* of

[14] R. Pintner, *Educational Psychology*, 1929, p. 265.
[15] H. A. Peterson, *Psychol. Rev.*, 1912, 19, p. 491.

their results are almost as numerous as the investigations themselves. Orata presents a summary of these interpretations, most of which in one way or another subscribe to the theory of identical elements, though some totally reject it.[16]

A detailed summary would serve no useful purpose here. Most of the experiments suffer from two serious weaknesses. For one thing, they often employ absurdly inconsequential tasks for training. To cross out *p's* and *q's* in a line of type, or to draw several hundred senseless designs, is a poor basis for a pronouncement concerning meaningful learning. A second weakness is the brevity of the experiments. Usually they are based on only a few days of training—a few months at the most. Optimal transfer—even normal amounts of transfer—cannot be expected under such conditions. In actual life, the development of skills and the building of personality take time; the process is continued for years. But whatever the demerits of the experimental approach, it is still necessary to appeal to evidence, such as it is, from this source when examining the case for partial identity.

If the theory of identical elements is to be defended at all, it must be defended in its *literal* meaning. It holds that mental life is composed of a certain number of well-defined habits, that these habits function independently excepting where some tangible, definable, testifiable "identical elements" connect them. This insistence upon "tangible, definable, testifiable" bonds is necessary in order to prevent proponents of the theory from slyly crawling out of the argument. All too often champions of the theory change their meaning of "identity" or of "element" in the midst of their discourse.

> Parenthetically it may be added that, strictly speaking, the term "transfer" ought never be used by those who believe in partial identity. Transfer suggests *change* of vehicle, whereas the hypothesis of identical elements should mean just what it says—*identical* vehicles. If one rides in the same vehicle throughout different territories one does not "transfer." The excursion unit is always the same. If it is the selfsame habits that function in different contexts, there is, strictly speaking, no transfer at all. But this difficulty with terms may be waived. It is more important to expose the central weaknesses of the theory than to recover a term from misuse.

[16] P. T. Orata, *The Theory of Identical Elements*, 1928, pp. 47-51.

HOW ELEMENTARY IS AN ELEMENT?

Thorndike likes to think of an element as very specific indeed, *e.g.*, "By identical elements are meant mental processes which have the same cell action in the brain as their physical correlate." [17] Likewise, "The general theory of identical elements—that one ability is improved by the exercise of another only when the neurones whose action the former represents are actually altered in the course of the exercise of the latter—is sound, and is useful in guiding thought. However, so little is known about which neurones are concerned in any ability that this general theory does not carry us far." [18] The image is one of identical neurone action.

We are told by Thorndike that a person's ability to estimate the length of 100 millimeter lines is essentially independent of his ability to estimate the length of 50 millimeter lines.[19] Since in experimental investigations it is found that training in one of these abilities does not appreciably affect the other ability, they are regarded as containing no appreciable elements in common. One wonders whether the abilities involved in estimating lines of 100 mm. and 75 mm. are still separate; and how about the abilities to estimate lines of 100 mm. and 99.999 mm.? In another connection we are told that there are "as many memories as there are facts to be memorized"; each memory is regarded as an element in itself. But what is a "fact to be memorized"? Is it a syllable, a word, a sentence, a sequence of sentences, an entire poem verbatim, or the general sense of the poem?

At the same time, extensive mental processes, such as "aims," "moods," "ideals," "knowledge of procedure," and such enormously complex functions as "esteem for truth wherever and however present" are alleged as elements.[20] If transfer can come about through such generalized components as these, the term element must lose its reference to "common cell action in the brain." To propose that a generalized sentiment, such as "regard for the scientific method," or "esteem for truth wherever and however present" has a rigid and specific location in the nervous system is to propose an absurdity.

[17] *Educational Psychology*, 1913, II, p. 359.
[18] *Ibid.*, II, p. 417.
[19] *J. Phil., Psychol. & Sci. Meth.*, 1909, 6, pp. 239 f.
[20] *Educational Psychology*, 1903, p. 81, and *Educational Psychology*, 1913, II, pp. 419 f.

Such alleged elements are not at all specific; they are extremely general; in fact, they are the utmost in trait-psychology.

At this point the conception of a truly elementary element is hopelessly lost, and for it is substituted the doctrine that transfer may be due to general attitudes, to concepts, or to traits, although this substitution is not recognized. It admits, without realizing the consequences, that whenever a generalized disposition is meaningful and relevant to two situations, it carries over from one to the other, exerting in both cases a determining influence upon behavior that makes the pattern of adjustment to one situation correspond in a meaningful way to the pattern of adjustment in the other. This is all that trait-psychology would maintain.

HOW IDENTICAL IS AN IDENTITY?

The question now arises as to where identities occur in the sequence of events from stimulus to response. Conceivably the identities might occur in the successive stimulus fields, or in neural processes, or in ideational activity (presumably reducible to neural processes), or in the final muscular contractions—or else in all these phases of the transfer situation.

Most champions of the theory stress identities in the stimulus fields. To react to identities in the midst of diversities, they say, is the crux of transfer (cf. Figure 19, *a* and *a'*). But is an *a* actually identical with an *a'*? Is one door identical with any other door? Do not these doors take their perceptual character rather from the whole situation in which they are embedded? A panther behind a cage is certainly a very different stimulus from a panther in front of the same cage. So it is with doors. The door to a neighbor's house can never be *identical* with the door to one's own house—neither objectively nor subjectively. Even the most persistent facts of nature, such as the sun setting in the west, or the shape of the figure 8, are never precisely the same in all respects. And especially are they dissimilar in their effects upon the organism at different times, depending on organic states of fatigue or desire, and on the contexts in which they occur.

The most one could argue in favor of objectively "identical" elements is that they sometimes seem to be *equivalent* for the purposes of the organism—functionally they can be substituted for one another. One friend may replace another as confidant or as partner at bridge. But in such cases it is not the objective identity that is responsible for the continuance of the same behavior, but rather the needs, attitudes, and traits of the person. It is these general dispositions that carry over from one situation to another *in spite of* the lack of identical elements in two stimulus situations.

Even if there were ascertainable identities in two stimulus fields, they certainly could not be regarded as automatically provocative of transfer. According to the theory, identities in the stimulus fields should *of themselves* arouse the habits to which they are bound. Yet it took centuries for men to discover the "identical element" in the behavior of the falling apple and the tides. Usually it takes years for students of psychology to see the manifestly common features between diverse schools of thought. One is seldom affected spontaneously by so-called identities. The scientist must *search* for identities in the midst of diversity. Only by hard work, and skillful analysis can he find identities (or equivalences), by which he may transfer his knowledge, acquired from one object, to like objects. There is nothing compulsive about identities; they do not automatically cause transfer. Only under the guidance of general concepts and volitional dispositions are they effective.

As for identities in the nervous system, they are even more elusive. Yet the belief that identical elements reside in identical *cell action* is basic to the whole theory. "In the same organism," writes Thorndike, "the same neurone-action will always produce the same result. . . ." [21] The picture he gives is one of definite neural grooves, capable of re-excitation in different response-patterns. Today such a picture is wholly untenable. Its fallaciousness from the point of view of cerebral physiology, and its complete inapplicability to the phenomenon of transfer, are disclosed by Lashley:

> The doctrine of isolated reflex conduction has been widely influential in shaping current psychological theories. . . . If learning is restricted to particular synapses, there can be no influence of training upon other activities than those actually practiced; any improvement in unpracticed functions must be the result of nervous connections which they have in common with the practiced activities. The rejection of doctrines of formal discipline seems to have been based far more upon such reasoning than upon any convincing experimental evidence.

[21] E. L. Thorndike, *Educational Psychology*, I, 1913, p. 7.

There is no evidence to support this belief in identity of nervous elements. On the contrary, it is doubtful if the same neurons or synapses are involved even in two similar reactions to the same stimulus. Our data seem to prove that the structural elements are relatively unimportant for integration and that the common elements must be some sort of dynamic patterns, determined by the relations or ratios among the parts of the system and not by the specific neurons activated. If this be true, we cannot, on the basis of our present knowledge of the nervous system, set any limit to the kinds or amount of transfer possible or to the sort of relations which may be directly recognized.[22]

As for identities of muscular contraction, they are still less suitable to serve as a basis for transfer. There are many ways of performing the same act; these ways may all be *equivalent* to one another, but clearly the muscular contractions are not *identical*. Writing with a crayon held in the right hand, left hand, toes, or teeth shows transfer effects, but the muscles involved in these cases are entirely different.[23] Furthermore, the acquisition of a specific muscular skill never helps in solving new problems in which the skill would be useful, unless the subject *sees the pertinency* of the skill to the novel situation (cf. p. 278). The employment of the same muscular movements is more likely to be a consequence of transfer, rather than a cause.

It seems, then, impossible to discover any "identities" sharp enough, tangible enough, or identical enough (!) to justify this theory of transfer. The theory is entirely explicit; it *says* identities and it *means* identities, but identities seem always to elude discovery. Thorndike himself is somewhat disturbed by this elusiveness, and speaks of "identities beyond our cognizance," but he believes that there is little trouble in reaching an "approximate decision" in those cases where training is of practical importance. This "approximate decision" is not so easily reached as Thorndike thinks. Furthermore,

---

[22] K. S. Lashley, *Brain Mechanisms and Intelligence*, University of Chicago Press, 1929, pp. 172 f.

[23] Considerable evidence proving that motor consistency in the *expression of personality* cannot possibly be due to the employment of identical muscular contractions, or for that matter, to identical nerve tracts is contained in G. W. Allport and P. E. Vernon, *Studies in Expressive Movement*, 1933. A typical finding: "The length of the walking stride and the area of the subject's normal writing correlate, $r = +.46$. In such dissimilar fields of behavior it clearly cannot be a question of identical nerve processes. It seems that each subject is simply maintaining what for him is a suitable and congenial level of activity. Somewhere between the minimum and maximum possible extent, there is an extent of movement natural to the subject, and this remains proportionately constant in very diverse situations whatever musculature is employed. The theory of identical elements is not equipped to handle a case of preserving a congenial proportionality in movement" (p. 156).

an approximate decision is not enough. If the theory is to be defended at all, the identities must be specifiable and not everlastingly shifting ground.

THE QUESTION OF PROPORTIONALITY

Thorndike's influential theory holds not only that transfer depends upon the presence of identical elements, but that the *amount* of transfer depends upon the *number* of identical elements present in two or more situations where transfer occurs. It is relatively simple to put this corollary to experimental test, although to determine the *number* of common factors involved it is again necessary to rely upon the "approximate decision," endorsed by Thorndike. To reach such a decision probably all would agree, for example, that the learning of two poems involves more processes in common than the learning of one poem and one set of nonsense syllables. However, in precisely this situation Sleight found no evidence of proportional transfer. A group trained in poetry showed as great an improvement in ability to memorize nonsense syllables as in ability to learn new poetry.[24] The results are typical of experiments on transfer.

Even the original experiment of Thorndike and Woodworth showed an embarrassing absence of proportional transfer.

> Individuals practiced estimating the areas of rectangles from 10-100 sq. cm. in size until a very marked improvement was attained. The improvement in accuracy for areas of the same size but of different shape due to this training was 44 per cent as great as that for areas of the same shape and size. For areas of the same shape, but from 140-300 sq. cm. in size, the improvement was 3 per cent as great. But for areas of *different* shape and *different* size (140-400 sq. cm.), the improvement was 52 per cent as great.[25]

The greatest transfer was secured with areas that *differed in both size and shape* from practiced areas! Results so contrary to expectation fail completely to justify the hypothesis of proportional transfer.

Other evidence is plentiful. Coover, after excluding so far as possible identical elements in two situations, still found transfer ranging from 25 per cent to 75 per cent; in other experiments he found transfer between dissimilar data greater than between similar data. Likewise in the work of Cole, Coover and Angell, McKinney and many

[24] W. G. Sleight, *Brit. J. Psychol.*, 1911, 4, 386-457.
[25] Cf. E. L. Thorndike, *Educational Psychology*, 1913, II, p. 397.

others the proportional transfer required by the theory is lacking.[26]

Not only in sensory-motor learning is the amount of transfer quite independent of the proportion of identical elements in two stimulus fields, but the same lack of ratio is clearly seen in other forms of learning as well. Take trauma, for example, where a single episode influences all the recesses of a life, not merely those habits to which it has been previously bonded. A traumatic change of one small item in a man's environment may make all the difference in the world to him, perhaps changing happiness into despair. What happens in trauma is that a single experience *saturates* the whole life and forcibly compels a re-structuration of the entire personality. There is no trace whatever of proportional transfer.

SO-CALLED IDENTITIES OF PROCEDURE

A classic experiment on transfer was that of E. Ebert and E. Meumann.[27] These investigators found such widespread improvement in the ability to memorize all sorts of material after training with nonsense material, that they felt compelled to postulate a *Mitübung* (a sympathetic exercise or spread) in all memorial capacities following training in one special type of memorizing. G. E. Müller objected to this interpretation as extravagant, claiming by contrast that various identities (of *Lernstoff*, *Lernmittel*, and *Lernweise*) would account equally well for the results.[28] Ever since this controversy it has been customary for the defenders of partial identity to join Müller in claiming, whenever identities of content are "beyond cognizance," that certain identities in *procedure* must be responsible for the results. Among these alleged identities of procedure are such complex mental states as "being aware that one has a problem," "distrust of opinion," "disposition to neglect irrelevant things," or the regarding of certain courses of action as desirable, beautiful, or false.[29]

Now such extensions of the theory of partial identity are fatal;

[26] L. W. Cole, *J. Educ. Res.*, 1928, 18, 32-39; J. E. Coover and F. Angell, *Am. J. Psychol.*, 1907, 18, 328-340; F. McKinney, *J. Exper. Psychol.*, 1933, 16, 854-864.
L. W. Webb correctly observes that objective similarity of stimulus patterns may not mean similarity of the neural activities involved, but adds, "To my mind herein lies the weakness of Thorndike's theory. Its validity can never be adequately tested. Any general agreement as to the degree of neural identity between any two complex problems is impossible." (*Psychol. Monog.*, 1917, No. 104, p. 57.)
[27] *Arch. f. d. ges. Psychol.*, 1905, 4, 1-232.
[28] *Zsch. f. Psychol.*, 1905, 39, 111-125.
[29] E. L. Thorndike, *Educational Psychology*, 1913, II, pp. 418 f.

they mean nothing less than its complete surrender. Take the "identical procedure," so often mentioned, of "getting to the heart of the problem directly." Such a complex mental attitude varies enormously, depending on the stuff of the problem. The irrelevancies that must be excluded in approaching the heart of different problems are not identical irrelevancies. "Habituation to discomfort and fatigue," "attentiveness," and "the disposition to maintain the scientific attitude," are never twice exactly the same. To maintain a scientific attitude, for example, requires many different associations, movements, and mental operations. The only common factor is a thoroughly generalized attitude or interest, versatile in expression, employing now this neural mechanism and now that, characterized by more flexibility than the theory of identical elements can admit with consistency is its own position.

The inclusion of general attitudes and volitional dispositions under the list of "identities" is a necessary but futile subterfuge to save the theory. The explicit thesis is that

> Training the mind means the development of thousands of particular independent capacities, the formation of countless particular capacities, for the working of any mental capacity depends upon the concrete data with which it works.[30]

This is the thesis and its proponents must stick to it. The scientific attitude, or a disposition to search for what is beautiful, or a general regard for truth, admitted by Thorndike as identities of procedure, are obviously not "particular independent capacities" specific to the concrete data to which they are applied!

Procedure in learning is indeed a crucial factor in transfer, but procedure depends primarily on *attitude, interest, aim, concept, ideal,* or an *understanding of principles.* All of these forms of mental organization result in transfer. But none of them is constituted of invariant habits or specific bonds.

Thorndike once found that certain pupils taught to square $x + y$ suffered a great deal of interference when asked to square $b_1 + b_2$. He concluded that squaring $x + y$ is an ability specific and independent of squaring $b_1 + b_2$.[31] Is it not perhaps the teaching that was at fault? A child often fails to see the *principle* of a computation, but the instruction is usually to blame. It is even possible to teach a young

---

[30] E. L. Thorndike, *Principles of Teaching*, 1906, p. 248.
[31] *J. Exper. Psychol.*, 1922, 5, 33-38.

child in such a way that his ability to count three pennies will not extend to the task of counting three apples, but such mischievous pedagogy proves only that under *unfavorable* conditions generalization will not occur.

The importance of forming a general concept in order to secure transfer, and the worthlessness of the blind recurrence of identical elements, is demonstrated in the well-known experiment of H. A. Ruger:

> A certain mechanical puzzle was so arranged that it could be presented in various forms. The manipulations for these various forms could all be comprised under a single formula. This general formula could be deduced from any one of these special forms. A number of subjects were tried with this puzzle. As soon as skill was acquired in dealing with one form of the puzzle it was changed to another form. The subjects who developed the general formula during the solution of the first form were able to use the specialized habits built up in the first form in the second. Those who formed merely the special habits without developing the principle attempted to carry over the habits without modification and were greatly embarrassed by the change.[32]

In another experiment, a group of students was taught geometry in the prevailing routine fashion, and another group by an improved technique devised to emphasize logical principles. The groups were equal in intelligence. After some months, the experimental group showed more persistence, developed more methods of solving new problems, secured higher examination grades, and even showed improvement on non-geometrical reasoning tests.[33] This experiment shows that as ordinarily taught geometry does not carry over to reasoning in general, but likewise that it may be so taught as to achieve this end. Many other investigations lead to essentially the same conclusions.[34] One study showed that training in neatness may or may not transfer to activities other than that in which neat habits were first established. Everything depends on the way training is given.[35] Transfer is not automatic, but depends upon insight into general principles. Good teachers know this is true.[36]

[32] "The Psychology of Efficiency," *Arch. of Psychol.*, No. 15, 1910, 18 f.
[33] E. P. Johnson, *Mathematics Teacher*, 1924, 17, 191-201.
[34] *E.g.*, H. Woodrow, *J. Educ. Psychol.*, 1927, 18, 159-172; G. P. Meredith, *Forum of Educ.*, 1927, 5, 37-45; W. W. Coxe, *J. Educ. Res.*, 1923, 7, 244-247.
[35] W. C. Ruediger, *Educ. Rev.*, 1908, 36, 364-371.
[36] "The conclusion is inevitable that when an individual is trained in mere routine fashion or drill, he gets fixed and mechanical habits which do not transfer. On the other hand, when he is trained consciously to organize his knowledge or pro-

GENERALIZATION

The theory diametrically opposed to the doctrine of partial identity is known, somewhat broadly, as the theory of *generalization*. Evidence for it is plentiful enough, but its detailed formulation gives more difficulty.

The experiment of C. H. Judd that led him and others to deny the theory of identical elements, and to offer a theory of generalization in its place, is well known. Two groups of boys were directed to throw darts at a target 12 inches under water. After one group had received instruction in the principles of refraction, the target was then placed four inches under water, and all the boys tried again. On this retest the uninstructed group had larger and more persistent errors, while the boys who had learned the theory adjusted very rapidly to the changed conditions.[37] Later, Alpert, working with preschool children, found that comprehension (insight) of a solution improved the subsequent solution of similar tasks, whereas trial and error solutions did not.[38] Ruger (whose experiments were cited above) concluded that "In general, the value of specific habits under a change of conditions depended directly on the presence of a general idea which would serve for their control." [39] Pear, with tasks involving low-grade motor skill in which conscious generalization was made impossible by the conditions, found little transfer. He concludes that there are two meanings of transfer, (a) that resulting from exercise of any particular function in two contexts (Thorndike's theory); and (b) transfer resulting from the extension of attitudes, sentiments, ideals, or knowledge of methods, where the particular function trained is a vehicle of these mental powers. He writes, "It now seems certain that (a) is rare, and that (b) definitely can occur." [40]

There is no need to multiply evidence. Time and again it appears that identical elements in themselves have no power to effect transfer. Only when a general principle is *understood as applicable* to two or more fields does the training in one carry over to the others. Fre-

cedure in such a way that general principles are formulated, the result is not a mechanical habit but generalization, or an adaptive and flexible form of behavior which by virtue of its flexibility transfers." P. T. Orata, *The Theory of Identical Elements,* 1928, p. 99.

[37] C. H. Judd, *Educ. Rev.,* 1908, 36, 28-42.
[38] A. Alpert, *T. C. Contrib. to Educ.,* No. 323, 1928.
[39] H. A. Ruger, *op. cit.,* p. 19.
[40] T. H. Pear, *Nature,* 1928, 122, 611-614.

quently this transfer occurs even when the subject is ignorant of specifically identical features in the various situations. He need have only a valid conceptual principle in mind. When introspections are taken it often turns out that the subject discovers identical features between his problems only *after* the transfer has taken place, and then merely because he is looking around for some means of rationalizing his first valid generalization.

One form of generalization aiding transfer, but utterly contradicting the hypothesis of identical elements, is the carrying over of an *abstract relationship* from one situation to another. For instance, in Köhler's work, many times verified, an animal trained to respond to the *brighter* of two grays by receiving food when the brighter is selected, will, when confronted with a *new* pair of grays, forsake the same gray (the specific element) with which food has been previously associated, in favor of one that is still brighter.[41] It is not the identical element that provokes the selection; the *identical* element with which food has been associated is actually abandoned. Monkeys, too, will choose the brighter, the squarer, the louder, the heavier, or the larger of two objects in their attempt to keep up with the experimenter's scheme for feeding them. It is impossible, of course, to argue that the relation between two stimuli is itself an element identical with the relation between two *different* stimuli, because in every such case wholly different sensory processes are involved.[42]

EQUIVALENCE AND SIMILARITY

To prove that transfer occurs, not through the re-activation of specific bonds, but through the perception of relations, through insight, and through the formation of general concepts, is important, but not altogether definitive. There are limitations to any individual's powers of generalization, and there are conditions and principles governing its occurrence, all of which need to be known, before the

[41] W. Köhler, *Abhandlungen der Preuss. Akad. d. Wissenschaft*, 1918, Phys.-Math., Kl., 2; also H. Klüver, *Behavior Mechanisms in Monkeys*, 1933.

[42] The case for partial identity looks even more hopeless in the light of Lashley's report on the transference of the ability to discriminate brightness from one eye to the other which had not been used during training. In this experiment the same sensory cells were certainly not stimulated in the formation of the habit. More remarkable still is the fact that this transfer took place in animals without a visual cortex, showing further that "identical cell action" is hardly the basis for the transfer. (*The Foundations of Experimental Psychology*, ed. by C. C. Murchison, 1929, p. 543.)

nature of transfer, or of the structural units of personality, can be understood.

Much help comes from the experimentalist's conception of *equivalence of stimuli*. This conception grew out of the discovery that changes in the environmental situation, sometimes even pronounced

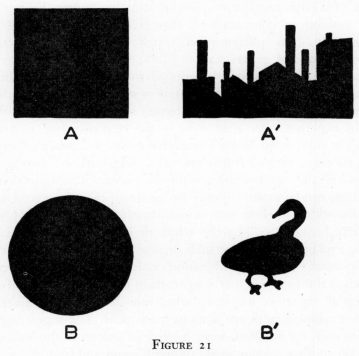

A   A′

B   B′

FIGURE 21

Equivalent and Non-equivalent Stimuli

Monkeys trained to respond positively to the square and to avoid the circle will transfer these responses to a wide range of equivalent relationships. These designs are reproduced through the courtesy of the experimenter, H. Klüver.

changes, do not essentially alter the nature of the response.[43] For example, night monkeys (Aotes), trained to respond favorably (in seeking food) to shape A (Figure 21) and to avoid shape B, will, when confronted with A′ and B′, select the former and avoid the latter. For them A and A′, B and B′ are equivalent.

To explain such remarkable transfer effects, the theory of identical elements helps not at all. There are no conceivable elements or

[43] H. Klüver, *op. cit.*, p. 4. The same author has given an historical account of the method of equivalent stimuli, and has pointed out its value in the investigation of personality, *Char. & Pers.*, 1936, 5, 91-112.

identities involved unless they be *curvilinearity* and *angularity*, but each of these is a *relationship* rather than an element. Further, the monkey responds to neither as separate from the other but only to a highly generalized cue, *viz., greater curvilinearity*. That the transfer is due to such a magnified degree of generalization is proved through the use of a large number of pairs of stimulus figures, having absolutely nothing in common save this greater and lesser degree of curvilinearity. The phenomenon which Klüver calls equivalence, therefore, is one of generalization.

The same principle can be applied to the dispositional units of personality. Suppose, for instance, one is studying the personality of a "super-patriot." One quickly discovers that to him many different items of experience are *equivalent* in the response they provoke: a red flag, a volume by Marx, a teacher's union, the peace efforts of a Yale professor, or the formation of a neighborhood co-operative. One and all they arouse the communist phobia. The equivalence of these items can be explained only by assuming that there is an underlying disposition of some sort, whose threshold of arousal is low and capable of being crossed by this whole diverse range of stimuli. How can one explain the fact that such diverse stimuli are equivalent (*i.e.*, not responded to with discrimination) unless one postulates a generalized personal disposition that *renders* them equivalent? This inference becomes all the more necessary when one discovers that diverse *responses* to these stimuli are likewise equivalent. The super-patriot in question may, on occasion, write a letter of protest to the local newspaper; on another, merely grow red with anger and bluster; or, again, he may join the vigilantes. What is manifestly constant is the *attitude;* it is because of the attitude that many stimuli and many responses are equivalent. Neither in the stimuli arousing the attitude, nor in the responses issuing from it, nor in the "cell-action of the cortex" is it possible to trace identical elements. The *meaningfulness* of the disposition, its significance in the life-pattern of the super-patriot, is the one and only stable feature.

The degree of generalization of such a disposition (which may here be called either a trait or an attitude) is measurable by the range of *equivalence*. Some people with an anti-communist attitude do not treat so wide a range of experiences as equivalent (with so little discrimination). Some likewise have a much narrower *behavioral* range within which responses may be regarded as equivalent. The degree of generalization, which is different in different persons, varies inversely with the degree to which stimuli and responses are discriminated. A finely discriminated disposition, one that is aroused only by some narrow and special class of stimuli, leading to a special kind of verbal or motor behavior, is likewise a unitary structure in personality, but far more specific than the widely generalized attitude just described.[44]

The welter of stimuli to which the individual is exposed fall for him, as it were, into *constellations*, every member of which is effective in producing some response. Correspondingly, the responses he makes, though almost infinitely varied, are not as diverse as they appear at first sight, for many of them are also equivalent in their personal significance. Thus, for a man with a disposition to be *polite*, innumerable environmental occasions are equivalent in their power to arouse this particular determining trait, and at the same time the polite gentleman finds innumerable *ways* of expressing his dominant trait (equivalent responses).

The application of the doctrine of equivalence to the problem of transfer is easily made. Transfer takes place whenever, and in whatever degree, a new stimulus field for a given individual is equivalent to another more familiar field. A child learning neatness will carry over this orderly behavior from the training situation to a new situation to the extent that the two situations are *for him* equivalent. If to him the fields are non-equivalent, there will be no transfer. And if in some way, the fields are conflicting or antithetical, negative transfer, or interference, will occur.

Related to this modern concept of equivalence is the ancient concept of *similarity*. For centuries "association by similarity" was regarded as a primary law of mental organization. In recent times, under the attack of specificity, partial identity, and related elementaristic crusades, this law lost its standing and was reduced to identities and contiguities. If, as we have argued, this reduction is impossible, then the concept of similarity again raises its bruised head.

To enter here into a full examination of this difficult problem would be impossible. Its reformulation with the aid of the many experiments on the equivalence and constancy of stimuli, and the

[44] Though both specific and general attitudes must be recognized as true dispositions, the latter type is ordinarily superior in duration and in motivational power. Cf. H. Cantril, "General and Specific Attitudes," *Psychol. Monog.*, No. 192, 1932.

equivalence and consistency of responses, is now gradually taking place. It is still premature, however, to regard the concept as fully reinstated to a central position in the explanation of transfer, or in the analysis of personality. But its status is improving.

Formulations in terms of *equivalence* are essentially behavioristic and operational. The investigator determines the range within which stimuli are equated, and the range within which responses are consistent. But the account in these operational terms is not complete without a corresponding formulation in phenomenological terms; for the *experience* of similarity, subjectively considered, is remarkably subtle and its role in mental organization cannot as yet be stated entirely in terms of operational equivalence.

Indeed the capacity of the human mind for sensing resemblances is astounding. Whenever two stimulus fields (however novel and different they may be) are for any perceiving mind, for its own purposes, classed together, a sense of similarity results. It is a highly individualistic matter, with the oddest of metaphors sometimes resulting. Someone's voice may be sensed as similar to blotting paper, someone's eyes as similar to twin ash cans just emptied, someone else's moral fiber as like a sponge. The capacity of mind for forming such analogies is almost limitless. Small wonder that William James was prompted to speak of the "lawless revelry of similarity."

For all its individuality of form, and for all its unpredictability, the sense of similarity is the subjective condition *par excellence* of transfer. If a student sees similarity between the Greek grammar at which he drudges and his own love of logic, mutual transfer results; if not, there is no such transfer. If for him there is some meaningful link between his instructor's criticism of his errors in English composition and his sloppy conduct outside the classroom, again transfer occurs (cf. p. 210).

To *some* students the study of English, psychology, or even of the much despised Latin, may have many valuable resemblances to life. For *others* these subjects are barren, not because they fail to possess elements that specifically overlap with life outside the classroom, but *because the persons can see no similarity*. For this group more "practical" subjects, such as business English or advertising, may kindle the undying flame.

Similarity is, then, seen to be a highly individual matter. Its operation is difficult to predict, and educationally it cannot be standardized.[45] To be sure, a teacher often points out resemblances between the experiences of his students inside and outside the classroom, but the results are unpredictable. Some remain impervious to the effort; others who have what James called "the electric aptitude for analogies," may perceive the similarities that the teacher points out and many more besides.

But is this revelry of similarity really *lawless?* It is conditioned by temperament and previous learning; it is certainly lawful enough if regarded from the point of view of the individual's life-history. Instead of lawless it would be more accurate to say that similarity is *personal.* And just because it is personal, the transfer value of any item in the school curriculum cannot be standardized or predicted. Neither for school children nor for adults are similarities *uniform.* Only in the sense that the transfer value of similarity evades standardization for the group is it lawless; in the sense that it always harmonizes with the individual life-history it is lawful.

Since similarity is essentially the subjective counterpart of equivalence, it plays a corresponding role in the structural arrangement of personality. To an artistic person, a sunset, a landscape, a sonnet, a threshing machine, a derelict in the sands, may all be similar: in that to him they all mean *beauty.* The wider the range of such conscious similarities, the more generalized is his esthetic interest.

It is not necessary to demonstrate again that such similarities cannot possibly be reduced to partial identity. *Resemblances* are never identities, not even *in certain respects.* If I say that you remind me of some friend, and you ask me why and wherefore, I may narrow down the resemblance to similar build or similar resonance of voice. But even in these respects you are not identical with my friend; your build or your voice is only *similar* to his. The search for the partial identity involves an infinite regress. Even should we come by analysis to some minute feature that seems virtually interchangeable between you and my friend, we then are forced to admit that this residual feature does not represent the original experience which was of a resemblance between him and you as *whole* human beings.

Every experience of similarity implies a paradox. There is both *sameness* and *novelty* in the experience. Two stimulus fields are compared, and though for certain purposes they may be subjectively equivalent, still they are known to be disparate and non-identical.

[45] And under certain special conditions of conflict and confusion, similarity may lead to negative transfer.

A sense of two-ness, not of identical one-ness, is always involved. The sense of novelty and of separateness in experiences of similarity enables us to escape from literal and stereotyped response. Even while we are reducing the limitless and confusing events of life to a manageable number—seeing analogies here and likenesses there—we find plenty of room for originality and discrimination in our adjustments.

The principles of equivalence and similarity (objective and subjective counterparts of the same mental process) are a great improvement over the theory of identical elements. The latter is a rigid, mechanical principle allowing only invariable "reactive" response; the former allow both for *stability* and for *flexibility* in conduct. As the individual develops he learns to economize his responses; a wide range of environmental demands take on, for him, the same significance (becoming equivalent and similar). Concepts are formed, likewise attitudes, and traits: these are for him stable *modi vivendi*, serving him as dependable principles of survival in a confusing world. Yet these concepts, attitudes and traits are not rigidly bound to the stimulus according to the principle of identical elements. If they were, a crude stereotyping of behavior would ensue, and personality would be far more machine-like than it is.

The reader can now see why this discussion has been a necessary prelude to a new and more adequate theory of the structure of personality. The true units of personality must be serviceable for survival. They must allow for both *stability* and *flexibility* in behavior. Even while the individual, through training, learns to behave to wide ranges of stimuli in essentially the same way (perceiving them as similar), at the same time he must constantly meet and master new demands. Hence, the units of personality, well structured though they are, cannot be fixed and changeless.

SUMMARY

The solution of the problem of the organization of personality will depend to a large degree upon the solution found for the problem of *transfer*. Both face the difficult question as to how the individual meets the succeeding events of his life through employing his relevant *previous* experience.

During the past generation the prevalent view of transfer has been in terms of hypothetical identical elements; and this doctrine, at the same time, has been widely accepted as an adequate theory of the structure of personality. Everything mental is said to be ruled by habit, and habits are conceived as insulated stimulus-response bonds, affecting one another and combining into patterns only to the extent to which they have some still more specific elements in common.

Such a conception must be rejected. Either, on the one hand, the search for elements becomes a matter of infinite regress, more and more minute (and more and more elusive) entities being sought; or else, on the other hand, the literal intent of the theory is sacrificed by positing highly generalized elements, such as "desire for truth," or "an attitude of going to the heart of any problem." In the latter case, no specific identities can be found. In spite of the explicit requirement of the theory, it is never able to specify the precise nature or location of any identity.

On the experimental side there is no evidence for proportionality of transfer, that is to say, for the contention that transfer occurs in proportion to the number of approximate identities between two fields of stimulation. The falseness of this contention is especially apparent in all cases where trauma or emotional learning is involved. In these instances, transfer passes all bounds of expectation. In such cases identities cannot be involved, for the whole personal life is *saturated* with the effects. All in all, experimental data, the discoveries of modern neurophysiology, the canons of theoretical psychology, and simple common sense, unite in rejecting this view of mental organization.

Evidence favors a theory of the opposite order, one in which integration and generalization play the leading part. Here transfer effects depend chiefly upon the equivalence of meaning to the individual of the fields that confront him. If they are similar, transfer takes place. Equivalence and similarity are not uniform for all; they are a personal matter, and hence it is impossible to predict for people en masse the transfer value of a single experience, or to arrange a program of school studies that will secure uniform transfer effects for *all* children.

To explain equivalence and similarity it is necessary to assume underlying focal dispositions within the latent mental organization of each individual. These dispositions must be of such an order as to account both for the stability and versatility of response. Upon the ground thus cleared, a constructive and detailed theory of the structure of personality may now be built.

CHAPTER XI

THE THEORY OF TRAITS

> We have the right and the obligation to develop a concept
> of trait as a definitive doctrine; for in all the activity of the
> Person, there is besides a variable portion, likewise a constant
> purposive portion, and this latter we isolate in the concept of
> trait.
>
> —*William Stern*

Scarcely anyone has ever thought of questioning the existence of traits as the fundamental dispositions of personality. In common speech everyone presupposes traits when he characterizes himself or his acquaintances. This man, one says, is *gruff* and *reticent*, but a *hard-worker;* that man is *fastidious, talkative,* and *penurious.* Normally the psychologist too talks in these terms. But as soon as he enters his laboratory or class-room he is likely to leave common sense behind him and to embrace one or another of the scientific theories discussed in the last two chapters. Rightly he thinks of common sense as a faulty guide. Yet in the matter of human traits common sense is remarkably well-seasoned with experience, and scarcely deserves the complete rebuff it receives.

For one thing the path of common sense would never have led into the thickets of specificity nor run the aimless course of the doctrine of identical elements. Such non-focal theories of organization are entirely foreign to it. On the other hand, common sense would not go to the opposite extreme and regard personality as a perfect unity, faultless in integration. It is between the levels of specific habit and complete unity that common sense locates the natural foci of personality. It is there that psychologists should search.[1]

---

[1] And physiologists likewise. Up to the present time there has been little work beyond rough speculation concerning the dynamics of "traces," of "cortical stresses," and "neurograms," all defined as multi-focal dispositions ready-organized to perform in some integrative fashion either at high tension or at low. (Cf. E. B. Holt, *Animal Drive and the Learning Process,* 1931; see especially pp. 167, 261, 263 for suggestive statements regarding this in-between level of analysis.) But in general so little is

ARE TRAITS BIOSOCIAL OR BIOPHYSICAL?

A certain metaphysical question is likely to arise at the outset of any discussion of traits, and if allowed to do so it bedevils the whole problem. The sooner it can be disposed of, the better. The question, in brief, is this: Are traits *bona fide*, veridical dispositions, or are they nothing more than nominal fictions, mere words, obscuring rather than clarifying the structure of personality? Some writers maintain the first position, some the second, and a few occupy a somewhat uncertain middle ground. The following quotations are typical of these three positions.

> My own view is that traits are only convenient names given to types or qualities of behavior which have elements in common. They are not psychological entities but rather categories for the classification of habits.[2] (BIOSOCIAL)

> A trait is a constant directing psychic force (*Richtkraft*) which determines the active and reactive behavior of the individual.[3] (BIOPHYSICAL)

> An individual is said to possess, or to be characterized by, a certain personality trait when he exhibits a generalized and consistent form, mode, or type of reactivity (behavior), and differs (deviates) sufficiently from other members of his social environment, both in the frequency and intensity of this behavior, for his atypicality to be noticed by relatively normal and impartial observers, themselves members of this same environment. . . . The definition tries to express the notion that the trait is a relation between the individual and his observers.[4] (MIXED)

The first quotation is compatible with the hypothesis of identical elements. If habits, connected by their common bonds, are the true elements of personality, then it follows, as the author asserts, that trait-names are merely designations for categories of habits. He considers traits not so much as residing in the individual himself, as *forms of perception* for an observer to use.[5]

known concerning the divisions and gradients of the neural process that a neurophysiological account of human traits is as yet scarcely possible. In time the story developed here from a psychological point of view will no doubt find its physiological counterpart.

[2] M. May, *J. Soc. Psychol.*, 1932, 3, p. 133.

[3] F. Baumgarten, *Die Charaktereigenschaften*, 1933, p. 15; also *Brit. J. Psychol.*, 1936, 26, p. 290.

[4] P. E. Vernon, *Psychol. Rev.*, 1933, 40, 542 f.

[5] The same author's suggestion that the total personality likewise be defined in biosocial terms, as "a man's social stimulus-value," was rejected in Chapter II.

Of course, traits *do* have stimulus value, but this does not mean that they are only "categories for the classification of habits." The fact that people can perceive, appreciate, name, and react to, the conduct of others, is not a legitimate reason why we must conclude that these others are *devoid* of traits. The perception or inference of traits by outside observers is a problem by itself, requiring later discussion (Chapters XVIII and XIX); but it has no essential bearing upon the question of the existence of traits.

The biosocial view of personality is likewise artfully expressed by Pirandello who never tires of pointing out that a man's personality seems to vary with the expectations and prejudices of his associates. To one he may be a saint, to another a sinner, a hated enemy or a trusted ally. Whoever chooses to view a character in a particular fashion is, in a sense, right (if he thinks he is). But wherein does the multiplicity lie? Surely not within the person himself. The variability lies rather in the fact that into their judgments of him many people project their own desires and biases. What is most noteworthy in research on personality is that different observers should agree as well as they do in judging any one person. This fact alone proves that there must be something *really there*, something objective in the nature of the individual himself that compels observers, in spite of their own prejudices, to view him in essentially the same way.

Another version of the biosocial view is "fictionism." One of its first representatives was Jeremy Bentham who was ever on his guard against substituting fictitious entities for real ones. Traits of personality he considered in the former category:

> Now disposition is a kind of fictitious entity, feigned for the convenience of discourse, in order to express what there is supposed to be permanent in a man's frame of mind.[6]

Bentham led a valiant fight against hypostatization through the reckless use of names, and no one can deny that obscurantism may result from their careless use. But this danger is not in itself sufficient grounds for a sweeping denial of the existence of traits. It indicates only the need for discrimination. As a matter of fact, on the page following the skeptical quotation, Bentham himself lays down the conditions under which the existence of dispositions may be securely inferred.

[6] Jeremy Bentham, *Principles of Morals and Legislation*, 1879 ed., chap. ix, p. 131.

A somewhat pragmatic compromise with fictionism is proposed by Thurstone who accompanies his doubts concerning the existence of traits with the admission that human beings certainly behave "as if" they had traits.[7] There is no real objection to this "as if" epistemology provided it is applied equally to all the data of psychology. It becomes objectionable only if it is used as a faint-hearted apology for traits as if for some reason they are to be regarded as less genuine than other forms of mental structure.

The second quotation on p. 287 represents a typical *biophysical* conception. A trait, it says, has more than nominal existence; it is independent of the observer, it is *really there*. Although it makes the unequivocal assumption that there are traits, or some corresponding neuropsychic dispositions, it leaves the problem of the criteria of traits and their discovery in particular cases to the critical procedures of psychology. In other words, this view does not hold that every trait-name necessarily implies a trait; but rather that behind all confusion of terms, behind the disagreement of judges, and apart from errors and failures of empirical observation, there are none the less *bona fide* mental structures in each personality that account for the consistency of its behavior. This view, the most worthy of endorsement, will be developed at greater length in succeeding pages.

The third quotation starts boldly enough with the recognition that there are such things as "generalized and consistent" forms of reactivity, but ends in the irrelevant sphere of social perception and judgment. It is a mixture of the biophysical and biosocial points of view. The first part of this definition is wholly satisfactory, but the biosocial additions are not. Why must a man's atypicality be noticeable in order that traits be attributed to him? Doesn't a person who is in no way outstanding or atypical possess traits as authentic as do conspicuous deviates? Distinctiveness is not the criterion of a trait. The author of this quotation likewise errs in assuming that a trait must be perceived by others, that it must represent some kind of relationship between two people. Did Robinson Crusoe lack traits before the advent of Friday? Will the last man to remain alive on earth abruptly lose his traits when his companions die?

[7] L. L. Thurstone, *The Reliability and Validity of Tests*, 1932, p. 101.

TRAITS AND DETERMINING TENDENCIES

Psychology has never been able to do without some conception of determining tendency (implying a readiness for response). Without such a conception it could never pretend to account for the manifest stability and consistency of behavior and experience. Determining tendencies, of course, are not matters of direct observation, but only of inference. The inference, however, is altogether compulsory, for not only do the observed data lead inevitably in that direction, but without it psychology could not advance beyond the stage of recording unintelligible discrete acts and separate states of consciousness. To accept traits requires no radical revision of the psychologist's creed, for traits are biophysical in the same sense that determining tendencies, attitudes, or other dynamic influences have always been considered by psychology as biophysical.

The phrase "determining tendency" has both a narrow and a broad connotation. In its narrower sense it refers specifically to a mental set that facilitates the solution of a special problem or the execution of a certain act. In its broader sense, it is *any* directive tendency or condition of readiness for response. The doctrine of traits may be ordered to this broader conception. All traits are directive tendencies, but conversely all directive tendencies are not traits. Some directive tendencies are far too narrow and specific in their reference, and too fleeting in time to satisfy the criteria of a trait. To be sure even a transient mental set may have some dependence upon personal traits, for traits often underlie the determining tendency of the moment. But in themselves traits are more generalized and more enduring, having less to do with fleeting mental sets than with lasting mental structures such as interests, tastes, complexes, sentiments, ideals, and the like.

There are two familiar classes of determining tendencies—habit and attitude—with which the concept of trait must be compared in detail.

Trait and Habit. Ordinarily the term *habit* connotes an invariable and inflexible type of response following the recurrence of a definite stimulus situation with which it is, by experience and practice, tied. The two previous chapters have explained at some length why this type of unit cannot be accepted as the sum and substance of mental organization. The units of personality must be more versatile both in respect to the situations that arouse them, and in respect to the responses they provoke.

In recent years some writers have sought to escape from the picture (bequeathed by William James) of the specific habit as a narrow task-master, and to put in its place a modified view, the doctrine of the *generalized habit*, or of a disposition that is not invariable in its mode of arousal or in its forms of expression.[8] This conception is sponsored by Dewey. While still employing the standard term, *habit*, he portrays a far more flexible disposition than was characteristic of usage in the generation after James.

> Repetition is in no sense the essence of habit. Tendency to repeat acts is an incident of many habits, but not of all. A man with a habit of giving way to anger may show his habit by a murderous attack upon someone who has offended. His act is nonetheless due to habit because it occurs once only in his life. The essence of habit is acquired predisposition to ways or modes of response, not to particular acts, except as, under special conditions, these express a way of behaving. Habit means special sensitiveness or accessibility to certain classes of stimuli, standing predilections or aversions, rather than the bare recurrence of specific acts.[9]

So far as it goes, Dewey's formulation of the generalized habit is in every particular equivalent to that of traits. Dewey does not deny the existence of some independent and specific habits, but these, he sees, are generally to be ordered under more inclusive dispositions. So much organization and coherence in mental life leaves no choice but to recognize great systems of inter-dependent habits, comprising generalized dispositions that grow in flexibility as they develop.

A young child may be regarded as forming a specific habit when he learns (with difficulty) to brush his teeth night and morning. For some years this habit may stand alone, aroused only by appropriate commands or by the appropriate environmental situation. With the passing of years, however, brushing teeth becomes not only automatic (as is the way of habits) but likewise firmly woven into a much wider system of habits, *viz.*, a trait of *personal cleanliness*. (If a more behavioral designation of the trait is desired, one can speak quite accurately though less conveniently, of a generalized tendency to remove all manner of dirt from one's person.) The adult is un-

---

[8] Cf. S. S. Colvin, *The Learning Process*, 1921, pp. 49 f.
[9] J. Dewey, *Human Nature and Conduct*, 1922, p. 42.

comfortable if he omits brushing the teeth from his daily schedule, not only because a single habit is frustrated, but because the omission violates a general demand for cleanliness.

This example implies, quite correctly, that a trait arises, in part at least, through the integration of numerous specific habits having in common not identical elements, but the same adaptive significance to the person. In addition to this gradual integration and conceptualization, the influence of personal temperament on the formation of traits must not be overlooked. As pointed out in Chapter IV, some styles of generalization are far easier for certain people to learn than others, depending upon innate influences of temperament, intelligence, and constitution. But however acquired, a trait is always a fusion of habits and endowment rather than a colligation or chain of habits alone.

By tracing the hypothetical history of another generalized habit, sociability, we can see the process more clearly. A young child finding that his mother is nearly always present to satisfy his wants, develops for her an early affective attachment (conditioning). But later other social contacts likewise prove to be conducive to this child's happy and successful adjustment: playmates, for example, or family gatherings, or crowds at the circus. Unless markedly timorous in temperament, or fearful and shy because of experiences of punishment or public ridicule, the child gradually comes to seek people, rather than to avoid them. A trait (not an instinct) of gregariousness develops. The child grows eager for social intercourse; he enjoys being with people. When isolated from them for some time, he misses them and becomes restless. The older he grows the more ways he finds of expressing this gregarious interest. He seeks to ally himself with groups of people at the lodge, at the theater, at church; he makes friends and keeps in touch with them, often entertains them, and corresponds with them. These separate activities are not habits. They are varied (but equivalent) aspects of a trait of sociability. On occasion this trait may become dynamic almost to the point of compulsiveness, leading to such excess of sociability that the person is morbid or unhappy unless with people.

Under guidance of this trait new and effective expressions may be found to satisfy the craving for social intercourse. Habits no longer dominate the trait; rather it is the trait that forces the formation of new habits, congenial and serviceable to the trait. The transformation of motives from the simple conditioned responses of infancy is complete. The trait has transcended its specific foci of origin. Neither conditioned response, nor specific habit, nor identical elements, nor instinct represents the condition that prevails. Sociability has become a deep and characteristic quality of this individual's personality. Its expression is variable; a wide range of equivalent stimuli arouse it. Furthermore its structure has changed with time; for not only has it become a pervading style of behavior, but also a motivational system basic in the structure of this personality. The trait has become autonomous.

Trait and Attitude. A trait is a form of readiness for response; so too is an attitude. A trait is individualized, distinctive of its possessor; so too may be an attitude. A trait guides the course of behavior, and may often become dynamic and compulsive as well; so may the attitude. Both may be regarded as biophysical in nature, combining, in any proportion, the fruits of heredity and the fruits of learning. Are trait and attitude, therefore, equivalent concepts?

There is indeed a great similarity, and there are instances where it is a matter of indifference whether a certain disposition is called an attitude or a trait. To take one example, *introversion* and *extroversion* have been regarded both as *traits* of personality and as *attitudes* toward reality. Either designation is acceptable.

1. Yet there are three distinctions. In the first place an attitude has a well-defined object of reference, either material or conceptual; whereas traits have no such definite reference to objects. One's point of view toward liquor or frog's legs, toward arctic exploration, divorce, or Fascism are attitudes, but one's conservative, radical, ascetic, indulgent, reserved, or expansive *manner* of behaving is a trait. The more numerous the objects that arouse an attitude, the more closely does the attitude resemble a trait. The more an attitude is specific and stimulus-bound the less does it resemble a trait.

2. As this last statement implies, attitudes may be specific as well as general; whereas a trait may be only general. According to psychological usage an attitude may be a narrowly limited state of readiness for response. The *determindierende Tendenz*, the *Bewusstseinslage*, the *Aufgabe*, as sensori-motor sets of the moment, are all specific attitudes. They are not traits. On the other hand, in the case of a more widely extended attitude, *e.g.*, toward the world at large (*Weltanschauung*), there is no real distinction between attitude and trait.

3. The term attitude, furthermore, usually signifies the acceptance

or rejection of the object or concept of value to which it is related. Ordinarily attitudes are favorable or unfavorable, well-disposed or ill-disposed; they lead one to approach or withdraw, to affirm or to negate. Traits as a rule have no such clear-cut direction. They are often merely stylistic, and their significance is often adverbial rather than prepositional. But here again there are cases where the terms are interchangeable. A well-integrated trait of patriotism, for example, might equally well be a highly generalized favorable attitude toward all objects and values subsumed under the individual's conception of nationhood. In such a case the only basis of preference is the context of the discussion.

Both *attitude* and *trait* are indispensable concepts. Between them they cover virtually every type of disposition with which the psychology of personality concerns itself. Ordinarily *attitude* should be employed when the disposition is bound to an object or value, that is to say, when it is aroused by a well-defined class of stimuli, and when the individual feels toward these stimuli a definite attraction or repulsion. In some cases either of the terms (trait or attitude) is correct, as in the case of extroversion or patriotism, previously mentioned, or conservatism or radicalism. If in the last two cases the object or value against which the person is rebelling, or which he is intent on conserving, can be specified, the term attitude is preferable. If, on the other hand, the radicalism or the conservatism is chronic and "temperamental," expressed in almost any sphere of the person's behavior, then the term *trait* fits the situation better. Narrow or specific attitudes are never traits. A man is fond of his dog: he has a kindly attitude toward it. But if in general he is thoughtful of, and sympathetic toward men and beasts, he has a trait of kindliness. The more generalized an attitude (the more difficult it is to specify its object or its polarity of affect), the more does it resemble a trait.[10]

Traits and Other Forms of Readiness. It is unnecessary to repeat here the distinctions drawn in earlier chapters between traits and *factors, needs, instincts,* and the array of both nomothetic and practical elements proposed by various authors as the basic units of personality. Nor need we say more about the opposition of traits to specific habits or to identical elements. All the demarcations have

[10] This comparison between attitude and trait is condensed from a more complete account of the significance of attitudes for social psychology and the psychology of personality: G. W. Allport, "Attitudes," in *A Handbook of Social Psychology* (ed. by C. C. Murchison), 1935, chap. xvii.

now been drawn. We are left with a concept of trait as *a generalized and focalized neuropsychic system (peculiar to the individual), with the capacity to render many stimuli functionally equivalent, and to initiate and guide consistent (equivalent) forms of adaptive and expressive behavior.*

This conception is not altogether novel. As previously pointed out, it has many approximate counterparts in psychological theory. Some of the dispositions listed below are virtually identical with traits, some represent special sub-classes of traits, and others are adumbrations of traits, proposed by authors having a point of view at least partially like the one here presented.

Psychological Concepts Equivalent to, Subordinate to, or Partially Overlapping the Concept of Traits

Charakterzug
complex
directional tendency
ego-system (Koffka)
Eigenschaft (Baumgarten, Stern)
foci of development
general attitude
generalized habit (Dewey)
ideal
inner-personal region (Lewin)
interest
linéament (Boven)
mode of adaptation

mode of adjustment
motor-perceptual region (Lewin)
need integrate (Murray)
Neigung (Lazurski)
phobia
Richtungsdisposition (Stern)
Rüstungsdisposition (Stern)
sentiment (McDougall)
style of life (Adler)
subjective value (Spranger)
taste
Triebfeder (Klages)
trend

TRAIT AND TYPE

Again we refer to the sharp contrast between the theory of traits and the doctrine (any doctrine) of types. Unlike traits, types always have biosocial reference. A man can be said to *have* a trait; but he cannot be said to *have* a type. Rather he *fits* a type. This bit of usage betrays the important fact that types exist not in people or in nature, but rather in the eye of the observer. Type includes more than is in the individual. Traits, on the contrary, are considered wholly within the compass of the individual. The crux of the distinction is that in type the reference point is always some attribute, or cluster of correlating attributes abstracted from various personalities, a biosocial reference defined by the interest of the particular investigator (cf. Figure 2, p. 15).

Many kinds of typology flourish. There are literary types, energy types, pathological types, constitutional types, eidetic types, statistical types, and ideal types. Whatever the kind, a typology is always a device for exalting its author's special interest at the expense of the individuality of the life which he ruthlessly dismembers. Every typology is based on the abstraction of some segment from the total personality, and the forcing of this segment to unnatural prominence. All typologies place boundaries where boundaries do not belong. They are artificial categories.

This harsh judgment is unavoidable in the face of the conflicting claims of various typologies. Many of them pretend to embrace the total personality, and to follow the cleavages that occur in nature. But the very typologies that have proclaimed themselves "basic," contradict one another. Compare, for example, the supposedly foundational types of Kretschmer, Spranger and Jaensch. Certainly not one of these typologies, so diverse in conception and scope, can be considered final, for none of them overlaps any other. Each theorist slices nature in any way he chooses, and finds only his own cuttings worthy of admiration.

Glance at the popular dichótomous types: extrovert—introvert, tough-minded—tender-minded, sensory—motor, masculine—feminine, subjective—objective, Apollonian—Dionysian, Philistine—Bohemian, sthenic—asthenic, and the like. What has happened to the individual? He is tossed from type to type, landing sometimes in one compartment and sometimes in another, often in none at all. The entire approach is external, directed toward abstracted points of similarity among men, rather than toward the integral neuropsychic make-up of any one individual man.

The present vogue of typology comes largely from the influence of psychiatry, which, for a long time following Kraepelin, had great interest in the classification of mental disease. Today, just at the time when many psychiatrists are turning away from classifications to the study of mental disturbance in the individual case, this discredited approach is sifting through to plague the psychology of normal personality. We may now, it is said, classify a person as cycloid, schizoid, melancholoid, manoid, paranoid, hypochondroid, hysteroid, imbeciloid, neurasthenoid, or epileptoid. And so we may, if we are interested in fitting him to the categories of mental disease. Quite as properly the same person may be classified as of the sensory or motor type, if we are interested in his style of reaction; or of the visual, kinesthetic, or auditory type, if we are interested in his imagery; Nordic, Alpine or Mediterranean, if we are interested in his race. But if, as psychologists, we are interested in him as an individual, his multiple memberships in these miscellaneous types are all seen to be factitious. Better to study him alive, to observe his own individual *traits* in action, and see what they signify in his own life, even if by this method we cannot always neatly place him in our favorite filing cabinet. If the information to be gained indirectly through fitting him to one typology or another is worth anything at all, it will be sure to appear, much more significantly, when his *traits* are analyzed.

INDIVIDUAL *versus* COMMON TRAITS

Strictly speaking, no two persons ever have precisely the same trait. Though each of two men may be *aggressive* (or *esthetic*), the style and range of the aggression (or estheticism) in each case is noticeably different. What else could be expected in view of the unique hereditary endowment, the different developmental history, and the never-repeated external influences that determine each personality? The end product of unique determination can never be anything but unique.

This evident fact is one that most psychologists have great difficulty in accepting. If individuals cannot be compared with one another in respect to the same traits, what is to become of the psychology of personality as a "scientific" (*i.e.*, nomothetic) discipline? Outraged at the prospect, one psychologist exclaimed, "I think it is nonsense to say that no two men ever have the same trait. I mean, of course it is true, but it is one of those truths that can't be accepted." The die-hard nomothetist feels that in sheer loyalty to science, he *must* search for nothing but common and basic variables, however great the resulting distortion of the individual structure. But if he will put aside those methodological fetishes that make manifest truths unacceptable to him, and adopt a more liberal conception of his science, he will see that the dilemma is not fatal. The case for the *ultimate* individuality of every trait is indeed invincible, but there is nevertheless a certain logic that justifies his search for comparable and mensurable units.

For all their ultimate differences, normal persons within a given culture-area, tend to develop a limited number of *roughly comparable* modes of adjustment. The original endowment of most human beings, their stages of growth, and the demands of their particular society, are sufficiently standard and comparable to lead to some basic modes of adjustment that from individual to individual are *approximately* the same. To take an example: the nature of the struggle for survival in a competitive society tends to force every individual to seek his own most suitable level of *aggression*. As the saying goes, everyone *must* be either a boot or a door-mat. One child as he matures finds that a constant effort to dominate his fellows is for him the most successful design for living; another finds that for him there is more satisfaction in a characteristic yielding or submission. Somewhere between the extremes of exaggerated domination and complete passivity, there lies for each normal individual a level of adaptation that fits his intimate requirements. The psychologist does well to recognize all these possible gradations and to postulate a common variable (in this case, ascendance—submission) which, though rough and approximate, permits quantitative scaling. He does not measure directly the full-bodied individual trait that alone exists as a neuro-psychic disposition and as the one irreducible unit of personality. What he does is to measure a common *aspect* of this trait, such a portion thereof as takes common cultural forms of expression and signifies essentially the same manner of adjusting within the social group.

To make the case quite concrete, let us suppose that the investigator wishes a scale for the purpose of comparing individuals in respect to the common (continuum) trait, ascendance—submission, mentioned above. He recognizes that he is concerned only with an aspect of neuropsychic dispositions that differ in each person. (There are endless varieties of leaders, dominators, aggressors, followers, yielders, and timid souls). What he does is to shut his eyes to the uniqueness of each case, and then seek a uniform schedule of test items that will force each individual into the same continuum. He selects plausible items from common cultural situations,[11] determines their diagnostic significance for the dimension he has in mind, standardizes and validates his scale as a whole, and emerges at last with a "personality test."

Measured in this way, ascendance—submission is not, strictly speaking, a trait at all. It is rather a bipolar directional scale or common continuum upon which a certain common aspect of true individual traits is measured.

[11] A selection of such "aspective" items is given on pp. 412 f.

In the strict sense of the definition of traits (p. 295) only the individual trait is a true trait: (a) because traits are always in individuals and not in the community at large, and (b) because they develop and generalize into dynamic dispositions in unique ways according to the experiences of each individual. The common (continuum) trait is not a true trait at all, but is merely a measurable aspect of complex individual traits.[12]

The question naturally arises whether common traits should be called *traits* at all. At first thought it seems confusing to speak of both biophysical dispositions (true traits) and empirical continua (products of abstractive analysis) by the same name. And yet for three reasons it seems best to let the term stand for both the individual and the common dimension.

1. In the first place, the term has a widely established generic usage. Hitherto it has not meant merely an individual trait (as in the definition on p. 295). In psychological parlance empirical continua are ordinarily called "trait scales"; and this usage must be respected. It is merely a step toward precision to speak of these continua as "common trait scales." To do so requires no radical change in usage.

2. The concepts of individual trait and common trait are complementary in the study of personality. What is unique and what is universal both need to be explored. Though the former approach is the more fundamental, the latter constitutes a large chapter in research (cf. Chapter XV). Hence, by preserving the term trait with its proper qualifying adjectives ("common" or "individual"), the two major methods of approaching personality are simultaneously covered, and a useful generic concept results. The psychology of personality is, in this sense, the scientific study of human traits.

3. There is an even stronger argument in favor of the epithet "common trait." Although it is undeniable that no two people have precisely the same trait, yet there are certain aspects of personality in respect to which all people in a given culture may reasonably be compared. It was shown above that ascendance and submission, to take two typical common traits, represent forms of adjustment which all individuals by virtue of biological necessity and cultural pressure must in varying degrees adopt. The same may be said for many other common forms of adjustment: gregariousness, talkativeness, tactfulness, radicalism, money-mindedness. Every *person* is also a *socius*. He

---

[12] This logic of traits agrees in all essentials with the position defined by F. H. Allport, "Teleonomic Description in the Study of Personality," *Char. & Pers.*, 1937, 6, 202-214. There is however a difference of terminology. This author means by "trait" what is here called a common trait, and for individual trait he proposes the designation "teleonomic trend."

must come to terms, though in varying degrees, with the demands of his culture. His basic traits are always his own, but they have a social aspect that is easily separated for analysis. Common traits, then, are not wholly arbitrary variables. They rest on an evolutionary and cultural logic. *Common traits are those aspects of personality in respect to which most mature people within a given culture can be compared.*[13]

The trap to be avoided is the erroneous assumption that the common trait ever corresponds exactly to the neuropsychic dispositions of individuals. Perhaps in occasional cases there may be a close accidental correspondence; but it is always precarious to measure common traits on the assumption that they are direct measurements of personal dispositions. A test has different meanings to different subjects, and their responses may have quite different significance. Time and again subjects in submitting themselves to a personality scale complain that the test does not fit them. They seem to sense that the scale misses their individual traits. There is no convincing reply to these critics. The best the psychologist can do is to assure them that the test is only a "rough measure," and that in individual cases it may indeed fall wide of its mark.

Since common traits are at best only convenient approximations, the psychologist should employ whatever technical aids he can to make his scale as serviceable as possible. By using statistical formulae he may determine the reliability of the scale; he may standardize it for various classes of people, making it more appropriate for vocational guidance or other practical uses. If by statistical analysis he finds his scale to be unreliable, he may discard the items found not to correlate with the remainder, and in so doing, of course, he alters to some extent his original conception of the common trait in question. In working out his scale he thus combines an initial conception of the trait with various empirical checks, and emerges with a somewhat mixed product that often gains through its applicability to a whole population of subjects what it loses in sensitiveness for the individual case.

In this process, factor-analysis is one of the statistical devices that

[13] At a higher level the distinction between the individual trait and the common trait is reflected in the distinction between the *person* and the *socius*. The former is the complete man, a unique biophysical product in whom cultural influences have been embedded in individual ways within a biological ground. The *socius* is the man viewed in reference to his social status. His beliefs, attitudes and traits are regarded as conforming to, or deviating from, societal standards. The frame of reference in the former case is the person himself; in the latter case, external social norms.

may assist in fashioning common traits for efficient measurement. The scaling of "pure" and "basic" factors—while unjustified from the point of view of the organic structure of personality—has undoubted utility for certain practical purposes. Occasionally too factor-analysis may succeed in cutting through certain complications of a priori conception, and shed new light upon problems of defining the common trait in question.[14] But one must be cautious lest the last state be worse than the first, for some factorial products are psychologically meaningless. Technical aids should never be allowed to lower the basic requirement of psychological intelligibility.

A nice illustration of the difference between common and individual traits is offered by Conrad's study of ratings. Three teachers were required to rate a number of children of preschool age upon 231 common traits, thus being forced to make the assumption that all the children did possess exactly these selfsame qualities in some degree. Proceeding on such a false assumption there was only a low agreement among the teachers, ranging from +.14 to +.78, with a median of +.48. Many of the children, it seems, were given ratings on the basis of sheer guesses, because the investigation *required* that each child receive a rating on every quality. But in the course of the same study, the teachers were instructed to *star* their ratings on such qualities as they considered to be of "central or dominating importance in the child's personality." On this part of their task the teachers agreed very well in their judgments: their ratings on such starred qualities correlated from +.93 to +.96.[15] This result shows that the low reliability of rating may often be due to the fact that the subjects are forced into a scale where they do not belong. In a few cases (the starred qualities) the common trait concept seemed to correspond fairly well to some striking individual traits, but in most cases the common designations fell wide of the mark.

Consistent with its nomothetic tradition, psychology up till now

---

[14] An instance is Guilford's reduction of introversion to certain component common traits. Two of these components (the principal factors) are *social withdrawing* and *emotionality*. Each is a meaningful trait, undoubtedly susceptible of measurement. In this case a concept that was troublesome to psychologists receives clarification. Jung's initial logic in respect to introversion, provocative though it was, turned out, at least for the purposes of measurement, to be amenable to improvement. Two, or perhaps more, separate scales, one for social withdrawing and one for emotionality, should probably replace the coarser omnibus scales hitherto relied upon to measure the somewhat amorphous common variable. (J. P. and R. B. Guilford, *J. Abnorm. & Soc. Psychol.*, 1934, 28, 377-399).

[15] H. S. Conrad, *J. Educ. Psychol.*, 1932, 23, 671-680.

has been more interested in common than in individual traits. (The clinician and the therapeutist are exceptions to this rule.) Yet nothing is more essential in the entire field of personality than an adequate recognition of individual traits. The methods adapted to the study of common variables do not readily transfer to the study of individual traits. New techniques are needed. No investigator, for example, would undertake to scale *paranoia* in the general population; yet paranoia *may* on occasion be the very core of personality. Nor would he attempt to scale *fastidious exhibitionism,* a trait for which Beau Brummell was famous. Goethe, who believed that there is always a sense in which everything is true, had a charming trait of listening to everyone without contradicting him. This is not a common enough trait to be scaled, but it is important in the understanding of *Goethe's* personality. Nor is its antithesis common—the negativism of those, who, like Benvenuto Cellini, or Samuel Johnson, are notoriously *contredisant.* When this uncommon trait does exist, it is exceedingly important, for every proposal, every assertion, almost every word, arouses a rejection. Dickens immortalizes the trait in Mr. Grimwig; but Grimwigs are rarely encountered.

There are many other characters, both in fiction and in history, known for a single outstanding trait: Uriah Heep for his sycophancy, Rose Dartle for her peculiar insinuations, Oblomov for his procrastination, Mrs. Jellyby for her presbyoptic philanthropy, Micawber for his empty optimism, Chesterfield for his self-conscious good breeding, the Marquis de Sade for his sexual cruelty. Our vocabulary has been enriched by the *naming* of individual traits after these celebrities. What better proof could there be for the existence of cardinal traits too rare to be measured as common traits in a general population?

A Partial List of Trait-designations Derived from the Names of Historical or Fictional Characters

Beau Brummell	Christ-like	Lesbian
Boswellian	Dantesque	Machiavellian
Byronic	Dionysian	Miltonic
Caliban	Don Juan	narcissistic
Calvinistic	Emersonian	Napoleonic
Cassandra	Falstaffian	Neronian
chauvinistic	Faustian	Oblomovism
Chesterfieldian	Homeric	Œdipus
Ciceronian	John Bull	Pantagruelian

Pecksniffian	quixotic	Scaramouch
Pickwickian	Rabelaisian	Shylock
Pollyanna	sadistic	Tolstoyian
Puckish	Sapphic	Xanthippe

The orthodox (nomothetic) psychologist will ask, "But what can psychology do with such individual traits? They cannot be measured; and they defy man-to-man comparison." Actually a great deal can be done. Individual traits, no less than common traits, are susceptible of genetic, analytical, and even experimental study, in the laboratory and elsewhere.[16] Almost any method of studying personality (cf. Chapter XIV), other than tests and common scales, is adapted to the study of individual traits. After all, the comparison of individuals is only *one* of the goals of the psychology of personality. Understanding the individual case and determining the laws of the individual's development are just as legitimate and even more important goals.

THE PROBLEM OF TRAIT-NAMES

There are approximately 18,000 terms (chiefly adjectives) in the English language designating distinctive and personal forms of be-

---

[16] Perhaps they may sometime, in a rather novel sense, be susceptible likewise of measurement. F. H. Allport suggests the possibility of developing an intra-individual continuum for each personality separately, in respect to which, one leading trait may be measured for its intensity and self-consistency without any reference whatsoever to other individuals.

The following instance suggests the approach: "There was a certain boy whose behavior at school was reported by his teacher as exemplary, while his home behavior was a cause of grave concern to his parents. At school he was orderly, industrious, and attentive, while at home he was noisy, unruly, and a bully toward the younger children. Rated upon a societally standardized continuum of degrees of a trait, *e.g.*, the trait of 'tractability,' we find the results immediately ambiguous. The intra-individual distribution for both spheres (home and school) together becomes bi-modal rather than normal. The [common] trait approach breaks down. When, however, we describe his behavior teleonomically, that is, in terms of what he is really trying (and we do not mean consciously trying) to do, we may find a basic consistency underlying the contradiction in these two fields of his behavior. For example, the boy might, in both lines of conduct, be acting to gain the attention of his elders. An hypothesis concerning a possible law of this individual's general behavior is thus provided, which can be subjected to the test of verification through wider sampling and measurement." (*Char. & Pers.*, Duke University Press, 1937, 5, pp. 206 f.)

The proposal is that every instance of behavior may be studied for its closeness to a hypothetical central trait in this boy's life, *viz.*, "trying to gain attention of his elders." If many acts clearly fall within this teleonomic continuum, then the trait is no longer hypothetical but empirically established, and its range and intensity may be statistically determined.

havior.[17] At first sight this vast array of verbal symbols seems chaotic and wholly outside the psychologist's field of interest. But the more these terms are studied, the more instructive and pertinent do they become.

There is no denying that trait-names bear a very complex relation to the underlying structural units of personality. As a first step in clarifying this relation let us consider their origin. They seem to have come into existence in response to two entirely different human needs.

In the first place men experience a desire to represent by name such mental processes or dispositions of their fellows as can be determined by observation or by inference. There is a demand for depicting personality as accurately and as faithfully as possible, for with a suitable term, corresponding to authentic psychological dispositions, the ability to understand and to control one's fellows is greatly enhanced. There is then reason to suppose that trait-names are not entirely arbitrary, that they are to some extent self-correcting, for there is little to gain by preserving through names an erroneous belief in merely fictitious or fabulous entities; there is everything to gain by using terms that designate true psychic structures. If this consideration were the only basis underlying our vocabulary of trait-names we should find the correspondence between linguistic convention and psychological truth very close, much closer than it actually is.

There is, however, a second influence determining our lexicon of trait-names, namely, the tendency of each social epoch to characterize human qualities in the light of standards and interests peculiar to the times. Historically, the introduction of trait-names can be seen to follow this principle of cultural (not psychological) determination to a striking degree.

Astrological superstition produced *lunatic, jovial, saturnine,* and *mercurial.* Galenian medicine which prevailed in England until the time of Harvey brought the term *temperament,* and with it quite naturally, *sanguine, choleric, melancholic, phlegmatic, good-humored, bad-humored,* as well as *cold-blooded, hearty, heartless,* and *cordial* (derived from the belief that the heart was the seat of the intellect and feeling). Following the Protestant Reformation came some of our

[17] Cf. G. W. Allport and H. S. Odbert: "Trait-Names: a Psycho-lexical Study," *Psychol. Monog.,* 1936, No. 211. This monograph was originally designed as an appendix to the present volume, but its length made separate publication necessary. The passages reprinted here represent an abbreviated summary of the study, but the original should be consulted for a full statement of issues insufficiently developed here, as well as for the complete list of 17,953 terms.

most indispensable trait-adjectives, reflecting the introspectiveness of the period, among them, *sincere, pious, bigoted, precise, fanatic*, also the substantives, *self-regard, self-assurance, self-love, self-confidence*, and *self-esteem. Selfish* is a term coined by the Presbyterians about 1640. To the aristocratic seventeenth century belong *fatuous, callous, countrified, disingenuous.* Political upheavals are responsible for such terms as *Tory, democrat*, and *radical.*

With the growing subjectivity of literature in the eighteenth century came numerous terms derived from self-analysis: *day-dream, depression, ennui, chagrin, apathy, diffidence;* and new (more subjective) meanings were attached to older terms, *reverie, excitement, constraint, embarrassment, disappointment* and others. In courtly circles in the eighteenth century persons were described as *prim, demure, gawky, enthusiastic, interesting*, and *boresome.* To recent years belong a surprising number of new expressions, still for the most part slang: *booster, rooter, knocker, hoodlum, climber, yes-man, four-flusher, crabber, cake-eater, chiseler, gigolo, flapper, racketeer, Babbitt. To this* ever-increasing vocabulary of human characteristics psychology has contributed its share: *introverted, extroverted, neurotic, regressive, psychasthenic, eidetic, cyclothymic, schizoid*, and the like.

It is therefore certain that trait-names are not univocal symbols corresponding throughout the ages to fixed varieties of human dispositions. In spite of the fact that the names probably would not have been invented unless there were something "really there" in the psychic make-up of individuals to call forth the new designations, still the symbols themselves are changeable and elusive. They are invented in accordance with current cultural interests; their meaning often varies, and some fall rapidly into disuse. (Although some trait-names become extinct, the tendency, in English at least, is for a rapid multiplication of terms designating human qualities, a reflection no doubt of the ever-rising interest in psychological problems.)[18]

The list of terms here under discussion is based on the 400,000 separate terms and derivatives included in Webster's *New International Dictionary* (edition of 1925). The exact number in the list is 17,953 words (obsolete terms excluded), or four and one-half per cent of the total English vocabulary.

The criterion for inclusion consists in the capacity of any term to distinguish the behavior of one human being from that of another. Terms representing common (non-distinctive) behavior are excluded, *e.g., walking* and *digesting*, whereas more differentiating and stylistic

[18] G. W. Allport and H. S. Odbert, *op. cit.,* pp. 1-3.

terms applied to these same activities, such as *mincing* and *dyspeptic*, are included. In many cases the application of this criterion involved a considerable degree of arbitrariness. In deciding doubtful cases the dictionary definition was followed: if in *any* of its meanings a term might be differentially employed in characterizing personal behavior it was admitted.

Adjectival and participial forms have been preferred throughout; nouns and adverbs appear only where no corresponding adjective or participle exists, or else in cases where their meaning is distinctive (*e.g.*, both *Quaker* and *Quakerish* are included).[19]

Having defined certain principles for the selection of terms, the next task is to determine whether a basis can be found for a *psychologically* significant classification of the terms. A division of the list into four parallel columns seems to fill the need.

Column I. In this column appear those names that symbolize most clearly "real" traits of personality. They designate generalized and personalized determining tendencies—consistent and stable modes of an individual's adjustment to his environment. Obvious examples are *aggressive, introverted, sociable*. These terms do not imply merely temporary and specific behavior as do the terms in Column II (see p. 309); they are more neutral and less censorial than those in Column III; and they are less metaphorical and remote in their applicability to personality than those in Column IV. On the other hand, since the decision is often arbitrary, *the investigator using the list is advised not to depend upon Column I alone, but to consult the parallel columns for added terms according to his needs and interests*. The intention of this first column is to provide merely a *minimum* list of trait-names and not a final list. The number of terms in this column is 4,504, or 25 per cent of the total list.

Column II. This column contains terms descriptive of present activity, temporary states of mind, and mood. The criterion for inclusion reads as follows: "Might the quality in question characterize a person's mood, emotion, present attitude, or present activity (but not his enduring and recurring modes of adjustment)?" Typical terms in this column are *abashed, gibbering, rejoicing, frantic*. The majority of these terms are present participles, derived from verbs signifying differentiative behavior. This column contains 4,541 words, about 25 per cent of the entire list.

Column III. This list is the longest of the four, and contains characterial evaluations. Typical examples are *insignificant, acceptable*,

[19] G. W. Allport and H. S. Odbert, *op. cit.*, p. 24.

worthy. The paradigm for inclusion reads "Might one judge a man as (*worthy*) without the man possessing a corresponding biophysical trait which may be symbolized with the *same* name?" It is obviously impossible to think of *worthiness* as resident in the structure of personality itself; it is altogether a social judgment. In this respect it differs decidedly from *benevolence, tolerance,* or *patience.* A person with three such biophysical traits would no doubt be *judged* as *worthy*, but he never could have a neuropsychic disposition of "worthiness." Some terms in this column imply no profound moral judgment but rather a social effect upon the emotions or moods of another, *e.g., dazzling, irritating.* These terms presuppose *some* traits in a man, but in themselves they are value-estimates and do not symbolize the psychological dispositions in him that cause him to have a dazzling or irritating effect upon others. This column contains 5,226 terms, or 29 per cent of the total list.

Strictly speaking, in the sense of the present volume, Column III is not a list of trait-names at all. It is, however, included for good reasons. In the first place, there are writers who consider personality to be essentially the social influence of an individual, and from this point of view these terms become especially significant; they represent not the reactions of the individual in question, but rather his "social stimulus-value." Furthermore, this vocabulary of social impressions and characterial judgment has a certain intrinsic interest for social psychology, sociology, and ethics.

Column IV. There are many terms of possible value in characterizing personality, even though they have no certain place in the first three columns. Since in one way or another they contribute to the total vocabulary of useful terms they are included in this miscellaneous column. More skillful editing might have made possible the assignment of some of these words to the first three columns. Subdivision is also possible. One sub-group might contain terms explanatory of behavior, past participles for the most part (*e.g., pampered, crazed, malformed*). Another sub-group could be made of physical qualities which are commonly considered to be associated directly or indirectly with psychological traits, *e.g., roly-poly, lean, red-headed, hoarse.* Still another group could be made of capacities or talents, such as *able, gifted, prolific.* Then there are many terms of allegorical and doubtful application to human personality, and still others that for various reasons are the despair of the editors. In all, this miscellaneous column contains 3,682 words, or about 21 per cent of the total list.[20]

[20] *Ibid.,* pp. 25-27.

Such a classification is of necessity approximate and to some extent arbitrary. Experiment proves, however, that different judges agree fairly well upon the use of these classificatory groups.[21] The most significant feature of the method is the separation of neutral trait-names in Column I from the evaluative or censorial terms in Column III. The psychology of personality must be kept free from confusion with the problems of evaluation (character). But the assignment of any given term to one of these categories rather than to the other is not always an easy matter.

> Concepts originating in social judgment, e.g., honest, unselfish, law-abiding, may and often do become ideals or guiding principles adopted by individuals. In this sense, the introception of an ethical ideal into subjective attitude turns a characterial designation into a true trait-name. The plan followed in the classification is to place such terms in Column I if it seems that the social ideal does with fair frequency become a personal ideal and become thereby a true trait of personality. But it is obvious that certain normative concepts, like fine, crazy, or perfect are too general or too unpsychological ever to correspond precisely to any veridical personal trait.
>
> In spite of our efforts to locate only neutral terms in Column I some of the terms appearing there do seem to imply censorial judgment. In America to say that John is self-assured, inventive, or decisive is to praise him; in some societies he would stand condemned. But in such cases as these it is clear that some definite psychological trait is the object of reference however much the flavor of judgment may cling to the trait-name employed.[22]

Such a list is not only a thesaurus of terms, but also of problems. Each word is a record of common sense observation regarding human behavior. As such, each term constitutes an authentic problem for psychology. With this list at hand, the investigator will not be too easily beguiled into an over-simplified theory of personality.

The list here presented is drawn from the full classification, and presents only an illustrative sample of terms. If the reader will note the "flavor" of the terms in each column, he will see why only Column I can be regarded as a list of names of traits in the strict sense in which the term is used in this volume.

21 G. W. Allport and H. S. Odbert, op. cit., pp. 34-36.
22 Ibid., pp. 28 f.

A Sampling of Terms Characterizing Personal Behavior and Personality

Column I	Column II	Column III	Column IV
		Weighted Terms Con-	*Miscellaneous: Desig-*
		veying Social or Char-	*nations of Physique,*
		acterial Judgments of	*Capacities, and Devel-*
	Terms Primarily De-	*Personal Conduct, or*	*opmental Conditions;*
	scriptive of Tempo-	*Designating Influence*	*Metaphorical and*
Neutral Terms Desig-	*rary Moods or Activi-*	*on Others.*	*Doubtful Terms.*
nating Personal Traits.	*ties.*		
abrupt	abashed	absurd	abrasive
absent-minded	ablaze	acceptable	absinthine
abstemious	absorbed	acclaimed	abstract
academic	accusing	accomplished	abysmal
accommodating	affrighted	addle-brained	accidental
accurate	affronted	admirable	acentric
acquiescent	aflame	adorable	Achillean
acquisitive	aflush	adulterous	acrid
active	aflutter	advanced	adept
adventurous	agasp	affected	adipose
aesthetic	aggrieved	agreeable	adroit
affable	aghast	aimless	Aesopian
affectionate	agitated	all-round, C.	afflicted
afterwitted	agonized	alluring	agitable
aggressive	alarmed	amazing	à la mode, F.
agile	alcoholic	ambiguous	alive
agnostical	altercating	ambitious	alone
à la militaire, F.	amazed	amiable	altered
alarmist, n.	andante	amoral	ambidexterous
alert	angry	amusing	ambivalent
amorous	animal-spirits	angelic	amoeboid
anarchistic	annoyed	annoying	amorphous
apathetic	appalled	antiquated	amphibious
applause-seeking	appeasing	antisocial	Anglican
appropriative	appreciative	appalling	angular
arbitrary	apprehensive	apparent	Apache
argumentative	aroused	appealing	Apollonian
artistic	arraigning	approachable	apoplectic
ascendant	ashamed	apt	aquiline
ascetic	ashen	arid	arctic
assertive	assuaging	aristocratic	arrhythmic
astute	astrut	articulate	asthenic
atavistic	a-tiptoe, adv.	artless	astringent
atheist, n.	attentive	asinine	athletic
atrabilious	averse	asocial	au fait, F.
austere	aweary	astonishing	autumnal
autocratic	awed	atrocious	avian
avid	awe-stricken	attractive	awakened

There remains the deeper metaphysical problem concerning the relation of any name to the unit-structures of nature. For centuries this problem has been disputed. The story is too long to be re-told here, but the solution suggested below is fully compatible with the biophysical view of traits advanced in this volume.

The theory we present then holds that trait-names are symbols socially devised (from a mixture of ethical, cultural and psychological interests) for the naming and evaluation of human qualities. Some of these terms are obviously censorial and as such have little utility for the psychologist. The non-censorial terms, however, are significant, for their common usage establishes a presupposition that some human beings possess actual dispositions or traits roughly corresponding to these symbols. There are, however, many more traits than any list of single names would indicate, for we often find neologisms, phrases, and metaphors called upon where trait-names are insufficient.

In scientific work no single trait-name can be accepted with assurance as applicable to a given personality until its correspondence with a true trait has been experimentally or clinically established. Traits cannot be called forth by fiat; they must be discovered.

The use of the same trait-name applied to any two different individuals signifies merely that the dispositions of both fall within a range of comparable judgments.

Although in some respects this theory follows the position of the Nominalists it does not agree at all with those extremists who in denying perfect correspondence between names and traits think they must also deny the very existence of traits. Traits exist in exactly the same sense in which any mental disposition or readiness-for-response exists. The naming of such intangible mental states is hazardous, but it is also unfortunately necessary. It would be absurd to allow the difficulties involved to lead us into the wholly untenable nihilistic position of denying mental organization and readiness altogether.

A trait-name is a range-name. Although traits are real enough entities, trait-names are essentially blankets, covering one trait in one person and other (similar) traits in other people. Though perceived as similar and labeled identically, the trait is never, strictly speaking, in two different human beings exactly the same.[23]

As inadequate as common speech may be in representing the complex structure of personality, it is several grades more adequate than the mathematical symbols and neologisms that psychologists sometimes employ. The nature of our problem forces us to seek out,

[23] G. W. Allport and H. S. Odbert, *op. cit.*, pp. 20 f.

to identify, dynamic mental structures and sub-structures, *and to name them*. And this is necessary even though the lexicon of any language is far from offering a perfect catalogue of the elements of mental life. To use trait-names, but to use them cautiously, is, then, our lot. Nor need we fear them simply because they bear the age-ong sanction of common sense.

CHAPTER XII

THE NATURE OF TRAITS

The constancy of a trait is merely an ideal or limiting concept—and for two reasons. One is that man is at no moment of his existence merely an adaptive, self-preserving creature; always there is in his behavior a spark of self-development and growth. For this reason his finished traits are never quite fin-·ished. In addition, a trait is never entirely independent of the world outside, but stands in constant active relationship to it. It indicates the way in which the person reacts to the world; but never are the stimuli that provoke the reaction entirely the same, and never therefore are the various expressions of one and the same trait completely in agreement with one another. The trait is each time slightly different because it confronts other determining conditions; and these conditions produce not only a special coloring in each act that a trait arouses, but also can influence the trait itself in a permanent way.
—*William Stern*

I N the last chapter the theory of traits was presented in broad outline. For the time being many special questions and complications were overlooked which now require full consideration. As Stern points out, the ever-changing nature of traits and their close dependence upon the fluid conditions of the environment forbid a conception that is over-rigid or over-simple.

HOW ARE TRAITS DISCOVERED?

The chief danger in the concept of trait is that, through habitual and careless use, it may come to stand for an assembly of separate and self-active faculties, thought to govern behavior all by themselves, without interference. We must cast out this lazy interpretation of the concept. For, to say the least, such psychological *dei ex machina* are more than a century out of date. *The basic principle of behavior is its continuous flow, each successive act representing a convergent mobilization of all energy available at the moment.* No single trait—nor all traits together—determine behavior all by themselves. The conditions of the moment are also decisive; the special character of the stimulus, the temporary distribution of stresses and tensions within the neuropsychic system, all demand a special form of adaptive response, perhaps never again required in precisely the same way.

Only one maximally integrated activity takes place at any one time, and this activity is the product of a final convergent path wherein all available energy, though not all potential energy, is channelized to meet the present demand. From moment to moment there is a redistribution of this available energy, with the result that consummatory acts are ever changing and are the product of the interaction of all manner of determining factors, of which traits are only one.

Unless full recognition is given to this continuous, variable and convergent character of behavior, the theory of traits will become a purely fanciful doctrine of "little men within the breast" possessing, by hypothesis, exclusive control over each and every separate activity. A kindly little man will be made responsible for initiating acts of kindness, and other homunculi will be credited with acts that are aggressive, vulgar, or avaricious. This, in principle, is the error of the older faculty psychology with its list of the "active powers of the mind." It is likewise an ever present peril for any dynamic psychology that conceptualizes the "forces" presumed to initiate and guide behavior, whether they be nomothetic forces, such as instincts, drives, wishes, needs, or more individualized dispositions such as traits.

Recognizing and admitting the danger, it can more easily be avoided. One precaution is the constant return to *the observable stream of behavior*, the only basic datum with which the psychology of personality has to work. Here the principles of continuity and redistribution and convergence rule supreme. Traits as such are not observable in the stream of behavior. What is observable is the succession of specific adaptive acts that follow one another in close array. Though traits themselves are never directly observed, they are *of necessity* inferred. For without some inference of a flexible underlying structure in personality it would be impossible to account for the recurrent quality of the separate observable acts. And yet to avoid personifying the separate traits, it is ever necessary before assuming their presence to return to the basic behavioral evidence, and to demonstrate that the inference is justified by strict adherence to the data.[1]

Traits, then, are discovered not by deductive reasoning, not by fiat, not by naming, and are themselves never directly observed. They are discovered in the individual life—the only place where they can be discovered—only through an inference (or interpretation) made necessary by the demonstrable consistency of the separate observable acts of behavior.

There are many technical aids that may be employed in the discovery of traits, but each is nothing more than a refinement of the method used by anyone in everyday life. The refinements reduce the likelihood of error, but the procedure is basically the same. In ordinary life a judgment to the effect that a certain man is a "zealot for justice," is based on observation of his conduct in situations where he is seen to be active and aggressive in demanding equity or in championing the underdog. The judgment, of course, may be mistaken; it may be based on some one impressive single instance which, divorced from the usual pattern of circumstances, is not at all typical of the man's ordinary behavior. Since common sense has no accepted criterion for the inference of a trait, erroneous first impressions are often the consequence. Though the psychologist also relies on observation and inference, he is never satisfied with unverified first impressions. It is his business to demand a more exacting demonstration.

The methods for establishing a trait depend upon the kind of trait that is the object of investigation, whether it be a common trait or an individual trait. In the latter case, the so-called clinical method is ordinarily used, especially by psychiatrists, psychoanalysts, consulting psychologists, and writers of case histories. The investigator makes a sustained study of a particular individual and on the basis of personal acquaintance with the case pronounces that such and such traits are outstanding.[2] Now, the objection to this method is that it

[1] This concession to the *operational* criterion for the validation of concepts may be made without subscribing to the entire creed of operationism which would brand as "meaningless" every psychological hypothesis or inference not instantly defined by objective evidence. Traits are more readily defined in operational terms than are certain other concepts equally indispensable to the psychology of personality, such as self-consciousness, similarity, intention, intuition, and other forms of mental activity belonging to the realm of immediate experience.

[2] This is likewise the method of biography. Cf. R. B. Perry's characterization of William James: "Turning to James's benign traits, I find four that are peculiarly pervasive: sensibility, vivacity, humanity, and sociability." *The Thought and Character of William James*, 1935, Vol. II, p. 682.

rests ultimately upon the "intuition" of the investigator and is without the benefit of objective verification. The clinical method stands next door to common sense in its reliance on subjective pronouncements. But in defense of the clinical method it may be urged that prolonged critical probing of many-sided material, even though executed by a single mind without external checks, tends to be *self-validating*. Erroneous first impressions are transcended and the true pattern emerges with acquaintance. This line of defense does not, of course, justify all dogmatic assertions concerning traits, nor does it deny the inherent danger of subjective diagnosis. It merely hints at the fact (more fully discussed in Chapters XIV and XIX) that direct, synthetic judgments have their place even in scientific studies of personality.

Experimentation also provides evidence for the existence of individual traits. Whenever diverse tasks set in the laboratory are responded to in uniform ways, whenever many stimuli and many responses are found to be equivalent, a trait is safely inferred.[3] Rating is another method, especially valuable when several judges are employed for the purpose of checking one another. The method of starred ratings (cf. p. 301) is particularly useful in the establishment of individual traits.

Serviceable especially in studying the traits of young children is the method of the time-sample. Two or more independent observers for short periods of time watch the natural and unrestrained activities of children. Each observation may last for no more than one minute. Through repetition, say, at intervals of one hour for several days, the accumulation of such observations gives a significant sampling of the behavior. When different observers agree on the frequent recurrence of certain forms of conduct an excellent basis exists for the inference of a trait.[4]

Time-sampling may be used either for the discovery of individual traits, or for the discovery of common (continuum) traits. In most researches to date the consistency of each child within a group has been studied with reference to the same common variable. There is nothing in the method, however, to prevent its being used for indi-

[3] Such laboratory demonstrations of traits can take place, however, only when the tasks set for the subject are diverse enough to permit the discovery of the equivalence of *many* stimuli and of *many* responses. Cf. G. W. Allport, *Char. & Pers.*, 1933, 1, 259-264.

[4] Cf. the work of F. L. Goodenough on such qualities as leadership, dramatic play, and reticence at the nursery school age. *J. Juv. Res.*, 1928, 12, 230-235.

vidual traits. A child who by intermittent observation is found always lost in fantasy, or vigorously active, or reading a book, may safely be said to have a certain trait or interest even if he is not directly compared with other children.

To aid in the discovery of *common* traits a variety of statistical devices may be used. Perhaps the most familiar are the various methods of determining the *reliability* of tests for some one trait. If a test, constructed of many items, and sampling a wide field of activity, is found to be reliable, this fact proves that subjects reply to the diverse items in a consistent way. If a test, for example, designed to measure *social withdrawing*, is reliable, it shows that subjects who "withdraw" in one situation (*e.g.*, who say that they keep a diary record of their inner life) are likely to "withdraw" in others (*e.g.*, admit being embarrassed when meeting strangers). If every response is positively correlated with every other it shows that the test is internally consistent, which means in turn, that the subjects, by and large, respond consistently and uniformly to the scale.

The contributions of statistical method to the demonstration of common traits are numerous; there are all manner of measures of correlation, contingency and association. Employed according to the needs of the special problem and the nature of the material in hand, each enables the investigator to determine the degree of co-variation of different forms of behavior. A demonstration of the persistence of association is always the first step in inferring the existence of a common trait.[5]

The procedure of assembling and examining the evidence for a trait, together with some of the difficulties involved, can be illustrated by reference to Dudycha's study of punctuality.[6]

The data for this study consisted of over 15,000 observations on the time of arrival of some 300 students at various exercises and collegiate gatherings (as diversified as basketball games, eight o'clock classes, vespers, private conferences, and college commons). Here is typical

[5] Any measure of association, to be sure, requires interpretation. Whether or not a given magnitude of association proves the existence of a trait frequently depends on the bias of the investigator who interprets the measure. Time and again, for example, correlational coefficients between various indices (presumably of the same trait) are no larger than +.35 or +.45. Having in mind the low predictive value of such coefficients one investigator will say that no trait can be inferred; another, aware of the intrusion of unwanted variables into his experiment, or having supplementary evidence in mind, may consider such low coefficients indicative. There is no certain criterion.

[6] G. J. Dudycha, "An Objective Study of Punctuality in Relation to Personality and Achievement," *Arch. of Psychol.*, 1936, No. 204.

raw material for the beginning of an extended study of traits. In this particular case, the problem was to determine whether punctuality (or earliness, or lateness) was a characteristic trait for every student.

After transforming into standard scores the records of earliness and lateness for each student for every occasion on which he was observed, the usual product-moment (Pearsonian) method of correlation was applied. The results were indecisive. There seemed to be only a slight tendency for students to maintain the same position of earliness or lateness in arrival. Eleven of the twelve coefficients of correlation were positive, but the largest (between arrival at entertainments and at college commons) was only $+.44$. From such evidence, the author, leaning to the side of caution, concludes, "We can hardly say that there is a general trait of punctuality—or its opposite, tardiness—which operates in the *whole* group."

Coefficients of correlation, however, have a propensity for accentuating *slight* variations in an individual's behavior, thus speciously reducing the evidence for traits, which of course require no such perfect correspondence of measures. The author makes this point, and explains his remedy in the following words: "Pearson r's do not clearly reveal *trait behavior* because the variations in that behavior are accentuated. Since in life situations we are not interested in slight differences of a few minutes, but rather in whether a person is early, on time, or late, fine differences in promptness or tardiness, for practical purposes, are of little significance. Hence we must employ such statistical tools as make use of broad categories, namely, *Chi square which is not a measure of the degree of association, but of the probability that association is or is not significant.* It must be emphasized further that *those variations which decrease the r's, as already noted, are largely within the broad categories selected and hence have no effect on the Chi squares.* Since Chi square reveals whether there is consistency in a fairly broad area of behavior, and since the obtained values indicate a significant association, on the average, *we must conclude that there is evidence in support of a general trait of punctuality,* when punctuality is not conceived of as referring only to isolated, specific events, but to a trait which is variable within limits" (p. 30). Thus does a different statistical tool lead to opposite conclusions!

The author continues his analysis. He points out the inescapable weakness of any conception of a common (continuum) trait: "The distinguishing characteristics of individuals are very effectively hidden when a whole group, distributed according to measures on a certain trait, is dealt with. In other words, since the largest part of any group, normally distributed, clusters about a central tendency, and since the individuals who compose this part of the group are not distinctive in the measured trait, those individuals who constitute the extremes of the distribution, and who are distinctive in the measured trait, are completely lost sight of because they constitute a minority. A far too common error which results from this lack of discrimination is the conclusion, that since the majority lack distinctiveness, there is none who possesses a general trait. This pitfall is avoided by using the method of contrasted groups, which is being used more and more generally in this type of study" (p. 41).

Using the method of contrasted groups, the picture again changes, this time more sharply favoring traits. Examination of cases of students falling within the extreme 20 per cent of earliness scores, and within the extreme 20 per cent of lateness scores, shows a remarkable consistency in their behavior. The early bird is nearly always early, the late comer usually late (though the evidence for a well-integrated trait of *earliness* is better than for *lateness*, due no doubt to the positive emphasis that social training places upon earliness. The early bird is *trying* to be prompt in every situation, but the late comer is not *trying* to be late. He is merely the victim of a thousand and one distractions. Hence it is that lateness is less well integrated than earliness).

According to Dudycha, "The unmistakable conclusion is: early students differ significantly from late students in punctuality in general and in specific situations; further they differ in both the *extent* and the *frequency* of earliness and lateness. . . . Further, since the contrasted groups include 40 per cent of the students observed, punctuality, or tardiness, is certainly found as a general attitude or trait in the behavior of at least two-fifths of the students; in the other 60 per cent it is less well organized, and exhibits less consistency" (p. 44).

This study demonstrates nicely the psychologist's procedure in the discovery of traits, and some of his dilemmas as well. Especially instructive is the finding that about two-fifths of the students in their own personal lives have well integrated habits of arriving early or late. Since time-of-arrival is essentially a matter of societal standards it is interesting indeed to see that in so large a percentage of cases a regular habit of behavior has been formed around these standards.

What then is Dudycha's dimension of punctuality? Is he dealing with common traits or individual traits? According to the terminology of this volume he has studied a hypothetical common trait. He has proved that consistency of behavior is not well marked for 60 per cent of his subjects, and therefore that no very reliable scale could be created for the measurement of earliness-lateness in the entire population. (It should, however, be remarked that many existent scales for common traits prove equally ill-adapted to the majority of cases.) As a common (continuum) trait therefore, punctuality leaves something to be desired, though it is perhaps no weaker than others of the same *genre*.

In the course of his investigations Dudycha found that about 20 per cent of his subjects were in one aspect of their behavior highly consistent and markedly similar to one another: they were always early. Now we cannot assume that all of the individuals in this group had precisely the same trait; not all the early birds were early for the same reason. They had, to be sure, uniform habits of earliness, but these habits may have "belonged" in quite different trait-patterns. In one student the habit of earliness may have been an adjunct to a trait of *ambition*, in others to a trait of *deference*, of *pride*, of *rivalry* or even *timidity*. Dudycha did not work on these more basic individual traits. But he does demonstrate clearly the fact that common cultural influences may set up habits in respect to which (by aspective analysis) many individuals may be profitably compared. In short, he has defined a common (continuum) trait and has established its range of applicability: all people *may* be ordered to his continuum, but with certainty and practical usefulness, only the extreme 40 per cent of the population. Such is frequently the situation with common traits.

THE DYNAMIC NATURE OF TRAITS: DO TRAITS DRIVE OR MERELY DIRECT?

Characteristic of the nervous machinery, says neurophysiology, is its arrangement in *levels*, the more complex higher levels standing in the dual role of driver and restrainer to the lower simpler levels.[7] Therefore, since traits, on the physiological side, are undoubtedly neural dispositions of complex order, they may be expected to show motivational, inhibitory, and selective effects upon specific courses of conduct. Brief as this statement is, it is the sum and substance of the present aid from neurophysiology. So far as it goes it suggests that the operation of a trait is dynamic, both in governing the reception of the stimulus and in directing the response. But the information is too meager to warrant at the present time a physiological account of the operation of traits.

[7] Cf. C. S. Sherrington, *Mental Hygiene*, 1923, 7, p. 13.

Two kinds of dynamic psychology were described in Chapter VII. One holds that the root motives of men are to be sought in the structure *underlying* the traits of personality, that is to say, in instincts, the Id, in certain original needs, wishes, or drives. Advocates of these theories are unable to envision traits as possessed of driving power. Psychoanalysis, for example, sees traits, not as systems of motivation, but as *symptoms* within the Ego, of driving power within the Id. For McDougall they are also individual ornamentations of propensities common to all men. Even Morton Prince, who regards traits as "obstinately persistent, enduring characteristics of the personality," and recognizes their determining influence on behavior, is of the opinion that the energy of the trait is ultimately always derived from the instincts.[8] According to these views instinctive or impulsive action takes place under the general guidance of the "contributory habituation" of traits. Traits themselves are mere formal (directive) determining tendencies, *styles of adaptation*, but not the mainsprings of actions.[9] This type of theory persists in making personal nature a mere incident in the universal pattern of human nature. It is not the attributes of a mind-in-particular that are dynamic, but those of the mind-in-general.

The other kind of dynamic psychology, advocated at length in Chapter VII, breaks with the nomothetic tradition completely, and regards motives as personalized systems of tensions, in which the core of impulse is not to be divorced from the images, idea of goal, past experience, capacities, and style of conduct employed in obtaining the goal. The whole system is integral. If biological drive plays a part (thirst, hunger, sex), it does so, not as *the* motive, but merely as an irritable state of bodily tissues set within an intricate and personalized psychophysical system.

For example, in the case of the motives commonly called sexual, there is, to be sure, a common biological capacity involved, but the concrete functioning of this capacity in each life is very different. It cannot be regarded as one and the same force in all personalities. It is not a single concrete motive, but is a factor, traceable in many

---

[8] M. Prince, *Clinical and Experimental Studies in Personality*, 1929, pp. 123, 127.

[9] A variant of this point of view stresses the redintegrative character of traits. Whenever a stimulus, or internal need, is effective in arousing any *portion* of the determining tendency, the trait as a whole is redintegratively activated. Thus aroused it directs the required response into characteristic channels. The trait *steers*, but the effective motives are still thought to be emotional tensions quite independent of the trait.

kinds of other dispositions (cf. pp. 187-189). Even a sub-classification of types of sexual interest does not suffice to mark off the individual case. To say, for example, that a certain man or woman is *homosexual* is by no means to characterize his or her motivation. There are myriad forms of homosexuality: overt, covert, active, passive, compulsive, sublimated, diffuse, specific, altruistic, gentle, sadistic, protective, adulatory, superficial, unconscious, temporary, lasting, esthetic, intellectual—ultimately, as many forms as there are individuals. The patterns are not directly comparable, for their significance in individual personalities is never twice the same. It is inexact to ascribe one underlying motivational system to all. What motivates each person is not some element common to all individuals, but his own particular pattern of tensions. We may perhaps learn something of the nature of this particular pattern from a study of the common biological capacity, but must not make the fatal mistake of assuming that it is the abstract capacity itself that does the motivating.

Only individualized patterns of motives have the capacity to select stimuli, to control and direct segmental tensions, to initiate responses and to render them equivalent, in ways that are consistent with, and characteristic of, the person himself.

But is the personalized trait dynamic in the sense of being self-active? does it in and of itself *initiate* behavior? Strictly speaking, no; any disposition must be *aroused* before it is dynamically active. According to the principles of convergence earlier described, at any one time energies are mobilized for purposes of adjustment as needed. Not every motivational system is at all times in a kinetic phase. The successive demands of living arouse first one region of stress, and then another. Only through an intricate course of stimulation and association are determining tendencies (including traits) raised from a state of potentiality to activity. Either external stimuli or segmental tensions of an organic order may arouse them; but such antecedent stimulation in itself is not the motive.

In another sense traits *do* initiate behavior. It is certainly not a ring on the telephone nor a friend's voice over the wire that causes an egotist to talk for half an hour unchecked about his latest exploits, or a gossip to recount at great length the doings of her neighbors. In these cases the response springs from deep-seated traits of personality, and not from a ring on the phone followed by a friend's voice over the wire. Traits may be even more self-active than these illustrations imply. The egotist and the gossip when alone may feel quite restless until they have sought out an opportunity to unburden themselves. They *seek* an excuse to talk, and put themselves *in the way* of stimuli that will release the flood. A sociable person, if he is quite as ready to listen as to talk, may be restless until he is among people. An author, a housekeeper, a public speaker, a reformer, a craftsman, a musician, if deprived of their favorite occupation, may "itch" to return to their work. In many such instances of "spontaneous" motivation it seems impossible to trace the precise train of stimulation or association that sets up the aggravated field of stress. The traits appear to be self-active, at least at times when they are not specifically inhibited by contrary courses of conduct.

A certain man, known to everyone as generous and open-handed, was preoccupied at a picnic in lighting a camp-fire. Someone suggested that for supper a half-pint of cream was needed, and that it could probably be obtained at a nearby farmhouse. Still preoccupied with his fire, the generous man reached into his pocket and handed over *two* one dollar bills. There was no reason why he rather than any other member of the party should have footed the bill, and certainly no reason for handing over so much money: not even a Yankee farmer could conceivably charge more than *one* dollar for half a pint of cream.

What had happened in this simple situation? Caught off-guard, the fire-tender fully revealed his trait of open-handedness. Normally, the specific demands of the occasion, and a hasty bit of mental arithmetic, would have brought forth a silver coin, or that lacking, *one* of the dollar bills. Being preoccupied with other duties, the half-heard suggestion crossed the ever-low threshold of his generosity. The response was perfectly in keeping with the disposition, though somewhat excessive and maladaptive in terms of the demands of the occasion. The fact that he offered the money at all, and the fact that he offered it in extravagant amounts, show the decisive influence of the trait, all the more decisive because it was not specifically controlled.

Was it the trait that initiated the behavior, or was it the semi-conscious suggestion that came to his preoccupied mind? The suggestion of course was prior in time, and was required to throw a latent system into action. But the same words spoken to a niggardly or unsocial person might have had no effect at all. Whether we say it was the words or the trait that initiated the behavior, there is no doubt that the trait played the decisive role.

Interests, ambitions, compulsions, phobias, general attitudes, inclinations, hobbies, values, tastes, predilections, and the like, are all traits, and are at the same time motives. Yet it is not correct to say that *all* motives are traits. The demands of some especially intense stimulation, such as pain, thirst, and the like, lead to immediate, and often reflex, adaptations not well integrated with other tendencies. Such motives are numerous, and quite specific, not at all resembling traits which are always complex and recurrent systems of stress.

Nor is it correct to think of all traits as motives—often they seem to have a defining or directive influence upon conduct, without true motivational significance. Some traits have less to do with *stress* than with *style*. Except in rare instances *politeness*, for example, seems not to be a motivational trait. One does not leave the house and seek out other people in order to be polite to them. One may seek out others because one is sociable and restless without their company; having sought them and being now in their company one may behave toward them in a polite *manner*. Nor is a man often *forceful* for the sake of being forceful; rather he employs a forceful style of behavior whenever he is, for other reasons, aroused to action. Such "directive" traits have been classed by Troland with the "praxiograms," cortical patterns that do not initiate but do regulate the character of response.[10] Some traits thus seem to have *motivational* (directional) significance, and some mere *instrumental* significance. The latter are primarily expressive in significance, and seem predominantly motor in their organization; they represent styles of behaving and, unlike the driving traits, are seldom involved in the profundities of emotional life. The distinction is clearly drawn by Stern who calls the driving traits *Richtungsdispositionen*, and the instrumental traits, *Rüstungsdispositionen*.

> Now the two factors of *Richtung* and *Rüstung*, however closely interwoven, have nonetheless a certain independence of one another, and the most varied relations to one another. We are therefore compelled to distinguish between those dispositions that have a prevailingly directional character from those that are principally an implemental character. The former are purposive, they have a "tendency to," the latter are capacities, and have a "potency for." [11]

This distinction is a useful one. But it must not be overworked. There is no sharp line between motivational traits and stylistic traits, between *direction* and *manner of expression*. Very often what was

[10] L. T. Troland, *Cerebration and Action* (Vol. III of *The Principles of Psychophysiology*), 1932, p. 321.
[11] W. Stern, *Die menschliche Persönlichkeit*, 1923 ed., p. 83.

originally a motivational trait (*e.g.*, interest in mechanics) becomes a mere instrument of expression (a skill serviceable in earning a living), or what was originally instrumental (*e.g.*, skill in seamanship) may become a passionate interest. This continual transformation of motives from the level of mechanism to the level of drives, or *vice versa*, has been discussed at length in Chapter VII.

Whether a trait is dynamic or directive is, then, a matter of degree. At one extreme are the compelling, seemingly spontaneous, unrestrained, obsessional traits of neurotics or psychotics.[12] Shading from these compulsive systems are the interests of normal people, which in turn vary from absorbing passions to mild predilections. Still less dynamic are the directive traits; nevertheless, having a certain steering capacity, they cannot be entirely divorced from motive. The dynamic pressure of these expressive traits often passes unnoticed until an individual is compelled, through outside constraint, to act contrary to his usual style. The resulting discomfort and maladaptation show to what extent his expressive behavior has been dynamic in character. His equipment, abilities, and style, he finds, are not wholly matters of implementation; they too have a certain *Drang*. In brief, the distinction between driving traits and directive, while useful for some purposes, cannot be sustained too rigidly.

GENOTYPICAL, PHENOTYPICAL, AND PSEUDO-TRAITS

It is obvious that what seems to be the *same* trait may, in different people, have quite diverse origins. Shyness in one person, for example, may be due to hereditary influences that no amount of contrary pressure from the environment has been able to offset; in another person shyness may stem from an inferiority feeling built by an abnormally exacting environment. In spite of dissimilar histories, in appearance and in effect, the shyness of these two persons may be very much alike. Conversely, two youths suffering some shocking experience of grief or bitter disappointment, objectively alike, may be

12 It may be well to remind the reader that such traits cannot be considered merely as *symptoms* of an unconscious conflict. Miserliness, scrupulosity, compulsive neatness, and similar traits are more than converted expressions of frustrated eroticism, infantile or otherwise. Even in cases where such unconscious components can be traced, these must be regarded not as the contemporary sum and substance of the motive, but merely as integral with it. Whether or not some initial repression took place, there have been elaborations and transformations in the focal character of the disposition until it must now be considered as rooted in the total life rather than in some one recess of the unconscious.

affected very differently. One of them becomes morose and ineffectual, lost in his trouble; the other stiffens his back and becomes more realistic and aggressive. The same fire that melts the butter, hardens the egg.

Lewin has shown this general problem of appearance *vs.* underlying cause to be of considerable importance in the investigation of personality. Descriptions in terms of here-and-now attributes are *phenotypical;* explanatory accounts, seeking underlying motives and stresses, are *genotypical.*[13]

This distinction, though valuable, has already been adequately implied in the foregoing discussion of the nature of traits. For one thing, common (continuum) traits are obviously conceived in phenotypical terms. When ascendance, perseverance, sociability, radicalism, punctuality, or neuroticism is measured for a whole population, with the intent of comparing all subjects in respect to the same trait, it is obvious that no account can be taken of the various reasons why different people are ascendant, persevering, sociable, or the like, nor can any attention be paid to the individual varieties of these traits. Stylistic (directive) traits also suggest Lewin's phenotypical classification, since they are more closely related to external conduct than to root motives. Conversely, driving traits must certainly be ordered to Lewin's conception of genotypical traits, for they are the very springs of conduct. The psychology of personality must deal with traits of *both* orders, if for no other reason than that in the course of development genotypes are often transformed into phenotypes, and phenotypes into genotypes. Chapter VII is a record of such transformations.

Another distinction of value is that drawn by Baumgarten between genuine traits and "pseudo-traits."[14] This writer points out that erroneous inferences are often made when behavior is observed superficially and interpreted only at its face value. A bearer of gifts may not be, in spite of all appearances, a truly generous person: he may be trying to buy favor. A person chaste in conduct may not be chaste at heart. Ever so many "virtues" may be simulated and mistaken by the unwary observer for true traits. "Pseudo-traits," then, are errors of inference, misjudgments that come from fixing attention solely upon appearances. The best way to avoid such errors is to find the genotype that underlies the conduct in question. What is

[13] K. Lewin, *Gesetz und Experiment in der Psychologie,* 1927.
[14] F. Baumgarten, *Brit. J. Psychol.,* 1936, 26, 289-298.

the individual *trying to do* when he brings his gifts? If his basic motive is known then the sycophancy of his conduct is understood and the pseudo-trait gives way to the true trait in the diagnosis. Baumgarten's distinction reminds us once again that the soundest methods and utmost of critical acumen are essential in diagnosing personal traits. It is only by its ability to separate true traits from pseudo-traits that psychology makes any advance over common sense.

THE INDEPENDENCE OF TRAITS

Probably nothing whatsoever in the structure of any human mind exists sealed up in completely independent systems. Segmental reflexes seem most nearly to approach this condition, but even these can be markedly altered in their functioning by concurrent activity or tonus prevailing in other psychophysical regions. Neither are the oft-mentioned "dissociated complexes" and "logic tight compartments" of the mind entirely separate; their boundaries are at least *semi*-permeable. Since this is so, the influences determining conduct are manifold and fluid. A single act may, and usually does, result from the mobilization of available energy through *many* channels. Consider the task of writing a letter; it requires the convergence of mental sets, habits, motives of the moment, skills, stylistic traits, as well as the deepest of personal convictions and values. Such adaptive behavior always demands the effective convergence of many determining influences, traits among others. Generalizing the illustration, it may safely be said that no single performance is ever a univocal product of any one single trait.

At the same time, since many different adaptive acts distributed in time show repeatedly the same telic and expressive character, it becomes necessary to assume some stable and continuous influences at work. A markedly loquacious person, who talks at great length on the slightest provocation, must have some psychophysical tendency that helps to stabilize his conduct in this direction. Loquacity, provoked so easily (by an equivalence of stimuli), leads to fluent speech wherein all manner of ideas and expressions may be employed (equivalence of responses). Though it is not easy to conceive in neural terms, there must be some system with a low threshold of arousal, readily crossed by many stimuli and by many associational currents. At any one time, to be sure, the form of the loquacity is determined not only by the disposition in question, but by the simultaneous functioning of ideational content, by special attitudes toward the topic under discussion, toward the interlocutor, and innumerable other concurrent conditions, both inner and outer.

The term "focalized" disposition, previously introduced, fairly represents the nature of this internal press. When latent, as when active, the barriers between these dispositions are not rigid, for often an impulse arousing one trait may at the same time arouse others. In fact the arousal of several dispositions in varying degrees seems to be the rule, each contributing to the convergent conduct in proportion to its degree of arousal. Figuratively, traits "overlap" with one another. They do not operate on an "all or none" principle. The situation is represented diagrammatically in Figure 17, p. 246, where *interdependent* traits are contrasted with *independent* factors.

The trait, then, is identifiable, not by clean-cut contours or boundaries, but rather by a nuclear quality, by its *focus*. This focus is essentially the *telic* significance of the trait, that is to say, its meaning to the individual as a mode of survival and mastery. The loquacious disposition of the talkative man is, for him, a *modus vivendi*. So too are all the other focalized (and interdependent) systems of his personality; his esthetic interests, his thriftiness, his timidity, his neatness, his affectionate attachments, and his political conservatism—they are all *modi vivendi*. In this same sense attitudes as well as traits are focalized dispositions.

By now it is clear why, either for the population at large or for the single individual, it is impossible, strictly speaking, to classify traits. Since the significant foci in any two lives are never precisely the same the most to be hoped for in the total population is an inventory of some of the *common* traits in which people may be roughly compared. (This procedure will be followed in Chapter XV where its value and its limitations will become apparent.) For the *individual*, since his traits are never wholly independent of one another, enumeration in terms of mutually exclusive units is not possible.[15]

This question of the independence of traits has important implications for the construction and interpretation of *tests*. Since the tests

[15] What usually happens in an attempt to list the basic traits of an acquaintance is that a *cluster* of trait-names is employed. One says of a friend, "She is one of the most tactful, sympathetic, and sociable people I know." Is only one focal disposition here intended, or two, or three? If more than one, then there is probably not independence among them, but some clustering tendency. Because of such clustering it becomes impossible to analyze a single life into wholly independent units.

are designed for the measurement of common traits, the interpretation of the score of any individual subject is an awkward task. When he answers the questions—or performs the acts—dictated by the test, he is behaving in a specific adaptive manner. If the reasoning of this chapter is sound, such adaptive behavior is unlikely to be the product of one and only one determining disposition. The test will not measure one and only one trait. It is rather a rough and approximate device whereby the investigator hopes to tap the trait in question along with he knows not what other variables. There is some justification for his belief that the sheer length of his scale will to a certain extent lead to a canceling out of the unwanted and intrusive variables. Further, if the test has a known reliability and validity, the investigator may with some assurance say that whatever extraneous reasons there may be for a subject's selection of responses, in the long run the trait itself probably has the most decisive influence on the selection and on the score.

But the problem becomes more seriously complicated when a test is designed (as many tests are) to measure not one trait, but *several*. Diagnostic weights, different for different traits, are assigned on the assumption, correct in itself, that a response is determined not by one single trait but by many. The simple uni-trait test is contented with *one* final score, admitting that many other determinants have gone *unmeasured*. The multi-trait scale (perhaps in the interests of efficiency or of that ever-recurring naive hope of finding one solution for all puzzles) expects to diagnose these other determinants (so far as they involve additional common-traits) all at one time.

Take, for example, Bernreuter's *Personality Inventory*, an omnibus of 125 questions, drawn largely from three pre-existing, "logical" scales each of which is intended to measure one and only one common trait.[16] With the aid of these 125 questions the scale attempts to measure simultaneously *four* common traits of personality: *dominance, self-sufficiency, introversion*, and *neuroticism*. Each answer receives four scores (some of them being zero), according to its empirically (*i.e.*, statistically) determined diagnostic value for each of the four traits. Thus, one question reads, "Do you often feel just miserable?" If your answer is "?," meaning either you don't know how you feel or else that you don't know what the tester means, you are scored —3 on introversion, —1 on dominance, and 0 for both neuroticism and self-sufficiency. Now such a response to such a question seems to bear a very tenuous logical relation, if any at all, to any of these four traits. Why should a person who sets a question mark against such an item be judged extroverted and submissive, but neutral in respect to neuroticism and self-sufficiency?

[16] R. G. Bernreuter, *J. Soc. Psychol.*, 1933, 4, 387-405.

In order to avoid such psychological confusion, it is much more wise to stick to the simpler conception of a scale, wherein a single response is evaluated only in its diagnostic significance for *one* trait, deliberately leaving unmeasured all the other determining influences affecting the score. In so doing the temptation to depart from the precincts of psychological intelligibility will be lessened.

A different attack on the dilemma created by multi-trait scales is to proceed in the direction of factor analysis as Flanagan has done in his treatment of the Bernreuter scale.[17] Bernreuter very soon found such a high correlation between his measures of neuroticism and introversion that he could not consider them separate common traits; hence for practical purposes he reduced his measures from four to three. Flanagan goes still further; eliminating the correlations between all scores, he pulls out as substitutes for the four original, interdependent traits, two new and *independent* factors, which he christens *self-confidence* and *sociability*. After this ceremony, it turns out that if ‣you "feel just miserable" you score $+4$ on Factor I, and o on Factor II. As the statistics grow better and better, the intelligibility grows less and less.—Contamination by statistical artifacts is not uncommon in scales of the multiple trait order. (From one highly sophisticated empirical scale comes this extreme instance: children who give the response word "green" to a stimulus word "grass" receive a score of $+6$ for "loyalty to the gang"—an example of empiricism gone wild.)

Unnecessary trouble springs from assuming, as some testers do, that *independent* factors are to be preferred to *inter-dependent* traits (cf. p. 245). What if certain scales do correlate with one another? (Correlations of the order of $+.20$ to $+.40$ are often found.) Each scale may still represent a well-conceived, measurable common trait (if it has demonstrated reliability and validity). No harm is done by overlap; indeed, overlap is a reasonable expectation in view of that roughness of approximation which is the very nature of the entire procedure (also in view of the tendency of certain traits to cluster). Well-considered scales with some overlap are preferable to ill-considered scales without overlap. To seek *intelligible* units is a better psychological goal than to seek *independent* units.

Constructive suggestions for avoiding such difficulties as we have been describing will be offered in Chapter XV where the logic of measuring common traits will be under discussion. For the time being it is sufficient to say that inter-dependent *traits* can be measured quite as successfully as independent *factors*, and, as a rule, much more meaningfully.

[17] J. C. Flanagan, *Factor Analysis in the Study of Personality* (Stanford Press), 1935.

THE CONSISTENCY OF TRAITS

The scientific evidence for the existence of a trait always comes from demonstration by some acceptable method of *consistency* in behavior (the consistency being not a matter of stereotyped habits, but of equivalent responses). It is simple enough to prove some people self-consistent: they are, for example, almost always *decisive,* or almost always *fastidious.* In other cases, however, the evidence is less conclusive. The degree of consistency that different investigators will demand before inferring a trait is a somewhat subjective matter. Aware of the difficulties encountered in framing pertinent tests, experiments, and rating scales, and aware of errors in measurement and of the unmeasurable and uncontrollable interplay of determining tendencies in the subjects themselves, one investigator may be content with relatively low measures of consistency; while another, unmindful of, or unimpressed by, these handicaps, may demand almost perfect correspondence among his measures before inferring a trait.

To argue against this latter position is not necessarily to lower standards of psychological investigation. Perfect consistency will never be found and must not be expected. There are many reasons why this is so. For one thing, in the same personality, traits often contradict each other. People may be both ascendant *and* submissive, perhaps submissive only towards those individuals bearing traditional symbols of authority and prestige; and towards everyone else aggressive and domineering. So-called guilt-behavior may betoken contradictory traits: the overt virtue may be compensatory for the hidden vice. Ambivalence in one's feelings of loyalty and affection also makes for contradictions in traits. Every person has conflicts, frequently expressed in antagonistic dispositions. The ever-changing environment raises now one trait and now another to a state of active tension.

Likewise harmful to perfect consistency is the omnipresent principle of convergence. No trait operates alone. The adaptive act of the moment is only partially a function of the one trait. It is determined as well by many other traits (even by contradictory traits, if the situation has dual "valence"), and by all manner of specific attitudes, by mood, and by momentary conditions. The excessively methodical person may become careless and demoralized in his haste to catch a train; the meticulously truthful person may lie if his life is at stake. Moreover, in every personality there are peculiarly specific dissociated habits. A person, otherwise polite and considerate, may, because of special prejudices, be rude to Jews, to red-heads, or to taxi-drivers.

A single inconsistency in behavior may mean very little. A vigorous executive who at the office, at home, or wherever he is in command, makes swift and emphatic decisions, may be reduced to virtual immobility when confronted in a restaurant with a tray of French pastry. Why? Perhaps it is just fatigue at the end of the day, or annoyance at being forced to decide so trivial an issue (in such cases the trait of decisiveness is not aroused); or his hesitation may be a throw back to some boyhood experience when the rod had inhibited the stealing of tarts. Such specific inhibitions may be at work, or the customary decisiveness may perhaps for this occasion be blocked by the activity of other deep-seated traits now functionally dominant, such as frugality or hypochondria.

> Or, take the case of Dr. D, always neat about his person and desk, punctilious about lecture notes, outlines, and files; his personal possessions are not only in order but carefully kept under lock and key. Dr. D is also in charge of the departmental library: in this duty he is careless; he leaves the library door unlocked, and books are lost; it does not bother him that dust accumulates. Does this contradiction in behavior mean that D lacks traits? Not at all. He has two opposed stylistic traits, one of orderliness and one of disorderliness. Pursuing the case further, this duality is explained by the fact that D has *one* cardinal (motivational) trait from which these contrasting styles proceed. The outstanding fact about his personality is that he is a self-centered egotist who never acts for other people's interests, but always for his own. This cardinal trait of self-centeredness (for which there is abundant evidence) *demands* orderliness for himself, but not for others.

For various reasons, therefore, simple statistical *correspondence* of measures is not the sum-total of the available evidence for traits. The more profound *congruences* of behavior emerge only after an intensive study of the organization of each personality.

And yet in arguing that the inner consistency of traits is often greater than surface explorations indicate, we must not commit the opposite error of presuming every trait to be organically self-consistent under all circumstances. As has been pointed out, traits are often aroused in one type of situation and not in another; not all stimuli are equivalent in effectiveness. Successful adaptation and mastery require a trait to remain loose-knit, so that its determinative influence may be modified or checked according to special demands of the moment. To serve as a successful *modus vivendi* a trait must remain plastic or lose its usefulness.

We conclude then that the consistency of a trait is entirely a matter of degree.[18] There must be some demonstrable relationship between separate acts before a trait can be inferred. Yet occurrence of dissociated, specific, or even contradictory acts is not necessarily fatal to the inference. Perfect and rigid self-consistency is not to be expected.

ARE TRAITS NORMALLY DISTRIBUTED?

The question of the distribution of traits arises, of course, only in connection with *common* traits. By their very nature individual traits cannot be scaled in a population.

Now, the investigator *wants* to think of any common trait as a single continuous variable with scores arranged according to a normal curve of distribution, corresponding to the probability (Gaussian) curve, so that he may treat the scores for any common traits according to convenient statistical principles. To have such a distribution facilitates the establishment of norms, the comparison of one individual with another, computations of correlations with other variables, and many other quantitative procedures dear to the heart of the tester. Without doubt, the most serviceable common traits are those whose distribution corresponds fairly closely to this requirement. Figure 22 illustrates the situation with one scale, the continuum in this case being Ascendance-Submission, constructed from a *pair* of traits, initially conceived according to the logic of biological adaptation and acculturation (cf. pp. 298, 410 ff.). Items designed to measure people on this continuum were scored in such a way that

[18] The reader should note how frequently it has been necessary to speak of various attributive characteristics of traits as a "question of degree." Earlier, the amount of driving or of directive stress in a trait was shown to vary from case to case (as well as from time to time); further, a common trait was seen to be common only to a certain extent and in a certain sense; then too, independence turned out to be only a relative attribute of traits; and now the self-consistency of a trait also seems to be a variable matter. Likewise, we shall soon see that the importance of a trait in an individual life may vary from a cardinal position to a minor and inconsequential one. Finally, the unity of personality itself, as the next chapter will show, is neither perfect nor wholly mythical; it too is a question of amount. No sharper distinctions or more final statements are possible, for the simple reason that mental organization in all its phases *is* a matter of degree!

they yielded a fairly normal curve of distribution, the extreme scores at either terminus of the linear scale signifying opposite modes of adjustment. Statistically considered, there is a *single* variable; psychologically, however, the composition of this variable is by no means simple.

In defense of the view that these linear continua represent a single psychological variable, it is customary to cite the supposed preference of nature for symmetrical distributions. So many minute genetic

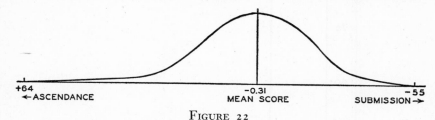

+64 ←ASCENDANCE   −0.31 MEAN SCORE   −55 SUBMISSION→

FIGURE 22

Distribution of Scores from a Test Designed to Measure
Ascendance-Submission

Constructed from the decile distribution of scores published in *Manual of Directions*, rev. ed., for "A-S Reaction Study," Form for Men.

influences determine the height of a man, for example, that the final stature attained by a large unselected male population will be found to vary about a central tendency as chance itself varies. When multiple causes are at work the normal curve of variation frequently found in biological measures is, therefore, the curve of probability. And this is why the native ingredients in personality, aspects of physique, temperament, and nervous plasticity, dependent as they are upon the composite determinants of inheritance, frequently yield symmetrical curves of distribution. The more any quality depends upon chance-biological determination the more likely it is to be normally distributed.

Traits, however, do not depend altogether on chance-biological determination. They depend also upon cultural determination, and here an entirely opposed principle is at work, for, roughly speaking, in so far as a quality depends on the mores, the *less* likely it is to be normally distributed. Folkways, civil laws, and all other exterior constraints tend to destroy the "natural" variation in behavior through their demand for *conformity*.

For example, motorists approaching an intersection without external control, will vary their behavior according to chance factors. The curve on a continuum from "Same Speed Ahead—Full Stop" is a normal curve. But only when strong social pressure is lacking does such a Gaussian distribution appear. Let an element of social constraint enter—"Stop" signs, red lights, a policeman, and the distribution of

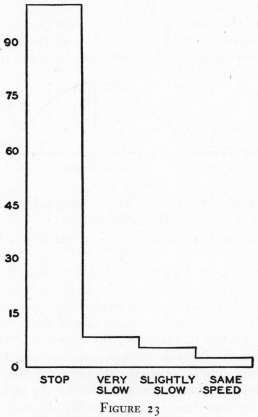

FIGURE 23

J-Curve of Conforming Behavior

Motorists' behavior at intersection, with no cross traffic approaching, but confronted with red lights and a traffic officer: 102 cases. After F. H. Allport, *J. Soc. Psychol.*, 1934, 5, p. 144, Figure 2.

speeds is no longer "normal." It is skewed markedly toward the side of *obedience*. A large number of instances of social conformity have been studied, always with the same result.[19] What appears in place of a normal (chance-biological) curve is a J-shaped distribution. The behavior of motorists confronted physically by stop lights and a policeman is represented in Figure 23.

[19] F. H. Allport, "The J-Curve Hypothesis of Conforming Behavior," *J. Soc. Psychol.*, 1934, 5, 141-183.

In many situations, a *double* J-curve is found. Some strong social pressure makes for conformity; every individual is expected to fit the same mold; and most of them do. But at the same time "uncontrolled" factors again enter to a sufficient extent to cause minor deviations from the norm. A good instance is found in the punching of the time clock in a factory, Figure 24. Here every incentive leads to punctuality, or if any deviation is permitted, it must be in the direction of earliness. The resulting distribution is sharply asymmetrical, with the mode falling upon the "punching time" set by the employer.

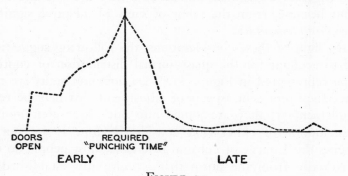

FIGURE 24

Double J-Curve of Conforming Behavior

Smoothed curve representing time of arrival at a factory: 1,277 cases. After F. H. Allport, *op. cit.*, p. 145, Figure 5A.

Underlying biological variation, then, makes for a distribution approaching the normal probability curve; cultural conformity, also operating in the case of common traits, tends, on the other hand, to make the distribution asymmetrical, with the mode at the terminal step defined by the norm itself. How can these opposed forms of distribution be reconciled?

Before attempting a solution of the puzzle, we must ask ourselves one other question: Is it more reasonable to suppose in the case of a given scalable variable that we are confronted with *one* common trait or with *two?* Taking Ascendance-Submission as typical, is one aspect of behavior here in question (as the hyphenated name for the continuum implies) or are two different aspects arbitrarily brought together for convenience of measurement? The second alternative is the more probable. For submission is not merely the absence of ascendance; a high score on the former does not mean simply an absence of the latter. Submission is a *positive* manner of adjusting, a positive as ascendance itself. Many people have a well integrated disposition to yield, to take the passive role in face-to-face situations; it is their style of life. The conception of a common trait of submission does its best to approximate this tendency as it is found in individual lives. And the same may be said of most other commonly scaled traits. Introversion is as positive (in the psychological sense) as extroversion; radicalism is as definite a common trait as conservatism. In such linear continua clearly *two* traits are involved.[20] Putting the two together is justified, not because they are one and the same trait, but because, from the point of view of adaptive significance, they are *complementary*.

In the light of these considerations, the following suggestions are offered to account for the quasi-normal distribution of continua of the type represented in Figure 22. *Two* common traits are present, but since they represent aspects of adjustment that may be regarded as complementary, they are joined into one linear continuum. The true distribution of either trait considered *alone* is not normal. It approaches the J-curve of cultural behavior: most people do not depart markedly from the norm that is culturally established; social pressure in these cases tends to produce moderation. Yet owing to special sets of influences (of which biological temperament is surely one) some individuals do deviate from the modal tendency.

In the case of Ascendance-Submission our hypothesis is that two separate distributions are represented in Figure 22. Most people are neither decidedly ascendant nor decidedly submissive; their average or near-average score on the test signifies as much.[21] When the two

[20] It is not true, however, that common traits, as conceived by testers, are always a combination of two opposite modes of adjustment. There are different ways of conceiving common traits. In some scales mere presence or absence of a tendency is measured, as, for example, in the case of esthetic, political, or religious *interests*, or in cases where the amounts of some prejudice or ambition are determined. In these instances a high score signifies the presence of the trait in question; a low score merely its absence. The present argument applies to scales, for either traits or attitudes, that are represented by hyphenated names, or could be so represented, *e.g.*, radicalism-conservatism, expansiveness-reticence, introversion-extroversion, fascism-communism, militarism-pacifism, and the like.

[21] An analysis of the reasons for the large proportion of average scores on the A-S Reaction Study reveals many contributing factors. In the first place the primary influence seems to be a tendency for the subject to select moderate responses to virtually every question; that is to say, he shows himself to be consistently "average" (neither ascendant nor submissive) in most situations. Here in all probability is a double effect: on the one hand, the social norms favor people neither markedly ascendant nor markedly submissive; on the other, the chance factors of temperament and other biological causes tend by and large in the same direction. A second, less frequent, cause of average scores is the cancellation of strongly ascendant

traits are put into a single artificial continuum, the result is a quasi-normal curve. If the distribution is still asymmetrical, as it often is, the inventor of the scale alters one item and another until a more satisfactory curve is obtained. The last step—so completely arbitrary—is often forgotten by the inventor when he interprets his results. He overlooks the fact that he personally has had much to say about the distribution which he blithely attributes to nature.

By way of summary: The whole problem of the distribution of common traits is exceedingly complex. Though for the present it is well to leave it open, a few suggestions have been made concerning factors influencing the distribution. For one thing the "normal" curve for common traits does in part reflect nature's preference for average (non-distinctive) levels; but in addition it reflects social pressure toward conformity with some accepted "average" level of conduct. The normal distribution often results from an arbitrary juxtaposition of opposite modes of adjustment into one linear scale. Finally, the distribution is to a certain extent affected by the inventor of the test who sees to it that successive revisions of his scale yield a more and more symmetrical scatter of scores. There is no serious objection to this last procedure, nor to the normal curve thus obtained, since in any case the scaling of common traits is but a rough way of approaching personality. In the interests of sound theory, however, it is well to realize the extent of the complications introduced into one "simple" variable for purposes of convenient measurement. Only by so doing can we avoid the fallacy of presuming, as more than one writer has done, that "everything in personality is normally distributed."

CARDINAL, CENTRAL, AND SECONDARY TRAITS

In every personality there are traits of major significance and traits of minor significance. Occasionally some trait is so pervasive and so outstanding in a life that it deserves to be called the *cardinal trait*. It is so dominant that there are few activities that cannot be traced

responses by an equal number of markedly submissive responses. In such cases, the scale is misapplied and misleading, for the subject obviously is not "average" in any intelligible sense of the word. He has two well integrated but entirely contradictory traits. Finally, an average score might result (though it seldom does so) from an entirely random series of responses, whereby this ascendant reply is cancelled by that submissive reply, with a number of non-diagnostic (moderate) responses thrown in, all as the theory of specificity would require. Thus there are many causes of average scores, and it is for this reason that an *average* score obtained by a single individual has little psychological significance.

directly or indirectly to its influence. The list of terms on pp. 302 f., derived from the proper names of historical and fictional characters, shows clearly what is meant by cardinal traits. No such trait can for long remain hidden; an individual is known by it, and may even become famous for it. Such a master quality has sometimes been called *the eminent trait, the ruling passion, the master-sentiment,* or *the radix* of a life.

It has been objected that the conception of a cardinal trait is essentially tautological, for, one asks, is not the cardinal trait identical with the personality itself? This objection cannot be admitted; however well integrated a life may be around the cardinal trait there remain specific habits, incidental and non-organized tendencies, and minor traits of some degree that cannot be subsumed functionally under the cardinal trait. Though pervasive and pivotal, a cardinal trait still remains within the personality; it never coincides with it.

It is an unusual personality that possesses one and only one eminent trait. Ordinarily it seems that the foci of personality (though not wholly separate from one another) lie in a handful of distinguishable *central traits.* (Cf. Perry's list of the four "benign" traits of William James, p. 314, ftn. 2.) Central traits are those usually mentioned in careful letters of recommendation, in rating scales where the rater stars the outstanding characteristics of the individual, or in brief verbal descriptions of a person.

One may speak, on a still less important level, of *secondary traits,* less conspicuous, less generalized, less consistent, and less often called into play than central traits. They are aroused by a narrower range of equivalent stimuli and they issue into a narrower range of equivalent responses. Being so circumscribed they may escape the notice of all but close acquaintances.

It goes without saying that these three gradations are altogether arbitrary and are phrased merely for the convenience of discourse. There are no criteria, statistical or otherwise, by which to mark off one grade from another. In reality there are all possible degrees of organization in a trait from the most circumscribed and unstable to the most pervasive and most firmly integrated. It is useful, however, to have these distinctions at hand when one wishes to speak roughly of the relative prominence of various traits in a given personality.

TRAITS AND THE TOTAL PERSONALITY

Since semi-separate traits are the most reasonable units for use in the psychological exploration of personality, it has been necessary to discuss them in some detail. It would, however, be unfortunate to give the impression that a personality is *adequately* studied when a list of these inter-dependent traits is assembled. The problem of sub-structures is not the same as the problem of total structure. Traits are merely the principal *Teilfunktionen* of personality; beyond them extends the problem of their inter-fusion. Various theories have been advanced to account for the homogeneity of the whole personality which Stern has so aptly characterized as an *unitas multiplex*. Thus far we have been considering theories that explain its multiplicity; the next question in order is its unity. Be it noted, however, that the theory of inter-dependent traits takes a long step in the direction of synthesis.

RÉSUMÉ OF THE DOCTRINE OF TRAITS

In everyday life, no one, not even a psychologist, doubts that underlying the conduct of a mature person there are characteristic dispositions or traits. His enthusiasms, interests, and styles of expression are far too self-consistent and plainly patterned to be accounted for in terms of specific habits or identical elements. Nor can the stability and consistency of behavior be explained away by invoking nominalistic theories; stability and consistency are not due to the bio-social arrangement of unrelated activities into categories with verbal tags. Traits are not creations in the mind of the observer, nor are they verbal fictions; they are here accepted as biophysical facts, actual psychophysical dispositions related—though no one yet knows how—to persistent neural systems of stress and determination.

Traits are not, like the faculties of old, abstractions derived from a theory of mind-in-general. There is no essential resemblance between impersonal faculties, as Memory, Will, and Sagacity on the one hand, and the focalized sub-structures of a particular mind (interests, sentiments, general attitudes) on the other. Faculties are universal, traits personal; faculties are independent, traits inter-dependent; faculties are a priori, traits must be ascertained empirically in the individual case.

The doctrine of traits differs also from the theory of factors or any other system of common dimensions into which every individual is fitted categorically. Conceptualized nomothetic units (factors, instincts, needs, and the like) stress what is universal in men, not what is organized into integral, personal systems. The doctrine of traits emphasizes concrete individuality.

Traits are not directly observable; they are inferred (as any kind of determining tendency is inferred). Without such an inference the stability and consistency of personal behavior could not possibly be explained. Any specific action is a product of innumerable determinants, not only of traits but of momentary pressures and specialized influences. But it is the repeated occurrence of actions having the *same significance* (equivalence of response), following upon a definable range of stimuli having the same personal significance (equivalence of stimuli), that makes necessary the postulation of traits as states of Being. Traits are not at all times active, but they are persistent even when latent, and are distinguished by low thresholds of arousal.

It is one thing to admit traits as the most acceptable unit for investigation in the psychology of personality, but another to determine authoritatively the precise character of these traits in a given life. In order to avoid projection of his own nature and many other sources of error, the psychological investigator must use all the empirical tools of his science to make his inferences valid. Traits cannot be conjured into existence; they must be discovered.

In naming the traits that are discovered, there are many pitfalls, the chief one being the confusion of personality with character through the use of eulogistic and dyslogistic terms. Whenever this occurs the existential pattern of personality becomes hopelessly entangled with social judgments of merit and demerit. It is possible, though difficult, to achieve a psychological vocabulary of noncensorial trait-names. Most of these terms antedate psychology by centuries; they were invented because they were needed. Simply because it is difficult to employ them circumspectly, the investigator is not on that account justified in dispensing with them altogether and attempting to put mathematical or artificial symbols in their place. Regrettable though it may seem, the attributes of human personality can be depicted only with the aid of common speech, for it alone possesses the requisite flexibility, subtlety, and established intelligibility.

For the purposes of comparison and measurement certain segments of behavior (by virtue of the similarity of human equipment and the common exigencies of the cultural and physical environments) may be considered as distributed in a general population. These *common* traits as conceptualized by the investigator may, in a rough and approximate way, be scaled on a linear continuum. The "normality" of distribution obtained for such traits is a complex product of chance-biological variation, cultural conformity, and artifact. However carefully conceived and scaled, a common trait is at best an abstraction, for in its concrete form, in each particular life, it operates always in a unique fashion. *Individual* traits cannot be scaled at all in a general population, and for that reason they have been hitherto neglected by all excepting clinical investigators.

Some traits are clearly motivational, especially those sub-classes ordinarily known as interests, ambitions, complexes, and sentiments. Other traits are less dynamic in their operation, having an ability to steer (to stylize) behavior rather than to initiate it. But often the traits that are at first directive acquire driving power, and those that are at one time driving become merely directive.

Traits are not wholly independent of one another; nor are any other neuropsychic systems. They frequently exist in clusters, the arousal of one portion tending to spread to all regions in readiness for communication. Throughout this elaborate interplay, different foci of organization can be detected, a fact that justifies the conception of a *manifold* of traits even where they clearly overlap.

As this segregation among traits is only relative, so too is their self-consistency. In fact, the usefulness of any trait to its possessor depends to a great extent upon its flexibility. Even while it stabilizes conduct and economizes effort, the trait must not be rigid in its operation; for effective adjustment and mastery require variation. The range of situations that arouses traits must be expected to change according to circumstances. Also in any personality one must expect to find some contradiction and conflict among traits, as novelists and clinicians never tire of telling.

Variable though they are, still in every mature personality certain *central* traits can normally be identified. So too can *secondary* traits, though these are less distinctive, less prominent, and more circumscribed in their operation. Whenever a disposition is so little generalized that it is aroused by only a narrow range of stimulus situations, it is more properly called an *attitude* than a trait. Somewhat rarely a personality is dominated by one outstanding *cardinal* trait, to which other dispositions serve as merely subsidiary, congruent foci.

As is the case with all other forms of mental organization, the structure of true (individual) traits is a question of degree. But however much they may vary in respect to their consistency, scope, and independence, they have—according to the theory developed in these chapters—certain essential characteristics. They are always biophysical in nature, concrete and personal in their organization, contemporaneous in their effect, capable of functional autonomy, but not structurally independent of one another; they are generalized (to the extent that the effective stimuli are equivalent, and to the extent that the resultant responses are equivalent). They are *modi vivendi*, ultimately deriving their significance from the role they play in advancing adaptation within, and mastery of, the personal environment.

CHAPTER XIII

THE UNITY OF PERSONALITY

> Made up of myriads of microscopic cell lives, individually born, each one of us nevertheless appears to himself a single entity, a unity experiencing and acting as one individual. In a way, the more far-reaching and many-sided the reactions of which a mind is capable, the more need, as well as the more scope, for their consolidation into one. True, each one of us is in some sense not one self, but a multiple system of selves. Yet how closely those selves are united and integrated to one personality!
>
> —*C. S. Sherrington*

In spite of the common preference of the psychologist for the analytical approach to any problem, he has not altogether neglected the task of accounting as well as he may for the idiomatic completeness of personality. Indeed, he has examined the problem from a great many angles, and has devised many theories and hypotheses, some of which he has submitted to empirical tests. Since the problem thus turns out to be many-sided, our treatment of it will of necessity be compendious and eclectic.

The only approach that may safely be excluded is the rhapsodic. Here we find theories that do little more than assert personality to be an "Indivisible Whole," "a total integrated pattern of behavior," an *Unteilbarkeit*, an *in sich geschlossene Ganzheit*. This rapturous literature of wholeness does not explore the unity that it apotheosizes; it merely contemplates and admires. Personality, it says, is like a symphony. Granted; but does not the comprehension of symphonic unity come only through an understanding of the *articulate weaving* of motifs, movements, bridge-passages, modulations, contrasts, and codas? Nothing but empty and vague adjectives can be used to characterize the work as a whole. If a totality is not articulated, it is likely to be an incomprehensible blur; it can then be extolled, but not understood. What is more fatal, the rhapsodic approach seriously over-simplifies the whole problem, under-estimating the conflicts and discords in every life. Unity, at best, is a matter of *degree*.[1]

RETROSPECT

The problem of unity, as we have said, is many-sided. Here and there in the last nine chapters it has been incidentally discussed. Before considering it from new points of view, a backward glance will recall the issues as they have thus far arisen.

In infancy there is marked evidence of a "dynamical unity" that seems never in later life to be of quite such striking degree. The young child responds pretty much "as a whole" whenever he reaches, retracts, or expresses emotion. The situation was represented after the manner of Lewin in Figure 14 (p. 133) where it appeared that few psychical systems are segregated in the earliest months, and that the barriers between these are weak. Even after the first months of life the child responds for a long while in what seems almost an "all or none" fashion, particularly when emotion is involved. He is incapable of delayed response, of discrimination, and of precise gradation. As he grows older and as *differentiation* within the psychical systems takes place this elementary dynamical unity is lessened, though vestiges remain throughout life in states of emotional seizure, and in the persistence of *synkinesis* (patterns of expressive movement undifferentiated from one another).

As if to offset the disunity that comes with differentiation, there is a compensatory process of *integration*. By virtue of the functional joining of psychical systems (through conditioning, generalization of habit, and all associational processes) integral units come into existence. For the most part these units represent coherent foci of development, found serviceable to adjustment and to mastery. Figure 15 (p. 141) represents this multiplicity of units in an hierarchical arrangement, and shows that these functional units though to some extent independent, tend, nevertheless, normally to converge into more embracing systems. Though perfect unity is never achieved, there may be said to be a constant progression in that direction,

[1] "The greatest difficulty in the scientific study of character comes with our realization that men by no means always behave as if their mental life bore a single stamp. Each performs acts or speaks words that are 'uncharacteristic,' seeming indeed to run counter to the character we ascribe to him. No man is a machine whose functioning is perfectly predictable and whose performance one may order to a mathematical formula. But despite all this, neither is man a wholly chaotic creation." R. Müller-Freienfels, *Lebensnahe Charakterkunde*, 1935, p. 13.

hindered however by the contrary formation and fixation of stereo-types, dissociated complexes, and primitive levels of adaptation.

While differentiation and integration are under way there develops gradually an important core of *self-consciousness*. Perhaps nothing contributes to the unity of personality as much as this subjective point of reference, by virtue of which the individual feels that there is coherence between his memories of the past and his plans for the future. Self-consciousness is necessary for self-esteem, for aspiration, and is a pre-condition of status in the social group (by which, in turn, it is profoundly modified). All these factors are unifying in their effects. Gradually the self extends in such a way that it is closely identified with personal possessions, with other people, and with introcepted ideals and cultural standards. The self becomes the center of an orderly psychological universe. Whether the self is regarded as the innermost nucleus of all conscious ego-systems (Koffka) or as the interplay of all conscious states (James), does not greatly matter. In either case the self is the subjective moderator of whatever unity the personality may have.

Many writers have stressed particularly the role of memory, pointing to its bridge-like character, reaching backward to provide easy communication between by-gone experiences. These bridges of memory can be completely broken only by an hysterical splitting of personality. And pathological dissociation of this type, as Sherrington says, bears important testimony to the inescapable unity of normal memory schemata:

> Even in those extremes of so-called double personality, one of their mystifying features is that the individual seems to himself at any one time wholly either this personality or that, never the two commingled. The view that regards hysteria as mental dissociation illustrates the integrative trend of the total healthy mind.[2]

In order to bind the past with the future, memory must be supplemented by *imagination*, another unifying capacity of the self. With its aid the human being may plan his life when he is young, and spend years of concerted effort in pursuit of his chosen goals.

Perhaps the most significant property of the self is the peculiar inward quality of emotional life, represented variously as the principle of Egoism, self-esteem, the sentiment of self-regard, or as the "up-

---

[2] C. S. Sherrington, *Mental Hygiene*, 1923, 7, p. 16. This quotation follows immediately the passage cited at the beginning of this chapter.

ward tendency of the Ego." Whenever the beloved ego is the object of regard, as it very often is, unity is enhanced, for at such moments all activities have a clear common point of reference.

Such selfishness, however, is not the whole story. An individual who devotes himself to one master-sentiment, whose personality is distinguished by one primary *Bestimmung* (Bühler) likewise finds psychological unity. In fact the pursuit of external goals can be more consistently maintained than the opportunistic pursuit of selfish ends which of necessity vary from time to time. This conception of *intention* as a principle of unification is related also to the conception of the *ego-ideal* (pp. 218-220). Whenever the ego-ideal is derived by virtue of introception from the ethics of culture, it helps to hold the individual within a single course of development. Any *Weltanschauung*, however derived, by engendering intelligibility upon the diversity of experience, serves as an important unifying influence.

Then there are the numerous balancing agencies in the body that preserve functional integrity in the course of growth: the homeostasis of the endocrines, the recovery or transfer of functions after injury, the remarkable adaptive properties of the sense-organs. All these *biological conditions of unity* must not be overlooked, for nature appears greatly concerned in preserving the integrity of the individual organism. This fact is the most basic of all the guarantees of unity. Hereditary endowment in terms of *temperament* contributes to this stabilizing of the course of development, with the result that as a personality changes it seems to change consistently with itself (cf. Figure 13, pp. 126 f.). Nature sets limits beyond which the variation in individual development may not extend.

In an entirely different sense, unity (of the moment) is guaranteed by the principle of *convergence*. At any one time the available psychophysical energies are mobilized in one maximally integrated course of conduct, through the medium of the final common path (p. 313). Important as this type of unification is, it has two limitations. In the first place, it does not mean, as is sometimes mistakenly held, that the "organism responds as a whole." Such a statement is an exaggeration (unless perhaps in the earliest days of infancy where mass action dominates the scene of behavior). Many concurrent activities can go along at one and the same time. A man may walk, smoke, dodge the traffic, digest his dinner, and at the same time be busy with his thoughts. The final common path means only that *one maximally integrated* activity occurs at a time. The man cannot be pursuing several different trains of thought at one and the same moment. The second limitation to the principle of convergence is that at best it guarantees unity only for the moment. In itself it does not account for the consistency between *successive* acts. To make good this lack, there must be an account of *structural* consistency whereby unity over a period of time is achieved.

The hypothesis of traits fills this need. Far better than any other doctrine of elements this hypothesis helps to account for consistency in personality wherever' consistency is found, and for inconsistency whenever conflict and discordance prevail. There is stability among traits; there is likewise contradiction; there are cardinal and central traits to which minor traits may be ordered as subsidiary foci, rounding out or specializing the operation of the principal traits; and there are dissociated traits. Further, the conception of equivalence supplies the elasticity necessary to account for the variability of behavior within a range. Unity is, after all, never mechanically rigid; it shows itself only within a *range* of equivalent conduct.

Most significant of all the attributes of traits for the problem of unity is their *interdependence*. Any theory of separate and independent elements will find itself hopelessly confused in attempting to represent the coherence among these elements (cf. Figure 17a, p. 246). Factorial psychology, for example, is faced with two alternatives, neither palatable. Either it may assume that personality as a whole is simply the sum-total of the independent factors, thereby committing the fallacy of the omnibus (bundle) conception of personality; or else it must find some cement to make the separate and unrelated factors cohere. With the assumption of *over-lapping* traits the task is easier, for the very conception itself contains the idea of *fusion*. Unity lies in the overlap of the traits with one another.[3] This

[3] A. Kronfeld has considered the various ways in which the *Teilfunktionen*, or traits, might be related to the total personality. The first possibility is the formal summation (omnibus theory) that he rightly rejects. The second is the view that each trait may contain, microcosmically, the essential qualities of the whole personality. This view seems to confuse convergence in action (the final common path) which is sound, with a curious and untenable principle of immanence, whereby the whole is regarded as resident in each part. It seems wiser to regard the dispositions as incomplete portions of the total personality, and to admit their convergence merely in action, where indeed one little act is often diagnostic of many qualities— as when we say, "That little gesture of his spoke volumes." The third possibility, according to Kronfeld, is the one here advocated, namely, that the unity of personality consists in the intricate functional inter-relationship of the traits, and their blended arrangement in hierarchies. A. Kronfeld, *Lehrbuch der Charakterkunde*, 1932, p. 35.

statement does not, of course, settle the issue for all time, since the nature of the overlap and its *raison d'être* need to be known. But intrinsically any hypothesis of *interdependent* traits is far more advantageous in the study of unity than an hypothesis of disparate and scattered elements.

All these considerations have been fully discussed in earlier chapters. They are important as factors making for coherence in personality. But they do not tell the whole story.

It is the three-fold argument of this chapter that the problem of unity must be approached from many sides; that the most significant contributions come with the aid of concepts from a somewhat more complex level than psychologists are wont to use; and, finally, that an empirical solution to many of the issues involved is possible. But before running the ever-present danger on the empirical road of losing one's way in a welter of detail, it will be instructive to hear what some of the rationalistic writers say concerning unity. Hypotheses originating with rationalists are often the best guides for psychologists when they enter new or only partially explored territory.

UNITY AS A PHILOSOPHICAL PRINCIPLE

As Chapter II made clear, there are many meanings of the term *personality* other than the special psychological meaning adopted in this volume. Metaphysically one might define personality as "the indestructible essence of individual being (the soul)." Such a definition would of necessity claim unity as an essential attribute of personality. This proposition, though it may very well be true, lies altogether in a nonpsychological realm of discourse. In deciding to dispense with the soul, psychologists cut themselves off deliberately from such speculative propositions of theology and philosophy. Unfortunately they fell at the same time into the rather shabby habit of declaring that all the metaphysical conceptions with which they refused to deal were *ipso facto* meaningless. It would be far wiser to concede that metaphysical unity may be a property of personality, while insisting that it is a different problem from the empirical unity that falls in the province of psychology.

Somewhat closer to the psychologist's interest are those philosophies of nature variously called organismic, systemic, or holistic. Such philosophies see nature as composed of coherent systems fraught with significance and survival value; they frequently cite personality as the supreme example. Such was the view of Fechner who regarded any organism as an expression of the primary law of the "tendency to stability." According to this principle any single system assumes a regular internal arrangement of its parts, and a regular external form whose stability is guaranteed by the very mandate of Nature.[4] Spinoza too had a philosophy of orderly systems, the key to which lay in his conception of *conatus*. In the material world an object at rest or in motion expresses its *conatus se conservandi* by resisting whatever would tend to change its state of motion or rest. In human beings the principle expresses itself rather as an active impulse toward growth and self-expression. Man is unique in that he alone is conscious of the possession of this *conatus*.[5] There are philosophies of system and order that regard the unification of personality as an illustrative event in a cosmos given to orderly and coherent arrangements; the philosophy of Whitehead being one of these.

Even physiologists often embrace a philosophy of "systematic relevance." The self-preserving, self-repairing, self-regulating processes of the body imply to them a root-tendency to maintain wholeness. In the constant return of all psychophysical systems to a state of equilibrium, some see a "wisdom of the body," others a "state of vigilance." The more prosaic refer merely to "homeostasis." But whatever terms they employ these physiological doctrines all assume an inherent tendency of every organism to form itself into one intricate homogeneous system.

Some philosophers, notably Keyserling, have commented upon the great difficulty, when compared with lower animals, that human beings have in achieving unity. Unity, they say, is attained only when all the possibilities of life have been realized. Lower animals are a comprehensive expression of their potentialities; human beings are seldom so. A kingfisher alertly catching food on the shores of a pond is a more perfect, if less intricate, unity than is a human being in quest of his daily bread.

UNITY AS STRIVING

Romantics of the nineteenth century were fond of saying, "A man is what he loves." Sometimes the adage was varied: "Everyman

---

[4] G. Fechner, *Einige Ideen zur Schöpfungs- und Entwicklungsgeschichte der Organismen*, 1873, chap. iii.

[5] B. Spinoza, *Ethics*, Bk. II, chap. iii. sec. 2.

bears the stamp of his favorite experience." In recent years there have appeared somewhat more technical versions of the same teaching. Psychiatrists, for example, tell us that the normal personality is one that is ever active in pursuit of chosen goals; whereas abnormality is characterized by apathy, by a deficiency in life interests. Without aspirations a life cannot be steered in a consistent course. In many of the neuroses and psychoses a pathological lethargy settles upon the patient, and a deadening of personality results.

Stating the case still more specifically, some writers find the unity of personality achieved in its life work. Burnham has pointed out that just as a concrete task (the *Aufgabe*) integrates available energy for the moment, so too, in the long run, a life work confers stability and consistency. Voltaire gave classic expression to the thought when he maintained that salvation for the individual lies in "cultivating his garden." The same view is upheld by John Dewey, who, however, hastens to add that there should be no fence about the garden, that the scope of one's devotion must be ever widening. Goethe, too, found eventual salvation for Faust in useful work that finally absorbed Faust's restless energies, and provided as nearly as possible the completeness that he sought.

In the course of striving it is natural that the "guiding image" or the ego-ideal should play a prominent part. A person centers his efforts on becoming what he wants to become, and develops consistently in ways that in his belief lead to that end. The guiding image fixes attention in one direction, dictates the skill that he must acquire, and prescribes the criteria by which all possible courses of conduct must be tested before they are engaged in. Even if the immediate details of a life are discordant, even if there seems to the outsider to be a bewildering clash of purposes, still there may be an imaginal unity among them that gives subjective coherence in spite of all visible disharmony.

Here is a curious fact: the attainment of unity depends more upon knowing what one wants than upon getting it. It is the striving towards the known goal that confers unity, not the successful arrival. Love of learning—to take an example—is more of a unifying force than the possession of learning, so too is love of art, of money, or of fame. Unity of intention offsets failure of accomplishment; it is a matter of what a man loves, not of what he has or acquires. Attainment may even be destructive of unity, for attainment forthwith abolishes the unifying desire. From this point of view unity lies only in the struggle for unity. It was Mephisto's wager that he could so beguile Faust that the latter would no longer struggle for completeness, but surrender to some tempting state of self-satisfaction along the way. Had Faust yielded to the illusion that his quest was ended he would have been damned. In the end he was saved because he ceaselessly strove for the completeness he never attained.

> *Wer immer strebend sich bemüht*
> *Den können wir erlösen.*

Faust, as the prototype of man, found that striving for completeness was not merely an abstract matter. The only practicable condition of unity that he discovered was the seeking of specific objectives related to a life work. When every moment of effort is directly or indirectly pointed to the same progressive series of goals, these moments are then bound to one another. Such an interlocking series of moments constitutes what Paulhan has called a "harmony of striving," and serves as the prime condition of unity in personality. The harmony is rarely perfect, for in most lives aims clash with one another quite as readily as they reinforce one another.[6] From the psychological point of view such a clash of purposes is inimical to unity.[7]

EMPIRICAL STUDIES OF UNITY

Many of the factors reviewed in the preceding pages can be submitted to empirical study. This is fortunately true, for since unity is a matter of degree, it is of considerable importance to have methods for determining in a given case what degree has been attained.

Empirical studies of unity, though still in the early stage of de-

---

[6] Lasurski rightly warns against mistaking pseudo-unity for true unity. The former is an illusory product of suppression and dissociation, "which consists in the fact that some inclination or group of related inclinations control all others, inhibiting them or suppressing them. Men who are given to self-denial and asceticism, often serve as examples of this specious unity." A. Lasurski, "Über das Studium der Individualität," *Pädag. Monog.*, 1912, No. 14, 27. Freudian psychology deals at length with the duplicity and lack of genuine unity in such personalities.

[7] Metaphysically, this statement may be denied. W. Stern has argued that since the clash of different aims takes place entirely within the person (he being in conflict with himself), the person, therefore, must be an embracing unity, capable of harboring all conflicts that occur. Likewise, says Stern, the existence of personal conflict presupposes an ideal of unity for the person, or else a state of prior unity or a unity of the future; otherwise a conflict could not be evaluated as such; it would have no meaning. *Allgemeine Psychologie*, 1935, p. 623. In other words, the person, ontologically considered, is more of a unity than he is from the empirical point of view. No doubt this is true, but it is only with the empirical (psychological) unity that we are here concerned.

velopment, have had the wholesome effect of exposing and correcting the exaggerations of unity ordinarily made in everyday life. As a
rule we stereotype our judgments even of our most intimate friends,
and see greater consistency in their behavior than we should. The
reason for this over-simplification, of course, is the reason for all
time-saving clichés: we cannot afford to think or to deal with objects in all their intricate and conflicting aspects. Hence we seek the
"essence," and in so doing often arrive no further than a pigeon-
hole.[8] It is for this reason that psychology with its corrective patience
may improve upon the too simple perceptions of common sense.

Empirically considered, the problem of unity is the same as the
problem of *consistency*. The latter term is for experimental work
much to be preferred, for it covers readily all approximations of unity,
and can be applied to part-structures as well as to the whole.

There follows a brief characterization of the principal methods
now employed in psychology in the study of personal consistency.

Prediction. Predictions of human conduct may be made under
three conditions. First, when people are viewed *en masse*, and only
the average behavior is of any interest. The experienced manager of a
restaurant or moving picture theater can predict remarkably well
how many people of the thousands who pass his establishment every
hour will turn in at his door. The insurance company predicts accurately how many people will die or be injured in a given year.
Such actuarial prediction, since it has nothing whatever to do with
the individual, has no direct bearing upon the psychology of personality. The second type of prediction, generally employed by the
psychologist, comes only slightly closer. It is based upon knowledge
of mind-in-general. The psychologist predicts that any man will
blink his eye if the cornea is touched, or that any normal individual
will show a gradual increase of proficiency while learning a motor
skill. Prediction of this type is possible through the knowledge of
the general properties of reflexes and habits; what is common in
human nature affords the basis of the prediction.

The third type of prediction, more relevant for the psychology
of personality, forecasts what *one* individual man (and perhaps no

---

[8] In biographies, even those that are full length, an inevitable exaggeration of
consistency occurs. "Irrelevant" activities and traits are discarded, and the act of
discarding makes for over-simplification. Particularly clear is the exaggeration in
the case of necrologies. The writer wishes to extract the "essence" or meaning of
the life. In so doing remarkable unity emerges, more than was ever present in the
animate person.

one else) will do in a situation of a certain type. Such prophecies pertain to mind-in-particular, and are absolutely indispensable in ordinary life. It is only by virtue of them that we are able to select gifts that our friends will like, to bring together a congenial group at dinner, to choose words that will have the desired effect upon an acquaintance, or to pick a satisfactory employee, tenant, or room-mate. That our predictions sometimes go awry is true, but the fact that they are so often successful is one of the principal lines of evidence for the existence of relatively stable dispositions in personality.

It is not, of course, the *exact* response of an individual that is predictable. It is only the *range* of his response. Rarely can we foretell the precise words our friend will use in expressing pleasure at the gift we have brought him, but that he will like it we are sure. With just what movements an aggressive person will show his nature in a given situation we do not know, but that he will be aggressive in some way we can safely wager. In other words we predict the operation of a *trait*, but allow for a fairly wide range of equivalent responses that will be called forth by other determinants prevailing at the time the behavior takes place.

It is not difficult to bring this type of prediction into the laboratory. One experiment based on this procedure was described on p. 254. The experimenter predicted with considerable success which of his subjects would violate the prohibitions contained in the directions for their part in the experiment, though in all probability the investigator could not have foretold precisely when and how the violation would occur. It will be recalled that in this particular experiment, a rather special condition was introduced, namely, the making of the prediction on the evidence of first impressions (five minute acquaintance). Even so, the predictions were correct in 69 per cent of the cases (chance = 50 per cent). Longer acquaintance, it may be assumed, would have enhanced the validity of the prediction.

Another experiment, based on longer acquaintance, was conducted by Bender.[9] After four one-hour conferences with each of eight subjects, this investigator predicted the scores that each would make in ten different "personality tests." When the tests were administered, and the 80 predictions correlated with the 80 performances, a coefficient of +.55 ±.05 was obtained.

After further acquaintance (sixteen one-hour conferences with

[9] I. E. Bender, *A Study in Integrations of Personalities by Prediction and Matching,* 1935 (Syracuse University Library).

each), Bender undertook with four new tests to predict not the total scores but the exact response each subject would make to every item. This feat, as pointed out above, is much more difficult than the prediction of total scores. Nevertheless the majority of the predicted responses were correct.

A further variation in this work consisted in using 100 judges not personally acquainted with the subjects. These judges had for their guidance sketches of the eight personalities prepared by the experimenter after his prolonged study of each case.[10] From each condensed portrait (called by the experimenter "integrational hypothesis"), the judges predicted what responses the eight subjects would make to a scale measuring various attitudes and interests (none of the attitudes or interests in question being mentioned specifically in the sketch). Even under this tenuous condition, success exceeded chance expectation to a marked degree.

These are only a few of the varieties of the many-sided method of prediction. It unquestionably demonstrates personal consistency in conduct, though it does not of course illuminate the question of the causes of consistency. As currently applied the method probably errs in the direction of under-stating the consistency of personality, rather than over-stating, for with the introduction of any *judge* into the research, his own failures to predict correctly may mistakenly be interpreted as a sign of inconsistency in the subject. Whenever judges are employed in investigations of personality it is found that they as human instruments vary greatly in their sensitiveness and skill (cf. Chapter XVIII).

Matching. A related method, employing likewise the *impression* of the judge, has come into wide favor in recent years.[11] It is the

---

[10] One example follows and illustrates the type of "thumb-nail sketch" that psychologists sometimes offer as a rough synthesis of a personality they have studied by analytical methods.

"K is characterized by a dignity of manner and bearing calculated to barricade her from certain contacts which she holds in disdain. She is interested in matrimony provided it will assure her economic security, luxury, travel and social prestige. Her reactions to people while often formal tend to develop into intensely personal contacts. With men, there is a high degree of sex-consciousness. She is selfish, *i.e.*, self-centered, pleasure-seeking, dilettante in her interests rather than profound. For the greater part she is dissatisfied and bored with life. There is a tendency to be moody and sometimes languid. She is neat to the point of being fastidious. Although introverted she is ascendant. Her high social intelligence is well integrated around her striving for social approbation. What her personality lacks in force and seriousness of purpose is redeemed by her physical attraction and her personal charm."

[11] Directions for using this method, as well as a valuable summary of research employing it, are given by P. E. Vernon, *Psychol. Bull.*, 1936, 33, 149-177.

attempt to match different records of *one* personality by a judge who is confronted with an assortment of records taken from *many* personalities. The records may be of any type: life-histories, photographs, specimens of handwriting, scores on various tests, artistic productions, or anything else.

> Bender, in the investigation cited above, used this method in addition to prediction. In one experiment, 91 judges were given the eight thumb-nail sketches ("integrational hypotheses") and a "percentile testograph" for each subject, constructed from the subject's scores on a series of tests. The number of correct matchings obtained was compared with the number of correct matchings expected by chance; in six of the eight cases the judges showed that they clearly were able to order the two sets of records correctly; they perceived the unity that obtained between the summary sketch and the test scores.

The method of matching has the advantage of permitting complex productions to be ordered with other complex productions, without first undergoing the destructive process of artificial analysis. To put the case another way, matching permits the quantitative study of qualitative patterns. Its utility will be further discussed in later chapters.

Correspondence of Measures. Both prediction and matching depend upon the ability of judges to order the records with which they deal. Some methods eliminate this source of error by comparing directly the record of an individual in one sphere of activity with his record in another. For example, through the use of correlation it is easy to determine whether the position of subjects relative to one another for one performance remains essentially the same for other performances. To take a typical instance: on p. 222 it was reported that for one group of subjects the correlation between measures of *insight* and of *humor* was +.88. Interpreted, this coefficient means that for most individuals in the population studied, both qualities were present (or deficient) to about the same degree. (In this particular case the measures used were ratings, in which an initial error of subjective judgment, perhaps a "halo," may be included, but some initial experimental error is possible, of course, even in objective measures.) Whenever the correlation between two or more qualities is high, consistency (barring initial errors) has been demonstrated between these qualities within the group as a whole; what is proved is that there is a tendency for the subjects to be consistent *in the same way*. (The degree of consistency any single individual has achieved cannot, however, be determined by this method.)

A somewhat similar form of correspondence was described on p. 316 where the *internal consistency* of any one scale for the measurement of a common trait was interpreted to mean that this trait (again within a total population) is self-consistent. This procedure, too, tells nothing about the individual pattern of unity, but only that some common trait, as conceived by the experimenter, is to a certain degree self-consistent for a whole population of subjects. Likewise, the products of factor-analysis, determined by an extension of correlational methods, are empirically self-consistent. But they too pertain only to the abstract average man, and not to single individuals.

Through a more elaborate use of corresponding measures attempts have even been made to determine whether consistency (or its opposite, variability) is itself a consistent attribute of personality. The individual's variability of scores about his own mean score for many tests is taken as a kind of "integration index." The conception is one of the "consistency of consistency" (or, its complement, the "consistency of variability"). Though offering a pretty problem for statisticians, this type of work has not as yet resulted in anything of psychological merit.[12] Since the unity of personality is not a matter of approximating the same "mean score" on many common traits, this procedure is maladapted to the problem in hand.

CONGRUENCE AND METHODS FOR ITS DISCOVERY

There is a wide gap between the type of consistency demonstrated by the correspondence of measures, and the radical (root) consistency with which clinical psychology deals. The former looks at a large group of people and aims to discover what common clusters of coherent qualities there are for this population; the latter is solely interested in the congruence of an *individual* life.

A young artist once took part in some psychological experiments in which many records were taken of his expressive movements, along with those of 24 other subjects. In seeking the correspondence of measures for all the variables studied, it turned out that the records of this particular subject were often "inconsistent." For example, the

[12] Cf. G. W. Allport and P. E. Vernon, *Studies in Expressive Movement*, 1933, pp. 123-133.

average pressure he exerted upon the point of a pencil in writing or upon the point of a stylus in tapping was 7th in the group; that is to say, the contact that he made upon a surface was somewhat *firmer* than the average. Yet records taken of the pressure he exerted in resting his *hand* upon the surface, showed that his rank order in the group for this performance was 19th. Obviously there was no correspondence between these two measures: the point pressure was heavy; the pressure of resting the hand, light. No correlation was indicated. Was there no consistency? Certainly not in respect to *pressure*. But pressure is a superficial variable, a concept originating in physics and not in psychology. Further consideration suggests that though the measures failed to correspond they are none the less congruent psychologically. Being an artist (and this is the unifying condition), this subject, following his customary style of execution, rests his hand lightly upon his work, but plies his crayons or brush with some firmness upon the surface he is using.[13]

This simple illustration of congruence has many counterparts in the study of personality. The routine search for the correspondence of measures in order to establish some preconceived dimension of unity (in the above case, *pressure*) is often disappointing. Sometimes it succeeds, but frequently does not. The weakness of this method is that it seeks consistency only in the horizontal dimension—between the peripheral activities of many people, and not in the vertical dimension, down through the structure of the single personality (cf. p. 11). By defining consistency only in terms of correspondence and never in terms of congruence a thoroughly one-sided picture (of specificity) is likely to appear.

A deeper consistency may often underlie superficially discordant activities. The case of D (p. 331) we recall as an instance in point. This man, a teacher, seemed one moment meticulous in his behavior, the next, careless and even slovenly. Measures of neatness in this case would certainly not correspond. But by looking further into the case, the illusion of specificity vanishes, for it appears that D is always orderly in respect to his personal possessions, and always disorderly in respect to other people's. The first step in the analysis of congruence, then, establishes the existence of two opposite traits. Pursuing the case still further, even these opposites are reconciled through their relation to a single essential quality of self-centeredness peculiar to D. This root quality "explains" the inconsistency in his expressive traits.

[13] This case is taken from *Studies in Expressive Movement*, pp. 137-141, by permission of The Macmillan Company.

At the same time it explains almost everything else in his nature, serving to reconcile other apparently discordant habits, traits, and attitudes. For such a cardinal trait, Wertheimer has proposed the designation *radix*. The radix may never be sought on the activity level, for it lies at the *root* of activities. And however inconsistent activities may seem to be, they are congruent so long as they spring from the

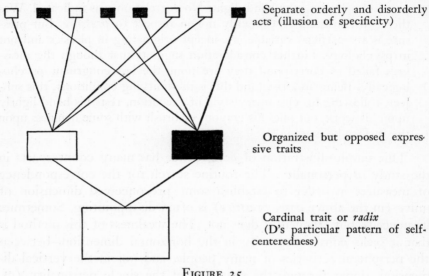

Separate orderly and disorderly acts (illusion of specificity)

Organized but opposed expressive traits

Cardinal trait or *radix* (D's particular pattern of self-centeredness)

FIGURE 25

An Illustration of Congruence

(The unity of personality becomes apparent as more basic dynamic systems are sought.)

same root. The argument as applied to the case of D may be illustrated with the schematic diagram in Figure 25.

The cardinal trait, or *radix*, has been represented in a slightly different way by H. A. Murray under the title of *unity-thema*. According to this conception, too, the dominant tendencies of a life are said to derive from a single central dynamic principle, which if properly understood would explain both the collaborating and the conflicting actions of the person. But according to Murray, the unity-thema often springs from fixations formed early in life, and can be accurately discovered only through psychoanalytic exploration. Here, then, is the principle of congruence with a Freudian rendering.

Yet the conception of congruence must not be carried too far.

To say that whatever occurs in a personal life is *ipso facto* consistent with everything else is going to a pointless extreme. The following statement is an example of such exaggeration:

> The unity of a person can be traced in each instant of his life. There is nothing in character that contradicts itself. If a person who is known to us seems to be incongruous with himself that is only an indication of the inadequacy and superficiality of our previous observations.[14]

The fallacy of this statement is its confusion of mere spacio-temporal unity (locality) with psychological unity.

It is difficult to keep a balanced footing. On the one hand there is no doubt that most experimentalists have under-estimated the consistencies of personality simply because their methods for determining consistency lack penetration. On the other hand, it is easy to *read into* discordant behavior some mythical unity, thereby mistaking an arbitrary interpretation for fact. In the case of the artist discussed above, there is no certain *proof* that his differential expressive behavior (his varying pressures) did in fact spring from one common root (his artistic style of work). To say so seems plausible enough, but in this particular case the congruence claimed has not actually been proved.

But are there any tests of congruence? Can it ever be objectively established? The strict positivist answers negatively. Congruence, he says, is always a matter of the investigator's interpretation; meaningful unity is impossible to demonstrate objectively. He complains because a psychoanalyst, for example, finds that the root of a certain life is an unquenchable, if unconscious, hatred for the father. How does the analyst know? Only because he "feels" that all the information he has obtained through the analysis "clicks" into place with this basic "integrational hypothesis." But might not another investigator feel the same satisfying click when he hits upon an entirely different hypothesis?

And how is it with the case study, the most available of all the methods of representing congruence? Dogmatic interpretation seems to be a danger whatever the variety we employ, whether biography, autobiography, the clinical record, the life-history, psychiatric summary, or the thumb-nail sketch. It is true that in practice the validity

---

[14] R. Franke, "Gang und Character" (ed. by H. Bogen and O. Lipmann), *Beihefte, Zsch. f. ang. Psychol.*, 1931, No. 58, p. 45.

of case studies is seldom checked. The assumption is that, given an accumulation of incident, the one true pattern of unity will emerge by sheer virtue of the "systematic relevance" of one incident to another. Thus the case study is tested only by its internal intelligibility, by its self-consistency. Such a test has been called the "logico-meaningful" criterion of integration.[15] Though unsatisfactory to a positivist, to many investigators it appeals as ultimately the soundest method.

Deferring to Chapter XIX more detailed discussion of this problem, we shall merely suggest here that the picture is not quite so dark as the positivist paints it. A pronouncement regarding the congruence of a life need not be merely an *ipse dixit* of the investigator, for which there is no possibility of proof or disproof. For one thing, there may be *many* investigators making the diagnosis. Should they all come to the same decision regarding congruence, the basic scientific requirement of agreement would be met.

In such a multiple diagnosis, it is, of course, scientifically desirable to have the investigators work in strict independence of one another. But because of the deficiency in the skill of the various investigators, to achieve agreement is hard. Perhaps the majority opinion may be incorrect, and the minority correct. Conceivably, too, only *one* judge may be right in his interpretations. To offset this danger, conferences between the investigators may be arranged, wherein they pool their evidence and try to reach a *synthetic* interpretation. The conference procedure sacrifices the strict check of independent diagnosis, but it gains something from the corrective influence of consultation. The best variety of the method might be one that permits consultation on *evidence* but secures independence of *diagnosis*.[16]

It is a problem for the future to perfect methods for establishing congruence in personality. There is need for criteria to determine whether the pattern that is held to be congruent is really so, or whether it is being "read into" the case. Some progress has been made. Both prediction and matching have a certain usefulness here. So too does the method of multiple diagnosis discussed above. More and

[15] P. A. Sorokin, *Rural Sociol.*, 1936, 1, 121-141, 344-374. The logico-meaningful method he defines as the determination of "the identity (or similarity) of central meaning, idea, or mental bias, that permeates all the logically related fragments" (p. 347).

[16] The method of multiple diagnosis is illustrated very well in the forthcoming experimental study *Explorations in Personality* by H. A. Murray, *et al.* This study attempts to preserve the benefits of consultation between judges along with certain controls making for independence of diagnosis.

more, psychiatrists and psychoanalysts are subjecting their diagnosis to checks. Even the case study will no doubt be improved and criteria evolved to determine its validity. This area of research is, without doubt, one of those most deserving of further exploration and methodological invention.

A GESTALT REPRESENTATION OF UNITY

Any school of psychological thought that aims deliberately to deal with *wholes* is bound to say something about the unity of personality. It is not surprising, therefore, that within recent years Gestalt psychology has made many contributions to this subject. Some of these (especially the contributions of Wertheimer, Koffka, and Köhler) are more appropriately discussed in other contexts, for they bear not so much on the problem of the unity of the total personality as on the unity of its sub-structures, on its patterns of expressive movement, and on the process of *apprehending* personality as an integral whole.

The question for the moment is whether the total personality may be considered *objectively* as a Gestalt: a Gestalt being defined as a "system whose parts are dynamically connected in such a way that a change of one part results in a change of all other parts." [17] To this question Lewin gives an affirmative answer, and justifies his position by a large number of experimental findings. Conceptually he represents his theory of the structure of the personal Gestalt with "topological" diagrams. One of these is reproduced in Figure 26.[18]

The person is regarded as a differentiated region separated by a permeable boundary from his external environment. In direct contact with the environment are certain perceptual-motor systems engaged in sensing and in acting adaptively. One of the most important processes of this region, for example, is speech which plays a principal role in the communication between the person and his social environment. As a rule the perceptual-motor region possesses a relatively high unity; its systems are fluid in that they readily interact, and the region as a whole is often called into play when adaptive acts are demanded.

Inward from this perceptual-motor region lie the peripheral

[17] K. Lewin, *Principles of Topological Psychology*, 1936, p. 218.
[18] Reproduced by permission from *Principles of Topological Psychology* (McGraw-Hill Book Co.), p. 177.

regions of the inner personality. These are more enduring and ordinarily better structured and more clearly segregated from one another than are the motor-perceptual regions. In some respects these peripheral regions seem to correspond to the directive or expressive traits discussed on pp. 323 f. When under tension they are regarded as *systems*, that may act either independently or—more likely

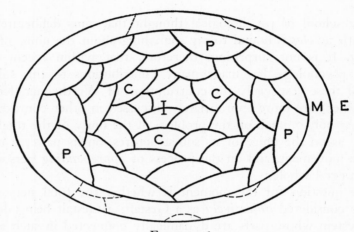

FIGURE 26

Topological Representation of the Structure of Personality

(*M*, motor-perceptual region; *I*, inner-personal region; *P*, peripheral parts of *I*; *C*, central parts of *I*; *E*, environment.)

—as parts of larger systems. It is a conception similar to the account given on p. 326 of the activation of interdependent traits.

Proceeding inward we find more central regions, representing, it seems, the principal driving traits of personality, the deeper motives and interests, and more lasting sentiments and prejudices. These central regions are not unlike the "central" traits described on pp. 337 f. Finally, at the heart of the inner-personal region lies the very most intimate zone of all, elsewhere called by Lewin the "core." It is this intimate center that is aroused in states of acute self-conscious emotion and is always involved in aspiration and in fantasy. It is the region that is most difficult for another to penetrate or to understand. Yet it is a region whose existence is attested not only by introspection but by a number of experimental researches.[19] This core, more than

[19] K. Lewin, *Principles of Topological Psychology*, 1936, p. 180.

any other single factor, guarantees the relative stability of the total structure. Though in some respects unique, Lewin's conception of the core of personality is not unrelated to the older principle of self-consciousness.

The sub-structures of personality here described are not to be regarded as rigid. Their boundaries are relatively permeable, and the whole organization is to some degree fluid, as shown by several facts. For one thing, any intense stimulation is more than likely to affect the state of the whole person, easily dissipating the otherwise effective functional barriers. Further, though the temporal dimension is not represented in topology, it is admitted that with time the regions alter greatly in their contours and scope. With time they tend to become finer and more segregated (the principle of differentiation), and tend likewise to restructure themselves in different patterns. "Young" systems may become stronger than the older systems, and may dynamically be quite independent of them (principle of functional autonomy). In regression, it is clear, there may be a return to older systems and a surrender of the newer.[20]

We have then a picture of personality as a stratified system, having a definite structure with distinguishable separate regions; but at the same time allowing for any degree of fusion and interdependence of the parts, for any amount of change—progressive or regressive—and for all kinds of individual differences. Personality, Lewin says in effect, is indeed a Gestalt, but it is a Gestalt that has *greater* or *less* unity, depending upon its own individual nature, upon the condition of the organism and the field in which it is behaving. Perhaps no other psychologist has succeeded quite so well in depicting at one and the same time so many of the intricate issues involved, and in demonstrating that the unity of personality is always a matter of degree.

An additional virtue of the topological method is its ability to represent the individual case, with all its peculiarities. Indeed it is one of the most insistent demands of topological psychology that the single case be accorded a position of highest respectability in psychological research. Lewin goes so far as to insist that scientific predictions can never successfully be made by a knowledge of general laws alone, derived as they are from abstractive analysis. The topology

[20] *Ibid.,* p. 190.

of the person in all its individual peculiarity must be understood before its true dynamic tendencies can be discerned.[21]

A further extension of the topological method adds a third dimension to the diagram, an "irreality level." By this means Lewin seeks to represent that in fantasy, in delusions, or in play, the structure of personality is somewhat altered. Whether this addition is of any great advantage may be questioned, for in all the regions of the personal life there are many aspects that might be called irreal. Yet the real and the irreal are bound into well-knit integral dispositions or systems. Ultimately it is impossible to know what in any psychological state is real and what irreal. For what, pray tell, *is* reality? Is an ambition real or irreal? and what about an ego-ideal or a guiding image?

The principal advantage generally claimed for the topological treatment of personality has not as yet been mentioned. It brings the person within the domain of the so-called "field theory," which endeavors to treat any psychological phenomenon in relation to its total setting. Roughly stated, the field theory of personality regards the total environmental setting as well as the inner structure of the person as decisive in the shaping of conduct. There is surely no objection to a statement as broad as this. But in practice, the field theory inclines to put too great emphasis upon the momentary determination of conduct without giving due credit to the enduring systems of personality, often quite unaffected by changes in surrounding conditions. One unfortunate consequence of the topological field theory is its rather contemptuous attitude toward any "class theory," that is, toward any theory that accounts for uniformities of behavior in terms of the properties of its contributing structures.[22]

It should be obvious, however, that the regions shown in Figure 26 are themselves "classes." They are the one and only guarantee of stability in personal conduct. Even though there are often alterations within the field, the regions themselves are relatively stable factors in the determination of behavior. Lewin himself admits that "a person's structure is often relatively constant over a long period of

[21] "If all the laws of psychology were known, one could make a prediction about the behavior of a man only if in addition to the laws the special nature of the particular situation were known." *Ibid.*, p. 11.

[22] See for example, J. F. Brown, *Psychology and the Social Order*, 1936, esp. pp. 34-41. This author though condemning class theories out of hand is quite unable to discuss the structure of personality without recourse to them. For example, he subscribes to the theory of the "normal distribution" of traits of personality, which obviously applies only to a "class" of phenomena, and not to a field.

time." [23] But a field theory is unable to take adequate cognizance of this fact. Traits, attitudes, habits, and sentiments are the guarantors of stability. They are class concepts, and it is impossible to write an adequate psychology of personality without their aid.

There is no need here to pursue this issue further. It is mentioned merely to show that topological psychology extends far beyond the narrower problem here under discussion, viz., the unity of personality. In most of its work topological psychology is concerned with the person only as he is behaving in some momentary experimental situation.[24] But for all its brevity, and perhaps incidental character, the topological treatment of the problem of unity is one of the most fruitful to be found in the entire literature of personality.

Of necessity this chapter has been eclectic in tone. A diversity of approaches to the study of consistency and unity has been described. Each was found to have merit, but none can be said to be the only way. The truth of the matter is that the total organization of personality is still a new and poorly formulated problem in psychology. It is a many-sided issue whose solution yet lies in the future.

[23] *Op. cit.*, p. 188.
[24] All of the work reported in Lewin's *Dynamic Theory of Personality*, 1935, is of this order, a fact which renders the title of the book somewhat of a misnomer.

Part IV

THE ANALYSIS OF PERSONALITY

CHAPTER XIV

A SURVEY OF METHODS

It is the mark of an educated man to look for precision in each class of things just so far as the nature of the subject admits.

—Aristotle

Pᴇʀsᴏɴᴀʟɪᴛʏ is so complex a thing that every legitimate method must be employed in its study. Excluded only are those fallacious ways that science has long since learned to avoid: hearsay, prejudiced observation, impressive coincidence, the overweighted single instance, old wives' tales, question-begging inductions and deductions, and the like. Such methods are used by charlatan characterologies (astrology, numerology, palmistry, and cranioscopy) as well as in uncritical everyday discourse. They lead nowhere. But apart from these, there are a great many *legitimate* methods of studying personality, each with a proper place in the armamentarium of the psychologist.

The basic method in psychology is the same as that employed by common sense, viz., *observation* of a datum, coupled with *interpretation* of its significance. The only difference is that psychology ordinarily follows the lead of the older sciences and makes use of ingenious and controlled techniques for securing observations normally not available to the layman; and in interpretation psychology is hedged in with various rules of evidence and logic which do not bind the layman or artist.

Figure 27 offers a graphic tabulation of the major methods employed in psychological investigations of personality. At the center lie the indispensable operations of observation and interpretation shared by science and common sense. One segment only is devoted to the method of common sense wherein observation and interpretation occur without the intervention of the special techniques customarily used by the psychologist. When not acting in his professional capacity the psychologist joins everybody else in understanding personality in the common sense way. Even in his professional capacity he does well to bring this simple "intuitive" type of understanding into the laboratory to supplement his "scientific" (inferential) understanding.[1]

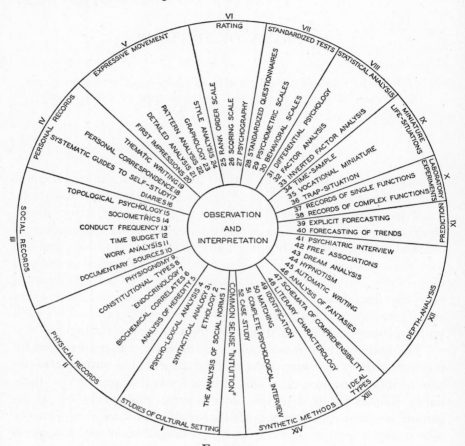

FIGURE 27

A Survey of Methods for Studying Personality

Excepting for the common sense segment, the diagram is taken up with specialized methods, technical aids variously employed. A number of these methods have been described in earlier chapters, but there is something to gain by reviewing them once more, this time in relation to one another. By so doing the reader can see how far, to date, empirical methodology has progressed.

[1] The relation between the inferential and the intuitive understanding of personality is too complex a subject to be discussed here; it is treated fully in Chapter XIX.

The circular arrangement is a convenient way of representing a rough continuum of methods ranging from those that are, generally speaking, external to the person to those that are internal, and at the same time differentiating those that deal with partial records of behavior from those concerned with the homogeneity and congruence of the personality as a whole. No strict logic of progression is implied, but it seems convenient to list the methods under fourteen main rubrics, proceeding roughly in the order just described:

1. Studies of Cultural Setting
2. Physical Records
3. Social Records
4. Personal Records
5. Expressive Movement
6. Ratings
7. Standardized Tests
8. Statistical Analysis
9. Miniature Life-situations
10. Laboratory Experiments
11. Prediction
12. Depth-analysis
13. Ideal Types
14. Synthetic Methods

Seldom is one method employed alone. Experimentation may be supplemented by statistics; studies of expression may borrow techniques and concepts from depth-analysis. The divisions are to a high degree arbitrary, but they will serve for the purpose of a rapid panoramic survey. To illustrate the 52 methods listed, excepting where they are clearly self-explanatory, one application, and usually only one, will be cited.

I. STUDIES OF CULTURAL SETTING

Under this head fall certain methods dealing not with personality directly, but with the social framework within which personality develops. The argument in their favor is obvious. Since personality is largely a matter of the introception and modification of social conventions, customs and codes, it is instructive to know to what cultural stimuli and models the individual is exposed in the course of his development. Knowledge of this social frame is essential to a full appreciation of his personality. Much of his nature will be found to be essentially a reflection of prevailing standards; but even his departures from these standards presume knowledge regarding them on the part of the investigator. For this reason it is always well to specify the racial, religious, and occupational groups to which a person belongs, as well as all other significant affiliations and memberships.

Yet a mere report on cultural setting and membership is never sufficient in itself; for no individual mirrors exactly and exclusively his social environment. Even within a narrow and homogenous cultural circle individuality is amazingly varied in form. Personality is more than "the subjective side of culture,"—a truth that sociologists and cultural anthropologists with their one-sided studies of "culture and personality" are likely to forget.

What culture does is to offer models both for common adaptive acts and for styles of expressive behavior. These models the individual may or may not adopt. In so far as he adopts them he fits the "cultural type"; in so far as he does not, his personality is sharply etched against the contrasting cultural ground.[2] No personality is an exact replica of prevailing cultural norms, but to understand the deviating as well as the relatively typical cases, knowledge of these norms is indispensable.[3]

A Southern white man who fraternizes with Negroes is, for example, a more striking personality than is the Northern white man who does the same thing. A rich banker's son who joins the Communist Party presents a different psychological problem from the son of a revolutionary leader who does the same.

There are innumerable special techniques developed in anthropology and sociology for the study of the cultural ground of per-

[2] An excellent study of the "typical" racial personality is that of K. Lewin, mentioned previously on p. 162 ftn. This author points out that the typical German is somewhat defensive toward, and therefore less open to, his social environment; whereas the typical American is on better terms with his environment, less confined within his ivory tower, with the result that the successive layers of his personality are more permeable. It is rare, for example, for a German official to leave his office door open, to permit newspapers to publish intimate details concerning his life, or to congratulate a victorious opponent in an electoral contest; whereas all these acts are common in the typical behavior within the American area of culture.

[3] Such knowledge has the same significance for the psychologist as knowledge of the prevailing style of penmanship has for the graphologist. Unless the graphologist knows in what country and according to what standards of "school copy" a person has learned to write, he cannot evaluate the individuality of a script.

sonality. Countless analyses have been made of primitive cultures, of civilized communities, neighborhoods, customs, professional codes, and the standards maintained by castes, creeds, and classes. Roughly grouped they may be said to constitute one propaedeutic technique for studying personality:

The Analysis of Social Norms   (1)

Since the procedures employed are not primarily psychological in nature, more detailed consideration of this method need not here be given.[4]

There is one special province of culture that bears a peculiarly close and many-sided relation to personality, viz., *language*. Language is a codification of common human experience, and by analyzing it much may be found that reflects the nature of human personality. One technique of analysis was described in Chapter III, *viz.,*

Ethology   (2)

Through the systematic study of proverbs, aphorisms, and literature, John Stuart Mill and his successors hoped to collect the data necessary to a science of character. Typical forms of character immortalized in language were to be classified, and, if possible, explained. Though Mill's proposal turned out to be sterile, yet in a certain sense psychologists as well as laymen make abundant use of proverbial wisdom. Since, in time, Mill's method may be improved and revived it deserves to be listed here.

Another linguistic method is that of

Syntactical Analogy   (3)

illustrated in the work of E. E. Southard.[5] This writer, a psychiatrist, has pointed to the resemblance between the four grammatical moods (the imperative, indicative, subjunctive, and optative) and the traditional temperaments (the choleric, the phlegmatic, the melancholic, and sanguine, respectively). He proposes further to use such grammatical rubrics as tense, voice, mood, person, and number in the depiction of personality. Southard believes that there is, of necessity,

[4] A significant theoretical treatment of the way in which social standards come to influence the mental outlook of the individual is given by M. Sherif, *The Psychology of Social Norms*, 1936. As concrete illustrations of the "impact" of culture upon personality, P. Freuchen's *Eskimo*, or C. R. Shaw's *The Jack-Roller* will serve.

[5] E. E. Southard, *Phil. Rev.*, 1916, 25, 424-455; *J. Abnorm. Psychol.*, 1916, 11, 189-202.

a close correspondence between the possible forms of linguistic structure and the basic characteristics of human mental life represented in the typical structures of personality.

Not only the grammar, but also the lexicon of a language show that personality is reflected in the evolution of language. One study (described on pp. 303-311) reveals that about four and a half per cent of the total English lexicon (or about 18,000 words) is concerned with characterizations of personal behavior and personality. This approach may be designated as

$$\text{Psycho-lexical Analysis} \qquad (4)$$

One of its merits is the aid it gives the investigator in preparing check-lists of descriptive adjectives, rating scales, and psychographs for deeper explorations. It leads also to special studies of synonyms, antonyms, trait-clusters, and may thus eventually yield a basic vocabulary for the study of common traits.

II. PHYSICAL RECORDS

In contrast to these methods of cultural analysis the study of physical and physiological features involves the investigation of a *single* life.

There are many techniques, for example, for the

$$\text{Analysis of Heredity} \qquad (5)$$

Record charts are used, obtainable from eugenic associations. Family resemblances are studied with the aid of these charts or by psychological tests. Foster children are compared with other children in order to determine whether common environment is as important as common heredity. The reverse technique is often used to determine whether identical twins reared apart are seriously affected by their contrasting environments.[6]

Another special field, and a large one, is the study of

$$\text{Biochemical Correlates} \qquad (6)$$

This approach appeals to physiologists and others whose interests lead them to attack the problems of personality from the bodily side.[7]

[6] Cf. Chapter IV, pp. 148 f.

[7] A good illustration is C. W. Darrow and L. L. Heath, "Reaction Tendencies Relating to Personality," in *Studies in the Dynamics of Behavior* (ed., K. S. Lashley), 1932.

There are studies that employ the psychogalvanic skin reflex, circulatory changes, blood composition, and "brain waves" (the Berger rhythm). There are others that attempt to correlate the amount of hydrogen-ion concentration in saliva with various traits of personality. Still others are concerned with the effects of the glands of internal secretion, and constitute a group of techniques that should be listed separately:

Endocrinology [8]   (7)

These various biochemical methods are often segmental, even atomistic, in their outlook, as when they seek specific correlations between blood pressure and humor, or hyperthyroidism and extroversion. But often they merge with the more totalitarian outlook as represented, for example, in studies of

Constitutional Type   (8)

This procedure, described in Chapter III, seeks to relate the total physical habitus of the individual with the broader functions of personality (as in the contention that a slender, asthenic physique is likely to be associated with an idealistic, dreamy outlook on life).
A related method is

Physiognomy   (9)

Under this heading falls a wide range of psychodiagnostic techniques, ranging from the study of psychic correlates of specific facial features to the reading of character by movement (often called pathognomy).[9]

III. SOCIAL RECORDS

No less important than physical records are social records. First among these are the available institutional records, or

Documentary Sources   (10)

such as are kept by social agencies, hospitals, parole officers, schools, or employers. From these documents valuable information may be obtained, though the records are often prepared merely for practical purposes without the intention of giving a well-rounded picture of the personality as a whole.

[8] Cf. Chapter IV, p. 120.
[9] Cf. Chapter III, pp. 65-78.

The investigator need not content himself with using such pre-existing records, but may himself make records according to his special interest. One example is the

Work Analysis (11)

If systematically studied, a person's behavior at work reveals many of his personal traits, *e.g.*, his characteristic types of error, his proneness to accidents, his punctuality, orderliness, initiative and dispatch.[10]

A method requiring the co-operation of the subject is the

Time Budget (12)

wherein a record is made of the time he devotes to his various daily pursuits.[11] Kept over a period of several months such time budgets are certain to betray significant interests as well as personal peculiarities of conduct (haste, procrastination, distractibility, and the like).

Instead of recording all types of daily activity, the method may be varied to give records of only one specific type of conduct. This technique has been used to study the frequency of laughter, or anger, or the susceptibility to moodiness, to suggestion, or to fear.[12] It may be designated as the analysis of

Conduct Frequency (13)

Another type of social record is represented by plotting in a topographical fashion the individual's *sphere* of conduct. An example is Muchow's study of the life-space of city children wherein their horizons, interests, personal contacts, and ambitions stand revealed.[13] To label this method we may borrow Moreno's term, employed for his own interesting "psychological geography" of circles of friendships and acquaintanceships.[14] Such studies he labels

Sociometrics (14)

Similar in some respects, though extending much further in its theoretical significance, is the method employed by Lewin in mapping many varieties of psychological relationships. He calls it

[10] Cf. B. Katzenstein, "Die eignungspsychologische Erfassung des Arbeitscharakters," *Zsch. f. ang. Psychol.*, 1932, 41, 69-137.

[11] Cf. J. D. Rankin, "The Use of Time in Farm Homes," *Univ. of Nebraska Agri. Exper. Stat. Bull.* No. 230, 1928.

[12] Cf. G. S. Hall, *Amer. J. Psychol.*, 1897, 8, 147-249.

[13] Cf. M. Muchow, *Der Lebensraum des Grosstadtkindes*, 1935.

[14] J. L. Moreno, "Who Shall Survive?" *Nerv. & Ment. Dis. Monog.*, 1934, No. 58.

Topological Psychology [15]   (15)

With its aid not only the social contacts of the individual are represented but likewise his personal attitudes toward his memberships
and toward the obstacles (resistances) he encounters in his environment.

IV. PERSONAL RECORDS

More intimate than social records are those documents prepared
by oneself for the express purpose of giving vent to one's feelings
and private thoughts. Special significance must be attached to

Diaries   (16)

These range in scope from semi-impersonal notebooks to intimate
self-revealing autobiographies, often of great value as psychological
data.[16] Although occasional documents have been analytically treated
by psychologists there has as yet been little attempt to systematize
such collections for comparative study.

More formal than diaries are the

Systematic Guides to Self-study [17]   (17)

These may range from informal casually arranged questions to be
answered by the subject in any way he chooses, to the standardized
pencil and paper test. In the latter case, the technique is so specialized
that it deserves separate listing (Section VII).

A neglected method is the analysis of

Personal Correspondence   (18)

Often series of letters to friends or relatives extending over many
years are available for study. Such collections have often been published, but chiefly for their belletristic value.[18] Psychologists have as
yet made little systematic use of such material.

A method used especially with school children is the *Aufsatz-
method* which in English may be called

[15] Cf. K. Lewin, *Principles of Topological Psychology*, 1936. The aspect of
topological psychology here described deals with "locomotion in life-space" and not
with the *structure* of personality which was discussed in the preceding chapter.

[16] Cf. W. Stern, *Anfänge der Reifezeit*, 1925.

[17] Cf. p. 236 ftn.

[18] For example, *The Letters of William James*, edited by H. James, two vols.,
1920.

Thematic Writing (19)

When a child is asked to write a school composition on such a topic as "What Hero I Should Like to Resemble," or "My Personal Ambitions," often a surprising amount of information comes forth. Some children favor religious or philanthropic heroes, others athletic or domestic heroes. One adolescent girl chooses a movie queen as her ideal, another her mother, a third Jane Addams. In employing this method, however, it is necessary to determine whether the writer is giving mere lip-service to conventional teaching or is revealing spontaneously his own guiding-image. The method may be used likewise with adults who in writing, for example, on their dislikes or "pet aversions" may betray a number of personal traits, among them fastidiousness, prurience, paranoia, irascibility, or humor.

V. EXPRESSIVE MOVEMENT

Too many forms of expressive movement are accessible for study to permit separate listing here.[19] In approaching this rich field five main procedures may be employed. The method of

First Impressions (20)

is discussed in detail on pp. 500-507. The advantage of employing "snapshot" impressions is that the relative weights of different expressive cues may thereby be determined. More thorough is the method of

Detailed Analysis (21)

which, usually with the aid of ultra-rapid motion pictures or other recording apparatus, studies the separate features of expression (*e.g.*, the face, gesture, or voice).[20]

Pattern Analysis (22)

covers more complex fields of expression, seeking to relate total sequences of movement to the structures and sub-structures of personality as a whole.[21]

In these investigations of expressive movement there are two quite

[19] A long list will be found in G. W. Allport and P. E. Vernon, *Studies in Expressive Movement*, 1933, especially pp. 24-35.
[20] Cf. W. A. Hunt and C. Landis, *J. Exper. Psychol.*, 1936, 19, 309-315.
[21] Cf. G. W. Allport and H. Cantril, "Judging Personality from Voice," *J. Soc Psychol.*, 1934, 5, 37-55.

different goals in view. The one is simply the study of activity in and for itself; the other is psychodiagnostic, directed to the discovery of the symptomatic value of expression for the "inner" qualities of personality. Both are legitimate goals, but progress toward the latter depends to a large extent upon the stage of advancement of the former (cf. Chapter XVII).

Graphology (23)

is a special method of psychodiagnosis, much more complex than it appears at first sight. Its commercial use is probably premature but it is an important field for research (cf. pp. 488 f.).

Style Analysis (24)

refers to the study of all types of *creative* activity of a person. Among the accessible products of creative effort are prose and poetic writings, musical composition, dress, ornamentation, room furnishings, drawing, scientific productions, recreation, public speaking, entertaining, and the like. (Very often a person's nickname is derived from his style of expression—"the duchess," "the brigadier general," "toughy," "the man on the flying trapeze," etc.) Literary critics have long been engaged in style analysis and its relation to the personality of the creator, but psychologists have lagged in this field of study.[22]

VI. RATING

The method of rating is used whenever one individual makes a quantitative estimate of the qualities of another. Although there are myriad refinements of rating scales it seems possible in principle to order them in two divisions.[23]

The Rank Order Scale (25)

compares two or more individuals in a relative manner. One person is judged as superior or inferior to another in respect to some single common quality. No statement is made about the absolute magnitude or intensity of the variable in question, neither for the individual

[22] One instance of successful research in this field is a study of "Written Composition and Characteristics of Personality," by F. H. Allport, L. Walker, and E. Lathers, *Arch. of Psychol.*, 1934, No. 173. This investigation will be described in Chapter XVII.

[23] For a more detailed discussion see pp. 436-447.

nor for the group with which he is compared. Relative position is all that counts.

The Scoring Scale (26)

uses definite intervals of judgment. The individual is scored at such or such a percentile, decile, quartile, or on a scale having three, five, seven, or more degrees as the case may be. Sometimes, as in the graphic rating scale, infinite degrees are possible, but in practice these are reduced to absolute units.

When ratings on several qualities for a single individual are available, they may be plotted on a profile, or

Psychograph (27)

The psychograph, to be sure, may be used to plot scores obtained by tests or any other quantitative method as well as by ratings. The construction of one psychograph will be described in detail in the following chapter.

VII. STANDARDIZED TESTS

Inspired by the successful use of intelligence tests many standardized scales for testing personality have appeared within the past fifteen years.[24] They are mostly of the order of

Standardized Questionnaires (28)

or "pencil and paper tests," wherein the subject selects a reply from various alternatives offered in the scale, thereby reporting the type of behavior or thought most characteristic of himself among these alternatives. Each alternative chosen is scored according to its empirically determined diagnostic significance. Usually such tests are designed to measure one and only one variable, though some yield scores on several. Sometimes they are called tests of *attitudes*, sometimes *interests*, or *opinions*, or *traits*. There is a growing tendency to use the ambiguous designation of *inventory*, leaving it to anyone who can to decide what it is the test tests!

These scales of necessity are limited to the measurement of common traits, and as has been repeatedly pointed out in this volume, the measurements obtained must be viewed as merely *approximate*,

[24] A convenient bibliography of tests is found in P. M. Symonds, *Psychological Diagnosis and Social Adjustment*, 1934.

since the significance of every trait is different in every life. Another serious limitation is the fact that virtually all pencil and paper questionnaires may be falsified by the subject if he chooses to do so, or if he is deficient in intelligence or insight. They have value therefore only when a competent subject is sufficiently motivated to give his replies honestly and carefully.

Personality may also be studied incidentally while using intelligence tests, or

Psychometric Scales (29)

The *way* in which a subject attacks a puzzle test, a maze test, or an ordinary verbal test varies according to temperament and other non-intellectual qualities. One individual is hypercautious, another is easily discouraged; a third may be impulsive and headstrong.

Following the tradition of psychometrics there has been evolved a varied group of

Behavioral Scales (30)

These include the word-association test which yields a score for the commonality or the idiosyncrasy of associational process; likewise various tests of imagery that reveal the fanciful, prosaic, fluent or inhibited characteristics of the subject's imaginal life.[25] Here too may be placed such standardized tests of movement as the Downey Will-Temperament test, or the Fernald test for strength of volitional decision.[26] This is a highly miscellaneous group, but common to all is the use of some relatively simple response on the part of the subject for the purpose of scoring the strength of one or more common traits. The weakness of these tests is that they pretend on the basis of the subject's performance in one *specific* situation to measure a *generalized* trait. Surely a person's interpretation of ink-blots, significant though it may be, is insufficient evidence for a judgment concerning his extroversion, his creativity, or his estheticism *in general*. In this respect the standardized questionnaire is superior, for its final diagnosis depends upon the individual's report of his behavior in *many* different types of life-situations.

[25] One of the most popular tests today is the Rorschach Ink-blot test. Vague and cloudy smears are interpreted in individual and often revealing ways by the subject when he is asked, "What might this be?" Cf. S. J. Beck, "Introduction to the Rorschach Method: A Manual of Personality Study," *Monog. Amer. Orthopsychiat. Assoc.*, 1937, No. 1.

[26] J. E. Downey, *The Will-Temperament and Its Testing*, 1924; G. G. Fernald, *Amer. J. Insanity*, 1912, 68, 523-549.

VIII. STATISTICAL ANALYSIS

Statistical analysis is only an *auxiliary* technique in the investigation of personality, for statistics can be applied only after data have been assembled by *other* methods. The value of statistical analysis in sorting, comparing, and determining the reliability of accumulated data is unquestionable; but so too is its power for mischief when the psychological aim and significance of the investigation become obscured in the sheer exuberance of digits.

Common statistical tools (*e.g.*, measures of central tendency, of dispersion, and simple correlation) are the backbone of

Differential Psychology (31)

This method, described in Chapter I, requires always a sizeable population of subjects whose performances (generally on some single function) are compared. The historical dominance of this procedure in psychology has led many psychologists to the false conclusion that the psychology of individual differences and the psychology of personality are one and the same thing. The reader now knows that the former method can only relate qualities in one person with the same qualities in other people; whereas the latter attempts to go further and relate certain selected qualities to all other qualities within the *same* person.

A modern and much respected representative of differential psychology is

Factor Analysis (32)

This method, discussed briefly in Chapter IX, attempts to discover non-correlating factors to account for the complex overlapping of scores or ratings usually obtained from any battery of measurements when it is applied to one and the same population of subjects. The British school of factor analysis, for example, has concluded that there is a factor w (strength of will) displayed by all people in greater or less degree, another factor p (perseverative tendency), and a third o (oscillation, variability). The conception of factors as contrasted with the doctrine of traits has already been discussed sufficiently (pp. 244 f., 300 f.), and the utility of factor analysis in formulating scalable (common) traits given due acknowledgment. Various criticisms of the method need not be repeated here, though it is well to stress again its excessive empiricism which often encourages the employment of "any old test" without prior regard for its significance and relevance.

In order to escape the failing shared by factor analysis and differential psychology—this exclusive interest in what is *common* to all men—an ingenious attempt has been made by Stephenson and others to establish an

Inverted Factor Analysis (33)

This method does not deal with one factorial variable at a time in a population of persons, but treats one person at a time for a population of variables.[27] Thus far, however, the method has yielded only a type-psychology (cf. p. 247). If it could be extended to show what clusters of variables within the *single* person exist, it would help solve the riddle of the *individual* hierarchical arrangement of traits. If a cardinal trait exists, it would emerge; also central and minor traits would appear, but there should be no assumption that all people must inevitably be compared in respect to the *same* clusters of traits. This accomplishment is a task for the future (cf. p. 247 ftn.).

IX. MINIATURE LIFE-SITUATIONS

To study natural behavior under controlled conditions is one of the important methods of investigating personality. A procedure especially favored in the study of children is the

Time-Sample (34)

To discover the habitual and consistent character of a child's behavior it is necessary to observe his activity for an extended period. But since the practical and intellectual confusion of *continuous* observation reduces its value, the time-sample may be used. A child is observed for a few seconds every five minutes, or perhaps he is observed for five minutes at certain stated intervals throughout the day. Whether he is idle or active, leading or following, laughing or crying, playing with materials or with children, can easily be determined. In the long run a convincing picture of the consistency of his behavior is obtained. But since very little can be observed at one time, and since the record is discontinuous, no *causes* of his behavior

[27] W. Stephenson, "Some Recent Contributions to the Theory of Psychometry," *Char. & Pers.*, 1936, 4, 294-304.

emerge clearly, nor any information concerning the *inter-relationship* of traits. But for restricted purposes the method has proved valuable.[28]

For many years psychotechnics has employed the method of the

Vocational Miniature (35)

The would-be watch repairman is tested for finger control, eye-hand co-ordination, and the like, not by sacrificing a watch to his manipulations, but by using apparatus that reveals in a parallel way the magnitude of his skills. The would-be aviator is first given tests for his sense of equilibrium, for visual acuity, and co-ordination before he is trained in an airplane. Not only may intellectual and motor competence be judged in this way, but in the process the subject may betray characteristics of his personality—for example, his irritability, distractability, orderliness, aggression, or suggestibility.[29]

A technique related to the miniature is the

Trap-Situation (36)

illustrated by the procedures employed by the Character Education Inquiry (cf. pp. 250-255). A child is given an opportunity to cheat, and unknown to himself makes a lasting record of his dishonesty; or occasions are presented leading him to disclose, unknown to himself, his dispositions toward helpfulness, perseverance, or untruthfulness.

X. LABORATORY EXPERIMENTS

Somewhat more artificial, but correspondingly better controlled, are the laboratory methods. They follow Galton's advice to "extemporize the emergencies of life" entirely under the supervision of the investigator. Many of the methods previously described may on occasion be brought into the laboratory, but there are still others that are exclusively products of experimental science. Some of them are devised to secure merely

Records of Single Functions (37)

[28] Cf. pp. 315 f.
[29] The vocational miniature is described by M. S. Viteles, *Industrial Psychology*, 1932, chap. xii; and by H. L. Hollingworth, *Vocational Psychology and Character Analysis*, 1929, chap. xvi.

One and only one type of behavior is studied; a single aspect of the personality stands revealed. For example, the characteristic imagery of the individual is determined; or his speed of judgment; or his tendency after a failure to blame the task, himself, the experimenter; or his characteristic "level of aspiration." [30]

Records of Complex Functions   (38)

are obtained when there is, for example, a hidden dictaphone, a motion picture camera, or a stenographer to record all of a subject's speech and behavior. From a subsequent analysis of these records a complex and patterned portrayal of the personality is possible. Needless to say no personality can be brought completely within the laboratory situation. Experiments vary between the two poles of narrow segmentalization and complex recording of several co-existing variables. Ordinarily the more behavioristic studies are the more segmental, while those involving lengthy introspections or verbal report are richer and more complete, though often more difficult to interpret.

XI. PREDICTION

It is part of the scientific ambition of the psychologist to be able to predict behavior. By attempting, at various stages of his investigation so to do, he is able to check the progress he has made in understanding the course of cause and effect, and the major traits of his subjects. In the preceding chapter two principal types of prediction were distinguished.

Explicit Forecasting   (39)

is illustrated by the experiments of Bender (pp. 353 f.) wherein an attempt was made to predict the exact responses of certain subjects to specific items in a measurement scale. Such explicit forecasting is at a serious disadvantage, for specific acts are far more difficult to predict than is the general trend of behavior. Where too great explicitness is demanded, prophecy fails. Biographies cannot be written in advance, at least not in detail.

Forecasting of Trends   (40)

[30] Cf. J. D. Frank, "Individual Differences in Certain Aspects of the Level of Aspiration," *Amer. J. Psychol.*, 1935, 47, 119-128.

is far easier, though more difficult to validate (because of verbal ambiguities and subjectivity of interpretation of the "meaning" of conduct). The prognosis given in the case of a paroled prisoner is a good example of this method. His conduct following release from prison is not prophesied in detail, but rather its probable social or anti-social *trend*. Another instance was given in Chapter IV, where the behavior of an infant of four months was used as a basis for forecasting his later *traits* (pp. 124-128). The psychologist hopes through the continuous modification of the weights assigned to one or another symptom to improve in time the accuracy of such prognosis.

XII. DEPTH-ANALYSIS

Methodology has been greatly enriched in recent years through the development of psychoanalysis with its intensive explorations of "the unconscious." There is, first of all, the

Psychiatric Interview (41)

which discovers through questioning and listening as much as possible concerning hidden motives and obscure sequences of behavior. Often this informal method is supplemented by auxiliary techniques, such as

Free Association (42)

Dream Analysis (43)

Hypnotism (44)

Automatic Writing (45)

To these familiar methods may be added a whole group of ingenious techniques for the

Analysis of Fantasies (46)

By all depth-psychologists fantasies are considered of primary importance in the investigation of personality. H. A. Murray gives a long list of techniques for their investigation.[31] Abbreviated, they are as follows: (a) questioning the subject about his day dreams; (b) questioning him about his favorite themes in plays, novels, literature; (c) word association tests; (d) free association; (e) induced visions (trance states); (f) similes test; (instruction to subject: "This

[31] *J. of Psychol.*, 1936, 3, 115-143.

is a test of verbal imagination. I am going to give you a number of adjectives, one at a time. Please respond to each adjective by giving as many apt or striking similes as you think of. They must be original with you"). The subject gives in a three-minute period as many similes as he can to complete the phrase "as unhappy as—," "as malicious as—," and the like. Additional methods include, (g) musical reverie test (associations aroused while listening to music); (h) picture completion test; (i) odor imagination test; (j) inkblot tests; (k) story elaboration test; (l) literary composition test (cf. *Aufsatz-method*). There is likewise (m) a word projection test, based on the use of B. F. Skinner's "verbal summator," a device that reproduces at low intensities various combinations of elementary vowel sounds to which the subject is invited to respond by telling what words he hears (in reality there are no "words").[32] The (n) thematic apperception test requires the subject to interpret a picture that depicts a person of the same sex and of about the same age as the subject in some dramatic situation.[33] Under such conditions the subject more likely than not reveals his own personality by identifying himself with the character in the picture. Similar is (o) the dramatic production test, for studying creative fantasies. A version of this latter method for juveniles is the "play technique" wherein the child is given toys, plasticine, or puppets, and his creative play is watched, and often found to disclose hidden conflicts or desires.

XIII. IDEAL TYPES

As pointed out on pp. 227-231, many investigators prefer to work in terms of ideal or pure types. These types, they find, serve them as

Schemata of Comprehensibility   (47)

The method they defend as an aid to understanding, for, they say, though no single individual fits perfectly the types drawn, still the purity and simplicity of these schemata accentuate the common forms of development which all personalities to some degree approximate.[34]

---

[32] *J. of Psychol.*, 1936, 2, 71-107.

[33] C. D. Morgan and H. A. Murray, *Arch. Neurol. & Psychiat.*, 1935, 34, 289-306.

[34] Cf. H. Klüver, *Psychol. Rev.*, 1924, 31, 446-462; *J. Phil.*, 1925, 22, 225-233; *J. Phil.*, 1926, 23, 29-36.

Not dissimilar is the tradition of

Literary Characterology (48)

described in Chapter III. Theophrastus, it will be recalled, used the method of simplification in order to represent certain universal forms of human conduct. To a lesser degree all literature depicts unified (and simplified) forms of personality with which concrete cases may be compared. In a certain sense ideal types may serve as paradigms in the scientific study of personality, though when used alone without empirical correction, they are scarcely to be considered as a method of science.

XIV. SYNTHETIC METHODS

Some writers express doubts concerning the ability of science to study the undivided personality. The whole, they say, is just *there*. Let the poet or the sentimentalist contemplate its untarnished perfection! To be treated scientifically it must be analyzed into parts. But, as the last chapter showed, the case is thus not quite fairly stated. Personality is never, strictly speaking, a perfect "whole"; it is always a matter of intricate and variable organization. As such it is quite as much the concern of psychologists as of poets.

Up to the present time segmental methods have been preferred to synthetic methods simply because elementary variables are more convenient to treat than complex ones. And yet, many of the methods described in this chapter (especially prediction and the techniques employed by psychoanalysis and psychiatry) are well adapted to the study of intricate levels of organization. To these must be added the various methods of dealing with the "unity" of personality described in the preceding chapter, and included at various points in the present survey. In addition there is

Identification (49)

a method employed whenever a series of complex records of personality (prose compositions, films, artistic creations, and the like) are studied by a judge with the purpose of identifying their authors.[35] The whole process of perception, judgment, recognition, takes place at an intricate level of organization; it is therefore a synthetic

---

[35] Cf. G. W. Allport and P. E. Vernon, *Studies in Expressive Movement*, 1933, pp. 226 ff.

method. The common experience of "spotting" the author of a literary passage or musical composition on the basis of previous knowledge of his creative style is an everyday instance of the method which undergoes refinements when brought into the laboratory. A variation is represented in the "guess who" technique, whereby fictitious sketches are used, and the judge is asked to "identify" the people to whom they apply.[36] In this way ideal portraits (e.g., of a leader, bully, coward, or popular wag) may serve to discover in a given group of individuals those who possess these particular prominent traits. The "guess who" technique is particularly applicable to studies of school children.

An extension of this approach, described on pp. 354 f., is the method of

Matching   (50)

Unlike the method of identification this method does not presume personal acquaintance of the judge with the subject. It is widely used in determining the perceptible similarity between various sets of data derived from a single subject within a group of subjects.[37]

The two foregoing methods permit quantitative treatment of qualitative data. The two following methods are wholly qualitative, and in Figure 27 fall closest to the initial common sense segment. Like common sense they are deliberately synthetic, although unlike it they attempt to select critically and systematize their data. The

Complete Psychological Interview   (51)

is designed to gather all possible information from the subject himself. It is thus a comprehensive method, though not easy to control. It is particularly valuable as a supplement and check to more objective techniques, since erroneous interpretation can often be forestalled if the psychologist obtains from the subject his *own* statements concerning his behavior. In Chapter XVIII methods for conducting a psychological interview are discussed, together with suggestions for its improvement and standardization.

There follows finally the preparation of the life-history or

Case Study   (52)

[36] Cf. H. Hartshorne, M. A. May, *Studies in the Nature of Character*, Vol. III, 1930, pp. 221-223.
[37] Cf. P. E. Vernon, *Psychol. Bull.*, 1936, 33, 149-177.

This method is logically the last in our series, for it is the most comprehensive of all, and lies closest to the initial starting point of common sense. It provides a framework within which the psychologist can place all his observations gathered by other methods; it is his final affirmation of the individuality and uniqueness of every personality. It is a completely synthetic method, the only one that is spacious enough to embrace all assembled facts. Unskillfully used, it becomes a meaningless chronology, or a confusion of fact and fiction, of guess-work and misinterpretation. Properly used it is the most revealing method of all.

The case study has not ordinarily been recognized as a psychological method, for, to date, psychology has had little interest in the complete person. It has been developed chiefly at the hands of clinicians and sociologists who find it valuable for the light it sheds upon maladjustments or upon the social influences surrounding the individual. Because psychologists have neglected the method it has fallen into the hands of specialists interested only in certain limited aspects of personality.[38]

The content of any case study is naturally restricted by the ulterior purpose of the writer. The social worker's case study is over-balanced by an unduly large number of facts pertaining to family budgets and to health; a probation officer is interested chiefly in the probationer's whereabouts and his misconduct; the employment manager stresses ability; the clinical psychologist tells more about illness than about health; and writers of journalistic case studies for the Sunday papers or popular magazines produce all manner of meretricious distortions. Taken in its purest form, as a medium of understanding (not of cure, reform, exploitation, statistical research, or entertainment) the case study is a method that falls primarily within the psychology of personality.

SUGGESTIONS FOR THE PREPARATION OF A CASE STUDY

The survey of methods in this chapter has of necessity been rapid and brief. To dwell for the remaining pages upon the case study is not meant as a disparagement of other methods. It is only because so little progress has been made in respect to this one most comprehensive technique that special attention is here given to it. Many of

[38] An instance of over-accentuation of the cultural and psychoanalytic significance of the case study is J. Dollard's *Criteria for the Life-History*, 1935.

the suggestions advanced in the following pages for preparing a case study are nothing more than practical applications of various abstract principles stressed throughout this volume.

Since individuality is never twice repeated, the form of the psychological case study must vary. It is impossible to prescribe in detail the information that it shall include or the exact manner in which it shall be presented. What is significant in one life may be insignificant in another; hence a form adapted to one case is ill-suited to another. There is only one inviolable rule, and that is *fidelity* to the life that is treated, including, of course, accuracy in all detail. There are a few additional rules, which if interpreted liberally, are serviceable guides.

Deal only with a personality that is known. It is essential that a case study be based upon long acquaintance or else upon unusually complete and dependable information from a battery of auxiliary methods including the psychological interview. It is important that there be no serious gaps in the writer's knowledge, no long periods of time for which information is lacking, nor important aspects of the subject's life (such as his sexual or religious attitudes) that are totally hidden. The events of childhood are likely to be most obscure, and require special care in reconstruction. Firsthand information is preferable; that lacking, the investigator must be critical of his sources. Ideally, two or more investigators should write independent studies of the same case, thus checking the facts recorded as well as the interpretations drawn.

Except in unusual cases a similarity in cultural and racial affiliations of the writer and his subject is desirable. Likewise, the less discrepancy in age the better. It is particularly difficult for a youthful writer to evaluate the experiences and attitudes of one older than himself, and few writers are able to portray accurately and convincingly a personality of the opposite sex. Ordinarily the closer one's mental life swings with that of another, the better is his understanding. In instances where the writer has unusual gifts of "artistic imagination" (that is to say, an ability to view another mental life as a unity apart), the requirement of similarity may be waived.

Write objectively and with directness. The less the intrusion of the personality of the writer into the case study, the better. Emotional bias is easy to detect and casts suspicion on the entire study. It is useless, for example, for a young man to attempt an objective study of his fiancée.

Smartness and eccentricity of expression are harmful; even high coloring and artistic accentuation should be avoided unless the nature of the case demands it. Apt phraseology, however, is an advantage; dullness and repetition a disadvantage.

Although length is a wholly secondary consideration, experience shows that the most successful studies are not so short as to exclude important information, nor so long as to include repetition and irrelevancy. Many excellent studies from the psychologist's point of view are between 4,000 and 8,000 words.

Describe the personality as it appears today. The study may well start by identifying the subject in respect to sex, age, occupation, race, and physical appearance. For most purposes use a pseudonym. Mere initials or such designations as "Mr. X" or "Mrs. Blank" are handicaps, since their impersonality suggests a hypothetical rather than a real individual.

Following, though not necessarily in the order here listed, there should be some report on the intelligence and temperament of the subject (to disclose the basic endowment permeating every trait). Also helpful as part of the identification is an initial thumb-nail sketch of the personality, as complete and well-proportioned a verbal portrait as is possible in a few words. This method serves to call attention at once to the central traits, and to the leading streams of thought and desire.

Following such an introduction there should be an account of the expressive traits, interests, values, tastes, and manners of the subject. In this part of the record a psychograph might help (pp. 402-430), but not merely as a record of quantitative estimates of predefined traits. Each of the common traits on the psychograph has its individual aspect, and this aspect *must* be revealed in a case study. Psychological terms for common traits and for common aspects of growth often seem stilted, and need not be used unless they actually succeed in expressing precisely the distinctions desired. A case study should not read like a textbook.

The descriptive portion of the study must include likewise an account of the subject's chief goals in life. For what is he living? What is he trying to do? Is he well organized in his pursuit of goals? There should be a mention of his primary likes and dislikes, his hobbies, admirations, his successes and failures. What is his humor like? Has he insight? Has he neurotic symptoms? What are his fantasies? In what social groups does he like to be? Is his manner in all groups the same? Is his "institutional behavior" different from his private behavior? What is his religion, and what his philosophy of life?

Use both general description and specific illustrations. It is not effective to write entirely in general terms nor entirely by incident. The best results are secured by giving a general statement of the attitude, trait, or conflict in question, and then following this statement with a specific and altogether *typical* illustration. It is a shrewd gift to be able to select incidents that are apt condensations of traits. General statements draw attention to the dynamic organization as a whole, while specific incidents by particularizing the operation of traits make them seem more personal and life-like. One without the other is incomplete; but specific incidents should be placed *after* the naming of the general trait which they illustrate. By comparing the four following characterizations one can see the superiority of the method of general statement followed by specific and typical illustration.[39]

> Tom was a poor white; he was originally lazy, but after his ambition was aroused, he traveled, and finally became an inventor.
>
> (Exclusively general statements)

> Tom's father could not read. They lived on the Mississippi. Tom liked to sit in a boat. His father died. He went to Pickleville, Ohio, and made a machine to plant cabbages.
>
> (Exclusively specific statements)

> Tom bought a book on mechanics; he went for long walks by himself, and though he spoke to no one he looked at people wistfully; all of which shows his hunger for human association and his desire to forget his loneliness.
>
> (Specific followed by general statements)

> Tom's basic traits are his hunger for human companionship and his determination not to let this longing defeat him. He will pass and repass a stroller in the

---

[39] It is an experimental fact that the optimum comprehension and memory-value result from the use of general characterization followed by specific illustration: H. Cantril, "General and Specific Attitudes," *Psychol. Monog.*, 1932, No. 192, chap. iv.

park in hope that the stroller will speak to him, and then he will return to his room and plunge grimly into his studies.

(General followed by specific statements)

Give all essential information concerning formative influences. Since, from the genetic point of view, all causes lie in past conditions, the longitudinal stream of a life must be traced with care. It is true that over-emphasis upon early events is the besetting sin of many psychologists who forget that the motive forces of the adult have undergone many transformations since childhood. Even though the importance of origins is often exaggerated, a knowledge of the course of development and of the process of transformation aids greatly in understanding. In order not to overlook important conditions the writer should consider the probable significance of such diverse influences as heredity, economic status, religious and moral background, disease and accidents, school history, play history, "weaning" from the home, subsequent relationships with parents, entrance into the world of ideas, early sexual experiences, feelings of inferiority, disappointments, suffering, crises, conversions, and significant successes.

Consider the personality also from the point of view of the future. What does the individual plan to do? Is there a *Bestimmung* (cf. p. 219), or is the life undirected? What trends are unmistakable; what general prognosis might be made and what specific predictions?

Many successful case studies seem naturally to fall into three sections: (a) a description of the present status, (b) an account of past influences and the successive stages of development, and (c) an indication of future trends. All three are important for understanding. Very often the prediction of the future serves admirably to define and to summarize tendencies that at present are diffuse and discordant. A prognosis seems, as it were, to establish for each man his own "ideal type." It makes a schema of comprehensibility whereby the significance of the present trends of development and conflicts become clarified. It is a method often employed in common speech: "He is going to be a successful stockbroker just like his father," or "Anyone can see that she will be a sweet little old lady who will crochet tea-cozies and give children sweet-peas from her garden." Such predictions tell something of the personality at the present time, as well as of its future.

The case study is the most complete and most synthetic of all methods available for the study of personality. Properly used it has the full value both of a work of science and a work of art. It can include data drawn from tests, experiments, psychographs, depth-analysis, and statistics; it can incorporate explanations derived from the general laws of psychology: genetic, comparative, abnormal. In short, it embraces both the scientific (inferential) and the intuitive aspects of understanding.[40]

One drawback of the case study must not be overlooked. As in every activity in which intuition plays a part, there is a danger that the interpreter will write his own message across the case and obscure it. Biographies, especially autobiographies, are frequently nothing more than characterological palimpsest. The picture which the interpreter desires to create is not the true picture. This is the reason why the case method should be employed only by those who are trained to avoid partisanship.

In preparing to use the case method valuable training comes from reading literature. From it the student learns to avoid preoccupation with the inconsequential, and to temper his interest in general laws with a feeling for individuality. He learns also that no personality is dull or trivial, but that each has a certain bigness if properly understood.[41]

GENERALIZATION OF CASE STUDIES

The value of the case study does not cease with its synthetic treatment of the single personality. By analyzing and comparing many such studies it is possible to pass to the construction of psychological laws and to new hypotheses. This wider use of case studies is well illustrated by an investigation issuing from the Psychological Institute of the University of Vienna.[42]

[40] Such was the conclusion of an experiment in teaching by the case method; to quote, "*The natural mental attitude in the study of personality is one which, even while it analyzes and compares, keeps its effort always directed toward the particular instance.*" G. W. Allport, *J. Abnorm. & Soc. Psychol.*, 1929, 24, 14-27.

[41] The following novels of character, biographies and autobiographies are samples of literary writing containing valuable psychological lessons for the student of personality: W. E. Leonard, *The Locomotive God*; Somerset Maugham, *Of Human Bondage*; Frank Norris, *McTeague*; Leo Tolstoy, *Anna Karenina*; Franz Werfel, *The Pure in Heart*; Theodore Dreiser, *Dawn*; Willa Cather, *My Mortal Enemy* and *Paul's Case*; James Joyce, *Ulysses*; Clifford E. Beers, *A Mind that Found Itself*; I. A. Goncharov, *Oblomov*; James T. Farrell, *Studs Lonigan*; H. G. Wells, *Experiment in Autobiography*; F. Dostoevsky, *The Brothers Karamazov.*

[42] Ch. Bühler, *Der Menschliche Lebenslauf als psychologisches Problem*, 1933; summarized in English by E. Frenkel, *Char. & Pers.*, 1936, 5, 1-34.

As a first step in this investigation, approximately two hundred life-histories of European and American figures of the past two centuries were prepared. The data for these histories were drawn from biographical accounts, from diaries and correspondence, as well as from the objective records of achievement. Prejudiced sources were avoided. The cases selected were chiefly eminent persons: Among the men, Goethe, Von Humboldt, Rockefeller, Carnegie, Stresemann, Wilde; among the women, Jenny Lind, Isadore Duncan, Belle Livingstone, Selma Lagerlöf, and Mary Baker Eddy.

These case studies are treated both as an end in themselves and as raw material for analysis and conceptualization. Interspersed with the life-histories are discussions of the generalizations to which they seem to lead. The method is thus in part intuitive and in part empirical and statistical. It is a contribution to the understanding of mind-in-general and mind-in-particular. It is, as the psychology of personality must be, both nomothetic and idiographic.

One generalization from this comparative study of these life-histories is the hypothesis that there are five distinguishable periods in the ascending and descending phases of life. Up to the age of 15 there is a period of rapid childhood growth; from 15-25 a period of growing reproductive capacity; from 25-45 maturity and prime; between 45 and 55 a turning point is reached and the recession of vital powers commences; and from 55 onwards there is a marked decline in physical powers. Is there a corresponding ascent and descent in *psychological* functions? The full capacity of athletes was found to coincide with the period of maximum biological power, or else to decline before this period ends. On the other hand, complete skill in hand-work is retained as a rule for a period of 10 years past the biological prime, and full capacity in mental work remains at least another 10 years.[43]

Besides the five biological phases there are five psychological periods in every career: (1) childhood and youth, during which time the question of what one shall live for does not seriously arise; (2) late adolescence, during which time the desire to live *for* something appears, and a provisional choice of careers is made; (3) early adulthood, during which time the decision becomes more defined, the life is arranged and planned, at first tentatively and then more definitely; (4) maturity, devoted to the pursuit of the chosen goal, to making results

[43] These findings are supported by the research of W. R. Miles in America (*Psychol. Rev.*, 1933, 40, 99-123). Miles found that physical strength, speed of response, memory, and sensory capacity are at their best in early adulthood, and show marked decline with age. Certain motor skills, on the other hand, such as appear in hand-work, remain at their maximum approximately up to the age of 50; and complex psychological functions, such as imagination, reasoning, judgment, and critical powers, remain on the maximum level nearly to the end of the individual's life.

correspond to ambitions; (5) old age, a period of retrospect and of waiting. This last phase lies beyond the "career" proper just as the first phase lies before it.

While there is nothing original in the attempt to order the period of human life into ages (Shakespeare chose seven, the Sphinx three), Bühler finds something rather final and ultimate in her five-fold classification. It does seem to serve well as a classification of the periods of life *work*. But work is not the only important factor in the *Lebenslauf*. It is often less significant than the love life, than disease, than avocations. If such factors were given their just weight these five divisions of life would break down. The "ages of man" exist only in respect to some one phase of existence, selected on occasion for special study.

Each career seems to be definitely ordered or steered toward a self-selected goal. Each man and each woman lives *for* something. Subjectively, this phenomenon appears as *Intention;* objectively as *Bestimmung* (cf. pp. 218-220). The ways in which careers may be ordered or steered are various. Some individuals stake their entire lives upon a single great objective; others have alternating goals; and still others, shifting goals. In a study of would-be suicides it was found that life becomes intolerable only to those who feel that there is nothing more *for* which they can live and *to* which they can aspire. The objectives which people adopt are generally vague at first and grow in definiteness. But in all the eminent careers treated in this volume, the presence of the steering-principle is detected; it is a precondition to maturity of personality. How far the principle is important in the ordinary lives of more average personalities Bühler does not say. Although a few life-histories of aged dependents are considered, the role of *Bestimmung* in these less colorful lives is not discussed.

Most individuals measure their satisfaction in life by the ratio of their objective success to their ambitions and pretensions (a formula identical with that offered by William James), but Bühler shows quite correctly that there are also many individual differences in self-esteem. Some individuals take their greatest joy in planning, some in working out their plans, and some in the accomplishment at the end. Ordinarily the subjective "high point of life," the period of the most intense sense of living, falls in early adulthood; in some individuals it comes in adolescence, and in some with more mental values, especially philosophers, it comes during later maturity.

Such are some of the generalizations that may result from an analysis and comparison of case studies. The interest of the Vienna investigators was weighted heavily on the side of life-work and careers, but their method could be applied to better rounded life-histories, more diversely chosen.

Briefly summarized the usefulness of the case study for the psychology of personality is as follows: (a) It furnishes an individual framework within which all relevant and significant data may be compiled and arranged, so that the investigator does not have on hand merely an embarrassing mass of scores and psychological debris that do not fit together. (b) It keeps attention always riveted upon a single concrete life—which is where the psychologist's attention should be riveted more often than it is. (c) By keeping the whole life in view, single acts and individual events can be more properly interpreted and evaluated by reference to their structural context. (d) By comparing many cases there may emerge evidence of common forms of response that leads to a fresh conceptualization regarding mind-in-general. New psychological generalizations thus evolved differ from most generalizations in that they are derived not from common segments of behavior viewed in isolation but from entire lives as they are actually lived, with all their intricate inter-relations fully exposed to view.

CONCLUSIONS

From this panorama of methods our principal conclusion must be that there is no "one and only" method for the study of personality. All methods have their value, most of them being adapted to the exploration of one special aspect of the problem. In respect to accuracy and reliability some of the segmental methods are to be preferred; in respect to *adequacy* of approach the various synthetic or relational methods are better.

Each method has its enthusiastic supporters. Unfortunately enthusiasm for one method often blinds the investigator to the merit of others. For example, one-sided and exaggerated claims are made for the diagnostic powers of the word-association test, for endocrine analysis, for the Rorschach test, for graphology, for psychoanalysis. Each is said to be the last word, making the use of any other method unnecessary. This is foolish. For some problems one method of attack is best, for others, different methods. The wise investigator will not place his faith in any one exclusively, but will use several to cover more ground, and at the same time to check the findings of one method against those of another.

As used in this chapter the term "method" has referred principally to ways of obtaining information, *i.e.,* to the treatment of data. In a broader sense, of course, "scientific method" involves the use of logical reasoning, of proper standards of verifiability, and independent confirmation of conclusions. All such safeguards are necessary, though it is not the task of this chapter to discuss them in detail. Procedures for obtaining data are worthless without standards for interpreting the data obtained. But it is something of a struggle to strike a balance between excessively rigid and perfectionistic standards (that accomplish nothing but a sterilization of research, limiting it to worthless fragments of behavior having no essential bearing upon personality) and loose standards that permit wanton assertions and extravagant claims to go without check or proof. It is this balance that Aristotle advocates in advising us to demand the highest degree of exactness that is compatible with adequacy of conception and clear perspective upon the problem in hand.

CHAPTER XV

COMMON TRAITS: PSYCHOGRAPHY

W̲ʜᴇɴ the psychologist chooses to study *common* traits he must be content with the best obtainable *approximations* to the structure of personality. He deliberately excludes from consideration *individual* traits and all individual coloring of common traits, and seeks universal molds into which to compress all personalities. If they do not fit his molds perfectly (and of course they will not), he can only grin and bear the consequences, admitting that dimensions are *dimensions* and persons are *persons*.

Having accepted this limitation the psychologist starts with as sensible a definition as possible of some one trait that he wishes to study differentially. It is essential to select only such a variable as, by virtue of a common humanity and common cultural influence, may be expected to serve as a comparable mode of adjustment, varying "normally," among all persons within a given area of culture (cf. pp. 297-303). It is wiser also to select a psychological rather than a characterial variable. To be avoided, for example, are such complex biosocial conceptions as "popularity," "attractiveness," "delinquency," "reputation," "social status," "leadership," and "pleasing personality." Normative concepts such as these, all pertaining to the individual's "social stimulus-value" are legitimate enough in social ethics, and furnish problems likewise for social psychology, but they are poor dimensions to use in the psychology of personality where only biophysical variables, devoid of social judgment, are in order.

Having selected some common trait according to these principles, the psychologist then submits it to empirical checks. With the aid of experiments, ratings, or tests he determines whether there are true individual differences in the trait in question, and whether his subjects are reasonably self-consistent in respect to this trait as he defines it, likewise what its range and form of distribution within his population of subjects may be. Unless the range is wide and unless it is "normally" distributed (cf. pp. 332-337), the usefulness of the dimension will be limited. If, after this preliminary study, the variable seems to be a promising one, he may then proceed with various technical aids toward the standardization of his scale for measurement. A "personality test" or an "attitude scale" ensues.

Finally, it will be necessary to consider the relation of this variable and scale to other similar variables and scales alleged by other investigators to cover the same area of personality. If one scale correlates highly with others, it may be a question of discarding all but the most efficient, or it may be a question of consolidating the scales (and the concepts) to effect a mutual improvement. But it is not always easy to tell which of several scales is most efficient nor which of several definitions of the variable is to be preferred. Ordinarily the investigator who "discovers" a variable will defend his brain-child against all competitors.

Partly for this reason it is impossible to say how many common traits there are, *i.e.*, to how many fundamental variables personality may be ordered (even admitting that there is much in every life that cannot be ordered to any common variables at all). In one sense there are as many possible common traits as there are non-censorial trait-names (cf. pp. 303-311)—at least 5,000, and more if compound words and phrases are employed as they often are (*e.g.*, "inferiority complex," "fair-mindedness," "civic attitude"). Any investigator with an interest in *any* common segment of human behavior, may, if he chooses, propose it as a common trait. There is scarcely any limit to the process. On the other hand, if only the tests and scales thus far proposed are considered, the count of common traits is much reduced. There are to date, speaking very roughly, about 300 common traits sufficiently treated to be considered in this connection.[1] The number shrinks still further if only those variables are counted that all psychologists accept as soundly demonstrated. In this case the tally is almost negligible. Such lack of agreement concerning "basic traits" is often deplored; yet it is inevitable so long as psychologists disagree concerning the *nature* of traits.

In this chapter certain common traits in which psychologists are now interested will be chosen for discussion. The selection is dic-

[1] Not more than sixty of these receive mention in this chapter. Others are listed in the following bibliographies: G. B. Watson, "Character Tests and Their Applications Through 1930," *Rev. Educ. Res.*, 1932, 2, 185-270; H. J. Baker *et al.*, same journal, 1935, 5, No. 3; G. H. Hildreth, *Bibliography of Mental Tests and Ratings Scales*, (Psychological Corporation), 1933; P. M. Symonds, *Psychological Diagnosis in Social Adjustment* (Appendix), 1934; *The Psychol. Bull.*, 1934, 31, 501-524; 1935, 32, 500-523.

tated partly by the relative prominence of these traits in present-day research, and partly by their conformity to the logic of traits developed in Chapters XI and XII. In listing these common traits, an illustrative psychographic scheme is employed. With the aid of this framework a number of important distinctions can be visualized, and the quantitative nature of common traits can be suitably emphasized.

CONSTRUCTION OF THE PSYCHOGRAPH

The term "psychograph" has several meanings. Sometimes it is synonymous with literary biography, sometimes with any random listing of disparate psychological facts concerning a given person (cf. pp. 10-12). It also may designate an orderly case study or life-history from the clinical point of view. But as used here, the term means simply a printed graph or profile upon which is plotted the actual magnitude of common traits attained by any individual.[2]

In the psychograph presented in Figure 28 it is assumed, and in most cases established, that the common variables there included are normally distributed in an average American population, or else that two separate traits are joined together in order to obtain a quasi-normal distribution (cf. pp. 335-337). Half the scores on each variable fall at or above the median line running through the center of the graph, and half at or below this line.

No vertical units are marked on the graph, since it is equally serviceable for any intervals that may be desired. Percentile or decile units may easily be placed against the left hand margin; or a seven point scale with 1 at the bottom, 7 at the top, and 4 exactly opposite the median line. For more refined recording, sigma-units or T-scores may be employed. Or if one group of subjects is used as the frame of reference it is possible to use the graph for rank-order comparisons, the most outstanding individual in respect to each variable receiving the highest plotting, the individual at the opposite extreme, the lowest. In such a case the number of intervals will be equal to the number of subjects in the group.

For clearest legibility the points should be plotted in the middle of the respective columns, and joined successively by straight lines, so that a jagged profile results. The points may be determined in a number of different ways: for some of the traits tests are available, yielding scores in percentile or decile ranks. Where only absolute scores are obtained from a test, they must be converted into percentile or

2 A standard discussion of psychographic methods may be found in W. Stern, *Differentielle Psychologie*, 3d edit., 1921, pp. 327-371.

PSYCHOGRAPH OF____

UNDERLYING PSYCHOBIOLOGICAL FACTORS								COMMON TRAITS OF PERSONALITY														
PHYSIQUE	VITALITY	INTELLIGENCE		TEMPERAMENT				EXPRESSIVE				ATTITUDINAL										
												DIRECTED TOWARD SELF		DIRECTED TOWARDS OTHERS			DIRECTED TOWARDS VALUES					
SYMMETRY	VITALITY	ABSTRACT (VERBAL)	MECHANICAL (PRACTICAL)	BROAD EMOTIONS	STRONG EMOTIONS	ASCENDANCE	EXPANSION	PERSISTENCE	EXTROVERSION			SELF-OBJECTIFICATION	SELF-ASSURANCE	GREGARIOUSNESS	ALTRUISM (SOCIALIZATION)	SOCIAL INTELLIGENCE (TACT)	THEORETICAL	ECONOMIC	AESTHETIC	POLITICAL	RELIGIOUS
HEALTH							SUB-MISSION	RECLUSION	VACILLATION	INTROVERSION											
DEFORMITY	LOW VITALITY	LOW ABSTRACT INTELLIGENCE	LOW MECHANICAL INTELLIGENCE	NARROW EMOTIONS	WEAK EMOTIONS						SELF-DECEPTION	DISTRUST	SOLITARINESS	SELF-SEEKING (UNSOCIALIZED BEHAVIOR)	LOW SOCIAL INTELLIGENCE (TACTLESSNESS)	NON-THEORETICAL	NON-ECONOMIC	NON-AESTHETIC	NON-POLITICAL	NON-RELIGIOUS	
ILL-HEALTH																					

FIGURE 28

An Illustrative Psychograph

some other relative units so that the plotting for all traits may be in uniform intervals. Where tests are lacking, the points may be determined by ratings (according to certain principles offered in the next chapter), or even by self-estimate.

So much for the method of using the graph. It is a highly flexible form, readily varied according to the needs of the investigator. Not only may the intervals and the methods of obtaining the scores be varied, but the content itself, arbitrarily chosen, can easily be changed. The common traits here inserted are merely illustrative, and some of them are tentative. The form of the graph, in short, is neither complete nor final.[3]

The choice of high and low extremes for each dimension is to a certain degree arbitrary. No implication of morality, desirability, or superiority is intended. From the psychological point of view all plottings are strictly objective and devoid of merit or demerit, approval or disapproval. In general, the arrangement of traits from top to bottom follows their tendency to correlate positively with one another, but there are exceptions to this rule; the matter being more fully explained on pp. 428-430.

Use immediately shows up the limitations of this psychograph (or of any other). However carefully the investigator plots the scores, he will find that no personality is accurately represented in a profile. In spite of its connecting lines, a psychograph fails to express the qualitative balance between two or more traits. A person whose profile dips in "ascendance" and rises in "expansion" has not merely low standing in one trait and high in another. There is a resultant blend in his behavior, colored also by all other co-existing traits, that eludes the psychograph completely. Discouraging as this discovery is, it follows inevitably from the false assumption that personality is the sum-total of plottings of scores on common variables.

Yet, psychography has a striking advantage to offset its limitations. It is a method particularly well suited to the *comparative* study of personality, which, of course, demands the use of common traits.

PSYCHO-BIOLOGICAL FACTORS

Excepting in the looser and more popular sense of the term, the first seven variables in the graph are not *traits* at all. They are rather

---

[3] Two previous editions of this psychograph have been published: the first in the *J. Abnorm. & Soc. Psychol.*, 1921, 16, 6-40; the second in A. A. Roback, *The Psychology of Character*, 1927, p. 427. An elaboration and revision of the second edition was published by Roback under the title of "Personalysis," *Char. & Pers.*, 1934, 3, 144-156. Reprints of our p. 403 can be bought in quantity from Henry Holt and Co.

underlying psycho-biological factors that represent the raw material from which traits develop. Placed to the left of the double vertical line in the graph, these factors call attention to the groundwork of personality in terms of its physical constitution, intellectual endowment, and temperament.

The array of possible dimensions in this field is almost limitless. One might measure and plot separately, height, weight, blood pressure, pulse rate, basal metabolism, various reaction times, sensory acuities, manual strengths, or the efficiency of each sensory-motor co-ordination. But such refinement of detail is not practicable in a psychograph, nor is it worth the pains. For a psychological schedule, coarser and composite ratings on physiological functions serve the purpose quite as well, for personality is not tied specifically to any one region of the body nor to any one physiological function. Subtlety in distinguishing the psychological *results* of organic conditions is more important for personality than is subtlety in diagnosing the physiological conditions themselves.[4]

Avoiding, then, too fine distinctions, the psychograph selects seven coarser variables that can be scaled quantitatively, each of which considered as a whole exerts a profound influence upon personality. The first three of these variables are grouped under the general rubric of *physique*, the next two under *intelligence*, and the final pair under *temperament*.

1. *Symmetry* (as opposed to deformity) is a variable requiring a composite score in respect to excellence of bodily form, including build, facial features, complexion, and normal use of the limbs. To some degree it is unavoidably a biosocial conception, including as it does, in part, judgments of beauty and ugliness. But its presence in the graph is demanded; for around this variable, more than any other, develop feelings of inferiority and their compensatory consequences (cf. pp. 173-181). The score on this variable often illuminates the plottings on other portions of the graph. To determine the score it may be possible to use a system of "points" objectively determined (after the manner of judges at a beauty contest), or ratings by associates.

2. *Health* is obviously a broad variable, that could be indefinitely subdivided. It is included in the psychograph for the same reason that

---

[4] Endocrinologists and physiologists generally reverse this emphasis. With technical precision they give an exact diagnosis of bodily states, but use only coarse and confused rubrics in representing personality.

symmetry is included. It is possible to obtain a composite score from a medical examination, perhaps with the aid of such a point scale as is sometimes used by life insurance companies.

3. *Vitality* is both obscure and important. It has sometimes been called "energy output"; more popularly, "vivacity" and "pep." Some people seem never to tire, to work ceaselessly and then to be ready for strenuous recreation. Others accomplish but little in a day, and that little fatigues them. To some extent this variable depends upon health, but to some extent it is likewise a permanent attribute of temperament, no doubt related to basic metabolic conditions. Its significance for the strength of "drive," for the energizing of expressive behavior, and for the development of all other traits, demands its inclusion. Physiological measures of tonicity and metabolism may help to establish the score on this variable, although it is one that can be approached fairly well by ratings since it issues unfailingly into overt activity.[5]

A second distinguishable group of common variables pertains to *intelligence*. Here again an extended subdivision is possible; indeed, most of the older psychographs included little else than intellectual functions. (Separate plottings were made for simple reaction time, associative reaction time, visual acuity, color discrimination, attention, rote memory, reasoning, and the like.) Just how many common factors there should be in this group is under active discussion among psychologists today. The common belief is that factor analysis will eventually provide a schedule of scalable and reasonably separate intellectual functions.[6] In the meantime the two following variables, somewhat old-fashioned, but still serviceable, will focus attention on two of the most important aspects of intelligence.

4. *Abstract or "Verbal" Intelligence*. The capacity to solve novel problems with the use of symbols (usually words) seems, within

[5] It is somewhat rare to find this variable discussed in psychological writing or its importance appreciated. An exception is W. B. Pitkin, *The Psychology of Achievement*, 1930, Bk. II.

[6] One factorial study suggests that the seven basic constitutents of intelligence are: facility with numbers, verbal fluency, visualizing, memory, speed in perceiving, inductive ability, and deductive ability (L. L. Thurstone, *Psychol. Bull.*, 1936, 33, 780 f.).

If this or some similar schedule is finally agreed upon, it could easily be substituted for the two-fold classification now included in the psychograph. The gain would be considerable, since these constituent functions would presumably be more clearly defined and more accurately measured. But the *personal* formations of intelligence would not be any more clearly illuminated by this method than by any other dimensional scheme, cf. p. 565 ftn.

limits, to be a homogeneous "power" possessed by each individual in a certain amount. (If this were not so there would be no possible justification for tests designed to measure intelligence.) With the many scales now available, nothing is easier than to plot a score for any individual on this particular variable. Nothing is easier, and nothing is more treacherous if the score is offered without interpretation, *i.e.*, without taking into account the *personal formation* of the intelligence in the life in question.

5. *Mechanical or "practical" intelligence* is a companion variable. It is sometimes called "ability in spatial manipulations," or "dexterity," and is measured with the aid of performance tests. It is not altogether independent of symbolic processes, and correlates with abstract intelligence often to an extent represented by a coefficient of $+.50$.[7] It is generally agreed, however, that it is sound procedure to keep the ranks on these two types of intelligence separate. As in the case of abstract intelligence, tests, rather than ratings, should be employed in obtaining a subject's score, and the score thus obtained should be interpreted in the light of special abilities and deficiencies, interests and training, and all other factors that mold mechanical intelligence into its myriad personal forms.

It has been suggested that a third major type of intelligence is found in an individual's ability to act effectively in *social* situations. But it is obvious that "social intelligence" cannot be an inherited capacity to the extent that abstract and mechanical intelligence may be. It is rather a *trait* developed through opportunity and through interest, upon the basis of a native general intelligence. Such being the case, we shall postpone discussion to its more logical place among the traits of personality, pp. 426 f.

The remaining common and primarily innate variables pertain to temperament. In Chapter II temperament was defined as

> the characteristic phenomena of an individual's emotional nature, including his susceptibility to emotional stimulation, his customary strength and speed of response, the quality of his prevailing mood, and all peculiarities of fluctuation and intensity in mood; these phenomena being regarded as dependent upon constitutional make-up, and therefore largely hereditary in origin.

Some of these aspects of temperament are too individualistic to be scaled. Two aspects however seem to suggest quantitative continua.

[7] Cf. R. Pintner, *Intelligence Testing: Methods and Results,* 2d ed., 1931, p. 62.

6. *Broad Emotions—Narrow Emotions*. A person with a wide "affective spread" is one who reacts emotionally to a broad range of objects and situations. The person of narrow emotional spread responds infrequently in an emotional manner; his behavior is usually of an even tenor, showing little variation of feeling. Pressey has proposed a test for measuring the range of emotional response, a simple device requiring the subject to cross out words which for him have emotional tone.[8] The method has point, but the principal difficulty with it is its low reliability; attitude or mood of the moment has marked influence upon the subject's response.

7. *Strong Emotions—Weak Emotions*. The characteristic *intensity* of feeling seems a different dimension altogether from emotional spread. Here is a question, not of how many situations arouse emotional response, but rather of the average degree of the response. Though every individual beyond the age of infancy is capable of grading his emotional reaction so that strong stimulations are reacted to strongly and slight stimulations but slightly, yet some individuals seem more *readily* raised than others to an intense degree of response, and their average level of response is higher. Objective measures can be used for this variable—among them such well-known indicators as blood pressure, pulse rate, and psychogalvanic skin response. Ratings seem to be particularly poor on this aspect of temperament, due no doubt to the voluntary masking of emotional expression in our culture. It should be added that this variable is only tentatively included in the psychograph; it can be readily displaced or modified if future research shows that it is not a true quantitative continuum as is here implied.

If the profile drawn upon the psychograph stands well above the average on both the breadth and strength of emotionality, the result suggests the ancient portrait of the *choleric* type; if the range is broad, but the intensity low, the *sanguine* type; if the range is narrow but the response intense, the *melancholic* type; if the emotional life is both narrow and weak, the *phlegmatic* type. On p. 65 it was pointed out that one reason for the longevity of the four ancient temperaments lies in their correspondence to these two simple quantitative scales. They represent the four extreme patterns of two common dimensions, emotional range and intensity.

Not included in the psychograph are a large number of common

[8] J. L. Pressey, *J. Abnorm. & Soc. Psychol.*, 1921, 16, 55-64.

variables related on the one hand to vitality, intelligence and temperament, and on the other to the expressive traits. Take, for example,
such a variable as speed of movement, the alleged factor of "psychic
tempo." It is (if it exists) obviously in part a function of biological
endowment, while at the same time influencing all acquired skills and
forms of expression, conferring upon them a characteristic temporal
style. Such a variable might be called a "psycho-motor" trait.[9] In the
case of "psychic tempo" it is doubtful whether there is such a variable sufficiently uniform for individuals to be reliably scaled upon it
as a single continuum. Few people seem to be uniformly slow or
uniformly fast in all their actions. Evidence favors rather the postulation of at least two common speed factors, each of which might be
separately scaled on the graph, viz., *verbal speed* (covering such
performances as talking, counting, reading, writing), and a *rhythmic
speed* (as in tapping, walking, and manipulating objects).[10] Further
research may show the need for still other categories of speed that
are scalable and self-consistent.

Another motility-variable is that of *impulsion-inhibition* (Downey) or *explosive vs. obstructed* volition (James). Some individuals, characteristically respond "on the trigger" (often before they
are really prepared to respond); others have inertia to overcome and
are obstructed in their movements.[11].

Three other psycho-motor traits have been derived from a study
of various natural styles of movement recorded under laboratory
conditions (writing, speaking, drawing, tapping, walking, reaching,
and the like). Individuals may, for instance, be compared with one
another in respect to *spacious vs. circumscribed* movement. Some
seem consistently to make expansive, spacious movements in writing,
walking, or gesticulating; their actions are sweeping and free. Others
are characteristically constrained and circumscribed in their actions.

[9] Variables of this order are not included in the psychograph, partly because as
"directive" traits they are less dynamic and motivational than the other traits included (cf. pp. 319-324), and for sake of uniformity of exposition the psychograph
is limited to traits of the latter type.

[10] G. W. Allport and P. E. Vernon, *Studies in Expressive Movement*, 1933,
pp. 100-108.

[11] Cf. J. Downey, *The Will-Temperament and Its Testing*, 1924. This book
contains a discussion of several other motility-variables as well. It too uses the
psychographic method. With the aid of a series of ingenious psycho-motor tests
(unfortunately not of high reliability) a Will-Temperament profile is constructed
for each subject. Downey's critics are right in pointing out that she too readily
identifies these psycho-motor variables with "inner" motivational traits of personality, without adequately demonstrating a correspondence between them.

Another distinguishable dimension is that of *emphatic-unemphatic* movement. Some people consistently employ more "psychological pressure" than others whether they are speaking, gesturing, or writing. A third common variable is *centrifugal-centripetal* movement. Some individuals display a predominant *outward* tendency in gesture and speech. Others seem on the contrary typically centripetal in their patterns of movement.[12] Though not finally established these variables probably represent the *kind* of dimensional analysis most suitable for the study of the motility aspects of personality. In principle it would seem simpler to reach agreement upon motility-variables than upon the more complex motivational traits; yet the fact is that less progress has been made in the former area of research than in the latter.

EXPRESSIVE TRAITS

Next on the graph is a group of three traits that may, a trifle ambiguously, be called "expressive." Like other traits on the psychograph they conform in every respect to the criteria of common traits as set down in Chapters XI and XII. They are dynamic modes of adjustment, generalized and distributed quasi-normally in the population at large. These three traits are expressive in the sense that they color behavior that is specifically motivated to some ulterior end. That is to say, in the pursuit of almost any goal, the ascendant person will be ascendant, the expansive person will be expansive, and the persistent person persistent. Thus these traits are "directive" (cf. pp. 319-324). Furthermore, each *may* also acquire a motivational character. The ascendant person usually *desires* to take the active role; the expansive person *seeks* opportunities to express his ideas; the persistent person *actively resists* interruption and interference. In comparison with the attitudinal traits that follow on the psychograph, however, these three are relatively overt in their manifestation, more directive than motivational, and it is for these reasons that they are grouped into one section of the graph and labeled *expressive*.

8. *Ascendance and Submission.* In every social relation there is, in a sense, a conflict of personalities. Whenever two individuals come face to face, one ordinarily must yield for the occasion, or for part of the occasion, to the other. In friendly relations as well as in unfriendly, one will dominate and be the "victor," and the other will

[12] *Studies in Expressive Movement,* pp. 109-117; *see* also Chapter XVII of the present volume.

yield and become the "vanquished." As the saying goes, one will be the boot, the other the doormat. Likewise, in non-social situations an individual must, as a rule, either become the aggressor toward his environment, or else submit to its pressure, giving up to the forces opposed to him. Thus, one man, finding that he has driven his car into a deep snowdrift, forces it onwards through the obstructing bank; another in precisely the same situation backs out in the tracks he has made, resuming the road in a roundabout, non-aggressive fashion. (Both may get to their destinations equally soon!)

Sociologists in the nineteenth century designated ascendance and submission as the two basic modes of social adaptation, no doubt because they fitted so well into the then current philosophy of evolution. When the first two beasts met in the forest—so the parody goes—they looked at each other appraisingly and each asked himself, "Shall I be dinner or diner?" The more ascendant beast decided that he would be the diner, and the other straightway resigned himself to being the dinner. Spencer termed this the Principle of Supremacy and Subordination, and saw it operating everywhere—in human society as well as in the forest. The Italian criminologist, Sighele, viewed partnerships in crime in essentially the same way; one party, the more ascendant, he regarded as the *suggestionneur*, the other, the more submissive, as the *suggestionné*. In criminal partnerships it is the former who plans and directs the crime; the latter executes it under orders. Later sociologists extended the principle for other dyadic relationships.[13]

The psychologist now comes on the scene and asks whether any person *habitually* takes one role or the other. Is the trait self-consistent? Is it not obvious that in certain situations where talents or experience fit a person for leadership he will become dominant; and, contrariwise, in other spheres of activity where he is inexperienced or incompetent, will he not of necessity be submissive? It is not unusual to see a man of affairs, titanic in his own occupational circle, thrust into the "passive voice" by his physician or his priest. Quite so; the traits of ascendance and submission are never fixed and con-

[13] A discussion of the dominance hierarchies among animals can be found in A. G. Skard, *Acta Psychologica*, 1936, 2, 175-232; see also R. M. Yerkes, *Almost Human*. 1925, pp. 153-155. Spencer's discussion of the subject is somewhat scattered, but a representative statement is in *First Principles*, pp. 366 f. S. Sighele's views are contained in *Le Crime à Deux*, 1892. Good discussions of dyadic groups are those of G. Simmel, *Amer. J. Sociol.*, 1902, 8, 1-46; also L. von Wiese and H. Becker, *Systematic Sociology*, 1932, chap. xxxix.

stant in every situation for any individual; and for that matter, neither are any other traits of personality (cf. pp. 330-332). Yet there is plenty of evidence that dominant and submissive behavior are far from being capricious or bound only to the specific stimulus-situation. Scales for the measurement of these traits are uniformly high in their reliabilities, and prediction of behavior in general is successful. Even though exceptions occur, it is the rule for each individual to find what for him is a "plane of ease" in respect to dominance and submission, and to maintain this plane in many and varied situations.

As pointed out on pp. 333-336, ascendance and submission are *separate* traits, even though for convenience they can be cast into a single continuum on the psychograph. Submission is not merely the absence of ascendance; it is a *modus vivendi* all by itself. By yielding, agreeing, placating, the submissive person indirectly gains his point. To some degree, of course, every individual has this trait. McDougall pictures it as a fundamental instinct, thus correctly emphasizing its *positive* character. Universal though it is, some people employ it less often than others, and employ the ascendant mode of adjustment more often. It is this differential frequency that is measurable. One test makes the measurement with the aid of such situations as the following, the subject being required to check the alternative answer that most accurately tells of his typical mode of behavior in each situation represented. The scale in question has thirty-five situations of the type here presented, and separate forms for men and women. Each alternative is scored according to its demonstrated diagnostic power.[14]

> Someone tries to push ahead of you in line. You have been waiting for some time, and can't wait much longer. Suppose the intruder is the same sex as yourself, do you usually
>
> remonstrate with the intruder ....
> "look daggers" at the intruder or make clearly audible
>   comments to your neighbor ....
> decide not to wait, and go away ....
> do nothing ....

[14] G. W. and F. H. Allport, *The A-S Reaction Study*, published by the Houghton Mifflin Co., Boston, and described in the *J. Abnorm. & Soc. Psychol.*, 1928, 23, 118-136. A revision of the scale for use in business is described by R. O. Beckman, *Person. J.*, 1933, 11, 387-392, and issued by the Psychological Corporation.

Do you feel self-conscious in the presence of superiors in the academic or business world?

     markedly ....

     somewhat ....

     not at all ....

Some possession of yours is being worked upon at a repair shop. You call for it at the time appointed, but the repair man informs you that he has "only just begun work on it." Is your customary reaction

     to upbraid him ....

     to express dissatisfaction mildly ....

     to smother your feelings entirely ....

In studying ascendance and submission, psychologists have found a number of interesting facts. The traits, it appears, are markedly constant even at an early age,[15] suggesting that temperament is an important factor in their formation. And yet, with sufficient influence they can be altered, both in children and in adults.[16] Deliberate attempts at modification, however, are much more successful in transforming submissive people into average or ascendant individuals, than in reducing ascendant people to average or submissive grade! Why should this be so? Perhaps ascendance is a more desirable norm (in our culture) and for that reason the experimental population of submissive individuals eagerly responded to their training, whereas those who were already ascendant are quite satisfied with their lot. Or, perhaps, this latter group was too dominant to be influenced by the hard-pressed experimenter. There is likewise a slight but persistent correlation between submissiveness and high grades in school and college; though which condition is the cause and which the effect is not easy to tell.

In vocational guidance and selection these traits have considerable practical importance. The ascendant woman would probably be badly placed as dressmaker, house-maid, private secretary, or under-librarian; she would do well, other things being equal, as professional hostess, tea-room manager, or teacher in a reform school. The submissive man would never do as a traffic policeman. In one system of chain stores it was found by the test just described, that there was a constant increase of ascendance in four grades of executive positions; from floormen (only average in the trait), through department

[15] Cf. L. M. Jack, *Univ. Iowa Stud. in Child Welfare,* 1934, 9, No. 3.

[16] M. A. McLaughlin, *Univ. Iowa Stud., Stud. Educ.,* 1931, 6, No. 5. M. L. Page. *Univ. Iowa Stud., Stud. Child Welfare,* 1936, 12, No. 3.

managers, store managers, and general managers (most ascendant). It is well, however, not to confuse ascendance with leadership. The latter is not a single scalable trait; for many abilities and traits are involved, and the requirements for leadership vary greatly from situation to situation. It is quite possible for a submissive person to be a leader, especially if he has executive lieutenants through whom he can exert practical as well as prophetic influence and control.

9. *Expansion and Reclusion.* Of all the common variables in the psychograph this pair of overt expressive traits is perhaps the easiest to identify. Our first meeting with a person gives the clue, and subsequent experience more often than not merely confirms our first judgments. What in popular parlance is often termed "personality" is little more than the trait of expansion in action. A person who is expansive projects himself into his social relationships; he talks readily, expresses his opinions frequently, and leaves little doubt as to his views on any subject. The reclusive person finds little to say; he relates his opinions briefly or not at all. He is reticent. Since these traits are by definition overt in expression, it is not surprising that several studies show them to be the most reliably rated of all the common traits of personality. Judges differ very little in their ratings, and subjects are as self-consistent in these traits as in any. A garrulous person seems almost always garrulous, and a "human clam" is under almost any circumstances hard to pry open. As in the case of ascendance and submission these traits seem to be self-consistent even at an early age. Young children, it is found, do a characteristic amount of talking, and can easily be scaled on this variable.[17] As socialization progresses the trait may, of course, be modified, though it is often constant throughout the entire life of the individual.

The concepts of expansion and reclusion should not be confused with ascendance and submission, nor with extroversion and introversion. Reclusion may appear in people who are fundamentally both ascendant and extroverted. Conversely, the expansive person may be compensating for a deep-seated submissiveness. To be sure his expansiveness may secure for him a certain temporary authority based upon an impression of personal force and intellectual fluency. He is often put upon committees or in a position of authority by mistake, and too late it appears that he is not able to "deliver the goods." There is always the danger that the abilities of the expansive person will be over-estimated. Many introverts are markedly expansive,

[17] Cf. C. T. Zyve, *Teachers College Record*, 1927, 29, 46-61.

partly because their inner life is so rich that it craves expression, and partly because they need a social compensation for deep feelings of inferiority and self-consciousness. Teachers, especially in college, are frequently expansive in the classroom and in conversation, though they are often fundamentally both introverted and submissive. There is nothing intrinsically desirable in expansion or in reclusion (nor in ascendance or submission). Whether they are charming or objectionable traits, depends upon the grade of intelligence, unselfishness, and breeding with which they are combined and modified in action, and upon ethical evaluations of the conduct to which they lead.

There is some evidence in favor of distinguishing two different dimensions of expansion and reclusion, the one a tendency to talk freely (or to be reticent) about *oneself;* the other, a tendency to speak freely (or to be reticent) on *impersonal* topics. Often people are found who seem to be expansive in one of these directions and reclusive in the other. Whether or not to make this distinction depends largely upon the degree of refinement desired for the psychograph. It is probably unwise to complicate the graph unduly, especially since the individual coloring of common traits can never be fully expressed in a psychograph no matter how many subdivisions are allowed. It is also true that the demonstrated self-consistency of this trait is high even when defined in the most inclusive way. It seems unnecessary, therefore, to split the variable into two.

The somewhat roundabout method of measuring traits by means of a standardized questionnaire ("pencil and paper" test) is not readily applied to expansion and reclusion, chiefly because of the difficulty in devising questions that are neutral in tone and unoffending to the subject. More direct methods may be employed.[18] One perhaps crude but surprisingly effective method consists in counting the number of instances during a given period of time in which an individual speaks of his personal views or of himself. Even a count of the frequency with which he uses the first person personal pronoun is surprisingly revelatory; though, of course, an ounce of social training correctly applied may set up the habit of avoiding the use of this pronoun without basically affecting the trait of expansion. In another test subjects may be asked to answer help-wanted advertisements from a newspaper as if they really were applying for the positions. It is remarkable what extreme variations in replies can be obtained to such advertisements as the following.

[18] Cf. F. H. and G. W. Allport, *J. Abnorm. & Soc. Psychol.,* 1921, 16, 6-40.

> Men wanted for detective work; experience unnecessary. Write *Herald*, Box 111.

> Wanted a young woman with tact, initiative and interest in her work to take charge of a library, circulating motion picture films to churches, schools, industries, etc. If interested write fully your experience to O. F. T., *Herald*, Box 112.

Some applicants give many references to their qualifications, to their ideas on the profession in question, and leave little doubt as to their own attitudes. Other replies are brief, meager, and uncommunicative. When this test is used along with other methods of determining expansiveness it usually agrees well with them, though it is unsafe to use it alone. A standardized battery of such performance tests has not to date been devised, but it should be a relatively easy task to do so.[19]

10. *Persistence and Vacillation.* One of the commonest characterizations of people is in terms of their characteristic level of perseverance. This person, we say, is tenacious, resolute, pertinacious, dogged, or steadfast, with "grit" or marked strength of will; another, we say, is inconstant, irresolute, fluctuating, capricious, an opportunist, easily deflected from his chosen course. In popular speech the traits in question reflect the possession of "will power" or its lack. But psychologists, terrified lest they find themselves mired in the problems of freedom of will, have preferred on the whole an indirect and less precarious conception of these important traits.

G. E. Müller was one of the first psychologists to call attention to the "perseverative tendency" (his own term) as a personal trait. He found that he himself was bothered by inability to leave tasks when an interruption came, also by the intrusion of nonsense syllables *previously* learned into a new series that he was attempting to learn. These phenomena he thought were related to his dependability when it came to a matter of carrying out resolutions and commissions of all kinds, no matter how trivial. Müller observed that there were marked individual differences in respect to this trait, and that some people, opposite in type to himself, were distinguished for their flexible, "associative" mode of adjustment that gained for them in adaptive versatility what it lacked in staying power.[20]

[19] It will be wise to watch for sex differences in norms. It is an experimental fact that women at the school age show in general a linguistic superiority over men, and in performing the same task use, on the average, more words. Such facts must be taken into account in devising a scale for expansion-reclusion.

[20] G. E. Müller and A. Pilzecker, "Experimentelle Beiträge zur Lehre vom Gedächtniss," *Zsch. f. Psychol., Erg.-Bd.*, 1900, 1, chap. iii.

Independently of Müller, but at about the same time, an Austrian psychiatrist, Otto Gross, became interested in the same traits. What Müller had called "perseverative tendency" he designated "secondary function," and to the opposite trait of oscillation or vacillation, he gave the name of "primary function." [21]

Following closely in the steps of Gross, the Dutch psychologist, Heymans, worked for many years upon the same problem. The secondary function he characterizes as a "relatively constant complex of factors which brings unity and coherence into life, and in the case of inevitable changes is able, through its restraining power, to effect a gradual veering about in the place of sudden shifts. The secondary function, when highly exaggerated, leads to melancholia and paranoia. It is often the cause of sterile brooding, a reduced sense of reality and lack of presence of mind, as well as low adaptability. The primary function, on the other hand, is to be associated with superficiality and incoherence." [22]

Müller's term "perseveration" prevailed over the less descriptive term "secondary function," and initiated a bewildering series of experimental investigations. These have been more numerous than fruitful, concerned as they are with only simple sensory or motor performances, such as the persistence of after-images, resistance to color fusions, adaptation to light or darkness, speed of tapping, of cancellation, of drawing, or of word associations, and inertia in changing one's pattern of movement to fit new tasks. By correlating the scores obtained for the subjects in such diverse tasks as these, certain investigators decided that perseveration, or "p," is a self-consistent factor that may be scaled for a general population; but other investigators conclude precisely the opposite.[23]

On the basis of his own investigations Shevach suggests an explanation of these contrasting conclusions: only for certain subjects, notably for children and for naive subjects, does perseveration (as operationally defined by the sensory and motor tests) possess any functional unity. In all other subjects the phenomenon is largely specific to the single test.[24] Perseveration thus seems not to be a common enough trait to be profitably scaled, though for certain subjects it may be both consistent and significant.

In all this work the difficulty, it seems, lies in the nature of the tests

[21] O. Gross, *Die cerebrale Sekundärfunktion*, 1902. A good account of this subject is given by A. A. Roback, *The Psychology of Character*, 1927, pp. 245-248.

[22] G. Heymans, *Die Psychologie der Frauen*, 1910, pp. 54 f.

[23] The literature favoring "p" is summed up by C. Spearman, *The Abilities of Man*, 1927, 291-307. Typical negative studies are those of H. H. Jasper, *J. Soc. Psychol.*, 1931, 2, 28-51; and R. M. Dorcus, *J. Gen. Psychol.*, 1935, 13, 345-356.

[24] B. J. Shevach, *J. Psychol.*, 1936, 3, 381-402, 403-427.

employed which, of course, define the trait. They are too trivial to tap the developed volitional functions of personality. Adaptation to light or darkness, for example, is primarily a retinal characteristic and bears but a tenuous relation, if any at all, to personality. More to the point would be tasks involving the overcoming of obstacles, resistance to suggestion, long-time planning and carrying through of plans. Fernald's ingenious test for determining how long by voluntary effort an individual could or would stand on his toes is more pertinent though somewhat artificial. The choice lies between *voluntary* persistence and *involuntary* perseveration. The former is a significant if unpopular concept; the latter is popular enough among psychologists, but relatively trivial and not unequivocally established as a scalable dimension. There is, as Lankes points out, little resemblance between these two conceptions.[25] But since perseveration has led nowhere, persistence should be given experimentally a fair trial.

There is already some evidence that persistence and vacillation, considered as "habits of will," may be considered as scalable common traits. Howells, for example, finds that persistence at tasks in the face of physical discomfort is a consistent disposition that shows agreement with other measures of tenacity.[26] Clark has developed a reliable test of persistence at the school age, setting various tasks for the pupils with instructions to them "not to give up until you are *sure* you have done all you can." [27] For adults, Wang has standardized a test comprising 111 questions, each of which has one answer that has been determined to be diagnostic of positive persistence. Questions deal with the subject's liking to take responsibility, his ability to stay by a task until it is finished, his withstanding of criticism, and other such behavior. The reliability of this scale is reported to be .91.[28] This type of evidence certainly favors the admittance of persistence to our schedule of common traits.

The belabored concept of involuntary perseveration was the psychologist's timid, half-hearted gesture toward a troublesome but inescapable problem in personality. The concept of persistence is far bolder, and in the long run should prove sounder. If so, it will take care, partially at least, of the thorny problems of "will power" whose inclusion in any psychological schedule of personality is as necessary as it is vexatious.

[25] W. Lankes, *Brit. J. Psychol.*, 1915, 7, 387-419.
[26] T. H. Howells, *J. Abnorm. & Soc. Psychol.*, 1933, 28 14-29.
[27] W. H. Clark, *J. Educ. Psychol.*, 1935, 26, 604-610.
[28] C. K. A. Wang, *J. Soc. Psychol.*, 1932, 3, 79-90.

ATTITUDINAL TRAITS

The distinction between an attitude and a trait is indefinite especially when the object toward which the attitude is directed becomes highly generalized (cf. pp. 293 f.). In the case of the expressive traits just described there seems to be no limitation whatever in the object of reference; they are stylistic and pervasive in the personality. Other traits, however, approach more closely the category of attitudes; they are modes of adjustment through which the person orients himself to some specifiable aspect of his life-situation. *Extroversion*, for instance, though it clearly conforms to the criteria of trait, is at the same time a generalized (exceedingly generalized) attitude toward "reality." Similarly, *self-assurance* is manifestly a personal trait, but at the same time represents a general attitude of the individual toward his own competence. The distinction between attitude and trait is not one of fundamental importance, at least so far as the psychograph is concerned.

11. *Extroversion and Introversion*. Without a shadow of doubt psychologists in the past twenty years have had more interest in these traits than in any others. Vigorously criticized and many times repudiated, they remain firmly rooted in the psychologist's store of concepts, and have found their way into common speech. Probably neither the psychologist nor the layman can ever again do without them. Prior to Jung's establishment of these terms, it was common to speak of "objective mindedness" and "subjective mindedness"; also James' parallel concepts of "tough mindedness" and "tender mindedness" worked their way into speech. But it was Jung's terms with their transparent etymology that finally won the day.

According to Jung a man is extroverted (or *extra*verted) "when he gives his fundamental interest to the outer or objective world, and attributes an all important and essential value to it; he is introverted, on the contrary, when the objective world suffers a sort of depreciation, or want of consideration, for the sake of the exaltation of the individual himself." To define by instances:

Extroversion implies	*Introversion implies*
preference for participation in the world of objective (social) reality, and in practical affairs;	preference for the imaginal world, which is rich and creative;

Extroversion implies	*Introversion implies*
realism the keynote in work and in communications;	productions and expressions clouded with subjective feelings; polarization toward the Ego rather than the Alter;
affective life not finely shaded;	general delicacy of feelings;
spontaneous and natural expression in the emotional sphere;	tendency not to express emotions immediately, but to delay expression or to vary it in unusual ways;
disregard for failures, and resolution of conflicts in action;	little overt resolution of conflicts, but a tendency to interiorize them, and to react in fantasy;
absence of prolonged self-analysis and self-criticism;	a large amount of self-analysis and self-criticism;
relative independence of the opinion of others;	sensitiveness to criticism; experiences of personal import retained long in mind, especially those involving praise and blame;
freedom from ideas of reference;	"touchiness" and a tendency to take all things personally;
tough-mindedness and a pragmatic outlook.	tender-mindedness and an idealistic outlook.

The extrovert usually considers the introvert a sick soul; the introvert is often of the opinion that the extrovert is a Philistine and a bore.

Such a characterization as this is an instance of the employment of "ideal types." Only thoroughgoing cases are described. It was, indeed, Jung's initial hypothesis that he was advancing basic psychological types, but most psychologists have concluded that they are not ultimate types at all, but merely the extremes of some kind of continuous variable, normal in its distribution.

Many tests have been advanced to measure this variable, nearly all on the order of the standardized questionnaire.[29] In recent years these tests have been submitted to extended critical study, with the conclusion that although the variable can be scaled with moderate success, it is none the less too coarse (too inclusive) to be helpful in giving a discriminating picture of the person. This fate of Jung's epic dichotomy might have been foretold. A concept broad enough to

[29] For references to, and descriptions of, these scales see P. M. Symonds, *Psychological Diagnosis in Social Adjustment*, 1934, pp. 241-246.

categorize all attitudes toward objective and subjective reality is of necessity loose and vague. As often defined extroversion embraces ascendance, expansion, persistence, and many other common traits as well. A narrowing of the concept was inevitable.

Specifically, the Guilfords' factor analysis of items included in many tests for extroversion-introversion shows that quite independent clusters of responses may be involved.[30] In place of one variable, the Guilfords suggest that there are at least three; S (social extroversion) makes a consistent and meaningful common trait of the unitary order. People characteristically show the same response in various kinds of social groups, either an outgoing or a withdrawing tendency. Separable from this is the E variable which seems less concerned with social shyness than with diverse forms of *emotional* dependence. To have one's feelings easily hurt, for instance, seems related to inclinations toward worry, toward day-dreaming and moodiness. The third factor, M (masculinity-femininity), is a vague factor confused with the altogether irrelevant consideration of sex. As much as anything it is an empirical counterpart of the more orderly variable described previously as ascendance-submission. Neither this factor nor certain minor factors discovered by the authors need be retained. But the first two of the Guilfords' factors might well be adopted and put in the place of the single variable, extroversion-introversion, now appearing in the psychograph. It seems not only empirically sound, but psychologically intelligible, to speak of *social* extroversion-introversion and *emotional* extroversion-introversion as distinct variables. There is, however, still some question whether the ingredients of the E factor can clearly be interpreted as emotional introversion and emotional extroversion. Elaboration of this point is needed. For the time being, but only for the time being, the single variable, extroversion-introversion, for all its excessive breadth, may be left in the psychograph in the form in which it is still most commonly accepted.

12. *Self-objectification and Self-deception.* As we have already emphasized in Chapter VIII, insight and humor are especially important in the development of the mature personality. Good insight not only prevents a person from being deceived by his own rationalizations, but forces him to face objectively the weakness and strength of his personal equipment. The sense of humor was there shown to

[30] J. P. and R. B. Guilford, "Personality Factors S, E, and M, and their Measurement," *J. Psychol.,* 1936, 2, 109-127.

stand both theoretically and empirically in such close relation to insight that psychologically it is not profitable to distinguish between them. For this reason an inclusive designation, *self-objectification*, has been chosen for these twin variables.

In the doctrine of traits no psychological disposition in and of itself is intrinsically desirable or undesirable. There are so many successful *modi vivendi*, so many ways of living adaptively and of living creatively, that no one but an ethical dogmatist could declare one trait to be always good and another always bad. Perfectionistic morality espouses quite different traits than does hedonistic morality, and the golden mean of Aristotle requires different qualities than does the storm and stress ethics of Faust. Yet it is interesting to note that most ethical teaching since the time of Socrates gives special commendation to self-knowledge. An impartial and objective attitude toward oneself is held to be a primary virtue, basic to the development of all others. There is but a weak case for chronic self-deception with its crippling self-justifications and rationalizations that prevent adaptation and growth. And so it may be said that if any trait of personality is intrinsically desirable, it is the disposition and ability to see oneself in perspective.

The range of distribution for this attitudinal trait is very great. Some people have a remarkable objectivity in their views of themselves; some, the psychotics, are completely deluded and totally devoid of self-knowledge. Probably most people fall within the somewhat ambiguous average range; this in spite of the tendency to overestimate oneself in self-ratings on both insight and humor.

The chief difficulty in measuring this variable is the lack of a sure criterion for insight (cf. pp. 220-222). A practicable way out of the difficulty is to study the disparity between the subject's self-rating on various traits and the average ratings of his associates judging him on the same traits. Such a method at least tells whether he sees himself as others see him; it does not tell whether he knows himself as he "really" is. If, however, the judges are skilled, and if there are objective measures of the personality to substantiate their judgments, the method is as good as any that can at present be found.

A graphic technique for studying insight employs a profile such as is presented in this chapter. On it may be plotted first of all the subject's self-ratings for all the traits. Then, superimposed upon this profile will be another, prepared from the composite ratings of the judges or from scores on available tests. The deviations of the subject's self-estimations from the criterion may then be determined, and may, if desired, be compared with the deviations of other people in their self-ratings; in this way a comparable "insight index" may be computed for each subject within the experimental population.

13. *Self-assurance and Self-distrust*. It might seem at first thought that a person's self-confidence in any sphere of activity would depend entirely upon his experiences and demonstrated skill within that sphere, and that as a consequence there would be no such thing as a generalized trait of self-assurance or self-distrust. Attitudes of confidence or misgiving would be specific to each situation. Yet in ordinary life we say that this man, though able, lacks self-confidence, another is self-disparaging, and a third is too sure of himself; and we mean thereby to characterize the whole range of conduct regardless of the grade of skill and competence involved.

There is experimental evidence to support this habit of speech. In studying tendencies in self-rating, for example, Shen finds that people usually judge their abilities *consistently* as high, low, or average. "It thus seems that the constant tendency of self-estimate depends more upon the individual than upon the trait" (which he is judging in himself).[31] It may be recalled in this connection that individual differences of a similar type were found in the "level of aspiration" (p. 385). Some people set their goals characteristically above their abilities, and some set them below. Furthermore, there are certain pencil and paper tests that might be cited as measures (or partial measures) of self-assurance and self-distrust, all of them yielding fairly satisfactory indications of internal consistency, viz., Bernreuter's test for *self-sufficiency*, Pallister's scale for the *negative or withdrawal attitude*, and Heidbreder's scale for *feelings of inferiority*.[32]

14. *Gregariousness and Solitariness*. This variable, like the two succeeding, but unlike those thus far discussed, is exclusively social in its reference. Gregariousness means nothing more than the desire to be present in social groups; solitariness, aversion to them. There are other, quite separate, aspects of "sociability," *e.g.*, unselfishness and social intelligence, that are sometimes confused with gregariousness, but should, more properly, be treated separately.

[31] E. Shen, *J. Educ. Psychol.*, 1925, 16, 104-107.
[32] R. G. Bernreuter, *J. Abnorm. & Soc. Psychol.*, 1933, 28, 291-300; H. Pallister, *Arch. of Psychol.*, 1933, No. 151; E. Heidbreder, *J. Abnorm. & Soc. Psychol.*, 1930, 25, 62-74.

Gregariousness is so familiar a trait that it is often mistaken for an instinct. That it cannot be so should be apparent from the fact that many people may be found who paradoxically lack the "instinct," much preferring solitude to company. It is best to think of gregariousness, as well as solitariness, as examples of dynamic (motivational) traits. Some people cannot bear to stay alone; they have a constant hunger for company, and are markedly restive when deprived of it. Conversely, the hermit or quasi-hermit goes to great lengths to find solitude, and is uncomfortable when in the presence of people. Most people, of course, have both sets of desires, usually in rotation; when satiated with company they long for solitude; when satiated with solitude they grow lonely. But the relative incidence of one desire over the other seems a suitable measure for the variable in question.

An approach to measurement may be made through the use of the time budget (cf. p. 376). The amount of time a person spends voluntarily in the company of others, together with an account of his social memberships, the size of his correspondence, his range of information concerning contemporary social life (sports, popular music, current gossip, and the like) all provide clues to gregariousness. A few tentative scales built in part along these lines have been proposed.[33]

In spite of these beginnings it is not yet customary for psychologists to conceive gregariousness and solitariness as common traits of personality, perhaps because the concepts are too much encumbered with the traditions of instinct and "social forces." The names, however, can easily be changed, and should be changed if by so doing psychological research on this important variable can be encouraged.

15. *Altruism and Self-seeking.* At first sight these traits may seem out of place in a psychological schedule, for their flavor is unmistakably normative and characterial. Unfortunately there are no wholly neutral and unweighted trait-names for the qualities in question, unless one adopts the cumbersome phrases *socialization of behavior* and *non-socialization of behavior.* Even these characterizations, neutral and technical though they are, seem to refer to static stages in development rather than to active modes of adjustment, and are therefore poor names for traits. Altruism is an acceptable desig-

[33] Cf. J. Hsaia, "A Study of the Sociability of Elementary School Children," *Teach. Coll. Contrib. to Educ.,* 1928, No. 322; J. J. Stauter and L. M. Hunting, *J. Soc. Psychol.,* 1933, 4, 377-380; also A. R. Gilliland and R. S. Burke, *J. Appl. Psychol.,* 1926, 10, 315-326.

nation provided it is taken to refer merely to the verifiable fact that some people do consistently modify their conduct to accord with the interests of other people, introcepting whatever current standards in their cultural area are considered conducive to the "social good." Self-seeking (a term less ambiguous than "egotism") may likewise be used without evaluation. Individuals who have failed to introcept social standards into their own personalities seek only their own good, generally at the expense of the interests of others. They may be aggressively selfish, even supporting their behavior with pejorative rationalizations, or they may be simply thick-skinned, unaware of the interests of other people.

To think of altruism and self-seeking as traits of personality is but to throw new light on an ancient problem. No infant is socialized though some temperaments seem from the beginning to respond to the socializing influences of the environment more readily than others. But in any case the development of an altruistic disposition takes time. Between the fifth and seventh year there is ordinarily a marked increase in co-operative behavior and a growing awareness of the rights of others; the process is linked to age throughout childhood.[34] The rules of social intercourse are learned; sympathy, courtesy, generosity are socially encouraged. In maturity it is not unusual to find individuals who have so completely transformed their original self-seeking impulses that they live primarily for the welfare of others. They are so far socialized that their own interests demand first of all a consideration for the interests of their associates. The reverse of this process is the tenacious holding to the stage of infantile selfishness, though elaborating and varying its expressions with the passage of time. The selfish person may develop a socially approved mask and some useful pseudo-traits, but there is little authentic socialization in his attitudes or in his behavior.

The degree of socialization attained by children at various ages has been measured by tests of "social maturity," "moral judgment," or "ethical discrimination." There are likewise tests of honesty, helpfulness, and generosity often based on observations of the children in concrete life-situations.[35] For adults it is much more difficult to devise a scale that is subtle, not inviting false report. A pencil and

[34] Cf. S. Baley, "Research on Ethics and Aesthetics of Children in the Preschool Age," *Polish Arch. of Psychol.*, 1936; the work of the *Character Education Inquiry* likewise establishes this point.

[35] References may be found in Symond's bibliography, *op. cit.*, pp. 277-208.

paper test does not serve the purpose; it is too easy to simulate social-mindedness and to misconstrue one's own motives, especially when pretense and rationalization have become set through habit. Only through objective records of behavior or through competent ratings can a plotting for this variable be obtained.

16. *Social Intelligence.* A term virtually synonymous with social intelligence, and in some respects to be preferred, is *tact*—the ready power of appreciating and doing what is required by social circumstances. Other equivalent expressions are "social insight," and "susceptibility to social stimulation." Psychologists prefer "social intelligence," though by so doing they risk the false implication that it is a matter of native endowment, as is "abstract intelligence." If any trait depends at all upon experience and training, social intelligence does so. The skillful hostess, high in social intelligence, has *learned* how to make people feel at home, to anticipate their needs, to draw them out in conversation, and how to be present-minded when minor social catastrophes occur.

There is no doubt that social intelligence is a generalized trait. Entirely different types of behavior may be called for depending on circumstance, and a flexibility in shifting from one to the other is the very essence of the trait. In an American home a tactful gentleman chooses an uncomfortable sofa if by so doing he leaves the more comfortable chairs for the ladies; but in Germany he learns quickly to avoid the sofa, however uncomfortable, for it is the seat of honor reserved for elderly matrons. In America he escorts a lady on the side nearest the curb; in Europe he will walk on her left. In an Eskimo's home he will belch heartily to show appreciation of a satisfying dinner; on Beacon Hill he will not. Social intelligence is not a matter of performing one act on all occasions, but of varying (even reversing) behavior to accord with circumstances. For this reason it is absurd to regard social intelligence as a congeries of specific habits (cf. pp. 260-262).

The chief puzzle concerning this variable is the nature of *low* social intelligence; is it merely a deficiency or is it a positive mode of adjustment? It seems difficult to conceive of social obtuseness or tactlessness as an active disposition, unless it is prompted by social rebellion or by contradictory values more highly prized by the individual. Here is an example of the arbitrariness involved in the construction of any common variable. Either two opposed traits are ordered to a single continuum, resulting in an artificial but serviceable normal distribution; or else, as seems true in this case, as with the variables of physique, intelligence, and all value-traits—the variable represents *presence* or *absence* of some characteristic. For practical purposes of measurement it does not matter how the scale is constructed so long as it is empirically sound, but in the interests of theory it is well to keep this question of *what* is measured on the empirical scale constantly in mind.

Various ingenious methods have been suggested for measuring social intelligence, including tests of memory for names and faces, of ability to select the socially "proper" act from a series of alternatives, of information concerning social codes and popular beliefs.[36] None of these tests is as yet wholly satisfactory; but the variable may provisionally be included both because of a priori plausibility and because of certain initial evidence suggested by these scales. More precise delimitation of the variable will follow improved methods of measurement.[37]

The last five variables on the psychograph relate distinctly to motivational traits or interests. No psychograph would be complete without some dimensions to represent subjective values which are the core of the dynamics of behavior, and play so large a part in unifying the personality. It is not necessary, however, to accept precisely the variables here proposed. Others might be preferred, such for example, as the four major types of occupational interest that Thurstone has distinguished, *viz.*, interest in *science*, in *language*, in *people*, in *business*.[38]

The interests included in the present psychograph are five of the six "directions of striving" described by E. Spranger, and defined in detail in Chapter VIII. They can be measured with a single scale, and each neatly fits the normal curve of distribution.[39]

[36] A convenient review of all available methods is given by R. L. Thorndike and S. Stein, *Psychol. Bull.*, 1937, 34, 275-285. The charge frequently leveled at these tests, namely, that they correlate with measures of general (abstract) intelligence, is not altogether relevant. General intelligence must be *expected* to influence the formation of this trait, and a moderate overlap is not injurious to the conception of social intelligence here advanced.

[37] The *definition* not only of this variable but of any other in the psychograph is largely in terms of the technique (or operations) by which the variable is measured. This concession to operationism, however, does not mean that rational criteria can be altogether dispensed with. It is still necessary for a variable to conform to some logic of traits.

[38] L. L. Thurstone, *Psychol. Rev.*, 1931, 38, 406-427; *Person. J.*, 1931, 10, 198-205. Other dimensions of interest, together with scales, are discussed by D. Freyer, *Measurement of Interests*, 1931.

[39] P. E. Vernon and G. W. Allport, "A Test for Personal Values," *J. Abnorm. & Soc. Psychol.*, 1931, 26, 233-248; also H. Cantril and G. W. Allport, "Recent Applications of the Study of Values," same Journal, 1933, 28, 259-273.

17. *The Theoretical Interest*
18. *The Economic Interest*
19. *The Esthetic Interest*
20. *The Political (Power) Interest*
21. *The Religious Interest*

Excluded from this list is the social interest which is not adequately defined and hence not satisfactorily measured by the scale in question. It has also been omitted because of its conceptual overlap with two other dimensions in the psychograph, *viz.*, *gregariousness* and *altruism*.

Some writers have proposed the addition of a *vital* or *hedonistic* interest to this series, and if it can be established as a scalable trait, it might well be included.

THE INTERCORRELATION OF TRAITS

One question remains. What is the relation of the variables listed in the psychograph to one another? Are they independent, or do scores on one variable ordinarily correlate with scores on others? The latter situation generally prevails. To take a few examples: tests for ascendance ordinarily correlate to a certain extent with tests for extroversion (+.30 to +.40); ratings on strong emotionality with ratings on introversion to an even higher degree; one test for ascendance correlates with a test for religious interest, —.23; a test for introversion with a test for theoretical values, +.32; in one study intelligence is associated positively with theoretical interests, +.23, and negatively with economic interests, —.41. Tests of social intelligence are found ordinarily to correlate around +.40 with tests of abstract intelligence. In general, there is a slight tendency for scores above the median line to correlate positively, and for scores below the median line to correlate positively; or, in other words, for the profile to be consistently high or low.[40] This fact suggests that there is evidence for the existence of a "strong" and a "weak" pattern of personality.

Yet the average intercorrelations are not high, and there are various ways of accounting for the slight associations that they do show. In part they undoubtedly result from experimental errors. In tests

[40] Certain reversals, however, tend to occur, as between "high" scores on emotionality and "low" scores on the expressive traits and on extroversion. The positive relationships seem to hold most securely for the nine traits grouped on the psychograph between and including ascendance and social intelligence.

there is often a duplication of questions or situations resulting in a spurious positive correlation among the scores for separate traits; in ratings there is the notorious "halo effect" or general impression that colors uniformly the judgments of any one rater on the separate variables. Positive correlations may likewise be due in part to overlapping initial conceptions and definitions of the variables. Investigators do not try to keep wholly separate dimensions in mind (unless they are seeking non-overlapping factors). But even allowing for these spurious aspects of the correlations, there is a genuine neuropsychic cause for the overlap—a tendency on the part of subjects who develop one strong trait to develop others, partly because all traits within the individual develop from a primordial matrix of temperament, vitality, and intelligence, and partly because of the principle of integration that tends to form ever more inclusive traits. In general, however, the evidence for the existence of "strong" and "weak" types of personality is too slight to have predictive value for any individual case, and is certainly too slight to displace the more discriminating method of studying personality with the aid of separate variables.

The question arises whether it is desirable to re-define all the traits on the psychograph with the aid of some statistical procedure that will render them "unitary," *i.e.*, wholly independent of one another. Factor analysis could accomplish this end. In certain instances where an ill-conceived variable is found to be too loose and too comprehensive, aid from factor analysis in suggesting separate components would indeed improve matters (cf. the Guilfords' analysis of extroversion-introversion)—or, conversely, where there is a large positive correlation, and it seems wise to combine the separately conceived traits into a single variable (just as insight and humor have been combined under self-objectification). But in other instances of *moderate* overlap the empirical re-definition of traits does not seem to be desirable, for empirical variables (unitary traits) often lose in psychological intelligibility what they gain in independence. By preserving the common variables in the graph the logic of traits remains intact; whereas by constructing artificial (statistical) factors, the purely psychological considerations (derived from clinical, laboratory, and everyday experience) as well as the rational logic of traits, are surrendered.

This argument does not imply that the search for more satisfactory common variables should cease. On the contrary all of the dimensions advanced in this chapter are admittedly tentative. New tests, improvements in the old, rational and empirical criticism, and judicious use of statistical analysis, should in time be able to remove some of the roughness from the variables here discussed, and establish new and improved dimensions for the comparison of one personality with another. But this progress will not come about unless intelligibility of a dimension is prized more highly than its independence of other dimensions. Strict independence is neither a vital, nor even a reasonable, requirement for human traits.

COMMON TRAITS NOT INCLUDED IN THE PSYCHOGRAPH

Only those variables are included in the psychograph that have been submitted by psychologists to considerable rational and empirical study, and at the same time fit well the conception of common traits advanced in this volume; but many other variables that fulfill as well (or almost as well) these same criteria might be added. Though it would be too long a task to examine each of these in detail, a few deserve special mention.

Radicalism-Conservatism is an attitudinal variable widely discussed in contemporary psychological writing. A thoroughly radical person is one who would alter every social institution and every convention in ways never before tried; a thoroughly conservative man is one who would preserve the status quo and resist *all* new ways. Such extremes, of course, are not found. The objects and customs toward which the individual might be radically or conservatively disposed are so numerous, that it would be remarkable indeed to find perfect functional unity in these attitudes at any constant degree of intensity. It is entirely possible for a man to be radical in morals and conservative in politics, or radical in art and conservative in religion.

Yet evidence shows that these attitudes as a rule are by no means specific. There is, in fact, an almost embarrassing breadth and internal consistency to radicalism, as well as to conservatism. In one study, for example, people favoring a socialistic government, are also internationalists, pacifists, atypical in religious beliefs, and rebels in morals. But consistency does not stop here. They are also, by and large, fond of poetry; they secure higher than average grades in school and college, and are freer from prejudice and misinformation than are conservatives. Where does the trait of radicalism stop? It seems to go on into an unnamable blend of tender-mindedness, conscientiousness, humanitarianism, and pioneering. Radicalism seems too narrow and misleading a designation; perhaps T. L. Kelley's designation for this complex variable, "Puritania" would serve the purpose better. Conservatism too is usually a highly generalized trait. If it were not so why should the judicial personnel of the United States Supreme Court be a matter of so great concern? The consistency in the liberal or conservative outlook of the various justices, whatever the case, is truly amazing. Every pleader before the Supreme Court begins his argument with an unspoken assumption that nothing he can say will turn certain of the justices against his client or win others over to his side.

. Numerous scales show that radicalism and conservatism, broad as they are, can be reliably measured.[41] Hence the variable is widely accepted. Should it not then be included in the psychograph? The only basis for hesitation lies in the indefinite position it gives to certain related attitudes, e.g., to "liberalism" and "reactionism." A liberal is not merely a mild radical; in many respects he has a wholly different outlook. Nor is a reactionary merely an ultra-conservative, for he resembles the radical in many respects: he too favors change (albeit toward the old rather than the new); he too is discontented, and in some studies seems to be as excitable and maladjusted as the chronic radical. All in all, the variable is not yet quite clearly enough defined for the psychograph.

Neuroticism. Favoring the inclusion of the neurotic disposition in the psychograph is its familiarity as a psychological concept and the existence of widely used scales for its measurement. Yet the case for neuroticism as a common trait is far from complete.

Neuroticism is generally measured by some scale consisting of many items, in part borrowed from pre-existing tests of introversion and submission. Such a scale results in very broad definitions of the variable. According to Thurstone neuroticism is the "failure to express imagination effectively on social reality." [42] This is an omnibus conception of doubtful value necessitated by a scale with too wide a

[41] Cf. G. B. Vetter, *J. Abnorm. & Soc. Psychol.*, 1930, 25, 26-39, 149-189; G. W. Allport, *Amer. J. Sociol.*, 1929, 35, 220-238. Of several available tests for this variable one of the most satisfactory is the "opinionaire" of T. F. Lentz, *J. Soc. Psychol.*, 1934, 5, 338-365.

[42] L. L. and T. G. Thurstone, "A Neurotic Inventory," *J. Soc. Psychol.*, 1930, 1, 3-30. A shortened form of the Thurstone scale is offered by R. R. Willoughby, *J. Soc. Psychol.*, 1934, 5, 91-97.

variety of items. Its correlation with measures of introversion is fatally high, so high that it is impossible to consider it a separate variable. Eventually neuroticism may be shown to be indistinguishable from "emotional introversion." It is apparently not related to the Guilfords' factor of "*social* introversion." But this regrouping of traits will of necessity wait upon the findings of further studies both of neuroticism and of introversion.

Another difficulty with neuroticism as a scalable trait lies in its asymmetrical distribution, most people having few symptoms, and some a great many. There is also a troublesome sex difference in norms, women being more neurotic than men (according to scale).[43]

As a common variable, then, the neurotic disposition is neither well enough defined, nor normally enough distributed to qualify for admittance to the psychograph. Though it fails as a common variable, neuroticism is exceedingly important as an *individual* trait in any life where it is found, but only in the peculiar form in which it is found.

Suggestibility-Negativism. This variable has many times been studied, and various scales have been devised, but with only doubtful success.[44] When the problem was discussed in Chapter VI (p. 168), the conclusion was reached that suggestion may best be regarded as an *aspect of growth*, a mental function operative in every human being, the degree to which it is operative varying with each situation. In only a few people do we encounter a nature generally suggestible or generally negativistic, and these cases of consistency are too rare to justify the construction of a measurable dimension of personality.

Masculinity-Femininity. The extended work of Terman and Miles upon this variable is an excellent example of the empirical establishment of a common dimension of personality, culminating in a scale for measurement.[45] Two forms of a test with over 400 items each are available. Each item carries a weight of *one* in the scoring, and is marked (+) if symptomatic of "masculinity," and (−) if symptomatic of "femininity." The diagnostic significance of the items is determined by a comparison of the percentage of each reply secured from male and female groups. The test-items cover such

---

[43] Cf. R. R. Willoughby, *J. Soc. Psychol.*, 1934, 5, 2-36.

[44] Cf. M. Otis, *Arch. of Psychol.*, 1924, No. 70; G. and L. B. Murphy, *Experimental Social Psychology*, 1931, pp. 155-168.

[45] L. M. Terman and C. C. Miles. *Sex and Personality*, 1936.

varied spheres of behavior as word association, ink-blot association, information, interests, emotional and ethical attitudes, and responses to personalities and opinions. For example, to associate "engine" with "train" is a masculine response, whereas to associate "gown" with "train" is a feminine one; fear of thunder is a feminine characteristic, and liking for chemistry, masculine.

Most striking is the discovery in this scale that so many items yield a significant sex difference. (It has been usual in recent years for psychologists to minimize the mental differences between the sexes.) Given, however, a high degree of culture and education, Terman and Miles do find that the scores for men and for women are brought closer together. They find also that male homosexual prostitutes have markedly feminine scores, a fact that contributes evidence for the validity of the test.

This variable could be included in the psychograph, provided of course, that the individual's score is plotted in reference to the mean score for his *own* sex. Yet masculinity-femininity (like neuroticism) is another broad omnibus conception somewhat lacking in incisiveness. Detailed patterns are covered up by the scores for "total" masculinity and "total" femininity. For example, it would seem misleading to score a male as "feminine" simply because he has a marked interest in language and literature and not in science. *The only certain fact here is that this man has an interest in language and literature (not that he is feminine).*

The proper interpretation of such an empirical variable is all the more difficult since cultural expectations for men and for women vary so widely in different social groups. Not until a much narrower biologically-rooted criterion is evolved will it be safe to speak of masculinity-femininity as representing "one of a small number of cores around which the structure of personality gradually takes shape." In short, a better logic of this variable is desired before admitting it to the psychograph.

We can close this discussion with brief mention of a few other common traits, all of which are dimensions proposed by active investigators. Though in most cases several psychologists have worked upon each of these variables, only a single reference is here given. To some degree all of these variables fulfill the criteria laid down for the selection of common traits, but each seems to need further attention. In some cases it is a matter of improvement in definition or in scaling, and in some cases it seems that there is an unnecessary overlap with other, better conceived variables.

Ambition (F. Baumgarten, *Prak. Psychol.*, 1922, 3, 333-349.)

Annoyability (H. Cason, *J. Abnorm. & Soc. Psychol.*, 1930, 25, 224-236.)

Art Appreciation (T. F. Karwoski and E. O. Christensen, *J. Educ Psychol.*, 1926, 17, 187-194.)

Carefulness (T. Valentiner, *Zsch. f. päd. Psychol.*, 1931, 32, 263-274.)

Co-operation-Competition (J. B. Maller, *Teach. Coll. Contrib. to Educ.*, 1929, No. 384.)

Depression-Elation (H. H. Jasper, *J. Abnorm. & Soc. Psychol.*, 1930, 25, 307-318.)

Emotional Maturity (R. R. Willoughby, *J. Soc. Psychol.*, 1932, 3, 3-36.)

Fair-Mindedness (G. B. Watson, *Teach. Coll. Contrib. to Educ.*, 1925, No. 176.)

Happiness (temperament) (G. B. Watson, *J. Educ. Psychol.*, 1930, 21, 79-109.)

Honesty (H. Hartshorne, M. A. May, *Studies in Deceit*, Vol. I in *Studies in the Nature of Character*, 1928.)

Inferiority Feeling (R. B. Smith, *Arch. of Psychol.*, 1932, No. 144.)

Inhibition (H. Hartshorne, M. A. May, *Studies in Service and Self-control*, Vol. II in *Studies in the Nature of Character*, 1929, pp. 437-439, 450.)

International-mindedness (general attitude) (H. R. Harper, *What European and American Students Think of International Problems*, 1931.)

Militarism-Pacificism (general attitude) (D. D. Droba, *J. Educ. Psychol.*, 1931, 22, 96-141.)

Money-mindedness (general attitude) (F. K. Shuttleworth, *Sch. & Soc.*, 1924, 19, 679-682.)

Nervous Mannerisms (motility) (W. C. Olson, *Univ. Minn. Inst. Ch. Welfare, Monog.*, 1929, No. 3.)

Originality (intelligence) (L. M. Chassell, *J. Educ. Psychol.*, 1916, 7, 317-328.)

Punctuality (G. J. Dudycha, *Arch. of Psychol.*, 1936, No. 204.)

Racial Prejudice (general attitude) (E. S. Bogardus, *J. Appl. Sociol.*, 1925, 9, 299-308.)

Studiousness (A. C. Eurich, *J. Appl. Psychol.*, 1930, 14, 577-591.)

Superstitiousness (G. E. Lundeen and O. W. Caldwell, *J. Educ. Res.*, 1930, 22, 257-273.)

Susceptibility to Monotony (L. A. Thompson, *Pers. J.*, 1929, 8, 172-195.)

CHAPTER XVI

ANALYSIS BY RATINGS, TESTS, EXPERIMENTS

> Psychology, in fact, proceeds like all other sciences, by
> analysis. It resolves the self, which has been given to it at first
> in a simple intuition, into sensations, feelings, ideas, etc., which
> it studies separately. It substitutes, then, for the self a series of
> elements which form the facts of psychology. But are these
> *elements* really *parts?* That is the whole question, and it is be-
> cause it has been evaded that the problem of human person-
> ality has so often been stated in insoluble terms.
>
> —*Bergson*

"ANALYSIS" means to loosen or unbind. Through analysis knowledge of some complex phenomenon is sought by considering it *in detail*. Since there are many ways in which any phenomenon—particularly a psychological phenomenon—can be examined in detail, there
are correspondingly many possible levels of analysis. Each is legitimate and suitable for some purpose, though in the study of personality, as Bergson indicates, certain levels are greatly to be preferred
to others.

A level of analysis is desirable when it reveals something significant concerning personality. It does this best when it deals with what
Bergson calls "parts" of personality and not merely with artificial
dimensions arbitrarily chosen by the experimenter. Unless the constituent units themselves are meaningful the investigator cannot expect an intelligible picture of the sub-structures of personality, nor
one that is convincing when it is re-set for inspection in the framework of the personality as a whole.[1]

According to this course of reasoning the most desirable level of

[1] Cf. the statement of W. Köhler, "From the standpoint of Gestalt psychology
there is after all *one* analysis which is perfectly genuine, allowed, and productive
in all cases, the simple description of the field in terms of real units and sub-units,
as their real parts in terms of their boundaries, sub-boundaries, etc." *Ped. Sem.*,
1925, 32, p. 705. For a helpful discussion of the various forms of analysis employed
in psychological investigation see A. J. Harris, *Psychol. Rev.*, 1929, 36, 1-12.

analysis is reached when the *individual* traits and attitudes of each person are studied separately and in combination. This objective should, then, be the primary goal of research in personality. However, it need not be the only goal, for legitimate likewise is the comparative study of personalities which can be accomplished only through the employment of different units of analysis (common traits).

The preceding chapter (together with Chapter XI) has shown that while common traits do not conform to Bergson's demand that only true "parts" of personality be segregated for study, still they are not without their significance and value. Common traits are meaningful segments of conduct often reflecting cultural forms of adaptation. Though these segments are embedded in unique and noncomparable traits, still they may from a special point of view be segregated for comparative study. Though not true dispositions of the *person,* they are, in a sense, true dispositions of the *socius* (cf. p. 300).

In the study of personality three of the most widely used analytical techniques are *rating, testing,* and *experimenting.* As generally employed the first two methods are adapted only to the study of common traits. (They are the two chief aids in determining the scores that may be plotted on the psychograph described in the previous chapter.) The method of experimenting, on the other hand, is adapted either to the study of common traits or to the study of individual traits.

The following discussion of these three techniques has a triple purpose: (1) to record some of the outstanding facts that have emerged from their use in the course of recent investigations; (2) to bring to the front certain practical rules that make for the most fruitful use of these methods; (3) to illustrate the general principle that techniques are most productive when they are applied at truly significant levels of analysis, *viz.,* to common traits or to individual traits as defined in this volume, or else to clusters and patterns of such traits (meaningful and relational analysis).

PRINCIPLES OF RATING

Rating is a formal and articulate estimate of the strength of one or more qualities in a personality made upon the basis of direct acquaintance with that personality. Teachers, army officers, foremen, personnel directors, and social workers are among those who use ratings extensively for practical purposes. But it is also a method indispensable to psychologists who are forced, in spite of their distrust of subjective judgments, to rely time and again upon ratings as basic criteria in their investigations.

Ratings yield quantitative comparisons of different people in respect to one variable at a time. Of itself the rating method gives no consideration to the setting of the rated variable in the personal life. It is a tool for aspective analysis and comparison, nothing more. But in spite of its limitation the method of rating has its uses, and many years of experience have shown how to make the most of it. The following rules sum up the story fairly well.

1. *Variables must be clearly defined.* A rating scale whose variables are not understood by the judges or, even worse, are understood in different ways, is worthless.

What variables the investigator will use, of course, depends upon his specific purpose. There is virtually no limit to the range of possibilities, for it is a peculiarity of dimensional analysis that any *aspect* of personality may be separated from the whole and viewed comparatively in a population according to the whims of the investigator. For purely practical purposes (hiring, firing, promoting, demoting) a schedule of "characterial" variables may be chosen, such biosocial dimensions as "personal charm," "leadership," "citizenship," "value to the business," and the like. But for the purposes of a strictly psychological analysis, a more orderly theory of the structure of personality is necessary, together with a guiding logic of common traits.

In defining variables for the raters it is possible (a) to give synonymous terms, (b) to describe in a general way the kind of behavior to which the variable pertains, (c) to give specific instances of its operation in overt conduct. In the preceding chapter a number of ratable variables were defined, usually with the aid of all three of these types of definition. Needless to say, it is a good plan to discuss the rating scale orally with the judges and to make sure in conversation that all have in mind precisely the same dimension for their judgment.

2. *There are two basic types of rating scales.* Of these the *scoring* scale is the more common. Here the subject is rated without direct comparison with other people in his immediate circle. To be sure, scoring, like any other quantitative judgment, requires *some* frame of reference in the rater's mind; but generally a somewhat vague

reference to the "general population" suffices. To put his judgment upon a scale the rater uses whatever units are prescribed. It may be a percentage score (which, however, requires such fine discriminations that he tends to rate only at round numbers, *e.g.*, 60%, 70%, or 80%). Or it may be a coarse scale in which only two intervals are employed, signifying merely the presence or absence of the trait. (The check-list of descriptive terms is essentially a two-interval scoring scale: a term checked signifying the presence of the trait.) More often some *odd* number of intervals is prescribed—five, seven, and nine being popular—probably for the reason that it is easier with odd numbers to express a judgment of "average."

In the *graphic* rating scale (a variant of the scoring scale), the judge makes as fine a discrimination as he chooses, placing a mark upon a straight line anywhere he wishes between the extreme of low and high. By this method the number of distinguishable intervals is theoretically infinite. In practice, however, since the graphic scale is more finely graduated than is warranted by its accuracy, it is always reconverted by the investigator into arithmetical or statistical units of some kind.

Studying the question of the relative reliability of scoring scales using few and many intervals, Symonds concludes that the optimum number of degrees is *seven*. Rating with a scale of more than this number of classes demands a grade of discrimination that does not yield a material increase in reliability. Rating with fewer intervals, on the other hand, suffers from a loss of reliability because of the coarseness of grouping.[2]

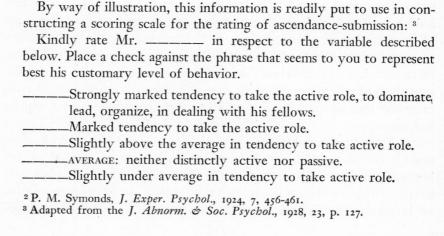

By way of illustration, this information is readily put to use in constructing a scoring scale for the rating of ascendance-submission: [3]

Kindly rate Mr. ———— in respect to the variable described below. Place a check against the phrase that seems to you to represent best his customary level of behavior.

————Strongly marked tendency to take the active role, to dominate, lead, organize, in dealing with his fellows.

————Marked tendency to take the active role.

————Slightly above the average in tendency to take active role.

————AVERAGE: neither distinctly active nor passive.

————Slightly under average in tendency to take active role.

[2] P. M. Symonds, *J. Exper. Psychol.*, 1924, 7, 456-461.
[3] Adapted from the *J. Abnorm. & Soc. Psychol.*, 1928, 23, p. 127.

_____Tendency to be passive in contact with his fellows, to be led rather than to be the leader.

_____Strongly marked tendency to be passive in contacts.

Remember: It is not necessary to give a "high" rating in order to compliment the friend whom you are judging. There is nothing intrinsically desirable about this variable. Excellent personalities stand below the average as frequently as above the average. You are not judging the general merit of your friend's personality, but simply one aspect of it for purposes of scientific research. So, BE OBJECTIVE IN THE RATING.

The rater checks the interval he selects; whereupon the investigator transmutes these checks into scores. Convenient in this case is a series of seven intervals, $+3$ to -3, with zero standing for a rating of "average." Note the investigator's concluding warning to the rater, an attempt to diminish the familiar "halo effect" in rating (cf. pp. 446 f.).

The *ranking* scale is used only when a whole group of associated individuals are to be rated in relation to one another. The judge places their names in serial order in respect to their status for a given variable. In such a scale there are no true arithmetical units, since it is impossible to demonstrate that the intervals between successive individuals in the rank-order are equidistant. If the distances *were* equal there would then be a rectangular rather than "normal" distribution of the variable, a most unusual situation. It is for these reasons that all ordinary statistical computations based upon rank-orders are precarious, though they are sometimes mistakenly attempted.

The usefulness of the ranking method is limited to such investigations as from start to finish employ one single group of subjects, and require no units other than the serial positions of these subjects. Whenever the method is applicable, it has the merit of being more concrete than a scoring scale. Each subject can be compared with every other subject before his final position is determined. Such tangible comparisons are sometimes thought to be more accurate than the "solitary" method of scoring. But whether or not this is so depends to a considerable extent upon the number of individuals included in the comparisons. The fewer the better. It is almost impossible to rank more than a score of people unless many ties are permitted. Extreme cases are likely to be reliably ranked, but the more moderate individuals receive their ranks almost by guesswork.

It is possible to combine the methods of scoring and ranking.

The man-to-man comparison scale used in the U. S. Army is such a scale. The rater assigns scores on a five-point scale, but in order to arrive at these scores he makes a concrete comparison between the subject he is rating and the five "scale men" selected as representing the variable in question, one at each of the intervals of the scale.[4]

3. *Judges require training.* To employ the method of rating most advantageously it is necessary to have three sharp implements: a well-defined and clear-cut schedule of variables, a proper scale with intervals neither too coarse nor too fine, and judges who are as talented and as well-trained as possible. Unless these three conditions are optimum it is not possible to obtain truly satisfactory ratings. The first two have already been discussed.

Judges differ greatly in ability, but whatever their inherent skill, to do his best each judge requires (a) instruction concerning the nature of the variables, (b) instruction concerning the intervals used, together with a warning not to place his ratings within too narrow a range, but to make free use of the scale, (c) instruction to make each rating a fresh and independent judgment unprejudiced by pre-ceding judgments. He also requires (d) adequate acquaintance with the subjects, (e) broad enough experience with people at large to provide a suitable range of reference for his judgments, and (f) suffi-cient time, patience, and incentive to work carefully and honestly.

4. *The reliability of ratings depends upon the extent of agree-ment among the judges.* Since it is seldom possible to decide which judge is "right" when judges disagree as to the score or rank of a given subject, the mean of all the judgments is ordinarily taken to represent the nearest approximation to the subject's true position. Yet if the judges have disagreed seriously with one another this mean position may be entirely worthless. (Thus if two judges rate a subject as $+3$ on a seven point scale, and two judges rate him -3, the averaged rating of o would be absurd, for whatever the subject may be he is manifestly *not* average.) Therefore, before using the mean rating of a subject as his true rating it is necessary to determine the extent of the judges' agreement. It is clear that if the mean variation (or average error) of the judges' ranks from the mean of their ranks is small, the judges have agreed with one another closely. On the contrary, a high mean variation (or any other measure of dispersion)

---

[4] For a more detailed description of this and other special varieties of scales see P. M. Symonds, *Diagnosing Personality and Conduct*, 1931, chap. iii.

points to confusion in the minds of the judges, or perhaps to contra-
dictoriness in the behavior of the subject—in any event to the unreliability of the ratings.

For example, eighteen judges, all well acquainted with one another,
spent five hours in ranking each other upon a set of common variables.
The mean variations for the variables were as follows:

Ascendance	2.88
Expansion	2.96
Social adaptability	3.02
Intelligence	3.07
Conceit	3.17
Selfishness	3.27
Conservatism	3.38
Emotional strength	3.51
Extroversion	3.60
Emotional breadth	3.66
Insight	3.75

The judges thus agreed with one another best in the cases of ascendance and expansion (the most reliably rated of the traits), and
least in the cases of emotional breadth and insight (the least reliably
rated traits). It is always a somewhat arbitrary act to set the degree
of agreement below which ratings are regarded as wholly unreliable
and undependable, though it is generally held by statisticians that before any reliance is placed in the composite rating, the agreement
should be at least three or four times that which might be obtained
by chance.

By the same method it is possible to determine for which subjects
there is most disagreement among the judges (the most "enigmatic"
and least reliably rated); for which subjects there is best agreement
(the most "open" and most reliably rated); also to determine which
judge deviates most widely from the mean in his ratings (presumably the least efficient judge), and which judge most closely approxi-
mates the mean (presumably the most efficient judge). By invoking
somewhat more elaborate statistical aids this method of studying reliability through agreement can be greatly extended, but it is enough
for present purposes to have the rudiments of the method in mind.[5]

[5] The reliability of ratings may likewise be studied in a variety of other ways,
such as repeating judgments after an interval of time, determining the agreement
between judges' ratings and self-judgment, correlations between the order of rankings
made by two or more judges, and the like. Discussions of these methods are given

5. *Variables that are overt in expression are more reliably rated than variables that are covert.* All investigators agree that the more objective a variable is, the better the agreement. Agreement is especially good when a variable can be judged on the basis of past and present accomplishment known to all the judges. In other words, behavior that leaves its mark, or influences external events, contributes greatly to agreement in rating. A safe generalization seems to be that variables pertaining to self-expression and to social behavior are among the most reliably rated, whereas variables pertaining to inner life and attitudes toward self are much less dependable.

In addition to the overtness with which a trait is expressed, Spielman and Burt find that actively *emotional* and *socially acceptable* qualities can be reliably rated (anti-social tendencies being masked by the subjects).[6] Especially good agreement was found for submissiveness, fear, assertiveness, sociability, self-confidence, energy and general emotionality; poor agreement for curiosity, acquisitiveness, and reliability. Wolf and Murray agree that variables involving emotion are reliably rated, provided the situations on which the observations are based afford suitable opportunity for emotional expression, and provided the variables are adequately defined and understood.[7] Specifically, these investigators find best agreement among clinical raters for *aggression, anxiety, impulsion, general emotionality*.

6. *The subjective certainty of the judges is an indication of the reliability of their ratings.* If judges are asked to indicate in conjunction with each rating the degree of certainty with which they have made the rating, it is found that judgments recorded with confidence are the most reliable. This is a well established fact upon which virtually all investigators agree.

As a rule, judges are most confident and most likely to agree on their extreme ratings. To interpret this fact it is necessary to refer

by P. M. Symonds, *op. cit.*, pp. 93-96; E. Shen, *J. Educ. Psychol.*, 1926, 16, 232-236; J. P. Guilford, *Psychometric Methods*, 1936, chap. ix.

Yet by none of these methods is perfect reliability to be expected. Each judge sees the subject in a different light, and each is fallible in his own way. "A reliability coefficient of .55 can be said to be typical for rating personality traits by ordinary judgment methods. Some traits yield higher reliability coefficients, others lower. It is easy to fall short of even this average figure of .55 if the raters are careless, if the traits are loosely defined, if acquaintance with those being rated is slight, or if there has been inadequate observation." (Symonds, *op. cit.*, p. 95).

[6] W. Spielman, and C. Burt, Industrial Fatigue Research Board, London, *Report No. 33*, 1926, pp. 57-72.

[7] R. Wolf and H. A. Murray, *J. Psychol.*, 1936, 3, 345-365.

again to the underlying theoretical weakness of all common traits. These variables are uniform and categorical, forcibly imposed upon the experimental population. It is no wonder that to a large number of persons, often to the majority, the variables simply do not apply. Only the extreme cases possess traits closely resembling the variable in question. All the other cases fall in the range of the meaningless mean. Whenever a variable is ill-adapted to a case, the judges are uncertain of their ratings.

7. *Some persons are more reliably rated than others.* There are "open" personalities about whom all judges agree exceptionally well; there are "enigmatic" personalities about whom they agree hardly at all. Who are these people? In one study (unpublished) eighteen subjects were arranged in rank order on the basis of the judges' agreement on all ratings. The relation of this rank order to the ratings for various traits was then studied. The only correlations of any interest were the following:

> Openness-Extroversion .... .61
> Openness-Social Adaptability .... .44
> Openness-Ascendance .... .29
> Openness-Expansion .... .24

The first coefficient suggests that the introverted person (who has a rich inner life) is the hardest person to agree upon; he is the most enigmatic. Grouping the four coefficients, it seems that open personalities have a "strong" pattern of traits (as defined in the preceding chapter) and that enigmatic personalities have a "weak" pattern.

A rather subtle problem here suggests itself. We find three variable factors contributing to the reliability of ratings, (a) the overtness or covertness of the variable rated, (b) the inherent skill of the judge, (c) the open or enigmatic quality of the subject himself. Which of these factors is the most important? In other words, to obtain valid ratings, is it more necessary to have overt traits, gifted judges, or open personalities? The problem has not yet been solved, but one experiment, described on pp. 507-509 indicates that under ordinary conditions of rating, the skill of the judge is the most important factor; then comes the nature of the variable; and finally the open or enigmatic character of the subject.

8. *Judges rate best those who are most like themselves.* It has often been shown that positive correlations exist between the posses-

sion of a trait in high degree and ability to judge it in others.[8] Commenting on their own finding that judges rate best those whom they resemble most, and rate poorly those whom they least resemble, Wolf and Murray write: "The best explanation seems to be the common one: that a man can only understand what he has already experienced. One might hazard the statement that without empathy a man cannot make an accurate diagnosis and he can best empathize with those whose responses resemble his own." [9] That this finding has important theoretical consequences will be shown in Chapter XIX.

9. *In self-rating there is a tendency to overestimate those qualities considered desirable and to underestimate those considered undesirable.* Subjects judge themselves especially possessed of certain qualities thought necessary for social success.[10] At least this overestimation is true for most self-judgments in our American culture, where self-assurance is so common a characteristic. For Chinese students, however, even for those studying in America, the reverse tendency holds. They underestimate themselves in desirable traits.[11]

But qualities not so desirable also show consistent over-estimation. In one self-rating study (unpublished) thirteen variables were persistently over-rated:

> Ascendance
> Emotional Breadth
> Emotional Strength
> Esthetic Appreciation
> Expansion
> Gregariousness
> Humor
> Insight
> Intelligence
> Introversion
> Radicalism
> Social Adaptability
> Unselfishness

[8] An early study to reach this conclusion is that of L. C. Cogan, A. M. Conklin, and H. L. Hollingworth, *Sch. & Soc.*, 1915, 2, 171-179. (The finding certainly holds so far as socially acceptable qualities are concerned. Whether the possession of anti-social tendencies makes one a better judge of the same tendencies in others is not so clear.)

[9] R. Wolf and H. A. Murray, *op. cit.*, p. 358.

[10] Cf. Cogan, Conklin, and Hollingworth, *loc. cit.*

[11] W. C. Trow and A. S. T. Pu, *Sch. & Soc.*, 1927, 26, 213-216.

To be sure, several of these characteristics are highly prized as socially desirable in our culture. But not all of them. In fact, radicalism, introversion, and emotionality are, if anything, obstacles to social success. Yet, in a sense, high self-ratings on introversion and emotionality may also be taken as a subtle form of self-flattery. By judging themselves high in these qualities most people imply thereby that their own inner lives are richer and more interesting than those of their fellows. But self-flattery aside, it is also true that each person *knows* his private desires, frustrations and turmoil at first hand, whereas his knowledge of others' is not only second-hand but comes through the veil of social taboo whose chief function is to dampen emotional expression.

Interesting likewise is the case of high self-rating on radicalism. Outwardly the subjects are conformists, else the ratings by associates would give evidence to the contrary, but inwardly the rebellion is strong. Each rater feels himself opposed to social restraints while he regards others as accepting and supporting them. In a sense each person is a potential revolutionist. That is to say, he is several shades less conventional than he appears to be, and consciously regards himself as more radical than the rank and file of his associates. What holds him in check is, in part at least, his mistaken impression that most of his associates are solidly conservative. Social upheavals are no doubt due in part to the sudden discovery by a large number of people that others (however staid their outward manner) have been thinking in private the same rebellious thoughts.

10. *In general, ratings are complimentary.* Unless prevented from so doing a judge is likely to give over-generous ratings. He assigns superior scores to too large a proportion of the subjects. Sometimes he does not use the "lower" end of the scale at all. This happens, however, only when he thinks of the high point in the scale as a *desirable* point. And it happens only in scoring scales, for a rank-order scale demands that the lower positions be occupied as well as the upper. The rater feels less guilty in giving unfavorable ranks than in giving unfavorable scores, for nothing is implied in a ranking scale concerning the *absolute* level of the rating. Even a choir of angels may have its least favored member.

The fallacy of generosity is found especially in the rating of friends.[12] It extends in marked degree also to the rating of members of one's own professional group, one's fraternal associates, and one's

[12] E. Shen, *J. Appl. Psychol.*, 1925, 9, 66-68.

own sex. That is to say, compliments are paid to those belonging to "in-groups" more readily than to those belonging to "out-groups."

Just why there should be so much generosity in rating is an interesting question. In the case of friendships and in-groups the explanation may readily enough be found in the phenomena of identification and self-esteem. But why are we as raters likewise well-disposed toward non-intimate associates? Is it fear of doing them an injustice, an application of the Golden Rule, or is it some peculiar type of "space error" that makes us cluster our ratings toward an attractive pole in the scale? Or shall we lay it to the American habit of boosting and outlook of optimism? There are a few judges who assign a preponderance of adverse scores: perhaps an over-correction for a tendency to rate too high, or perhaps a misanthropic outlook on mankind. In any case, both the judge who flatters and the judge who depreciates, themselves deserve to be studied as problems of personality.

To reduce the systematic error of flattery the experimenter may (a) prescribe the number of subjects who must be assigned to each interval in the scale, to the low degrees as well as to the high; (b) allow the judge to use any range he chooses but transmute his ratings into some standard scores in relation to the mean of the judge's own ratings, thereby correcting for his systematic prejudice; (c) use variables that are not evaluative but entirely neutral, so that flattery is impossible. It is peculiarly difficult, however, to follow this third road, for the judge reads merit and demerit into almost any trait according to the bias he has acquired from his culture, or according to some particular prejudice of his own; thus he confounds his ratings with censure.

11. *The "halo effect" prevents the giving of strictly independent judgments on the separate variables.* Rugg in his discussion of the U. S. Army Rating Scale defines the halo effect as follows: "We rate or judge our fellows in terms of a general mental attitude toward them"; and, "there is dominating this mental attitude toward the personality as a whole a like mental attitude toward particular qualities." [13] The general impression thus influences any one specific judgment; and in turn some impressive specific observation may be the source of the general impression. For example, a superficial physical attribute, such as a slight deformity may set up a "halo" and may

[13] H. O. Rugg, *J. Educ. Psychol.*, 1922, 13, p. 37.

color the judgment of all the psychological traits, even to the extent of rendering them quite worthless.[14]

The halo effect appears with monotonous uniformity in nearly all studies of ratings, and its magnitude is often surprisingly great. The judge seems intent on reporting his final opinion of the strength, weakness, merit, or demerit of the personality as a whole, rather than on giving as discriminating a rating as possible for each separate characteristic. Whenever the variables have moral connotation the halo effect is larger, for it is a striking fact that a general attitude of approval or disapproval toward the subject colors every single judgment concerning his single vices and virtues. The halo effect is also large when any single variable is not easily observed in action or when it is ill-defined; in such cases the judge substitutes his general impression for the variable that he cannot rate directly.

The halo has considerable theoretical significance. Its existence is proof positive that in perceiving and reflecting upon a personality we rapidly structure our impressions into a self-consistent totality. The structuring is far more rigid and coherent than it should be. Though it dulls our discriminative capacity it demonstrates for us one of the essential characteristics of intuitive knowledge, namely, its tendency toward totalized structures (cf. Chapter XIX).

Though impossible to eradicate completely, there are many ways to diminish the halo effect, viz., (a) by specific warning against it, (b) by employing distinctive and well-defined variables, (c) by using alert and trained judges, (d) by avoiding characterial and censorial variables, (e) by so varying the presentation of the qualities to be rated that a fresh and independent consideration of each is demanded, (f) by avoiding haste and perfunctoriness in making the ratings, and (g) by averaging together the ratings of several judges so that to some degree the prejudices of the several judges will cancel one another.

In conclusion it should be said that for all its inherent limitations the method of rating is of permanent value. Of all the techniques of analysis it is the easiest to employ. It is likewise the most venerable, for comparative judgments of individuals are as ancient as human society, and will presumably endure as long. The contribution of psychology lies in the critical development of improved rating scales based upon the principles here described. Nor are the improvements yet at an end.

[14] Cf. C. Landis, J. Pers. Res., 1925, 4, 7-19.

PRINCIPLES OF TESTING

Boring has defined a *mental test* as "an abbreviated experiment upon an individual in which his behavior is observed in order to determine his capacity with respect to some biological use." The definition serves for the field of personality testing provided the crucial concept of "biological use" is understood somewhat broadly. It is not necessarily mere success at biological adaptation that a test of personality intends to measure; it may be some mode of self-expression, some social attitude, or some private aspiration. Like any mental test a test of personality is a brief standard experiment designed to measure capacity, but the capacity in question is *disposition* rather than mere biological *ability*.

Tests of personality, as explained on pp. 380 f., are of two types: *standardized questionnaires* (pencil and paper tests) and *behavioral scales* (performance tests). Since both alike are psychological experiments the basic principles of experimental analysis should apply to their construction and use. Behavioral scales are ordinarily specialized in their content (*e.g.*, word-association, inkblot interpretation, behavior in some miniature situation). Their greatest danger is that unsafe generalizations will be made on the basis of too specific a type of conduct (the fallacy of monosymptomatic diagnosis). A certain character analyst was in the habit of pausing during his interview with a client to attempt to sell him a book. If the client resisted, the diagnosis was "stubborn"; if he yielded, "compliant." An abbreviated experiment, to be sure, but a poor one since one instance of behavior fails to demonstrate trait consistency. A *battery* of behavioral tests should always be used rather than one alone.

Though less objective than behavioral scales, standardized questionnaires have the merit of sampling a much wider range of behavior, through the medium of the subject's report on his customary conduct or attitudes in a wide variety of situations. These pencil and paper tests are popular for a number of reasons. For one thing they are fun to construct and fun to take. Students find them diverting, and teachers accordingly use them as agreeable classroom demonstrations. Furthermore, the scores on the tests can be manipulated in diverse ways, and when the quantitative yield of coefficients and group differences is complete, everyone has a comforting assurance concerning the "scientific" status of personality.

But are the tests of any more solid value? Do they give true aid in understanding personality, do they represent any improvement over the more venerable methods of the interview, the letter of application, or rating? Are they a modern aid to educators, employers, mental hygienists? The answer is only partially affirmative. When employed cautiously, the better scales probably justify themselves both theoretically and practically in much the same way as psychometric scales for measuring intelligence have done. But they have certain inherent limitations.

One of these is that the items in any test have to be standardized according to their average significance for people at large. The stimulus-situation is assumed to be identical for each subject, and his response is assumed to have constant significance. A test will assume, for example—and with some justification in terms of statistical probability—that a person who conspicuously takes a front seat at church or at an entertainment should as a rule receive a plus score for ascendance. But the fact of the matter is that this person *may* seek a front seat not because he is ascendant but because he is hard of hearing. Or a test will assume again, with statistical (empirical) justification, that a person who confesses to keeping a diary is introverted; yet upon closer inspection (which no test can give) it may turn out that the diary is almost wholly an expense account, kept not because of introversion but because of money-mindedness. It is a fallacy to assume that all people have the same psychological reasons for their similar responses. At the level of personality it can not be said with certainty that the same symptoms in two people indicate the same trait, nor that different responses necessarily indicate different traits. All mental tests fail to allow sufficiently for an individual interpretation of cause and effect sequences.

The only possible answer to this objection against tests is the one given by Binet, "Let the items be crude if only there be enough of them." One hopes through sheer length of a series that the erroneous diagnoses will to a certain extent cancel one another, and that a trustworthy residual score will remain. But even this assumption is so hazardous that it is necessary to admit once and for all that test scores are at best coarse approximations, and should not be given over-precise interpretation, nor elaborated unduly through statistics.

A related limitation is the fact that in testing common traits attention is necessarily diverted from the individual subject to his mere rank within the total population. The variable is unchanging, and to it all subjects are categorically ordered. It does no good for the critic to protest that the natural lines of cleavage in personality do not follow the lines of the assumed common trait. In testing, everyone must receive a score whether or not the variable applies to him. It is no wonder that the score that emerges from this machine-like process often bears only a faint resemblance to the person for whom it was obtained. The reply to this objection is that high reliability in a scale is *ipso facto* demonstration that by and large subjects do reply in consistent ways to the test, standing at a constant level for most of the items contained in the test. Yet reliabilities are never so perfect as to guarantee that every single individual is appropriately tested by the scale.

Another severe criticism lies in the ability of the subject to fake the test if he chooses to do so. In this respect tests of personality are at a disadvantage compared with tests of intelligence. Anyone by trying can (on paper) simulate introversion, conservatism, or even happiness. And if he thinks he has something to gain he is quite likely to do so. It is for this reason above all others that the practical use of scales in personnel work is limited. Many people, especially the young or suggestible, will give the replies they think are desired or expected. Prisoners, ever suspicious of the motives of the "psycho," often give untrustworthy replies. Even well-intentioned subjects may fail in insight or slip into some systematic error or bias that vitiates the value of their answers.

To reduce these hazards, scales are usually given a misleading title that veils their true purpose from the subject; or irrelevant questions ("jokers") may be introduced to throw the subject off guard. A few scales are so elaborately disguised that their basis of scoring lies entirely beyond the subject's power of comprehension or control. But these deceptions often interfere with the validity of a test, and on the whole work much better with children or stupid people than they do with alert adults for whom the tests are usually designed.

Much better than reliance on deceptive tricks is a straightforward effort to secure honest and unstinted co-operation from the subjects. Over-much talk about the nature of the scale before it is used will set up prejudicial attitudes, but without biasing the subject it is usually possible to motivate him to give his honest effort to the experiment. Also it is usually necessary to assure him that the outcome will not be to his disadvantage. (It is because this assurance cannot be given in cases where hiring, firing, or promotion depends upon the results of the test, that scales are of limited value in personnel work.)

The experimenter may use a number of incentives in securing the co-operation of the subject.[15] He may pay him for his services or, if the subject is a student, may give him credit as for any other type of class exercise. This economic incentive secures a *quid pro quo* in respect to the time and attention devoted to the test, but does not guarantee wholly honest or conscientious responses. It is far better to take the subject into the game by a promise to make the results of the test available to him. People are seldom unwilling to talk frankly about themselves if some such incentive is skillfully presented. Other excellent incentives are the subject's interest in the material of the test and his desire to see how objectively he can report his own behavior, or his genuine concern for the success of the experiment as a scientific undertaking. As a rule college classes or comparable groups are most easily motivated, and at the same time have the greatest capacity for self-objectification. They make the best subjects. But even in these select groups it is necessary to avoid, excepting under unusual conditions of rapport, questions that are too intimate or impertinent. Questions pertaining to sexual behavior or anti-social conduct are under too strong a taboo to be included in any general test. Investigations in these areas of conduct must be undertaken by entirely different methods of study. Relative to this matter of approachability, interesting cultural differences occur; different nations and social groups differ markedly in their reticence and in their readiness to resent or accept personal questions.

The three major limitations of testing then are (a) the categorical ordering of all subjects to the same variable; (b) the fixed interpretation of each response in terms of its average (empirical) significance for the variable in question; (c) the necessity for co-operative and competent subjects in order to use the test at all. In addition there are many mechanical weaknesses in current tests, but by constructing them according to the following principles these weaknesses can be markedly reduced.

1. *The variables must have psychological significance.* That is to say, the variables should be drawn from significant levels of mental organization. They must not be so broad as to be vague and intangible, nor so narrow as to be unmeaningful or trivial. Let the logic of

[15] Cf. P. E. Vernon, *J. Appl. Psychol.*, 1934, 18, 165-177.

common traits prevail throughout. Furthermore, every item in the scale should be significantly related to the chosen variable, thus contributing in an intelligible way to its definition.

2. *The scale must have a rational construction throughout.* Not only should the variables and the items be psychologically significant, but the alternative replies permitted to the subject should always bear a reasonable relation to the trait. In the following item, for example, it is impossible to interpret an encircled question mark.

> Have you ever seen a vision? YES NO ?

Does it mean that the subject is not certain whether he has had a vision, or does it mean that the definition of "vision" in this question is unclear to him? And what if he encircles the question mark in the following item?

> Do you often become discouraged? YES NO ?

Does he mean that he does not know whether his state of mind would be called discouragement? Or does he mean that he is unable to decide what the investigator means by "often" (certainly a reasonable query)? A question mark is too ambiguous. Statistical measures of internal consistency may show that those who encircle the question marks in these cases are by and large to be suspected of neuroticism. But sheer empiricism can never make clear what is inherently ambiguous.

Even the most carefully worded items and alternatives occasionally give the subject difficulty. For this reason the subject should be allowed to omit questions that are unclear, or that are for some other reason unanswerable. This also helps to eliminate worthless scores, and spares the subject a feeling of irritation that may prejudice him against the entire scale.

A finely graded series of alternatives (multiple choices) is preferable to categorical replies Yes or No, partly because the diagnostic weights can be more varied, and partly because any subject hesitates to commit himself to an all-or-none answer.

3. *Items must be diagnostic.* Important as it is for the experimenter to show a meaningful relationship between every item, every alternative, and the purpose of the scale as a whole, he cannot determine on a priori grounds alone the trustworthiness of any single item. Especially is he unable to assign out of hand diagnostic weights to the various alternative answers. Statistical aid at this point is indis-

pensable, for it alone can show whether every item contributes its share to the total score. If the item does not do so it must be discarded. Likewise each alternative answer must justify itself. None should be so extreme or unattractive that all subjects avoid it, nor so popular that it fails to differentiate. Statistical analysis is a valuable check upon the experimenter's initial skill in selecting and phrasing items and alternatives.

4. *The scale must be reliable.* The reliability of any instrument has been defined as "prediction of itself alone." If all items in a scale are diagnostic of the same trait it is obvious that each item will correlate positively with every other, and the scale will be internally consistent; that is to say, it may be depended upon to measure whatever it measures with some degree of regularity. Unless this condition prevails the test lacks cohesion and is worthless.

Reliability may be determined not only by relating each item to the whole but by correlating halves of the test with one another, or by using equivalent and interchangeable scales of the same construction, or by repeating the test as a whole on the same group of subjects after an interval of time. The last method has certain weaknesses, chief of which is that the subjects themselves may change in the meantime, thus giving a false impression of unreliability in the scale; or, conversely, they may remember the test and reply to it consistently for that reason, thereby spuriously raising its reliability. Generally speaking, the more methods used for demonstrating the reliability of a scale the better.

5. *The scale must be valid.* A reliable scale does no more than agree with itself, whereas a *valid* scale has the power of predicting behavior beyond the immediate range of items contained in the scale. Though a test may be reliable without being valid, it can scarcely be valid unless it is first of all reliable.

To determine validity it is necessary to adopt some external criterion of the trait in question. For this purpose one may use ratings by the subject's associates; or better still, direct proof of their habits of conduct. In validating a scale for measuring interests, for example, it may be discovered that an occupational criterion will serve, and that the test correctly differentiates between groups of teachers, ministers, salesmen, artists and politicians. Or it is external validation to find that a test for introversion obtains its highest scores among patients known to be suffering from dementia praecox. There are many such sources of external validation for tests, depending on the nature of the variable under investigation.

To be valid a scale must also be sensitive. It can scarcely differentiate one group from another unless it permits a wide latitude of responses. There must be free play for individual differences, with the extremes of the scale occupied as well as the middle range. A test that does not initially yield a normal distribution of scores should ordinarily be altered until it does so.

6. *A test should be simple.* Many sources of error plague the construction and administration of tests. For this reason scores can be regarded only as crude measures. They cannot sustain hair-splitting diagnoses nor too precise interpretation. And their bluntness makes over-refined statistical treatment out of place. In other words, tests should be of simple construction and applied without intricate qualifications.

Simplicity requires first of all the employment of clear-cut common traits, rather than ill-defined empirical variables. Simplicity requires furthermore, that the wording of questionnaires be direct, unambiguous, and that the alternatives be clearly understood by the subject, and uncomplicated by double meanings and prolonged qualifications. Particularly hazardous to simplicity is the confusing process of assigning several scoring weights to any one alternative on the dubious assumption that it is possible to distinguish the relative contributions of each of several traits to any one verbal response (cf. pp. 327-329). Even in a single trait-scale undue weight should not be placed upon small differences in scores; and average scores (within the range of the "meaningless mean") ought ordinarily to be discarded as virtually impossible to interpret (cf. p. 336). Simplicity means that no score should be made to sustain a judgment upon personality as a whole, but should be interpreted only when its true position in the personal (not populational) setting is known. It means, in short, less intricate and elaborate instruments, and more caution in their use.

The rules for the construction and use of tests have been stated briefly and in general terms. But the reader who has followed the argument of the preceding chapters will have no difficulty in understanding the theoretical basis of each rule, or in applying it in specific instances.

The place of testing in the study of personality is as secure as that of rating, though the movement is much younger, and the margin of blunders much wider. To discuss in detail the hundreds of scales that have been published within the past two decades is beyond the scope of this volume.[16] Historically considered the extension of mental measurements into the field of personality is without doubt one of the outstanding events in American psychology during the twentieth century. The movement is still in its accelerating phase, and the swift output of ingenious tests has quite outstripped progress in criticism and in theory. Hence the rules and the caveats of the present section.

PRINCIPLES OF EXPERIMENTATION

Not long after psychologists first learned to use experimental techniques in their study of elementary mental phenomena Sir Francis Galton proposed that the same methods be applied to the investigation of human character (cf. pp. 93-95). He advised psychologists to "extemporize the emergencies of life" in so far as they reflected character, and to examine them under controlled conditions. The proposal seemed at the time too audacious. More than a generation was to elapse before psychologists were well enough trained in basic laboratory methods and sufficiently fortified with courage and imagination to follow Galton's advice. Now at last the tide of experimental investigations has begun to rise, and with such remarkable force that it (like testing) has become one of the most conspicuous events in modern psychological progress.

Two attributes of experimental procedure give it the position of preference among all analytical methods. These are its *objectivity* and its *exactness*. In an age of science it would be superfluous to extol these manifest virtues. But it is not superfluous to point out certain dilemmas that these very virtues create.

The demand for objectivity puts many problems of personality beyond the radius of experimental technique. By no means all of the emergencies of life can be extemporized or controlled. How shall we experiment with the influence of grief upon personality, or with first love, guilt, religious conversion, loneliness, or despair? How experiment with gradual changes extending throughout the course of life, or for that matter with sudden traumatic changes? Where are ob-

---

[16] Bibliographical sources are cited on p. 401 ftn. An additional source is J. B. Maller, *Descriptive Bibliography of Character and Personality Tests* (Teachers College), 1937.

jective methods for the study of self-consciousness, inventive imagination, loyalty, hate? Many delicately balanced forms of thought and feeling, ambition and misgiving, hope and dismay, are too subtle for heavy-handed laboratory probing. Experimentation is not yet ready, and perhaps never will be ready, to supplant the half-hundred other approved methods listed in Chapter XIV.

The second ideal of experimental analysis, *exactness*, has forced the psychology of personality into a serious dilemma. Briefly stated, the desire for precision, laudable though it is, has misled many investigators to work exclusively upon processes so elementary that they run their course entirely on a *sub-personal level*. Devotion to the quantitative ideal has led these investigators to shun the complex patterned forms of behavior and thought even though *it is only in these forms that personality can be said to exist.*

Instances of such misguided research are numerous. One investigator, thinking to study the masculinity of his subjects, correlates the width of the hips or shoulders with play interests and knowledge of sports. Others, to find the correlates of intelligence, carefully compare the I.Q. in childhood with the number of teeth present, or with height, or with the hydrogen-ion concentration of saliva. Others with a biochemical interest compare free acid per body weight with perseverance, phosphorus per body weight with good-naturedness, or amount of urine excreted with leadership. Still others, approaching (but not really entering) the field of psychodiagnostics, determine the relation between length of *t*-bars in handwriting and ambition, or convexity of the profile and optimism.[17]

In such psychophysical researches as these the magnitude of the physical attributes are generally obtained with microscopic exactness; likewise by averaging ratings or other criteria, a definitive, though less reliable, estimate is obtained for the personality variables in question. With these magnitudes in hand the investigator executes a correlation with the maximum of precision, often carrying out the coefficient to three decimal places. The probable error is then determined, and (is it surprising?) usually found to be about as large as the coefficient of correlation itself.[18]

[17] Many more examples might be drawn from D. G. Paterson's valuable survey, *Physique and Intellect*, 1930. This book unfortunately tends to accept such researches at their face value, and fails to challenge the *adequacy* of the methods to the problems they purport to study.

[18] For much research in personality the use of correlation is itself an over-refined method. It gives too much weight to non-significant differences. Cf. Dudycha's discussion of this point, p. 317.

The experiments are exact and the results are negative. Why? Much too hasty is Paterson's conclusion that the results "should go a long way toward counteracting the view that there is a functional unity between mind and body." Correlations between such separate and elementary variables as most of these experiments deal with are not to be expected. Until experiments are designed to allow *complex* physical expressions to show their *complex* relations to *inclusive* and *patterned* dispositions of personality, judgment should be suspended. The point is that many investigators are more interested in the exactness than in the adequacy of their methods. Accordingly, they have overlooked the complexities of pattern, and have either created artificial variables for study or have fallen back upon infra-personal levels of analysis.

The paradox is, then, that the more exact methods of research generally yield the least information. Vernon goes so far as to suggest that high reliabilities may even be regarded as indicative of a *poor* method, for high reliabilities are ordinarily secured only for data so elementary as to be of no significance for the understanding of personality.

It is known, for example, that excellent reliabilities can be obtained in the records of independent observers who simultaneously count the number of "physical contacts" that occur between children in a playground, whereas judgments concerning the *nature* of these contacts, *e.g.*, whether they betoken teasing, bullying, or affection, are considerably less reliable. But "physical contact" means nothing psychologically. Shall one choose high reliabilities obtained at an infra-personal level of conduct, or lower reliabilities at the personal level?

1. Recapitulating the discussion thus far, the first and most important rule for experimental analysis may be phrased as follows: *The study of narrow ("molecular") aspects of conduct, though often exact, yields results that are of little value in understanding human personality. Far more significant is research at complex ("molar") levels where the structured forms of personal organization are freely manifested.* In support of this rule three instances of research will be cited. All these have deliberately employed *two* levels of analysis, one relatively elementary (though not necessarily "molecular") and one complex and well patterned. In all three the superiority of the second level is demonstrated.

The first example is quoted verbatim from the experimenter's own account of his work.[19] "As part of a wider investigation of personality, 20 to 25 subjects, American college students, were observed by the writer and by two other experimenters while they were engaged on various performance tests. These three experimenters, who either observed separately or in pairs, embodied their impressions of the subjects' personalities in interpretative sketches, and in ratings upon four traits—'intelligence,' 'quickness,' 'extroversion,' and 'emotional stability.' When the ratings by the different experimenters were intercorrelated, the average of the twelve coefficients was 0.44 ±.032. In addition, the experimenters attempted to identify or match one another's sketches with their own impressions, and were successful in 23.3 per cent of the cases. It would have been better if the sketches had been split into smaller groups and matched, say, 5 at a time; 20 or 25 are far too many to deal with conveniently. Thus a greater proportion of correct matchings might have been obtained had the technique been more fully worked out at the time of this experiment (1930). Nevertheless the contingency coefficient which corresponds to the 23.3 per cent of successful matchings is 0.72 ± .055. This indicates that the experimenters agreed more closely in their general structured impressions of the subjects than in their ratings on separate traits."

A second example is taken from an investigation of the ability of judges to estimate personal qualities from voice alone.[20] In this study three voices, speaking identical words, were heard successively over the radio. In various experiments 15 different speakers were used and 8 groups of judges (an average of 63 in each group). The judges were asked to match the 3 voices with three records of information. For example, after hearing the 3 speakers the judges attempted to tell which of 3 specimens of handwriting fitted each voice, also which of 3 ages, heights, photographs, and descriptions of complexion. The voices were likewise matched with statements concerning the vocation and political preferences of the speakers; and with the results (previously obtained from the speakers) of 3 personality tests (for extroversion, ascendance and personal values). Finally, the *same* items of information were combined into a summary sketch for each speaker, giving thus a patterned description of his personality; the judges then attempted to match these sketches with the voices they heard.

The results of these experiments are quite decisive. Least successful

[19] P. E. Vernon, "Can the 'Total Personality' Be Studied Objectively?" *Char. & Pers.*, Duke University Press, 1935, 4, pp. 7 f.

[20] G. W. Allport and H. Cantril, *J. Soc. Psychol.*, 1934, 5, 37-55.

of the matchings were voice with records of handwriting, complexion, and height. Somewhat more successful were matchings with age and photographic appearance. Still more successful were matchings with vocation, political point of view, extroversion, ascendance and dominant life-values (the Spranger list, cf. pp. 228-230). Most successful of all were matchings of voice with the *summary sketches*.

Computing the contingency coefficients for these data, Vernon shows clearly the progressive enhancement of the validity of matchings as the features to be matched with voice proceed from the more physical and segmental attributes to the more complex psychological traits and patterns.[21] The final figure in the series shows how markedly the *grouping* of isolated characteristics into a single picture of each individual enhances the validity.

DESCRIPTION OF EXPERIMENT	C and P. E.
Three voices reading the same passage matched with the ages of the speakers, their height, and their complexion (*i.e.*, physical characteristics). Average of 6 experiments with 4 different sets of speakers.	0.13 ±.042
Voices matched with appearance in photographs or appearance in person (after the reading); 9 experiments, 6 sets of speakers.	0.20 ±.058
Voices with political preferences, and with dominant values (*i.e.*, scores on the Allport-Vernon *Study of Values*); 10 experiments, 7 sets of speakers.	0.25 ±.050
Voices with scores on (Heidbreder) Extraversion-Introversion, or (Allport) Ascendance-Submission scales; 13 experiments, 7 sets of speakers.	0.29 ±.047
Voices with brief character sketches made up of the above characteristics; 6 experiments, 5 sets of speakers.	0.41 ±.048

A third experiment, employing a different method, but with similar results was performed by von Bracken who asked several adult judges to "deduce" certain unknown characteristics of children's personality from two sets of data: (1) free descriptions of the children's personalities, and (2) a list of 26 separate characteristics pertaining to each child presented in the typical manner of a school report, each characteristic being listed separately. The judges made many deductions whose correctness was passed on by the authors of the original descriptions. In every experiment it was found that deductions from the free

[21] P. E. Vernon, *Psychol. Bull.*, 1936, 33, p. 170.

descriptions were more accurate, more comprehensive and more preg-
nant than the deductions made from the segmental descriptions.[22]

These experiments all prove in different ways that more valid
judgments, more accurate predictions and deductions, are obtained
when analysis is not pressed to the lowest molecular levels. Organization, pattern, molar processes, must be kept in view if the experiment is to yield optimum results. Indeed, unless they are kept in view
the experiment is in danger of slipping to some sub-personal region
where it cannot properly be said to deal with personality at all.

2. *Experimental analysis may be applied to the single subject no
less appropriately than to a group of subjects.* In other words, differential experiments are not the only legitimate types of experiment.

Lewin has reported that the question most frequently asked of
him following a showing of psychological films based on the behavior
of a single child, is whether *all* children behave in the same way.
It is as though the single case, however convincing and clear it may
be, is of no interest to most people unless it serves as an instance of a
general law. As Lewin says, his questioners seem to feel that the individual case is "fortuitous, unimportant, scientifically indifferent."
They overlook the truth that a scientific law of development may
be no less of a law for applying only to one individual.[23]

Many familiar experimental methods may be applied to the single
individual alone. Prediction is one of them. It is quite possible to fore-
cast (and then objectively to verify) what a certain person will do
without at the same time predicting the conduct of others. Similarly,
through time-samples it is possible to determine the consistency of
an individual's behavior without comparing the frequency of his
conduct with that of others. And almost any method of controlled
observation may lead to the establishment of cause and effect sequences that hold for one individual but for no other.

The proposal is made by F. H. Allport to extend still further
experimentation upon the individual through the application of
"intra-individual statistics." [24] This author believes that it would be
possible to scale for the single individual the frequency with which
his single acts of behavior conform to what he "seems to be trying

---

[22] For a brief report of this work see P. E. Vernon, *Char. & Pers.,* 1935, 4,
pp. 4 f. The original study is by H. von Bracken, *Jenaer Beitr. zu Jugend-und
Erziehungs-Psychologie,* 1925, 1, 1-50.

[23] K. Lewin, *J. Gen. Psychol.,* 1931, 5, p. 151.

[24] "Teleonomic Description in the Study of Personality," *Char. & Pers.,* Duke
University Press, 1937, 5, 202-214.

to do." To refer to the example previously used, a certain child seems to have a dominant trait of attempting to gain the attention of his elders in whatever way he can. At first this diagnosis is made merely as an hypothesis. Through repeated observations (by several judges) separate acts are scored for their relevance or irrelevance to this hypothesis. In time the existence of this trait is established or disproved. Its range and intensity of expression are determined. By extending this method the relative prominence of this trait in the life of the child is established in comparison with other major trends of his personality. This procedure is thoroughly quantitative even though it never involves behavior of more than one person.[25] The author of this proposal comments on its theoretical significance as follows:

> There exists among psychologists a peculiar aversion to the individual case study. This aversion is based upon the wholesome scientific principle that one must not generalize from a single instance. But it must not be forgotten that scientific data may be composed of events of many different kinds. An "instance" does not need to be an individual; it may equally well be a single act of behavior of an individual. And a fair sampling of the behaviors of an individual represents not a single item but a large number. Hence as long as the generalization made from this sample does not transcend the field of data from which it was obtained, that is, so long as it is made to apply to this one individual's behavior and to no other, such a generalization involves no violation of sound scientific procedure. And the attempt, in this way, to discover laws of individuals is precisely what we mean by the scientific study of personality.[26]

3. A third principle of experimentation may be stated as follows: *Since exact reproducibility of experiments is never possible in the field of personality, maximum reliability should be assured through the use of several experimenters, supplementary methods of investigation, and as much repetition as the case permits.* The point of this rule is to secure as much accuracy in all investigations as it is humanly possible to obtain. Broadly construed it is a warning against careless procedures and hasty and inaccurate interpretations of results. After all, in spite of the critical tone of portions of the pre-

---

[25] This proposal is identical with the suggestion made on p. 303 ftn. that *individual* traits may be scaled no less successfully than *common* traits, though in a wholly different way,—the continuum being individual rather than societal.

[26] *Loc. cit.*, pp. 203 f.

ceding discussion, the basic canons of laboratory science do apply to the study of personality as well as to any other psychological research. Methods must be adequate, but they must also be as accurate as possible.

4. The final principle is a plea for simplicity and flexibility in method. *The conditions of the experiment should invite activity as spontaneous and natural as possible.* If apparatus is used the instruments should be unobtrusive or else the subject should be fully adapted to their presence. If the experimenter himself is a decisive factor in the experiment there is danger that the results may be a function only of one special form of social relationship. Furthermore, the subject's attitude toward the experiment as a whole is often crucial in determining his responses.[27] All these variables should, if possible, be controlled, or in any event their influence fully allowed for.

Responses indicative of personality are ever changing. So far as possible these changing responses should be studied with a changing instrument. An analogy might be made between experimentation and natural conversation. To "draw a person out" the interlocutor asks successive questions which vary according to the nature of the preceding response. An experiment should, where possible, do the same. In this way the responses *unfold* and do not become rigid or stereotyped. To alter the course of an experiment at each successive stage is by no means easy to do, but it represents none the less an ideal of flexibility that experimenters will do well to have in mind.

In the field of human personality, where the experimental method is so new, the invention of novel techniques deserves every encouragement. The four principles here set forth are probably liberal enough to embrace significant advancement in the future. But neither they nor any other set rules should be invoked to restrict inventiveness and freedom of exploration.

The obscurantists of any generation, says Whitehead, are in the main those scientists who practice relentlessly the dominant methodology, failing to speculate freely upon its limitations and possibilities for its improvement. From this point of view, the present chapter, concerned wholly with the methodology of rating, testing, and experimenting, may be considered partly as a protest against current

[27] Cf. S. Rosenzweig, "The Experimental Situation as a Psychological Problem," *Psychol. Rev.*, 1933, 40, 337-354.

obscurantism in the scientific study of personality. But with the passage of time, the principles here set forth may in turn become outmoded. If so, they should then be altered or discarded lest they in turn obscure the path of progress.

CHAPTER XVII

EXPRESSIVE BEHAVIOR

Chacun fait son salut comme il peut.

WHEN the psychologist speaks of "expression" he may be referring to any one of three classes of phenomena. He may (and usually does) mean *emotional* expression, as reflected in involuntary visceral and skeletal changes of the body—in blushing, contraction of the brows, dilation of the pupil, clenching of the fist, or quaking of the knees. Such involuntary manifestations of emotion generally comprise the whole of the chapter on "expression" in textbooks of psychology, probably because it was this problem that engaged the interest of four great investigators in the nineteenth century: Bell, Piderit, Darwin, and Wundt. As K. Bühler has shown, their formulations have held the center of the stage for a hundred years.[1]

The second meaning of expression is less specialized and more familiar to the layman. We say that a man "expresses" an opinion, or a preference, an attitude, or a point of view. In such statements we imply that we are learning something about the man's personality from the content of his behavior. He tells us something directly about himself. His expression need not be verbal. The fact that he is frequently seen at ball games, or that he is a regular patron of the public library, also "expresses" his interests as truly (perhaps more truly) than his verbal communication.

The third meaning of the term is somewhat subtler, though the most important for the purposes of the present chapter. It refers to *involuntary* aspects of behavior that reflect more than they directly disclose. One's *manner* of communicating is not wholly determined by what one is saying. It is marked by an individuality that is superimposed upon the volitional activity. Individual peculiarities in the manner of performing adaptive acts are often called *expressive movement*.

[1] *Ausdruckstheorie,* 1933.

Both the second and third forms of expression tell a great deal about personality. The fact that a man walks to the ball park on every free afternoon expresses his interest in the game; but his *gait*, whether steady and firm or uneven and slipshod, is likewise revealing. The *fact* that a person takes every opportunity to talk about his job is unquestionably symptomatic; but so too is his apprehensive, arrogant, jocular, or wistful *manner* of talking.

In this chapter the topic for discussion is the elusive problem of *expressive movement*. The reflex display of emotion (in its merely transitory aspects) is disregarded; so too, though not to such an extent, is the question of *what* the person is doing, that is to say, the revelation of his attitudes and motives from the *content* of his adaptive acts. The separation of the *what* and the *how* is difficult to maintain rigidly, but that it is justifiable the following discussion will show.

EXPRESSIVE *versus* ADAPTIVE BEHAVIOR

Every response is the resultant of many determinants; it is the natural culmination of some stimulus acting upon many muscular and glandular effectors through the intervening medium of what are called "central determining tendencies." Since the final act is integral and convergent, it is only through a somewhat arbitrary analysis that its two primary phases may be distinguished. Never does expression exist as an isolated phenomenon. It is merely an undercurrent in the stream of behavior.

Yet, in the interests of analysis, one may distinguish two classes of determining tendencies that contribute in varying degrees to the ultimate effector process. One set of determinants pertains to the special adaptive performance prescribed by the task in hand. Something must be done: a lock must be repaired, a question answered, a doctor summoned, or a tree cut down. The resulting action is purposive, skillful, voluntary, and specific in reference to the demands of the occasion and to the special tensions created. But this adaptive performance seldom stands alone. Not merely are a task-attitude and pertinent skills aroused, but likewise a host of subtler, deeper, and less specific determinants. Many are the *ways* in which the lock may be repaired, depending upon the interest, patience, and mechanical-mindedness of the repairer. Many are the ways in which a question can be answered, depending upon the tact, courtesy, self-assurance or humor of the answerer. All activities, even the blinking of an eye, represent both *adaptive* performance and *expression*. Essentially, of course, the blinking of the eye is an adaptive response provoked by irritation of the cornea, but there enter into this simplest of responses subtle contributory influences from the "higher" (more integrated) areas of personality. Some people blink with regularity, others in uneven rhythms; some close their eyes completely, others do not.[2] Judging from the records of the cinema Mussolini blinks not only infrequently but also "deliberately," as though his self-styled "in-

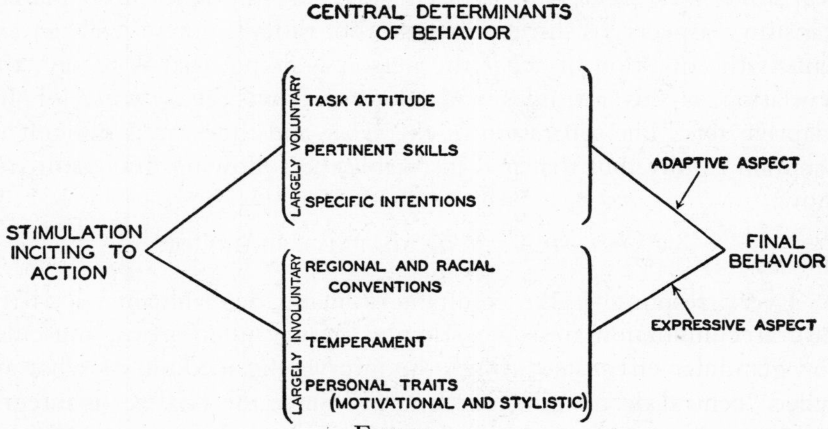

CENTRAL DETERMINANTS
OF BEHAVIOR

LARGELY VOLUNTARY

TASK ATTITUDE

PERTINENT SKILLS

SPECIFIC INTENTIONS

STIMULATION
INCITING TO
ACTION

ADAPTIVE ASPECT

FINAL
BEHAVIOR

LARGELY INVOLUNTARY

REGIONAL AND RACIAL
CONVENTIONS

TEMPERAMENT

PERSONAL TRAITS
(MOTIVATIONAL AND STYLISTIC)

EXPRESSIVE ASPECT

FIGURE 29

Behavior as a Confluence of Adaptive Performance and Expression

domitable will" were exerting itself in even this remote corner of his adaptive conduct.

The expressive portion of conduct results, then, from deep-lying determinants, functioning, as a rule, unconsciously and without effort. The adaptive portion, on the other hand, is a more limited system, circumscribed by the purpose of the moment, closely dependent upon the stimulus and upon voluntary effort or upon habits of skill. The *reason* for a present act of conduct is to be sought in the present desires and intentions of the individual (though these in turn may arise from deep-lying personal traits and interests); but the *style of execution* is always guided directly and without interference by deep and lasting personal dispositions. Figure 29 represents the situation schematically.

Generally speaking the adaptive performance is more efficient the less it includes of involuntary expression. Particularly is this true in

[2] E. Ponder and W. P. Kennedy, *Quart. J. Exper. Physiol.*, 1927, 18. 89-110.

all tasks that have been standardized to conform to the domination of the machine. To run a milling or stamping machine and turn out innumerable copies of the same model, allows less play for individuality of expression than did the handcraft of workmen in former times. Before the advent of the machine the style of a product was a clue to its authorship; cabinets, churches, saddles, chessmen, all were stamped with the individuality and style of their makers. At the present time, however, not only artisans and factory workers, but also policemen, printers, librarians, radio-announcers, and even teachers, are trained to do the same things in the same way. Precision in their performance is valued above individuality of style. The expressive factor is thus sacrificed in the interests of more efficient adaptive performance.

Though the adaptive and expressive determinants of behavior are confluent with one another, still they stand in an opposed relationship. The exercise of volition tends to suppress involuntary expressive movement.[3] Effort to do a task *correctly* destroys the impulse to do it stylistically, and any deliberate attempt to disguise expression markedly inhibits its individual character. Extreme examples of such attempts are the poseur, the mimic, the character actor, and the forger, who make conscious effort to divest their performance completely of the spontaneous forms of expression. In these instances voluntary determinants predominate to such an extent that the naive personal idiom is altogether suppressed.

To sum up, no single act of behavior can be designated exclusively as expressive, and none as non-expressive. Every act has both an adaptive (*zweckmässig*) and an individual or stylistic (*ausdrücklich*) character. The former masks the latter even while it converges with it. Under certain circumstances the expressive significance of an act sinks to a minimum degree, when, for example, there is deliberate disguise, or when there are exacting requirements of efficiency, standardization and conformity.

[3] According to Klages this antagonism is the most basic principle in the science of expression. The precise adaptive functions of volition and skill he ascribes to the high development of *Geist* in the modern man; the diffuse, affective, primitive character of expressive behavior to the elemental surging of the *Seele*. The antagonism between these two principles, mind and soul, is complete. The former acts as a restrainer, an impediment, even as a destroyer of the basic rhythms that are the carriers of vital expression. To perceive the individuality of expressive behavior it is, then, necessary to look beyond the specific intent of the act, beyond conscious control and the manifestations of convention and skill. L. Klages, *Der Geist als Widersacher der Seele*, 3 Vols., 1929-1932.

This two-part analysis of the determinants of behavior, sound so far as it goes, is somewhat over-simplified. It is not enough to make allowance for the exigencies of the immediate goal, for deliberate intent and efficiency of performance, and then to regard the residue of the act as expressive of personality. To do so would be to lose sight of still other determinants:

a. racial tradition
b. regional convention or fashion
c. transitory emotional states or moods, not characteristic of the person at other times
d. conditions of strain and fatigue
e. age
f. sex
g. peculiarities of native muscular structure and bodily build
h. conditions of health and disease
i. accidental deformations of the body
j. special habits arising from special training (*e.g.*, elocution, dramatics, military training) which may overlay and mask subtler individual expression
k. accidental conditions of the physical environment (*e.g.*, pen, ink and paper in writing; the ground and climatic factors in walking).

All of these determinants are important, and all seem, at least at first sight, to fall outside the twofold classification thus far discussed. Yet their roles may be quickly established in relation to this classification. They fall into four clusters (factors *a* and *b*, factors *c* and *d*, *e-i*, *j* and *k*).

The first two factors, racial tradition and regional convention or fashion, have already found their place in Figure 29; they are there classed among the determinants of *expressive* movement, for their influence is involuntary, deeply ingrained, and permanent, depending not at all upon conscious and deliberate intention of the moment.

Conventional styles of expression, for all they are standardized, are none the less *personal* determinants. The child adopts (intro-cepts) the cultural norms of expression as he does all other social standards. To a newcomer in a culture this adoption of a common "ground" of expression is most obvious. Indeed only after consider-able adaptation to this cultural ground can he discern the play of individuality, or appreciate the range of personal variation.

It is, of course, not only the forms of expression that are standardized within a culture, but likewise to a certain extent "racial character" itself. All expression—even that which is conventional—must have a basis in underlying psychological dispositions. Schopenhauer points to this correlation between racial expression and common racial traits in his observation that, "The English have a peculiar scorn of gesticulation and hold it to be something unworthy and common; it appears to me that this is only one of the examples of English prudery." Schopenhauer's diagnosis may be in error, but he is right in assuming that there must be *some* basis for the peculiarity in question.

For the psychology of personality the situation is best stated as follows. What is called "racial character" is the *socius*. The socius is that aspect of each personal life that is standardized and uniform within a culture (cf. p. 300 ftn.). Convention in expression is the outward and visible reflection of the nature of this socius. The personalities of some individuals within the culture conform more closely than do others to the ideal type for the culture. In some instances of marked conformity it might almost be said that the socius *is* the personality; but such a degree of typicality is rare. Only in part does the person take on the character of the socius, and only in part do his expressions conform to standard.

Nevertheless, such conformity as exists is immediately apparent to a newcomer. Only with time will he perceive the play of individuality beyond the confines of convention. Oddly enough in one's own culture the standard pattern is taken for granted and seldom remarked, a fact that has fatally narrowed the outlook of many social psychologists.

Factors *c* and *d*, dealing with the temporary conditions of mood and fatigue, are often decisive in conduct. They too must be classed as *expressive* determinants, though in this case the expression is of transitory personal states, and not of enduring dispositions. How important mood is under normal conditions is a problem discussed on pp. 485 f.

Factors *e* to *i* represent certain structural and organic influences upon the course of behavior. A woman, light in weight, cannot have as heavy a tread, as strong a grip, or as deep a voice, as an average male. A hand crippled by arthritis will show itself in gesture and script. A heavy, pyknic physique cannot poise itself lightly and delicately on the edge of a chair. Infirm age does tremulously what youth does with vigor. It is difficult to classify such influences wholly as adaptive determinants or as expressive. In part they affect movement via their special influence upon skill; in part they are related to changes in personality and therefore are expressive of personality. It is the inherent ambiguity of these items that causes some character analysts (graphologists, for example) to demand that information concerning these determinants be made available to them before they undertake an interpretation of expressive movement.

The final factors, *j* and *k*, are properly regarded as special instances of *adaptive* determinants. Especially is this true of conditions in the physical environment. On a hot day or on uneven ground, anyone is likely to slacken his pace or reduce his stride; with a scratchy pen anyone is likely to write with uneven pressure. Somewhat more subtle is the operation of special habits of skill (the trained voice, the military demeanor). To some extent of course such training directly influences personality, and therefore becomes incorporated into the expressive phase of action. But often it confers a type of mask-like skill that overlays rather than reveals the personal qualities of the individual. It is, for example, more difficult to judge correctly, from voice alone, the personalities of radio-announcers than it is to judge the personalities of untrained speakers. Special training in this case quite obscures the natural expressive character of the voice.

GENESIS OF EXPRESSIVE BEHAVIOR

Reverting for a moment to the discussion in Chapter V, we recall that in early infancy movements of the body are ordinarily diffuse and massive. The baby lying in his crib reaches for an object not with one hand but with two, and often with the legs as well. As he grows older and acquires precision in the use of limbs and voice, this diffuseness recedes. Before he is very old a mere knitting of the brows may signify as much pain as the random thrashing and screaming of early life, a slight shake of the head as definite an avoidance as the retraction of the whole body. This refinement comes about not only in adaptive performance but in expressive movement as well. The irritable child shows his irritability in nearly all his movements, but as a rule the adult learns control so that the only clues to his state of mind may be fidgeting fingers or abrupt speech.

This fact that expression tends with growing maturity to become confined to limited regions of the body has important consequences for psychodiagnostics. For one thing it means that various features of expression are of unequal significance in different people. Some faces are more revelatory than others; so too are some voices. In some cases gestures are merely conventional or perhaps absent altogether; in others they are significantly individual. Sometimes a style of clothing or of handwriting will seem "just like" the person; in other cases entirely non-expressive. One person reveals himself primarily in speech, another in posture and gait, a third in gesture and handwriting, a fourth in clothes and ornamentation. Each life has a different *Schwerpunkt* of expression. Hence it happens that many efforts at diagnosis fall wide of the mark, especially in cases where the observer looks only for his favorite cues, to the eyes perhaps, or to the hands, or script.[4]

In spite of psychomotor differentiation with advancing years, there remains throughout life a certain consistency of expression. Temperament obtrudes at all stages of development. Ordinarily the child who laughs gaily and readily is also gay in his expression in later life; whereas the solemn child is more apt to be a solemn adult. All native factors in expression are resistant to change. Identical twins are remarkably similar in mannerisms and in style of handwriting, even when they live apart. Family resemblances in mannerisms, ways of tilting the head, of thrusting out the chin, of holding the hand, can often be traced through grandparent, parent, and child; though in such cases, it must be remembered, imitation rather than inheritance may be responsible.

There is also the role of convention. Each child introcepts standard forms of expression that conflict with, and to a degree suppress, his individuality of movement. He learns to write from a copy-book, to play the piano or to dance according to rules, and to do his manual training only in the approved way. But as his skill develops he breaks away in part (but only in part) from his stereotyped models. His handwriting acquires "graphic maturity," his musical interpretation and his dancing steps are his own, and his handwork takes on individual style. Even the stenographer in time modifies her system of shorthand, and the physician, when he is no longer an interne, comes to practice his art in his own manner.

Klages, as we have seen, makes much of the constant battle that

---

[4] It is this consideration that leads W. Stern to repudiate what he calls "monosymptomatic" methods of psychodiagnosis, and to recommend that any one method, graphology, for example, be supplemented by the study of facial expression, gait, posture, gesture, and the like. "Ausdruck und Leistung," in *Die Wissenschaft am Scheidewege von Leben und Geist* (L. Klages Festschrift), 1932, pp. 219-223.

goes on between the requirements of skill and convention on the one hand, and the pressure from within, the *Gestaltungskraft,* on the other.[5] People differ greatly in the degree to which they are able to break through the prescriptions of training and convention, and to place their own stamp of individuality on every activity.

The role of *imitation* in the development of expressive behavior must not be overlooked. The little boy envying the maturity and worldliness of the grocery clerk imitates his nonchalant manner of tilting his cap and spitting. The adolescent girl wears her hair or her clothes in obvious tribute to her favorite actress. The college student apes the mannerisms of some lecturer or athlete whom he admires (cf. pp. 156-158).

Such external imitation is of considerable psychological interest. It is obvious that the youthful admirer does not imitate directly what he most covets: the competence, maturity, and inner poise of his hero. It is even doubtful whether he fully understands what he does covet. The office boy has a vague sense that his employer has worldly wisdom and experience to his credit, but these attributes are beyond the boy's immediate competence to attain. So he imitates his boss's neckties and haircuts. The lad cannot hasten the long process of training and experience. The most he can do is to attempt to short-circuit the process. These features are for him an outward and visible sign of the inaccessible qualities he desires. A *pars pro toto* substitution takes place. The accessible symbol is taken in place of the unattainable success.

With maturity many of these imitative mannerisms are abandoned, sometimes because the individual no longer admires the hero, and sometimes because he is now able to replace these partial imitations with others more complete and appropriate. The office boy grown up to worldly wisdom can wear whatever necktie he likes; he no longer needs the external tokens.

But maturity does not always efface mannerisms even though the personality may have changed and outgrown them. Take the case of a youth suffering from extreme self-consciousness who develops a certain furtiveness of movement; he blushes readily, shows

[5] The term *Gestaltungskraft* is used by Klages to signify the force making for ripeness or finish in expressive individuality. High *Gestaltungskraft* "fills the frame of every act with expressive significance." A low degree makes for indecisiveness of expression. The productions of children or of immature people—beset by convention—are likely to be "cloudy," to lack individual force and rhythm. Cf. *Ausdrucksbewegung und Gestaltungskraft,* 4th ed., 1923.

embarrassment or timidity before strangers, and perhaps possesses a number of compensatory mannerisms. As he grows older he may gain greatly in self-assurance; still this furtiveness lurks in his expression. Even without feelings of self-consciousness he may blush freely. His expression is a reflection of traits he once had. The traits themselves are lost or transformed, but the forms of expression remain as functionally autonomous systems. Hence it comes about that expression often reveals what a personality *has been* rather than what it is now in the present.

We have not yet mentioned the part played by mental conflict in the creation of expressive mannerisms.

A fastidious house painter who feels that his occupation is far beneath him, betrays his conflict through scrupulous care of his finger nails which during work he polishes and inspects at frequent intervals.

Another young man has a peculiar habit of jerking his arms whenever he thinks of embarrassing things. This habit has been traced back to a time when he had unpleasant compulsive thoughts of striking people on the street. At such times he would jerk his arms to throw off the impulse. With time this habit came to be used on other occasions where freedom from unpleasant thought was desired. Though freed from the initial compulsion, the gesture remained, and finally came to express and symbolize new conflicts.

To movements of this order Krout has given the name *autistic gestures*.[6] They are "self-directed" with only unconscious meaning for the subject, and no meaning at all (unless carefully studied) for the observer. They originate in some experience of frustration and occur in any situation that touches, however remotely, upon this frustration. In his experiments Krout found that similar stimulus words (related to the same constellation of meaning) were often accompanied by the same symbolic gesture. Thus one subject examined her finger nails or else clenched her hands whenever "work" or some related word occurred in the stimulus series. Upon investigation it was found that a "complex" had been tapped, the subject being against her will self-supporting, and for that reason inclined to resentment and self-pity.

Krout's theory of autistic gestures, following the Freudian line

[6] M. H. Krout, "Autistic Gestures: an Experimental Study in Symbolic Movement," *Psychol. Monog.*, 1935, No. 208; also "The Social and Psychological Significance of Gestures," *J. Genet. Psychol.*, 1935, 47, 385-412.

of thought, is based upon the concepts of blockage and conflict. If tabooed, an impulse is not allowed full motor expression. The individual must not complain of his lot, admit fear, or confess shame. At times when these adaptive activities would normally be invoked they are summarily blocked. A conflict occurs. The impulse to speak or to act is initiated, but is promptly reduced to a mere vestigial state—to a rudimentary gesture. This gesture recurs in all situations where the conflict is active.

One of the peculiarities of such autistic gestures is the fact that they are ordinarily perceived neither by the actor nor by the observer. Unless very striking in type or in frequency they are allowed to pass. The twisting of a ring, the sniffling of the nose, or a glance over the shoulder, are so common and seem so trivial that no one gives them second thought. And yet they may be, as Krout has shown, significant of conflict in the deeper recesses of the personality.

But beware of suspecting hidden meanings where none exist. A temperament that is "high strung" may engender many useless synkinetic movements without their having any symbolic significance. Some gestural patterns are simple motor habits set into play through fatigue, cramp, or through some remote cross-conditioning by endogenous or exogenous stimuli. People with an excessive number of nervous mannerisms may be singularly free from repressions or conflicts; whereas others who suffer greatly may be outwardly perfectly placid.

PSYCHODIAGNOSTICS

Psychodiagnostics is the technical term for what is popularly called *character reading*. Throughout the ages it has ranked among the chief interests of man. A quaint eighteenth century statement in its favor is found in *Tristram Shandy:*

> "There is," continued my father, "a certain mien and motion of the body and all its parts, both in acting and speaking, which argues a man well within; and I am not at all surprised that Gregory of Nazianzen, upon observing the hasty and untoward gestures of Julian, should foretell he would one day become an apostate; or that St. Ambrose should turn his amanuensis out of doors, because of an indecent motion of his head, which went backwards and forwards like a flail; or that Democritus should conceive Protagoras to be a scholar, from seeing him bind up a faggot, and thrusting, as he did it, the small twigs

inwards. . . . There are a thousand unnoticed openings," continued my father, "which let a penetrating eye at once into a man's soul: and I maintain it," added he, "that a man of sense does not lay down his hat in coming into a room, or take it up in going out of it, but something escapes, which discovers him."

Entirely comparable are many writings in the twentieth century. Take, for example, the following passage which sounds not unlike Tristram's father:

> There are human hands that look like a monkey's paws, and sometimes, if bones and sinews be prominent, like the claws of a bird of prey. They seem to proclaim a deep-seated selfishness, a regardlessness for others, a tendency to grasp with greed and to hold with tenacity. They convey an impression of animal or elemental behavior, a lack of all the finer shades of restraint. Some hands look not greedy or grasping, but decidedly cruel. . . . From the hands in repose we tend to infer the breeding of men and women, by which we here mean their blood and race, the degree of their sensibility for others, their restraint or undiscipline of nature. . . . Again, we infer artistic power and appreciation of beauty. . . . The movements of hands will tend to emphasize these points, and to make them even clearer. We all know and recognize gestures and movements—do we not all occasionally astonish ourselves?—that express ruthlessness, violence, gentleness, self-centeredness, grace, sensitiveness, love of beauty.[7]

The history of psychodiagnostics was reviewed in Chapter III; there it was pointed out that two paths are open. One is the road of dogmatic assertion, charted with shrewd observation and brilliant *apperçus*. The two preceding quotations are of this order. Their captivating insights may delight the reader, but at the same time leave him wondering as to their trustworthiness.

The second road is much more tedious, the path of experimental study wherein, up to the present time, little progress has been made. Experiments are few in number and many of them are flimsy in conception and in execution, designed merely to disprove the claims of charlatans. As a result of these crusading studies we know that many common psychodiagnostic practices are unsound and that many popular beliefs are unfounded. But we do not know what positive results may be expected in this field, nor how to go about producing them.

[7] J. G. Vance, *A Mirror of Personality*, 1927, pp. 113 ff. Quotation by permission from the publishers, Williams and Norgate, London.

Negative demonstrations, to be sure, have some value. It is perhaps well to know, for example, that blondes and brunettes as classes are not appreciably distinct in temperament; that certain detailed signs in handwriting, such as the length of the *t*-bar or the height of upper and lower projections have no simple point-to-point correspondence with measured qualities of personality; that letters of application make markedly different impressions upon different judges; and that very little agreement can be obtained in judgments from photographs. It is well to have a demonstration that one way in which character analysts secure a reputation for success is through the employment of ambiguous terms that may apply to any mortal person. Through the use of a flattering *Universalscharakteristik* the analyst is credited with acumen because the client is pleased.[8]

Still other failings of popular character analysis were discussed in Chapter III. The time is at hand when psychologists must dwell not upon what is wrong in psychodiagnostics, but rather upon what is right. Francis Bacon averred that the study of expression had made little progress since the time of Aristotle. The study of expression has likewise made little progress since the time of Bacon.

One would like, of course, to see a full and systematic guide, based entirely upon experimentally verified principles, that would enable the psychologist and layman alike to read personality from external signs. But such a demand is premature, for no branch of psychology is more complex than psychodiagnostics, nor more backward. For the present we must be content to help lay its foundations by gathering together pertinent knowledge concerning the genesis of expressive movement, its consistency, and such other experimental evidence as is at hand.

THE CONSISTENCY OF EXPRESSION

To what extent do the expressive features of the body agree with one another? Is it true, as Lavater asserted, that, "one and the same spirit is manifest in all" (cf. p. 77)? Or is there marked specificity in expression, so that one feature has little appreciable relation to another? Do facial muscles reflect only fleeting inclinations; is handwriting merely a *manual* habit; is posture a separate neuromuscular function; and are all these features quite unrelated to voice and speech? Should the latter situation hold, the case would look dark

[8] Cf. O. Bobertag, *Zsch. f. ang. Psychol.*, 1934, 46, 246-249.

indeed for psychodiagnostics, for the interpretation of one feature might be negated by the interpretation of another. Even if the features that serve as the *Schwerpunkt* of the personality were correctly identified, there would be no dependable supporting evidence from other features, and the whole task of interpreting traits from external signs would seem vain.

Fortunately this problem is accessible to experimental study in two ways. The first is the method of comparing objective measurements obtained from separate expressive features. The second is the method of impression, determining the degree to which diverse features of expression seem to observers to be related (*e.g.*, by finding the extent to which they can be correctly matched with one another). Both methods have been employed. Described elsewhere at length they require only a brief illustration here.[9]

> The method of direct comparison is accomplished by taking a representative group of subjects, and securing from them under like experimental conditions records of many forms of movement. In one such study twenty-five male subjects were used, eighteen to fifty years of age; they were required to write, walk, draw, count, read, tap, stroll, estimate distances, and perform many other simple tasks, always at their own speed and in their "usual way." Measurements were obtained with the aid of suitable instruments and timing devices at several different experimental sessions.[10]

> By correlating the measures obtained it was found that any one individual subject tended to maintain the same position among the twenty-five in respect to various "dimensions" of movement. To take a single example: by correlating all measures that seemed to bear upon "expansiveness" of movement an average coefficient of $+.33$ was obtained, which for nine composite measures implies a corrected internal consistency of $+.82$. The relationship may likewise be expressed as a series of correlations between each single composite measure and the sum of all other eight composites dealing with this "areal" or expansive factor in movement.

> Area of Total Writing .... .69
> Total Extent of Figures .... .67
> Area of Blackboard Figures .... .64
> Slowness of Drawing .... .52

[9] See G. W. Allport and P. E. Vernon, *Studies in Expressive Movement*, 1933. Also in the present volume see pp. 355-367.

[10] For a complete account of this experiment see *Studies in Expressive Movement*, chaps. ii-v.

The average correlation between each component and the sum of the other eight is $+.51$.[11]

These results, applied to the single case, mean simply that a subject who writes large *tends* also to cover much space in his drawing (whether with hand or foot), to overestimate angles, to walk with a lengthy stride (in proportion to his height), and even to place elongated check marks on a paper when asked to check his personal traits.

In the same way, through correlation, other consistencies besides expansiveness were established, *viz.*, in respect to the emphasis or force of movement, and its prevailing centrifugal or centripetal character.

This method of comparing quantitative records of movement is applicable only to *groups* of subjects; it is a product of *mass* investigation. As such it demonstrates that all subjects tend to be consistent with themselves *in the same way*. The degree of consistency is established by the *correspondence* of measures. It is noteworthy that the evidence for consistency by this method is as marked as it is, for, as has been previously shown, all studies that rely upon the correspondence of measures have stringent limitations.[12] At best correspondence demonstrates only group consistency. One must turn to different procedures to establish congruence or true personal consistency.

One of these methods is *matching* (cf. pp. 354 f., 458 f.), a highly serviceable device in spite of its substitution of fallible judges for the direct comparison of measures. The signal advantage of matching is that it permits the ordering of *any* records of expression with any other records, however complex they may be and however incommensurable from the mathematical point of view. Photographs (which cannot be measured) may be matched with the total formquality of a specimen of script (which also cannot be measured), or

[11] *Op. cit.*, p. 110.

[12] For example, on pp. 250-252, where it was pointed out that lack of correspondence of measures cannot be taken as evidence against the existence of self-consistent individual traits; likewise, pp. 456-458, where the concept of correspondence was found inferior to the concept of "congruence" in representing the consistency of the individual personality.

one part of a photograph with another part, or complex artistic creations with case histories of the artists' lives.

Credit for the first use of this valuable method belongs to M. Wertheimer and his pupil Arnheim.[13] Recently a distinct improvement in the method has been made by Vernon who offers a technique for expressing the results of all matching experiments in standard terms (contingency coefficients).[14] This author likewise presents a tabulation of the results of many experiments dealing with the perceived consistency of expressive movement. A few illustrative samples follow, the names of the original experimenters appearing at the end of each entry.

DESCRIPTION OF EXPERIMENT	C and P. E.
Four photographs of bodies (with heads removed) matched with 5 photographs of heads; (the latter were taken at a different time, when different clothes were worn). (Vernon)	0.42 ±.046
Pairs of drawings of a house and a man by 490 children (10-13 years), arranged in 70 sets. Each set of seven matched with a time limit of 30 seconds by educated adults. (Vernon)	0.59 ±.062
Handwritings matched with phonograph records of the voices of the writers. (Wolff)	0.39 ±.042
Photographs of hands matched with silhouettes of profiles. (Wolff)	0.14 ±.052
Handwriting specimens matched with portraits of the writers. (Arnheim)	0.25 ±.055
Eight themes written by 70 students matched with one or more other themes by the same authors. Two judges matched groups of 5 authors at a time. The result is the average of 112 experiments. (Allport, Walker, and Lathers)	0.60 ±.142
Judges were given 9 sets of 5 "incidents" (including test scores, probable vocations, quotations from essays, etc.). They had to sort out all the incidents into 5 "congruent" groups. Thus each set was, in effect, matched with 8 other sets. (Vernon)	0.34 ±.045
Handwriting specimens and kymograph curves of point pressure matched with thumbnail character sketches. (Allport and Vernon)	0.38 ±.056

[13] R. Arnheim, "Experimentell-psychologische Untersuchungen zum Ausdrucks-problem," *Psychol. Forsch.*, 1928, 11, 1-132.

[14] P. E. Vernon, *Psychol. Bull.*, 1936, 33, 149-177.

C and
P. E.

Handwritings of Leonardo da Vinci, Raphael, and Michel-
  angelo, matched with the names of these artists.[15] (Arn-   0.59
  heim)   ±.020

Experimental evidence, then, both by the method of correspondence and congruence, demonstrates that considerable consistency
exists among the expressive features of the body. To the experiments here cited one might add other testimony.[16] But enough has
been said to justify three major conclusions.

1. The expressive features of the body are not independently
activated. Any one of them is affected in much the same way as
any other. Hence, to a degree Lavater is justified in saying that "one
and the same spirit is manifest in all."

2. The consistency, however, is never found to be perfect. One
channel of expression is not an exact replica of all others. If this were
so, monosymptomatic methods of psychodiagnostics would be fully
justified. The complete personality would be betrayed equally well
in every feature. Handwriting would tell the whole story, so too
would the eyes, the hands, or the limbs. The amount of agreement
that has been demonstrated does not justify so simple an interpretation of the case.

3. The unity of expression turns out, as we would indeed expect,
to be entirely a question of degree, just as the unity of personality
itself is a matter of degree. The expressive features of the body
should not be expected to reflect more consistency than the personality itself possesses (nor should they be expected to reflect *less*).
Expression is patterned in complex ways precisely as personality
itself is patterned. There are major consistencies and secondary consistencies, much congruence and some conflict and contradiction.

[15] The last two experiments show that matching may be used not only to study
the consistency of different features of expression, but likewise to determine the
psychodiagnostic significance of expression. A further instance was given on p. 459,
where it was shown that the sound of voices could be matched fairly successfully
to the traits, vocations, and to pen portraits of the speakers.

[16] For example, (a) experiments on cross-education, whereby it is shown that
both adaptive and expressive behavior first trained in one limb of the body transfers without specific practice to other limbs (cf. T. W. Cook, *Psychol. Rev.*, 1936,
43, 149-178). (b) Experiments on affective disorganization and emotional disturbance
which show their influence not only in speech, but in steadiness of motor performance and tonus of unused muscles (cf. A. R. Luria, *The Nature of Human
Conflicts*, trans. 1932). (c) Certain typological studies that establish for contrasting
groups of subjects marked consistency in a wide variety of motor performances
(cf. W. Enke, "Die Psychomotorik der Konstitutionstypen," *Zsch. f. ang. Psychol.*,
1930, 36, 237-287).

Psychodiagnostics must then proceed as any other branch of the psychology of personality proceeds, to the study of *complex* phenomena at a *complex* level.

EXPRESSIVE FEATURES

Any mobile region of the body in rest or in motion is expressive—eyes, mouth, head, trunk, shoulders, hands, fingers, legs. And any of the innumerable activities of these regions may be analyzed for their expressive significance: standing, walking, gesticulating, running, jumping, strolling, dancing, sitting, lying down, sleeping, talking, laughing, weeping, shaking hands, handwriting, smoking, painting, musical performance, scientific work, play, dress, ornamentation. All these activities and more besides are accessible to study, separately or in combination.[17] To consider here all of these channels of expression would be impossible, or to consider any one exhaustively. But since the present purpose is merely to point out the path of constructive research, it will be sufficient to single out certain representative channels for special comment.

The Face. Richly supplied with nerves and striated muscles the face is capable of the most varied expression. Because of its endowment with distance receptors it is the region where the person meets the world, as it were, head-on. Not only is it the region where most impressions are received, but its exposure to the outer world makes it the station for signals of rejection, threat, or invitation to others. Perhaps for this reason it is the center to which we give our chief attention when we are observing others. It is likewise the principal focus of emotional expression, and the region where most people locate their sense of selfhood. Its intimate connection with feeding and with vocal communication are further reasons for its strategic position among the expressive agents of the body.

By psychologists the face has been studied chiefly for its reflections of temporary emotional states, not for its revelations of the lasting qualities of personality. It is true that the practice of *physiognomy* reaches far back into the past. But until very recent years the psychologist's role in relation to this art has never been constructive; he has contented himself with the position of critic, challenging the legendary signs of "high brow," "weak chin," "sensual lips," and

[17] A more detailed classification will be found in Allport and Vernon, *op. cit.* pp. 24-35.

"sensitive nostrils," and doing little more. But the rapid growth of the psychology of personality has led to the discovery that the province of physiognomy is richer than psychologists had suspected, and well worth exploring.

A few representative topics for research will suggest how the scientific study of the face may proceed, and how this study may be related to basic questions in the psychology of personality.

1. Does the bony configuration of the face have a significant relation to one class of personal qualities, and muscular sets to another? In ancient times the author of *Physiognomonica* wrote, "That which is durable in the form expresses what is immutable in the nature of the being; that which is mobile and fugitive in this form expresses that which, in this nature, is contingent and variable." Cast into modern terms this hypothesis holds that the native factors in personality, such as temperament and intelligence, are reflected in the bodily form and structure; whereas acquired traits are represented in muscular sets and changes (see pp. 69-78).

2. Why do the eyes seem to us, as Köhler observes, the "visible center of another man's personality"? Is it because we obtain most of our information concerning him from our own eyes, and through some curious act of projection regard his eyes as equally important in the process of understanding? Is it because many of us locate our own sense of selfhood midway between our eyes, and seek, as it were, to fix our attention on the "self" that confronts us? Or is it because the subtleties of glance and ocular movement (including the motion of the lids and neighboring brow) are especially rich in expressive significance? Experimental work thus far seems to favor the mouth rather than the eyes as the principal agency of expression.[18] Why then are the eyes the focus of our attention?

3. Can patterns of facial expression (whether fleeting or set) be analyzed into the contraction of separate muscles? Or can the contribution of each feature or combination of features within the total pattern be specified? Experiments show that features in isolation are not nearly as intelligible as the total expression, and yet it is obvious that in some way the total pattern is *composed* of these very same features. Might it be possible through quantitative analysis to determine what combinations of features give rise to critical differences of patterns?

[18] Cf. K. Dunlap, *Genet. Psychol. Monog.*, 1927, 2, No. 3.

An ingenious beginning with this problem has been made by Brunswik and Reiter.[19] The six schematic faces in Figure 30 are selected from an experimental series containing 189 similar drawings, each constructed in such a way as to secure an irregular series of small quantitative variations in respect to (a) distance between the eyes, (b) height of brow above the eyes, (c) position of the nose, (d) length of nose, (e) height of mouth. Judges were asked to rate each face in the series of 189 according to certain biophysical and biosocial characteristics (*e.g.*, intelligence, mood, age, occupation,

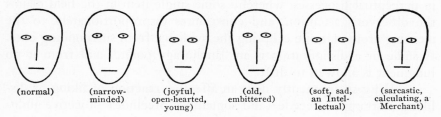

| (normal) | (narrow-minded) | (joyful, open-hearted, young) | (old, embittered) | (soft, sad, an Intellectual) | (sarcastic, calculating, a Merchant) |

FIGURE 30

Brunswik's Schematic Faces

Employed for the quantitative determination of the influence of various features (separately and in combination) upon physiognomic judgments. (Courtesy of Franz Deuticke, Vienna)

beauty, energy, likeability). In the figure are given the modal judgments for six of the faces obtained in this manner. One finding of particular interest is the fact that the height of the mouth has the greatest significance among the variables used, a high mouth sometimes creating an impression of youth and joy, sometimes of dullness and lack of energy, depending upon the pattern of other features with which it is associated. The pre-eminence of the mouth in expression, it will be remembered, was also established by Dunlap.

The implications of such a method of research are far reaching in significance. Patterns (simple ones to be sure) are here actually reduced to a matter of quantitative variation. Complex relationships between features are scrutinized in more detail than has generally been thought possible. Furthermore, for the first time an experimental wedge is here driven into the problem of the *arrangement* of cues whereby psychodiagnostic judgments are made. The process, at least on a simple level, seems thus to be not so unanalyzable as some have held. There have been previous investigations of the psychodiagnostic

[19] The brief account here given is taken from a short preliminary report contained in E. Brunswik, *Wahrnehmung und Gegenstandswelt*, 1934, p. 221.

significance of separate features of the body, but not as here a quantitative study of the inter-relation of these features.[20]

4. Why is the smile so disarming a pattern of expression? It is a familiar experimental fact that a smiling face is judged as more intelligent than one that is serious, and is credited with all social virtues and graces. Smiles arouse so favorable an affective attitude in observers that impartial judgment is virtually impossible. Conversely, disfigurations and asymmetries of the face make for adverse judgments. Here is an instance of the undue constraint found frequently in perceptual processes, whereby some single item in the field claims the observer's attention, and contributes disproportionately to the meaning aroused, quite eclipsing the evidence from surrounding cues. A smile or a disfiguration is an "anchorage point," and from it no judgment is allowed to drift.

5. Why so frequently does an affective reaction of liking or disliking a stranger precede (and sometimes preclude) objective judgment? New acquaintances often arouse such strong feelings of favor or disfavor that rational inferences concerning their personalities are inhibited. In such cases is there an unconsciously perceived resemblance to another person toward whom we have strong feelings? If so, why is the *affective* judgment swifter than the conscious recognition of similarity?

6. If, as the work of Landis suggests, patterns of expression differ markedly from individual to individual, while remaining consistent for each person, how does it happen that we are able to judge other people as well as we do? If each new face has a unique pattern of expression, not one that we have encountered before, ought we not find it quite unintelligible? All inferential judgments require experience; but here is a face with which we have had no experience! Do we judge on the basis of the nearest related experience, or is there another factor involved in the process—something called "intuition"? If so, what is the nature of this mysterious function? Chapter XIX will discuss this problem in greater detail.

[20] A possible exception is the interesting study by Blake. Using full-length photographs of an actor in several emotional poses, this investigator finds that the most accurate judgments result when the whole body including the face is visible; next in value is the whole body excluding the face; then the torso including arms and hands; then the feet, knees, legs and hips (the entire lower portion of the body); least valuable are the head and shoulders with the face blocked out. (The relative value of the face alone was not determined.) W. H. Blake, "A Preliminary Study of the Interpretation of Bodily Expression," *Teachers College Contrib. to Educ.*, 1933, No. 574.

Gesture, Gait, Handwriting. In the movements of the limbs one can usually trace the influence of the three primary factors: task, convention, and personality. The traffic policeman stops the flow of vehicles with his left arm and motions to the pedestrians with his right. In this case the constraints placed upon these movements by the nature of the task and by convention are the predominant factors in his behavior; but over and above these prescribed movements one perceives a subtle individuality of expression, sometimes suggesting friendliness, sometimes impersonality, or perhaps arrogance and egotism.

The presence of these three factors is clearly demonstrated in an experiment of Giese's. His subjects were given batons and asked to beat time to various musical compositions as recordings were played. The room was dark and a flashlight bulb at the end of the baton permitted the photographing of the movements on a cinema film. From these records it was possible to identify the effects of sheer convention (previous training in beating time or imitation of orchestra leaders), a common interpretative type of motion according to the style of composition for any single composer or for the composers of a given epoch (the prescriptive or adaptive aspects of the task), and finally a definite individuality in movement (expressive only of the subject himself).[21]

A more detailed analysis of gesture would no doubt reveal the influence of other determining factors, such as age, sex, bodily build, and conditions of health and disease; but these factors, as shown on pp. 468 ff., can in turn be ordered with fair success under the major determinants of task, convention, and personality. The influence of passing emotion or mood, however, does require special mention, for under certain circumstances depression, fatigue, or elation may be so marked that it dominates the motor region and completely obscures the normal course of movement. But under ordinary circumstances the influence of transient states of feeling, fatigue, or passing mood is not decisive.

Some evidence on this point is contained in the experiment described on pp. 477 f. All measurements repeated within the *same* experimental session had an average repeat-reliability of $+.75$. When these measurements were repeated after several weeks, the reliability fell to $+.64$. The difference between these two coefficients suggests the part

[21] F. Giese, "Individuum und Epoche in Taktierbewegungen bei verschiedenen Komponisten," *Arch. f. d. ges. Psychol.*, 1934, 90, 380-426.

that temporary factors, such as mood and the subjects' "attitude of the evening," plays in determining expressive consistency. Though the part is appreciable, it is by no means large. Far more influential are the lasting dispositions that place their stamp on movement over long periods of time.[22]

In speaking of gesture, one ordinarily has in mind the use of arms and hands. But in a broader sense the term includes as well postures of the body, and these are especially significant since they are seldom the object of voluntary control. The postures of one person are characteristically tense and swiftly changing, of another relaxed, or even toneless. Sometimes there is a surcharge of vitality, sometimes a chronic weariness or else a forced animation.

There are interesting studies of posture and change of posture during sleep. With recording instruments and cameras Johnson and Weigand have discovered marked individual differences in the manner of sleeping, reaching the conclusion that "the way a person sleeps is a very stable personal characteristic—as stable as his strength of grip or his speed and accuracy in mental arithmetic." [23] This research pertains only to the *consistency* of expressive movement; it says nothing concerning the psychodiagnostic significance of postures in sleep. Adler, however, is bold to suggest that pessimists may be recognized by the posture they assume in sleeping; they tend, so he asserts, to curl themselves into the smallest possible space and to draw the covers over their heads.[24] To the establishment of this point, however, psychodiagnostic research has not yet progressed.

Also in observations of *gait* psychodiagnostics seems in the lag. Impressionistically one would expect gait to be one of the most revealing forms of movement. Vance writes,

> Thus a walk easily indicates determination or weakness of purpose, self-esteem or self-abasement—each forms in its own way of self-assertion—buoyance of spirit or dullness, a vivid or sluggish temperament, reflective quickness of action, impulsiveness or irresolution, while many walks give valuable indices of pride, courage, and restraint.[25]

These assertions may all be correct, but as yet none is scientifically proved.

[22] Cf. *Studies in Expressive Movement*, pp. 98 f.
[23] H. M. Johnson and G. E. Weigand, *Proc. Penna. Acad. Sci.*, 1927, 2, 43-48
[24] A. Adler, *Understanding Human Nature*, 1927, p. 176.
[25] J. G. Vance, *A Mirror of Personality*, 1927, p. 20.

The most satisfactory method of studying gait is through cinematographic records. When subjects are dressed in loose fitting garments, with heads covered or blocked out in the film, it is possible to control all extraneous cues, and to proceed experimentally to study the significance of the gait alone.

Using this method Wolff made a striking discovery concerning the subjects' recognition of their own expressive behavior. With considerable promptness all subjects recognized their own gait, whereas they failed in 70 per cent of their attempts to identify the gait of their friends. This is a curious finding inasmuch as one seldom *sees* oneself walk (never, unless some reflecting surface is present), but often sees the gait of one's friends. Frequency of visual impression cannot account for the results. Furthermore, it turned out that although self-recognition in gait is universal, it is much less frequent in other features of expressive behavior. Time and again Wolff's subjects failed to identify their own voices when mechanically reproduced in a series with other voices; they did not recognize their own styles of retelling a story, nor pictures of their own hands, and sometimes not even their own profiles if these were photographed without their knowledge. All these self-recognitions are inferior to the recognition of corresponding features in one's friends.[26]

These results indicate the high importance of postural *empathy* in the process of self-recognition. The person unerringly identifies himself with the total movement of trunk and limbs, but not with the finer and more precise productions of single regions of the body. There is a certain "total swing" to gait that bears some peculiarly intimate relation to the self.

Though gait has indeed a total swing, it invites none the less attempts at analysis. Wilsmann proposes seven measurable attributes: regularity, speed, pressure, length of stride, elasticity, definiteness of direction, and changeableness or variability.[27] To this list, however, Wilsmann hastens to add an eighth (non-measurable) attribute, the qualitative pattern of the whole that he calls *rhythm*.

Time and again, in every sphere of expression, the problem of

[26] W. Wolff, "Zuordnung individueller Gangmerkmale zur Individual-charakteristik," in *Gang und Charakter* (ed. by H. Bogen and O. Lipmann), *Beihefte zur Zsch. f. ang. Psychol.*, 1931, No. 58, chap. vi. Also, *Char. & Pers.*, 1933, 2, 168-176; *Imago*, 1934, 20, 104-122.

[27] A. C. Wilsmann, "Charakterologische Bedeutung von Einzelmerkmalen," in *Gang und Charakter, vid. sup.*, chap. iv. For a still more refined analysis of gait and a description of "microscopic" techniques for its study, see G. Kreezer and A. D. Glanville, "A Method for the Quantitative Analysis of Human Gait," *J. Genet. Psychol.*, 1937, 50, 109-136.

"rhythm" recurs. It is a poorly defined concept. Often it means periodicity in respect to some detailed feature of expression; but quite as often it means the unanalyzable effect created by the whole pattern of movement. Many investigators do as Wilsmann does, first list such aspects of expression as can be analytically treated, and then fall back upon "rhythm" to cover the *co-existence* of these aspects which must be taken into account in addition to the separate constituent factors.

This seems to be Klages' point of view regarding rhythm in handwriting which, he insists, is the most important of all the features of graphic movement. It is something not reducible to the detailed (and for the most part, measurable) attributes: It is not a matter of pressure, speed, width, slant, connectedness, direction, emphasis on initial letters, overlining, distribution of spacing, pastosity, cultural conformity, or regularity. Especially is it not a matter of mere regularity which is wholly a production of the "will," reflected in uniformity of spacing, size, slant and mechanical composition. Rhythm in script expresses the underlying vital force (*Seele*) of the individual, and is not to be confused with the regulating control of the *Geist*. Rhythm has to do with recurrent impressions of strength or weakness, esthetic quality, *Gestaltungskraft* (cf. p. 472). It means the similar reproduction of *similar* features, but not the mathematically exact repetition of measurable features. In Klages' opinion there are no precise objective criteria of rhythm; it is always a matter of impression and evaluation.[28]

Many thoughtful students of personality, and not professional graphologists alone, consider the analysis of *handwriting* to offer the best of all channels for psychodiagnostics. They argue that handwriting is after all "brain writing," and that nothing about it is accidental or peripheral, that it is "crystallized gesture," far finer in detail and more precisely recorded than are the gross and fugitive movements of the limbs.

It must be admitted that the a priori case for scientific graphology is excellent. But so too is the a priori case for scientific physiognomy or for any other branch of psychodiagnostics based upon the study of voice, gait, posture, or any expressive muscular behavior. The

[28] Cf. T. Stein-Lewinson, "An Introduction to the Graphology of Ludwig Klages," in a forthcoming issue of *Char. & Person.* This reference serves as the best available account in English of the science of expression as formulated by Klages.

best case, however, is for a comprehensive science of psychodiagnostics that will embrace *all* manifestations of personality and avoid one-sided preoccupation with any one. Part of the enthusiasm for graphology springs naturally from the easy access of the records, but this fortunate accident is not sufficient justification for a monosymptomatic approach to expression.

Graphic movement is an exceedingly complex subject, that should be thoroughly explored or let alone; in such a subject partial understanding and half-truths are more damaging than helpful.

This problem has been omitted here in view of the somewhat detailed account available in *Studies in Expressive Movement*, often cited in this volume. Besides an historical survey of the subject, the *Studies* contain a report of several experiments, which led the authors to the following general conclusions:

"The results show that practicing graphologists seem on the whole to give better judgments and to make more correct matchings than do untrained persons. Even at best, however, the results do not establish professional graphology on a certain basis; by our criteria the results are still nearer to chance than to perfection. But in favor of the graphologists it may be urged that psychological criteria are far from perfect, that many items in an analysis may be predictions which time alone can affirm or deny, that the conditions of our experiments have been so stringently controlled as to be prejudicial to the free exercise of the graphologist's talents.

"Regarding the value of commercial graphology the authors have no final opinion. Probably too much has been claimed for it by graphologists and too little by psychologists. Practically all lines of research reported have been favorable to a slight degree. The success of professional graphologists seems usually to exceed chance, and occasionally to show brilliance. Some experts appear to give better readings than others, although each seems to be irregular and variable in the aptness of his judgments." [29]

STYLE

Style represents the most complex and most complete form of expressive behavior. It concerns the whole of activity, not merely special skills or single regions of the body. It has been termed the

[29] Reprinted by permission of The Macmillan Co., from *Studies in Expressive Movement*, pp. 246 f.

"personal idiom" in conduct; the French adage has even said, "The style is the man himself." Each painter has a style of his own, so has each composer, pianist, sculptor, dancer, poet, dramatist, actor, orator, photographer, acrobat, housewife, and mechanic. From style alone we may recognize compositions by Chopin, paintings by Van Gogh, and pastry by Aunt Sally. Style enters whenever well integrated and mature behavior of the personality is involved.

It is apparent that style is one of the most embracing concepts with which psychology has to deal. It involves the very highest levels of integration, reminding one of the concept of the "total personality." Already in Chapter VIII we have discussed the dangers of a merely rhapsodic use of such "high level" concepts, and have proposed a more discriminating treatment of the phenomena of unity (or near-unity). As alternatives to the exaggerated doctrine of perfect wholeness, there were offered more articulate points of view—as the theory of master-sentiments, the theories of the radix, the unity-theme, the core, the cardinal trait, congruence, and inter-relationship among traits.

It is not necessary to discuss style in relation to each of these structural concepts, but whatever the theory finally accepted as representing the structural *consistency* of personality, it will be necessary to regard style as the external aspect of this consistency; for style is intimately bound to the structure of personality, changing as the structure changes, and reaching its full development only when personality itself is mature.

Style is a problem of great interest to esthetics as well as to psychology. In literature, we are told, style seems to be a product of peculiarities of sentence structure, vocabulary, the number and variety of syllables, their arrangement and accent, alliterative and other devices to obtain "tone color," favorite imagery, suggested associations, the use of metaphor and all manner of characteristic rhetorical figures. Sometimes there is added likewise the principle of "rhythm" to draw attention to the fact that these separate attributes of style rely for their effect not upon their successive impact but upon their co-existence. Yet an esthetic analysis of style is not adequate.

Such an esthetic analysis as has been outlined calls attention to the mechanical carriers of style. It fails to depict style in the only way it can be fully understood, as an expression of central traits of personality. The following psychological experiment will make this fact clear.[30]

This study employed the English themes of 70 college students. Nine themes were gathered from each student, three in October, three in January, and three in May. The topics for the themes were prescribed and were uniform for all students.

. After being typed and divested of all identifying signs, two experimenters attempted to sort these themes carefully so that they might from style alone group all the themes written by the same student. For both experimenters the results were strikingly positive, well above chance (Vernon's calculation of the success of this experiment in terms of contingency coefficients is given on p. 479).

The point of interest here is the method by which successful matchings were made. Occasionally, to be sure, some striking mechanical feature caught the eye and aided in identifications. Addiction to semicolons would mark the writing of one student, or some other oddity of punctuation or spelling. But most of the identifications were not made on this basis but through a diagnosis of the *personal traits* of the writers. "The investigators found themselves searching for a 'form-quality' of the individual." They felt in each production a reflection of certain complex qualities in the writer himself. Now these qualities were different in each case and difficult for the experimenter to reduce to words.[31]

In spite of the difficulty of expressing these hypotheses of "form-quality" in words, the fact remains that they (and not mechanical features) were ordinarily the basis of judgment, and likewise that the judgments were to a significant degree successful.

It is of interest to note some of the bases upon which this matching proceeded. The productions of one student, for example, would be felt always to reflect "a feeling for atmosphere; a well-balanced sense of humor; a quiet, amused tolerance of social relations and situations." Another showed in all his themes "a positive self-assurance; definite, but neither prejudiced nor opinionated; sense of humor." A third was "constantly bored. Looks at life as a monotonous experience in which one follows the easiest course of action." A fourth had a "simple,

---

[30] F. H. Allport, L. Walker, E. Lathers, "Written Composition and Characteristics of Personality," *Arch. of Psychol.*, 1934, No. 173.

[31] "A significant fact about the process of matching themes is that the identifying characteristic one is seeking is too elusive to be stated adequately in language. It is too highly individualized to be expressed fully in the common and universal meanings attaching to words. When a word is used to describe it, there is usually a unique connotation attaching to that word in that particular instance which would be lost or altered if the same word were applied to another individual." Allport, Walker, Lathers, *op. cit.*, p. 69.

optimistic attitude toward life and people; simple, direct, declarative sentences."

One concludes that style is not a matter of mechanical arrangement of grammatical and rhetorical figures. It is simply the personality expressed in writing. *Le style est l'homme même.*

A brief but revealing instance of style comes in an individual's narration of events he has seen or of books he has read. This familiar situation has been turned to account as an experimental technique. By reading to all the subjects the same passage, a short story, let us say, and asking them after an interval of time to retell the story in their own words, striking individual differences are found. In one case the retelling is meager and colorless; in another, elaborate and inventive; always there is the introduction of the personal factor. In ordinary life-situations this phenomenon may be observed in even more marked form. An individual has read a book; hundreds of pages of impressions have filled his mind. Now within a few sentences he recounts in a highly selective way the "main features" of the book he has read. We learn something of the book, to be sure, but we learn even more about his own mind through which the pages have filtered.

Style is a characteristic not only of verbal expression, but of any articulate complex-level of activity as well. It is ever present in music. There is no way to account for the style developed by individual composers unless their own lives are searched. There was a lyrical but tragic quality in Schubert's life as well as in his music; Handel was said to be as majestic in his behavior as he is in his music; the perfectionism and order in Bach's compositions were not adventitious; nor was the combination of rhapsodic and religious feeling in the music of Brahms.

A certain well-known violinist whose style of playing is tender, possessed of a distinctive *vox humana* quality, shows in his personal life corresponding traits. He believes, for example, that his talent should not be used for financial gain. From his large income he reserves only enough money to provide a modest living for himself and his family, giving the balance of his earnings to charity for the care of neglected children. In this case the artistic style is an obvious expression of inner attitude. Again, the style is the man himself.

Style enters not only into verbal and artistic activity, but into economic behavior as well. There are, for example, styles of *error*, springing perhaps from a characteristic haste or superficiality of thought, or from an imaginativeness or personal prejudice.[32] There are styles of *setting to work*, in one case with a modest goal in view, well under the level of one's ability, or in another case with an aspiration that is quite excessive, bound to lead to failure.[33] There are *occupational styles* that cling to the performance of any individual in the course of his daily work.

An interesting study of occupational styles was made by Katzenstein among office clerks in a large department store. These clerks were given all manner of psychological tests (for arithmetical, associative, linguistic, and motor abilities, for concentration, information, and professional judgment). None of these tests of common abilities betrayed the style of work. Two clerks with identical scores in all abilities, and of equal effectiveness as workmen, might be entirely different in their manner of working. One would show an uneven nervous performance, consistent with a moody temperament and severe mental conflict. He would be agreeable, witty, the center of attention on one occasion; disagreeable, rude, and morose on another. A second individual with a similar occupational profile would be an even-tempered, unimaginative plodder. In no two cases were the styles of work the same, and in no instance did any standard test or combination of tests reveal the style.[34]

Style is an expressive form of slow growth; it is not something ready-made, picked at random to be donned mechanically. It develops gradually from within; it cannot for long be simulated or feigned. Behind the manifestations of an individual's style stretches a whole life history, back to the cradle and his first departures from the schedule prepared for him and all other infants. Style is the gradual externalization of the inner peculiarities and unique characteristics of the individual. Convention and fashion may set limits upon style, prescribing the frame of the moment within which one's style (of clothing, writing, painting, script, conversation, music, recreation, and what-not) must be constrained. For the time being these limits are rigid; only a genius is able to tear loose from the current frame of mode or convention and create a new idiom (that will determine the frame of the future). But even within these limits no personality, whatever the culture, repeats exactly the style of another.

There is an esthetics of being oneself, even in those stern re-

[32] A. Kiessling, *Vjsch. f. Jugendkunde*, 1932, 2, 232-236.
[33] J. D. Frank, *Amer. J. Psychol.*, 1935, 47, 119-128.
[34] B. Katzenstein, *Zsch. f. ang. Psychol.*, 1932, 41, 69-137.

pressive cultures intent on destroying every trace of individuality. In the long run such destructive effort is vain, for individual style cannot be extinguished, any more than individual physical identity can be extinguished. The person is the fundamental and unique unit of all activity, and the individual style expresses that fundamental uniqueness. For this reason there are as many styles of expression as there are mortals who live; they cannot be compressed into one mold. *Chacun fait son salut comme il peut.*

SUMMARY

Expressive behavior is an accompanying phase of adaptive behavior. It is the latter that gives the primary clues to the structure of personality: *what* a man is doing, or what he is *trying* to do, gives the fundamental testimony as to the nature of his traits. But unless there is deliberate volitional suppression, one finds expressive behavior entering into nearly all adaptive acts. Expressive behavior is unconsciously determined. It often sheds additional light upon the very same traits that are being revealed in the adaptive behavior, but often it reflects quite different deep-lying personal qualities not directly concerned with the act of the moment.

The genesis and the self-consistency of expression are among the basic psychological problems in this area of investigation. Then, too, separate channels of expression are studied, such as facial set and movement, gait, voice, handwriting. Yet exclusive pre-occupation with any of these channels is likely to lead to a dangerously narrow method of monosymptomatic diagnosis. The discovery of the significance of these external expressive signs for inner qualities of personality is called psychodiagnostics, a modern scientific extension of the ancient arts of physiognomy.

The study of expressive behavior *requires* the doctrine of traits, for the only secure interpretation of expression seems to be in terms of stable personal dispositions. Expressive movement, in brief, is the external aspect of inner structural consistency.

The most complex form of expression is called "style"—the particular individualized manner of execution that permeates any highly integrated volitional activity. Though most conspicuous and most celebrated in the fields of esthetic creation, style is also apparent in economic, domestic and social conduct—wherever, in fact, the fundamental traits of personality are operative. Though the roots of style are no doubt to be traced to native temperament, the interaction of mature traits with one another, and their confluent effect upon creative and adaptive acts, are the immediate sources of the stylistic idiom.

Part V

UNDERSTANDING PERSONALITY

CHAPTER XVIII

THE ABILITY TO JUDGE PEOPLE

There is hardly any person living concerning some essential part of whose character there are not differences of opinion even among his intimate acquaintances; and a single action, or conduct continued only for a short time, goes a very little way toward ascertaining it.

—John Stuart Mill

No person can understand any other person completely, for it is impossible for one human being to share directly the motives, thoughts, and feelings of another. This unbridgeable chasm between mind and mind has led philosophers to ponder the egocentric predicament of the human race, and poets to lament the ultimate solitude of each soul. It is, they assure us, only through circuitous routes and through the study of "shadows" that we are able to achieve our imperfect glimpses of one another. Since psychology can do nothing to change this "metaphysical solitude," it must recognize at the outset that the problem of understanding people is always a problem of *partial* understanding. We may understand one another *relatively* well but never completely.

From the psychologist's point of view some of the most important problems involved in judgments of personality are the following: (1) the nature and reliability of first impressions, (2) the chief factors involved in judging, (3) the value of interviews, (4) the question whether ability to judge people is general or specific, (5) the qualifications of a good judge, (6) the relative excellence of men and women as judges, (7) the types that are best known to us, and (8) common sources of error in judgment. These problems will serve as a topical outline for this chapter.

FIRST IMPRESSIONS

Mr. A and Mr. B meet for the first time. They discuss the weather, the last ball game, and the condition of the stock-market. After five minutes they part without having revealed directly any information of a specifically personal nature. Nevertheless each carries away an impression of the personality of the other. A may think B is straightforward, jolly, well-informed, dependable, and friendly; B may think A modest, tactful, conservative, and reclusive, "a good sort when once you get to know him." Such first impressions are often quite definite, but unfortunately, as John Stuart Mill pointed out, are frequently not as trustworthy as they seem.

In the brief period of first meeting there is little chance for contradictions to appear, or for the judge to ascertain which traits are central and which are incidental in the personality. Some features are hidden entirely, especially those that are asocial; the *persona* is not easy to penetrate at first meeting, even though its presence may be suspected. Nevertheless a brief acquaintance often does result in amazingly rich impressions, many of which are proven upon further acquaintance to be correct. Such successful judgments are significant because, lacking personal information, or a telltale context of conversation, the cues are derived almost entirely from expressive movements—from appearance, gesture, and manner of speaking.

The astonishing rapidity with which first judgments are made can easily be demonstrated. While riding in a public conveyance close your eyes and turn your head toward some fellow passenger not previously observed, perhaps someone sitting obliquely opposite. Open your eyes for a brief glimpse lasting two or three seconds, and then with the eyes closed introspect upon the impressions as they arise. Here is a person, never before seen and completely unknown. With but the briefest visual perception, a complex mental process is aroused, resulting within a very short time, thirty seconds perhaps, in judgments of the sex, age, size, nationality, profession, and social caste of the stranger, together with some estimate of his temperament, his past suffering, his "hardness," his ascendance, friendliness, neatness, and even his trustworthiness and integrity. With further acquaintance many of the impressions would no doubt prove to be erroneous, but the exercise serves to call attention to the swift "totalizing" nature of our judgments. The fact that one perceives a personality at first contact, not by fragments pieced together with painful slowness but with swift "intuition," is, as the following chapter will show, a matter of considerable theoretical importance.[1]

The reliability of first impressions has been studied experimentally. Using a somewhat generous allowance of time (half an hour) Spielman and Burt examined the agreement of two independent investigators interviewing 16-year-old children.[2] Each investigator used a five-point rating scale. For "primary instincts" (McDougall's list) the agreement ranged from +.85 for *submissiveness* and +.75 for *fear*, down to +.37 for *curiosity* and +.23 for *acquisitiveness*. Among "secondary qualities" the range was from +.77 for *self-confidence* and +.64 for *energy*, down to +.44 for *punctuality* and +.36 for *reliability*. The authors conclude that the qualities more reliably rated on the whole are those that are emotional and "instinctive," and likewise those that are socially acceptable. Anti-social qualities are concealed behind the *persona* during the first interview, and are therefore impossible to rate. Nothing is established in this experiment concerning the validity of these impressions, and the agreement of the judges with one another seems on the whole rather higher than in most studies of a similar nature.

On the basis of extremely short interviews, lasting only 30 seconds, another investigator made estimates of the probable abilities of apprentices in the printing trade. Checked against a long series of aptitude tests, half the cases, it is reported, showed "good" agreement, and the other half only "fair" or "poor" agreement.[3] This study illustrates one way in which first impressions may be *validated*, but it unfortunately does not express its results clearly or objectively.

Still another investigation studied both the agreement (between two judges) and the validity of first impressions gained from brief interviews with 25 subjects. The average correlation between the two sets of ratings for such qualities as *expansiveness, neatness*, and *emotionality* was about +.40. Such an agreement compares favorably with many rating-studies where judges have had the advantage of long acquaintance with their subjects. The interviewers employed questions that were not directly personal in nature, and each inter-

---

[1] *Intuition* as used in this connection means simply *a unitary perception resulting from a complex pattern of inter-related cues.*

[2] W. Spielman and C. Burt, *Indust. Fat. Res. Bd. Rep.*, 1926, No. 33, pp. 57-72.

[3] W. Englemann, *Indust. Psychotech.*, 1928, 5, 307-310.

view was terminated at the end of the ninety seconds. At the close of the interview the judge made his ratings. He likewise predicted the type of behavior which the subject would show in certain subsequent experimental situations. These later experiments were conducted by a third investigator, in this way providing a validation for the "snap" predictions. In many respects, especially in the prejudgments of *impulsiveness, verbosity, co-operativeness,* and *originality,* the predictions of the subjects' behavior were borne out. On the whole the predictions of one of the interviewers were more successful than those of the other.[4]

In interpreting all experiments of this type it must be borne in mind that by its very nature the short interview tends to put the subject on his guard. Generally during the first few moments of *any* interview he does not behave in a natural way, but wears his protective mask. Experimental interviews therefore are not well suited to eliciting spontaneous and unpremeditated behavior.

Natural settings are better testing-grounds for first impressions, even though the judgments are much more difficult to express. Let us take one example. The following protocol was written by a woman attending for the first time a summer school course in dramatic literature in a western university. The instructor was totally unknown to her. She sat in the rear of the room, and during the fifty minutes occupied by the first lecture made the free-running notes which are presented here in a somewhat condensed form. Even though they have necessarily been edited to some extent, the notes indicate the way the mind may work while forming its first judgments.

FIRST IMPRESSIONS OF PROFESSOR D

Entrance: late—quiet and firm; passes out papers; fixes cuffs and coat; does not face class in speaking. Slightly condescending feeling toward class as "undergraduate." Some shyness—much more composed with back to class.

Ethnic type uncertain; name Brythonic in origin, but found all over British Isles. Thought him at first Irish type, but closer observation changed, probably South Wales, maybe Cornish. Features rather fine, but small—lack of force here. Head brachycephalic-mesocephalic, but face oval and long. Slightly more curve than common in pure Celtic

---

[4] This work is described by H. S. Odbert, *The Consistency of the Individual in his Imaginal Processes* (Cambridge: Harvard College Library), 1934.

type—face disharmonic with cephalic index. Lips thin: these deny the sense of delicacy of perception that rest of contour might suggest. Never really smiles, but slight widening of lips. He compresses these with an animal-like hint of ire. Thin lips: self-discipline good.

Graceful in spite of chunky build. Gestures good. Self-confidence in knowledge of subject much greater than in self.

Middle west provenance? R's rather burred (says "pervailing" for "prevailing"); tries to use English accent but his early training betrays him.

Self-indulgent; indifferent to dress—coat too short, trousers unpressed. Standards of personal neatness not high; skin of face clear but not hands. Moderately well-kept, but one does not have sense of cleanliness about him; uses pomade. One feels that he likes his gray hair and thinks it a distinction. Conservative trend—does not like shaggy-haired dramatists, and yet a contradictory tendency here for he obviously prefers romantic literature.

Lecture confused as he goes on. Sternness and severity of pedagogic attitude grows stronger. Poetic appreciation submerged in critical attitude. Poor ear for speech sounds.

Witty but acid—remarks not really funny. Would be best company when slightly drunk—inhibitions removed. Fond of satiric remarks toward world in general, especially women, but possibly not unfair or unjust in general reaction.

Type more feminine in some ways than masculine. Nervous fussiness—scratches himself—sits like a woman. Probably likes to play around women, but very conscious underneath of essential superiority. Could be conventionally attached to wife—or might leave her for a temporary attachment that he would rationalize as a "cerebral affinity."

Whom does he resemble? Some memory of L. E. W. (set of eyes— he has not *yet* squarely seen his class). Sadistic strain as in Y. T. who had similar expression around mouth and eyes. Bodily planes wholly avertive, hands soft, inclined to paddiness at tips. Not a common homosexual type—except for one thing: unpleasant aspect of torso.

Feeling of strong inhibitory conflict, much mask. No large expressive movements; maybe due to dislike of teaching—certainly some conflict. Rather subtle and complex, not sensitive to class, cynical, even satiric toward whole business. He is a type found at times in faculties of women's colleges. Very few professors seem so indifferent to class.

Not a type I like. Recall now L. E. W., J. P. J., and L. L. at similar age (*cir.* 40), and another I can see clearly but whose name I cannot at present recall, though his character is strong in memory.

General reaction—introversion. Not as much ability as he would like to have—ambitions above power; critical and mathematical, rather than artistic approach. Esthetic appreciation is for small things—fine structure rather than total effect—large poetic feeling beyond him. Rather easily bored. But that is a long and deep-seated defense. Careless pronunciation and lack of tonal variation in voice make poor background probable, which he has sought to overcome, but not successfully. Cannot see faults clearly enough, yet not markedly conceited; a sad world, and he doesn't quite know why. Endocrine maladjustment?

Has a subtle truculence of bearing, as if he did not think the world had treated him well. Conceals many of his opinions toward the world, but might become quite expansive and confidential given a few cocktails; very sensitive to such stimulus. Changeable and moody. Might be expansive too when something awakens his sense of power. Not wholly reliable.

Probably good bridge player, but not for high stakes,—no daring or roving in his eyes. Philosophy of life materialistic and mechanistic. Politically, a diluted radical; under some types of emotional stimulus would get a great kick out of direct action—vicarious compensation for imagined personal wrongs.

Lecture ended as it began, no enthusiasm, no warmth—poorest lecture on subject I have ever heard. Students coming up with papers. Took paper from middle-aged teacherish person without looking at her; plain girl also not seen; pretty fair haired girl, feminine eyes at work—bare glance. Two fair calf-like males—no reaction. Tall dark handsome boy—bodily planes change instantly—the one looked for? First real smile he has allowed—attention instantly centered. Others crowd around and ask questions—face immobile, but eyes still seek the one he apparently knows and likes.

From this sketch several interesting facts appear. First impressions seem to be remarkably rich, and to have almost innumerable ramifications in thought and feeling. They are also disorderly, probably much more so than the sketch itself, for the very act of writing forces some form upon the chaos of impressions. It also appears that first impressions are laden with the affective attitude and value-judgments of the observer. It is not only the *personality* of the professor which is described, but his *character* as well: he is considered to be unreliable, rather incompetent, and on the whole not a likeable person.

It is evident that the observer's interest in ethnic and anthropometric matters constitutes for her a framework for "character analysis." She is likewise particularly attentive to hands and to postures. When she makes detailed reference to anatomical and expressive features it does not mean that each single feature reveals some separate trait, but rather that the feature acts as a "point of condensation" in her mind for judgments which are so elusive and complex that their basis cannot be fully recognized. The fact that she makes many judgments without stating any basis for them shows likewise that impressions arise from unanalyzable patterns of movement and speech. A single physiognomic feature may often *suggest* a trait, but other features usually are consulted to see whether they reinforce, modify, or contradict the suggestion. One thing is quite certain, and that is that the observer is unable to tell the *entire* basis for her judgments of Professor D's personality.

It is interesting to note how the observer's mind swings from a quite specific observation to a broad generalization, and then back again to some detail. At the opening of the sketch, a few rather colorless and specific acts are noted, suddenly followed by a judgment of two traits, "condescension" and "shyness." First impressions seem characteristically to be made up of just such an irregular alternation between detailed and "totalized" observations.

As the protocol advances it seems to deal somewhat more with broader and more fundamental traits, and correspondingly less with detailed observation. The phenomenon of personal *congruence* becomes clearer. So it always seems to be in approaching a new personality. At the very beginning the contours are dim. It is much like watching the coastline of a strange country from the deck of an approaching vessel. The structure is not at once grasped; objects have no sharp boundaries or clear coloration; what is taken for a mountain may turn out to be a cloud. The attention lights first upon one confusing detail and then upon another. But in the course of time the contours gradually become sharper and well articulated; substructures appear; what was strange and blurred becomes clear as soon as it can be brought into focus.

The sketch shows likewise the important part played by imagery and associated ideas in the process of judgment. Inferences extend beyond the direct evidence offered in the classroom; there are conjectures concerning D's sensitivity to liquor, his attitudes toward bridge, politics, and philosophy, and even concerning his marital fidelity. Occasionally the writer compares him explicitly with individuals whom he seems to resemble. Such trains of association serve as a basis for prediction and generalization beyond the limits of the immediate perception. But in addition to the play of associated imagery and inference there seems to be much in the sketch that is intuitive. No elaborate train of associations is needed to explain the perception of gracefulness, boredom, disorderliness, condescension, or inner conflict. These are qualities so intrinsic in his behavior that they seem to be as readily perceived as are the physical features themselves.

A few apparent contradictions occur in the sketch; for example, inconsistent statements are made concerning his conceit, self-control, and sexual adjustments. But whether these are based on errors of observation or indicate the complexity of D's personality cannot be determined without a suitable method of validation which in this case is lacking. Ordinarily the only way to validate first impressions is through further acquaintance.

Within limits, however, a pen portrait, such as we have here, may be considered to be self-validating. If it creates a convincing and meaningful picture, if it has the ring of "systematic relevance," it is accepted; but if the author seems arbitrary or confused in her judgments, it is rejected. This is the only test applied to character-portraits in literature. No one requires more of Hamlet than that, with all the complexity of his nature, he be self-consistent. When his mood changes it must change in ways that still are congruent with the underlying currents in his life. The writer of the sketch of Professor D may not be correct in all her judgments—especially since she confesses to a bias of dislike for his "type," but she has nevertheless sketched a personality that seems in the main plausibly self-consistent.

Would a different lecture or a meeting with D under other circumstances lead to the same judgments? On the morning of the lecture D may have been unprepared, preoccupied, or perhaps ill. Another day he might be more orderly, more interested, and more friendly. Or it may be that his professional behavior is quite different from his behavior outside the classroom. To see D under different circumstances would be the only possible way to distinguish his permanent traits from temporary moods and from habits that are specific to the situation of the classroom. But many of the "constitutional" qualities noted in the sketch, such, for example, as his introversion and conflict, his effeminateness, are in all probability not temporary or specific. Further acquaintance would undoubtedly discover new characteristics and correct erroneous judgments, and yet, as is usually the case with first impressions, a residuum of valid judgment would no doubt survive.

THREE BASIC FACTORS INVOLVED IN JUDGING PERSONALITY

An experiment dealing more explicitly with the validity of first impressions will next be described in order to illustrate the roles of the three basic variables involved in any judgment of personality (whether based on first impressions or on long acquaintance).

The experiment is that of S. G. Estes.[5] This investigator used short (two-minute) motion picture records of behavior of subjects whose personalities had been intensively studied by a group of twenty psychologists over a period of one academic year. In these films the subjects performed briefly certain "expressive" tasks (such as divesting themselves of coat, tie and shirt; playing slap-jack and wrestling with an opponent; holding a lighted match as long as possible, and building a house of playing cards).

In one portion of the experiment film-records were employed for eight subjects upon whom extraordinarily complete criteria-data were available. Thirty-seven judges watched the films (each shown twice, making a four minute "first impression"). These judges were all psychiatric social-workers having at least two years' practical experience in addition to their formal training. The judges' ratings were made with the aid of the same schedule of variables that had been employed in the intensive one year investigation of the personalities of the subjects. Hence it was possible to make a direct comparison between the judgments based on film-records and upon the prolonged experimental and clinical study.

In such a situation the excellence of the judgment is found to vary

(1) with the inherent ability or shrewdness of the judge,

(2) with the nature of the variable (trait) rated,

(3) with the "open" or "enigmatic" character of the subject.

In reference to the first of these factors (which seems likewise to be the most important), it was found that the 10 best judges were uniformly better than the 10 poorest judges for *all* the variables and for *all* the subjects. The average efficiency (correctness) of the 10

[5] S. G. Estes, *The Judgment of Personality on the Basis of Brief Records of Behavior* (Cambridge: Harvard College Library), 1937.

best judges was 33 per cent higher than that of the 10 poorest; and the record of the best single judge averaged 62 per cent better than that of the poorest judge. The conclusion is inescapable that even in a homogeneous and highly trained profession such as psychiatric social work the difference in ability to "size up" individuals on brief acquaintance from appearance alone is very striking. What personal qualities make one judge more capable than another is an intricate question considered later (pp. 513-518). Suffice it here to say that Estes found within the age-range of his judges (25-52) no influence of age, no relation to length of professional service, sibling status, nor to the fact that the judge had himself been psychoanalyzed, as half of them had been.

The second factor concerns the variable or trait in respect to which the subjects are judged. With considerable uniformity for all the subjects certain qualities were rated well above chance, viz., *inhibition-impulsion, apathy-intensity, placidity-emotionality, ascendance-submission*. It is clearly evident that these qualities are overt; they are "expressive" traits which represent the individual's characteristic mode of adaptation to the world around him. Poorly rated variables included such covert qualities as *objectivity-projectivity* (*i.e.*, realism-paranoia), *desire for change*, and the "need" for *rejection* (*e.g.*, snobbishness), the "need" for *play*, and the "need" for *nurturance* (*e.g.*, "parental instinct"). These badly rated traits are obviously not of the type that the situations used in the film-records would reveal, and likewise they seem less well-defined and therefore less easily understood by the judges than the traits correctly rated.

In brief, the evidence here supports the conclusion reached on p. 442, that in order to be accurately judged traits should be overt, expressive and well-defined. Poor judgments are to be expected when the quality is hidden, not issuing readily into ordinary action, or when it is ill-defined and therefore confusing to the judge. The best-rated trait (*inhibition-impulsion*) was judged by the thirty-seven judges 28.2 per cent more accurately than the poorest-rated trait (need for *nurturance*).

The third important factor in the judgment-situation is the "openness" of the subject (cf. p. 443). For one of the eight subjects these 37 judges agreed with the criterion ratings on the average 25 per cent better than would be expected by chance, but on another (the most enigmatic) of the eight, only 5 per cent better than chance. Both the best judges and the worst judges had the same relative difficulty. Although their ratings were of unequal accuracy, both found the same subjects easy to rate, or hard to rate. Considering the results of all the judges together on all of the variables rated, the correctness for the most "open" personality was 22 per cent better than for the most "enigmatic" personality. We are forced to conclude that at first meeting the *persona* of some individuals is definitely a handicap to the judges, whereas the expressive behavior of other individuals is relatively transparent.

In summary, to secure the most trustworthy judgment from first impressions (and probably from long acquaintance as well), it is necessary to have *a gifted judge, applying his skill to certain overt and readily accessible traits in a subject who is himself not deceptive or enigmatic.*

THE INTERVIEW

Unlike first impressions which, as a rule, are obtained incidentally in the course of an impersonal relationship, the interview seeks to secure directly as much information of a personal nature from the subject as is relevant to the interests of the interviewer. The method is age-old, but still is of paramount importance in most fields of social investigation.[6] Scientific studies of interviewing are as yet few in number, and are for the most part artificial and unsatisfactory, for a good interview requires variation and spontaneity, and only with difficulty can it be reduced to rules and formulae.

Although interviewing is an art, it clearly involves the same three factors as do all judgment-situations. There is first the skill of the interviewer (probably the most important and most complex factor of all). Secondly, there is the openness or enigmatic quality of the subject himself. Thirdly there is the selection and framing of questions that will reveal significant and trustworthy information concerning the subject.

In considering the third factor, one must first know what the goal of the interview is. Significant questions for a psychiatrist to ask might be immaterial for a census-taker. But assuming that the goal of the interview is *psychological, i.e.,* to obtain the fullest and most accurate knowledge possible of a personality, how should the interviewer proceed? He may use various published guides for the study

[6] A serviceable manual for interviewers has been prepared by W. V. Bingham and B. V. Moore, *How to Interview,* 1934.

of personality.[7] Or he may have at hand a list of topics with the aid of which he can frame specific questions according to the progress of the interview. Or he may proceed in a planless way, letting one line of inquiry suggest the next. Ordinarily the second plan is most satisfactory, neither as rigid and mechanical as the first nor as loose and precarious as the third. The following brief schedule of topics has been found satisfactory in guiding interviewers who wish to follow this plan. It is fairly comprehensive, though it can readily be expanded or contracted to fit the individual case. There is no inviolable sequence. For one person a given topic may yield nothing of significance; for another the same topic may contain the most important clues, and for that reason require expansion. Needless to say, the interviewer must be on his guard to distinguish conventional and self-protective answers from those that are frank and genuine.

A BRIEF SCHEDULE FOR A PSYCHOLOGICAL INTERVIEW

1. Age
2. Nationality
3. Degree of education
4. Sicknesses and accidents
5. Occupational history and plans
6. Hobbies
7. Cultural interests
8. Ambitions (*e.g.*, what he hopes to accomplish within the next two years)
9. Personal attachments (*e.g.*, who has influenced him most)
10. Daydreams
11. Fears and worries
12. Humiliations and disappointments
13. Marked aversions
14. Sex experience
15. Neurotic difficulties
16. Religious experience
17. Philosophy of life

These topics deal in approximately equal proportion with the life-history, the present situation, and the subject's outlook into the future. They provide an aid in *understanding* the subject rather than

[7] A list of several available schedules is given on p. 236, ftn.

in describing him. For a fuller "cross-sectional" record of the person-ality as it is today, the interviewer may supplement his observations and notations by tests for attitudes and traits, by ratings obtained from the subject's associates, and may perhaps find assistance in the psychograph (Chapter XV).

Certain items in the above schedule pertain to the social status of the subject. Information of this order is essential; for only by knowing the "frame of reference" within which a personality has developed can the interviewer understand fully his subject's pre-conceptions and codes. In recording the cultural frame, however, the interviewer should not fall into the erroneous assumption of many social determinists that the subject will, of necessity, in his own personal life hold to each and every norm that characterizes his race, religion, or social class.

The success of an interview depends not only upon properly framed questions, but likewise upon the attitude of the subject. The interviewer must seek to remove antagonism and suspicion, and to create a situation in which the subject feels encouraged to speak, and confident that his interests are protected. But where the subject is unintelligent or reticent or disingenuous, this is easier said than done. It is ordinarily more satisfactory to interview a person of high intelligence and good cultural background than of low intelligence and inferior social position. Yet, the person with a brilliant mind, if neurotically defensive or inclined to deception, is perhaps the most difficult of *all* types to deal with. In general the method of the inter-view is satisfactory only when the subject possesses a reasonable degree of intelligence, has some insight, and above all is willing (preferably, eager) for the interview to take place.

The third and most complex factor in the situation is the skill of the interviewer. The psychologist cannot at present include in a single formula the intricate combination of abilities that makes a good judge of people, nor can he tell anyone how to become all at once a great "character reader." He can, however, offer an analysis of some aspects of this skill, and can pronounce upon some of the qualifications displayed by successful judges.

IS THE ABILITY TO JUDGE PERSONALITY GENERAL OR SPECIFIC?

Most mental abilities are neither entirely general nor entirely specific. A person with "artistic ability" is not as a rule equally

proficient in drawing, painting, music, dancing, and writing. Training, experience, and taste, as well as native gifts, run in narrower
channels. On the other hand, artistic ability is not entirely specific.
It is unheard of for a man to be able to sketch a good boat but an
unrecognizable lighthouse, or to be able to produce one original
melody and not others. It would be unreasonable, therefore, to expect a judge of people to be uniformly successful in estimating every
quality of every person, or conversely to be successful only in understanding but *one* quality in all people, or perhaps all qualities of
one personality. In common speech one man is said to be "an excellent judge of character" and another to be "continually taken in
by people," but the ability and the disability here spoken of are
probably not absolutely uniform.[8] There are limiting conditions of
perceptual powers, of memory, experience, interest, and social intelligence that produce individual clusters or ranges of the ability.

On the basis of experimental evidence, Vernon suggests three
such typical ranges: there are those, he finds, who understand *themselves* well; there are others who have specially good knowledge of
their *friends* and acquaintances; and there are still others who excel
in judging *strangers*. Individuals in the first group are characterized
by high intelligence and a sense of humor. Good judges of friends
and associates are on the average less socially inclined and less intelligent than good self-judges, but more artistic. Good judges of
strangers are distinctly high in intelligence and in artistic gifts, and
tend to be unsocial in certain respects.[9] These qualifications are logical enough. The good judge of self must have not only high intelligence but also that humor which is almost invariably associated with
insight (cf. p. 222). Within limits the good judge of acquaintances
may make up in experience what he lacks in intelligence, but he
must have the distance and objectivity in his point of view that
usually go with artistic and asocial tendencies. The good judge of
strangers must have the same distance, but in addition more intelligence, since the cues upon which he bases his judgment are fewer
and more transient. It is precisely this latter combination of qualities
which seems to make a good writer of fiction or biography: he must

[8] It seems more of an error, however, to consider the ability entirely specific
than to consider it entirely general. The reader will recall the experiments of Estes
which showed considerable uniformity of ability for his various judges whatever
subjects and whatever traits they judged (cf. pp. 507 f.).

[9] P. E. Vernon, *J. Soc. Psychol.*, 1933, 4, 42-58.

be intelligent, artistic, and asocial enough to be *detached* in his view of people.

QUALIFICATIONS FOR A GOOD JUDGE OF OTHERS

Combining the findings of Vernon with the results of other investigations, published [10] and unpublished, a summary statement may be made of the qualifications for a good judge of people, so far as they are at present understood.

1. *Experience*. A good judge requires first of all maturity, which means not only the attainment of thirty years or so in age, but likewise a rich store of experience with human nature in its varied and more intricate forms. The youth sees people in the narrow perspective of his limited experience, and when forced to judge those whose lives differ markedly from his own, frequently resorts to such callow and inadequate clichés as "a good sport," "an old stick-in-the-mud," or "queer." The jargon of adolescents contains any number of such characterial clichés. In spite of the protest of each younger generation that the elder fails to understand it, the chances are vastly in favor of it misunderstanding the elder.

Without a broad and long-continued acquaintance with all manner of people, the elementary basis for logical inference is lacking. Each judgment partakes of previous judgments, and is corrected by them. For each of the innumerable expressions of personality, the experienced person has at his disposal a rich apperceptive chain of well-tested interpretations. Even if association and inference do not represent the only mental processes involved in understanding people, if—as is probable—some concession must be made to the theories of intuitive understanding, still the solid foundations of experience are the first and most essential requirement, for intuition cannot occur in an experiential vacuum.

2. *Similarity*. Another important, but not unexceptionable, requirement is that the judge in his own nature resemble the individual whom he is attempting to judge. According to Klages, "understanding is possible only by virtue of *some* similarity between the perceiving self and the perceived object; and as dissimilarity

[10] E.g., H. F. Adams, *J. Abnorm. & Soc. Psychol.*, 1927, 22, 172-181; C. W. Valentine, *Brit. J. Psychol.*, 1929, 19, 213-238; H. Gross, *Criminal Psychology*, trans. 1918; G. W. Allport, *The Family*, 1930, 11, 124-128; H. L. Hollingworth, *Vocational Psychology and Character Analysis*, 1929.

grows, understanding gives way to a failure to understand." [11] This requirement is simply a corollary of the first. Experimental studies have shown that it is indeed a fact that the best judges of a trait in another person are those who themselves possess the trait in a high degree. But the correlation is not perfect, and the situation is far from simple: flexibility of imagination in one judge may be worth more than stores of unused experience in another.

Similarity, it will be noted, is a special case of "experience." The more an associate resembles me, the more experience, so to speak, have I had with *him*. It is for this reason that members of the same racial, religious, or occupational group are ordinarily the best judges of one another. A capitalist understands a capitalist, a communist a fellow-communist, more adequately than members of one group understand members of the other. And it is not merely for reasons of democracy that Rotarians call one another by their first names; there is genuine fellow-feeling to justify the familiarity.

3. *Intelligence.* Experimental studies have found repeatedly that some relationship exists between superior intelligence and the ability to judge others. The positive correlations hold even within the high and narrow range of intelligence which characterizes the selected groups of judges employed in most of these experiments. Vernon, it will be recalled, found that high intelligence is a characteristic especially of good self-raters and of good judges of strangers, but that for raters who are well-acquainted with the subjects, experience can to some extent be a substitute for exceptional intelligence. On the average, however, good intelligence is necessary, and the reason is simple enough. Understanding people is largely a matter of perceiving the relations between past and present activities, between expressive behavior and inner traits, between cause and effect, and intelligence *is* the ability to perceive just such relations as these.

4. *Insight.* The proper realization of our own anti-social tendencies, of our own hypocrisies and inconsistencies, and of our own complex motives can usually prevent us from making too conventional and too simple a diagnosis of our fellowmen. Blindness and blunders concerning our own natures will automatically carry over to our judgments of others. A compulsive neurosis (or any other quirk) not understood in oneself, is bound to enter as a projection or as a value-judgment into one's estimate of others. In the practice of

[11] *The Science of Character*, trans. 1928, pp. 43 f.

psychoanalysis the prerequisite of self-knowledge has long been recognized. Before the analyst can unravel the knots of other personalities he must first disentangle his own.

5. *Complexity*. As a rule people cannot comprehend others who are more complex and subtle than they. The single-track mind has little sympathy for the warring of interests of the cultured and versatile mind, and the Philistine devoid of emotional conflicts is helpless in the face of the turbulent confessions of a Barbellion or a Marie Bashkirtsev. Two souls dwelt within the breast of Faust, and but one within the breast of his famulus, Wagner; it was Faust only who was able finally to gain an understanding of human life.

It follows that the psychiatrist, since he deals with exceedingly complex mental conditions, should benefit by the possession of a complex nature; and if he has neurotic difficulties of his own and manages them well, they may even add to his qualifications. This is not to say that there is no place for the buoyant, uncomplicated psychiatrist whose role is not so much the understanding as the encouraging of patients caught in the snares of a depression. Therapeutically it is often more valuable to radiate health and good spirits than to enter sympathetically into the distortions and complexities of the patient's mental life. Perhaps there are two types of successful psychiatrists: those who cure by the tortuous reconstruction of personality, and those who cure by radiant suggestion.

6. *Detachment*. Experiments have shown that there are generally certain asocial trends in the personalities of the best judges. Introversion is more common among them than extroversion, and the best judges tend themselves to be enigmatic and hard to judge. On the average, too, they stand low in social values. Those who are preoccupied with social values have little time to consider others dispassionately; they feel sympathy, pity, love, or admiration, but they do not detach themselves sufficiently from the emotional relationship to gain an impartial view. An individual, on the other hand, who does not at every moment participate, but who can stand aside and observe, "never missing a trick," is likely to make more valid judgments. It frequently happens, as in the case of novelists, that the good judge may participate heartily enough at times, but that afterward he withdraws, and in retrospect considers events and people with an almost grim detachment.

7. *The Esthetic Attitude*. Frequently associated with asocial characteristics is the esthetic attitude. As a qualification it seems to stand

above all others, especially in the case of the most gifted judges. The esthetic attitude seeks always to comprehend the intrinsic harmony of any object that is the center of attention. The object may be as trivial as an ornament or as substantial as a human being; in any case the singleness and the symmetry of the structure are what interests the esthetic person. This attitude is indispensable to the novelist and biographer. When highly developed it may to a certain extent offset limitations of experience, of intelligence, of insight, of similarity and complexity. But when it is combined with these qualifications it enormously enhances a judge's skill.

8. *Social Intelligence*. This qualification is not indispensable. The novelist and the artist often lack it. The interviewer, on the other hand, must possess the "social gift," for his function is most complex: he must listen quietly and yet probe, encourage frankness and yet never seem shocked, be friendly and yet reserved, patient but prodding, and through it all never seem bored. Such a delicate balance of accomplishments requires in high degree any and all traits making for frictionless personal relations. To do and to say the tactful thing requires a prognostication of a person's most likely responses. Hence social intelligence is linked with the ability to make swift and almost automatic judgments of people. On the other hand social intelligence is not identical with *Menschenkenntnis*, for it does not necessarily imply *deep* knowledge of an individual, nor the capacity to systematize and to express one's judgment. Social intelligence lies at the behavioral rather than at the conceptual level. It leads to social adjustment, but not necessarily to profound understanding.

SEX DIFFERENCES IN ABILITY TO JUDGE PEOPLE

The proverbial "intuition" of woman is supposed to manifest itself especially in her judgment of people. The business man brings a prospective client home to supper for his wife's opinion of him, and she gives it swiftly and with decision. When new neighbors move in, she is quick to size them up, and her opinions have a ring of certainty. Returning home from a dinner party her husband perhaps reports as the extent of his observation that the hostess looked rather pretty in her new green dress. Whereupon the wife may add that the dress was not new, that it was formerly white, and that it had been lengthened with tulle to bring it into style; furthermore, that the hostess is worried about money-matters and about her husband's drinking, that she is having trouble with the new maid, that she has dyed her hair, and that she is something of a flirt, but nevertheless jealous of her husband's stenographer, and all things considered, that it would not be surprising if there were a divorce in the family within the year.

Yet the case for woman's superiority may easily be exaggerated. Experimental studies, so far as they go, establish only a slight margin in favor of women. It is somewhat rash to call upon native sex-differences of mental "type." [12] A simpler explanation for such slight superiority as exists, comes from the signal importance of personal relationships in women's lives. The girl or woman who is economically dependent finds that the attentions she receives depend less upon her objective accomplishments than upon her personal conquests. Subtle indications of favor and disfavor, of rivalry and defeat, are therefore of utmost importance to her. Even the woman who is economically independent usually finds that her success still depends upon the attitudes of people toward her. It is important for her to know, for example, whether her male associates in business have an antagonistic, jocular, patronizing, or fair-minded point of view regarding her presence in their profession. She must develop skill in understanding them.

Another reason for the woman's superiority may lie in the nature of her sexual life which is more particularized and personal than that of men.[13] The entire force of her sexual interests, therefore, may lie behind her judgments of people. In a society where double standards of morality prevail it is necessary likewise that a woman be more observant and circumspect about the qualities of her friends and associates. Finally, in accordance with the principle of autonomy, there may arise from some of the basic influences here mentioned, a genuine interest in people which becomes an incentive to study them and a source of satisfaction. Such an interest might easily become integrated with the esthetic value which is known on the average to stand higher in women than in men, and which as we have shown is indispensable to accurate judgments of personality. All in all, there

[12] Koffka, however, makes a case for the theory that women are superior to men in judgments of other people because they more readily identify themselves with situations that surround them. Their "egos are less separated from the environment." On this account they are able to sense immediately the shades of feeling in other people. (*Principles of Gestalt Psychology*, 1935, p. 361.)

[13] Cf. K. Dunlap, *Social Psychology*, 1925, chap. ii.

are plenty of reasons to account for woman's superior judgments of personality. The wonder is that their superiority over men is not more marked than it is.

WHOM DOES ONE KNOW BEST?

It has been pointed out that *similarity* between the personality of the observer and that of his subject is one of the conditions for a successful judgment. We seem to understand best those who are most like us, those who speak the same language. One author goes so far as to declare that we can understand *only* those who stand near to our own mental type, and since this is so, no psychologist should ever undertake to write an interpretation for any type other than his own.[14]

The situation, however, does not seem to be so simple. In the first place, one often seems to be able with considerable success to understand natures directly opposite to one's own. The frank nature, writes Klages, "understands the liar by virtue of its own frankness," for "Every impulse which urges me to *do* something affords the mind means of judging the inhibition which might cause me to *refrain* from doing it." [15] The older associationists likewise pointed out that a train of ideas consonant with our own natures must include ideas that are antithetical, for are not opposites essentially similars? Dostoevsky believed that each man possesses a "double" representing unconsciously the qualities directly opposite to those that he discloses. Jung's theory of the role of the unconscious is very similar. The introvert for all his incessant self-reference and brooding has latent tendencies which permit him to understand well enough the reckless and extroverted frame of mind he cannot attain. It is often said that "opposites attract." If this is so, it may be because of this unconscious sympathy for what is suppressed and latent in oneself.

In general it seems to be true that men understand the personalities of men better than they do those of women, and, correspondingly, that the personalities of women are best understood by women. Anyone who has read many case studies of personalities has observed that it is very rare indeed to find an entirely successful and assured study whose author is not of the same sex as the subject. Even expert novelists seldom seem to be able to give convincing portraits of

[14] R. Friedmann, *Arch. f. d. ges. Psychol.*, 1913, 27, 195-203.
[15] L. Klages, *op. cit.*, p. 52.

characters of the opposite sex. The women in Dickens are mostly fainting caricatures of the sex, and the women in Trollope and Meredith are idealizations. The men created by Jane Austen and Charlotte Brontë are puppets. A few great exceptions come to mind, perhaps Sigrid Undset, Tolstoy, Anatole France, and Flaubert; the success of these authors, however, is often limited to portraits of one type of the opposite sex. Opinions may differ on the illustrations here employed, but the reader is not likely to dissent from the rule.

If the male student of personality is able to free himself of his own self-consciousness in relation to the opposite sex, if he discounts his own idealistic or cynical bias and is able to escape from his "mother image," if he has no preconceptions of the proper social and economic role which women should play, he will achieve a certain objectivity that will improve his judgments of women. And if he is able through some intricate combination of personal traits to take the feminine point of view, he will do even better. Conversely, the woman who seeks to become a good judge of men must have a corresponding flexibility in her mental life. Provided either judge is free from restraints and prejudices, there is sufficient similarity between the sexes to provide a basis for considerable mutual understanding. But there remains one unbridgeable chasm, namely, the role of the specific sexual functions. In so far as these are a decisive factor in the genesis and maintenance of emotions, of traits and attitudes, they can be a matter merely for speculation and not for direct understanding.

The most general rule is that one understands best those personalities that are like one's own; similarity in race, in sex, in age, in traits, and in outlook are of great assistance. But since similarity, to some extent, embraces also contrasting qualities, there is likewise a basis for understanding traits opposite to one's own. The general rule has many exceptions. Long-continued practice, for instance, may to some degree offset lack of similarity, as in the case of the male psychiatrist who specializes in the nervous disorders of women, or in the case of the female teacher who understands successfully the adolescent boys in her class. Exceptions must be allowed likewise for judges who have developed a special interest, as a naturalist might, in unusual types of people. In such cases, to be sure, there may be unrecognized similarities or unconscious affinities, but it is also true that interest and imagination, unsupported by subjective resemblance,

may aid a gifted person in understanding personalities quite different
from his own.

COMMON SOURCES OF ERROR

Almost every conceivable way of committing an error in thinking is at the same time a way of making erroneous judgments of
people. Superficial observation, faulty memory, errors in premises,
mistaken inferences, *non sequiturs*, superstitions, prejudice, rationalization, and projection; the number of possible blunders is too great
to classify. There is, however, one sort of error so typical of judgments of personality, so persistent, and seemingly so unavoidable,
that it should be constantly borne in mind. For convenience it may
be called the fallacy of *over-simplification*.

Neither the longest novel nor the most elaborate case-history can
give a complete portrait and explanation of a character. Briefer and
more selective records, of course, over-simplify still more, and common everyday characterizations, mentioning only one or two of an
individual's central qualities, are almost caricatures. Even though we
are usually well enough satisfied with our crisp characterizations of
other people, we object strenuously to having ourselves disposed of
with a well-turned phrase. Each person knows that he himself is too
complex to be briefly accounted for, and he rather suspects that
no novel, even in three volumes, could quite do him justice.

Over-simplification has two major causes. The first is the inherent
limitation of the human intellect. It is impossible to hold as many variables in mind as there are aspects of any single personality. The heterogeneity of motives and the variety of expression are baffling. The
range and duration of our cognitive processes are simply unequal to
the task. So we are forced to be content with aphoristic and inadequate judgments.

The other cause of over-simplification lies in emotional prejudice
of various kinds. Sentiments such as awe, love, admiration, envy,
distrust, or hate simplify and distort judgment. A certain tone of
voice or accent, a colored skin, manners which we consider uncouth
or affected, a style of clothing, or a smiling face frequently arouse
an affective bias that becomes a focus for our judgments. We become
inattentive to other cues or discount them in favor of one outstanding impression. Experiments have shown that when individuals are
handsome, healthy, neat, and have smiling faces, they are generally

judged to be intelligent, although there is very little relation, or none at all, between these features and intellectual ability. Nearly all analyses of ratings on traits of personality show the same "halo effect." One outstanding "good" or "bad" quality in a person casts its reflection upon all judgments pertaining to him.

Historical or public personages become greatly simplified in perspective, and are remembered for only one accomplishment or one trait; they virtually become personifications of some single abstract quality. In most people's minds Nero, Napoleon, Casanova, Abraham Lincoln and Calvin Coolidge are fables rather than personalities. It is true also that the character of our dead friends and relatives seems not only to improve with time, but to become very simple and well structured.

The term *stereotype* is most often employed to designate the paralyzing effect of simplification upon the process of judgment. The causes and the consequences of stereotypes have often been discussed in psychological literature.[16] The phenomenon is by no means confined to judgments of personality, although its presence in this field has been frequently recognized.[17]

Another common source of error in judging personality is called the "central tendency of judgments."[18] It has been shown, for example, that schoolteachers and parents have a marked tendency to overestimate the intelligence of retarded children, and to underestimate the intelligence of superior children. The same phenomenon appears in the rating of traits. Judges avoid the extreme values on rating scales, as if their uncertainty and doubt could be compensated through the selection of *average* points on the scale. This tendency, marked enough in single judges, becomes greatly magnified when the ratings of several judges are pooled, for then such deviations above and below the median as exist tend to cancel each other. It is for this reason that a composite judgment of "average" is always difficult to interpret, unless the dispersion of the individual ratings is known.

[16] For a theoretical discussion of the problem consult W. Lippmann, *Public Opinion*, 1922; G. W. Allport, "Attitudes," in *Handbook of Social Psychology* (ed. by C. C. Murchison), 1935; R. T. La Piere and P. R. Farnsworth, *Social Psychology*, 1936, chap. ix.

[17] Pertinent studies are those of S. Rice, *J. Person. Res.*, 1926, 5, 267-276; O. F. Litterer, *J. Soc. Psychol.*, 1933, 4, 59-69; L. Gahagan, *J. Soc. Psychol.*, 1933, 4, 128-134; M. Sherif, *J. Abnorm. & Soc. Psychol.*, 1935, 29, 370-375; M. Zillig, *Zsch. f. Psychol.*, 1928, 106, 58-106; G. W. Allport and H. Cantril, *J. Soc. Psychol.*, 1934, 5, 37-55; G. Ichheiser, *Zsch. f. ang. Psychol.*, 1929, 33, 273-287.

[18] Cf. H. L. Hollingworth, *op. cit.*, pp. 124 f.

In general, the central tendency results in judgments that are timid and colorless.

This "pallid mean" is further complicated by the kindly tendency of most people when in doubt about a rating to give a complimentary judgment (cf. pp. 445 f.). There is, therefore, a preponderance of meaningless judgments of a slightly better-than-average order. Nearly all rating scales show this double tendency to level off, and to level up, estimates of personality. Ways of avoiding this and other persistent sources of error were discussed on pp. 446 f.

This chapter has dealt with practical rather than theoretical problems. It contains a summary of psychological investigations and a few additional principles drawn from everyday experience. But no psychological discussion of the ability to judge personality is complete with merely a report of empirical facts. It must consider likewise the mental operations involved in the *process of understanding*. To this more abstract, but at the same time more basic, problem, the following chapter is devoted.

CHAPTER XIX

INFERENCE AND INTUITION

We perceive no living man without also perceiving *that* he is a living man, which means that we do not only perceive a body in movement, but in and simultaneously with it, something alive: and we do not only perceive something alive, but, in addition, something alive in a personal manner.

—L. Klages

THERE are two contrasting explanations of the way in which each of us obtains knowledge of other human beings. For convenience they may be called the theories of *Inference* and *Intuition*. Each theory has many variations, but the distinction between the two is fundamental, and to psychologists familiar enough; for the first mirrors the doctrine of association and the second the doctrine of configuration. The first is essentially a special case of the "context theory" of meaning, and the second of the theory of "insight."

INFERENCE

The question has often been asked, "How is it possible for human investigators to comprehend the minds of infra-human animals?" The answer most frequently given is that such comprehension comes from man's ability to reason by analogy and inference. When animals behave as the observer would behave under like circumstances, he feels entitled to ascribe to the animals mental processes and conscious states similar to his own. The fact that dogs are capable of jealousy is established by the resemblance of their behavior to that of jealous human beings; but the fact that they frequently move in circles before lying down has no human counterpart, and this bit of ritual is therefore consigned to the *terra incognita* of animal-instinct or ancestral habit. Other human beings are supposed to stand in the same analogical relation to ourselves as animals: if they behave as we have behaved under similar circumstances, we understand them, if not, they must remain unintelligible.[1]

The process of reasoning by analogy or inference has been treated with the utmost deference by the sciences of logic, epistemology, and psychology ever since Aristotle first stated the conditions of the syllogism. Starting with an undisputed experience, it needs only to be shown that a new event is an instance of this class of experience, in order that the event itself shall be endowed with the same significance. If it is our experience that all men are mortal, and if Socrates belongs to the class "men," then he too must be mortal. Or, if in my experience all tall and thin men have schizothymic temperaments, it follows in my reasoning that this new acquaintance who is likewise tall and thin will possess the same temperament.

Now it is true that we are seldom *aware* of reasoning in the manner of the syllogism. The statement of the process as given by *logic* is not quite the same as that offered by psychology. The *psychological* theory of inference is more familiar in terms of the process of association, as a single example will show. Most people are familiar subjectively with the postures and facial expressions accompanying a state of despair. In themselves they have associated feelings of despair with its various forms of expression. When now they perceive the outer manifestations of despair in another, their own experiences of this state are (perhaps unconsciously) aroused, and the mood of the other becomes intelligible. If the observer is so young or so buoyant in his own temperament that he has never experienced despair, the significance of its manifestations in another is necessarily lost to him. The essential formula of understanding according to this point of view is

$$\text{Sensory core} + \text{association}_1 + \text{association}_2 + \text{association}_n = \text{Understanding}$$

Some writers, troubled by the mosaic nature of this formula, have added within the equation a "feeling of relation" (James), or a *Gestaltqualität* (von Ehrenfels). But in these cases the inference theory is not modified; in fact, even the mosaic itself remains.

One variation of the associational theory is the doctrine of redin-

---

[1] "Any experience or mental process in another organism can be inferred from structure, situation, history, and behavior only when a similar experience or mental process is or has been associated with similar structure, situation, history, and behavior in oneself; and the probability of the inference will be proportional to the degree of similarity." D. K. Adams, "The Inference of Mind," *Psychol. Rev.*, 1928, 35, 235-252.

tegration,[2] or as it is sometimes called, *ecphory*.[3] This doctrine refers to the power of a sensory cue, even when it occurs in a new and unfamiliar context, to restore the original total meaning which was once associated with this cue. A fleeting facial expression, a slight contraction of muscles, or the use of a certain word in speech, may be sufficient to reactivate whole stores of antecedent experience. Although the process is not fully conscious, it is as though one says to oneself, "Here is Mr. X using a certain vulgarism of speech. I have heard it employed by Mr. A whose personality I know quite well. Mr. A is this type of person: he is uneducated, uncouth, and insensitive, although he thinks he makes a good impression upon his listeners by using what he regards as virile and unaffected language. All these attributes I shall ascribe to X, at least until such a time as contrary evidence forces me to modify my inference."

The associational theory is also held by behaviorists who fit it to the rubrics of the conditioned response. A hypothetical case-history will illustrate the argument. As a child S had the experience of being whipped by a neighbor whose orchard he had invaded. The chastisement was a natural cause of shrinking, which is the motor (and operational) equivalent of "fear." Associated with the fear-response was the physical appearance of the surly-faced avenger. In later years, S encounters a man whose features have the same cast ("identical" stimulus elements). Owing to the intensity of the original conditioning this new face has the power of re-arousing the original shrinking and fear. But in the meantime the child has grown to be a man, and the original response has undergone "efferent modification." He no longer cries out or shrinks in a childish manner, but does respond with covert visceral changes which have been substituted for the original overt fear response; the "meaning" remains the same. Through a process of verbal cross-conditioning, laryngeal habits are aroused which, blended together with the affective responses, constitute the judgment of the stranger's personality. Without recognizing the basis of the judgment, S declares, "I do not like him"; "he is cruel"; or "he is not to be trusted." The theory is presented in diagrammatic form in Figure 31.

The virtues of the theory of inference are apparent; it accounts admirably for many of the conclusions reached in the preceding chapter. It explains forthwith why people know best those who are

[2] H. L. Hollingworth, *The Psychology of Thought*, 1926.
[3] R. Semon, *Mnemic Psychology*, trans. 1923.

like themselves, why a long-continued experience in life is essential for sound judgment, why personalities subtle in structure are not well understood by observers who are themselves uncomplicated, and finally it accounts for the unbridged chasms which lie between the two sexes, between races, and between types of persons who have incompatible points of view, *e.g.*, between esthetes and athletes, Fascists and Internationalists, Philistines and Bohemians. But though

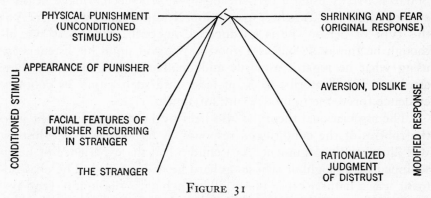

FIGURE 31

A Conditioned Response Interpretation of a Judgment of Personality Through Inference

the inference theory accounts for the requirements of *experience* and *likeness*, it fails to account adequately for the *process* of understanding, for it suffers from the same theoretical weaknesses as does the old-fashioned doctrine of association itself.

CRITICISMS OF INFERENCE

1. *The inference theory receives little support from introspection.* If meaning is the "accrual of an associational context to a sensory core," why should there be so little conscious awareness of the fact? If I read in another's face that he is suffering, why am I unable to factor out the components that must be present according to the inference theory: the lines in *his* face + *my* own experiences? Introspection reveals only that *his* face and *his* suffering are all of one single system. I do not perceive a face *there* and add a meaning *here;* the process has exclusively an objective reference.

Aware of this dilemma, associationists have postulated "unconscious inferences" and "rapid abridgement of conditioned reflexes" to explain the lack of introspective support. It has also been said that there is some selective process in the mind which obliterates specific memories but leaves nevertheless an associational trace that can be employed in future inferences. I may forget, for instance, that on certain dates in 1920, 1924, and 1930, I had definite experiences in which the perception of facial lines like those of my present acquaintance were associated with my personal suffering. Only the "effect" of the original association remains, forming the basis of the unconscious inference I am now making. This forgetting of causes while the memory of the effects remains is said by Leuba to explain a great many experiences usually regarded as marvelous intuitions.[4] It is a fact that in the course of a psychoanalysis, forgotten associations are sometimes recalled to mind that seem to account nicely for otherwise inexplicable likes and aversions.

Whatever the role of unconscious inferences may be, it remains nevertheless true that introspection strongly favors an hypothesis not of inference but of immediacy and objectivity in perception. Describing her meeting with George Bernard Shaw, Helen Keller wrote, "I shook Shaw's hand; it bristled with egotism." Köhler, too, has pointed out that when we say a man is *melancholy, embarrassed*, or *big-hearted*, it is clearly *he* and not we ourselves who seems to have these qualities; the expressive features are indissolubly tied to the traits of *his* personality and not to our own subjective life.[5] Even the little experiment of glancing at a stranger on a subway train (cf. p. 500) proves that judgments are too immediate and too objective to be accounted for entirely by tortuous chains of experience, however unconscious and abridged they may be.

2. *Understanding seems to occur in the absence of relevant previous experience.* The attack on associationism becomes more radical when its fundamental premise, the indispensability of experience, is called into question. It is almost impossible to deny this premise if it be interpreted liberally. Somewhere in the dim recesses of his mind every person has stored away a vast amount of vague experience which, if the laws of assimilation and similarity are generously construed, may in some way be relevant to almost any encounter. But it is a question whether such experience is not too remote and too approximate to assist in the swift and sure perception of *novel* patterns of personality. It seems difficult to explain in terms of relevant ex-

[4] J. H. Leuba, *The Forum*, May, 1928, 694-704.
[5] W. Köhler, *Gestalt Psychology*, 1929, pp. 234-268.

perience why the plumed knight who swings his medieval lady up to his saddle and gallops across the drawbridge with a defiant flourish of his lance at the furious and frustrated griffin, should be so completely understood by the schoolboy who has never ridden a horse, nor carried a lance, and whose acquaintance with medieval ladies and frustrated griffins is decidedly limited.

Even when experience is available, the ease and certainty of our judgments are not always directly proportional to it. An inference "stamped in" and justified through experience in ninety-nine cases, may fail entirely to occur to us in the hundredth case because of some unfamiliar sign which seems to alter the entire objective situation. Suppose a friend tells us that he is feeling well, that he has no worries, and that he is happy, and suppose his behavior is in virtually every respect circumstantial support for his statement, by the laws of association, we should accept his statements, and make our corresponding inferences regarding a well-adjusted life. But it sometimes happens that a trivial incident, the absence of a familiar tone in the voice, or an unusual tenseness in the face, may belie the obvious. What he tells us and most of what we see, together with all our habits of inference, *are discounted in favor of slight and less familiar evidence*. An unusual or unique mannerism in speech or behavior may take precedence over all the common experience which according to the law of "exercise" should be dominant. Nor is it some mental capriciousness that leads us to make the unorthodox judgment. Something about the man *himself*—unfamiliar though it be—tells what type of judgment we must make. The force of such constraints seems to set aside all the laws of association.

One of the most telling arguments against the inference theory comes from the observation of infants. At the age of one year or less they often show an appropriate type of response to expressions with which they have had no conceivable experience. The child who has suffered no actual punishment ("biologically adequate cause") may respond with astonishing pertinency to a scolding or to a scowling face. Even though this is a field where assertions are frequently invalid because of prejudiced observation, nevertheless there is excellent authority for the statement.[6] No one who has observed in-

---

[6] Cf. W. Stern, *Psychology of Early Childhood*, trans. 1924, pp. 101-104, 133 f.; also S. M. Blanton, *Child Guidance*, 1927, pp. 26-30. Köhler (*Mentality of Apes*, trans. 1927) gives many instances of apes' understanding of expressions (*e.g.*, masks)

fants closely will doubt their responsiveness to emotions in others.

Even after the period of infancy, the inference theory encounters difficulties. For many years the child is inclined to view his own subjective life as no more authentic or personal than the innumerable objects with which he deals both in animate and inanimate nature. This tendency toward animism, a well-known characteristic of the child-mind, makes it difficult for theories which regard understanding as a piecing together of subjective experience.

3. *The understanding of emotional behavior does not, as the inference theory would require, arouse similar feelings in the observer.* According to the doctrine of inference, the cue, the conditioned stimulus, or the identical element (as the redintegrative stimulus may variously be called) should tend to reinstate the *full* original experience with which it was associated. Perception of an angry face should arouse an angry frame of mind in us, gestures of a sensual nature should awaken concupiscent feelings in ourselves. But instead of doing so in the nicely logical way required by associational theories of meaning, such expressions may provoke either no feelings at all, or else quite contradictory feelings, as amusement or disgust. No elaborate theory of associational conflicts or of cross-conditioning seems quite adequate to account for the almost universal detachment of our objective comprehension of another person from feelings of resemblance to him.[7]

All in all, it appears that the inference theory does not offer a satisfactory account of the mental processes involved in understanding people. Certain associationists themselves have realized the fact, and have proposed modifications which are supposed to supply the needed flexibility. Wundt, for example, concluded that knowledge of another person demands, in addition to inference, a process of re-thinking (*umdenken*) of one's own personality in terms of the other's. This type of mental activity he held to be common among

with which they could have no clearly relevant experience. Köhler argues that the "sensory field" itself, without the help of association, dictates the spontaneous emotional comprehension which the apes display.

[7] This fact presents difficulties not only for the doctrine of inference in its simpler forms, but also for theories of "imitation" and of the "sympathetic induction of emotion" which introduce an instinctive factor into the inferential process. These theories too require that the feelings of the observer should be like those of the person whom he observes. Since this requirement is contradicted by fact, neither an "instinct of sympathy" nor a theory of "emotional contagion" will account for our understanding of others.

historians, actors, and others whose business it is to understand people. Although Wundt regarded this process of "putting oneself into another's Ego" as one of the major problems of psychology, he did not himself offer a closer analysis.[8] Wundt never abandoned the inference theory, but he realized its shortcomings.

It has also been suggested that certain neglected laws of association, if more generously employed, would lend flexibility to explanations in terms of inference.[9] The "law of acquaintance" for example holds that mere acquaintance with an item, irrespective of its previous associative connections, may give the item facility in entering new contexts and in creating novel meanings. Acquaintance with smiling faces, for example, does not mean the establishment of fixed and inviolable bonds of association, so that a smile must always mean affability. Familiarity with smiles enables us also to interpret them more readily in new contexts where their significance is certain to be modified. Experience with an item, instead of engendering a stereotyped meaning, adds to its versatility in association. The "law of assimilation" is likewise a flexible law, for it permits associations to occur on the basis of tenuous and remote similarities. According to this law virtually any previous experience, however distantly related to the perception of the moment, may supply its "meaning."

No matter what tinkering the inference theory undergoes, the results never seem satisfactory. When associations play a part at all, they seem, at least in consciousness, only to reinforce and to verify a judgment which is made immediately under the dictates of external factors. Whatever form the inference theory takes, the mystery of the *objectivity* of judgment remains.

EMPATHY

The imitative assumption of the postures and facial expressions of other people plays a greater part in ordinary life than is commonly realized. Figure 32 offers an illustration of this fact.* The camera has recorded the strains and stresses induced in spectators watching an athletic event. Were it not for this graphic evidence it would be hard to believe that many watchers had unconsciously lifted their legs, in some instances as much as two feet off the ground, or had shown intense strain upon their faces and in their arms.

[8] W. Wundt, *Logik*, III, 1895, chap. ii, sec. 5.

[9] E. S. Robinson, *Association Theory Today*, 1932, esp. pp. 117-119, pp. 81-93.

* Figure 32, opposite, is reproduced by courtesy of *The Dartmouth Alumni Magazine*.

FIGURE 32

Empathy

Some writers have maintained that our understanding of other people is derived from our capacity to imitate, usually in imperceptible ways, the behavior of the person we are trying to understand.[10] Such motor mimicry has been given a systematic setting in the theory of *empathy* which according to its author, Theodore Lipps, gives the most satisfactory account of our knowledge of other people.[11]

It has often been said by the advocates of empathy that the understanding of a personality is like the understanding of a work of art. Contemplation of a work of art involves innumerable slight movements of brows, the eyes, the trunk and limbs, as well as internal changes which elude observation. Graceful, uninterrupted, but not too simple, empathic movements are said to give rise to judgments of pleasantness and beauty; movements that are jerky, asymmetrical, or over-simple make the object seem disagreeable or ugly. When one says that the Gothic spire *soars* heavenward, that the arch of the nave is *exalted*, that a waterfall *leaps*, or that a storm cloud *weighs heavily*, it is in reality one's own kinesthetic response that is being reported. Similarly, empathic elements are apparent in many judgments of people, as, for example, when one says, "her placidity has a calming effect," "his movements are invigorating to watch," "his mirth is irresistible," or "his depression weighed me down."

Watch the facial expressions of a sympathetic audience—the chances are they show strains, smiles, and changes like those of the speaker. It often happens that actors and mimics are exceptionally good judges of people. Using the experimental method, one investigator finds that the interpretation of facial expressions is more accurate for many judges when they actively imitate the expressions than when they perceive them passively.[12] Graphologists, when confronted with new and strange formations of script, sometimes trace these formations with a dry pen in order to obtain kinesthesis which will enable them to reconstruct for themselves, and in some degree, the affective and motor impulses of the writer.

[10] Kempf writes, "When we can't imitate an individual's behavior we are at a loss to understand it." *The Autonomic Functions and the Personality*, 1921, p. 134.

[11] "There are three spheres of knowledge. I know about things, about myself, and about others. The first type of knowledge has its source in sensory perception. The second in inner perception, that is to say, in the retrospective view of the self with all its qualities, feelings, and relations to its contents and to objects. The source of the third type of knowledge is empathy (*Einfühlung*)." *Leitfaden der Psychologie*, 1903, p. 187. A fuller account of Lipps's theory is contained in his article "Das Wissen von Fremden Ichen," *Psychol. Untersuchungen*, 1907, 1, 694-722.

[12] F. H. Allport, *Social Psychology*, 1924, p. 229.

In the simple form in which it has here been described, the doctrine of empathy is merely a special case of the inference theory. Kinesthetic cues were originally associated with subjective experience, and now when the cues recur in an imitative response they reinstate the same original experience. Empathy becomes simply "kinesthetic inference." [13]

Lipps, however, had a more complex view of the nature of empathy. It is to be sure an *inneres Mitmachen,* but it is also inseparable from the outer object itself. Even though empathic meaning is dependent upon our own past experiences, it has exclusively objective reference. Since there is no recognition that the activity is located in one's own body, it should not be considered to be a merely imitative process. There is no duality between the strain, the pride, the sorrow, or the playfulness which I feel empathically, and the personality of the one whom I am seeking to understand. "A unitary object demands a unitary perception." [14] The unity is not a synthesis of associations, but is something demanded by the unity of the object itself. Lipps does not explain why we realize that the conscious life apprehended by empathy is the conscious life of *another* self. This objectivity is simply a "given" attribute inherent in empathy, marking it off from the ordinary process of inference.[15]

One apparent limitation of the doctrine is that a strong quality in myself would prevent my assumption of an opposed expression. Feeling grief, I cannot empathize with my friend's elation; I may, however, understand it well enough. To answer this objection Lipps

[13] Freud makes the interesting suggestion that empathy is an activity which plays a part only in the understanding of what is essentially *foreign* to one's ego. People who have no particular emotional significance for us are understood through empathy, but those who are especially similar to ourselves or in some way have emotional value for us, are understood through a process more properly called *identification.* Empathy is an intellectualistic endeavor to understand by mimicry and inference those activities which are not immediately intelligible; identification is emotional and unconscious, and requires no specific mimicry. *Group Psychology and the Analysis of the Ego,* trans. 1921, p. 66.

[14] *Leitfaden der Psychologie,* pp. 188 f. The view that unity of apperception is required by the unity of the object itself is further developed in *Einheiten und Relationen,* 1902.

[15] Baldwin's theory of imitation and Mead's theory of role-assumption emphasize likewise the subtle part played by muscular imitation in our understanding of others. The dilemma concerning the objectification of the inferential judgment is met by Baldwin through the positing of a separate mechanism of "ejection." Mead, on the contrary, agrees with Lipps that the empathic act *presupposes* the consciousness of another self, and that this other self, as *given,* becomes *intentionally* the object of knowledge.

postulates somewhat obscurely a "negative" empathy which takes place, as it were, against resistance, but which yields a true understanding even while it is accompanied by a sense of conflict and displeasure.

Other objections to empathy seem still more difficult to meet. For example, it should follow from the theory that the blind, who are less able to empathize, should be inferior judges of people, and that paralytics should to some degree lose their capacity. Neither of these consequences seems at all certain.

In spite of Lipps's desire to remove empathy from the simple realm of inference, he has been criticized for not having achieved his purpose. According to phenomenologists, who are his philosophical critics, empathy is acceptable as an explanation of our knowledge of other people only if it is regarded as a pure "theoretical act" which involves neither motor mimicry nor any other subjective states, but presupposes only the complete objectification of the *fremdes Ich*. It is not enough to admit that empathic knowledge achieves a unity through a welding of the objective and the subjective; it must be assumed that the knowledge of others has complete priority over self-knowledge and therefore over the possibility of inference. The original awareness is of the *Thou*, and this awareness always takes precedence over the meager contribution of motor empathy.[16]

From the point of view of the inference theory Lipps is guilty of adding an intuitive element in the perception of the *fremde Seele;* from the point of view of the philosophical intuitionist, he remains too close to the psychology of association. Actually, he stands midway between these views. The theory of empathy is a peculiar blend, and must in fact be regarded both as a theory of inference and as a theory of intuition, depending somewhat upon the coloring given it by different authors.

INTUITION

In the mind of the average psychological reader the concept of "intuition" is encrusted with connotations of mystery and obscurantism, and is therefore suspiciously viewed. It is, however, the only concept that contrasts properly with "inference," and that can be applied to a wide variety of related theories, all of which hold knowledge to be, in one way or another, immediate and direct. The term

[16] Cf. E. Stein, *Zum Problem der Einfühlung,* 1917.

insight is a fairly accurate equivalent, but since in this volume insight has been reserved for self-knowledge, *intuition*, in spite of its connotations, must be used. Although there are several varieties of intuitionism, all of them agree that knowledge of people is not derived solely from inference and analogy.

1. *Direct Perception.* One of the simplest of the intuitional theories, and one not ordinarily designated as intuition, is that which places personality in the same class as all objects clearly defined in sensory space. According to this view, less is added by experience, and more is given in the original presentation than is allowed in the theory of inference. The perception, however complex, is always well-structured under the dominant constraints of the outer field. A person is like a geometrical line drawing: it is usually impossible to view the design in any but *one* way. If previous experience is involved at all, the sensory configuration dictates what part it shall play. Experience itself is not strong enough to overcome spontaneously the arrangements that are originally presented to the senses. The role of inference, when it is employed, is merely to support or to verify the judgment which itself is immediate. Koffka is one exponent of this view; [17] Köhler is another:

> I think it was Nietzsche who occasionally said that somehow the "you" is earlier than the "I." This seems to apply most of all to our knowledge of "character" and "personality," since it is extremely difficult to get a definite picture of our own character from our subjective experiences, whereas the main traits of the character of others may sometimes be strikingly apparent in their attitude.
>
> I do not think that the language of others is our main or most trustworthy cue, in the sense that the content of it might be taken as a description of their experience. [*I.e.*, inferences from verbal cues are not a primary guide to understanding.] People do not talk sincerely about their subjective experiences, and we ascribe to them pomposity or modesty, friendliness or coldness, without their telling us a single word about such traits. In a foreign country, we appreciate to a great extent that others are "provocative" or "kind," though we may be absolutely unable to understand their language. Where we do under-

---

[17] K. Koffka, *Principles of Gestalt Psychology*, 1935, especially pp. 655-661. Koffka speaks of external "physiognomic characteristics" in the behavior of others which have a demand-character for our own perception. We cannot help realizing their objective pattern. The emotion or mood that we perceive being devoid of our own "Ego ground," is not a true emotion but a *perceived* emotion (p. 407). The self is not involved. Thus it is that we know others without feeling as others feel.

stand their words, their *manner* of talking is often a better cue, and we trust it more than the content of their talk. Also a certain kind of silence can occasionally tell us more about others than any number of words could reveal in the same situation.[18]

Köhler also points to our capacity for perceiving immediately in our associates such states as hesitation and lack of inner determination, perturbation, growing emotional excitement, attitudes of avoidance or withdrawal and sudden changes of mood. These directly observable activities correspond to dynamic tendencies, not within ourselves, but within the person we are observing.

There is a certain assumption in this Gestalt doctrine of understanding, not usually explicit, that throws it definitely into the class of intuitional theories. The assumption is simply that meanings themselves are somehow present in the outer world. *Embarrassment, softness, melancholy*, to use Köhler's own illustration, reside in the object which is perceived. This theory clearly represents a *biophysical* view of personality, for it considers personality to be completely independent of the observer. What the observer does is to try to obtain an understanding of the qualities of another as these are in and of themselves.[19] The observer does not *create* the meaning, he *receives* it.

This view must not be understood to deny altogether the contribution made by analogy and inference to the process of understanding. Köhler's illustrations are drawn very largely from transitory emotional states or moods, and not from the realm of deep-lying and permanent traits. He seems for the most part to be speaking of the perception of a *frame of mind* rather than of *personality*. Direct perception never reveals the relation between *distant* causes and *present* effects, whereas understanding a person requires a knowledge of just such relations. Understanding requires acquaintance, stores of experience, the use of causal and structural analysis—

[18] W. Köhler, *Gestalt Psychology*, Liveright Publishing Corp., 1929, pp. 234 ff.

[19] According to the *Gestalt* theory meanings are presented objectively not only in the case of personality, but in every other sphere of perception as well. A good example may be taken from music. In a certain experiment, C. C. Pratt required a large number of judges to listen to a typical composition of each of four composers. Few of the judges recognized the compositions or the composers, but over 90 per cent selected the adjective *stately* as best characterizing the composition by Brahms, *sprightly* for Mendelssohn, *wistful* for Mozart, and *vigorous* for Tchaikowsky. Such unanimity, Pratt argues, must spring from the "intrinsic character of the composition rather than from extrinsic and variable association." *J. Phil.*, 1934, 31, 38-45.

all of which obviously involve a wide range of associational activity. In short, evidence from inferential processes is as necessary as evidence from the "sensory field."

2. *Innate Knowledge and Identity.* A different type of intuitionism is the Platonic, according to which understanding requires a cooperative activity between external impressions and innate ideas. There are a priori conceptions in the mind, archetypes as it were, of the qualities which human beings possess, and these become aroused by, and confer intelligibility upon, the activity of the senses. Understanding results when "the light within meets the light without."

A variation upon the Platonic theory is the Hegelian. For Hegel, understanding is possible because of the essential universality of mind. Each person is but a single incarnation of a common mental life, and he must therefore share the essential structure and attributes of the minds of all his fellow-mortals. Mutual understanding rests ultimately upon men's possession of a common mind. *Es ist der Geist selber, der in seinen Individuationen sich selbst versteht.*

Not dissimilar are the theories of the *racial unconscious* (C. G. Jung) and of the *subliminal self* (F. W. H. Myers). In both of these is the belief that certain portions of one's own mind are co-extensive with the minds of others. A common inheritance, a common civilization, or a common humanity (according to the variant of the theory) enable all those who share it to understand one another sympathetically.

Theories of this type are out of fashion among psychologists, for, by assuming innate ideas and the existence of an over-individual mind, they deny the basic tenets of empiricism. These theories are, in fact, only the more extreme varieties of intuitionism, although they are sometimes mistakenly thought of as its only representatives.

3. *Immediate Knowledge.* According to Bergson, intuition is that sympathetic attitude toward reality outside of us that makes us seem to enter into it, to be one with it, and to live it.[20] Intuition stands in contrast to the artificial attitude of the scientist who treats facts and things as entirely outside himself, as external entities to be analyzed and dissected and compared until they are made to yield laws and generalizations of a purely conceptual order. The knowledge arising from this operation of *intellect* (as opposed to *intuition*) is indirect, and like the record of a cinematograph, is composed of a succession

[20] H. Bergson, *An Introduction to Metaphysics*, trans. 1912.

of fixed states. The combining and recombining of these states constitute inferential or associational knowledge, foreign to normal intuitive understanding which is more immediate and far more vital.

The theory of Lossky is similar.[21] This writer regards intuition as the capacity for knowledge of an object in its original form. Consciousness is able to take immediate possession of whatever configuration is presented to the senses. But the senses alone are unable to mediate the unity of the perception. It is possible for me to see the color of an orange, or to feel its shape, or smell it, or taste it, but it is impossible to see, feel, touch, or taste its *unity*. Unity is not a sum-total of these sensory aspects. It is something original in the object, and is taken possession of directly by consciousness. Similarly, to understand a personality it is necessary first, last, and all the time to grasp its underlying unity, not through analysis, but through intuition.

The reason why it is difficult to explain the operation of intuition, or to communicate its revelations, is that verbal analysis itself is a tool of inferential reasoning and a product of association. Intuition cannot be explained; it simply exists. If an attempt is made to explain it, it appears perversely enough to be only a subtle form of inference. According to Bergson, the work of the artist is proof enough that intuition exists, for it demonstrates that the artist's understanding involves a kind of coincidence between himself and the object of his attention. The intuitive method of the artist, unlike the scientist's, does not lead to reasoned *explanations*, to a *cognitio circa rem*, but more directly to an understanding of the phenomenon itself, to a *cognitio rei*.

4. *The Perception of Individuality*. Croce's theory of intuition, like those of Bergson and Lossky, also regards intuition as the method by which one gains an understanding of the *systematic relevance* of an object or an event. Croce too lays stress upon intuition as the perception of *particularity*. Science, he says, deals only with concepts. Concepts being generalizations are inimical to the understanding of the peculiar harmony which the single object possesses. Concepts are formed through images and associations, and images and associations never yield unity. "The dilemma is inexorable: either keep associationism and give up unity, or keep unity and give up associationism. No third way out of the difficulty arises." [22] With

[21] N. Lossky, *Rev. Phil.*, 1928, 53, 50-87.
[22] B. Croce, *Aesthetic*, trans. 1909, p. 171.

Bergson, Croce regards art as the purest form of intuition, for it deals always with individuality which is never repeated. Since a person, like a work of art, is an individual and never a repeated event, he too must be understood with the aid of intuition and not through science.

Intuition for Croce is not, however, a merely passive appreciation of individuality; it must itself be a form of expression. "In reality, we know nothing but expressed intuitions; a thought is not a thought for us, unless it be possible to formulate it in words." Croce does not agree with those who consider intuitions to be ineffable. Verbal, pictorial, or mimetic expression is the criterion of true intuition. A successful judge of personality must be able in some way to react adequately and intelligibly to the individuality which he perceives. By nature, though not necessarily in talent, he should be an artist, as experiment, in fact, shows that he often is.[23]

5. *Verstehen.* The forms of intuitionism thus far described are general theories of knowledge; they do not have exclusive reference to the understanding of *people.* There is one vigorous and influential school of thought which has busied itself more directly with the question, *How does one understand the personality of another?* This school, generally known as *Verstehendepsychologie,* has its chief center in Germany, and its voluminous literature is written almost entirely in the language of that country. It is peculiarly difficult to render the theories of this school into English. To illustrate the dilemma, it is only necessary to list some of the German equivalents and variants of the awkward and almost solitary English verb "to intuit." Each of these terms has been employed by one or more German writers with a systematic connotation distinguishing it from all the rest.

ahmen	sich heineinfühlen
deuten	sich heineinversetzen
einleben	sinndeuten
einsfühlen	umdenken
intuitives erfassen	verständlich machen
intuitives umfassen	verstehen
kapieren	wesenserfassen
nachfühlen	wesensfühlen
sich hineindenken	wesensverstehen

[23] Estes' experiment (pp. 507-509) showed that psychologists' judgments of personality from motion picture records were much *less* valid than those of artists.

In the absence of accurate verbal equivalents the task of representing such subtle shades of thought is too unprofitable to undertake. The general point of view of this school, however, is of such importance that it must be described if only in rough outline.[24]

THE PSYCHOLOGY OF "VERSTEHEN"

The doctrine of *Verstehen* is the pivotal conception of the school of psychological thought established toward the end of the nineteenth century by the philosopher Dilthey. A devoted student of biography, Dilthey held the conviction that each individual is unique and ineffable. Certain sequences in a man's life may be *explained* in terms of natural science, but his life as a whole can be *understood* only by the method of mental science. The method of the mental sciences (*Geisteswissenschaften*) must transcend the analytical procedures of traditional psychology. The model of the natural sciences is irrelevant for the study of individuality, because experimental, physiological, and genetic analysis result at best in the construction of uniform laws, and uniformity is the very antithesis of individuality. Dilthey proposes that a new descriptive psychology elevate the individual to the central place of interest.[25]

Dilthey's thought has been developed by his disciple, Eduard Spranger. Maintaining the same sharp distinction between *explanatory* and *descriptive* psychology, Spranger too favors the latter which "does not go back to the last distinguishable elements, but remains on a higher level of concepts and apprehends inner processes as intelligible wholes which belong to a total mental situation and from it take their significance." [26]

[24] Discussions of *Verstehendepsychologie* in English are given by A. A. Roback, *Psychology of Character*, 1927, chaps. xviii, xxiv; A. Wenzle, *Monist*, 1928, 38, 120-157; D. Klein, *Psychol. Rev.*, 1932, 39, 552-569; E. Stern, *Psyche*, 1923, 3, 358-366; H. Klüver, *Appendix* to G. Murphy's *Historical Introduction to Modern Psychology*, 1929; G. W. Allport, *J. Abnorm. & Soc. Psychol.*, 1924, 19, 132-141; 1929, 24, 14-27.

All these discussions suffer from the lack of adequate terminology. The verb "to understand" lacks an adjectival form; the noun "intuition" has the awkward and unpopular verb-form "to intuit"; and "intuition" itself is a much-abused and unsatisfactory term. Roback proposes a new word *perilepsis* as a class name for all the theories which deal with the grasping of personality as a complex meaningful whole.

[25] The most pertinent of Dilthey's writings are his "Ideen über eine beschreibende und zergliedernde Psychologie," (1894) and "Beiträge zum Studium der Individualität," (1895) in *Gesammelte Schriften*, Vol. V.

[26] E. Spranger, *Lebensformen*, 1922, p. 11.

It is only when the life and actions of another are intimately and intelligibly bound together that I *understand* him. To observe fragments of behavior, and then to reason by analogy (which really means binding these fragments to the lives of *other* people), will never yield an understanding of individuality. *Verstehen* is the only mental process guided by a consciousness of structure. Spranger defines it as the mental activity that *"grasps events as fraught with meaning in relation to a totality."* [27]

Now it is impossible to apprehend events in "relation to a totality" unless there is some focus in personality which provides a point of anchorage for the observer's attention. What should the observer look for first, and to what must he refer each observation? The answer lies in the discovery of the individual's direction of striving, that is to say, in his constellation of personal values (cf. pp. 225-231). Dilthey had proposed three forms of *Weltanschauung* which serve as a basis for the unity of the personalities of great philosophers. There is first the materialistic or naturalistic outlook (represented by Democritus, Hobbes, and Hume), secondly, transcendental idealism (represented by Plato, Kant, Fichte), and finally objective idealism (Goethe, Schopenhauer, Hegel). Such typical *Lebensverfassungen* pervade not only the writings of these philosophers, but their personal lives as well. A man's philosophy of life reflects itself in his speech, his conduct, his mannerisms; "it is one with his character." *As soon as an individual's philosophy of life is known, his personal activities, which taken by themselves are meaningless, become understood.*

Not content with the three-fold classification which Dilthey proposed, Spranger developed as his "schemata of comprehensibility" the six famous "ideal types" described on pp. 228-230. These types must be regarded merely as theoretical guides in understanding people, for no individual is a pure representation of a single type. Ultimately each individual is unique, and yet the understanding of the ideal forms which human values may take will assist greatly in the comprehension of concrete, "mixed" cases.

The unity of a man's life, therefore, is not understood through reference to his nervous processes, nor to the temporal course of his life, but rather through its approximation to an ideal scale of over-individual values (the theoretical, economic, esthetic, social,

---

[27] E. Spranger, *Proceed. Eighth Internat. Congress of Psychol.* (Groningen), 1927, p. 148.

political, and religious). The individual is viewed as striving to fit himself into the objective *Geist* which in itself embodies these values. Hence, to understand him it is first necessary to comprehend the "spirit of the times" and the "spirit of the culture" in which he lives.

This final step in the argument, resting upon Hegelian metaphysics, is perhaps the reason why so many dissenting interpretations of the process of *Verstehen* have arisen, particularly among psychologists who find distasteful the assumption of a super-individual mind. All of these alternative interpretations agree with Dilthey and Spranger that inductive or inferential knowledge is not the only type of knowledge involved in understanding personality, but most of them strive to soften somewhat the opposition, which in Dilthey and Spranger is irreconcilable, between psychology conceived as a *descriptive* and as an *analytical* science.[28]

One example of the conciliatory view may be cited. Ewald believes that whenever psychologists work with the problems of practical life they inevitably employ *Verstehen*.[29] But this method is not unmixed with empathy and with inference. It is, in fact, only through *associative* activity that a verification of understanding is possible. Uncontrolled intuition yields mere dogmatic conviction, and suffers from the common errors of prejudice and projection. The psychologist must use inferential thinking to raise his judgments above the level of mere common sense.

Nor is Ewald willing to follow Spranger in dispensing altogether with "elements." Even though personality has a uniqueness of structure, it consists none the less in certain elements: drives, feelings,

[28] Among the more significant discussions of the problem may be mentioned:
G. Kafka, *Arch. f. d. ges. Psychol.*, 1928, 65, 7-40. (Considers *Verstehen* to be the central problem in psychological methodology.)
R. Müller-Freienfels, *Zsch. f. ang. Psychol.*, 1928, 31, 410-470. (Shows that *Verstehen* takes many forms according to the nature of the investigator's interest and purpose.)
W. Peters, *Zsch. f. Psychol.*, 1929, 112, 379-444. (Considers the valid portions of the doctrine to be already recognized in the practice and theory of dynamic psychology.)
G. Heymans, *Zsch. f. Psychol.*, 1927, 102, 6-34. (Regards *Verstehen* in the last analysis as a subjective structuration of associative content.)
S. Bernfeld, *Zsch. f. ang. Psychol.*, 1932, 42, 448-497. (Discusses the psychoanalytic equivalent of *Verstehen*, viz., *Deutung*.)
There are several volumes devoted largely to the problem, among them, T. Erismann, *Die Eigenart des Geistigen*, 1928; K. Jaspers, *Psychologie der Weltanschauung*, 1919; G. Roffenstein, *Das Problem des psychologischen Verstehens*, 1926.
[29] G. Ewald, *Zsch. f. Psychol.*, 1927, 103, 228-241.

traits, and habits. The complete understanding of an individual necessitates a study of his constitution under the guidance of physiological and genetic analysis, but also, of course, an appreciation of the significance and meaning of his behavior through the process of *Verstehen*. Intuition is an authentic and indispensable avenue of knowledge, but it is not, and should not be, separated and opposed to critical and inferential mental activity.[30]

CRITICISMS OF INTUITION

Hard-headed naturalists remain unconvinced by all the arguments. Störring says that the theories of intuition are all cloudy and obscure, only wordy renderings of the vulgar psychology of common sense; that the doctrine of *Verstehen* is nothing more nor less than a glorification of the observer's failure to recognize the associational relationship between sensory evidence and subjective inference.[31] Essentially the same point of view is expressed by Leuba: "The formula for 'intuition' of this kind is simple: Do not remember how you came by a certain bit of knowledge—forget! Thus, the pudding will seem to have been made without any ingredients." [32] Such rebuttals, of course, are only re-statements of the theory of inference, and do not answer specifically the charges against it.

Bechterev, on the other hand, although an uncompromising associationist, is willing to admit the consequences of his position.[33] He concedes that inferential knowledge must always be indirect and inaccurate. Since words and gestures never *carry* the meaning of another personality to me, but only *awaken* in me my own ideas of their significance based upon my past experience, the resulting interpretation that I give is likely in many particulars to be erroneous and will certainly be incomplete. *Jedes Verstehen ist ein Nichtverstehen.* Knowledge of others is inevitably so partial and so subjective that it would be better to abandon all attempts to re-create their personalities in our imaginations, and to confine our efforts to the study of

[30] W. Stern's solution of the problem is similar: "It is erroneous to place *verstehende* psychology as an independent discipline in opposition to psychology as a natural science. There is only one unitary psychology which seeks to know its objects in their elementary nature and in terms of the conceptual laws under which they may be subsumed, as well as in their totality as concrete value-structures possessed of unique significance." *Weltphilosophie*, 1924, p. 380.

[31] G. Störring, *Arch. f. d. ges. Psychol.*, 1927, 58; 1928, 62.

[32] J. H. Leuba, *op. cit.*, p. 696.

[33] V. M. Bechterev, *General Principles of Human Reflexology*, trans. 1932, chap i

elementary forms of behavior, such as are accessible to objective methods. Bechterev thus arrives at skepticism which, as Hume long ago proved, is the logical destiny of simon-pure associationism.

So much for the clash of theories. There are those who believe to the bitter end in analogy and inference; there are those who are convinced that associative processes are irrelevant to the understanding of personality, and that some type of immediate and direct understanding is possible; finally there are the conciliators who believe in both inference and intuition. Most of what is said by the proponents and opponents of each theory sounds sensible enough. What does the controversy signify?

It does no good to assert that this controversy is merely an epistemological snowball fight, and that psychologists should forget it and return to their tests and measurements to collect *facts*. Facts do not speak for themselves. Every fact concerning a human person, regarded *as* a person, requires interpretation, and interpretation is likely to involve the use of both inference and intuition. The proportion of each and the way in which these processes may be combined in the course of an investigation are matters of extreme methodological importance. The psychologist who studies personality must use every legitimate method, but particularly must he know how to *combine* methods in order to secure the optimum understanding. Up to the present time (in English speaking countries) he has placed his confidence almost entirely upon those methods of investigation which tell him more about *populations* of people than about concrete personalities. His restricted standards of scientific experimentation have blinded him to certain obvious truths to which the doctrines of intuition call attention. Accordingly he suffers a dissociation in his own mental operations, using one method in his professional investigations and another method in everyday life. The question now to be considered is how he may regain his mental integrity, seasoning his knowledge *about* people with an understanding *of* them.

THE PLACE OF INTUITION IN THE STUDY OF PERSONALITY

In recent years a revolution has occurred in the psychology of *perception*. A counterpart of this revolution is now due in the psychology of personality. Before the present generation psychologists overlooked the most significant characteristics of perception, *viz.*, its order and organization. The story was told altogether in terms of sensation plus association. Perceptions were represented as a matter of colligation or mosaic; today they are treated in their proper state as unified, articulated, mental structures.

The outmoded view of perception has a perfect replica in the theory of understanding personality by inference, which too is a mosaic theory. Light waves reflected from your face and clothes, sound waves from your larynx, other forms of physical energy exciting my organs of touch or smell, force upon my brain an array of elementary sensations. By themselves these sensations are a meaningless turmoil. But as I have developed in years, other sensory impacts have left traces in my brain. These traces with all their ramifications of associated experiences are aroused to provide a "meaning" for the new light and sound waves as they impinge. The result is that I *assemble* you, as it were, with lightning rapidity from light and sound, touch and smell vibrations. I know you (in so far as I do) because of my previous experience with similar vibrations. You are not *you*. You are merely a source of physical energy. I give you all the meaning you possess for me. *I* assemble you, *I* construct you, and *I* unify you. Such are the assumptions of a pure inference theory.

This view is as erroneous as is the corresponding associational theory of perception. Just as broken and incomplete figures in the perceptual field tend to be seen as solid and single, and just as geometrical designs are perceived as one unit rather than as an assemblage of discrete lines, so too is there a compulsive tendency for the mind to form patterned judgments concerning people. We cannot help view a personality as one single—if many-sided—structure. There is a constraint from the sensory field itself that forces us to apprehend all cues as related *to one another*. The constraint is objectively determined. Never am I able to think of you as a mere source of physical energy, as devoid of complex states, nor am I able to regard you as a mere projection of myself. *You*, and not I, are grieving; it is *you* who are shy, sensitive, boisterous, or domineering—not I. *Unity* and *objectivity* pervade the whole process of understanding.

It is a misfortune if "intuition" connotes any greater mystery than objectivity and unified structuration, which are attributes that most psychologists now recognize and accept in their accounts of perception.

So far as the understanding of personality is concerned, intuition implies three simple facts—none of them really questionable: (1) Personality is a biophysical structure—something objective that is capable of being understood, with greater or less accuracy; (2) the sources of physical energy through which manifestations of personality are communicated act upon the observer in a patterned manner rather than atomistically, creating in him structured rather than chaotic impressions; (3) the interest and attention of the observer are bent, not upon generalization and conceptualization of the impressions received, but upon an understanding of the singular *objective* structure which for the moment is presented to the mind. This final factor, the attitude of the observer, is important, for he *may*, if he wishes, negate this normal intuitive activity in favor of conceptual analysis, but in proportion as he does so, he loses his grasp upon the individuality of the structure.

In a word, intuition in the study of a personality means simply the *comprehension of organization under a sustained interest in the structure of the personality itself*. In this definition the word "comprehension" is used rather than "perception" in order to avoid the danger of referring merely to the momentary experience aroused by the present conduct of the person. It is correct to speak of the perception of emotion—as Köhler does—but it is scarcely accurate to speak of the perception of personality; for personality is not all given at any one time. The structuration of the outer field is *more* significant in momentary perceptions than in the comprehension of personality, though it plays a dominant part in both.

Intuition exists at the very outset in our efforts to understand another person. Our first glimpse is of a complete individual. We do not understand all the angles and facets of his nature at once, but we never from the beginning lose our firm conviction that he is a mortal like ourselves whose conduct has a certain relevance if only we can comprehend it. The first intuition is the guide to subsequent study. A psychiatrist, a counsellor, or an interviewer, has no idea how to frame his questions and his inquiry until he comprehends, however dimly, the manner of individual with whom he is dealing.

In the same way, by the use of naive intuition the psychologist obtains his initial understanding of his problem. Without it he can have no idea of the best means to his end. Unless he first senses the pattern of the personality which he is attempting to study, he runs the risk of not studying it at all. This danger is not at all hypothetical. More effort has been wasted in the study of personality from the use of irrelevant variables and artificial conceptualizations than from any other cause. Many a time an assortment of percentile ranks or sigma scores on the most fantastic variables is offered (without a smile) as a psychological portrait of a person. The blunder would not occur if a psychologist sensed in the beginning the nature of the personal structure he is attempting to analyze.

Intuition is indispensable not only at the outset of an investigation, but likewise at every subsequent stage. When the psychologist feels that his investigations are becoming mired in methodology he can do no better than return to a simple intuitive view of the structure he is attempting to study. When his results are complete, the most convincing validation (for him) is to check them in the same way. Do the factors he has extracted "make sense"? Does the psychograph he has prepared really resemble the person?

In intuition, the life of another person is necessarily viewed from *his* point of view. A whimsical couplet by Pope expresses the thought:

> A perfect judge will read each work of wit
> With the same spirit that its author writ.

It is the *author's* interests, intentions, pretensions, plans, ambitions, values, aversions, strivings, and hopes, that vitalize and confer meaning upon what he says and does. So it is in personality. To study experimentally expressive traits, abilities, nervous symptoms, physiological changes, popularity, adaptability, originality, forcefulness, deceitfulness, and any other qualities, is ultimately vain unless these features can be related to the life-stream of each separate personality studied. Intuition is the crucial method for appreciating such congruences, even though other synthetic methods (cf. Chapter XIV) may have to be used for communicating these intuitions to others.

Does intuition differ from the "esthetic attitude" discussed on pp. 515 f.? The concepts are indeed almost equivalent. In both cases there is a "set" to apprehend the structure that is given. There is likewise in both a constraint exerted by the object over its phenomenal representation in consciousness. If there is any difference at all, it lies in the tinge of pleasure accompanying the esthetic attitude. As our attention wanders throughout the day from particularity to particularity, we are using intuition (as opposed to analysis). When we say, as it were, "Hold, this is something good which I must enjoy for its own sake," we are using that special form of intuition known as the esthetic attitude.

Can intuition be taught? The child does not have to be taught to be interested in objects, to perceive figures upon grounds; he does so by virtue of his native perceptual capacity. No one can be taught to *hear* a tonal pattern, but one can be taught to *listen to* and to *look for* significant features in the pattern that is instinctively heard. It is an interesting fact that instruction in the appreciation of art is almost altogether a matter of dissection and analysis. The student cannot be taught to appreciate the whole, but he can have his mental equipment so enriched that his intuitive apprehension may be sharper and more discerning. In the same way, the student cannot be taught to understand personality, but he may have his attention called to significant details, and to laws and principles which if known may be employed to sharpen and enrich the comprehension.

THE EMPIRICAL-INTUITIVE NATURE OF UNDERSTANDING

It would not have been necessary to discuss at such length the part that intuition plays in the understanding of personality were it not for the fact that the psychologist (of all people) tends to forget about it. The psychologist delights in the use of recording instruments—galvanometers, kymographs, and scales of all kinds. Yet strange to say he discredits the most delicate of all recording instruments—himself. The human mind is the only agency ever devised for registering at once innumerable variables and for revealing the *relations between them*. It is the one and only instrument capable of comprehension. Failing to employ intuition the psychologist unduly limits his resources. Without it he starts with analysis and ends with conceptualization; on the way he sacrifices his chance to understand living people.

From all that has been said it should now be obvious that *the process of understanding personality requires both intuition and inference.* There are indeed sensory cues, empathic responses, redintegrative activity, and swift associations—all as asserted by the theory of inference. But it is also true that these processes are normally subservient to the structuring activity of the mind that takes place whenever it is guided by external pattern and by an interest in what is concrete.

In any given act of understanding it is not possible to distinguish products of intuition from products of inference. The original sensitivity to form is certainly an a priori possession of each individual, as is his capacity for sustained interest and concern with this form. On the other hand, the employment of associational thinking and analogy is likewise an intrinsic part of the process of understanding. (The reader will recall from the last chapter that *experience* is an indispensable qualification of a good judge of personality.)

Our understanding of personality comes, then, partly from without, but partly also from within. The first cues come from the structuration of the outer field; where these prove insufficient (as they usually do) then memory, imagination, and abstract conceptualization come to aid the process. We obtain what organization we can from the outer field and supply the remainder from within.

The value of analysis and inference is especially apparent when the smooth course of comprehension is interrupted. When my friend puzzles me with his behavior, I am likely to ask, "Now, what made him do that?" It was an act out of character, and as such it disrupted my previous understanding of his nature. The pattern I had formed is broken into, and a desire arises to repair the structure. I feel disturbed until a new judgment is formed. I seek parallel conduct in my friend's earlier behavior, or that failing, draw some inference from the behavior of myself or others under like circumstances. But even while I try one analogy after another and draw tentatively upon this generalization and upon that, my interest is always directed toward an intuitive understanding of my friend as a single individual.

CHAPTER XX

THE PERSON IN PSYCHOLOGY

THE swiftly rising tide of interest in the systematic study of personality carries with it a denial of the traditional belief that individuality is beyond the limit of science, or at least beyond the limit of psychological science. Implicit in the modern point of view is the demand that psychology expand its boundaries, revise its methods, and extend its concepts to accommodate, more hospitably than in the past, the study of the single concrete mental life.[1]

This demand is thoroughly radical. It is directed against the practice in general psychology of drawing the blood and peeling the flesh from human personality, leaving only such a skeleton framework of mind as is acceptable to the sparse canons and methods of nomothetic science. By stripping the person of all his troublesome particularities, general psychology has destroyed his essential nature. The newer point of view reverses the perspective. The person is no longer regarded as a neutral tinted background upon which the all-important design of mind-in-general stands out. Quite the reverse: the uniform design traced by general psychology becomes the ground upon which the integral, three-dimensional, and unique individual emerges as the salient feature.

This modern revolt has two distinguishable fronts. The first is the aggressive doctrine usually known as *personalistic psychology*. The second front of attack is *the psychology of personality*, as represented in the present volume. The shafts of the former are heavily

---

[1] The definitions of psychology offered by Wundt, James, and Titchener are of considerable interest in this connection. The first wrote: "*It* [psychology] *investigates the total content of experience in its relations to the subject.*" The second: "*Psychology is the science of finite individual minds*"; and the third: "*Psychology is the study of experience considered as dependent on some person.*" Yet none of these eminent authors developed his account of mental life to accord with his definition. All were pre-occupied with the merely uniform aspects of mind. Some vague feeling of propriety guided them in framing their definitions: they *knew* that mind (as a psychological datum) exists only in finite and in personal forms. Yet their historical positions—the spirit of the times in which they worked—prevented them from following their own definitions consistently to the end. Had any one of them done so, the psychology of the person would have had early and able sponsorship.

supplied with metaphysical barbs; the weapon of the latter is empirical necessity. Though the two lines of attack have something in common—namely, their insistence that the person be given more adequate recognition in psychology—it is well to consider them separately, and to mark their differences. In the next section the principal arguments of the personalistic school will be outlined. In the succeeding section there will follow a rapid review of the main tenets established in this volume for the concrete empirical study of personality.

PERSONALISTIC PSYCHOLOGY

There are several versions of personalistic thought, but they all do agree that the individual person as a many-sided unity must serve as the center of gravity for each and every investigation and formulation of theory undertaken by psychology. The intention is to rewrite the science of mental life entirely around this new center of emphasis (cf. pp. 18 f.). Note well: the goal is not merely to free the study of personality from over-rigid conceptual barriers drawn by general psychology, but to demolish and reconstruct the entire edifice of general psychology from the ground up. In this respect personalistic psychology is more extreme than the psychology of personality which is content to play its role *within* the many-sided science of psychology.

Why should such thoroughgoing reconstruction be demanded by the personalists? The reasons they advance are too numerous and too intricate to be given here in full. A brief hint of certain of their arguments will suffice.

1. Without the co-ordinating concept of Person (or some equivalent, such as Self or Ego), it is impossible to account for, or even to depict, the interaction of mental processes upon one another. Memory affects perception, desire influences meaning, meaning determines action, and action shapes memory; so on, indefinitely. This constant interpenetration takes place within some *boundary*, and the boundary is the Person; it occurs for some purpose, and the purpose can be represented only in terms of service to the Person.

2. The phenomenon of mental *organization* can have no significance unless it is viewed as taking place within a definite framework. Mental states do not organize themselves nor lead independent existences; their arrangement always constitutes part of a larger

arrangement—the personal life. "Everything mental is a totality or a part of a totality."

3. Such concepts as *function, adaptation, use,* and *adjustment* are of no significance without reference to the Person. An adaptation must be the adapting *of* something *to* something; so with adjustment. Use and function likewise imply an interested personal agent.

4. Above all, it is in immediate experience that the case for a central co-ordinating agent becomes unanswerable. The central position of Self is implied in all states of consciousness. Descartes' dictum *Cogito ergo sum* can hardly be refuted. This argument, though cast in metaphysical terms, has psychological support in the vivid sense of the self present in experiences of strain, conflict, and choice.[2]

5. Another argument stresses the *creative* properties of the Person or Self. Every system of thought originates with someone. The most objective of scientists, no less than philosophers, ultimately create or "will" the canons of their own science. Disagreements result in the last analysis from the individuality of their own minds. So too with psychologists. If they embrace a nomothetic positivism and empty the personality of all its bothersome individuality, they do so ultimately because they *want* to. Thus a prior act of volition is responsible for the austere limits they place upon their own speculation. We all build our scientific world from the symbols taken from our own personalities. Which then is the prior fact, the creative person or creed he creates?

Such are some of the philosophic arguments whereby personalistic psychologists and self-psychologists state their case for the reconstruction of psychology. They do not object to the existence of impersonal (natural) sciences for the exploration of limited problems. They do agree, however, that *psychology* whose task it is to treat

[2] To be sure, the sense of self is a peculiarly elusive datum for introspection. To catch it for direct examination in consciousness seemed to James like trying to step on one's own shadow. In Brentano's terms, the Self, though ever present, is a matter of "secondary" awareness. Primarily I am conscious of the object to which I attend: a tone, a landscape, a menacing gesture; only secondarily am I aware that it is *I* who am apprehending, admiring, or fearing these objects.

The situation becomes even more elusive when the Self is regarded not only as Knower (reflected to itself somehow in a "secondary awareness") but also as the *ground* for that which is known. I not only know that it is *I* who perceive an object, but I feel that this object has some special significance for *me*. (Cf. discussion of Koffka's Ego, p. 159, ftn. 2.) The intimacy of the whole conscious process is baffling, a cause of consternation to philosophers and psychologists alike. The point is that this very intimacy is one of the chief arguments in support of personalistic psychology.

the whole of mental life cannot possibly discharge its duty without relating the states and processes it studies to the Person who is their originator, carrier, and regulator. There can be no adjustment without someone to adjust, no organization without an organizer, no memory without self-continuity, no learning without a change in the person, no knowledge without a knower, and no valuing without someone possessed of desires and the capacity to evaluate. Psychology must take seriously James's dictum that every mental operation occurs in a "personal form," and must take it more seriously than James himself did.

It is not uncommon in contemporary works on general psychology to find wedged into the last chapter a separate and rather abrupt treatment of personality, as if to placate the reader bored by excessive abstraction. Personalistic psychology would reverse the procedure. Personality, or at least the Person, would form the *point of departure* for every treatise in general psychology. Within this frame of reference initially established, every subsequent fact would be ordered.

A concrete instance of such a reconstruction of general psychology is contained in W. Stern's *Allgemeine Psychologie, auf personalistischer Grundlage.*[3] In addition to subscribing, in the main, to the above general arguments in favor of the personalistic system of thought, Stern makes many concrete applications of his point of view to detailed psychological problems. Since the question at hand is the *way* in which the personalistic method would reconstruct general psychology, a survey of some of these applications is advisable.[4]

> *The Person-World Dimension.* However unified and self-contained the person may be in the metaphysical sense, he is actually open at every moment to the surrounding world. He acts upon and is acted

[3] *General Psychology, from the Personalistic Standpoint*, trans. 1938 (The Macmillan Co.).

The following brief digest of this work is condensed from a longer review: G. W. Allport, "The Personalistic Psychology of William Stern," *Char. & Pers.*, 1937, 5, 231-246 (by permission of Duke University Press).

[4] It should be noted that for Stern psychology is only one branch of a broader discipline of personalistics. Psychology is the *science of the Person considered as having experience or as capable of having experience.* But experience is limited. Personalistics embraces the whole realm of personal existence. For Stern, as for Aristotle, there are higher persons and lower persons: the Godhead, humanity, a folk, a family; and at the other extreme, cells, molecules, atoms. Common to them all are unity, individuality, and telic activity. In their midst stands the *human* person, a connecting bond between lower persons and higher persons. Such a conception, as Stern himself asserts, leads far beyond the domain of psychology proper and need not affect in any way the merits of the more limited doctrines of personalistic *psychology.*

upon by the environment; a tension always exists. When the tension is most acute there is a resultant state of consciousness. The most important of all facts about consciousness is that it is graded; sometimes it stands out, as it were, against the diffuse background of personal life. It is *salient* (*abgehoben*). Whenever we are acutely aware of objects or when we are self-conscious there is this sharpness. At other times, as in many states of mere feeling, consciousness is embedded (*eingebettet*) more deeply; there is less clearness, less salience. Salience represents an act of pointing, a directedness of the person toward something that at the moment has special significance for him. The more salient an experience, the greater is its objective meaning; the more embedded, the greater is its subjective meaning. Complete embeddedness is of course unconsciousness. Embeddedness is marked particularly within the province of vital processes. For instance, the experiences produced through the lower senses, *viz.*, through smell, taste, and the organic modalities, are characteristically embedded. Vision and audition on the contrary, because of their superior capacity for making contacts with the outer world, usually yield salient experiences; touch is in this respect an intermediate modality. Experience is embedded likewise when it is emphatic, when it is introceptive (cf. pp. 217 f.), or when it bears a "physiognomic" correspondence to the surrounding events in the environment (cf. p. 534).

Perception. The historic category of "sensation" receives as scant treatment in personalistic psychology as it does in Gestalt theory, for "sensation" is not only an elementaristic conception but is nonpersonal as well. Both schools agree that it is only at the level of sensory *perception* that problems become psychological. In spite of this initial agreement personalistic psychology deviates widely from the Gestalt approach. Stern fears that if Gestalten are made the fundamental phenomena in perception and endowed, as it were, with their own laws (*e.g.*, "self-distribution") the danger of a new elementarism arises; for then the Gestalten themselves may be regarded as elements out of which all mental activity is composed, just as was formerly true of sensations. For Stern there can be no Gestalt without a person who forms Gestalten (*Keine Gestalt ohne Gestalter*). On occasion, of course, the Gestalt is dominanted by features of external constraint; the objective stimulus situation determining by its very definiteness of boundaries the type of salience that arises in experience; but even here the significance of the phenomenal Gestalt is invariably its relevance to the person in his intricate process of adaptation to the complexity of the world. In the last analysis Gestalten require some active participation of the person himself; they are never self-sufficient. It depends upon *me*, for example, whether I arrange the ticking of my watch into three-part or four-part rhythm, or see the cloud in the sky as a menace or as a negligible factor on the day of a picnic.

Furthermore, not every experience is salient; the category of *Ungestalt* (embeddedness) is quite as important as is the category of *Gestalt*. Its significance is especially apparent in the domain of feeling with which Gestalt psychology is ill-equipped to deal. In various respects, then, the boundaries of personalistics are wider than those of Gestalt theory.

Both theories are much interested in the phenomena of intersensory perception. The personalistic approach holds that experience mediated by the separate modalities is "dissociated" from the non-specific total perception that is deeply embedded in the person, and originally represented by a state of diffuse feeling. "Sharpness," for example, in smell, taste, hearing, and touch is not to be explained by the association of various specific sensations. It is a prior total experience that under certain conditions may become ascribed primarily to one modality or another. The Gestalt theory of course does not take into account the unifying substratum of the person, nor does it imply, as does Stern's theory, a genetic process of differentiation among modalities.

The experiences of space and time are instances of inter-sensorial perception. There are no special "spaces" for each sensory modality, but only one personal space. The locality and volume of a tone may seem to be a spatial experience of a predominantly auditory nature, but the space *in* which these impressions exist is not a sound-space, but *my* space, the same space that is the common ground of my visual and tactual experiences as well.

The recasting of the experiences of space and time is one of the most original features of personalistic psychology. What impersonalistic psychology is able, for example, to give an intelligible setting to the fact that "my seat-mate in the street car is distant from me while the friend toward whom I am riding is already near me"? The essence of space and time, psychologically considered, is their *personal relevance*. Events are distant when they lack such relevance; near when they possess it. The synthesis of space and time is likewise possible on the basis of personalistic theory, for there is at the center of my experience the feeling of *here-and-now*, an unanalyzable blend of space-time.

Memory. Memory too brings up the problem of personal time which, of course, is much more irregular than the unidimensional schema of objective time. Thus, a segment of life that is ten years behind me may be far nearer to me subjectively than a period two years ago; or vice versa, some act that I performed yesterday may today appear incomprehensible to me, a totally foreign element in an otherwise continually unfolding past.

The significance of memory is found in the mid-position it occupies in personal life between the function of instinct (the conservational factor) on the one hand and the function of intelligence (the progressive factor) on the other. Memory conserves the past, providing salient features of experience for the present in the service of future goals. It is thus not merely a matter of re-activated traces. Without memory each present state would be self-sufficient and rigid; having lost its connection with the total person, it would be meaningless.

In most acts of memory remembrance of self and remembrance of the outer world are not differentiated; even attempts at critical analysis never give a wholly separate picture of what occurred in the world around us and what occurred in ourselves. The entire episode has become embedded in the substratum of personal existence. It is for this reason that objective recall never possesses complete fidelity. Conversely, an individual's recall of his personal states is inevitably colored by his present experiences of the world.

Thought. Personalistic psychology finds a suitable place for all facts known concerning imagery, insight, attitude, fantasy, and intelligence. It arranges these facts, however, under teleological principles. Thought takes place whenever our personal world seems insecure, that is, whenever occasions arise that cannot be taken for granted; herein its function differs from that of instinct, habit or memory. Thought thus has survival value; it facilitates adjustment. But that is not all. Thought is not merely reactive; it is spontaneous and creative as well. It reaches out, as it were, *looking* for trouble. The person not only adapts in a passive sense, but having the capacity for self-development, for asserting himself against the world, he has therefore an active *need* for thought.

There is a special role assigned to pre-categorial thinking and to fantasy. Purely objective and rational thinking is brittle and artificial. It is so salient that it is ever in danger of becoming de-personalized. It is *too* objective; it is far from life, and lacks *understanding*. The most comprehensive and adequate products of thought, the works of art, religion, literature, and metaphysics, are a result of embedded experience that comes from feeling, from empathy, and from "physiognomic" understanding, quite as much as from sharply salient, rational analysis.

Feeling. Since of all types of experience feeling is "nearest to the person" one would expect personalistic psychology to be most productive in this province. And it is. The dimensions that it uses are exceedingly numerous, and more distinctions are turned up than other schools of psychology ever dreamed of. Wundt's tridimensional framework is made to look like a bony scarecrow.

Although all feelings are embedded, some are relatively more salient than others, *i.e.*, some pertain to objects, some, like mood, to mere passive existence. Some are near and some distant in their reference (*e.g.*, terror *vs.* grief). There are feelings of expectancy and of retrospect, of alienation for the world (anxiety) and of harmony with it; there are feelings of familiarity, of unfamiliarity, of premonition and recollection; there are positive and negative feelings toward the future (hope and dread). There are feelings of success and of failure, of the expansion or of the negligibility of the self (as in various esthetic experiences), of preparation for action or reflection after action. Some feelings are broad, some narrow, some intense or weak, some lasting or temporary. They possess depth or shallowness, genuineness or disingenuousness, seriousness or playfulness; they may pertain to cultural or to vital functions, and may lead to adaptive action or to expressive action. All these are recognized and used in addition to Wundt's dimensions, pleasure and unpleasure, strain and relaxation, and excitement and calm.

Motivation. The emphasis is upon personal goals and personal striving. In order to represent the great diversity of motivated behavior Stern has recourse to virtually all the available concepts of dynamic psychology: instinct, impulse, motive, need, disposition, urge, interest, inclination, wish, drive, goal-striving, and will; not to mention more inchoate principles such as entelechy and "personal energy." By virtue of this array the author establishes the important personalistic principle that the individual is not merely a reactive creature, seeking passive adaptation to the environment. He is creative, and capable of spontaneous as well as reactive behavior. Problems of intention, attempt, effort, and that distinctive human ability for *conscious planning*, are all prominent in personalistic thought, though generally neglected by psychology at large.[5]

---

[5] Abandoning at this point the expository method, a certain criticism of Stern's treatment of motivation is in order—one that will serve to call attention to an important distinction between his point of view and the standpoint of the present volume.

By employing all the conventional rubrics of motivation Stern places himself in the class of those who think of motivational systems within the individual as merely special instances of universal motivational systems. This type of dynamic psychology was criticized at length in Chapter VII. To be truly personal, motives must not be regarded as changes rung upon standard themes. There is a vast difference between a flexible doctrine of authentic personal motives (interests, desires, inclinations, tastes, attitudes, and traits) and stereotyped reliance upon instinct,

In this section we have implied that personalistic psychology and self-psychology are very much alike in their points of view. And so they are. The principal characteristics of the Self, as Calkins defines them, turn out to be characteristics that Stern likewise recognizes as highly central in the Person.[6] The Person, like the Self, is *persistent; changes* as it develops; is *unique;* is *many-sided;* is the *groundwork of all its own experiences;* and is *related to its physical and social environment.*

There is, however, a difference, though not a vital one for present purposes. Calkins sees a sharp cleavage between mental and bodily events. The Self, she holds, is not made of body-mind, but rather it *is* mind and *has* a body. This dualism results in strong emphasis upon the role of self-awareness, and upon introspection as a method of psychological study. Stern's Person, on the other hand, is "psychophysically neutral." It cannot be characterized as *mental,* because mind in turn has no significance excepting in terms of its position within, and service to, the Person.

Space does not permit the discussion of other personalistic doctrines, those, for example, of Bowne, Ward, Müller-Freienfels, and Klages. Nor is this the place to consider objections that have been raised against this line of thought.[7] The present purpose is simply to show *in what way* general psychology may be influenced to advantage by an orientation that regards the Person as the central fact in

drive, need, and universal wants. It is impossible to build up a concrete structure of motives from abstractions.

The principle of the functional autonomy of motives, it must be admitted, finds a minor place in Stern's system—witness the following quotation: "As is the case with inclinations, indirect or mediated interests may become immediate. Many a man who at first has concerned himself with chemistry because he wanted to be an apothecary has become more and more absorbed in the problems of chemistry as such, and has found complete satisfaction in pursuing them." But Stern does not follow this line of thought to its logical conclusion. Had he done so a more radically personalistic theory of motivation would have resulted.

[6] Cf. M. W. Calkins, *Psychol. Rev.,* 1917, 24, 279-300.

[7] Perhaps the most common objection is that personalistic and self-psychologies say little that is not self-evident. The critics say, "To be sure, mental life takes personal forms, but what of it? Animals too have personal forms, but this fact does not compel us to reconstruct zoology as a science. Classification, abstraction, generalization are still justified." Two replies to this objection are in order: (1) So far as psychology is concerned, its classifications, abstractions, and generalizations might be far more realistic and useful if they rested upon the personalistic mode of analysis. The dimensions chosen would be less artificial. (2) Granted that aspective analysis is justified, it ought not be so rigid in its methods and concepts as to exclude consideration of mind-in-particular. For if the Person is self-evident then all the more reason to remove barriers against those who would explore the peculiarities of this self-evident datum.

mental science. The following section will show that this book, while not averse to the personalistic reconstruction of general psychology, has attempted a somewhat different task.

THE PSYCHOLOGY OF PERSONALITY

Somewhere in the interstices of its nomothetic laws psychology has lost the human person as we know him in everyday life. To rescue him and to reinstate him as a psychological datum in his own right is the avowed purpose of the psychology of personality. To aid in this re-establishment a number of unfamiliar but important tenets have been proposed. Their import is not essentially iconoclastic. They do not aim to destroy the traditional structure of general psychology, but rather to expand it. Let psychology pursue its analysis in any way it finds helpful and instructive, so long as it allows also for analysis in terms of *natural* cleavage: personal forms must be as admissible as impersonal constructs.

The intent of the preceding chapters thus has been to limber up the frame of psychological science, so that it will no longer exclude the direct study of individuality. To this end particular stress has been given to the following somewhat novel principles.

1. The proposition that psychology seeks laws has not been denied, but it has been shown that *a general law may be a law that tells how uniqueness comes about*. Part II of this volume is especially devoted to a discussion of laws of this order, the central one being the principle of the functional autonomy of motives. This law—altogether basic for the psychology of personality—accounts, as no other principle of dynamic psychology is able to do, for the concrete impulses that lie at the root of personal behavior.

In still another sense the psychology of personality deals with laws. One may say (with penetrating accuracy) that each personality is a law unto itself, meaning that each single life, if fully understood, would reveal its own orderly and necessary process of growth. The course of each life is a lawful event, even though it is unlike all others of its class. Lawfulness does not depend upon frequency nor upon uniformity, but upon necessity. There is a necessary patterning in each life, separate from every other life. The preceding chapters have attempted to help free the psychological mind, and so instruct it, that this lawful patterning may be more accurately understood.

2. As in any science *prediction* is one of the goals of the psy-

chology of personality. It is axiomatic that prediction can proceed
only by virtue of prior *generalization*. But what *kind* of generalization? All the general laws of human behavior taken together cannot
possibly tell the psychologist what his best friend will do come Christ-
mas. Such prediction is possible only from knowledge of the individual alone. The necessary knowledge is, of course, in a sense generalized, but the generalization pertains to the *equivalences* in the
behavior of one person, not to the uniformities of behavior among
human beings at large. If ability to predict behavior in concrete instances is the test of scientific skill, the honors go not to traditional
psychological method but to the psychology of personality.

3. In Chapter II the possibility of approaching personality from
many angles was admitted—poets, religionists, philosophers, novelists,
biochemists, sociologists, welfare workers, and politicians, all having
their preferred points of view. It was admitted likewise that each acquaintance sees a person in a different way. Yet all this biosocial variability has not been allowed in this volume to obscure the existential
definition adopted in Chapter II. Biosocial impressions are like reflecting mirrors in an amusement park. Each distorts the face and figure in
a different way—lengthening, shortening, expanding, and contracting
it—while still keeping some sort of likeness. But all the while there is
only *one* person present; he remains single however much the reflecting images may multiply. The psychology of personality proceeds
from the point of view of the person himself. It asks what *he* is like in
his essential nature. If he is like many things, if he changes from environment to environment, very well and good. It is always *he* who
changes; and the range and forms of his variations can be determined. He himself is the datum; he *is* something and *does* something
(or if one prefers, he is *many* things and does *many* things); but we
can still find out what they are, viewed from *within*, from the person's *own* point of view.

4. Having accepted the biophysical conception it is vital to follow it up with the principle that *the analysis of personality shall proceed at significant levels only*. What are its natural units or substructures? They are certainly not specific habits nor identical elements,
nor are they abstract dimensions gleaned from a comparison of mind
with mind. The units of personality are complex neuropsychic dispositions, in this volume generically called *traits*. They are internally
generalized, flexible, interdependent dispositions, attuned to a range

of equivalent stimuli and issuing into an equivalent range of responses. It is their function to guarantee stability and economy in personal life.

It is not only in the doctrine of traits that this volume shows a preference for relatively complex levels of analysis. This preference runs throughout the whole exposition. For personality appears only when individuals possess sufficient variety and multiplicity in their make-up to warrant a high degree of complex organization. Not only our theories but our methods must be adapted to the existence of inclusive patterns. Microscopic techniques lose sight of the only levels at which personality can be said to exist at all.

5. What is true of substructures is true likewise of total structure. The problem of the *unity* of personality is as much a subject for psychological concern as are its elements. Chapter XIII showed that this many-sided issue is most effectively approached by the empirical method under the guidance of rational hypotheses. To be sure unity is never perfect, but only "high level" concepts of consistency are capable of depicting adequately such unity as exists. The common devices of correlation and other measures of correspondence are not sufficient. To express total organization new and more adequate formulations are needed.

6. Preference is given throughout to those concepts that savor of individuality. Certain terms, long freighted with nomothetic significance, can never serve as adequate "bait" for the strictly individual forms of mental life. The following list, though not complete, will serve to call to mind the class of concepts that the preceding chapters do *not* favor. Most of them are adapted only to the representation of dull uniformity, allowing at best for quantitative variations upon some standard pattern. Many are likewise static, overlooking the fact that in personal life there is absolutely no return to, or perfect repetition of, processes that have once occurred. These concepts do not allow for the constant change and growth that take place. Some imply an over-simplification of personality, reducing it to too few standard variables or types. And some stress uniform and early genetic sequences, forgetting that the normal mature personality is post-instinctive and post-infantile.

Concepts which as commonly used in psychology have little
individualizing value:

abnormality	nomothetic law
attribute	normal distribution
average	Oedipus complex
correspondence of measures	prepotent reflex
cultural determination	qualities of character
dimension	sex drive
factor	situational determinant
Id	specificity of habit
identical element	standard deviation
instinct	Super-ego
intelligence quotient	type (of any order)
mental faculty	uniform stages of development
need	uniform variable

The list is not complete, but it serves as a reminder of some of the
critical discussions in earlier chapters. With it one may contrast the
following list of terms that help to extend the traditional limits of
psychological thought so that it may embrace more adequately and
concretely the study of the individual.

Concepts which as used in this volume have marked individualizing
value:

attitude	interest
Bestimmung	introception
case study	intuition
configuration	life-history
congruence	need-integrate
differentiation	part
ego-ideal	radix
ego-system	self-consciousness
equivalence of response	structure
equivalence of stimuli	style
focal disposition	subjective value
functional autonomy	substructure
guiding image	trait
integration	unity thema

7. Though the primary goal of the psychology of personality is to aid in the understanding of individual forms of mental life, it has as a secondary goal the comparison of one person with another in respect to their *common traits*. In Chapters XI and XV the logic of this comparison was worked out in detail. Its novelty consists in its juxtaposition of certain cultural and evolutionary principles that render human beings comparable even while, in the stricter sense, they remain unique.

8. The psychology of personality is essentially nothing more than a modern codification of knowledge concerning human nature in its concrete aspects. It is made possible through the application of the high standards of fact collecting and critical induction evolved by its scientific predecessors, particularly by experimental psychology during the past sixty years. Therefore, accuracy of observation and freedom from prejudiced interpretation are among its primary aims. Fidelity to fact is its goal.

At the same time some of the most brilliant insights into personality, and some of its most valuable hypotheses, come not from the activity of the laboratory, but from adjacent fields of study. Many provinces of human thought are entered. Out of the remote past come well tested bits of wisdom, and from older psychological formulations comes unexpected aid. For this reason the approach of this book is marked by a strong *historical orientation*, not only in Chapter III, its longest single section, but in all other chapters as well. If there seems to be partiality for the support that the humanities can give—for the contributions of literature and philosophy—it is because in them one finds the richest and most full-bodied accounts of the subject.

9. Another somewhat novel principle is the *empirical-intuitive theory of understanding*, developed in Chapters XVIII and XIX. Its special significance lies in the fact that it does for the level of impression what the remainder of the book does for the objective level of study. Existentially considered, personality is a many-sided structure. It is also *perceived* as such (within certain limitations imposed by the process of judgment). To equate in this way the objective and subjective representations of personality is a step toward the conceptual unification of the field as a whole.

10. Above all, to revert to the statement of the preface, *adequacy of depiction* represents the goal of these chapters. Every legitimate method available at the present time finds a place. Hospitality is ex-

tended also to many rationalistic doctrines and to common sense, generally with suggestions as to how their contributions may be recast into more certain empirical formulations. Since at the present stage of our knowledge finality is not possible, it has been our goal to avoid pedantry, letting the new science be as flexible as its subject. Only through such liberality of outlook is it possible to throw the maximum light upon the main business in hand.

PERSPECTIVE

There are those who would say that the epithet, "the psychology of personality," is a mere tautology. They would insist that psychology in all its branches deals with personality and with nothing else. Personalistic psychologists would say so; so too would certain dynamic psychologists interested only in the deep-rooted personal forms of mental life. But this is not the view of the present volume.

Not every problem in psychology is a problem of personality. Most of the questions raised by animal psychology are not, nor are all the problems of psychophysiology, of sensory psychology, of applied, social, or developmental psychology or psychometrics. In these branches, and in still others, there is a place for that historic abstraction, "the generalized mind." Work in many fields progresses best with the aid of this construct even though it takes account of merely average or majority behavior. Individuality is not always the object of interest.

The validity of any construct can be tested only by its fitness to the purpose for which it was devised. Since the *purpose* of much psychological work is what it is, it would be unfair to apply personalistic standards to its impersonal objectives. Any constructs are allowable if they aid in the comprehension of certain chosen classes of phenomena.[8]

[8] "The constructs in terms of which natural phenomena are comprehended are man-made inventions. To discover a scientific law is merely to discover that a man-made scheme serves to unify, and thereby to simplify, comprehension of a certain class of natural phenomena. A scientific law is not to be thought of as having an independent existence which some scientist is fortunate to stumble upon. A scientific law is not a part of nature. It is only a way of comprehending nature. . . .

"The criterion by which a new ideal construct in science is accepted or rejected is the degree to which it facilitates the comprehension of a class of phenomena which can be thought of as examples of a single construct rather than as individualized events." L. L. Thurstone, *The Vectors of Mind*, University of Chicago Press, 1935, pp. 44 f.

The most frequent cause of pessimism regarding the future of psychology as a science is its ceaseless war of terminologies. Each writer who builds a system invents his own constructs, and these are as a rule promptly rejected by all but a narrow circle of followers. Yet according to the above argument these competing constructs are all justified so long as they serve the purpose for which their authors intended them. It is the most noteworthy characteristic of mind that it may be surveyed and divided in an infinite number of ways. The only legitimate question that can be asked about the proposed divisions is whether they represent adequately the surveyor's intentions. In most cases they do.

The existence of many schools of psychology is, therefore, not an evil. It is rather a demonstration of the richness of mind. Each competent surveyor has his own point of departure, and maps out as much of the territory as he is qualified to explore. His sense of boundaries and connections (in other words, his constructs) is his own, and may serve admirably for the map *he* is preparing. The penalty of undertaking the systematic study of mental science is the necessity of learning many maps by heart. No two are drawn from the same point of view, nor have they the same objectives in mind. Often they do not even overlap one another's territory.

A quarrel can arise only when a map-maker who has surveyed the ground with one objective in view pretends that his chart will lead as well to a wholly different goal. This has happened whenever unsuitable constructs have been applied to the study of mental individuality. All of the critical portions of the preceding chapters have been devoted to the exposure of this false claim. *It is not the nomothetic constructs as such to which exception is taken but the pretense that they cover the phenomenon of individuality.*

Many of the teachings of general psychology contribute significantly to the understanding of personality. In fact, they are indispensable. To mention only a few upon which this volume has leaned: adjustment, autism, compensation, conditioning, co-variation, differentiation, empathy, equivalence, final common path, halo effect, imitation, inference, inferiority feeling, integration, intelligence, learning, methods of measurement, prediction, rationalization, reliability, repression, similarity, socialization, sublimation, temperament, trauma.

Often these concepts, and others like them, have received somewhat special interpretation to make them serve the purpose in hand. But their profusion demonstrates sufficiently the close dependence of the psychology of personality upon much that has gone before it in laboratory and clinical research.

The influence should be reciprocal. To keep the individual in mind is to enrich research in any department of mental science. Some may argue with the personalistic school that every aspect of psychological thought should be recast about the person. They may point to Stern's reconstruction of the psychology of perception, thought, memory, feeling, and emotion as an example of hopeful reform.

To give one other illustration of the improvements that might come from taking more serious account of the personalistic orientation: the problem of intelligence will serve. The present impasse in this field of study is due to the search for *universal* constituents in mental ability. If the personalistic view were taken, the whole search would be shifted (no doubt with profit) to an attempt to account for the highly individual patterns of intellectual power. Although the concept of "general intelligence" has proved of value *for certain purposes*, and has therefore a certain validity, still, as everyone knows, it makes for distortions. Some intelligences can only be aptly characterized by saying that they are "poetic," or "mathematical," or "domestic." One man, we find, is intelligent in literary, social, and horticultural lines; another is keen in mechanics with odd blind spots for electricity and plumbing. Another is quick in matters of music, trade and interior design. There are peaks, valleys, and plateaus in everyone's abilities. To express them by an I.Q. is the roughest kind of approximation. To be sure, the abilities enumerated above are complicated by the presence of interests and training. But to separate intelligence from interest and training is perhaps one of those misleading abstractions which a more personalistic view of mental life would remedy.

According to the argument of this chapter the personalistic account of general psychology is desirable inasmuch as it introduces one more valid point of view, and a particularly wholesome one, into the many-sided science of mind. The multiplication of points of view is not evil so long as they are allowed to act upon one another, thus enriching our comprehension of mental life. The more ways we have the better. None that can stand the tests of fidelity to fact and self-consistency should be excluded. Only the narrow creed which says that psychology by its constitution is forbidden to take note of individuality is rejected.

Thus there are many ways to study man psychologically. Yet to study him most fully is to take him as an individual. He is more than a bundle of habits; more than a nexus of abstract dimensions; more too than a representative of his species. He is more than a citizen of the state, and more than a mere incident in the gigantic movements of mankind. He transcends them all. The individual, striving ever for his own integrity, has existed under many forms of social life—forms as varied as the nomadic, feudal, and capitalistic. He struggles on even under oppression, always hoping and planning for a more perfect democracy where the dignity and growth of each personality will be prized above all else.

INDEX OF SUBJECTS

INDEX OF SUBJECTS

INDEX OF NAMES

INDEX OF NAMES